THE LEGAL PROCEDURE OF CICERO'S TIME

BY

A. H. J. GREENIDGE, M.A.

LECTURER AND LATE FELLOW OF HERTFORD COLLEGE
LECTURER IN ANCIENT HISTORY AT BRASENOSE COLLEGE, OXFORD
AUTHOR OF 'INFAMIA IN ROMAN LAW'

THE LAWBOOK EXCHANGE, LTD.
Clark, New Jersey

ISBN 978-1-886363-99-1 (hardcover)
ISBN 978-1-61619-473-4 (paperback)

Lawbook Exchange edition 2000, 2015

The quality of this reprint is equivalent to the quality of the original work.

The Lawbook Exchange, Ltd.
33 Terminal Avenue
Clark, New Jersey 07066-1321

Please see our website for a selection of our other publications and fine facsimile reprints of classic works of legal history:
www.lawbookexchange.com

Library of Congress Cataloging-in-Publication Data

Greenidge, A.H.J. (Abel Henry Jones), 1865-1906.
The legal procedure of Cicero's time / by A.H.J. Greenidge.
p. cm.
Originally published: Oxford : New York : Clarendon Press : H. Frowde, 1901.
Includes bibliographical references.
ISBN 1-886363-99-4 (cl. : alk. paper)
1. Procedure (Roman law) I. Title.
KJA2700.G74 1999
340.5'4—dc21 99-26771
CIP

Printed in the United States of America on acid-free paper

THE LEGAL PROCEDURE OF CICERO'S TIME

BY

A. H. J. GREENIDGE, M.A.

LECTURER AND LATE FELLOW OF HERTFORD COLLEGE
LECTURER IN ANCIENT HISTORY AT BRASENOSE COLLEGE, OXFORD
AUTHOR OF 'INFAMIA IN ROMAN LAW'

OXFORD UNIVERSITY PRESS
LONDON: At The Clarendon Press
1901

TO

J. L. STRACHAN-DAVIDSON

TO WHOSE INSTRUCTION AND ENCOURAGEMENT MY

STUDIES IN ROMAN LAW ARE DUE

THIS BOOK IS GRATEFULLY

DEDICATED

PREFACE

THE leading design of this book is to furnish students of Cicero's writings with a clue to the chief legal difficulties which they will meet with in their reading. These difficulties are far more numerous in the sphere of procedure than in that of substantive law; and, as it was quite impossible to write a work of moderate compass which dealt with both branches of the subject, I have thought it better to confine my attention mainly to the former; although, as will easily be understood, it has proved impossible to deal thoroughly with the procedure of the period which I have treated, without touching on many questions of pure law; so intimately are these bound up with the forms in which they were presented to the courts.

When I had chosen the procedure of the Ciceronian period as my subject, there were two methods of treatment which lay open before me. One was to write a series of brief commentaries on Cicero's speeches, either singly or in groups; the other was to adopt a systematic and historical treatment of the civil and criminal procedure of his time—to present as complete a picture as the material permitted of the courts of law of the later Republic, and to employ the works of Cicero as the material for and the illustration of this picture. I came to the conclusion that the first method of treatment, although far the easier, would be both tedious and incomplete: tedious, because it would necessarily involve repetitions and irrelevant digressions; and incomplete, because it would leave gaps, capable of being filled up from other literary records, which might be employed in a general discussion of the subject but which it would be difficult to introduce into a mere commentary on the speeches. I therefore adopted the plan of a systematic treatment. The danger of this course, of which I have been keenly sensible, is the necessity of dependence for many important details, about which Cicero tells us nothing, on other and for the most part later sources. But the difficulty is only real with respect to civil procedure. Cicero's speeches on criminal matters afford ample material for the reconstruction of the criminal courts of his time; on the other hand, his four speeches on matters of private law, with the numerous passing references to civil procedure which are contained in his other works, often supply hints and suggestions rather than principles or facts. How these suggestions fit into the scheme which is detailed for us by Gaius and other lawyers of the imperial period, is one of the chief problems which the first book of my treatise attempts to solve. Personally, I am convinced that the danger is smaller than it at first appears. A knowledge of the changes wrought by the constitution of the Empire can be employed to eliminate irrelevant elements: the principles of Roman process can be shown to be one of the most durable things in Roman history, and the *onus probandi* usually rests on one who would deny the prevalence in the Ciceronian period of a legal rule enunciated by Gaius. Those readers, however, who do not feel such confidence as I do in the continuity of Roman procedure, may observe with satisfaction that, where Cicero or some republican source is not the authority, I have generally stated the existence of an institution as a probability and not as a fact.

But, if in some respects Cicero's evidence on civil procedure is too narrow, in others it is too wide. None of the speeches on criminal matters contain such obscure and subtle points as the four which deal with questions of private law. To consider such questions in the text or the notes would have spoilt the proportions and symmetry of the work. I have, therefore, treated these speeches in an appendix, and have devoted a brief commentary to each in turn.

The length of this book has far exceeded my original anticipations: but I intended it to be a work of reference, and, as compression would have spoilt it for this purpose, its growth was inevitable. I could not afford to neglect the full citation in the notes of any passage that had an intimate bearing on the text; nor could I omit passages which, though not necessary for proof, would appeal to a reader as not less difficult than those which were. The notes had to be compiled with an eye to the index of passages in Cicero which will be found at the end of the volume.

During the long time which I have spent in the correction of the proofs my knowledge of subjects already treated has often been increased and my views have consequently been sometimes modified. The new views thus gained could not always be incorporated in the text, as the book was passing through the press. Hence the necessity for the additional notes which will be found printed after the appendices. They contain both second thoughts of my own and ideas that were suggested by friends who looked through my pages. I have been particularly fortunate in the assistance that I have received from the latter source. The book was read in manuscript by Professor Pelham, who made many valuable suggestions, especially as to its form. The proofs have been read by Mr. Strachan-Davidson, whose helpful criticism has enabled me to correct errors and clear up obscurities. I am also grateful for assistance on special points to Professor Goudy, Mr. W. Warde Fowler and Mr. A. C. Clark. In the final verification of the references in the later portion of the work I am greatly indebted to a former pupil, Miss Muriel Clay of Lady Margaret Hall.

A. H. J. G.

OXFORD,
January, 1901.

CONTENTS

PAGE

INTRODUCTION 1–14

BOOK I. CIVIL PROCEDURE.

PART I.

THE COURTS OF THE MONARCHY AND EARLY REPUBLIC 15–78

§ 1. Theory of Civil Procedure at Rome; the Magistrate and the *Iudex* 15–49

§ 2. The Magistrate 18–37

(*a*) At Rome 18–32

(*b*) The Municipal Magistrate 32–36

(*c*) The Magistrate in the Provinces . . 36–37

§ 3. The *Iudex* 37–49

§ 4. Procedure *in iure*; the *Legis Actio* 49–78

PART II.

THE COURTS OF THE CICERONIAN PERIOD 79–296

§ 1. The Relation of the Magistrates to the Laws. . 79–82

§ 2. The Magistrate 82–132

(*a*) At Rome 82–99

(*b*) The Municipal Magistrate and Municipal Jurisdiction 99–109

(*c*) The Provincial Magistrate and Provincial Jurisdiction 109–132

§ 3. The Action 132–181

(*a*) Preliminaries to Action 132–141

(*b*) The Summons 141–145

(*c*) Proceedings *in iure* 145–149

(*d*) The Formula 150–161

(*e*) The Formula and the *Legis Actio* . . 161–175

(*f*) Dangers of the formulary system . . 175–177

(*g*) *Actionis* or *Formulae Editio.* Discussions connected with the *Postulatio* . . . 178–181

PAGE

§ 4. The Different Kinds of Action 182–210
(a) *In rem actiones* 182–195
(b) *In personam actiones* 195–206
(c) *Actiones Poenales* 206–210
§ 5. The Interdict 210–227
§ 6. Defence; *Exceptio; Praescriptio* 227–235
§ 7. Representation 235–243
§ 8. The *Litis Contestatio* 243–251
§ 9. Confession 251–254
§ 10. Neglect of Defence 255–258
§ 10.* The Oath 259–263
§ 11. The *Iudex* and the *Iudicium* 263–277
§ 12. Execution 278–286
§ 13. Appeal and reversal of Sentences 287–296

BOOK II. CRIMINAL PROCEDURE.

§ 1. The Criminal Procedure of the Earliest Times . 297–307
§ 2. The Criminal Procedure of the Early Republic . 307–326
§ 3. The Jurisdiction of the Tribune and of the *Plebs* . 327–331
§ 4. Magisterial *Coercitio* 331–338
§ 5. The Jurisdiction of the different Magistrates and the separate *Comitia*. The *Triumviri Capitales* 338–344
§ 6. The Procedure of a *Iudicium Populi* and of the *Provocatio* 344–349
§ 7. Survivals of popular jurisdiction in Cicero's day . 349–366
§ 8. Domestic Jurisdiction 367–373
§ 9. Religious Jurisdiction 373–380
§ 10. Special Commissions 380–397
§ 11. Martial Law 397–406
§ 12. Italian and Municipal Jurisdiction 406–410
§ 13. Provincial and Military Jurisdiction 410–415
§ 14. The *Iudicia Publica* or *Quaestiones Perpetuae* . . 415–428
§ 15. The Presidents of the *Quaestiones Perpetuae* . . 428–433
§ 16. The *Iudices* of the *Quaestiones Perpetuae* and the *Leges Iudiciariae* 433–456
§ 17. The Course of the Trial in a *Quaestio Perpetua* . 456–504
§ 18. Execution 504–516
§ 19. Appeal and Restitution 516–525

APPENDIX I.

PAGE

The *Nexus* and the *Vindex* 527–529

APPENDIX II.

Commentaries on Cicero's Speeches for Quinctius, Roscius the Actor, Tullius and Caecina 530–568

(1) *Pro Quinctio* 531–541

(2) *Pro Roscio Comoedo* 542–551

(3) *Pro Tullio* 551–556

(4) *Pro Caecina* 556–568

APPENDIX III.

The Conditions of the *Provocatio* 569–572

APPENDIX IV.

On the Position of Pompeius as sole consul in 52 B.C. . . 573–574

ADDITIONAL NOTES.

Page 13, note 1 575

„ 58 575

„ 102 575

„ 115, note 3 576

„ 262, „ 4 576

„ 319, „ 2 577

„ 356, „ 3 577

„ 363 577

„ 395 578

INDEX OF SUBJECTS 579

INDEX TO PASSAGES IN CICERO 592

INTRODUCTION

PROCEDURE may be defined as a series of symbolic actions, generally accompanied by words, and, in developed societies, by the exhibition of written documents, by means of which rights or liberties guaranteed by a society are reasserted by its individual members. Reassertion is the essence of procedure; for in the sense in which we shall use the term—the sense of regaining before a competent court a status that has been lost or questioned—it assumes an already violated right. It is true that active processes of a similarly symbolic character are often necessary for the mere attainment of rights; the acts, for instance, by which possession was acquired in Roman Law, assert an uncontested claim and imply no voluntary contractual relation between two parties; but the Procedure of Contentious Jurisdiction, which is our present subject, implies more than assertion or aggression on the part of an individual; it implies a controversy. Sometimes the controversy is between the State and the individual, and the gradual solution of this contest, which is generally of a highly unequal kind, is manifested in the successive stages of the Administrative or Criminal Procedure of the community. More often the controversy lies between individuals, and the State is called in as an arbitrator and exponent of the right in question. The great end to be attained in both these cases is the formation and expression of a judgement by the supreme authority or its representa-

The nature of Procedure.

The end which it attains.

tives—a judgement which shall reassert a principle of right presumed to be already in existence[1]. This reassertion of rights by means of judgements is the end for which the whole judicial organization of a State exists. The means to the attainment of this perfect truth is the series of symbolic acts, each expressive of a partial verity, which we denominate Procedure. It is true that the assertion of a judgement does not always terminate a controversy. Compulsion is sometimes necessary to bring the individual will into harmony with the verdict of the supreme authority; in other words, Judgement must often be followed by Execution. But execution adds no new element to the settlement of the question of right; it is merely an assertion of the very obvious truth, recognized by all governments worthy of the name, that a right about which there is no controversy shall be immediately enforced by the State. In certain cases, it is true, the very process of execution may demand a new judgement and therefore a new procedure; the determination of a debt, for instance, may give rise to the question how, under the circumstances of the case, this debt can or should be liquidated. In such cases it would be truer to say that the original judgement was no final judgement at all—as little final as the verdict 'Guilty' would be in the criminal law before it is known whether the consequence of the verdict will be imprisonment or death. But, in an excessively cumbrous and involved system such as that presented by the Civil Procedure of Rome, clearness can be at times attained only by sacrificing logical accuracy to considerations of convenience. Sometimes the determination of a civil suit is so protracted that its stages seem to create several distinct trials, each with its own procedure, rather than one continuous process. Execution here almost takes the form

Judgement and Execution.

[1] For procedure (*actio*) as the means of realizing *ius* see Cic. *pro Caec.* 11, 32; 13, 37; 14, 40. An action is a means 'iuris persequendi' (ib. 3, 8).

of an independent trial. At other times the final stage is so automatic, so little the subject of controversy, that the methods by which the judgement is reached and its execution is attained are easily separable. But, separable as they sometimes are, the connexion between the two elements is too close to make it possible to ignore Execution in a treatise on Procedure. It is an integral part of the subject, but it is the less important part. The highest aim of procedure is to attain a true judgement on a controverted question of right.

Relation of Procedure to Right.

The relation of Procedure to Right may be looked on from many points of view. It may be of some value to glance at two aspects of this relation which are specially manifested in the history of Roman Jurisprudence. Procedure is always a symbolic manifestation of right; but it is not only the process as completed in a judgement which has this character; the success attained at every step in the procedure is itself the assertion of a right. It is not, it is true, the ordinary symbol of a right; such symbols are furnished by the unimpeded acts of daily life. But it is its symbol in the last resort, and it is one which bears a curiously varying relation to its original. It may happen that the modes of formulating rights which are cultivated by a community are far less perfect than the rights themselves, although it would be difficult to furnish from history any instance of the counter-case, where the rights are inferior to the procedure by which they are made good. The Athenian legal system furnishes an instance of excellently adjusted legal relations combined with a procedure which erred in the direction of a too great striving after simplicity. The judicial system of the Roman Empire with its over-strained centralization and its infinite stages of appeal reacted most injuriously on the law, or rather systems of law, which it attempted to control. In certain modern states the absence of codification, and the consequent costliness of litigation, has sometimes rendered almost nugatory the possession of rights which are at least tolerable. Amongst undeveloped systems we may cite Germanic Law as an instance of a highly developed legal sense, more ethical because more individualistic in character than that possessed by either Roman or Greek, associated with the barbarisms of ordeal and trial by battle. In truth the growth of Jurisprudence in a country is always two-fold, never simple. It is, firstly, the growth of its material law, and, secondly, the growth of the forms by which it is asserted. And the march of the two systems is by no means made with equal step. As a rule perfection in procedure—the happy mean that lies somewhere between the over-conscientious complexity of the old and the cheerful simplicity of the infant state—comes far later in a nation's history than perfection in legal relations. The laws of Romulus, who lived, as Cicero tells us, in a literary and enlightened age[1], show a nice respect for the rights of women, but punish the husband who has sold his wife, by having him 'sacrificed to the infernal gods[2]'; and at a much later date the *elegantia* of the language and laws of the Twelve Tables[3] was combined with an extraordinary complexity of procedure. In the particular case of Rome various reasons can be assigned for this inequality of development. The earliest movements of plebeian agitation took the form of a demand for the publication of a code, not for a reform of the official hierarchy. The code when produced embodied the simpler plebeian law, but the ordinances of procedure were still the clumsy acts of patrician ceremonial; the military heads of the State, on whom had devolved the judicial duties of the king, were almost wholly dependent for their knowledge of the

Material and formal law; slower development of the latter.

[1] Cic. *de Rep.* ii. 10, 18 'Romuli autem aetatem . . . iam inveteratis literis atque doctrinis, omnique illo antiquo ex inculta hominum vita errore sublato, fuisse cernimus.'

[2] Plut. *Rom.* 22.

[3] Cic. *de Rep.* iv. 8, 8 'Admiror, nec rerum solum, sed verborum etiam elegantiam.'

forms of action on the rulings of the pontifical college, while the petrifying influence of religion and the pride of exclusive knowledge kept the members of the guild from relaxing the rigour of these ancient rules. Again, stiffness of form gives security in an age when written documents are scarce; the formalism of business transactions naturally found its counterpart in the courts, and the song of the *legis actio* must have been as sacred to the ears of the litigant as the *carmen* of the Twelve Tables. The general thesis that formalism haunts the law-courts long after it has quitted the market and the hearth is too obviously true of early states of society to need further illustration; but yet, when the initial difficulties have been overcome—when religion has been relegated to its proper place, when *fas* has a sphere distinct from *ius*, when the exclusive privileges of the legal guild or other interpreter have been broken down, and writing can be used for documentary evidence and for instruction—then the development of procedure is one of the surest signs of the development of law. We shall have ample illustration of this when we come to deal with the praetor's edict—a compendium of judge-made law expressed through rules of procedure. At present a simple negative example may suffice. Criminal procedure at Rome long lagged far behind the civil, and this rudeness of procedure was but an expression of the vagueness of the law. There were exceedingly good and sound reasons, which we shall examine elsewhere, for keeping the criminal law in this vague condition, as long as Rome remained a city state. But the fact remains that the chaotic nature of the law was reflected in the procedure and that, at the time of the institution of the *quaestiones perpetuae*, the codification of the former was followed by a regulation of the latter.

A developed procedure the true test of a developed legal system.

So far we have touched on procedure as the reflection of the aggregate of rights known as law. But the second idea that every step in procedure is the assertion of a right, and that the completion of the steps perfects the right was equally familiar to the Romans. 'Right' and 'court' are with them synonymous; *ius petere* is to seek what is 'right' or 'fitting'[1]; *in ius ire* is to go before the magistrate[2]. We shall find a still more perfect exemplification of this view in the theory evolved by the jurists, that the definite appearance before a court and submission to its will is the renewal (*novatio*) of the obligation out of which the case has arisen.

Differences in procedure spring from differences in the rights to be enforced.

The most strongly marked differences in procedure spring naturally from the varying character of the rights to be enforced. One class of rights consists of those possessed by individuals in a private capacity; they are enforced by the organs of state, but only on the motion of the individual. This—the sphere of the Roman *ius privatum*—was the subject of what we should now call civil procedure. A second class of rights are those enforced by the State on individuals; when the enforcement of these rights possesses a penal character, or when the activity of State is called forth in consequence of wrongs done by individuals to one another which it is its recognized duty to repair, we have the subject of what we generally call criminal procedure. But it is hardly necessary to remark that the spheres of civil and criminal jurisdiction of no modern state correspond exactly to those of Rome, nor indeed were the spheres marked out in precisely the same manner at different periods of Roman history. The variations in forms of procedure in different countries, or at different times in the same country, may be either material or formal. Material differences are furnished by the classes

Material differences between the civil and criminal law.

[1] *Ius* is perhaps connected with the Sanskrit *ju* (to join), and has the same root as *iubere*. For the meanings of the word see Nettleship, *Contributions to Latin Lexicography*, p. 497; Clark, *Pract. Jurisprudence*, pp. 16-20; Bréal, *Sur l'origine des mots designant le droit en Latin* in Nouvelle Revue Historique de Droit, vol. vii (1883), p. 604 ff.

[2] Nep. *Attic.* 6; Ter. *Ph.* v. 7, 43 'in ius ambula.' Cf. the phrase 'in ius vocare' (Cic. *in Verr.* ii. 76, 187).

of cases which are brought respectively before the civil and criminal courts. In Rome, for instance, the neglect of family obligations was in the earliest times a matter for the criminal jurisdiction of the religious courts; theft was, throughout the whole of the Republican period, treated, not as a subject for criminal cognisance, but as a delict for which compensation was to be recovered by civil process; adultery, on the other hand, was not a subject for action but for criminal prosecution[1] Such material differences are part of the general legal history of nations or ages; they are based on ethical conceptions which alter from land to land or from time to time. In a history of procedure we must assume them, but it is not our business to examine into their causes. Far more important are the formal differences exhibited by the structure of the courts themselves. This structure changes from time to time in a nation's history, sometimes in obedience to a change in the conceptions of material law, but oftener still from considerations of pure convenience or from alterations in the administrative machinery of government directed by wholly political, often external, considerations. The civil and criminal courts may at one moment be kept widely apart, at another they may seem almost to be merged into one another. The Romans grasped, as few nations have done, the fundamental distinction between public and private law, and they regarded criminal law as a part of the former. Had a fixed and lasting constitution been given them by a legislator of the Greek type, the spheres might have been kept permanently apart. But, as it was, their procedure like their law was made by the 'genius of many,' not of one[2]. Symmetry was sacrificed to convenience, and a series of experimental improvements resulted in

Formal differences between civil and criminal procedure.

[1] In early times before a family court; by the *lex Iulia* (perhaps of 17 B.C.), before a *quaestio*.

[2] Cic. *de Rep.* ii. 1, 2 'nostra autem res publica (in contrast with the Greek polities) non unius esset ingenio sed multorum, non una hominis vita sed aliquot constituta saeculis et aetatibus.'

a composite structure in which the lines of civil and criminal procedure were ever crossing. So closely interwoven were the two that it is difficult to study one branch intelligently without a considerable knowledge of the other. A brief anticipatory sketch of the chief epochs in the history of procedure at Rome may furnish a justification for the choice of the Ciceronian period as the best available standpoint from which to view the changes.

Sketch of procedure at Rome. First period: Early religious law.

In the earliest times the appeal to religious law is almost universal. The Roman State was nearer a theocracy than any European community of which we possess records. The king may have been himself the head of the religious guild of pontiffs; but, whether he was or not, the pontifical college was at least his judicial council. With them rested the knowledge of 'divine' or 'family' law (*ius divinum*), and of the mode in which retribution (*poena*, *ποινή*) should be exacted for sin. The ordinary civil and the ordinary criminal law are entrusted to the same hands; yet it appears that from the first a clear distinction was drawn between the procedure meant to secure the adjustment of private claims and the process by which penal pronouncements were made in consequence of such a violation of private and religious right as could be looked on as a sin. Civil and criminal procedure are even now distinct, and there was a third department of the judicial organization of the State which emphasized still further this distinction.

Early military law.

A strict discipline is enforced by the king as the military head of the community; the pontiffs have no authoritative voice on such conceptions as those of treason (*perduellio*). They are for the king and his delegates alone. He may, if he pleases, submit such charges on appeal to the people, and in such references we have at least some of the germs of the late popular jurisdiction. But, whether the jurisdiction be the king's or the people's, the important fact is that from the first we have evidences of a court whose proceedings are untainted by religious law.

We cannot give very definite limits for what may be called the second great period of Roman procedure. It begins with the revolution which overthrew the monarchy (509 B.C.), it gathers strength with the codification effected by the Law of the Twelve Tables (451 B.C.), it culminates with the publication of the forms of action (*circa* 304 B.C.), and it may be said to last down to the middle of the second century B.C., when great reforms were effected, in criminal procedure by the introduction of the *quaestiones perpetuae*, in civil procedure by the supremacy of the written *formula* over the verbal *legis actio*. During this period the pontifical assistance in civil jurisdiction and the pontifical sanctions in criminal jurisdiction became extinct. In civil procedure, although the *legis actio* still remains as a burdensome legacy of religion, cases are decided by reference to purely secular authorities. Some of the criminal procedure of the *pontifices* has taken a wholly different and exceedingly useful form. Many of the sins which they visited with their awful bans are now made the grounds of political disability by the censors; other offences, which the community was obliged to treat as crimes, have been taken up by the secular arm; they are tried in what had been the royal courts (*iudicia regia*), now the courts of the magistrates and people combined (*iudicia populi*). In this period there was a greater correspondence than ever before or after between civil procedure and private law, criminal procedure and public law. But it was a correspondence that was destined to be transitory.

Second period: Secularization of law. Separation of civil from criminal procedure.

In the third period, which commences with the middle of the second century B.C., the civil courts are in their main characteristics unaltered, but a great simplification of procedure has been introduced, partly through the influence of the praetor, partly through law, by the use of a simple written *formula* in place of the verbal plaint of the *legis actio*. Criminal procedure, on the other hand,

Third period: Simplification of civil procedure and influence of civil on criminal procedure.

has undergone a radical change. The State has proved itself unequal to the task of protecting its citizens and its subjects by its own initiative. This protection is relegated to the initiative of private individuals, who voice their complaints before courts—the *quaestiones perpetuae* or *iudicia publica*—whose constitution recalls the structure of the civil far more than that of the earlier criminal *iudicia*. With the growth of a scientific jurisprudence civil and criminal law were more distinct than ever, but never perhaps was there a greater approximation of the principles of civil and criminal procedure to one another. Yet one important difference still remained. The criminal courts could for the most part be set in motion by any citizen, not merely by the party directly interested. Criminal jurisdiction is thus still an activity of the State, still a part of *ius publicum*.

Importance of Cicero's epoch for this final change.

For the first of these three periods accurate and detailed reconstruction is of course impossible; it is a period that belongs, not so much to the epoch of the monarchy as to the earlier portion of that epoch. Even here Cicero, in his constitutional writings, is one of our best and earliest guides. But for the other two periods the epoch of Cicero is the best worth studying, if we are to choose an epoch or an author at all. Even if we set aside the obvious fact that nowhere but in Cicero's works do we come face to face with the courts of the Republic at all, we find that the times of the orator's life and writings correspond to two great changes in procedure. In civil process they mark the transition period from the *legis actio* to the *formula*; they exist side by side in Cicero's day. In criminal process the new system of *quaestiones perpetuae* has not yet stamped out all relics of the older system of the *iudicia populi*. The new procedure is nearly triumphant, but not quite.

Final differences between civil and

Although in the Ciceronian period there was, as we have said, something like a fusion of the principles of civil and criminal procedure in one particular department of jurisdiction, yet there are certain external marks which enable us to distinguish a civil action from a criminal prosecution.

criminal procedure.

The right of taking action.

(i) The first series of differences is connected with the right of taking action. In a civil suit only the party directly interested, or a duly accredited representative could bring the action. In a criminal case, the right to prosecute was in nearly all cases open to every citizen, subject to certain disabilities of age or sex, standing or character. A civil action is never undertaken by the State, except the State has a pecuniary interest in the matter to be decided; the action then becomes an outcome of Administrative Law, which belongs to a distinct category and demands a separate discussion. In this particular case the State may appear as both accuser and judge, but this is the only case of their identity in a non-criminal process. In early criminal procedure at Rome the *rôles* of accuser and judge were sometimes played by the same individual, the magistrate undertaking the criminal investigation; but the tendency of development even in the criminal law was to separate the parts, and by the period of the epoch of the *quaestiones perpetuae* they have become quite distinct.

The recipient of the satisfaction.

(ii) Another difference lies in the recipient of the satisfaction finally given by the judgement. In civil procedure the plaintiff is the recipient; and this is the case even where civil procedure is applied to delicts such as theft. Incidentally the State may gain some material advantage from a stage in the process; thus in the 'action by oath' (*actio sacramento*), the *sacramentum* (as the fine deposited for the perjury came itself to be called) went to the State. But this is only an incident in the process, a means of securing the main issue for one or other of the litigants. In criminal procedure, on the other hand, the satisfaction is appropriated or inflicted by the State, according as it takes the form of a fine or of some other punishment. It is true that in some *iudicia publica*—those e.g. for extortion and peculation—the individual plaintiff or the clients he represents may gain compensation for damage; but care was usually taken to separate the criminal from the civil aspect of these courts. In their final form they present the appearance of criminal courts which give rise to a civil *iudicium.*

Administrative jurisdiction. Its two departments.

For purposes of simplification administrative jurisdiction has been omitted in the foregoing sketch, as, from its too close connexion with public law, it must be exempted from detailed discussion in this work; but it is of some importance to consider how far such jurisdiction can give rise to anything resembling a civil or criminal process. By Administrative Jurisdiction should be meant the Jurisdiction consequent on ordinances which the government has issued for the support of the state machinery, or else that consequent on obligations or claims which the government has had to meet or enforce for the same purpose. The first kind of jurisdiction must be always of a coercive or quasi-criminal kind; the second will always have something of a civil character.

Enforcement of state-sanctions.

The most frequent example of the first kind of jurisdiction at Rome is furnished by the means adopted for the enforcement of monetary penalties which form the sanction of administrative ordinances. When the sanction of a law creates penalties for disobedience, two modes of enforcing these penalties are possible. They may be enforced on the individual transgressor by the direct action of the State operating through the power of coercion (*coercitio*) of its magistrates. This procedure—especially in cases where an appeal from the penalty to the sovereign people is allowed—gives rise to a *iudicium* of a criminal character. But the penalty may also be exacted by a more indirect act on the part of the State. The delinquent may be the object of an action brought before the ordinary civil judge either by a magistrate or by any citizen representing the community. In this case a *iudicium* resembling that of ordinary civil process is established[1]. Thus modes of procedure analogous to those of the ordinary civil as well as of the ordinary criminal courts are possible in this department of coercive or quasi-criminal administrative law. The procedure differs according as the State takes on itself the *rôle* of plaintiff or of judge.

Enforcement or satisfaction of claims or obligations of the State.

It is evident, when we turn to the second department of administrative law, that there is an extension of the parts that the State may play. In enforcing claims it is a plaintiff, in meeting obligations it is a defendant. The only question is whether it shall, in both cases, be judge as well. Although evidence on the subject is extremely slight, it is possible that at Rome the State, through the cognisance of the magistrate, may originally have taken upon itself the right of deciding cases in which it was personally interested[2]; but the alternative procedure—the sure sign of an advancing political civilization—of forcing

[1] This stage is illustrated by the procedure enjoined by the *lex Bantina* (*circa* 130 B.C.), ii. 9-11. It is enjoined 'eam pequniam quei volet magistratus exsigito. Sei postulabit quei petet, pr(aetor) recuperatores . . . dato . . . facitoque ioudicetur.' By the side of the new we have the old method of enforcing the legal penalty, for it is prescribed (l. 12) that 'Sei quis mag(istratus) multam inrogare volet . . . liceto.' For instances of the later procedure in Cicero's time we may cite the *multa* exacted from C. Junius, the president of the court which condemned Oppianicus (Cic. *pro Cluent.* 33, 89-91), and from a *iudex* in the same process (ib. 37, 103). Such a *iudicium publicum* was conducted before Verres in his urban praetorship (Cic. *in Verr.* i. 60, 155 'Atque etiam iudicium in praetura publicum exercuit... Petita multa est apud istum praetorem a Q. Opimio, qui adductus est in iudicium . . . quod, cum esset tribunus plebis, intercessisset contra legem Corneliam'). The powers given to the ten commissioners under Rullus' bill in 63 B.C. seem to have conferred very wide powers of penal administrative jurisdiction (Cic. *de leg. agr.* ii. 13, 33 'datur cognitio sine consilio, poena sine provocatione, animadversio sine auxilio'). Where *recuperatores* were not employed a *consilium* was usual (Cic. *in Verr.* v. 21, 53). For a *multa* of the kind enforced by such processes see Cic. *pro Caec.* 33, 98. The chief sphere of administrative law illustrated by Cicero's writings is that found in provincial jurisdiction. It is treated in Book I, Part II, §§ 2 (b).

[2] According to Mommsen (*Staatsr.* i. p. 172) this was the ruling principle.

the State or its representatives to adopt procedure either ordinary or analogous to that of the ordinary civil law, seems to have prevailed. In such cases the representatives of the State may have continued to possess some privileges as plaintiffs, and even as defendants; for it is difficult to eliminate even from the most democratic community such relics of the theory that the State is something more and higher than the citizens.

In the exercise of administrative jurisdiction of this second character it is possible to have another party to the suit besides the State and its immediate plaintiff or defendant. In inquiries undertaken by the government concerning the tenure of land, the possessor may have played the part of defendant, a claimant other than the State that of plaintiff[1]. Although the extraordinary nature of such commissions makes them a part of administrative jurisdiction, the procedure followed in such cases would in all probability have been that of the ordinary civil courts.

Thus Administrative Jurisdiction is at every point in such constant contact with the ordinary civil and criminal procedure, that it cannot be wholly ignored in a treatise on these subjects. To exclude it would be to forget the fact that the determining characteristics of the Roman government were largely due to its courts, and that, though their sovereignty was non-existent in the eye of the law, and they remained mere agents of the people, the necessity for their practical supremacy so strongly appealed to the Roman legal mind that their principles were followed even in departments to which their powers did not directly extend.

[1] In the jurisdiction enjoined by the *lex agraria* of III B.C. (ll 36–39), the *publicanus* is the plaintiff. In other cases one who claimed to be *dominus* might have brought an action for recovery before the commissioners.

BOOK I

CIVIL PROCEDURE

PART I

THE COURTS OF THE MONARCHY AND EARLY REPUBLIC

§ 1. *Theory of Civil Procedure at Rome; the Magistrate and the Iudex.*

The essentials of a Roman civil court.

THE immediate essentials of an act of civil procedure are the parties to the action, the methods which they adopt, and the court which gives the judgement. Of these three the last is often the most significant, as giving the key to the theory of the jurisdiction exercised, and as it is the primary condition of justice being done at all, and as its character is less variable than that of the other two elements, it demands an early consideration. The Roman civil court has the first characteristic which we have mentioned in an exceptional degree; its constitution in itself expresses a theory of justice, and its composite character contains the germ of that distinction which has now become well-nigh universal—the distinction between judge and jury, law and fact. From the very earliest times to which tradition carries us we find a fundamental division of competence between the magistrate on the one hand and the *iudex* or *iudices* on the other; the utterance of the first gives *ius*, the utterance of the second makes

Magistrate and *iudex*; *ius* and *iudicium*.

this *ius* into a *iudicium*. The original theory which underlay this division of power between the skilled interpreter and the layman of practical common sense, which, whether it actually exercised an influence on the development of the modern jury-system or not[1], was yet one of the revelations of new principles that Roman Law has given to the world, has not unnaturally been the subject of much investigation and conjecture. We may at once set aside the view that it is the outcome of any abstract principle of justice, of a desire to separate for ideal ends the province of interpretation from that of principle. For, even assuming that the unskilled is a better applier of principle than the skilled, the supposition that the primitive Roman mind was perplexed with the solution of such an abstract difficulty is wholly inadmissible. Theories of its origin based on the assumption of practical or political difficulties demand more respect. It has been thought that the object was to create an essential division of the judicial power for the purpose of guarding against unjust and arbitrary sentences on the part of the magistrate[2]. In this case the institution of the *iudex* would be akin to the collegiate principle which was introduced into the magistracy, and would have been regarded as an added safeguard to the constitution[3]. This view, apart from the somewhat anachronistic idea of the '*essential* division of the judicial power,' is closely akin to another which represents the institution of the *iudex* as the outcome of a desire for popular control; the simple *cognitio* of the magistrate did not content the parties; hence the creation of the special *iudex* and of the boards of *decemviri* and *centumviri*[4]. This theory represents the institution of the

Theories as to the origin of these distinctions.

[1] On this point see Brunner, *Entstehung der Schwurgerichte*, p. 16 ff.

[2] Puchta, *Inst.* §§ ii. 175, note n.

[3] It may be noted that the democratic king Servius Tullius is said to have contemplated putting the monarchy into commission (Liv. i. 48), and to have instituted the *iudex* (Dionys. iv. 25).

[4] Bernhöft, *Staat und Recht d. Königszeit*, p. 230; cf. Merkel, *Gesch. d. klass. Appellation*, p. 127.

iudex as analogous to that of the appeal to the people; it brings it into relation with the *provocatio* and with the later institution of the *iudices* of the criminal courts. Savigny takes a still more practical view. The division was introduced merely to lighten the burden of the praetor's duties: for without the *iudex* civil jurisdiction could not have been transacted by two civil praetors at Rome. His appointment was necessary only when doubtful facts had to be settled; where there was no doubt as to the matter of fact the praetor delivered the judgement himself, for, in this case, 'he could pronounce a judgement as quickly and as certainly as he could draw up a *formula* for the *iudex*[1].' The questionable character of the latter part of the statement we shall examine later; but it is obvious that the motive here given for the institution of the *iudex* in connexion with the praetorship applies with equal force to the period when the consuls were the supreme heads of the judicature, and *a fortiori* to the epoch when the *rex* was the only judge. The element common to all these explanations is that they represent the division of the judicial authority as an artificial institution, introduced at a time when the State had a definite political organization. But it is possible that the *iudex* is a more ancient institution than the magistrate, perhaps even than the State. It has been held that, so far from being an institution of the State, he is an arbitrator chosen by compact between the parties, his appointment by them being based on the notion of self-help which is so prominent in early Roman, as in early Greek Law[2]. It is true that a public official assists in his appointment, but the idea that the consent of the parties was necessary to the validity of the choice never died out of the Republican law of Rome[3].

Probable early origin for the Roman *iudex*.

Here in all probability we have the real origin of this

The *iudex* is an arbi-

[1] Savigny, *System*, vi. p. 287.
[2] Ihering, *Geist*, i. p. 169.
[3] Cic. *pro Cluent.* 43, 120.

BOOK I.

trator and a relic of clan life.

peculiarity of the Roman Judicature. The *iudex* is a legacy from the life of the clan (*gens*), and of the village (*vicus*), which preceded the life of the State. In these communes the headman may have presided at the solemn ritual of action; but, once this ritual has been performed, the issue is placed in the hands of an arbitrator (*arbiter* or *iudex*[1]) chosen by the litigants. The communes are finally united under the headship of a strong military monarchy, supported by the religious wisdom of a body chosen from the Patriciate. Tradition says that the

His later subordination.

monarch at times dispensed with the arbitrator[2]; even when he gave him, it was necessarily under stricter conditions than before. A strong government knows of no right of private judgement in matters of law; even of customary law the king and the magistrate is the guardian and exponent[3]. Hence the secondary position of the *iudex* as an interpreter of facts. But, secondary as his position was, his existence was of profound significance for the character of Roman procedure. By facilitating the business of the courts he rendered possible that unity of jurisdiction which gave the world the praetor's edict; he is a salutary, sometimes a galling restraint on the caprice of the magistrate[4]; he is an embodiment of popular liberty, a guarantee that the common sense of the market shall modify the science of the law-court in the discussion and decision of private claims.

§ 2. *The Magistrate.*

(*a*) *At Rome.*

The king.

Rome, in the earliest period of which we have any certain knowledge, possessed but a single magistrate, who

[1] Cf. Cic. *pro Mur.* 12, 27. [2] Dionys. iv. 25.

[3] Cic. *de Rep.* v. 2, 3 'nec vero quisquam privatus erat disceptator aut arbiter litis, sed omnia conficiebantur iudiciis regiis.'

[4] The litigant might complain to the *iudex* of the praetor's conduct; see Cic. *pro Tull.* 16, 38 'in iudicio queri praetoris iniquitatem, quod "de iniuria" (in formula) non addiderit.'

bore a variety of titles. He was known as *Dictator*, a word of uncertain meaning, as the 'master of the people' (*magister populi*), more generally as the 'Regulator' of things human and divine (*Rex*), and by titles with which we are more expressly concerned, for they mark him out as the supreme head of jurisdiction, those of *praetor*[1] and *iudex*. The king, although the true head and representing the active intelligence of the State, exercising, in Cicero's language, an *imperium* of the reason over the passions of the body politic[2], yet cannot be regarded as more than the magistrate and the minister of the people. Indications of popular sovereignty appear on every hand. According to the best tradition, the Roman people is the source of law, and, though the initiative for an act of legislation can come only from the king, yet the validity of a standing ordinance of a general character rested on the votes of the Assembly[3]. Tradition also affirms the *Populus* to have been the source of honour. Even the royal *insignia*, borrowed from Etruria, and adopted by the kings of Rome, could be assumed by them only after ratification by the senate and people[4]; and, although officers appointed for special purposes were not magistrates but strictly delegates of the king, yet the permission to exercise such power of delegation could be gained only through a law of the Comitia of the Curiae[5]. The people, too, possessed a share in criminal jurisdiction; whether their intervention took the form of an exercise of the truly sovereign right of pardon, or whether it was due to a long-standing privilege of trying criminal cases as a final court of appeal, the existence of the *provocatio* in the regal

Relations of the king to the people.

[1] Varro, *L. L.* v. 80 'Praetor dictus, qui praeiret iure et exercitu.' It is possible, however, that this title is a purely military one.

[2] Cic. *de Rep.* i. 38, 60.

[3] Dionys. ii. 14.

[4] Dionys. iii. 62; Cic. *de Rep.* ii. 17, 31.

[5] For the appointment of the earliest *quaestores* in this fashion see Tac. *Ann.* xi. 22; Ulpian, in Dig. i. 13.

BOOK I.

period is assured[1]. The shackles of the regal authority created by these popular rights made the king's command of his subjects an *mperium legitimum*[2]. Possibly a more absolute rule in the days when king Romulus is said to have 'lorded it over his burgesses as he pleased[3],' by the close of the monarchy it had been so thoroughly encased in a net of precedents, of conventions, even of ordinances elicited by progressive kings from the people and 'meant to be binding on future monarchs[4],' that freedom from these restraints—a freedom attempted by the Tarquins—was an act of revolution, and prepared the way for the counter-revolution which introduced the Republic[5].

The *imperium.*

Yet the *imperium*, even with these limitations, was a mighty power, unparalleled in the magistracies of any other than the early Italian Republics[6]. The unity of power it expressed, symbolized by the variety of titles borne by its possessor, made the king the sole executive authority in the State[7]. The sole right of jurisdiction in the first instance, the sole authority in war, are signified by the word, and, whether directly comprised in it or not, the sole right of laying matters before the people for their approval or dissent was possessed by the holder of the *imperium*[8].

[1] Liv. i. 26; Cic. *de Rep.* ii. 31, 54. On this early *provocatio* see Book II.

[2] Sall. *Cat.* 6.

[3] Tac. *Ann.* iii. 26 'nobis Romulus, ut libitum, imperitaverat.'

[4] Tac. *ib.* 'praecipuus Servius Tullius sanctor legum fuit, quis etiam reges obtemperarent.' 'Sanctor' and 'Sancire' are not used solely of self-given ordinances; cf. Tac. *Ann.* i. 6, and Puntschart, *Grundgesetzliches Civilrecht*, i. p. 3.

[5] Dionys. iv. 43; cf. Cic. *de Rep.* ii. 24, 44.

[6] Aristotle's reference to the *αὐτοκράτορες μόναρχοι* amongst certain *βάρβαροι* (*Pol.* vi. 10, 2) is perhaps not so much a reference to the Dictatorship of Rome as to the similar governments in Italy.

[7] It is in this sense that he could be said to possess πᾶσα ἀρχή (Plut. *Ti. Gracch.* 15).

[8] In later Roman history this power became in certain cases dissociated from the *imperium*. But the *auspicia* are the religious side of the *imperium*, and no one not in possession of the auspices can lay matters before the people.

PART I.

Respective shares of the king and the people in legislation.

The initiative in legislation lies with the king, but laws are, at least in the main, the utterances of the people. It has been held that the law asked for by the magistrate and granted by the people (*lex rogata*) is a two-sided act, an agreement between the magistrate on the one hand, and the people on the other [1]. This conclusion is based on the analogous uses of the word *lex* in other connexions where it seems always to imply a contractual relation [2]. But, because an ordinance when established must imply a contractual relation, it is not quite a justifiable conclusion that its creation implies the co-operation of two parties The primary meaning of the word is something that is laid down [3], and this may be the work of a single authority. That most of the general ordinances of an important character which were introduced during the monarchy were laid down by the people was certainly the view of most ancient inquirers; but it is modified by the idea that there also existed régal *instituta* independent of the *leges* of the community [4]. The true line of separation between the spheres on which the people and the king could respectively pronounce with authority would probably have been between the province of *ius* on the one hand, and those of *fas* and *res militaris* on the other. Any fundamental alteration in what was then regarded as *ius*, whether public or private, might have demanded the consent of the citizens; but it does not appear that the king, as the head of religion and the army, was subject in any way to the popular will. Many of the ordinances which gave rise to civil jurisdiction may have come under the head of *ius*, but it must be remembered that a great many relations which were in later Roman history subjects for

Ius and *fas*; the *leges regiae*.

[1] Mommsen, *Staatsr.* iii. pp. 304–312.

[2] e. g. in business we have *leges censoriae*, *leges locationis*: in corporations a *lex collegii*. In augury the answer of the gods to a request is *legum dictio*. See Mommsen, *l. c.*

[3] Connected with the German *legen* (Gothic *lagjan*) as *θεσμός* with *τίθημι*.

[4] Cic. *Tusc. disp.* iv. 1, 1.

the investigation of the civil courts came at an earlier period under the head of *fas*. Now it is with these relations that the so-called royal laws (*leges regiae*) seem chiefly to have been concerned. A collection of such ordinances dating from the monarchy is said to have been made at a very early period by one Papirius, a member of the college of pontiffs; a commentary on this collection written by Granius Flaccus, a jurist of the age of the dictator Caesar, preserved it from oblivion, and it was much drawn on by later writers. The fragments of the contents which have been preserved show that it dealt largely with family relations, and almost exclusively with religious law [1]. It was the product of the pontifical college with the king either as its exponent or as its head. But, if we may trust tradition, a secularising spirit was at work even towards the close of the Roman monarchy. Servius Tullius, the representative of the lay and reforming spirit amongst the Roman kings, is said to have been the originator of fifty laws on contracts and delicts, and these he ratified before the assembly of the curiae [2].

The king as the authentic interpreter of law,

But, whatever might be the ultimate source of the civil law, there is no doubt that the king was its authentic interpreter. He was the 'guardian of the laws and ancestral customs [3],' the guardian in the sense of keeping them and doling them out to applicants when they were required. The interpretation given by active and unfettered jurisdiction is one of an extraordinarily elastic kind. This is especially the case in an age when the conceptions of law are concrete, when the special utterance, rather than the principle that underlies it, seems the 'law.'

[1] See the references in Bruns, *Fontes Iuris Romani*.

[2] Dionys. iv. 13 τοὺς νόμους τούς τε συναλλακτικοὺς καὶ τοὺς περὶ τῶν ἀδικημάτων ἐπεκύρωσε ταῖς φράτραις· ἦσαν δὲ πεντήκοντά που μάλιστα τὸν ἀριθμόν.

[3] Dionys. ii. 14 νόμων τε καὶ πατρίων ἐθισμῶν φυλακὴν ποιεῖσθαι. Puntschart (*Grundgesetzl. C. R.* i. p. 19) compares Cicero's language about the praetor (*de Leg.* iii. 3, 8) 'iuris civilis custos esto.'

PART I.

In fact the utterances of the kings are themselves *leges*; his *formulae* take the place of the principles on which they are based[1]. So great is the power of the interpretation of the king that we are almost justified in calling him the source of law in the form in which it reached the community[2]. But though the king was formally the only authentic exponent both of *ius* and *fas*, both he and the litigants must have been bound to make constant appeals to the body which preserved not only the secrets of law but the mysteries of procedure. This was the college of pontiffs which may perhaps be regarded as the judicial *consilium* of the kings in matters of private and religious law. There was a difference of opinion in antiquity as to whether the king was himself the titular head of this college[3]; but the facts that five pontiffs are said to have been instituted in the regal period[4], and that by the year 300 B.C. the number had sunk to four[5], may show that the king himself was reckoned a member of the college, and that the abolition of the monarchy reduced the number of the board by one[6]. Even so it is by no means certain that the king bore the title *Pontifex Maximus*, and it is possible that he delegated some of his powers as the undisputed head of the state-religion to an official of that name[7]. But, whatever may have been his position in the college, the transitory king must have been very greatly dependent on the permanent board for his knowledge of

assisted by the pontifical college.

[1] Dionys. x. 1 *τὸ δικαιωθὲν ὑπ' ἐκείνων τοῦτο νόμος ἦν.* Cf. Liv. i. 26 'Lex horrendi carminis.'

[2] Cic. *de Rep.* v. 2, 3 '(nihil esse tam) regale quam explanationem aequitatis, in qua iuris erat interpretatio, quod ius privati petere solebant a regibus.'

[3] On the one hand Livy (i. 20) speaks of King Numa selecting Numa Marcius as the pontiff; on the other Plutarch (*Numa* 9), Zosimus (iv. 36) and Servius (*ad Aen.* iii. 81) make the king pontiff.

[4] Cic. *de Rep.* ii. 14, 26.

[5] Liv. x. 1.

[6] Bouché-Leclerq, *Les Pontifes de l'ancienne Rome*, p. 9.

[7] This may be the truth reflected in Livy's account. See note 3.

the law and the peculiar ceremonies that were necessary to put it into action.

The theory that all courts are the king's.

Yet of the ceremonial as of the law the king was in theory the undisputed lord; 'all judicial business was transacted in the king's courts[1],' and how it was transacted must have depended much on the power of the crown and on the personality of the reigning monarch. The institution of the *iudex* was, as we saw, probably older than the monarchy itself; but we are told that a succession of kings had exercised a purely personal jurisdiction in all cases until Servius Tullius again restored the balance between the royal prerogative and the liberties of the people. 'Public' cases (by which are probably meant cases of administrative as well as of criminal law) he reserved wholly to his own court. But for private suits he established *privati iudices*, to whom he gave the formula expressing the law and itself the *lex* under which the case was to be decided[2].

Delegation of jurisdiction.

Another power of delegation must have played a considerable part in the monarchy—the delegation, that is, of the power of giving '*ius*.' It is doubtful whether civil jurisdiction was entrusted to any official during the king's presence in Rome[3]. During his absence his *alter ego*, the praefect of the city (*praefectus urbi*), exercised jurisdiction as part of the general executive power with which he was entrusted[4].

Creation of consuls.

The change from king to consuls produced no essential

[1] Cic. *de Rep.* v. 2, 3 'omnia conficiebantur iudiciis regiis.'

[2] Dionys. iv. 25 *ἐκεῖνος διελὼν ἀπὸ τῶν ἰδιωτικῶν (ἐγκλημάτων) τὰ δημόσια, τῶν μὲν εἰς τὸ κοινὸν φερόντων ἀδικημάτων αὐτὸς ἐποιεῖτο τὰς διαγνώσεις, τῶν δ' ἰδιωτικῶν ἰδιώτας ἔταξεν εἶναι δικαστάς, ὅρους καὶ κανόνας αὐτοῖς τάξας, οὓς αὐτὸς ἔγραψε νόμους.* Cf. the *formula* employed in criminal jurisdiction when the case was delegated (Liv. i. 26). *τὰ δημόσια* cannot include capital cases, for Dionysius (iii. 22) believes that these were tried before the people from the time of Tullus Hostilius.

[3] The delegation of the trial of minor delicts (*ἀδικήματα*) is made by Dionysius (ii. 14) one of the privileges of the king.

[4] Tac. *Ann.* vi. 11.

Modifications of the regal jurisdiction.

alteration in the theory of civil jurisdiction. The single head of the State was replaced by two, invested with the *imperium* and with its accompanying powers of jurisdiction both criminal and civil. They too are, like the kings, *praetores* and *iudices*[1]. The general form of procedure was the same as it had been in the time of the monarchy: the magistrate decided what special rule of procedure was applicable, and the facts were decided by a *iudex* chosen by the parties. But there were three peculiarities of the new magistracy, as compared with the older one which it had replaced, which had an important influence in modifying the character of civil jurisdiction. These were the dual number, which expressed the new fact of colleagueship and therefore of conflicting authority introduced into the higher branches of the constitution, the annual tenure of office, and the fact that the consuls were not, like the king, either members of the college of pontiffs or in any way official heads of the state-religion. The effect of the first peculiarity was to introduce the principle of appeal (*appellatio*) from one colleague to the other on questions of law for the first time into Roman civil process—an innovation which was important in principle, although the facts that the appeal had to be made to the magistrate in person and that one of the consuls was usually absent from Rome could not have made it very effective in practice. The result of the two other peculiarities was to make the new magistrates far less of an independent authority and of an originative fount of law than the king had been. It was impossible for annually changing officials with no previous legal training in law (for law had not yet become a lay profession), and much occupied with administrative and military business, to profess a full knowledge of *ius*

Appellatio.

[1] Cic. *de Leg.* iii. 3, 8 'regio imperio duo sunto iique praeeundo iudicando consulendo praetores iudices consules appellamino'; cf. *de Rep.* ii. 32, 56. Varro (*L. L.* vi. 88) cites from the 'commentarii consulares' the old formula used in summoning the 'comitia centuriata':·'Accensus dicito sic "Omnes Quirites ite ad conventionem huc ad iudices."'

BOOK I.

Dependence of the consuls on the pontiffs.

or of the complex forms of action. Hence a great increase of authority to the college of pontiffs. For two hundred years (509–304 B.C.) they continued to possess the exclusive knowledge of the inner mysteries of procedure, and we have every reason to suppose that long before the publication of the Twelve Tables there originated the device for bringing this religious college into co-operation with the civil judges, which Pomponius describes as existing after this codification was effected. Since the formularies of action could be repeated correctly only by the aid of the college, this body annually appointed one of its members to 'preside over private suits[1].' By this 'presidency' is not meant the power of judgement; the pontiff is never a judge in civil law. His duty was to act as an adviser to the magistrate (perhaps even to the parties) and to be a witness to the correctness of the performance. This co-operation of the religious with the civil power was in no way weakened by the publication of the Law of the Twelve Tables. Startling as that code is in its thoroughness, its modernness, its frank recognition of the supremacy of plebeian law, it preserves a most curious reticence on the inner side of the working of the courts. It was the 'consummation of equal law[2], it revealed the Triad of the

Relations of the pontiffs and the civil judges.

[1] Pompon. in Dig. i. 2, 2, 6 (after the Twelve Tables) 'ex his legibus . . . actiones compositae sunt, quibus inter se homines disceptarent: quas actiones ne populus prout vellet institueret, certas sollemnesque esse voluerunt . . . omnium tamen harum et interpretandi scientia et actiones apud collegium pontificum erant, ex quibus constituebatur, quis quoque anno praeesset privatis.' One is surprised to find that the delegate of the college was not the Pontifex Maximus himself. Puntschart (*Grundgesetzl. C. R.* i. p. 42) explains the annual appointment by the desire of the college that each of its members should be in touch with practical life. The calendar was as secret as the actions (Cic. *pro Mur.* 11, 25 'Posset agi lege necne pauci quondam sciebant: fastos enim vulgo non habebant. Erant in magna potentia qui consulebantur, a quibus etiam dies tamquam a Chaldaeis petebatur'). For the importance of the pontifices in the development of law, even after its secularisation, see Cic. *de Orat.* iii. 33, 134; *de Leg.* ii. 19, 47 'ex patre audivi pontificem bonum neminem esse nisi qui ius civile cognosset.'

[2] 'Finis aequi iuris' (Tac. *Ann.* iii. 27).

iura[1],' it was the 'fountain of all public and private right[2],' but it was not a source from which any one who willed could draw the rules which would enable him to conduct his own case without flaw in word or action. Its rhythmic language (*carmen*)[3] recalled the *actiones* but did not reveal them. We find, indeed, that the simplest rules of procedure are laid down in the law; there are directions for the summons of parties and witnesses, and for the length of the trial; but the forms of action were nowhere found, these were still hidden with the pontiffs. Their revelation did not come until after many changes had been introduced into the source of civil jurisdiction. The great censor Appius Claudius Caecus is said, doubtless in his capacity of pontiff, to have 'systematized' (perhaps recorded in writing) forms of action[4], which were published by his clerk Cn. Flavius[5]. Publication, although a sign of the secularisation of jurisprudence, was of little practical use for lawyers until it showed and explained the relation of the actions to the written law. No work of this kind was produced until the end of the third or the beginning of the second century. Then appeared (*circa* 200 B.C.) the *Tripertita* of Sextus Aelius Paetus, classed by Cicero amongst the 'old interpreters' of the Twelve Tables[6]. The book gave in three divisions the text of the Tables, an explanation of them, and the form

Revelation of the forms of action.

Publication of the relation of the forms to the law. The beginnings of jurisprudence.

[1] Auson. *Idyll.* xi. 61–62:—

'Ius triplex tabulae quod ter sanxere quaternae,
Sacrum, privatum, populi commune quod usquam est.'

[2] 'Fons omnis publici privatique est iuris' (Liv. iii. 34).

[3] Cic. *de Leg.* ii. 23, 59 'discebamus enim pueri xii, ut carmen necessarium, quas iam nemo discit.'

[4] Pompon. in Dig. 1, 2, 2, 7 'Postea cum Appius Claudius proposuisset et ad formam redegisset has actiones, Gnaeus Flavius scriba eius libertini filius subreptum librum populo tradidit.'

[5] Pompon. in Dig. *l. c.*; Cicero (*ad Att.* vi. 1, 8) speaks of a view that Cn. Flavius, besides publishing the Fasti (cf. *pro Mur.* 11, 25) 'actiones composuisse.' Cf. *de Orat.* i. 41, 186 'expositis a Cn. Flavio primum actionibus.'

[6] 'Veteres interpretes' (Cic. *de Leg.* ii. 23, 59).

of procedure applicable to each case. Aelius is also said to have added new forms of action which were published in a more popular work known as *ius Aelianum*[1]. The introduction of new forms to meet the increasing demands of a widening civic life shows the expansiveness of procedure in the hands of the secular lawyers.

Meanwhile great changes had been at work in the presidency of the civil courts. Mixed motives, partly of necessity, partly of political sentiment, had led to the practical abolition of the consulship. The office was suspended, and the three, four or six military tribunes with consular power (*tribuni militum consulari potestate*) succeeded in 445 B.C. to the *ius*, *imperium* and *potestas* of the consuls. This provisional government, and the almost contemporaneous institution of the censorship (443 B.C.) show a recognition of the necessity of dividing up the military, judicial and registrative duties of the supreme magistrate with as little disturbance to the constitution as possible. The necessity for this division is proved by the fact that, out of the seventy-seven years extending from 444 to 367, twenty-two show consular *collegia*, fifty-one those of military tribunes. At the close of this period (the epoch of the Licinio-Sextian rogations which secured a share in the consulate to the plebeians) a permanent solution of the difficulty was at last reached. A third colleague was given to the consuls, who bore their early title of *praetor*, and two curule aediles were added to the early plebeian officials of that name to assist them in the police duties of the city. To the praetor is given the whole charge of civil jurisdiction. The contentious jurisdiction of private law is no longer exercised by the consul in Rome or Italy; but this is rather because the power is dormant

The military tribunate.

The praetor and the curule aediles.

[1] Pompon. *l. c.* § 7 'augescente civitate, quia deerant quaedam genera agendi . . . Sextus Aelius alias actiones composuit et librum populo dedit, qui appellatur Ius Aelianum.' For the distinction of this work from the *Tripertita* see Huschke in *Zeitschr. f. gesch. R. W.* xv. p. 177 ff. Cicero speaks also of 'Sex. Aelii commentarii' (*de Orat.* i. 56, 240).

than because it is extinct. The praetor, even as president of the civil courts, is not entirely out of relation to his greater colleague (*collega maior*). An appeal from the praetor to the consul in a matter of jurisdiction is theoretically possible, and there is at least one instance dating from the Ciceronian period (77 B.C.) of its actual exercise[1]. The consul, in this case, vetoes a decision of the praetor urbanus with regard to the granting of an inheritance—the possession of goods (*bonorum possessio*) given by praetorian law. The act of the praetor here (although in accord with the civil law) is an outcome of his *imperium*; the case affords little ground for thinking that the strict processes of *ius civile* were in any way supervised by the consul, and indeed consular interference with praetorian jurisdiction of any kind must have been extremely rare.

Survival of consular jurisdiction.

The single praetor, thus created, was for over a hundred years (366–242) the sole civil magistrate of Rome, and his sphere of jurisdiction increased as Rome's conquests spread. Not only did the Roman citizen colonies planted in Italy and the various communities on which the private rights of Roman citizenship had been conferred come within this sphere, but foreigners from communities which had treaty relations with Rome must have frequently appeared before his court. The processes of Roman civil law could not be applied to these strangers. It was not so much that the Roman would not grant it as that the stranger would have hesitated to accept the gift. Dispatch in his business before the courts was what was wanted by the busy Carthaginian trader at Rome, and this could not be gained

[1] Val. Max. vii. 7, 6 'appelatus Mamercus (Aemilius Lepidus, cos. 77 B.C.) a Surdino, cuius libertus Genucium heredem fecerat, praetoriam iurisdictionem abrogavit, quod diceret Genucium, amputatis sui ipsius sponte genitalibus corporis partibus, neque virorum neque mulierum numero haberi debere.' Savigny (*System* vi. p. 494) suggests that the disability was based on an analogous application of the *lex Voconia*, the eunuch being something less than a woman.

Growth of the *ius gentium.*

through the *legis actio.* As the *ius gentium*—the mixed Roman and peregrine code—must have originated ages before Rome dreamed of Empire and at least a century before the institution of the special foreign praetor, so we must suppose that some simple verbal procedure—the prototype of the later *formula*—must have been devised by the single praetor of early days to meet the wants of these foreign litigants. When the same judge administers two different types of laws, his ruling in one court is not unlikely to effect his ruling in the other, and the simplification of Roman law and Roman procedure through the *ius gentium* must (in spite of the inevitable absence of literary evidence of the fact) have begun at a much earlier period than the year 242 B.C. In this year the press of foreign business became so great that a second praetor was appointed whose duty it was to decide cases between *peregrini* and between members of this class and Roman citizens. The necessities of provincial administration subsequently increased the number of these magistrates, and, as the praetor's specific title was derived from his department of administration (*provincia*), of the two original 'home' praetors one was known as the *praetor qui inter cives ius dicit* or (in the colloquial phrase which became titular) as *praetor urbanus*: the other as the *praetor qui inter peregrinos ius dicit*, finally known as the *praetor peregrinus.* But both the home praetors were often spoken of as having *urbanae provinciae* and exercising *urbana iurisdictio*; their rank was higher than that of their provincial colleagues, and of the two the *praetor urbanus* was considered to hold the more distinguished position[1]. The business of his court was naturally much greater than that of his colleagues, and explains the law which prohibited him from being absent from Rome more than ten days during his year of

Appointment of the praetor peregrinus.

[1] App. *B. C.* ii. 112; cf. Cic. *pro Mur.* 20, 41 (of the urban praetorship) 'egregia et ad consulatum apta provincia.'

office[1]. The *insignia* of the praetor are in a modified form those of the consuls; as a magistrate armed with general administrative power he has the right to six lictors, and appears with the full number in a province; but as president of the courts of Rome he employed, or was allowed, only two[2]. The consideration of the praetor's method of jurisdiction must be deferred until we treat of the Ciceronian period; at present we pass to a magistracy, created at the same time, which also exercised civil jurisdiction although within a more limited sphere.

The aedileship and aedilician jurisdiction.

The new curule had been fused with the old plebeian aedileship into something like a single magistracy; but the limited civil jurisdiction of the aediles belonged to the curule members of the board alone. It is strange that it should have been so, for the curule aediles are as devoid of *imperium* (the usual source of jurisdiction) as their plebeian namesakes. But the jurisdiction is anomalous and must have been conferred on them by special enactment. It was connected partly with their care of the city (*cura urbis*), partly with that of the market. In their first capacity they gave the *formula* and appointed the *iudex* or board of assessment (*recuperatores*) in the case of damage done by wild beasts which were being led along the public roads[3]; in their second capacity they performed the same functions for the return of slaves and cattle sold under false pretences[4]. Their rulings on these subjects are

[1] Cic. *Phil.* ii. 13, 31 'cur M. Brutus (urban praetor in 44 B.C.) referente te legibus est solutus, si ab urbe plus quam decem dies afuisset?'

[2] The praetor is *sexfascalis*, *στρατηγὸς ἑξαπέλεκυς* (Polyb. iii. 40; App. *Syr.* 15), and appears with the full number in his province (Cic. *in Verr.* v. 54, 142 'sex lictores circumsistunt'); but in the exercise of his jurisdiction within the city he employs only two. Censorinus *de Die Nat.* 24, 3 'M. Plaetorius tr. pl. (of unknown date) scitum tulit, in quo est: praetor urbanus, qui nunc est quique posthac fuat, duo lictores apud se habeto usque supremam iusque inter cives dicito.' Cf. Cic. *de Leg. Agr.* ii. 34, 93.

[3] Dig. 21, 1 (Edict of the curule aediles), 40–42 'Ne quis canem, verrem vel minorem aprum, lupum, ursum, pantheram, leonem . . . qua vulgo iter fiet, ita habuisse velit, ut cuiquam nocere damnumve dare posset.'

[4] Gell. iv. 2 'In edicto curulium aedilium, qua parte de mancipiis

BOOK I. preserved for us in fragments of their edict as codified under Hadrian.

(b) *The Municipal Magistrate.*

Organization of Italy.

While Rome was extending her sway over Italy, the sphere of the jurisdiction of her magistrates kept pace with her conquering arms; for her policy of occupying conquered land by means of colonies of her own citizens, as well as her earlier policy of absorbing vanquished states wholly or partially into her own community, demanded an extension of central government beyond the limits of the purely Roman domain. On the organization of Italy, the first stage of which may be said to have been completed after the close of the war with Pyrrhus[1], the peninsula forms a vast military alliance of which Rome is the head, and its states (*civitates*) stand in varying degrees of dependence to the central power. Most of them fall under the general designation of military allies (*socii*) of Rome. These allies are either states who have received a charter of independence (*libertas*) from Rome, and are hence called *liberae civitates*, or who are in the still better position of having concluded a sworn treaty with Rome which recognizes their independence. The latter are the *foederatae* or *liberae et foederatae civitates*: and prominent amongst this second class, from certain peculiar privileges which they possess, are the *Latini*. Each member of

The *socii*.

vendundis cautum est, scriptum sic fuit: "Titulus singulorum scriptus sit curato ita, ut intelligi recte possit, quid morbi vitiique cuique sit, quis fugitivus errove sit noxave solutus non sit."' This edict (Dig. 21, 1) had reference to the sale of 'mancipia' (§§ 1, 1) and of 'iumenta' (§ 38). In both cases the promise is made 'Iudicium dabimus.' Cf. Cic. *de Off.* iii. 17, 71 'etiam in mancipiorum venditione venditoris fraus omnis excluditur. Qui enim scire debuit de sanitate, de fuga, de furtis, praestat edicto aedilium.' The jurisdiction of the curule aediles, based as it was on edict, could hardly have been earlier than the introduction of the *formula*. It can scarcely date back to the time when the *legis actio* was the sole form of action.

[1] The second stage was that effected by the social war. For this see Part II.

these two classes of *socii* is, in its corporate capacity, entirely exempt from Roman jurisdiction; for the *libertas* common to both implies even a modified degree of external sovereignty, far more that condition of internal control of their own affairs which the Greek states similarly gifted designated by the word *αὐτονομία*. Individually a member of a free or a free and allied community is a *peregrinus*, but a *peregrinus* who is no longer a *hostis*, for his state stands in treaty relations with Rome. While sojourning at Rome he appears before the court of the praetor peregrinus, and his case is settled by an appeal to that higher *ius gentium* which applied to the communities of Italy[1].

The *Latini*.

The Latins are on a different footing. It is true that as members of allied communities they possess their own laws, their own magistrates and their own jurisdiction; but the individual Latin who comes to Rome is, from the point of view of private law, a *civis*, and appears, like a Roman citizen, in the court of the praetor urbanus. For one of his peculiar privileges is the possession of the *ius commercii*, and the power to employ Roman methods of acquisition or transfer of property implies the necessity—for to the foreigner it is a necessity rather than a right—of having disputes arising from his business transactions at Rome settled by the ordinary processes of the *ius civile*. We do not know the rules which regulated the double jurisdiction to which members of the free and the allied communities were subject; analogies in the provincial world would seem to show that the court of the defendant (*forum rei*) was chosen as the scene of the trial[2]; but there is also evidence that, in the early relations of Rome

[1] Even before the extension of the franchise the *socii* of Italy stand on a higher plane than those of the provincial world. Their exemption from taxation implies that they possess ownership of their soil. It may not yet have been called *dominium ex iure Quiritium*, but it distinguishes them from the *possessores* in the provinces. Even the free provincial towns have only *libera possessio* (*Lex Antonia de Termessibus*, l. 20).

[2] Cic. *in Verr.* iii. 15, 38 'ne quis extra suum forum vadimonium promittere cogatur.'

with the old Latin communities, the place of judgement was the locality where the contract had been concluded (*forum contractus*)[1].

Extension of Roman law without Roman jurisdiction to the allies.

The increasing closeness of the relations between Rome and her Italian allies dictated the effort to induce them to accept many enactments of the statute-law of Rome. The effort was successful, and Cicero mentions innumerable civil laws 'quas Latini voluerunt adsciverunt[2].' But this extension of Roman law did not mean an extension of Roman jurisdiction. The acceptance was based on the voluntary consent of a sovereign community. The Roman law in this case becomes a part of the law of the accccepting state and is administered as such by the native magistrates.

But outside the circle of the *socii* stand a number of towns which Rome had either created out of her own citizens, or had, in pursuit of her earlier policy of incorporation, absorbed wholly or partially into herself.

The *coloniae* and *municipia*.

To the first category belong the towns which had been formed from colonies of Roman citizens (*coloniae civium Romanorum*); to the latter the towns possessing the private rights of Roman citizenship (*civitas sine suffragio*) and known in early times as *municipia*. Occasionally the incorporation had been carried further, and a few cities not settled from Rome possessed the full rights of *civitas*. To these we must add certain units smaller than cities scattered through Italy and composed either of full or of partial citizens, which were known as *fora*, *vici* and *castella*.

Direct Roman jurisdiction exercised by delegation.

The four types fall equally under the jurisdiction of the praetor urbanus. But a personal jurisdiction exercised by this magistrate was out of the question; many of the cities or districts were too far from Rome to

[1] Dionys. vi. 95 (in the treaty supposed to have been concluded with the Latins in 493 B.C. was found the clause) τῶν τ' ἰδιωτικῶν συμβολαίων αἱ κρίσεις ἐν ἡμέραις γιγνέσθωσαν δέκα, παρ' οἷς ἂν γένηται τὸ συμβόλαιον.

[2] Cic. *pro Balbo*, 8, 21.

render it possible for their occupants to bring their suits to the central State, and the praetor was chained to his tribunal in the capital and could not go on circuit[1]. The solution adopted was that of delegated jurisdiction. Every year praefects (*praefecti iuri dicundo*) were sent to the communities of full, or of half-burgesses to administer Roman law[2]. Some of these—namely the *quattuorviri praefecti Capuam Cumas* were elected by the *comitia tributa* and were reckoned amongst the minor magistrates of Rome; the others were appointed by the praetor urbanus under conditions fixed by the laws[3]. It is somewhat difficult to determine the character of the jurisdiction of these delegates; it could not have rested on a division of competence between the praetor at Rome and the praefect in the municipal town; of such a division there is no trace before the epoch of the social war and the enfranchisement of Italy, and the fixing of such a division would imply an incredibly early date for central municipal legislation. Nor can it be held to be jurisdiction springing,

Theory of this jurisdiction.

[1] A recollection of early attempts of the praetors at personal jurisdiction in Italy is contained in Gell. xx. 10, 9 'Sed postquam praetores propagatis Italiae finibus... proficisci vindiciarum dicendarum causa [ad] longinquas res gravabantur &c.'

[2] Festus, *s. v.* 'praefectura' (p. 233). The passage does not furnish evidence that all of the colonies of Roman citizens were *praefecturae*; none of the colonies mentioned by Festus are of an early date; on the other hand most of the *municipia* are very early, e. g. Caere (353), Atella, Calatia, Suessula (338), Acerrae (332), Anagnia (306), Arpinum (303). But it is obvious that there must have been delegated jurisdiction of some sort in all the colonies. Of the *fora*, *Forum Clodii* is known to have been a *praefectura* (Plin. *H. N.* iii. 8; *C. I. L.* xi. 3310 a); see Mommsen, *Staatsr.* iii. p. 581 n. 4.

The relations of Rome to some of the higher class of *municipia* were rather those of ἰσοπολιτεία: e. g. Capua kept its own supreme official the 'Meddix tuticus' (Liv. xxiv. 19), and the Roman and native law probably existed in such cases side by side.

[3] Festus, *l. c.* 'alterum (genus praefecturae), in quas solebant ire praefecti quatuor [qui] viginti sex virum numero populi suffragio creati erant... alterum, in quas ibant, quos praetor urbanus quodannis in quaeque loca miserat legibus.' Mommsen (*Staatsr.* ii. p. 609) thinks that the quattuorviri were not appointed by popular election until 124 B.C.

BOOK I. not from law but from the *imperium* of the praetor, such as the civil jurisdiction of the *imperator* in the camp[1]; for we are told that even those praefects who were nominated by the praetor were sent in accordance with the laws[2]. It must be regarded rather as purely urban jurisdiction anomalously extended beyond the limits within which such jurisdiction should properly be kept. These limits were fixed by the first milestone outside the city (*primum milliarium urbis Romae*). In theory the operation of the *legis actio* is confined within this limit; but there is ample evidence, which we shall examine elsewhere, that every form of action could be employed in the municipal communities of Roman citizens. We must conclude that the laws which gave the praetor the power of delegation also gave him the right to summon any case from a municipal town to Rome; that for this reason the early municipal jurisdiction, like the later, was properly regarded as the jurisdiction of the capital; and that the procedure of the *ius civile* applied in all its strictness to the Roman citizens scattered over the peninsula[3].

(c) *The Magistrate in the Provinces.*

The provincial praetors.

The need for new judicial magistrates did not end with the creation of the two city praetors. The provinces of Sicily and Sardinia, acquired as a consequence of the first Punic War, opened up a new field for jurisdiction, and two additional praetors were created to meet this want about the year 227 B.C.; two more were added in 197 B.C. for the two recently acquired Spanish provinces, thus bringing up the full number to six. A *lex Baebia* (*circa* 180 B.C.) enacted that four and six praetors should be elected in

[1] Val. Max. iii. 7, 1 a; Liv. *Ep.* 86. [2] 'Miserat legibus' (Festus, *l. c.*).

[3] From certain words in a *formula* of contract given by Cato (*R. R.* 149 'Si quid de iis rebus controversiae erit, Romae iudicium fiat') it appears that parties from municipal towns might by agreement bring a case to Rome. This voluntary resort to the courts of the capital seems to show an identity between their procedure and that of the municipal towns.

alternate years, probably for the wise purpose of making the government of the difficult Spanish provinces biennial; but this regulation was not long in force, and six praetors continued to be elected annually until the time of Sulla (81 B.C.). The reason for this limitation in spite of the increase in the number of provinces was that the praetorship was ceasing to be a provincial post. The principle of administration by ex-magistrates who had held the *imperium*, proconsuls and pro-praetors, originally a system of consular delegation, but one now asserting itself in the form of prolongation of an already-existing command (*prorogatio imperii*), was ever gaining fuller recognition. The praetors became, like the consuls, more and more home officials, whose duties were confined to Italy and the capital; and the necessity for the further increase of their number to eight, which was effected by Sulla, came from the rapid growth of the new system of criminal courts which required their presidency.

§ 3. *The Iudex.*

Judicial reform attributed to Servius Tullius. Final recognition of the *iudex*.

The tradition which we have already glanced at[1], that the prehistoric institution of the arbitrating *iudex*, whose free power of decision and even existence had been imperilled by the growth of the strong military monarchy, had been restored and placed on a more definite basis in the great epoch of reform associated with the name of Servius Tullius, is one of the most credible of the legends connected with the name of the democrat king. The time was not yet ripe for a popularization of the law, or even of the forms of procedure; but a liberal readjustment of the constitution, such as took place at the end of the sixth century B.C., could not but be accompanied by a recognition of one of the oldest privileges of the people. Renewed recognition of privilege almost always entails its greater

[1] p. 24.

BOOK I.

fixity, and this restoration of the judicature seems to have been no exception to the rule. Whereas of old the king *might* employ a *iudex* in certain cases, now he *must* employ him. The cases were vaguely defined as those which touched private interests only, and the general rules or individual judgements given by the king still decided when the *iudex* should be summoned or dispensed with. But the statement of the principle, perhaps accompanied by a clearer definition than we are at liberty to furnish of the demarcation between the two spheres of jurisdiction, was sufficient to make the old judicial delegate a new part of the Roman constitution. The qualification for the *iudex* was in all probability the mere possession of the rights of citizenship independent of status and of rank. When we consider the voluntary character of the acceptance of the *iudex* by the litigant, it is inconceivable that a member of the *plebs* should have been forced to seek arbitration from a patrician; still slighter is the probability that senators, still perhaps chosen from the Patriciate and in no way members of a recognized *ordo*, should at this early period, when the two communities were hardly welded into one, have claimed that right to the judicial bench which they seem to have asserted in the later period of oligarchic rule[1]. We shall soon have occasion to discuss two standing panels of judges known respectively as the *centumviri* and the *decemviri*. If we are led to attribute the existence of these boards to this early epoch of reform, their popular constitution contains a decided proof that no aristocratic qualifications were required for the new partner of the magisterial jurisdiction.

Qualification of the *iudex*.

The *iudex* and the *arbiter*.

The partner himself, as an isolated unit, appears under

[1] Polybius (vi. 17) says that from the senate *ἀποδίδονται κριταὶ τῶν πλείστων καὶ τῶν δημοσίων καὶ τῶν ἰδιωτικῶν συναλλαγμάτων, ὅσα μέγεθος ἔχει τῶν ἐγκλημάτων*. He does not assert, therefore, that, even at the period of highest senatorial ascendency, senators had even a practical monopoly of the bench. From a legal point of view the standing of the *iudex* must have depended wholly on the magistrate and the parties.

two forms; sometimes he is a *iudex*, sometimes an *arbiter*[1]. The distinction between their functions and the ethical character of their jurisdiction is unfolded for us in a splendid passage of Cicero, to which we shall presently give a detailed examination; the essence of the distinction which he deduces is that while the appeal to the *iudex* is for a fixed sum (*pecuniae certae*), that to the *arbiter* is for an amount indefinite (*incertae*), to be fixed by an estimate of circumstances; it is a distinction that widens into that between law and equity and has led to the modern contrast of judgement and arbitration. It is not impossible that there was always a truth in this distinction, although how little evident it was even during the later period of the growth of Roman law is shown by the hesitation of learned jurists as to when the word *iudex* and when the word *arbiter* should be employed[2]. But its origin is to some extent accidental; it was a distinction of locality rather than of principle (although the latter was involved in the former) that differentiated the *arbiter* from the *iudex*. Etymologically the former word may mean a man 'who goes about' or a man 'who is approached[3]'; in either case it implies nearness to the litigants or to the object of litigation. In popular Latin phraseology *arbiter* often means a 'witness[4].' Here we get the most primitive type of juryman; the man who knows the circumstances, who can get ocular or oral demonstration of the truth. He is a man who can take account of all the surroundings of a case and offers a strong contrast to the judge (*iudex*), fixed in the capital and led

The *arbiter* as a witness.

[1] Cic. *pro Rosc. com.* 4, 10. The *arbiter* of purely private extra-judicial arbitration must always have existed and of course survives into Ciceronian times (*ib.* 9, 26).

[2] Cic. *pro Mur.* 12, 27 'Iam illud mihi quidem mirum videri solet tot homines tam 'ugeniosos post tot annos etiam nunc statuere non potuisse utrum . . . iuuicem an arbitrum . . . dici oporteret.'

[3] From *ad* and *betere* or *bitere*; see Eisele, *Beiträge*, p. 2 ff.

[4] Cic. *de Off.* iii. 31, 112; *ad Att.* xv. 16 a.

BOOK I. by instructions and by pleadings to a judgement in strict law (*ius strictum*). The magistrate, and later the law, decided when that weighing of circumstances was necessary which should make the *arbiter* replace the *iudex*. It is no accident that the Twelve Tables enjoined *arbitri* for the cases where an inheritance was to be divided (*familiae herciscundae*), or where an injury done by rain-water was to be averted (*de aqua pluvia arcenda*[1]).

By the side of the individual *iudex*, acting in either of these capacities, we find established in later times two panels of jurors, which may be a survival of the same great epoch of reform. The attribution of the courts of the Hundred and the Ten (the *centumviri* and *decemviri*) to the period of the late monarchy or even of the early Republic is based partly on the interpretation of the doubtful language of a single legal enactment, but with more probability on the consistency of their structure and functions with the needs of the primitive political society of Rome. The Valerio-Horatian laws of 449 B.C., while pronouncing the tribunes and aediles of the plebs to be inviolable, further recognized the sacredness of the persons of the *iudices* and the *decemviri*[2]. The collocation of the Latin words affords a slight possibility of these two classes of officials being identical; but it was a possibility not recognized by the ancients themselves, some of whom were

The *centumviri* and *decemviri*.

[1] Cic. *pro Caec.* 7, 19; *Top.* 9, 39; cf. *pro Mur.* 9, 22. The evidence is indirect; but both these actions belonged to the Twelve Tables and both necessitated *arbitri* in later times. So in a controversy about the fixing of boundaries (*finium regundorum*, cf. *pro Mur. l. c.*) the *arbiter* is employed (Cic. *de Leg.* i. 21, 55 'e XII tres arbitri fines regemus'). When Cicero writes (*de Rep.* iv. 8, 8) 'Iurgare igitur lex (duodecim tabularum) putat inter se vicinos, non litigare,' this action is probably meant. It is not impossible that when the Tables said SI IURGANT (Cic. *l. c.*) they referred to arbitration, not to litigation.

[2] Liv. iii. 55 'Consules . . . L. Valerius, M. Horatius . . . cum religione inviolatos (tribunos plebis) tum lege etiam fecerunt sanciendo ut qui tribunis plebis, aedilibus, iudicibus, decemviris nocuisset, eius caput Iovi sacrum esset, familia ad aedem Ce.eris, Liberi Liberaeque venum iret.'

driven to a conclusion, unwarranted by the historical circumstances of the enactment, and by the later facts of constitutional history, that *iudex* here had its old sense of *consul*[1]. The tribunals protected by these laws had clearly been established in the interest of the *plebs*, or were at least of a popular character. Why this character should have attached to the decemvirs is easily understood when we discover that even to the close of the Republic they are the arbitrators on the question of freedom. The typical story of Verginia which ushers in this legislation gives a peculiar point to the need for the inviolability, which is the Roman expression for the independence, of the men who pronounced on the *status* of the citizen. If we can discover that the *centumviri* also satisfied some great popular need, their identification with the *iudices* of the Valerio-Horatian laws becomes at least possible. Cicero's detailed description of the functions of the centumvirs in the generation just preceding his own[2] sets one fact beyond dispute: *viz.* that their jurisdiction was concerned mainly with rateable property, with the goods taken account of in the census. If it was the judgement of the decemvirs that made or unmade the citizen, it was the vote of the centumvirs that made or unmade the voting member of the *comitia centuriata*. One of the greatest political questions of the fifth century of Roman history was that of the *census*, and the court which decided about *nexa* and *mancipia*, which unravelled the mysteries of *usucapio* and the intricacies of intestate inheritance to the *gentiles* and *agnati*, was engaged in assigning individuals to centuries and classes or denying them participation in both. As the Servian census was a strictly national institution, as it equally concerned patricians and plebeians and was

Primitive character of these courts; their importance for public law.

[1] Liv. iii. 55 'Fuere qui interpretarentur eadem hac Horatia lege consulibus quoque et praetoribus, quia iisdem auspiciis quibus consules crearentur, cautum esse: iudicem enim consulem appellari.'

[2] Cic. *de Orat.* i. 38, 173.

BOOK I.

in fact the means by which two states were first welded into one, there is no reason to believe that the judges engaged in deciding those controversies, which concerned the property which formed its basis, were drawn exclusively from the plebeians. Yet as the *census* was the guarantee of rights but lately assigned to the plebs, this body had a peculiar interest in conserving any institution of a popular character connected with it; hence the plebeian blessing embraces the centumvirs, and the plebeian curse rests on their oppressors.

Antiquity of the centumviral court.

The symbol and formulae of this court also point to a remote antiquity. The lance (*hasta*) was set before the assembled *centumviri*—the 'symbol of true ownership,' if we are to credit Gaius [1], who associates it with the wand (*festuca*), perhaps the primitive weapon of hardened wood, with which the plaintiff had through the ages vindicated his claim to the lordship (*dominium*) of a thing. Whatever its meaning, it is certainly a survival from a remote past, for the lance did not figure in the ordinary courts of Rome. The procedure before the court of the centumvirs, as before that of the decemvirs, was by oath or wager (*sacramento*), a form of action which was disappearing in Cicero's time and which, by its being the only form applicable to their jurisdiction, proves that the courts were instituted when no other *formulae*, either for recovery or for the assertion of liberty, were in current use. Of the two courts, that of the *decemviri* suffered most change in its character, perhaps also in its functions, although

The decemvirate becomes a magistracy.

its primary object still survived in Cicero's day. The language used by the orator himself leaves little room for doubt that the *iudices* of the decemviral period had in course of time risen to the rank of a minor but independent magistracy—a growth of subordinates into state

[1] Gaius, iv. 16 'Festuca autem utebantur quasi hastae loco, signo quodam iusti dominii: . . . unde in centumviralibus iudiciis hasta praeponitur.'

officials which finds a parallel in the *triumviri capitales*, the masters of the mint and the military tribunate—and that this increase in their position was, as their later name (*decemviri stlitibus iudicandis*) signifies, accompanied by an increase in their civil competence[1]. There is nothing surprising in the fact that patricians are known to have been members of this magistracy[2], for, like the *centumviri*, the original decemvirs were probably chosen from the whole people. In the days when they were still but *iudices* they were probably selected by the magistrate (king, consul, praetor); when they were enrolled in the magistracy, this selection was doubtless replaced by the suffrage of the *comitia* of the Tribes.

The centumvirs remain *iudices*.

The members of the court of the *centumviri* (*centumvirale iudicium*) always remained true *iudices*, and were probably, like other standing panels of jurors, selected for a fixed period of service by the magistrate, throughout the main period of the Republic no doubt by the praetor urbanus. The size of the court always approximated to, but perhaps at no period ever exactly realized, the number of a hundred implied in its designation. The principle by which these jurors were selected in the later Republic, three from each of the thirty-five tribes[3], which produced a board of One Hundred and Five, cannot be earlier than the year 241 B.C., when the number of the tribes attained its full complement; but modes in which the nominal number might have been attained with an equal or almost equal approximation to the truth, may easily be imagined for the earlier period. The four tribes and twenty-six pagi of Servius Tullius may have furnished ninety judges, or the twenty-one tribes of the decemviral period, if five

[1] Cic. *Orator*, 46, 156; *de Leg.* iii. 3, 6 *litis contractas iudicanto.* In the latter passage the decemvirs are classed amongst the *minores magistratus.*

[2] Mommsen, *Staatsr.* ii. p. 607.

[3] Festus, p. 54 'cum essent Romae triginta et quinque tribus . . . terni ex singulis tribubus sunt electi ad iudicandum, qui centumviri appellati sunt'; cf. Varro, *R. R.* ii. 1.

and not three members were chosen from each, the later number of a hundred and five.

Employment of the *unus iudex* and the *arbiter*.

When these two special panels of *iudices* were instituted, their spheres must have been accurately defined. But this could not have been the case with the *unus iudex* and the *arbiter*. The increasing stringency of laws which enjoin this fundamental division of competence in spheres to which it had not yet been applied shows how much this institution must have depended at first on the nature of the case and the discretion of the magistrate. The necessity for his presence, and his freedom of judgement when he had been assigned by the magistrate and accepted by the parties, depended on the character of the controversy which called for settlement. It is improbable (although we cannot say, impossible) that private delicts with their quasi-criminal character and savage modes of execution—the assignment to servitude (*addictio*) of the thief caught in the act, the right of one who has received bodily harm to inflict corporal injury of a similar kind on his aggressor, the capital penalty for libel—ever came under the cognizance of the *iudex*; the penalty might have been inflicted, the right to self-help maintained by the voice of the magistrate alone. In personal actions, where they took the form of recovery by *sacramentum*, the *iudex* may have been employed, but his presence could scarcely have been necessary when the question was one of execution by arrest on the part of the creditor (*per manus iniectionem*); in the *actio sacramento*, where the statement of claim and the refutation were rigidly expressed in the formulae, his functions would have been confined to an estimate of evidence alone. Sometimes his discretionary power must have been greater, and grounds of equity have dictated a freer judgement, for one form of action at least *required* the praetor to grant a *iudex* or an *arbiter*. Later legislation, by making the granting of a *iudex* in certain cases obligatory, extended the duality of procedure. This was done by the *lex Pinaria* of uncertain date in cases where pecuniary claims up to a certain value were in question[1]. Later still the *condictio*, introduced by the *Lex Silia* for the recovery of a definite sum of money (*certa pecunia*) and extended by the *Lex Calpurnia* to the recovery of every *certa res*, made the appeal to the *iudex* an integral part of the procedure[2].

Increased frequency of the employment of the *iudex*.

Arbitria.

The functions of the *arbiter* or of the *iudex* in an arbitrating capacity (for the two terms were not sharply distinguished) were still more extended. All cases where property had to be divided amongst kindred claimants, or the limits of ownership were to be defined (*arbitria familiae herciscundae, finium regundorum*) were submitted to the 'adjudication' of the *arbiter*[3]. The settlement of obligations, which were not incurred according to such forms of strict law as the 'mancipation' and the 'stipulation,' also required his cognizance, as soon as they could be made actionable at all[4]. Most of these did not involve merely the specific delivery of an object; as in the contract of *Fiducia*, which created obligations connected with the use and return of a thing lent on trust, they involved a delicate adjustment of counter-claims, which would have weighed heavily on the time of the magistrate and which the previous neglect of such contractual relations by the State had long relegated to the category of *arbitria*.

The estimate of damage (*noxia*), which fell short of the injury to which the laws had affixed a penalty, was also the subject of the discretion of an investigator chosen by the advice of the magistrate and the consent of the parties. Doubtless at all periods of Roman history the choice of both was theoretically free; but we are not surprised to find that, by the close of the Second Punic War, the

[1] Gaius, iv. 15. [2] *ib.* 18, 19. [3] See p. 40, note 1.

[4] An informal loan (*mutuum*), which probably was not originally a ground for action, is an exception to this rule. It belongs to the *iudicium*, not to the *arbitrium*; the reason for its assignment to *ius strictum* being that it did not obviously involve a counter-claim.

Later senatorial qualification of the *iudex*. His quasi-official position.

exclusive tendencies of the oligarchy had led the magistrates to seek the fitting *iudex* or *arbiter* chiefly in the senatorial body[1], and that the people accepted this restriction of their own choice. This was one of the results of the quasi-official position which the *iudex* had ever held. Always in theory a friend appealed to by the parties, he was yet responsible to the State. He was a sworn official, bound by oath to observe not only the truth of the facts but the letter of the law; for legal arguments were by no means exhausted in the praetor's court: the *iudex* was often an interpreter, expanding and explaining the mere outline suggested by the ruling of his superior[2]. The danger threatened by the possible bribery of this powerful delegate, whose judgement was subject to no appeal, was keenly felt. It was met by the enactment, created or renewed by the Twelve Tables, of a capital penalty against the corrupt juror[3].

International jurisdiction.

International jurisdiction naturally engaged a great deal of the attention of the early government of Rome. Its leading principles have already been briefly sketched[4]; but it remains to notice the general character of the procedure and the court which grew out of these principles. If we exclude from the map of Italy the communities which possessed the Roman citizenship in whole or in part, we are left with an aggregate of *peregrinae civitates* which in the earliest times possessed only treaty relations with Rome. But these treaty relations were, from the dawn of Roman history, by no means confined to States within the peninsula. We have positive evidence for a commercial treaty with Carthage dating from the beginning of the Republic[5], and similar relations may be

[1] p. 38, note 1.

[2] Cf. Cic. *in Verr.* ii. 12, 31 'iudex, homo et iuris et officii peritissimus.'

[3] Gell. xx. 1, 7 'duram esse legem putas quae iudicem arbitrumve iure datum, qui ob rem dicendam pecuniam accepisse convictus est, capite poenitur.'

[4] p. 29.

[5] Polyb. iii. 22.

assumed between Rome and commercial communities with which she was early brought into contact, such as Syracuse and Massilia. Commerce involves the jurisdiction of Private International Law: and it was to meet this obligation that a new code and a new procedure were created. The code was necessary because it was seldom that the relations between Rome and a foreign State were so close as to lead to a mutual acceptance of the full jurisdiction of each other's courts and therefore of each other's law according to the simple principles of the *forum contractus* or *forum rei.* The former was recognized in the early relations between Rome and the Latins, but only because Latium was the twin-sister of Rome. A more distant relation or a stranger shrank from the rigour and the narrow local character of the Roman law, and the feelings were reciprocated by Rome. A compromise was necessary and was arrived at. The simpler principles that already prevailed in the commercial intercourse of men of different towns—principles which reduced law to sensible perceptions, which regarded actual physical transfer as the essence of conveyance, the spoken word (apart from a special language or a special *formula*) as the essence of contract, and which cemented these with the consciousness of the obligation of good faith (*bona fides*)—were recognized as the guiding principles of the international courts. It was natural that this *ius gentium*, 'that which was fitting for a man as a member of the nations,' should be carried out by composite courts. But this composite character could not be found in the magistracy, for the magistrates of distant states could not be ever meeting to settle disputes between their respective citizens; consular representation was unknown, and the amalgamation of personnel, to balance that of law, was sought in the judicial bench and found in the court of the 'Recoverers' (*Recuperatores*). It is true that history furnishes us with no instance of such a mixed panel,

The recuperatores:

BOOK I.

first an international court.

but the belief that this court sprang from the needs of international jurisdiction was held in the ancient [1], and has met with general acceptance in the modern, world [2]. The reason for the absence of the representative idea, at the time when the court is historically known to us, is twofold. It is due in the first place to the cessation of such treaty relations, which were replaced by the principle of state jurisdiction in Italy and the favoured towns abroad, and by actual domination throughout the provinces: and in the second place to the absorption of the *recuperatores* into civic jurisdiction. But it is difficult to explain the plurality of this court except on the hypothesis that it was a mixed tribunal [3]. The *recuperatores* were sometimes three, sometimes five in number. Possibly the State whose tribunal established the *iudicium* was permitted the majority of the judges: possibly each city provided equal numbers and the court was supplemented by representatives from some third community agreed on in the treaty. When the stage was reached at which these courts ceased to represent Rome's allies and were composed of citizens alone, their connexion with the interests of the *peregrini* remained for long unaltered. The *unus iudex* was supposed to be the product of jurisdiction dependent on law (*lex*); but, though the justice administered to the foreigner might be based on a command of the people in the sense of a *lex data* or charter, it did not rest on the civil law of Rome; the *iudicium* was in this sense not *legitimum*; here *recuperatores* could alone be given, and the gift of these jurors with the instructions

[1] Cf. Festus, p. 274 'Reciperatio est, ut ait Gallus Aelius, cum inter populum et reges nationesque et civitates peregrinas lex convenit quomodo per reciperatores reddantur res reciperenturque, resque privatas inter se persequantur.'

[2] The chief opponent of this ruling theory is Hartmann, *Der ordo iudiciorum*, Thl. i. p. 229 ff.

[3] Unless, indeed, the *unus iudex* was a peculiarity of Rome and, in international jurisdiction, she assimilated her courts to those of other states.

Iudicia quae imperio continentur.

committed to them were the outcome of the *imperium* of the praetor peregrinus. The idea of a court constituted by 'imperium' (*quod imperio continetur* [1]) with its freedom from the trammels of law and its indefinite possibilities of equity, was the starting point of a progressive jurisprudence.

Employment of recuperatorial courts for urban jurisdiction.

The recuperatorial courts had also been marked by a rapidity of constitution and procedure, originally devised in the interest of the migratory foreigner, which made them peculiarly suitable for the trial of those civil suits in which dispatch was an important consideration. These advantages led to their recognition by the urban praetor: yet their international character was not forgotten. Besides the constant reminder of their origin latent in their employment by the 'foreign' praetor, as late as the year 171 B.C. we find them given by the magistrate to assess the damages claimed by Spanish provincials from their extortionate governors [2].

§ 4. *Procedure in iure; the legis actio.*

The idea of an 'action'; *actor* and *reus*.

A violated right, when immediate satisfaction has been denied to the party who claims to have been injured, can only be readjusted, according to the Roman mind, not so much by a mere plaint to a higher authority, as by the individual who claims to have been wronged setting in motion a process for the recovery of the thing. This process is accomplished throughout in his own person; he becomes again the subject of the right if it is accomplished without hindrance from his adversary. As the beginner of the process the plaintiff is said to act (*agere*), and to be an *actor*; the counter-action of the defendant is neither denied nor obscured, but his relative passivity leads to his description as a person 'with whom the action is taking place' (*is cum quo agitur*). At any moment it is possible

[1] Gaius, iv. 109.

[2] Liv. xliii. 2.

for the latter to perfect the action of the plaintiff and to interrupt his own; he can confess before the court (*confiteri in iure*), he can effect a compromise (*pactum*); it is only if he persists in his contention, that the solemn attestation of a controverted matter (*litis contestatio*) results and that a new and formal agreement is entered on to abide the decision of the court. It is possible that even early Roman lawyers, such as the jurists of the Ciceronian period, felt the contractual nature of this situation; the feeling may explain the designation of both parties, of plaintiff as well as defendant, as equally bound, as mutually debtors (*rei*[1]), although later terminology, dwelling rather on the motive than the situation, distinguishes the plaintiff as the prime agent (*actor*), and dwells on the potential indebtedness of the defendant (*reus*).

The *legis actio*. Meaning of the phrase.

The whole procedure (the part played by the defendant as well as by the plaintiff) was called an action: but an action 'of law' or 'of the law' (*legis actio*) is the name which has been handed down for the early process by which a Roman recovered his rights in his native courts. The meaning is obscure. Of the alternative explanations furnished by Gaius, that they were so called either because they were *given* by the laws or because they were *adjusted* to the very wording of legal enactments[2], the first lacks evidence and historical analogy and is in conflict with the tradition that new forms of action might be devised by pontiffs and lawyers without assistance from the legislature. The second explanation, which he illustrates by an appeal to the rigidity of these forms, seems to contain a larger element of truth. The fact that the plaintiff who demanded compensation for the cutting of his vines could not employ the word *vites* in his plaint, because the Twelve

[1] The Twelve Tables referred to *iudici arbitrove reove* in connexion with excusable grounds for non-appearance (Festus, p. 273).

[2] Gaius, iv. 11 'Actiones quas in usu veteres habuerunt legis actiones appellabantur, vel ideo quod legibus proditae erant. . . . vel ideo quia ipsarum legum verbis accommodatae erant.'

Tables had spoken only of trees (*arbores*[1]), while it illustrates the well-known tendency of an unlettered society to attach enormous importance to words, also shows the great influence of the Code of Civil Law on the terminology of the courts. Before the Twelve Tables there was no body of law that could be denominated a *lex*; after the publication of this code there was—it was the *lex centuriata* of these Tables themselves. Originally the Romans may have spoken of an 'action' simply (for to interpret *legis* in some more primitive sense than 'law' is to stray widely from the direct path both of evidence and of probability): after the publication of the Tables they spoke of the 'actions of *the* law.'

Number and forms of the *legis actiones*.

The number of these forms of action appears to have been limited only by the discretion of the Pontifical College that gave them validity and sometimes birth. Even in the Ciceronian period there was a probable survival of certain forms which were not identical with the five types furnished by our authorities. But it is probable that the multiplicity of the *formulae* was gained by the development and adaptation to new purposes of some of these types. We must say 'some,' because an inspection of the five forms of action described by Gaius shows that there are only two, or at most three, which can really be primitive. These are the actions *sacramento, per manus iniectionem* and *per iudicis postulationem*. The antiquity of the third depends on our view of the antiquity of the legal recognition of the *iudex*. The first was at once the most primitive in character and associations and the most generic in its use of all the forms; it was the supplement of all the others—the one employed where no special provision had been made[2]. It was the normal mode of recovery, as the action *per manus iniectionem* was the normal mode

[1] Gaius, iv. 11.

[2] Gaius, iv. 13 'Sacramenti actio generalis est: de quibus enim rebus ut aliter ageretur lege cautum non erat, de his sacramento agebatur.'

BOOK I. of execution. Of the remaining actions that *per pignoris capionem* was apparently a development from certain rules of administrative law, while the late date of the *actio per condictionem* is testified by Gaius.

The *legis actio sacramento*. The *legis actio sacramento* is an example of the primitive method of deciding the merits of a case by an appeal to a wager. The bet was advanced by the plaintiff, met by the defendant; the stakes were taken by the representative of the State. It was this representative that in the earliest times decided the issue; later there came the mutual agreement to appear before a *iudex*, or before one of the two great standing panels, the decemviral and centumviral courts. This was the meaning that was certainly read into the action in historical times, and it was an interpretation which profoundly influenced the further development of Roman procedure; it suggested the use of the mutual *sponsio*, which we shall treat in connexion with the second epoch of Roman procedure, and it contained within itself the idea, afterwards elaborated, of a praejudgement (*praeiudicium*), that is of the possibility of reaching a verdict which was not concerned with the main issues of the case but which implicitly decided those issues.

Meaning of *sacramentum*. But if this was the original meaning of the action, how came the wager to be called a *sacramentum*? Two explanations were suggested by Roman antiquarians. While some thought that it derived its name from its deposit in a sanctuary (*in sacro*[1]), others held that its use by the State for the maintenance of religious ceremonial had given it this derived appellation[2]. The explanations, though not devoid of an historical foundation, are not in

[1] Varro, *L. L.* v. 180 'Ea pecunia quae in iudicium venit in litibus, sacramentum a sacro . . . qui iudicio vicerat, suum sacramentum e sacro auferebat, victi ad aerarium redibat.'

[2] Festus, p. 344 'Sacramentum aes significat quod poenae nomine penditur, sive eo quis interrogatur, sive contenditur . . . sacramenti autem nomine id aes dici coeptum est quod et propter aerari inopiam et sacrorum publicorum multitudinem consumebatur id in rebus divinis.'

accordance with the normal meaning of the word. *Sacramentum* may mean the thing deposited as a *sacratio*, a substitute for the self devoted to a god in cases where such a substitute was allowed; it means too a voluntary oath, and the meanings are reconcilable, since the oath accompanies the dedication[1]. The primitive ceremonial of challenging an opponent *by* oath (*provocare sacramento*) to prove his claim was accompanied by a deposit on the altar of the god. This deposit was forfeited if the oath turned out to be unfounded (*iniustum*); it was the expiation (*piamentum*) for the involuntary perjury, the means of averting the wrath of the god for the injury done to his name. The perjury was never regarded as deliberate; in this case the perjurer's life would have been forfeited. It must always have been felt that it was not a fact, of which the swearer would have full knowledge, but a claim which was the mere subject of belief, that was being asserted on oath. The wrong done to a divinity by calling on him to attest a claim and then discovering that his assistance had been invoked in vain, was regarded as an expiable offence. At a later period the State took from the priesthood the considerable sums that flowed from this source into the various shrines, it ordered them to be collected by the *tresviri capitales*[2], but it had the decency not to devote them to secular purposes; they were now expended under government supervision on things divine. But it was inevitable that, as the course of years brought with them the almost complete divorce of the religious from the secular law, the original meaning of the *sacramentum* should be forgotten. It was known only as a wager, recovered by the winner but forfeited

[1] Danz, 'das Sacramentum und die lex Papiria' in *Zeitschr. f. R. G.* vi. (1867) p. 339 ff.; *der sacrale Schutz*, p. 151 ff. For the different views that have been held as to the nature of the *sacramentum* see the above-cited article by Danz. Jobbé-Duval has lately maintained the older theory that the procedure is a simple wager (*Études*, i. p. 16).

[2] Festus, *l. c.*

BOOK I.

by the losing party to the State, by which a right was asserted or lost[1].

Amount of the wager.

The amount of the deposit was fixed by the Twelve Tables at 500 asses for objects of the value of 1000 asses or more, and at fifty asses for all things of smaller value; one important exception was made; in all controversies concerning the freedom of a man, his value was of no account. For the purpose of encouraging the friendly assertor of liberty (*adsertor in libertatem*) the minimum of fifty asses was all that was demanded in such a case[2]. In earlier times the money had been deposited at the time of (perhaps even before) the challenge, but at a later period personal securities (*praedes*) were accepted by the praetor for its liquidation[3].

The *actio sacramento* is both *in rem* and *in personam*.

The adaptability of this *legis actio*, due to its praejudicial character, made it as efficient a means of asserting a right against the whole world as of maintaining a claim against a given individual. The assertion of a right against the world is expressed by the later Roman law in terms of a phenomenal object which is claimed without any particular regard to its protesting possessor; it is

[1] The wager is such an obvious method of settling a dispute that we need not suppose all instances of the *sponsio* to have sprung from the *actio sacramento*. It might be employed in political life to settle a question of honour (Cic. *de Off.* iii. 19, 77 'Fimbriam consularem audiebam . . . iudicem M. Lutatio Pinthiae fuisse . . . cum is sponsionem fecisset NI VIR BONUS ESSET'; cf. Val. Max. vii. 2, 4)—a use which Jobbé-Duval (*Études*, i. p. 45) compares to that of 'un jury d'honneur.' A man might use the *sponsio* to prove mitigating circumstances connected with a criminal offence (Val. Max. vi. 1, 10). The challenge to a *sponsio* might be made as a means of proving, and giving the accused or a third party the means of disproving, a misdemeanour or a crime (Cic. *in Verr.* iii. 57, 132 'cum palam Syracusis, te audiente, maximo conventu L. Rubrius Q. Apronium sponsione lacessivit NI APRONIUS DICTITARET TE SIBI IN DECUMIS ESSE SOCIUM'; cf. 58, 135. *ib.* v. 54, 141 'Cogere eum coepit (Verres), cum ageret nemo, nemo postularet sponsionem . . . facere cum lictore suo NI FURTIS QUAESTUM FACERET. Recuperatores se de cohorte sua dicit daturum. Servilius et recusare et deprecari ne iniquis iudicibus, nullo adversario, iudicium capitis in se constitueretur'). In such a *sponsio* all the forms of law might be observed, but its employment was strictly extra-judicial.

[2] Gaius, iv. 14.

[3] Gaius, iv. 13, 16.

an action directed towards a thing (*in rem actio*). The maintenance of a claim against an individual is an action which aims at infringing the existing rights of a given legal personality (*in personam actio*).

Actio in rem or vindicatio.

In the pursuit of a thing, the pursuer asserts his right to power over the object; hence the name *vindicatio rei*[1], and to assert this vindication the *legis actio sacramento* was originally the only means. The positive nature of early Roman law subordinated the right to the object; whatever was claimed was a corporal thing (*res corporalis*) of given dimensions and qualities. But definition was not sufficient: actual production was demanded of land or house or slave. In the case of moveable objects (*mobilia et moventia*) the production could be literally fulfilled; they were seized wherever found by the plaintiff and produced in court[2]. Denial by the possessor of his control of the object justified the plaintiff in searching for it as a stolen good (*res furtiva*); he prosecuted his search in the house of the defendant in the light attire prescribed by law and in the presence of two witnesses[3]. It was only moveables that had become fixtures, such as beams or stones forming part of a building that could not be directly produced; an action for the recovery of double their value (*actio tigni iuncti*) was prescribed by the Twelve Tables; yet even these objects must in early times have been visited and inspected by the court.

Production of moveables in court.

Visitation of immoveables.

This visitation was, in fact, the process adopted for immoveables. At the time of the Twelve Tables the praetor and the parties visited the spot, and the *legis actio* was begun *in* the locality which was the subject of dispute. But as the bounds of the Roman land (*ager Romanus*) extended, the presence of the magistrate in

[1] Cf. Cic. *de Orat.* i. 10, 42; *pro Mil.* 27, 74; *ad Fam.* vii. 32, 2.

[2] Gaius, iv. 16 'mobilia quidem et moventia, quae modo in ius adferri adducive possent, in iure vindicabantur.'

[3] Gaius, iii. 186, 192, and 193.

BOOK I. the disputed territory became impossible. The parties with their witnesses (*superstites*) visited the site and returned to the court bearing a fragment—a clod of earth, or a tile from a building—which symbolized the object in dispute [1]. Thus the summons to action in the court (*in iure*) became a summons outside its precincts (*ex iure*) [2], but the main condition, that the thing vindicated should be present (*in rem praesentem vindicatio*) [3], was satisfied. By Cicero's time a further advance had been made. The parties had brought their symbolic burden before the suit began; in the few paces that lay between it and the tribunal the praetor's injunction to go and return, the necessary preliminary of the legal contest, was fulfilled [4].

Opening of the contest.

The contest itself [5] was opened by the plaintiff as vindicant; grasping the thing with one hand he touched it with the staff (*festuca*), the symbol of power, held in the other, asserting at the same moment his legal right to the object. The *vindicatio rei* thus completed, the defendant appeared on the scene. His rôle was not fulfilled by a mere denial of the plaintiff's right; he too grasps the thing and wields the staff and repeats the same solemn claim of right. When this *contra-vindicatio* had been completed both parties had their hands on the object of dispute or were touching the clod with their feet.

Then the praetor intervened in the interests of peace. At the words 'both of you release that man' or 'both of you quit that field,' the parties separated and the symbolic strife was at an end.

Then began the peaceful assertion of the grounds of

[1] Gell. xx. 10, 9 'institutum est ... ut litigantes ... profecti simul in agrum, de quo litigabatur, terrae aliquid ex eo, uti unam glebam, in ius in urbem ad praetorem deferrent et in ea gleba, tanquam in toto agro, vindicarent'; Gaius, iv. 17 'Si qua res talis erat ut (*non*) sine incommodo posset in ius adferri vel adduci ... pars aliqua inde sumebatur; deinde in eam partem, quasi in totam rem praesentem, fiebat vindicatio.'

[2] Cic. *de Orat.* i. 10, 41; *pro Mur.* 12, 26.

[3] Gaius, *l. c.*

[4] Cic. *pro Mur.* 12, 26.

[5] Gaius, iv. 16.

claim. 'Why have you vindicated?' asks the plaintiff. 'Because it was my right' replies the defendant. 'Your vindication is unjust' is the retort; 'I challenge you by a sacrament of 50 (or 500) asses;' 'And I repeat the challenge to you.'

Interim possession.

The case was now ripe for a settlement on its merits; but before it could proceed an important step had to be taken; this was the assignment of the *interim* possession of the object claimed. This lay in the discretion of the praetor; he gave the thing itself and its produce (was it capable of such) pending the settlement of the case to which ever litigant he pleased[1]. A careful cognisance must have been necessary for this act, because to some extent it prejudged the merits of the case. The normal procedure must undoubtedly have been to allow the existing possessor (who in most cases would be the defendant) to detain; it could only have been when the grounds of existing possession were, according to the usual ruling of the praetors, manifestly inequitable, that the privilege was transferred to the non-possessor. In every case the *interim* possessor thus constituted by the praetor had to furnish sureties for the surrender of the thing and its fruits to his adversary in case his wager should be pronounced unjust.

The praetor's assignment of temporary possession seems to have had no influence on the structure of the case. We are never told that the party to whom he assigned it became the defendant and that the party-rôles could thus be changed. Nor is the supposition that both *sacramenta* could be declared 'unjust,' which, if the praetor had assigned possession to a non-possessor, would have shifted the practical attributes of ownership from one litigant to another, borne out by our authorities. The 'justice' of

[1] Gaius, iv. 16 'Postea praetor secundum alterum eorum vindicias dicebat, id est, interim aliquem possessorem constituebat, eumque iubebat praedes adversario dare litis et vindiciarum, id est, rei et fructuum.'

BOOK I. the *sacramentum*[1] was probably a relative one; the course of the evidence might prove both claims to be unfounded; but the burden of proof probably lay on the original vindicant; the injustice of his claim established the relative justice of his rival's, who retained ownership and recovered (if he had ever lost) possession.

The *iudicium*.

The appeal to the *sacramentum* was followed, in the period when *iudicia* in the strict sense had been fully established, by a mutual challenge and agreement by the parties to appear on a given day before the Centumvirs or Decemvirs according to the nature of the case, or to present themselves before the praetor's court again after thirty days for the acceptance of a *iudex*.

The legal drama. Utterances of the parties and the praetor.

The legal drama, whose stages we have briefly sketched, is capable of partial reconstruction from fragmentary notices of Cicero and Gaius. Assuming as object in dispute Cicero's typical instance of a Sabine farm, the utterances of the *dramatis personae* are as follows:—

Plaintiff. FUNDUS CORNELIANUS QUI EST IN AGRO QUI SABINUS VOCATUR, EUM EGO EX IURE QUIRITIUM MEUM ESSE AIO. INDE IBI EGO TE EX IURE MANUM CONSERTUM VOCO.

Defendant. UNDE TU ME EX IURE MANUM CONSERTUM VOCASTI, INDE IBI EGO TE REVOCO.

Praetor. SUIS UTRISQUE SUPERSTITIBUS PRAESENTIBUS ISTAM VIAM DICO. INITE VIAM.

(The parties advance with their witnesses to the symbol of the object in dispute.)

Praetor. REDITE VIAM[2].

(The parties return with the symbol.)

Plaintiff. HUNC EGO FUNDUM EX IURE QUIRITIUM MEUM ESSE AIO SECUNDUM SUAM CAUSAM, SICUT DIXI: ECCE TIBI VINDICTAM IMPOSUI.

Defendant repeats these words.

Praetor. DISCEDITE AMBO[3].

(The parties lay down the symbol.)

[1] Cic. *de Orat.* i. 10, 42; *pro Caec.* 33, 97; cf. *pro Mil.* 27, 74.
[2] Cic. *pro Mur.* 12, 26.
[3] Or, in the case of a personal object, MITTITE AMBO HOMINEM.

Plaintiff. POSTULO ANNE DICAS QUA EX CAUSSA VINDICAVERIS[1].

Defendant. IUS PEREGI SICUT VINDICTAM IMPOSUI.

Plaintiff. QUANDO TU INIURIA VINDICAVISTI, D (*or* L) AERIS SACRAMENTO TE PROVOCO.

Defendant. SIMILITER EGO TE.

The action implies the assertion of ownership.

A strict interpretation of the foregoing *formulae* reveals a singular limitation of the applicability of this action to the ordinary needs of life. The vindicant claims to be the owner of the thing and, the contra-vindicant repeats the claim *verbatim* on behalf of himself. Hence it would seem that none but the actual owner could contest such an action. Legal representation was unknown in the *legis actio* which concerned a private right[2], and the *bona fide* user or detainer of a thing—the son under power, the man who holds it as a deposit or the lessee—cannot claim to be its owner. It is, indeed, by no means certain that a man's assertion that a thing is 'his according to law' (*suum ex iure Quiritium*) necessarily implied a claim to full ownership; if it did not, then, though neither of the two rights were absolute, the better may have prevailed. But in a small community it would not be difficult to trace derived possession to its source: underived possession would count as ownership in default of a better title being adduced by others, and the close family organization made the *dominium* of the household's head easily determinable. In the case of newly acquired ownership the title was protected by the possibility of summoning the source (*auctor*) of the litigant's acquisition. This vendor could be requested by the purchaser (the defendant in the case) to intervene and prove his right, and

[1] Cic. *pro Mur.* 12, 26.

[2] Gaius, iv. 82. Cicero's words in a letter to Volumnius (*ad Fam.* vii. 32, 1 and 2), 'parum diligenter possessio salinarum mearum (i. e. the authenticity of his witticisms) a te procuratore defenditur . . . pugna, si me amas . . . ut sacramento contendas mea non esse,' might, if taken seriously, assume representation in the *legis actio sacramento.* But the whole passage is a mixture of legal metaphors. These words are immediately followed by an appeal to the interdict.

BOOK I.

a stereotyped phrase, which doubtless conveys the *formula* of summons, has been preserved[1].

Other employments of the vindication.

The vindication, which was the essence of this action, could be employed not only in other spheres where absolute ownership was asserted, such as the right to an inheritance or the possession of a son under power, but to the assertion of rights in things which fell short of ownership, such as the enjoyment of powers over alien property which are called servitudes. In one instance the vindication assumed the exceptional form of the assertion of a right that was not the litigant's; this was the *vindicatio* or the *contra-vindicatio in libertatem*, the claim that a man was free or the answer to the claim that he was a slave.

Hereditatis vindicatio.

The *hereditatis vindicatio* was thought of as a claim to a unity as perfect as that represented by a corporeal object; for the *familia* which was claimed was a unit which might even be transferred by purchase. In early times the *hereditas* may have been represented by some symbolic portion which was visited by the litigants; later it sufficed if a mere fragment of the property was brought within the precincts of the court. The claim to a son was equally a claim to property, but here the *potestas* was asserted rather than ownership.

Vindication applied to servitudes.

Ownership was still less apparent where a servitude, or freedom from a servitude was claimed. Here the statement and counter-statement must, unlike that of the ordinary *actio in rem*, have been respectively an assertion and a negation. It has been supposed that the opening words of the *actio confessoria*, or action asserting a servitude, may have run somewhat as follows:—

Plaintiff. AIO MIHI IUS ESSE EUNDI AGENDI IN FUNDO TUO.
Defendant. NEGO TIBI IUS ESSE, &c.;

[1] QUANDOQUE TE IN IURE CONSPICIO (Cic. *pro Caec.* 19, 54; *pro Mur.* 12, 26) POSTULO ANNE FUAS AUCTOR (Probus). The penalty of non-intervention by the *auctor* was that an *actio auctoritatis*, which was *in duplum*, might be brought against him by the purchaser. See Girard in *Nouv. Rev. Hist. de droit*, vol. vii (1882) p. 180 ff.

while in the *actio negatoria*, which asserted the freedom of property from such burdens, the order of the statements would have been reversed, e. g.:—

Plaintiff. NEGO TIBI IUS ESSE or AIO TIBI IUS NON ESSE EUNDI AGENDI, &c.

Defendant. AIO MIHI IUS ESSE, &c.

The mutual challenge to the *sacramentum* would then have followed.

Vindicatio in libertatem.

In that form of vindication which most closely touched the citizen's rights, the assertion of slavery or freedom, the champion of the latter (*adsertor in libertatem*) could not by the nature of the case assert any personal right in the object, and the *formula* must have contained a mere statement that the individual was free. This object was produced in court by a praetorian command, was grasped by the litigants and struck by the staff, and its *interim* possession was granted by the praetor according to the general rules of the action.

The *actio sacramento in personam.* **Applied to** *certa pecunia* **and** *certa res.*

The *legis actio sacramento* was as fitted to enforce a claim against a person as a claim to a thing, but only on one condition. Unless assisted by further procedure, it could deal only with an obligation that was fixed and definite (*certum*), one that entailed the payment of *certa pecunia* or the transference of a *certa res*. The contract out of which the obligation sprang had also to be one that was formally recognized by law; the defendant was one who, it was asserted, ought to give (*dare oportere*) something to the plaintiff, and the ground—perhaps the only ground—of the 'ought' in early Roman law was the solemn form of *sponsio* or *stipulatio* which it shared with so many other kindred systems, the agreement which opened with the question *spondesne dari?* and closed with the answer *spondeo*[1]. In this action

[1] The contract of *nexum*, although creating an equally formal obligation, probably did not give rise to the *actio sacramento*. It was enforced by a form of *manus iniectio*.

the plaintiff stated the obligation, the defendant entered a formal denial (*infitiatio, negatio*). Then followed the mutual challenge by *sacramentum*. The proceedings *in iure* were somewhat as follows:—

Plaintiff. AIO TE MIHI MILLE AERIS (or HOMINEM STICHUM or TRITICI AFRICI OPTIMI MODIOS CENTUM) DARE OPORTERE.

Defendant. NEGO ME TIBI, &c.

Plaintiff. QUANDO NEGAS, TE SACRAMENTO QUINGENARIO (or QUINQUAGENARIO) PROVOCO.

Defendant. QUANDO AIS NEQUE NEGAS TE SACRAMENTO, &c., PROVOCO.

The decision of the *sacramentum* was then made by the magistrate or, in later times, relegated to a *iudex*. In cases of small debts it was ordered by the *lex Pinaria* that the parties should appear again before the praetor after thirty days *ad iudicem capiendum*[1].

The rigidity of the action is clear from the formula. It gave no room for any estimate of indebtedness other than that which was formerly stated: it did not permit the *iudex* to strike a balance between the wholesale assertion and the wholesale denial. If 1000 asses were demanded and the debt of 500 was proved, the plaintiff lost his case.

This was the case also with the *certa res*; but here a further difficulty presented itself; the thing might have disappeared or been consumed and its monetary value alone could be recovered. But as there was no statement of monetary value in the formula of the action, the reduction of the thing to this form awaited the decision of another court. This complement of the sacramental action was probably the work of an arbitrator for valuing the thing in dispute (*arbiter liti aestimandae*).

Estimate of the value of a *certa res*.

If we admit the existence of such a *litis aestimatio*, it seems difficult to deny the *possibility* of a specific promise to do something (*facere*) being enforced by the *sacramentum*. The promise to perform might of course

Question whether the action could enforce a *facere*.

[1] Gaius, iv. 15.

be backed by a monetary penalty at the time of the sponsion (*poenae stipulatio*); but, if this precaution had not been taken, its enforcement is conceivable by an action claiming the performance, followed by an *arbitrium* which prescribed the pecuniary compensation for its loss.

Application of this action to delicts.

The varieties of this *personal* 'actio sacramento' were perhaps best exhibited in its application to delicts or quasi-delicts. In so far as summary penalties or the privilege of retaliation (*talio*) were not prescribed for wrongs, compensation for delict such as Theft and Assault took the form of money penalties[1]. These could be recovered by the *legis actio sacramento*, but with *formulae* varying from that of the simple *actio in personam*. Thus in the action for theft (*actio furti*), the phrases that survived into later times—

OPE CONSILIOQUE TUO FURTUM AIO FACTUM ESSE[2],
(Aio te) PRO FURE DAMNUM DECIDERE OPORTERE[3],

were probably utterances of the plaintiff in the *legis actio*.

The *legis actio per iudicis postulationem*.

The second form of *legis actio*[4] was characterized by the request made to the praetor for a *iudex* or an *arbiter*, the only part of its *formula* which is known being the words IUDICEM ARBITRUMVE POSTULO UTI DES. The determination of its scope turns very largely on the question whether the *iudex* and the *arbiter* specified in the form of words were originally distinguishable. Jurists, we

[1] Even where *talio* was prescribed 'si reus . . . iudici talionem imperanti non parebat, aestimata lite iudex hominem pecuniae damnabat' (Gell. xx. 1, 38).

[2] Cic. *de Nat. Deor.* iii. 30, 74.

[3] Gaius, iv. 37. On the phrase see Jordan, *de praedibus litis et vindiciarum* p. 13 'Decidere enim idem fere est quod transigere vel pacisci, damnum decidere itaque idem significat quod transigendo poenam dare . . . nequidquam tamen condemnatione reus damnum decidere iubetur, sed potius absolvitur vel omnino actione non tenetur quia sua sponte pro fure damnum decidendo adversario satisfecit.' Bethmann-Hollweg, on the other hand (ii. p. 301), takes *damnum* as equivalent to the 'injury,' not the 'compensation.' According to this interpretation the phrase would mean 'must, as a thief, make good the injury' (i. e. by process of law).

[4] *Per iudicis postulationem* (Gaius, iv. 12).

BOOK I.

have seen, hesitated about their identity in certain applications[1], and yet Cicero has no doubt that the connotation of *iudicium* is that it deals with a *certum*, of *arbitrium* that it is concerned with an *incertum*[2]. It is probable that a form of action which dealt not only with *all* 'incerta,' but with *some* 'certa' that were not actionable *sacramento*, was necessary as a supplement to that form of procedure, and hence that the *iudex* and the *arbiter* were, if originally identical, at least distinguishable at an early period of the history of the action. Amongst claims that could be classed as *certa* would be those for the return of an informal loan (*mutuum, commodatum*), of a deposit (*depositum*), or of a pledge (*pignus*); for a *bona fide* contract, with its clauses carefully guarded by such phrases as:—

Did it deal with *certa* that were not actionable *sacramento*?

UT INTER BONOS BENE AGIER OPORTET or,
UTI NE PROPTER TE FIDEMVE TUAM CAPTUS FRAUDATUSQUE SIEM[3],

although classed by Cicero as the subject of *arbitria*, need not always have involved the modification of a strict claim; in itself it suggests the demand for the return of a definite amount. The sphere of *arbitria* (if used with the connotation of a discretionary judgement) is clearer. Three arbiters had been enjoined by the Twelve Tables to settle disputes about the bounds of property: others had been recognized by the same Code for the division of an inheritance or disputes about a water-course; and family relations which gave rise to the actions for the recovery of a dowry (*actio rei uxoriae*) or for getting a ward's property from a guardian (*actio de rationibus distrahendis*) also required arbitration in the strict sense[4].

Its dealings with *incerta*; *arbitria*.

[1] p. 39.

[2] Cic. *pro Rosc. com.* 4, 10 'Iudicium est pecuniae certae, arbitrium incertae.'

[3] Cic. *Top.* 17, 66; *de Off.* iii. 17, 70. The second must be an utterance of the party. It is doubtful whether the first was used by the party or the praetor. See Bekker in *Zeitschr. f. R. G.* v. p. 345.

[4] Cic. *Top.* 17, 66; *de Orat.* i. 36, 166, 167. The latter case was a *tutelae*

Of the consensual contracts partnership (*societas*) must always have been of the latter class, but sale, lease, and commission (*venditio, locatio, mandatum*) may have hovered between the two. It must be remembered that these conceptions were in a state of flux when the action which we are discussing was in full working force; it must have depended on the nature of the claim and the request of the litigants whether the praetor gave the one individual known as the *iudex* or the one to three individuals known as *arbitri*. Yet the indefiniteness of the claim, leading to compromise and adjustment, is the main feature which distinguishes this second *legis actio* from the first.

Probable formalism of the language of this action.

This indefiniteness probably did not extend to the language used by the litigants. It may have been as rigid and formal as that employed in the *actio sacramento*. A tiny fragment of a *formula* employed in one of its applications—the *actio familiae herciscundae*—has survived in the words HERCTUM CIERE, 'to challenge or summon to a division [1].'

The *legis actio per condictionem*. The *condictio*.

The third form of *legis actio*—that *per condictionem*—marks a later stage of development in procedure; it was called into existence by no new relations that required legal recognition, but was a definite attempt to simplify the cumbrous procedure by which a claim to a *certum* had been maintained. The *condictio*, from which it derived its name, was a formal notice (*denuntiatio*) made by the plaintiff to the defendant that both should appear in court (*in iure*) at the end of thirty days for the purpose of selecting a *iudex* (*ad iudicem capiendum*). The pro-

iudicium and one of the litigants 'plus lege agendo petebat quam quantum lex in XII tabulis permiserat.' It is just questionable, however, whether *lege agere* is here used in the strict sense of the *legis actio*.

[1] Cic. *de Orat.* i. 56, 237. The words in Festus (p. 249) which were employed 'in iudice' conlocando, SI ALIUM PROCAS NIVE EUM PROCAS (i. e. iudicem poscis)' have been attributed to this action. They appear to be a fragment of the utterance of the magistrate who gives the iudex or arbiter and refers to the choice by the parties.

cedure was introduced by two laws, by the *lex Silia* for *certa pecunia*, by the *lex Calpurnia* for *omnis certa res* [1]. Gaius' wonder that it should have been considered worth while to invent a new form of action for a sphere already covered by an old, has been successfully shown by modern inquirers to rest on a misconception of the object of the innovation. The intention was primarily to create a greater rapidity of procedure, and perhaps secondarily to make the granting of a *iudex*, hitherto dependent on the discretion of a magistrate, obligatory for the future. The simplification of the process becomes manifest if we hold the view that the *Condictio* or *Denuntiatio* was made before the appearance of the parties in court [2]. In the sacramental process the *request* for a *iudex* was made thirty days *after* the formal proceedings *in iure* [3]. And not only were these thirty days saved, but the whole of the cumbrous proceedings which distinguished the first stage of the *legis actio sacramento* was omitted. It was only when the parties had presented themselves before the court that the *sacramentum* was mimicked and an appeal to a wager made. This indeed we are never told, but in a manifest survival of the *condictio*—the later action *de certa credita pecunia*—the mode of procedure was *per sponsionem*. The plaintiff challenged the defendant

Reasons for the introduction of this action.

Procedure *per sponsionem* in case of *certa pecunia*.

[1] Gaius, iv. 18–20 'haec quidem actio proprie condictio vocabatur; nam actor adversario denuntiabat ut ad iudicem capiendum die xxx adesset. . . . Haec autem legis actio constituta est per legem Siliam et Calpurniam: lege quidem Silia certae pecuniae; lege vero Calpurnia de omni certa re. Quare autem haec actio desiderata sit, cum de eo, quod nobis dari oportet, potuerimus sacramento aut per iudicis postulationem agere, valde quaeritur.' For *condicere* in the sense of an oral invitation or command to accomplish a certain act by a certain day see Festus, p. 64 ('condicere est dicendo denuntiare'), 66 ('condictio in diem certum eius rei, quae agitur, denuntiatio'), and Gell. x. 24, 9 ('Sacerdotes quoque populi Romani, cum condicunt in diem tertium, "diem perendini" dicunt').

[2] Keller, *Civilprocess*, § 18. The opposite view of a *denuntiatio* in court is taken by Bethmann-Hollweg, i. p. 152.

[3] p. 58.

to a wager of the third part of the sum in dispute[1], while he bound himself by a counter-promise (*restipulatio*) to surrender the same amount in case he should fail to establish his claim. In accordance with the secular spirit of the new jurisprudence the stake which was lost went no longer to religion or to the State, but to the victorious adversary. The decision pronounced on the new *sponsio*, like that on the old *sacramentum*, was a *praeiudicium* on the main issue of the case.

Procedure in case of *certa res*.

But though survivals establish this procedure for *certa pecunia*, there is no trace of a similar practice in later times for the recovery of a *certa res*. It is supposed that, in the procedure introduced by the *lex Calpurnia*, the praetor gave instructions to the *iudex* as to his finding, and if this supposition is correct, a very near approach to the later 'formulary' process was reached in this action. It was possibly this *iudex*, and not an *arbiter* subsequently appointed *liti aestimandae*, that valued the object in dispute in case of condemnation.

Both the remaining *legis actiones* agree in being executive processes undertaken by an individual outside the precincts of a court (*extra ius*) for the purpose of enforcing a right. They begin by being acts of self-help, but the self-help is regulated by law and convention, and conditioned by precise *formulae*, and both processes entail an ultimate appearance before the regular judicial authorities.

The *legis actio per pignoris capionem*.

Gaius tells us that to the first of these[2], which derived its name from its leading feature of the seizure of a pledge (*pignoris captio*[3]) the title *legis actio* was assigned by some, denied by others. The ground for the former view was furnished by the use of precise phraseology (*certa verba*) in the accomplishment of the seizure: for the latter

[1] Cic. *pro Rosc. com.* 5, 14 'Pecunia petita est certa, cum tertia parte sponsio facta est'; 4, 10 'Pecunia tibi debebatur certa, quae nunc petitur per iudicem: in qua legitimae partis sponsio facta est.'

[2] *Per pignoris capionem* (Gaius, iv. 12, 26).

[3] Gaius, iv. 28.

by the facts that the seizure was effected outside the court, often in the absence of the adversary, and was valid even on *dies nefasti* when no action at law was possible[1]. The solution of the doubt may be that the procedure dwelt on was only a *part* of a *legis actio*, constituting the mere preliminaries to an appearance in court, in which the justice of the seizure would be contested and an attempt would be made to recover the pledge. If no such attempt were made by the victim of the seizure, the pledge would remain in the hands of its captor and the preliminary procedure, in this case final, would be considered of itself to be a *legis actio*, a kind of pro-jural execution.

Originally a part of administrative law.

Although this procedure was extended by the Twelve Tables to certain relations of an unimportant character affecting the general mass of citizens, there can be no question that it was originally a part of Roman *administrative* law affecting the servants of the State sometimes to their profit, sometimes to their disadvantage. The soldier could use this means of distraining on his officer for arrears of pay, the knight for drawing the money destined for the keep and purchase of his horse from those who owed it, the *publicanus* for securing the payment of the revenues owed him under a *lex vectigalis*[2]. It is not known whether it originated as a boon to the soldier or the middle-man, but it survived longest as a privilege enjoyed by the latter.

The *legis actio per manus in-*

The last of the actions—that by personal arrest (*per manus iniectionem*) was not in its developed form primarily

[1] Gaius, iv. 29 'certis verbis pignus capiebatur et ob id plerisque placebat hanc quoque actionem legis actionem esse; quibusdam autem (*non*) placebat: primum quod pignoris captio extra ius peragebatur, id est, non apud praetorem, plerumque etiam absente adversario, cum alioquin ceteris actionibus non aliter uti possent quam apud praetorem praesente adversario; praeterea nefasto quoque die, id est, quo non licebat lege agere, pignus capi poterat.'

[2] Gaius, iv. 27, 28; cf. Cic. *in Verr.* iii. 11, 27.

PART I.

iectionem: really a form of execution.

a mode of asserting a controverted right, but of gaining fulfilment of one which had been admitted, either by the defendant or by a court. The right secured by this means was always one against a person, never against a thing: and this *legis actio* was, therefore, a form of execution following on *actiones in personam*. It is true that it had other applications, some guaranteed by custom, others by law, and these applications sometimes bring it into harmony with the other actions as a means of asserting and not of enforcing a right. But properly it is a mode of execution: and symmetry demands that we should neglect it for the moment and fix our attention on the mode in which the judgements consequent on actions in respect to things (*actiones in rem*) were enforced.

Execution following *actiones in rem.*

In such a case the recognition of the right by the magistrate and its enforcement under police protection followed immediately on the successful *vindicatio*. The symbol of state-consent to the successful litigant's absolute enjoyment of the right was the formal approbation (*addictio*) of the magistrate. The utterance of the word 'addico' enabled him to enter on the land, to enjoy the servitude, to take away the slave. The resistance of the defeated litigant to this command necessarily entailed magisterial assistance to the victor and the assertion of further rights by him. He could seize with his own hand (*ducere, abducere*[1]) the slave that had been *addictus* and could refuse the equivalent in money. If the defeated litigant had been accorded *interim* possession of the thing in dispute and now refused to restore it, the personal securities for the thing and its fruits (*praedes litis et vindiciarum*), which he had been compelled to furnish at the time when his possession was recognized, were now the objects of the victor's attack. No action was required; he could, in virtue of his already recognized right, seize and in early times sell these sureties. Later

Addictio.

Sale of *praedes*

[1] Cic. *de Orat.* ii. 63, 255; cf. *pro Quinct.* 19, 61.

BOOK I.

and counter-rights of the sureties.

the sale of their property superseded the sale of their persons[1]; but the harshness of the security in early times was alleviated by the circumstances that the securities could employ the summary method of *manus iniectio* against their debtor[2], and that the man whose *praedes* had satisfied his debt was probably *infamis*[3]. Although some have thought that this appeal to securities was the sole method of enforcing a claim to a resisted debt in an *actio in rem*, it is probable that the seizure of the thing itself, if it was practicable, was permitted to the successful litigant under protection of the magistrate. Did the thing bear produce, and had this produce been consumed, the Twelve Tables allowed the praetor to appoint three *arbitri* to assess these *fructus* and to condemn the defendant in double their value[4].

Execution following *actiones in personam*. The *manus iniectio*.

The execution in personal actions is for obvious reasons not analogous to that in an *actio in rem*. The claim in the latter case is to the whole of the thing, in the former case it is not primarily to the whole of the person but to a part of the personality; it is only when this part is not surrendered, that the claim takes the form of a conditioned right to the person itself. This is the essence of the procedure *per manus iniectionem*, and we must carefully distinguish the use of this action as the means for carrying out a judgement with its use as a means for carrying out an already admitted right based on something resembling a contract. It is only the former use that really concerns us here, but the historical and legal

[1] Jordan, *de Praedibus*, pp. 23, 34; Mommsen, *Stadtrechte*, p. 471 n. 41.

[2] Gaius, iv. 22 'Postea quaedam leges ... pro iudicato manus iniectionem in quosdam dederunt, sicut lex Publilia in eum pro quo sponsor dependisset, *si* in sex mensibus proximis quam pro eo depensum esset non solvisset sponsori pecuniam.' Cf. § 25.

[3] Amongst the cases involving *infamia* in the *Lex Iulia Municipalis* (45 B.C.) is that of one 'pro ... quo datum depensum est erit' (l. 115).

[4] Festus, p. 376 'et in xii.: Si vindiciam falsam tulit, si velit is ... *praetor* arbitros tres dato: eorum arbitrio ... fructus duplione damnum decidito.' See Jordan, *de Praedibus*, p. 13.

connexion between the two demand a brief notice of the *manus iniectio* based on contractual grounds.

The *manus iniectio* based on contractual grounds. *Nexum*.

This was the mode of enforcing one of the manifold forms of *nexum* or binding obligation created by the copper and the scales (*per aes et libram*[1]). A borrower was allowed to sell himself, i.e. his own services and those of his *familia* (for the family is the juristic unit) to his creditor conditionally—the condition being the non-repayment of the debt within a given time. It is probable that this form of *nexum* was, like one kind of testament, a *conditioned* mancipation or formal sale. The creditor may have been the *mancipio accipiens* or purchaser, the formal announcement of the conditions (*nuncupatio*) being made by him. The *mancipatus* may have been purchased with the whole amount of the loan or perhaps later with the symbolic 'single coin' (*nummus unus*) which appears in the *mancipationes fiduciae causa* which have been preserved[2]. As an illustration of the procedure we may give the following conjectural *formula*, modelled on one that survived into historic times:—

Creditor and *Purchaser*. EGO TE NUMIS C. or NUMO I FIDI FIDUCIAE CAUSA MANCIPIO ACCEPI.

Then would follow the *nuncupatio* closing with the words:—

SI PECUNIA SOLUTA NON ESSET—TUM UTI EGO TE MANCIPIO HABEREM.

When the prescribed time had elapsed without repayment of the debt, the debtor and his whole *familia* passed into the power of his purchaser. He became his bondsman (*nexus*) until the debt had been paid by his labour. The *nexus* remained a citizen and was not in public law a

[1] Cic. *de Orat.* iii. 40, 159; cf. *Top.* 5, 28. In *de Har. Resp.* 7, 14 and *ad Fam.* vii. 30, 2 *nexum* and *mancipium* seem to be used indifferently to express the same obligation. In the former passage full acquired ownership, in the latter full ownership seems to be implied.

[2] Bruns, *Fontes*, p. 294.

BOOK I.

slave; but the line that separated such serfdom from the condition of actual slavery was a very thin one. It seems clear that no judicial process was necessary to create this servitude or to empower the creditor to effect the arrest of his insolvent debtor. The simple proof of the debt and its conditions (perhaps given before a magistrate) by the witnesses to the contract was all that was required.

The *manus iniectio* based on the judgement of a court.

It is possible that the *legis actio per manus iniectionem*[1], with which we are more immediately concerned, may have originated from this contract of *nexum*, although it is equally possible that it had an independent origin, both being based on the same primary conception that the right against a person *must* be fully satisfied, even if the whole personality be ultimately involved. The point that differentiates the *legis actio* from the procedure already described is that it assumes a judgement, and not a contractual debt: that it must, therefore, be preceded by the judgement of a court or by the confession of one of the parties in a court. When the issue had been decided[2] the *iudicatus* or the *confessus* was allowed thirty days' grace for the purpose of finding the money in settlement of the judgement debt[3]. When this time had lapsed the creditor could lay hand on the debtor, wherever he met him, with the words:—

Formula of the creditor and protest of the debtor.

QUOD TU MIHI IUDICATUS SIVE DAMNATUS ES[4] SESTERTIUM X MILIA, QUANDOC NON SOLVISTI, OB EAM REM EGO TIBI SESTERTIUM X MILIUM IUDICATI MANUS INIICIO.

[1] Gaius, iv. 12, 21.

[2] In the case where the object in dispute was, not *certa pecunia*, but a *certa res*, the *iudicatum* was not reached until the value of this had been assessed by a *iudex* or an *arbiter liti aestimandae*.

[3] The Twelve Tables enacted 'Aeris confessi rebusque iure iudicatis triginta dies iusti sunto. Post deinde manus iniectio esto, in ius ducito. Ni iudicatum facit aut quis endo eo in iure vindicit, secum ducito, vincito aut nervo aut compedibus. Quindecim pondo ne minore aut si volet maiore vincito. Si volet suo vivito. Ni suo vivit, qui eum vinctum habebit, libras farris endo dies dato. Si volet plus dato' (Gell. xx. i. 45).

[4] Or, in the case of *confessio in iure*, CONFESSUS ES. For *quandoc* Eisele would

But the act gave no immediate power over the debtor; the arrested man was brought before the praetor; there were yet two possibilities of escape, payment of the debt or protest against its being due. It is to the possibility of this protest that the singular cumbrousness of Roman executive procedure is due, but it was a necessary result of the original recognition of self-help as a mode of enforcing obligations. The protest, however, could not be made by the creditor himself after the *manus iniectio* had been completed. It must be made through a representative who, possibly from the fiction that he was an individual with a prior claim on the person of the debtor, was called *vindex*[1]. Did the *vindex* fail in his defence, he was himself liable to the payment of double the amount of the original debt.

The *vindex*.

Consequences of arrest.

This payment may have freed the original debtor[2]. In default of such defence he must submit to the consequences of arrest. He is taken to the house of his creditor with the formal consent (*addictio*) of the magistrate. But still for a time he is treated only as a pledge; the *addictus* can still compound with his creditor, and for sixty days the precarious state continues. During this interval he is produced on three successive market days before the magistrate, the amount of the debt is cried in the *comitium*, and any who will may be his ransomer. It is only after this appeal has been made in vain that the creditor can exercise his extreme rights. The captive might be put to death, sold into slavery beyond the Tiber, or kept like the *nexus* in a lasting servitude[3]. In theory he was perhaps working out his debt, but we hear of no estimate

read *quando te* (*Beiträge*, p. 22). The suggested phrase would, however, suit the contract of *nexum* better than the obligation of a judgement debt.

[1] *Vindex* connected with *vindico* (*vim dico*) meant primarily a man who 'claimed' a thing, not who 'defended' it. He defended it only because he claimed it.

[2] See Appendix, note I.

[3] Gell. XX. 1, 42-48; Gaius, iv. 21.

BOOK I.

by the State of the amount of labour necessary for the satisfaction of a claim. A concourse of creditors with conflicting claims could divide the debtor's body[1], a primitive anticipation of the later division of his property.

Possible modification of this mode of execution by the *lex Poetilia*.

It is possible that the harshness of this procedure was at a comparatively early period mitigated by law. The *lex Poetilia* of 313 B.C.[2], which practically abolished the older rights springing from the contract of *nexum* and spoke of the 'goods' where the older law had spoken of the 'body' of the creditor, perhaps improved the lot of the *iudicatus* as well. It is true that the *manus iniectio* still continued until the praetor had devised a substitute for it. The creditor was still arrested, led to his debtor's house, even put in bonds; were he wholly insolvent he may still have had to work for his creditor, although perhaps under better conditions and with a stricter estimate of the requisite labour than before. But the law, although it did not abolish judicial as it did contractual servitude, suggested that the seizure and sale of the debtor's goods (*bona*) should be effected before proceedings were taken to effect his detention.

Manus iniectio perhaps applied to a form of *in iure cessio*.

Hitherto we have treated the *manus iniectio* as a consequence of a judgement, or of its equivalent, a confession. It would have been a slight step to make it the consequence

[1] Gell. xx. 1, 48.

[2] Varro, *L. L.* viii. 105 'Liber, qui suas operas in servitutem pro pecunia quam debet dat, dum solveret nexus vocatur, ut ab aere obaeratus. Hoc C. Poetilio Libone Visolo (*Lachmann* for C. popillio vocare sillo) dictatore sublatum ne fieret: et omnes, qui bonam copiam iurarunt, ne essent nexi dissoluti.' *Qui bonam copiam iurarunt* probably means 'who swore that they had reasonable hopes (literally "means") of ultimately satisfying their creditors.' C. Poetilius was dictator in 313 B.C., but the change referred to is doubtless that mentioned by Livy (viii. 28) in connexion with the year 326: 'iussique consules ferre ad populum ne quis, nisi qui noxam meruisset, donec poenam lueret, in compedibus aut in nervo teneretur: pecuniae creditae bona debitoris, non corpus obnoxium esset.' Cf. Cic. *de Rep.* ii. 34, 59 'Fuerat fortasse aliqua ratio maioribus nostris in illo aere alieno medendi . . . cum sunt . . . omnia nexa civium liberata nectierque postea desitum.'

of a quasi-judgement based on confession, and it may have been the mode of executing a personal obligation analogous to that of the *in iure cessio*. The cession in court is an undefended *vindicatio in rem*. If we suppose that in a personal as well as in a real action, one party might assert a claim and the other by agreement raise no protest and thus incur a *debitum*, the latter might have been considered the *confessus* of contentious jurisdiction, and the *manus iniectio* might have been applied to enforce the claim which he had admitted.

Other applications ordained by law.

Other and more certain applications give it a still greater appearance of an independent action. The *lex Publilia* granted it to the security (*sponsor*) against the principal debtor, if the latter had not reimbursed him within six months. A *lex Furia* further allowed sureties this means of recovery against those who had exacted from them more than the amounts for which they were individually liable[1]. In these cases the fiction of a *iudicatum* was assumed and the action was known as *manus iniectio pro iudicato*; a *vindex* was necessary to contest the action, and the penalty of his unsuccessful denial was the doubling of the debt. It was distinguished from a few applications of the action which were known as *manus iniectio pura*[2]; here the person arrested could defend the action without the intervention of a representative, but the penalty of denial was the same. The survival of this *poena dupli* in later Roman procedure may, in most cases where it occurs, attest the original employment of this form of action[3].

§ 5. *The Interdict.*

Meaning of *interdicta*.

The *actiones* formed in theory the whole of the proceedings *in iure*, when the reassertion of a violated right was in question, and it is probable that the incidental

[1] Gaius, iv. 22. [2] *ib.* § 23.

[3] e. g. in the *actio iniuriarum* springing from the *lex Aquilia* (Bethmann-Hollweg, i. p. 163).

BOOK I.

commands of the magistrate, e.g. for the exhibition of a thing or for the peaceful recovery of a possession, were originally treated as parts of the action, for without these it would have been ineffective and incomplete. It is just possible that such occasional remarks of the magistrate to the two parties may have been spoken of as 'interlocutions,' for such is the nearest approach to a translation of the word *interdictum*; which means an intervention of the magistrate *between* two people accompanied by a remark addressed to both of them[1].

They transcend the sphere of the *legis actiones*.

But long before Ciceronian times, and therefore well within the period of the *legis actio*, both the name and the practice had extended far beyond these limits. The praetors had long been prohibiting violence or ordering restitution in a manner quite independent and outside the scope of the older actions. In the Ciceronian period the praetor's command was meant to invite and prepare an action, which was itself of praetorian growth. It was intended to supplement the narrowness and to simplify the elaboration of the older forms of procedure. To what sources can this remarkable development of a form of procedure never contemplated in the constitution be assigned? Three may perhaps be specified.

Origin of the interdicts: (i) police regulations.

(i) A glance at the interdicts shows that a large number are of the nature of injunctions meant to secure the safety and comfort of the public, and even to protect its religious

[1] Gaius, iv. 139 'Certis igitur ex causis praetor aut proconsul principaliter auctoritatem suam finiendis controversiis interponit: quod tum maxime facit cum de possessione aut quasi possessione inter aliquos contenditur; et in summa aut iubet aliquid fieri aut fieri prohibet.' For the relation which the interdict assumes between two parties see Cic. *de Orat.* i. 10, 41 'qui aut interdicto tecum contenderent'; cf. the reference to the interdict *uti possidetis* in *de Rep.* i. 13, 20 'nisi forte Manilius interdictum aliquod inter duos soles putat esse componendum, ut ita caelum possideant, ut uterque possederit.' The character of the interdict is clearly expressed in its supposed (and probably correct) etymology (Justin. *Inst.* iv. 15, 1 'obtinuit omnia interdicta appellari, quia inter duos dicuntur.' Cf. Theoph. *ad h. l.* Ἰντερδίκτον ἐστιν ὁμιλία πραίτωρος μεταξὺ δύο τινῶν).

susceptibilities. They are the orders of a Police Commissioner or of an Ecclesiastical Court. We should expect an order against blocking a river or building on its bank to come from a purely executive magistrate, the consul or the aedile: while a command against the desecration of a sacred place would seem more appropriate to the pontifex than to the praetor. Yet they are injunctions which in the historical period are issued from the Civil Tribunal of Rome. The reason for this appears to be two-fold. In the first place we must remember that an executive magistrate occupied the tribunal, and as such injunctions, which are generally of the nature of prohibitions, are always issued *ex post facto*, the court and the court-days were the most fitting place and time for their expression. Secondly, the tendency of the administrative, like that of the criminal, law of Rome was to make the individual citizen the guardian of the welfare of the community; the magistrates were exponents but not inspectors, and the protest of a citizen against a breach of public order which affected himself would not unnaturally be heard before the civil court.

(ii) Commands to protect undefended rights.

(ii) The function of the interdict as an *interim* command necessary to facilitate the course of justice offered an irresistible inducement to its extension. The order for the production of an individual under power by some one who was detaining him must always have been in vogue, although not necessarily in its later interdictal form; when written testaments came into use, a similar 'exhibitory' interdict had to be framed to effect their production. There were some spheres of right which, so far as we can see, could only be enforced by praetorian command, e. g. the prohibition of violence being used against one who cut down a neighbour's tree which impended on his house. Such spheres were ever increasing in fact though not in strict law. One of the newest and greatest of these facts with which the magistrate had to cope was the growth of a theory of 'possession' which fell short of perfect ownership. The extension of the 'restitutory' and the framing of the 'prohibitory' decrees which protected such occupation were a necessary means of defending by interdict what was not defended by law.

(iii) Provisional rules preparatory to a *iudicium*.

(iii) And this growth of a new praetorian Jurisprudence —for the protection of rights is nothing less—introduces us to another probable source for the extension of the interdictal procedure. The praetor wanted new forms of action to defend the rights which he was creating. The original defence was in the *imperium* alone, but the estimate of the merits of the case must always have required some magisterial cognizance (*cognitio*). But in an age familiar with the jury-system and to a magistrate burdened with the cases of Romans dwelling now between the Padus and the straits of Messina, this system was burdensome and unsatisfactory. The praetor wished to state a case for *iudex* or *recuperatores*, and one of the simplest modes of effecting this was to frame an interdict and then ask the *iudicium* to decide whether there had been 'exhibition,' 'restitution,' or 'violence,' as the case might be, within the meaning of its terms. The praetor had, as we shall see, many devices for framing new actions, but the interdict was perhaps the simplest of them all.

PART II

THE COURTS OF THE CICERONIAN PERIOD.

§ 1. *The Relation of the Magistrates to the Laws.*

PART II.

Shares of the magistrate and the law in the increase of civil rights.

THE history of the public is in one respect very different from that of the civil law of Rome. In the domain of administrative or of criminal jurisprudence the tendency is to increase the citizen's liberty by limiting the magistrate's power through legislation. In the civil law, on the other hand, we find the growth of new rights unaccompanied by any very marked development in legislation, and it is hardly too much to say that the freedom of intercourse, the abolition of vexatious trammels, the recognition of natural claims were not only accompanied by, but were actually the product of, an enormous increase in the power of the judicial magistrate. It is important to determine how far there was, in Ciceronian times, a recognition of this power, how it was defended when recognized, and how it was supposed to be adjusted to the 'rule of law.'

Rights as the outcome of *lex*,

It is possible to collect a series of passages from Cicero's philosophical and oratorical works which, taken alone, would tend to exhibit the Roman constitution and the Roman judicature as resting wholly on a basis of statute law (*lex*). In one passage the magistrate seems to be regarded as the mouthpiece of *lex*; he is a 'speaking law' as the law is a 'mute magistrate[1]': in another the *im-*

[1] Cic. *de Leg.* iii. 1, 2 'magistratum legem esse loquentem, legem autem mutum magistratum.'

BOOK I.

perium is the correlative, perhaps it even implied the outcome, of *lex*[1]. The *lex* is the guiding power of the State as the mind is of the body; the magistrates are the ministers of the laws (*legum ministri*), the *iudices* their interpreters, the commonalty their slaves[2]. Like Aristotle Cicero represents law as the passionless reason, the calm immobility of which should be imitated by the guiders of the Republic[3]; like him again he believes that right (*ius*) can be obtained through the rule of a personality; but the age for this soon passes; a refinement of justice has been attained when *leges* have been invented 'to speak with all men ever with one and the same voice[4].' Sometimes these utterances may be due to an unconscious imitation of Greek originals, sometimes they are the outcome of the exigencies of the moment; but while they emphasize the fact that every activity of the State can be found to have somewhere or other its basis, or at least its partial foundation, in a statute, they can hardly be pressed to mean much more than this. In the last-cited passage he has risen to a higher plane than *lex*—to *ius* itself, of which he clearly conceives law to be, if an essential, only a partial expression[5].

of ius and of mos maiorum.

A full, if popular, summary of the grounds of civic liberty is to be found in the juxta-position of the three phrases *ius*, *mos maiorum*, *leges*[6]. The two latter are partial expressions or modes of manifestation of the first; yet even the second does not adequately

[1] Cic. *de Leg.* iii. 1, 3.

[2] Cic. *pro Cluent.* 53, 146 'Legum ministri magistratus, legum interpretes iudices, legum denique idcirco omnes servi sumus ut liberi esse possimus.'

[3] Cic. *de Off.* i. 25, 89.

[4] *Ib.* ii. 12, 41, 42; cf. *Top.* 25, 95 'quoniam lege firmius in controversiis disceptandis esse nihil debet, danda est opera ut legem adiutricem . . . adhibeamus.'

[5] So procedure (*actio*) springs from *ius*; 'ius actionemque' (Cic. *pro Caec.* 11, 32) are right and the means by which it is enforced.

[6] Cic. *pro Sest.* 34, 73. A fuller classification of the grounds of *ius civile* in its widest sense is given in *Top.* 5, 28 'si quis ius civile dicat id esse quod in legibus, senatus consultis, rebus iudicatis, iurisperitorum auctoritate, edictis magistratuum, more, aequitate consistat.'

convey the idea deeply rooted in the Roman mind that there are rights which form the background of the structure of the State and which even the law of the State dare not infringe. This belief finds a striking expression in the scruple which led Roman legislators to append to their enactments the saving clause:—

SI QUID IUS NON ESSET ROGARIER, EIUS EA LEGE NIHILUM ROGATUM.

The clause safeguarded a law against being a breach of some ultimate religious obligation: but it might recognize, if we follow Cicero on a point on which many jurists of the time were in agreement with him, a right hardly less sacred than one supported by religion. When Cicero read this clause from the law of Sulla which disfranchised Volaterrae and many other towns, he asked 'Is there a *ius* which the people cannot command or forbid?' 'This ascription declares there is,' he answered; and he agreed, for it guaranteed, in spite of legislation, the citizenship of his client, Caecina the Volaterran[1].

Ius wider than *lex*.

If we transfer this idea to the sphere of private rights its content is manifestly increased; it is so clear, to use Cicero's own expression, that a *iudicium* is about a *ius*[2]; it is only an incident if it is also concerned with a *lex*. The *ius*, to be validly upheld, must of course have claimed universal or at least authoritative recognition: but the Roman mind does not seem to have regarded it as necessary that this recognition should be based on statute. The courts of Rome, like those of every other aristo-

[1] Cic. *pro Caec.* 33, 95; cf. *pro Domo* 40, 106 'Quae tua fuit consecratio? Tuleram, inquit, ut mihi liceret. Quid? Non exceperas ut, si quid ius non esset rogari, ne esset rogatum?' An apparent denial of the supremacy of *Fas* over law in international relations is contained in the words of the *pro Balbo* (15, 35) 'Sacrosanctum enim nihil potest esse nisi quod per populum plebemve sanctum est.' But it is only apparent, the meaning merely being that a definite legal sanction is required for a thing to be *sacrosanctum*. Cf. Festus, p. 318.

[2] 'ius de quo iudicium est' (Cic. *pro Caec.* 4, 10). Cf. *pro Tull.* 18, 42; *de Off.* ii. 12, 42.

cratically governed state, are a combined reflection of the popular mind and of the higher practical tendencies of the rulers. Now the popular mind hardly recognized such a thing as a body of statute laws at all; even the learned had to ferret the *leges* out of the archives by means of skilled assistants[1], and perhaps there never was a State in which the laws sank so rapidly into desuetude as at Rome. The people had got their *ius* from authority, from the pontifices, the consuls and the praetors. But this was only possible on the condition that the magistrate kept pace with the demands of the time; and the higher minds of Rome were eminently suited to fulfil this hardest of all tasks. Their conviction of the necessity of the rigidity of law—a conviction which finds expression in the intense dislike to codification and in the antiquated structure of even their more recent statutes—combined with a genuine belief in the existence of rights wider than those recognized by *leges*, gave an impulse to interpretation which has not found its equal in history. External causes—the world empire, perhaps even the Stoic philosophy—had their influence on the judge-made law of Rome; but they were only added *stimuli*, in no sense true causes. The Roman had grasped the difference between form and spirit long before either of these tendencies had begun to influence his life.

The power of interpretation: judge-made law.

§ 2. *The Magistrate.*

(a) *at Rome.*

The magistrates at Rome with civil jurisdiction.

There were but three magistracies at Rome which had any claim to the exercise of ordinary civil jurisdiction: and two of these demand but a passing notice. We have already seen that the jurisdiction latent in the consular *imperium* could occasionally be excited, not however in the form of cognizance in a court of first instance, but only

[1] Cic. *de Leg.* iii. 20, 46 'Legum custodiam nullam habemus. Itaque eae leges sunt quas apparitores nostri volunt: a librariis petimus.'

as a controlling power meant to stay, but not to supersede, the rulings of the praetor[1]. The jurisdiction of the curule aediles, although it took the form of actual cognizance of cases *ab initio*, was limited to a certain narrow class of legal relations and delicts[2]. The ordinary jurisdiction was vested wholly in the two courts of the urban and the foreign praetors. In spite of the differences in their spheres of administration all that we shall have to say about praetorian jurisdiction applies equally to both these magistrates, with one exception. This occurs in the mention of *ius civile*, the rights only possible to citizens, with which the peregrine praetor had no immediate concern. Yet an analogous treatment of the two magistrates is possible even with respect to their relation to the fixed laws of Rome; for wherever statutes bound the praetor peregrinus he was subject to the same limitations which the urban praetor experienced from the trammels of the *ius civile*.

PART II.

The praetor as the exponent of the civil law.

The praetor, says Cicero (and he means pre-eminently the urban praetor), is to be the guardian of the civil law (*iuris civilis custos*)[3]. Although it is undoubtedly true that, from an ideal standpoint, the praetor's mind should be a treasure-house of the material or substantive law of Rome[4], yet this custody was pre-eminently a guardianship of forms. In the earlier period of the history of the procedure of his court he was the keeper of the *legis actiones*, in the later period he was the keeper of the *formulae*, which the statute law of Rome permitted to replace the older forms of action. These *formulae* of the *civil* law of Rome[5] constituted, as we shall see, the ground

The *formulae* of the civil law.

[1] p. 29. [2] p. 31.

[3] Cic. *de Leg.* iii. 3, 8 'Iuris disceptator, qui privata iudicet iudicarive iubeat, praetor esto. Is iuris civilis custos esto.'

[4] Cic. *de Leg.* i. 5, 17 'Non ergo a praetoris edicto, ut plerique nunc, neque a XII tabulis, ut superiores, sed penitus ex intima philosophia hauriendam iuris disciplinam putas.'

[5] For such *formulae* of the civil law see Cic. *de Nat. Deorum*, iii. 30, 74

of what was known as a *iudicium legitimum*, i. e. a court composed of a single *iudex* and trying cases which had formerly been provided for by a *legis actio*. But the custody of forms of law had long been accompanied by their publicity, and the praetor's mode of exposition was to write up the still surviving *legis actiones* and the *formulae* on a whitened board (*album*) that any one who chose might come and claim the particular vehicle of his rights. These skeletons of cases must have had rubricated headings to make them in the least degree intelligible, but there is no evidence that they were furnished with either explanation or commentary [1]. The ground on which the particular *formula* was to be selected could be sought only from a skilled lawyer; and it is possible that the praetor, though bound to give what was asked, may have lent his assistance in the choice. Nor is it at all likely that these *civil* 'formulae' were preceded by any ruling in law, by any promise of an action, or in fact by anything of the nature of an edict [2]. For the praetor could not promise where he could not refuse, and the ruling was not his but that of the *ius civile*. So far the praetor professes to be only an exponent of something beyond and behind him. It is true that, even in this department, his predecessors had been creators (for the elaboration of these *formulae* had been their own work), but these forms of the *ius civile* were limited to a definite sphere, and a fixity was attained which made the praetor little more than the mouthpiece of the civil law.

In strong contrast with this position stands what we may

'iudicia (which, in Cicero, are practically equivalent to "formulae") de fide mala, tutelae, mandati, pro socio, fiduciae: reliqua, quae ex empto aut vendito aut conducto aut locato contra fidem fiunt.' The *formulae* of all these *bonae fidei iudicia* are *in ius conceptae*, and belong to the *ius civile*.

[1] Wlassak, *Edict und Klageform*, pp. 119, 123.

[2] The words of Cicero (*de Fin.* ii. 22, 74) 'est enim tibi edicendum, quae sis observaturus in iure dicendo,' cannot refer to the forms of the civil law, for the observance of these was binding on the praetor.

The *ius honorarium*.

call his *edictal* authority[1]. He was the source of what was known as 'magistrates' law' (*ius honorarium*), a term which the jurists employ in marked contrast, either expressed or implied, to the *ius civile*. It is briefly described as 'that which we are told by the perpetual edict to do or to leave undone[2].' The motive for the creation and recognition of this great body of judge-made law was, according to Papinian, 'to help, to supplement, to correct the civil law for the sake of public utility[3].' If any sharp distinction can be drawn between these three means of modification, the 'help' might refer to the cognizance of cases not provided for by the civil law at all, e. g. the rights of 'possession,' the 'supplement' to the employment of new means in reaching an old end, e. g. the recognition of damages in place of retaliation in cases of *iniuria*, the 'correction' to a change in the end itself, e. g. the recognition of cognatic as well as agnatic relationships in the transmission of inheritances. Such a vast supplement to the civil law suggests at first sight immense creative energy and a boldness of design and of innovation such as we do not generally associate with the Roman character. The creative genius, which is here more than a mere faculty for adaptation, is undeniable, and the receptive or passive elements in the *ius honorarium* only

[1] Justin. *Inst.* i. 2, 7 'Praetorum quoque edicta non modicam iuris optinent auctoritatem. Haec etiam ius honorarium solemus appellare, quod qui honores gerunt, id est magistratus, auctoritatem huic iuri dederunt.' Pompon. in Dig. 1, 2, 2, 10 'Eodem tempore et magistratus iura reddebant et, ut scirent cives quod ius de quaque re quisque dicturus esset, seque praemunirent, edicta proponebant; quae edicta praetorum ius honorarium constituerunt: honorarium dicitur, quod ab honore praetoris venerat.'

[2] Modestinus, in Dig. 44, 7, 52, 6 'Iure honorario obligamur ex his, quae edicto perpetuo vel a magistratu fieri praecipiuntur vel fieri prohibentur.'

[3] Papin. in Dig. 1, 1, 7, 1 'Ius praetorium est quod praetores introduxerunt adiuvandi vel supplendi vel corrigendi iuris civilis gratia propter utilitatem publicam.' For the contrast between *ius civile* and *ius praetorium* see Cic. *pro Caec.* 12, 34; for that between *lex* and *edictum* see *Top.* 5, 28.

BOOK I.

exhibit the wise moderation with which it was guided. It cannot be treated as a carefully thought out code, but must be regarded as a modest necessity of the times in so far as it was a means of meeting the growing demands of life without legislation—to the Roman always the last resort—and in so far as it was suggested by obvious *lacunae* in the civil law. The result of these self-imposed limitations was a fortunate avoidance of conflict between the two systems. There is no confusing concurrence between 'honorary' and civil actions. It is true that a civil action was sometimes replaced by an honorary (one of the aspects of the 'correction' spoken of by Papinian), but, where it was allowed to stand, the praetor did not offer another as an alternative, and the Roman jurists are surprised and perplexed when they sometimes think they discover the possibility of alternative modes of procedure. 'It is a ground for wonder why an honorary action should have been introduced when civil actions apply here[1].' 'What was the good of the praetor promising an action when the case is covered by the *lex Aquilia*[2]?' are the kinds of expression they use when such an anomaly meets their eyes.

No concurrence between *ius civile* and *ius honorarium*.

A point in the *ius honorarium* could find expression only through an edict. The *edictum* was the proclamation through which the Roman magistrate communicated with the public and expressed his commands, prohibitions and offers of assistance. But, while some edicts were merely occasional announcements, others, such as those of the praetors, curule aediles, and provincial governors, were

The *edictum*, a collection of rulings (*edicta*).

[1] Ulp. in Dig. 4, 9 (*nautae*, etc.) 3, 1 'Ait praetor; "nisi restituent, in eos iudicium dabo." Ex hoc edicto in factum actio proficiscitur. Sed an sit necessaria, videndum, quia agi civili actione ex hac causa poterit . . . miratur igitur (Pomponius), cur honoraria actio sit inducta, cum sint civiles.'

[2] Ulp. in Dig. 7, 1 (*de usu fructu*), 13, 2 'Denique consultus (Iulianus) quo bonum fuit actionem polliceri praetorem, cum competat legis Aquiliae actio, respondit, quia sunt casus quibus cessat Aquiliae actio.' See Wlassak, *Processgesetze*, i. p. 13.

'continuous' (*perpetua*), i.e. intended to have a permanent character, and were transmitted through successive holders of the office (*tralaticia*)[1]. But the *edictum* itself was not properly a body of rules: it was an utterance on a single point, however general that point might be[2]. The body of praetorian law was thus a collection of separate *edicta*, which subsequently became clauses in a tabulated *ius honorarium*. From this primitive sense a second was soon developed. It became usual to speak of the whole table of praetorian law as '*the* edict,' and sometimes to speak of the separate rulings as heads (*capita*)[3] or clauses (*clausulae*)[4] of the whole document. But this is the limit to the proper application of the word; it should only designate the praetor's rulings in whole or in part.

The *album*.

But these rulings were written on the *album* which contained the *formulae* of both civil and praetorian law, and, although in strict legal terminology the *album* was distinguished from the *edictum*, it was not unnatural that the name of the most striking portion of the *album* should be employed to designate the whole, although it is difficult to determine in any given case whether the *formulae* of *civil* law are included or excluded where this usage is found[5].

Contents of the *album*.

The great notice-board of the praetor must have contained three distinct things: first, the *legis actiones* that had survived and the *formulae* of civil law, where these

[1] For these terms, as applied to the praetor's edict, see Ascon. *in Cornelian.* p. 52 (cited p. 97) and Cic. *in Verr.* i. 44, 114 'in re tam usitata (the praetorian *hereditatis possessio*) satis est ostendere omnes antea ius ita dixisse et hoc vetus edictum translaticiumque esse.'

[2] Cic. *pro Quinct.* 19, 60; 29, 89; *in Verr.* i. 41, 105, 106; 43, 110; 44, 114; 45, 115; 48, 125; ii. 13, 33, 34; iii. 10, 25, 26; *pro Caec.* 16, 45.

[3] Cic. *in Verr.* i. 46, 118; *ad Fam.* iii. 8, 4.

[4] Cic. *in Verr.* iii. 14, 35.

[5] *Edictum* (Cic. *in Verr.* i. 43, 112; 45, 116; 46, 118); *album* (Cic. *de Leg.* i. 5, 17; *Lex Rubria*, c. 20, *ll.* 24, 25, 34, 35; Labeo, in Dig. 2, 13, 1; Gaius, iv. 46); *edictum* for *album* (Gaius, iv. 118 'Exceptiones . . . in edicto praetor habet propositas').

BOOK I.

had replaced the older actions: secondly, the praetor's new rulings: and thirdly, the praetorian *formulae* which were consequent on these rulings, and which are said sometimes to be in the edict (*in edicto*)[1], but are more properly described as springing from the edict (*ex edicto*)[2]. The *civil* 'formulae' must have stood alone unsupported by promise or commentary, but it is difficult to determine the relative places in the *album* of the praetor's edict and the praetorian *formulae*: to determine, that is, whether the *edicta* formed a complete whole and the *formulae* another whole, or whether each *formula* followed its appropriate edict. The *album* itself must have formed a series of numbered tables, such as were employed for the publication of municipal laws at the close of the Republic[3], and the different portions of the praetor's work may have appeared on different tablets. The arrangement of the *edictum perpetuum*, however, by Salvius Julianus in the reign of Hadrian, suggests that each action was brought into close juxtaposition with its appropriate edict, and although this system may have been a change due to the compiler, it must always have suggested itself as the more logical treatment and the one which was easier for litigants, and it may for these reasons be assumed to have been the praetor's original design. But still the *formulae* and the *edicta* must be considered two very different parts of the *album*, which did not always come into being at the same time and had different significations when they were created. While the edict is the rule, the *formula* is the skeleton outline of its application: and it is almost idle to discuss the relative importance

Relative positions of the *formulae* and the *edicta*.

[1] Gaius, ii. 253 '(utiles actiones) in edicto proponuntur'; iv. 31 '(stipulatio), quae in edicto proposita est.'

[2] *Ex edicto* (Cic. *Top.* 4, 18; *pro Cluent.* 60, 165; *ad Fam.* vii. 21; *in Verr.* i. 48, 125; *pro Quinct.* 6, 25; 14, 45; 15, 48, 50; 19, 60; 20, 65; 22, 73; 24, 76; 25, 79; 26, 83; 29, 88, 89).

[3] The table which we possess of the *lex Rubria* is numbered IIII (Bruns, *Fontes*, p. 98).

of the two, for while the value of the first appealed more strongly to the legal and scientific mind, the latter must have had far more importance in the eyes of the average litigant. Historically the *formula* might, and perhaps generally did, come first, for it is easier to frame a case than to make a rule; the praetor might not know whether the temporary assistance which he was offering might need to be permanent: or he might borrow a *formula* from some contemporary edict (that, for instance, of a provincial governor) without ever converting it into a rule of law. The action of mortgage (*actio hypothecaria*) seems to be an illustration of the last-mentioned tendency. It was perhaps taken from the provincial edict of some Hellenised province where ὑποθήκη was in use, and is always appealed to as a *formula*, no mention being made of an edict on which it rested[1]. The multiplicity of *formulae* dwelt on by Cicero[2] shows what extreme difficulty there must have been in reducing a mass of case-law to a general principle. The praetor, in the perfection of his *ius honorarium*, must have generally proceeded from the particular to the general: and Cicero's constant references to the *edicta* and to the principles of the *album* show that this work must have been very fully accomplished by his time. When the stage of an edict had been reached, there can be no doubt as to its preponderance over the *formula*, from a juristic point of view. It is true that no argument for its superior importance can be drawn from the commentaries of the later jurists: for, when they wrote, the formulary procedure was in its decay or no longer in use; but an argument may be drawn from the way in which the *edictum* is treated both in juristic writings and in general literature. It is placed side by side with *lex*, with particular *leges*, with *senatus consulta*, with the code of the Twelve

Historic priority of the *formula*: juristic priority of the *edictum*.

Functions attributed to the *edictum*.

[1] Wlassak, *Edict und Klageform*, p. 130.

[2] Cic. *Top.* 8, 33 'si stipulationum aut iudiciorum formulas partiare, non est vitiosum in re infinita praetermittere aliquid.'

BOOK I. Tables as a source of authoritative law[1]. The edict commands, forbids, prohibits, punishes, restrains, has, in short, all the external applications of a law: and it is possible for a man to be bound by an edict, to fall under it, and to act contrary to its provisions[2]. The edict is treated as the origin of actions; and a praetorian action springs *ex edicto*, as a civil action might spring *ex lege*[3]. In all these cases the actions are contained in and expressed through *formulae*, and the ultimate subordination of the latter is, therefore, manifest. This secondary character of the *formula* may be still further exhibited by a glance at the wording of the *edicta* as they appeared in the *album*. Most of the clauses are permissive of actions and conclude with the words *actionem* or *iudicium dabo*. But others are of a negative character, e.g. the clause about the oath as an alternative to action (*de iure iurando*) declares that, in the case of the man who has sworn or, when prepared to swear, has had his oath remitted, *no* action will be granted (*neque in ipsum neque in eum ad quem ea res pertinet actionem dabo*); others, again, issue commands which contain no reference to any particular kind of action, e.g. the edict *de postulando* which prohibits certain persons from appearing as representatives of others, the edicts which guarantee interim possession to a creditor (*missio in possessionem*), or which promise, under certain circumstances, to treat a condemnation as null and void (*in integrum restitutio*). It is only the first class of these injunctions that could be followed

[1] Cic. *pro Caec.* 18, 51 'Quae lex, quod senatus consultum, quod magistratus edictum . . . non infirmari ac convelli potest, si ad verba rem deflectere velimus.' *Cf. de Leg.* i. 5, 17. Gaius, iii. 82 'successiones quae neque lege XII tabularum neque praetoris edicto . . . introductae sunt'; cf. iii. 78. Modestinus, in Dig. 34, 7, 52 'obligamur . . . aut lege aut iure honorario.'

[2] 'adversus edictum' (Cic. *pro Caec.* 16, 45); 'contra edictum' (*in Verr.* iii. 10, 25).

[3] See p. 88, note 2, and compare 'iudicium ex edicto' (*in Verr.* iii. 11, 28; 12, 29; 13, 33; 65, 152; *pro Flacco*, 35, 88).

by *formulae*, and here the *iudicium dabo* of the praetor—i. e. a promise in the edict—is the basis of the action.

Final relation of *edictum* to *formula*.

The edict, in fact, is rather a part of substantive law, the *formula* of procedure. The latter is a concrete expression of the law, and was used by the jurists (as the praetor himself, perhaps, meant it to be employed) as a mode of interpreting the edict. It is even possible that the typical illustrations and representative personalities, found in the legal text-books, were employed by the praetor in his *album*, that the *patera aurea* of the *actio furti*, the *sestertium X milia* of the *condictio certi*, were due, not to the writers of these books, but to him. But the *formula* was something more than a mere example or illustration; it was the actuality of the law, its realization in practical life, and it often repeated the very words of the edict[1].

The praetor's edict as the embodiment of customary law.

The nature of this praetorian code, so far as procedure is concerned, will become apparent in our future discussion of the formulary system: but certain of its general characteristics, more intimately connected with the edict than with the *formula*, may be considered here. Cicero says that much the greater part of the praetor's edict embodied customary law (*consuetudo*)[2], and by customary law he understands all that has been approved by common consent of long standing and has not been ratified by statute. It was those rights conferred by customary law which age had established on a sure foundation that were above all

[1] Compare the edict for *vi bonorum raptorum* in Dig. 47, 8, 2 'Praetor ait: "Si cui dolo malo hominibus coactis damni quid factum esse dicetur sive cuius bona rapta esse dicentur, in eum, qui id fecisse dicetur, iudicium dabo,"' with the formula for *vis hominibus armatis* (the older form of this action) in Cic. *pro Tullio*, 3, 7 'quantae pecuniae paret dolo malo familiae P. Fabi vi hominibus armatis coactisve damnum datum esse M. Tullio.'

[2] Cic. *de Inv.* ii. 22, 67 'Consuetudine autem ius esse putatur id, quod voluntate omnium sine lege vetustas comprobarit. In ea autem quaedam sunt iura ipsa iam certa propter vetustatem. Quo in genere et alia sunt multa et eorum multo maxima pars quae praetores edicere consuerunt.'

to be found in the edict. Cicero's statement is undoubtedly correct, and it is only those who would deny his definition of customary law and refuse the name to anything which has been fixed in writing that would cavil at it. It is merely against the danger of inverting Cicero's proposition that we have to guard, of supposing that all even of the definite customary law (*certa consuetudo*)[1] of Rome found expression in the edict. That this was not the case is clear from the fact that much of the *civil* law and procedure of Rome was based on custom, and was not to be found in statute[2]. The development of the *legis actiones* themselves was, in fact, largely due to the jurists. That, in spite of their rigidity, they were adaptable to the growing needs of the time is shown by the facts that new ones could be composed and that a jurist as late as Sextus Aelius found it worth while to re-edit them with modifications of his own[3]. That the praetor, their later channel, may have had some influence in moulding their form is probable, although they do not belong to that department of his work known as *ius honorarium*. But certainly when the law-making faculty of the praetors had been recognized, when they had come to feel the possibilities of the edict, that edict did become the main, if not the only, embodiment of *fixed* customary law, which

But the civil law also rests on *consuetudo*.

Final recognition of the praetor as the channel of customary law.

[1] Cic. *l. c.* 'Quaedam autem genera iuris iam certa consuetudine facta sunt; quod genus, pactum, par, iudicatum,' i.e. informal agreements, equity ('in omnes aequabile') and the respect for precedents.

[2] Cic. *Part. Orat.* 37, 130 'propria legis et ea quae scripta sunt et ea quae, sine literis, aut gentium iure aut maiorum more retinentur.' But by *lex* Cicero may conceivably understand here any official expression of *ius*. The main contrast in the passage is between *lex* and *natura* as sources of *ius*. Papin. in Dig. i, 1, 7 'Ius . . . civile est quod ex legibus, plebis scitis, senatus consultis . . . venit.' 'Venit ex' does not mean 'is directly based on' but 'flows from.' Gaius, iv. 118 'exceptiones . . . vel ex legibus, vel ex his quae legis vicem obtinent, substantiam capiunt, vel ex iurisdictione praetoris proditae sunt.'

[3] Pompon. in Dig. 1, 2, 2, 7 'quia deerant quaedam genera agendi . . . Sextus Aelius alias actiones composuit et librum populo dedit qui appellatur ius Aelianum.' See p. 28.

PART II.

was now defined in terms of a newer *ius gentium*[1]—the old private international law which had passed through a long refining process in the edict of the praetor peregrinus—and even in terms of a more abstract and ideal natural right[2].

When this recognition and this consciousness arose it is impossible to say with certainty. Cicero refers vaguely to the time *posteaquam ius praetorium constitutum est*[3]. The two concluding words, which convey the idea of public if not of official recognition, have been interpreted as a reference to some great 'constitutional law, through which new spheres of jurisdiction in the sense of *potestates edicendi summae* were conferred on the praetor urbanus and the praetor peregrinus, in consequence of which the *potestas legum interpretandarum* of the Pontifex Maximus and the presidency possessed by the delegated pontifex in the civil courts must also have been conferred on the praetor urbanus[4].' The chief objection to this theory is the entire absence of evidence to support it. No ancient writer who touches on the praetor's edict knows of any such enactment, although its far-reaching effects would have made it second in importance to none of the constitutional laws of Rome. The only important measure dealing with the praetor's jurisdiction is a *lex Aebutia* of uncertain date, and all that we are told of it is that it tended to replace the *legis actio* by the formulary procedure[5]. We shall consider later the mode in which this effect was probably reached, but, whatever be our views as to its tenor, our information about this law would lead us to suppose that it enabled the praetor to

This recognition probably not effected by statute.

[1] Cic. *Part. Orat.* *l. c.*

[2] Cic. *l. c.* 'Quae autem scripta non sunt, ea aut consuetudine aut conventis hominum et quasi consensu obtinentur. Atque etiam hoc in primis, ut nostros mores legesque tueamur, quodammodo naturali iure praescriptum est.' The preservation of moral, that were not yet legal, obligations was a main function of the praetor's edict.

[3] Cic. *in Verr.* i. 44, 114.

[4] Puntschart, *Grundgesetz. Civilrecht*, i. p. 114.

[5] Gell. xvi. 10, 8; Gaius, iv. 30.

BOOK I. modify the *civil* actions, and that it had no reference to *ius honorarium* at all. The objection might also be raised that the praetor's edictal jurisdiction, if based on a *lex*, could hardly be spoken of as customary law; but a still more serious flaw in this hypothesis is the absence of all analogy for such constitutional legislation as is here imagined. Constitutive power was sometimes conferred by law, as on the decemvirs and on Sulla, but only for a given purpose or for a given time; the conferment of interpreting power, other than that inherent in jurisdiction, is unknown until the time of the Principate, and was only then adopted to attach a quasi-sovereign right to one who was not a sovereign. On the other hand, almost every great office in the Roman constitution furnishes an analogy for a wide power of interpretation springing from the *imperium*; it appears in administrative law and in that power of magisterial coercion (*coercitio*) which was the source of much of Rome's criminal justice; and to the Roman mind the exercise of higher jurisdiction seems at all times to have been inconceivable without it.

The legal validity of praetorian law.

The legal validity of praetorian law rested, therefore, on the acceptance by an existing of the rules made by a pre-existing *imperium*. It was this acceptance which in theory secured the continuity of the edict, for the rules made by a magistrate with *imperium* were valid only for his year of office. 'Those who attribute most to the edict speak of it as only an annual law (*lex annua*),' says Cicero, and he concludes from this limited validity that the edict can not be retrospective, i.e. change a particular legal relation existing before its publication[1]. He also holds (possibly on the same ground) that the praetor cannot during his year of office spring a ruling upon the world to meet

[1] Cic. *in Verr.* i. 42, 109 'Qui plurimum tribuunt edicto, praetoris edictum legem annuam dicunt esse. Tu edicto plus complecteris quam lege. Si finem edicto praetoris afferunt Kal. Ian., cur non initium quoque edicti nascitur a Kal. Ian.? An in eum annum progredi nemo poterit edicto quo praetor alius futurus est: in illum quo alius praetor fuit regredietur?'

a case not provided for in his already published edict[1]. It is very questionable whether the first conclusion follows from its premiss. The 'annual law' of the praetor could only influence the jurisdiction of his year of office, not the legal relations concluded within that year. It was quite possible theoretically for a contract to be concluded under one law and settled, after a controversy, under another; and we find Cicero himself, as a provincial governor, seriously infringing, in accordance with the terms of his own edict, the conditions of a bargain that had been concluded under the rule of his predecessor[2]. This danger, in fact, could only be averted by the practical continuity of the edict. The second irregularity, of *ex post facto* ordinances, seems to have no inherent connexion with the annual validity of the edict; the edict itself must have grown out of such ordinances. If such acts were illegal they were made so, *after* this criticism of Cicero's was delivered, by a *lex Cornelia* which enjoined that the praetor should adhere to his once-published edict. But it is by no means clear that even the *lex Cornelia* prohibited the praetor from issuing new edicts which did not conflict with those already published.

PART II.

Limitations. Theoretical lack of continuity.

Ex post facto ordinances.

Unfortunately the case out of which Cicero's points arise do not exhibit the working of *ius honorarium* at all. A certain P. Annius Asellus had died and left his daughter sole heiress. As he was a wealthy man the will was invalid in consequence of the *lex Voconia*, which enacted that no one enrolled in the *census* as having a property of 100,000 asses (perhaps by later interpretation or enactment changed to sesterces) should make any woman his heir. The law was supposed to be evaded in this case by the fact that the defunct man had never, or at least

Cicero's criticism of Verres' edict in respect to such ordinances.

[1] Cicero, in criticizing the *fecit, fecerit* of one of Verres' rulings (cited p. 96), says (*in Verr.* i. 41, 107) 'Quis umquam edixit isto modo? quis umquam eius rei fraudem aut periculum proposuit edicto, quae neque post edictum reprehendi neque ante edictum provideri potuit?'

[2] Cic. *ad Att.* v. 21, 11.

BOOK I.

not since his property had reached this amount, been assessed at a *census*. But the spirit of the law, when it spoke of the *census*, was clearly to obtain proof of the amount of the property; and this proof might be obtained in a court of law as well as at the registration. Accordingly Verres, the praetor urbanus, refused to grant possession of the estate (*hereditatis possessio*) to the girl, and he took the occasion of raising his judgement into a general rule in the words:—

> *Qui ab A. Postumio, Q. Fulvio censoribus*[1] *postve ea fecit fecerit* (sc. *heredem virginem sive mulierem*)[2].

The words are in essentials a mere reproduction of the terminology of the law[3], and it is clear that the praetor, although he may have been wrong in not adopting the literal sense of one portion of the enactment, only conceived himself to be putting into force a part of the *ius civile*, and was making no addition to the *ius honorarium*.

Local extent of the praetor's jurisdiction.

The other possible limitation to the validity of ordinances is that of space. But by this the praetor's rulings were not affected. The urban praetor, the magistrate *qui inter cives ius dicit*, could give valid decrees for Roman citizens all over the world; the decree of possession (*bonorum possessio*), issued by the praetor in favour of the creditor of Cicero's client Quinctius, applied as much to the latter's estates in Narbonese Gaul as to his chattels at Rome. It is true that, in the case of a praetorian injunction which is carried out in a province, it is the duty of the provincial governor to see that the proceedings are legal, and the praetor is dependent on his co-operation. But the governor cannot contest the validity of the act, if the executive proceedings are regular. In the case in question Quinctius found strong support against the execution of the decree

[1] These were the censors just preceding the passing of the *lex Voconia* in 169 B.C.

[2] *In Verr.* i. 40, 106.

[3] *ib.* 42, 107, 108.

from C. Flaccus, the governor of Gaul; but this was due to the conviction of that *imperator* that the proceedings of Quinctius' creditor on the Gallic estate were marked by violence and irregularity[1]. The writ of the praetor peregrinus, in a case that came properly within his cognizance[2], would undoubtedly have travelled as far as that of the urban praetor.

Practical continuity of the edict.

Amongst the limitations of the praetor's edictal authority must be reckoned the short tenure of his power; but the practical continuity of the edict, the certainty that any sound and workable rule would be embodied in the *album* of his successor, made this theoretical rather than practical.

Collegiate intercession.

A stricter limitation was the veto (*intercessio*), often exercised by his colleague, more rarely by the possessor of a superior power, of which we shall have to speak in the section dealing with the appeal. But it was found that the conflict of authority, which at Rome was generally supposed to be enough to keep a magistrate within bounds, was not sufficient to secure a due observance of the edict even by the magistrate who had issued it. The extreme flexibility of its rulings, and the uncertainty of their source, must have offered many opportunities for the indulgence of spite or favouritism. The attempt to limit this discretionary authority was one of the valuable contributions to reform made by the democratic party.

Limitation on the edict imposed by the *lex Cornelia*.

A *lex Cornelia*, a tribunician *plebiscitum* of the year 67 B.C., enacted that the praetors should administer justice in accordance with their *edicta perpetua*[3]. It is difficult to grasp all the bearings of this ordinance. Did it limit the praetor to the *formulae* exposed in his *album* as well as to the *edicta*

[1] Cic. *pro Quinct.* 7, 28; 29, 90. See Appendix II.

[2] A case e. g. that should not have been reserved to a free city.

[3] Asc. *in Cornelian.* p. 58 'Aliam deinde legem Cornelius, etsi nemo repugnare ausus est, multis tamen invitis tulit, ut praetores ex edictis suis perpetuis ius dicerent; quae res summatim (*Mommsen*, cunctam *Baiter*, eum aut *MS.*) gratiam ambitiosis praetoribus, qui varie ius dicere assueverant, sustulit'; Dio Cass. xxxvi. 23; cf. Cic. *de Fin.* ii. 22, 74 (see p. 84, note 2).

exhibited there? By the time that the law was passed the two portions of the *album* were so intimately connected that the fixity of the one implied in all probability the fixity of the other. We have already stated the unanswerable question whether the *lex Cornelia* prohibited the praetor from issuing occasional decrees (other than those necessary to the enforcement of a law), which were not in conflict with, but were as certainly not contained in, the edict which he had issued at the commencement of the year.

Praetor limited to proceedings *in iure.*

A further limitation, one based on custom rather than on law, arose from that fundamental division of the civil judicature into *ius* and *iudicium*, on which we have so often touched. One of the leading principles of the courts of the Ciceronian period is that the magistrate should not, in his utterances on the law, prejudge a question of fact. It is not, for instance, on the reality of a debt that he decides, but merely on the legal conditions under which the debt may be held to have been incurred[1]. The reality of the obligation, as exhibited not only by evidence of facts, but by proofs of the applicability of the praetor's ruling, is first established by the decision of the *iudex*. It is true that at times the praetor does have to decide, without the assistance of a *iudex*, a matter which raises at once both a question of law and a question of fact. Such praetorian or 'extraordinary' cognition (*cognitio praetoria, extraordinaria*) had reference to guarantees which he demanded from litigants, to modes of execution, or to the proof of the grounds of assistance which he offered. The demand for *satisdatio*, the putting of a creditor into the possession of the goods (*missio in possessionem*) of his absconding debtor, the quashing of an inequitable sentence (*in integrum restitutio*), were all decided on personal cognizance. Yet the challenge and the test of the result of such cognizance might be fought out in a case remitted to a *iudex*. The

Cognitio praetoria, extraordinaria.

[1] Cic. *ad Q. Fr.* i. 2, 3, 10 'praetor solet iudicare deberi?'

praetor, for instance, allows Cicero's client Quinctius to appeal on a wager (*sponsio*), and to attempt to prove before a *iudex* that there was no adequate ground for the *missio in possessionem* under which he laboured[1]. PART II.

(b) *The Municipal Magistrate and Municipal Jurisdiction.*

Our last glance at Italy showed a twofold status enjoyed by its communities. The greater part were free or allied members of the military confederacy; the rest were colonies (*coloniae*) or partners in the civic rights (*municipia*) of Rome. The possession of *libertas* everywhere carried with it a jurisdiction independent of that of the praetor's court; the possession of *civitas* everywhere entailed a strict limitation of autonomy on the states which enjoyed the right, and subjected them to the judicial control of Rome. But, even before the great revolution in the condition of the Italian towns created by the Social War, there had been a tendency towards the levelling-up of the absorbed communities in the direction of a fuller independence. A new and truer theory of *municipal* life, which has influenced the history of the whole world, had begun to dawn upon the Roman legal mind. This was the theory of the possibility of combining an active local life with the possession of full civic rights in a central state. The conferment of full citizenship on the town of Arpinum in 188 B.C. and the enrolment of its citizens as voters in the Cornelian tribe were not followed by the deprivation of its communal autonomy, and its *comitia* was still legislating in 115 B.C.[2] Here we have a foreshadowing of the new

Fuller autonomy granted to communities of Roman citizens; growth of the municipal idea before the social war.

[1] See Appendix II on the *pro Quinctio*.

[2] Cic. *de Leg.* iii. 16, 36 'avus quidem noster . . . in hoc municipio . . . restitit M. Gratidio . . . ferenti legem tabellariam . . . Ac nostro quidem . . . Scaurus consul (115 B.C.) "Utinam," inquit, "M. Cicero, isto animo atque virtute in summa republica nobiscum versari quam in municipali maluisses."'

type of *municipium*, which was to be perfected by the consequences of the Social War. It is, indeed, questionable whether, in the typical instance of Arpinum, any increase in the powers of local jurisdiction was immediately granted to the town. It remained a *praefectura*, and its magistrates in Cicero's time were still only *aediles*, a title which conveys no idea of higher jurisdiction. But Italian towns were notoriously conservative in the retention of names that had once signified their status—as indeed Arpinum's preservation of the name *municipium* proves—and in preserving the old titles of their magistrates; and as Arpinum possessed aediles, even *after* the Social War[1], no certain conclusion can be drawn as to their limited jurisdiction. At the same time we possess evidence of the existence of magistrates called *duoviri* in *coloniae* before the Social War. They are found at Puteoli as early as 105 B.C.[2]; the name probably signifies *duoviri iuri dicundo*, not *duoviri aediles*, and therefore implies the possession of a jurisdiction inconsistent with the condition of a true *praefectura*.

Consequences of the Social War.

The Roman mind had, therefore, to some extent been prepared for the great problem which awaited solution after the *lex Iulia* had conferred the *civitas* on those of her allies who had remained faithful during the great struggle[3], i.e. all the Latin States and some of the *foederatae civitates*, and the *lex Plautia Papiria* had completed the work by gradually incorporating the rebel states in some manner unknown[4]. Yet the situation

[1] Cic. *ad Fam.* xiii. 11, 3.

[2] *C. I. L.* i. n. 577. Cicero speaks of *duumviri* as the most ordinary title for magistrates of *coloniae* (*de Leg. Agr.* ii. 34, 93), but the reference is to a period after the Social War (83 B.C.); cf. the quattuorvirs at Cumae in 49 B.C. (*ad Att.* x. 13, 1).

[3] Cic. *pro Balbo*, 8, 21.

[4] The only clause of this law known to us is one of minor importance, referring to domiciled strangers (*incolae*) who had been enrolled on the registers of federate states as citizens of those communities (*foederatis civitatibus adscripti*; cf. *ad Fam.* xiii. 30, 1). It was enacted that, if at the

presented many anomalies, and two main difficulties stood in the way of removing them. The first was the still surviving sense of the fundamental inconsistency of *libertas* with *civitas*; the second, the real inequalities in the amount of communal independence possessed by the incorporated towns. The first was much more than a sentimental difficulty: to the municipal mind the surrender of the local law, even if the extinction of the local courts was not required, seemed a terrible break with the past, and communities such as Heraclea and Neapolis, from this fear as well as from that of added administrative burdens, shrank from the troublesome gift of the *civitas*[1]; while the Roman was perplexed with the combined problems of saving the supremacy of the Roman courts, of avoiding the adoption of new administrative machinery, and of preserving the fact of municipal independence. By the side of such questions the gradual levelling of the condition of the Italian towns was a minor difficulty that might be left to time and to isolated action.

Adaptation of central to local jurisdiction.

We know that the harder of the two problems had been solved by the Ciceronian period; but it is not easy to point to the method of solution. The old principle of the delegation of praetorian jurisdiction to *praefecti* was not resorted to, although the name *praefecturae* was still retained by states to which these officers had been sent, and the *quattuorviri* still went on circuit in their Campanian district[2]. It has been held that the policy adopted by the Roman government was the very characteristic one of *laisser faire*, that the states were allowed to retain their own jurisdiction as though they were *liberae*, and that an adjustment of the local to the central courts was

time of the passing of the law they had their domicile in Italy, they might receive Roman citizenship by making a *professio* to the praetor within sixty days (Cic. *pro Arch.* 4, 7).

[1] Cic. *pro Balbo*, 8, 21 'In quo magna contentio Heracliensium et Neapolitanorum fuit, cum magna pars in iis civitatibus foederis sui libertatem civitati anteferret.'

[2] p. 35.

BOOK I.

not attempted until the calm of the Augustan rule gave opportunity for systematic legislation [1]. The slight evidence which we possess points to the conclusion that this view is in the main correct; but it also shows such a slender modification of the jurisdiction of the municipal towns as might be effected by statutes of the most general character—either the laws that conferred the citizenship or a *lex municipalis* which made no attempt at elaborate reconstruction. The sole notice which we possess of a division of jurisdiction between the praetor at Rome and the local magistrates in Italy for this period is contained in a reference of Cicero to municipals appearing before the court of the praetor urbanus in accordance with the mutual guarantees which they had made for their appearance (*vadimonii causa* [2]). It has been assumed that this denial of the jurisdiction of the local courts was voluntary, and that any two parties could enter into a *vadimonium* to appear instead before the praetor at Rome [3]. But why should it have been voluntary? May not the presence of municipal litigants at Rome point to a line of demarcation having been drawn between the competence of the local magistrates and that of the praetor, such as we shall soon find the *lex Rubria* ordaining for Cisalpine Gaul?

But no uniformity in the constitutions of the municipal towns.

The negative evidence is against the view of any thorough remodelling of the towns between the close of the Social War and the dictatorship of Caesar; and indeed the turmoil of these times was hardly favourable to constructive legislation. There is some slight evidence for an adjustment of a constitution here and there, such as might be undertaken by commissioners having the authority of senate and people [4]; Arpinum, for instance, was being

[1] Wlassak, *Processgesetze*, p. 197.

[2] Cic. *in Verr.* v. 13, 34 'ut nemo tam rusticanus homo L. Lucullo et M. Cotta consulibus (74 B.C.) Romam ex ullo municipio vadimonii causa venerit,' &c.

[3] Bethmann-Hollweg, ii. p. 24.

[4] Cic. *in Verr.* ii. 49, 121 'Quas enim leges sociis amicisque dat is, qui

remodelled in 46 B.C.[1] The object of these efforts was perhaps the increase of the power of the local magistrates to a level with that of the officials of the more favoured communities; but no effort was made to secure uniformity in the titular designations of towns or magistrates[2], and the *lex Iulia municipalis* of 45 B.C. shows how much remained to be done in the way of securing uniform principles in the administrative system.

The lex Iulia municipalis.

It is difficult to determine the place that we should assign to this law of Caesar's in the unification of Italy. The fragment that we possess can scarcely be said to contain a single original idea; but it aims, in a somewhat haphazard way, at tightening the bonds of administrative community between Rome and all other communities of Roman citizens both in Italy and in the provinces. The law shows incidentally that detailed reconstruction was going on[3], but unfortunately not a single clause that we possess refers directly to municipal jurisdiction, or to the extent of the judicial power of the local magistrates.

General type of municipal organization.

We can, however, form from scattered sources an incomplete picture of the communal life of these towns. The typical Italian constitution of magistrates (*magistratus potestatesve*), senate (*senatus, curia* composed of *decuriones conscriptive*), and popular assembly (*comitia conciliumve* composed of *municipes* and sometimes of *incolae*) was

habet imperium a populo Romano, auctoritatem legum dandarum a senatu: hae debent et populi Romani et senatus existimari.'

[1] Cic. *ad Fam.* xiii. 11, 3. Sulla's violent interference with the constitution of Larinum, and his establishment of a provisional government there (Cic. *pro Cluent.* 8, 25) can scarcely be taken as evidence of readjustment on a deliberate plan.

[2] Cf. Cic. *in Pis.* 22, 51 'Neque enim regio ulla fuit, nec municipium neque praefectura aut colonia, ex qua non ad me publice venerint gratulatum.' *Lex Iulia municipalis*, l. 84 'Queiquomque in municipieis coloneis praefectureis foreis conciliabuleis c(ivium) R(omanorum) II vir(ei) IIII vir(ei) erunt aliove quo nomine mag(istratum) potestatemve sufragio eorum, quei quoiusque municipi . . . erunt, habebunt.'

[3] ll. 159, 160 'Quei lege pl(ebeive) sc(ito) permissus est fuit utei leges in municipio fundano municipibusve eius municipi daret,' &c.

BOOK I.

still preserved. Where the commune was not large enough for municipal organization it was attached to a town, or formed a circuit court for the Roman prefect. Some of the magistrates bear titles such as dictator or praetor, which reveal a constitutional development as long as that of Rome[1]; but the more usual, perhaps in many cases a mere generic, name was that of *quattuorviri.* The aggregate of officials so designated were usually divided into two magistrates with higher jurisdiction (*duumviri iuri dicundo*), to whom it is difficult to deny something resembling the Roman *imperium,* and two police magistrates and commissioners (*duumviri aediles*[2]).

Jurisdiction of the municipal magistrate.

The evidences referring to Italian jurisdiction are so scanty that it is impossible to determine the extent of the judicial power possessed by the higher municipal magistrates. The right of declaring bankruptcy (*missio in possessionem*) was one of the highest of the powers created and employed by the praetor; it was at the close of this period denied to the local magistrates of Cisalpine Gaul, and the mention in the *lex Iulia municipalis* of the *bona ex edicto eius, quei iure deicundo praefuit praefuerit, possessa proscriptave*[3] furnishes no warrant for attributing this function to the magistracy of the Italian towns. Like the Roman praetor the *duumviri* administered justice from a *tribunal*; those of the Roman colony of Urso in Spain were accompanied by the retinue of a Roman magistrate[4]—two lictors (the number enjoyed by the praetor in the capital) with *accensi, scribae, viatores* and others. The lictors may in some cases have borne the *fasces*; it is no argument against this view to point to the fact that in certain older Roman colonies the

[1] Wilmanns, *Index,* p. 618.

[2] The whole board might be designated *quattuorviri iure dicundo*; sometimes, where only aedilician power existed, we find *quattuorviri aediles* or *aedilicia potestate* (Wilmanns, *Index,* p. 622).

[3] l. 115.

[4] *Lex Ursonensis,* c. lxii.

attendants of the magistrate were only permitted the use of staves (*bacilla*)[1].

Ius and iudicium.

The fundamental division of jurisdiction into *ius* and *iudicium* had probably been recognized in most Italian towns long before the Social War. When after this period a *iudicium* finds mention in municipal legislation it must be assumed to be a process heard before a *iudex*, *arbiter*, or *recuperatores*. Had this custom not existed before, it would have been an inevitable consequence of the extension of the praetorian edict, with its constantly reiterated *iudicium dabo*, to the municipal towns. The *lex Rubria* shows the immense debt of the towns of Cisalpine Gaul to the edict and the *formulae* of the praetor; everywhere a copy or a paraphrase of a portion of it, adapted to the limited jurisdiction of the local magistrates, must have accompanied the extension of Roman civil law to the Italian municipalities. The praetor's edict had by this time attained a fixity which rendered its local application possible; but provision must have been made that further changes in the *ius honorarium* of Rome would be reflected in the law of the municipal towns.

Influence of the praetor's edict on municipal jurisdiction.

The subsequent extension of Italy to its natural boundary, the Alps, seems to have established the municipalities of Cisalpine Gaul on precisely the same general footing as those of the rest of Italy. This extension had been foreshadowed at the close of the Social War by the gift of Latin rights to the towns beyond the Padus[2]. This gift, while it rendered the cities *foederatae civitates* and as such independent of Roman jurisdiction, must have familiarized their citizens with the forms of Roman law and made the body of this law the inevitable *exemplar* to be copied in

Inclusion of Cisalpine Gaul in Italy.

[1] Cic. *de Leg. Agr.* ii. 34, 93 (of the colony established at Capua in 83 B.C.) 'Deinde anteibant lictores non cum bacillis sed, ut hic praetoribus [urbanis] anteeunt, cum fascibus duobus.' In a transmarine colony such as Urso there would be a more independent jurisdiction, and this might be signified by the *fasces*. For *bacilla* cf. *ad Att.* xi. 6, 2.

[2] Asc. *in Pisonian.* p. 3.

their local jurisdiction. The promise contained in this grant seems to have been fulfilled by the democratic party under Cinna or his successors; but the gift of full *civitas* was never recognized by the government restored by Sulla. This was enough to lead Caesar, during his ten years' monarchy of Gaul, to prepare the way for the effective exercise by these towns of administration on the Italian model, at the moment when the inevitable recognition should come. In the year 51 B.C. constitutionalists at Rome were startled by a rumour that the proconsul had ordered the towns to create *quattuorviri*[1]; that is, that he had given them a magistracy of a purely Italian type. The only magistrates of this title known to have been actually created by Caesar are *quattuorviri aediliciae potestatis*[2], but this does not exclude the possibility of his having, either then or two years later, created the higher quattuorvirate *iuri dicundo*. It is at this latter date (49 or 48 B.C.) that the gift of *civitas* was renewed; but its universal extension to the district may be questioned from the fact that Cisalpine Gaul still remained a Roman province. If it was universal, the maintenance of the governorship must have been merely provisional and a sign of incompleteness in the execution of the scheme, for a *provincia* of Roman citizens on the borders of Italy is inconceivable as a permanent form of organization. It was not until after Philippi (42 B.C.) that Octavianus, perhaps from fear of this dangerous provincial governorship, as much as from respect to his uncle's wishes, gained the consent of the Senate to its 'autonomy' and incorporation with Italy[3].

[1] Cic. *ad Att.* v. 2, 3 'eratque rumor de Transpadanis, eos iussos IIII viros creare. Quod si ita est, magnos motus timeo.'

[2] *IIIIvir aediliciae potestat. e lege Iulia municipali* at Patavium (Wilmanns, n. 2130).

[3] App. *B. C.* v. 3 *τήν τε γὰρ Κελτικὴν τὴν ἐντὸς Ἄλπεων ἐδόκει Καίσαρος ἀξιοῦντος* (i. e. Octavianus after the battle of Philippi) *αὐτόνομον ἀφιέναι, γνώμῃ τοῦ προτέρου Καίσαρος.* Cf. iii. 30, where the intentions of the

The *lex Rubria*; its date.

We possess a fragment of a *lex Rubria*, which regulates in minute detail the jurisdiction of this district. It is uncertain of which of the two epochs of settlement it is a product. In favour of its attribution to Caesar is the use of the expressions *Gallia Cisalpeina* or *Gallia cis Alpeis*[1] to describe the district, although these would not necessarily be inappropriate to the time of Augustus who was *incorporating* a country thus territorially designated into the Italian name. An evidence of the attribution of this law to the Augustan epoch has been sought in the fact that it makes the central authority in jurisdiction not the proconsul but the chief judicial magistrate of Rome (*praetor isve quei Romae iure deicundo praerit*)[2], and it would certainly have been strange had the military administration of the provincial governor been associated with this attribution of higher civil functions to the praetor.

Object of this law; division of jurisdiction which it recognizes.

But, to whichever date we assign the law, its object is manifestly to extend an already existing Italian system to the new district. The main characteristic of this system is a fundamental division of competence between the praetor at Rome and the municipal magistrates, who are spoken of as duumvirs, quattuorvirs, and praefects, the type of the last-mentioned magistrate which is chosen being the praefect of the old citizen colony of Mutina (*praefectus Mutinensis*)[3]. The division may have been of a manifold character, but only two points are specified in our fragment. One is that the right of *missio in possessionem* is reserved for the praetor; provisional arrest of the debtor may be ordered by the local magistrate, but he cannot exercise the right of declaring the bankruptcy

Senate, when it was proposed to give Cisalpine Gaul to Antonius, are described and it is said ἦσαν δ' οἱ καὶ τὸ ἔθνος ὅλως ἐλευθεροῦν ἡγεμονίας ἠξίουν. The statement assumes that some of it was 'free' before, i.e. rendered autonomous by Julius Caesar. Dio Cass. (xlviii. 12) attests its complete liberation for 41 B.C.

[1] cc. xxii. and xxiii. [2] cc. xxi. and xxii. [3] c. xx.

of an individual[1]. Another principle of division is based on the amount of the matter in dispute. In the action for the recovery of a fixed loan (*condictio certae creditae pecuniae*) and in those arising from certain other obligations, all cases involving an amount over 15,000 sesterces are to be remitted to Rome, the local magistrate having the right to enforce on the parties *vadimonium* for their appearance there[2]. One of the most interesting features of the law is the extreme care and minuteness with which praetorian *formulae* are written out for the benefit of the local magistrate: even typical names (Q. Licinius, L. Seius) are supplied, and to the *formula* for *damnum infectum* is appended the curious interpretative clause that these fictitious names are not to be taken seriously[3]. The other main principle of praetorian jurisdiction is as abundantly illustrated as the *formula*; the magistrate has not only *ius dicere, decernere* but *iudicia dare, iudicare iubere*, and here as at Rome he is mainly a guiding authority, limited by law as the praetor by his edict[4].

Extension of the conception of a *legitimum iudicium*.

One effect of this centralization of jurisdiction was that the conception of a *legitimum iudicium* was extended to the whole of Italy, to Cisalpine Gaul, and even to isolated citizen colonies beyond the sea. For throughout this sphere the competence of the urban praetor, the possibility of the *legis actio*[5], the application of the *formula* which replaced it and the cognizance of the *unus iudex* extend. There is, in fact, no interval between the 'legal' jurisdiction of the praetor at Rome and that based on the *imperium*

[1] cc. xxi. and xxii.

[2] Cf. Cic. *in Verr.* v. 13. 34 'unum illud, quod ita fuit illustre notumque omnibus, ut nemo tam rusticanus homo L. Lucullo et M. Cotta consulibus (74 B. C.) Romam ex ullo municipio vadimonii causa venerit quin sciret iura omnia praetoris urbani nutu . . . Chelidonis . . . gubernari.' See p. 102, note 2. Cf. *Fragmentum Atestinum*, l. 15.

[3] c. xx.

[4] c. xxiii.; cf. *Fragmentum Atestinum*, l. 5.

[5] In the form of the *manus iniectio* it is found in the *Lex Ursonensis* (c. lxi).

of a pro-magistrate in the provinces. Jurisdiction in Cisalpine Gaul or at Urso does not fall under the latter category: it must, therefore, belong to the former. The mile-limit of praetorian jurisdiction has been vastly extended, but the early fiction which máde the *municipia* a part of Rome was capable of the widest application. Rome now includes every *civitas* with the Roman citizenship, but perhaps not all in an equal degree; for it is impossible to conceive that such close judicial relations as existed between Cisalpine Gaul and Rome prevailed also between the capital and such distant outposts of citizenship as Gades and Urso. Here the competence of the local magistrate must have been greater, the power of the urban praetor proportionately less.

(c) *The Provincial Magistrate and Provincial Jurisdiction.*

Abandonment of the theory of delegated command.

We have seen that the provinces became gradually emancipated from the control of the home magistracy and were subjected to the government of their delegates, the pro-consuls and pro-praetors[1]. But the theory of delegation was soon lost sight of, if it had ever been seriously applied to the pro-magistracy when operating alone in a province. The principle of appeal, which usually accompanies the theory of delegated command, was never resorted to in the relations between the pro-magistrates in the provinces and the magistrates at home, and the turn of events would have made its continued employment constitutionally impossible if even it had existed. No appeal could have come from a proconsul to a praetor, for the former could not easily be looked on as a delegate of the latter; the consuls were too busy to be invested with supreme jurisdiction over the provincial world, and the Senate shrank from interference with justice which

[1] p. 37.

BOOK I.

Hence no central jurisdiction.

was the function of the *imperium* alone. A refusal to recognize a central authority, whether personal or impersonal—an incapacity, in fact, for complete organization—was one of the weaknesses of the Republican mind; it was a fragment of the undying belief in the all-sufficiency of the *imperium* wherever found.

The unfettered *imperium* in the provinces.

Its effect, as applied to provincial governorship, was to make each *imperator* a king in his own domain. Many of the limitations which hemmed in the *imperium* at home were non-existent here[1]. The governor had no colleague and was, therefore, limited by no power of veto; a Roman public opinion—the only one for which a Roman cared—did not exist, or if by chance it did, it was often represented by classes of men—the governor's own staff, the tax-farmers of the provinces—whose interests were adverse to those of the provincials. Even the theoretical limitation of the tenure of command to a single year was at times inoperative; the provinces had grown faster than the magistracies and the vacancies were often more numerous than the candidates. Verres in Sicily, Q. Cicero in Asia, and Fonteius in Narbonese Gaul, each held their provincial command for three years in succession.

Limitations on the governor's jurisdiction.

It is of great importance, therefore, to consider the actual restrictions which were held to be imposed on the judicial power of a provincial governor; for the Romans, in spite of their dislike to an organization so detailed as to fetter discretionary power, never contemplated the rule of caprice even in this department. Amongst these limitations we may neglect for the moment the criminal responsibility of the governor, which will find a more fitting exposition in the second portion of this work.

[1] Cic. *in Verr.* ii. 12, 30 'Dubium nemini est quin omnes omnium pecuniae positae sint in eorum potestate qui iudicia dant et eorum qui iudicant . . . si . . . praetor improbus, cui nemo intercedere possit, det quem velit iudicem, iudex nequam et levis quod praetor iusserit iudicet.' Cf. *ad Q. Fr.* i. 1, 7, 22 'ubi nullum auxilium est, nulla conquestio, nullus senatus, nulla contio.'

PART II.

Rights guaranteed to certain states. ***Foedus* and *libertas*.**

The rights guaranteed to certain states within the provincial area were the first limitations on their power. The grant by which these rights were conferred were either embodied in a sworn treaty (*foedus*) ratified, in the early Republic, by senate and people, in the later, by either of these powers[1], or by the conferment of a charter of privileges (*lex data*), which during the Republic was usually based on a legislative act (*lex rogata*)[2]. In either case the grant raised the state or people on whom it was conferred to the level of the Italian communes and ensured its members control of their own finances, a free possession of their land which exempted them from the payment of tribute, and above all a use and enjoyment of their own native law[3]. The states which were *liberae* and those which were *liberae et foederatae* may often have differed only in the important particular of the basis of their rights. While the free states had only a charter which the Roman government might at any moment revoke[4], the allied cities rested their claims upon a *foedus*, a breach of which by Rome was the violation of an oath and an act of war.

But both kinds of cities agree in being entirely outside the sphere of the governor's jurisdiction; juristically they are not a part of his *provincia* at all; he could enter such

[1] Mommsen, *Staatsr.* iii. p. 1171. Even in the post-Sullan period, when the ratification of a treaty by the senate alone seems to have been regarded as permissible, Cicero insists on the necessity of the popular will (*pro Balbo*, 15, 34, 35 'Gaditani, M. Lepido, Q. Catulo consulibus [78 B.C.] a senatu de foedere postulaverunt. Tum est cum Gaditanis foedus vel renovatum vel ictum. De quo foedere populus Romanus sententiam non tulit, qui iniussu suo nullo pacto potest religione obligari. Ita ... quod publica religione sanciri potuit, id abest. Populus enim se nusquam obligavit').

[2] The grant of *libertas* to Termessus (see next note) is conferred by a *plebiscitum*, that to Chios (p. 112 note 1) by a decree of the senate.

[3] See the grant of *libertas* conferred on Termessus in Pisidia in 71 B.C. (Bruns, p. 94), especially the clause which confers autonomy 'so far as is consistent with this charter' (i. 1, l. 7 'eique legibus sueis ita utunto ... quod advorsus hanc legem non fiat').

[4] δίδωσι δ' ἡ βουλὴ ... μέχρι ἂν αὐτῇ καὶ τῷ δήμῳ δοκῇ (App. *Hisp.* 44). See Marquardt, *Staatsverw.* i. p. 77.

BOOK I.

a city only as a guest, and although convenience dictated that great central cities which were also free states, such as Antioch in Syria or Thessalonica in Macedonia, should be the chief residence of the governor, the anomaly might in these cases be witnessed of a magistrate holding a court in a town whose citizens were exempted from his jurisdiction. Even cases in which Roman citizens were engaged could not call for the attention of the governor; the Romans domiciled in Chios were subject to the local laws and the local jurisdiction of the town[1]; the Roman trader did business with the free cities at a greater risk than with the subject states, for the favour of the governor was here of no avail.

Reassertion of the rights of the free cities; occasional infringement of these rights.

Such was the practice that had always accompanied the recognition of sovereignty external and internal (*libertas* and *αὐτονομία*) possessed by these communities; but both theory and practice were growing weaker in the Ciceronian period[2] and required to be buttressed up by law. The rights of the free cities were asserted afresh by one of the *leges Iuliae* passed by Caesar in his first consulship (59 B.C.)[3]: but it is the father-in-law of the author of this protective legislation that Cicero attacks for a wanton disregard of the guaranteed privileges during his government of Macedonia. 'He held a court in a free city in violation of the laws and the decrees of the senate' is one of the gravest of the charges with which Cicero assails Piso[4]; but it appears that the transgression was constitutional rather than legal. The *plebiscitum* of the tribune Clodius,

[1] *C. I. G.* ii. n. 2222 (Extract from a Senatusconsultum of 81 B.C.) ἡ σύγκλητος εἰδικῶς ἐβεβαίωσεν ὅπως νόμοις τε καὶ ἔθεσιν καὶ δικαίοις χρῶνται ἃ ἔσχον ὅτε τῇ 'Ρωμαίων φιλίᾳ προσῆλθον, ἵνα τε ὑπὸ μηθ' ᾡτινιοῦν τύπῳ ὦσιν ἀρχόντων ἢ ἀνταρχόντων, οἵ τε παρ' αὐτοῖς ὄντες 'Ρωμαῖοι τοῖς Χείων ὑπακούωσιν νόμοις.

[2] Cic. *in Verr.* iii. 89, 207.

[3] Cic. *in Pis.* 16, 37 'lege Caesaris iustissima atque optima populi liberi plane et vere erant liberi.' It may have been the *lex Iulia Repetundarum*, or (less probably) a *lex de iure magistratuum*; hardly (with Bethmann-Hollweg ii. p. 37), a *lex de provinciis*.

[4] Cic. *de Prov. Cons.* 3, 6.

which had conferred on Piso the government of Macedonia, had specifically allowed him the right to exercise jurisdiction on loans (*de pecuniis creditis*) over the peoples which still enjoyed *libertas*[1]. It is possible that this extended jurisdiction was meant to apply only to claims in which Roman citizens were involved; but, whatever its extent, its legality was questionable. The law of Caesar, it is true, could not be adduced against a later law; but it is possible that a charter was supposed to require a specific repeal, and that the abrogation of a portion of it (where this portion was not definitely stated to be held on an insecure tenure)[2] was held to be irregular as the result of occasional legislation.

The subject states; the *lex provinciae*.

When we pass from the narrow circle of free and allied communities to the unprivileged states (*stipendiariae civitates*) which were directly under the governor's jurisdiction, we find that here too the *imperator* was limited by charter, but by vaguer and wider grants conferred on the *provincia* as a whole. The so-called law of the province (*lex provinciae*) was always a *lex data* but had ceased, at a comparatively early period of Roman history, to be necessarily a *lex rogata*. It was often the work of the conquering general himself, assisted by a commission of ten appointed by the senate; had the co-operation of these senatorial delegates been dispensed with, ratification by the senate was required to ensure the validity of the work of the organizer. But the charter perpetuated the name of the founder or refounder of the province, and the *lex Rupilia* for Sicily[3], the *lex Aemilia* for Macedonia[4], and

[1] *de Prov. Cons.* 4, 7 'Emisti a foedissimo tribuno plebis (Clodio) . . . grandi pecunia ut tibi de pecuniis creditis ius in liberos populos contra senatus consulta et contra legem generi tui dicere liceret.'

[2] Such as the exemption from the quartering of troops in the charter of Termessus. It is valid only 'nisei senatus nominatim utei . . . in hibernacula meilites deducantur decreverit.'

[3] Cic. *in Verr.* ii. 13, 32; 15, 37; 16, 39; 24, 59.

[4] Liv. xlv. 17 and 32.

the *lex Pompeia* for Bithynia[1] recalled the periods at which the aggregate of states comprising the province in question had been endowed with a new political life or with a partial revival of the old.

Regulations about jurisdiction created by these *leges*.

The regulations affecting jurisdiction are the only features of these charters with which we are immediately concerned. Besides the creation of territorial districts, to which, in their character as centres for courts of assize (*fora, conventus, διοικήσεις*), we shall refer elsewhere, they contained regulations on certain general principles of judicial procedure, especially on that portion of procedure which was most expressive of popular liberty—the hearing of the case by a *iudex* (*iudicium*). Details of such regulations have been preserved only for the province of Sicily, and although in the organization of subject peoples certain general principles of freedom came to be recognised, yet the problems of organization were so various in different provinces, that these rules of the *lex Rupilia* cannot be considered wholly typical. Sicily, with its highly developed Greek civilization, possessed an elaborated charter of rights, the chief clauses of which, in reference to jurisdiction, were as follows:—

Rules applied to Sicily.

Rules based on the nationality of the parties.

1. 'In a suit between two citizens of the same state, the trial should be held in that state and according to its laws[2].' This admitted competence of the laws of the city to which the parties belonged does not necessarily imply the competence of their courts. It certainly meant that the *iudex* in this case should be a native of the town, but it could not have prevented the Roman pro-praetor from interpreting the native law, from giving it as his *ius*, and from applying to it all the forms expressed in his edict. The local law and the local *iudex* are the rights guaranteed in this clause: and the appeal which the party

[1] Plin. *ad Trai.* 79 (83), 1.

[2] Cic. *in Verr.* ii. 13, 32 'Siculi hoc iure sunt ut, quod civis cum cive agat, domi certet suis legibus.'

actioned can make to the magistrate 'to send him back to his own laws' (*ad leges suas reiicere*)[1] implies a claim to both. The appeal was neglected by Verres in the case of an action brought by the commonalty of Bidis against a certain Epicrates, a native of that town, for the recovery of an inheritance, and in a subsequent action between the same parties, in which Epicrates was charged with falsification of the public registers. Whether Verres had a shadow of legal ground for the refusal depends on whether we interpret the words *civis cum cive* literally or not. An action brought by the government of a town might seem to Verres not to come under this clause, but to be one of the *ceterae res*, for which a Roman *iudex* was provided[2].

2. 'If a Sicilian sues a Sicilian of another state, the praetor is to furnish by lot a *iudex* or panel of *iudices* in accordance with the decree of P. Rutilius[3].' The principle observed in this case probably was that the *iudex* should be a Roman citizen.

Suits between individuals and communities.

3. 'In a claim made by a private individual' (of one state) 'from the commonalty' (of another state) 'or by a commonalty from a private individual, the senate of some other state shall be chosen as judge, when each party shall have exercised the right of challenging the senate proposed[4].' In this case three senatorial bodies may have been proposed by the parties and the praetor, and the plaintiff and defendant have had each the right of challenging one of these[5].

4. 'When a Roman citizen sues a Sicilian, or a Sicilian

[1] Cic. *in Verr.* ii. 24, 59; 25, 60.

[2] This is contemplated in the alternative request of Epicrates (*in Verr.* ii. 24, 59) 'ut se ad leges suas reiiciat aut ex lege Rupilia dicam scribi iubeat.'

[3] Cic. *l. c.* 13, 32 'quod Siculus cum Siculo non eiusdem civitatis (agat), ut de eo praetor iudices ex P. Rupilii decreto . . . sortiatur.'

[4] Cic. *l. c.* 'quod privatus a populo petit aut populus a privato, senatus ex aliqua civitate, qui iudicet, datur, cum alternae civitates reiectae sunt.'

[5] It is by no means clear, however, whether the whole of this selected

a Roman citizen, the *iudex* shall be of the nationality of the defendant[1].'

5. 'In all other matters judges chosen by the magistrate (*iudices selecti*) shall be appointed from the Roman citizens dwelling within the precincts of the assize[2].'

6. 'In all disputes between husbandmen and the tithe-collectors the *iudicia* shall be organized according to those conditions regulating the collection of corn known as the *lex Hieronica*,' i.e. those conditions which the Romans found already in force when they effected the occupation of Sicily[3].

7. A further provision related to the allotment (*sortitio*) of the *iudices*. The *lex Rupilia* provided that the *iudices* should not be chosen until thirty days after the claim had been entered[4].

Change of venue.

8. The tenor of some of the preceding enactments, which are careful to provide that the *iudex* shall be of the defendant's city, is still further expressed in the rule that no one shall be forced to give security for his appearance outside the limits of the circuit (*forum*) in which he is domiciled. This privilege was of necessity limited to the defendant, and cannot have applied to either plaintiff or defendant in the case (clause 3) where a senate from some other state was called to intervene between two litigants. But its application was wider even than the rules about the nationality of the *iudex*. It ought to have held good even in the exercise of administrative jurisdiction (under clause 6), where the *iudex* was a Roman

senatus sat in judgement, or whether a *iudex* was chosen or *recuperatores* empanelled from it.

[1] Cic. *in Verr.* ii. 13, 32 'quod civis Romanus a Siculo petit, Siculus iudex datur, quod Siculus a civi Romano, civis Romanus datur.'

[2] Cic. *l. c.* 'ceterarum rerum selecti iudices ex civium Romanorum conventu proponi solent.'

[3] Cic. *l. c.* 'Inter aratores et decumanos lege frumentaria, quam Hieronicam appellant, iudicia fiunt.'

[4] Cic. *l. c.* 15, 37, 38.

citizen. The change of venue was probably forbidden by the *lex Hieronica* itself as well as by the more general clause of the *lex Rupilia*, and Verres was probably wrong in law as well as in equity in making the wretched Sicilian husbandman appear wherever it suited the convenience of the *decumanus* to summon him[1]. A very similar provision to this clause in the Sicilian *lex* is mentioned by Cicero as applying to Cyprus. This island was included in the government of Cilicia at the time of Cicero's tenure of that province, and he remarks that he has sent a legate there to try the suits in which the few Roman merchants were involved; for he has no power to summon (*evocare*) the Cypriotes from their island[2].

Local jurisdiction permitted by the governor.

The amount of judicial autonomy guaranteed by the *lex provinciae* was at times increased by the governor's regulations. In the cities of the Hellenic or Hellenized world, where the developed judicial organization had never been destroyed by Rome, it was for two reasons beneficial that this permitted autonomy should be enjoyed by the *civitates*. One was economy of time and labour; for the Roman staff was not large and no good purpose could be served by its undertaking duties which could be performed as efficiently by the local courts. Another and greater advantage was the feeling at once of loyalty and of quickened life evoked in the minds of the provincials by this enjoyment of their own laws and their own courts. Cicero, in his government of Cilicia, seems to have made good use of this discretionary power[3]. He followed the edict of Mucius Scaevola, governor of Asia (*circa* 98 B.C.), which

[1] Cic. *in Verr.* iii. 15, 38 'Iam vero illud non solum contra legem Hieronicam nec solum contra consuetudinem superiorum, sed etiam contra omnia iura Siculorum, quae habent a senatu populoque Romano, ne quis extra suum forum vadimonium promittere cogatur. Statuit iste, ut arator decumano, quo vellet decumanus, vadimonium promitteret.'

[2] Cic. *ad Att.* v. 21, 6.

[3] Cic. *l. c.* vi. 2, 4 'omnes (civitates), suis legibus et iudiciis usae, αὐτονομίαν adeptae, revixerunt.'

BOOK I. granted a large amount of judicial liberty to the subject states. It is probable that the permit of Scaevola and of Cicero allowed jurisdiction by the local magistrates as well as the use of *peregrini iudices*[1]; it is needless to say that any decision of these magistrates could be overridden by the governor, for this jurisdiction is permitted and therefore delegated; but the enjoyment by the cities of their new 'autonomy' must have rendered such requests for revision infrequent. Magisterial jurisdiction was, however, not a prominent feature of courts organized on the Greek type; an independent court of δικασταί must often have decided the merits of a case with or without the interpreting authority of the governor.

Modes of expressing substantive law in the provinces.

The regulations of the provincial *lex*, although, by such clauses as appear in the Sicilian law about *vadimonium* and the *iudex*, they compelled the governor to administer justice in the *conventus* to which the defendant belonged, seem to have imposed no limitations on his manner of expressing the substantive law *in iure*. Even the first clause of the Sicilian *lex*, if it contained no reference to jurisdiction by a local magistrate, left the interpretation of the native law wholly to the Roman pro-praetor. The edict of the pro-praetor or proconsul, which we shall now proceed to examine, clearly could not express the native law of each particular state under his jurisdiction; but its generality and its expansiveness admitted, as we shall see, of an application of Roman forms to the substantive law of any particular city. The value and necessity of the edict were, however, greater when it provided for cases that, in modern terminology, would come under the two heads of (1) private international, and (2) administrative law. Illustrations of the first are furnished by suits between citizens of different states in the same

[1] Cic. *ad Att.* vi. 1, 15 'multaque sum secutus Scaevolae; in iis illud, in quo sibi libertatem censent Graeci datam, ut Graeci inter se disceptent suis legibus . . . Graeci vero exsultant quod peregrinis iudicibus utuntur.'

province, or between Roman citizens and provincials; of the second by the *iudicia* springing from the claims of the *publicani*. PART II.

The *edictum provinciale* differed for each separate province and bore a name drawn from the area to which it applied; that for Sicily, for instance, was the *edictum Siciliense*[1]: and, although there were faint inter-relations between the edicts of different provinces, no attempt was made in the Republic to evolve a common type which could be described as *the* 'edictum provinciale.' Like that of the Roman praetor it was transmitted from governor to governor (*tralaticium*) and was supposed to possess something of the permanent character of the urban edict[2]. In the interval that elapsed between his appointment to a province and his assumption of his command the governor had ample time to frame his edict at Rome and to decide how far he should follow the rulings of his predecessor, how far he should seek other or earlier precedents, and to what extent he should introduce innovations of his own. The rulings of his predecessor, especially those dealing with administrative law, were by no means slavishly followed, and Cicero, by asserting that the only addition which he had made to his edict after quitting Rome was to incorporate into it *totidem verbis* a clause from that of his predecessor in the province[3], confesses the chaotic character of provincial administration which even in essentials might change from year to year. Radical changes might be made the ground of private complaint by the departing governor[4], but there was no legal remedy against them. Even when alterations were introduced, a certain continuity might be effected by going back to earlier precedents set by some governor whom

The *edictum provinciale*.

Its continuity and variations.

[1] Cic. *in Verr.* i. 45, 117. [2] Cic. *ad Fam.* iii. 8, 4; *ad Att.* v. 21, 11.

[3] Cic. *ad Fam.* iii. 8, 4 (to Appius Claudius, 51 B.C.) 'Romae composui edictum: nihil addidi nisi quod publicani me rogarunt . . . ut de tuo edicto totidem verbis transferrem in meum.'

[4] Cic. *ad Att.* vi. 1, 2 (from Cilicia, 50 B.C.) 'Appius enim ad me ex itinere bis terve . . . literas miserat, quod quaedam a se constituta rescinderem.'

BOOK I.

the new occupant of the post admired. The edict of the province of Asia had no doubt formed the model for those of the newly-created provinces of Syria and Cilicia. But portions of it had been omitted by Cicero's predecessor in Cilicia, perhaps even by later governors of Asia; and Cicero prides himself on the introduction of a famous plea in bar of suit (*exceptio*) invented by Mucius Scaevola [1], which had also appeared in a modified form in the edict of the contemporary governor of Syria. We have already noticed Cicero's adherence to Mucius' liberal permission of local jurisdiction [2], which seems to have been a novelty in Cilicia. Since many provincial magistrates had been the highest civil judges of Rome, the influence of the *edictum urbanum* was necessarily very great; even to those who had not held this post it must have appealed as the great *exemplar* of equitable, and therefore universally applicable, law, and of orderly procedure [3]. The extent of this indebtedness can best be estimated by a glance at the outlines of a provincial edict which Cicero has preserved.

Cicero's provincial edict: its divisions.

Cicero begins by remarking on the brevity of his edict [4], a brevity due to his recognition of a leading principle that an edict should fall into two divisions: one of a purely local character, concerned with the administration of the province, the other of a more general character and dealing with procedure that could be universally applied. It is the absence of specification in the latter department that no doubt led mainly to the brevity which he admires,

[1] This exception was *extra quam si ita negotium gestum est ut eo stari non oporteat ex fide bona* (Cic. *ad Att.* vi. 1, 15). For an instance of the transference of a formula from the urban to the provincial edict see Cic. *in Verr.* iii. 65, 152 'quam formulam Octavianam (on *vis* and *metus*) et Romae Metellus habuerat et habebat in provincia (Sicilia).'

[2] p. 118.

[3] Hence Cicero's reproach to Verres for not making his rules of *hereditatis possessio* the same as those of Rome; in this matter 'video non modo ceteros sed te ipsum totidem verbis edixisse quot verbis edici Romae solet' (Cic. *in Verr.* i. 46, 118; cf. i. 45, 117).

[4] Cic. *ad Att.* vi. 1, 15.

although the amount of local jurisdiction which he permitted must have contributed not a little to the shortening of his edictal work. But, in spite of this twofold division, he actually distinguishes three portions of his edict, of which the third is vaguer even than the second. To this we can add a fourth department, as essential as the others, which, unnoticed by him, is drawn from other sources.

1. The first part is called 'provinciale' *par excellence*[1], for it would have no application outside a province. But we are surprised at the anomalous character of its contents. It spoke of the financial relations of the states, about debts, about the rate of interest, about bonds, and contained all the provisions that the edict needed to frame about the *publicani*. The greater portion of this department of the edict was concerned with administrative law, with the public and chiefly with the financial relations of the states of the province to the Roman government and to its agents. But even matters which seem purely connected with private law assumed, in a province, an administrative aspect that they never presented at Rome. Cicero would have left the local courts to pronounce by native law on debts, interest or bonds that had been incurred or concluded within the sphere of any given state; but such legal relations between individual provincials, or more often provincial corporations on the one hand and Roman bankers or companies of *publicani* on the other, required special regulation. Fixed rules of law, based on statute or even, in Cicero's province, on custom, did not exist for such cases. Here the governor creates or transmits perhaps the only purely substantive law which appeared at all in the edict.

2. Cicero describes the second portion of his edict as dealing with certain rules of procedure by which the

[1] Cic. *ad Att.* vi. 1. 15 'unum (genus) est provinciale, in quo est de rationibus civitatum, de aere alieno, de usura, de syngraphis; in eodem omnia de publicanis.' Cf. *ad Fam.* iii. 8, 4; *in Verr.* iii. 10, 25; *ad Att.* vi. 1, 16.

BOOK I.

rights of individuals are perfected[1]. That they required, as he says, edictal notice is due to the facts that the assertion of the rights was of a quasi-public character and that their completion, as affecting the status of individuals, had to be regulated by certain fixed forms. He gives as instances the right to assume inheritances (always in the Greek world something more than a private right), and the declaration of bankruptcy (*missio in possessionem*) with its accompaniment of the sale of the debtor's goods by auction.

3. While the two former portions of the edict were committed to writing, he describes the third portion as possessing only a potential existence[2]. It was a body of unwritten law, the outline of which was suggested by the *edicta* of the praetor urbanus at Rome. As cases arose he meant to fit them into this outline by means of special decrees. Evidently if the Cornelian law aimed at putting a stop to such special *decreta* at Rome[3] its spirit had not penetrated to the provinces.

4. Another portion of the edict, as we learn from the proceedings of Verres in Sicily, dealt with the formal rules of jurisdiction.

An attempt to fill up the blank spaces in Cicero's outline is peculiarly difficult, for we have no other description of the provincial edict of Republican times; but scattered notices enable us to amplify or interpret to some extent the branches of jurisdiction which he has sketched.

The *edictum provinciale* in the narrower sense;

1. The *edictum provinciale*, in the narrower sense of the word, contained for the most part rules of administrative law, most of which gave rise to a *iudicium*, i. e. to cognizance by a *iudex* or *recuperatores*. We may take as the first

[1] Cic. *ad Att.* vi. 1, 15 'alterum, quod sine edicto satis commode transigi non potest, de hereditatum possessionibus, de bonis possidendis vendendis, magistris faciendis: quae ex edicto et postulari et fieri solent.'

[2] Cic. *l. c.* 'tertium, de reliquo iure dicundo, ἄγραφον reliqui. Dixi me de eo genere mea decreta ad edicta urbana accommodaturum.'

[3] p. 95.

instance the relations between the Roman tax-gatherers (*publicani*) and the occupants of the land (*aratores*). From the regulations made by Verres in Sicily we find that it was possible for an administrative decree of the Roman magistrate (operating perhaps through native officials) to be concurrent with the promise of a *iudicium*. This mode of dual enforcement is at least represented by Cicero as having accompanied what was in itself a very equitable regulation made by Verres. While granting a *iudicium* against the too exacting *decumanus* for eight-fold the amount of his extortionate demands (*in octuplum*), he gave one against the recalcitrant *arator* for the recovery of fourfold of his deficit (*in quadruplum*)[1]; but he accompanied the promise by a decree that the Sicilian magistrate should exact from the farmer the amount which the *decumanus* said that he owed[2]. The two regulations, if really concurrent, are open to Cicero's criticism; but we have no means of interpreting their relation to one another. The second decree may have offered a means of administrative assistance to the *publicani* for the collection of arrears when time had elapsed, and the *arator* had raised no protest against the illegal nature of the exaction, and again the *quod decumanus edidisset* of this edict simply states the fact or nature of the claim, and by no means excludes inquiry into its justification. The investigation of the magistrate might elicit the existence of a counter-claim and bring about a *iudicium*[3]; and an action by the *arator* against the *publicanus* must have been possible even after the

PART II. rules of administrative jurisdiction.

[1] In neither case probably was the penalty a multiple of the whole sum demanded or the whole sum owed, but of the excess over the rightful claim. It was the excess alone that constituted the quasi-theft.

[2] Cic. *in Verr.* iii. 13, 34 'qui in decumanos octupli iudicium se daturum edixit, idem habuit in edicto se in aratorem in quadruplum daturum . . . edixit ut quod decumanus edidisset sibi dari oportere, id ab aratore magistratus Siculus exigeret'; cf. 29, 70.

[3] Cic. *l. c.* 14, 35 'ita scribit, *si uter volet recuperatores dabo.*'

exaction had been effected. We have here a trace of administrative law, of assistance rendered to a class which is regarded as serving the state and denied to the private individual, which suggests the *pignoris capio* of the *publicani* in early Rome—a form of *legis actio* which itself survived in some modified form, even to Cicero's day, as a right of the tax-farmers in Italy and in the provinces [1].

Most administrative decrees enforced only by civil process.

But most of the administrative decrees in the provincial edict seem to have been capable of enforcement only by ordinary civil process. The return of lands (*professio iugerum*) by the *aratores* of Sicily gave rise to such a *iudicium*. If the *decumanus* maintained that the returns had not been made in full in accordance with the edict, he supported his claim by a civil action. The governor gave *recuperatores* (to be chosen in this case from the Roman citizens at the *conventus*) with a *formula* to the effect that 'If it should appear that the acres of this particular farm are more in number than have been professed by the occupier (whether lessee or owner), then the occupier should be condemned [2].' This reasonable procedure was disfigured by two weak points. The *recuperatores* were Roman citizens and the governor could, like Verres, pack the jury with members of his own staff of personal assistants or privileged 'bandits,' as Cicero prefers to call them; and it was possible for the governor, again like Verres, to declare no fixed penalty (*poena certa*) for a wrong *professio*. An absolutely fixed penalty might have been inferior to one graduated to the amount of falsity in the returns; but even a scale of indebtedness was not fixed by the governor of Sicily: 'all the corn in his threshing-floors' was the condemnation pronounced either in the edict or in one particular *formula* [3]. The judgement

[1] Cic. *in Verr.* iii. 11, 27. Cf. p. 68.

[2] Cic. *l. c.* 22, 55. It was an enforcement of the edict 'ut aratores iugera sationum suarum profiterentur' (*ib.* iii. 15, 38).

[3] Cic. *l. c.* 21, 54 'Nulla erat edicti poena certa. Frumenti eius omnis, quod in areis esset.'

of the *recuperatores* was, therefore, on a *certum*, although this fixed amount, determined by the governor and inserted by him in the *formula*, differed in each particular case. The amount recovered was a penalty (*poena*) and may have been supposed to fall to the state; the successful prosecutor may have shared in it[1], and the *decumanus* derived from the action the advantage of a renewed claim on the additional debt of tithes made apparent by the emended *professio*.

Rules regulating the *pactiones* of the *publicani*.

Hitherto we have been considering the relations of the tax-farmers to individuals, as regulated by the edict. Cicero's letters from Cilicia show a far more complicated series of relations which they entered into with the *civitates* of a province. It appears that the arrangements made by the home government with a company of *publicani* were only of the most general character, and did not exclude a series of special agreements made by the agents of these tax-farmers in a particular province with the states of that province. These agreements (*pactiones*) were probably of a very varied character. It is possible that some states may have wished to compound by a money payment for their tithes of corn; more often, perhaps, they asked for time, and it was granted under the condition of a heavy rate of interest. An irregular practice seems also to have sprung up by which a company of *publicani* lent money to a state, receiving in return not only an exaggerated interest on the loan, but sometimes the right of collecting the *local* taxes, which had no connexion with the imperial revenue, as security for its repayment[2]. As the validity

[1] Cicero (*in Verr.* iii. 21, 54) seems in one case to imply that the prosecuting *decumanus* took the whole of the *poena*. It is possible that the company which purchased the tithes had, as representing the state, a claim to the penalty.

[2] This is probably the true explanation of Cic. *ad Att.* v. 16, 2 'Audivimus nihil aliud nisi imperata ἐπικεφάλια (in Cilicia).' These 'personal' taxes (*tributa capitis*) must have been local, not imperial, for Cilicia is a *vectigalis provincia*. When Q. Cicero writes (*ad Q. Fr.* i. 2, 6) 'renuntiari . . . Licinium plagiarium . . . tributa exigere,' he is, perhaps, describing the

BOOK I.

of these *pactiones* rested wholly on the governor's edict, we can understand the importance which Cicero gives to *aes alienum, usurae* and *syngraphae* in the edict which he describes as specially 'provincial.' The governor was unlucky who came to a province at the beginning of the quinquennial period, during which the leases made by the home government with the tax-farmers ran. He then found these agreements in process of conclusion, and his acceptance or repudiation in his edict of the principles that they involved made him a marked man to the equestrian order, whose friendship or hostility might ultimately decide his fate or that of his party at Rome[1]. Cicero not only escaped this great trial and was content to ratify in the main his predecessor's acts, but found the task of steering between the interests of the tax-farmers and provincials easier than he had anticipated. His chief remedy was a moderate rate of interest, on condition of early payment of the debt. While remarking that even the great Isauricus had recognized and upheld the interest of the *pactiones*, he describes his own rule as '12 per cent. if the debt is paid before the close of a tolerably long interval which I have fixed: the interest of the agreement, if paid after this time[2].'

Discretionary power of the governor.

The governor, therefore, can in his edict actually upset the conditions of contractual relations entered into under the rule of another edict, i.e. under another law. For Cicero never treats his great panacea as simply a prospective

agent of a company of *publicani* imprisoning his debtors. In the affair between Atticus and the Sicyonians (Cic. *ad Att.* ii. 1, 10 'Quod Sicyonii te laedunt, Catoni et eius aemulatori attribues Servilio. Quid? ea plaga nonne ad multos bonos viros pertinet?') we may see the phenomenon of the taxes of a free city given as security for a debt. Atticus was not a member of a company of *publicani*, but he might have taken such a security. The 'injury' is connected with Cato's campaign against the *publicani* in 60 B.C.

[1] Cic. *ad Q. Fr.* i. 1, 11, 32.

[2] Cic. *ad Att.* vi. 1, 16 'Diem statuo satis laxam; quam ante si solverint, dico me centesimas ducturum; si non solverint, ex pactione.'

remedy. In his long controversy with the *negotiatores* of Cilicia over the debt owed by the Salaminians of Cyprus his position is that the special decree of the senate did indeed make the illegal bond valid, but that it was never meant to validate the illegal rate of interest (48 per cent.). The illegality of this rate seems, however, to have been due to Cicero alone and to have been no bar to the validity of the bargain at the time of its conclusion [1].

The second portion of the edict; rules furnished by the *imperium* on inheritance and bankruptcy.

2. The rules which Cicero mentions as embodied in the second portion of his edict may have been suggested by Roman forms but were not necessarily expressive of Roman law. In one of his typical instances, the *hereditatis petitio* and *possessio*, the practice of proving a right to an inheritance before a magistrate had long been customary in Greek communities; its value was chiefly felt in the declaration of the order of succession to intestate inheritances, and, when the Roman magistrate stepped into the place of the local officials, there is no reason to suppose that the Roman order of succession, simplified and natural as it was, was made to replace those of the subject communities. The rules were probably so framed as to be applicable to every kind of local law: to the rights following an adoption by the native forms of Patrae in Achaea [2], to the particular principles of intestate succession recognized at Bidis in Sicily [3], or to the rights and duties of the sons of concubines, which were valid in parts of the Eastern world [4].

[1] Cic. *ad Att.* v. 21, 11 'cum ego in edicto tralaticio centesimas me observaturum haberem cum anatocismo anniversario, ille ex syngrapha postulabat quaternas. "Quid ais?" inquam, "possumne contra meum edictum?"'

[2] Cic. *ad Fam.* xiii. 19, 2.

[3] Cic. *in Verr.* ii. 22, 53.

[4] From an Egyptian papyrus of the year A. D. 124 it appears that the concubine's child could institute none but his father as heir during the lifetime of the latter (Mommsen in *Zeitschr. der Savigny-Stiftung* xii. 284 ff.). The provision is probably typical of the *ἄγραφος γάμος* of Graeco-Asiatic 'Volksrecht'—an institution with which the governor of an Eastern province must often have come into contact. See Meyer (P.) *Der Römische Konkubinat*, pp. 116, 117.

When Cicero reproaches Verres with not inserting his clause about heiresses in the Sicilian edict [1], he chooses to forget that the obvious answer to the charge is that the *lex Voconia* did not apply to Sicily.

The other typical instance mentioned by Cicero—the *bonorum possessio, proscriptio, venditio*—may have been more Roman in character. When this bankruptcy was the result of contentious jurisdiction, it was an integral element in civil procedure, a part of the conception of an *actio*, and would therefore be tinged with the Roman colouring of the whole. The advanced and humane character of bankruptcy procedure in Cicero's time must have been a modifying influence on the more rigorous law of parts of the Graeco-Eastern world, where enslavement for debt was probably still in vogue [2].

The unwritten portion of the edict.

3. The unwritten portion of Cicero's edict can by its very nature not be illustrated. Here, as we have said, the urban edict formed a background of principles of substantive law, possessing much the same influence that the developed Roman law has sometimes exercised on the decisions of English courts. Cicero may have carried this practice of the use of principles, absorbed but not expressed, to a point unusual in his day; but that it was not an uncommon feature in provincial jurisdiction is shown by his sarcastic explanation of the suppression by Verres of a customary ruling:—'You wished to decide a given case as it arose by a sudden application of the urban edict [3].'

Rules about forms of jurisdiction.

4. Rules about the forms of jurisdiction also appeared in the provincial edict; and even provisions that the *lex*

[1] Cic. *in Verr.* i. 43, 112; 46, 118.

[2] Diod. i. 79 *μέμφονται δέ τινες οὐκ ἀλόγως τοῖς πλείστοις τῶν παρὰ τοῖς Ἕλλησι νομοθετῶν, οἵτινες ὅπλα μὲν καὶ ἄροτρον καὶ ἄλλα τῶν ἀναγκαιοτάτων ἐκώλυσαν ἐνέχυρα λαμβάνεσθαι πρὸς δάνειον, τοὺς δὲ τούτοις χρησομένους συνεχώρησαν ἀγωγίμους εἶναι.*

[3] Cic. *in Verr.* i. 43, 112 'Tu ipse ex Siciliensi edicto hoc sustulisti. Voluisti, ex improviso si quae res natae essent, ex urbano edicto decernere.'

provinciae had made for procedure were sometimes further emphasized here. Thus some of the rules made by the *lex Rupilia* for the selection of *iudices* appeared in the Sicilian edict of Verres[1]. It also contained a provision as to the hours that should elapse on the stated day of trial before condemnation was pronounced on one who was absent and undefended[2]. Throughout the edict there was the constantly repeated promise to grant a case in the form of 'giving' *iudices* or *recuperatores*[3]; sometimes, to settle a question of administrative law (as in the controversies between the *aratores* and the *publicani*), the promise was made to either party in the words *si uter volet, recuperatores dabo*[4].

The governor's jurisdiction either personal or delegated; the circuit-courts.

The civil jurisdiction of the governor, which was based on the edict, could be exercised either personally or by delegation. In both cases it was a jurisdiction that required the successive visitation of certain circuits. The number and limits of these *conventus* or διοικήσεις[5] were generally determined on the formation of a province, and the governor held a court (*forum egit*) in each of them in turn[6], the amount of time which he passed in the circuit being determined by the amount of business to be transacted. All the preliminaries to the actions and the programme of the judicial business (*actus rerum*) were drawn up and submitted to him before his departure from the capital or the camp, so that he could determine with some accuracy how much time it was necessary to devote to each *conventus* and the date of his arrival at the various centres[7].

Jurisdiction delegated

But the tasks of provincial administration were so complex that personal jurisdiction was in many cases impossible. The theory of delegated authority was fully recognized[8], and for this vicarious jurisdiction the governor

[1] Cic. *in Verr.* ii. 15, 37. [2] *ib.* ii. 17, 41. [3] *ib.* iii. 13, 32. [4] *ib.* iii. 14, 35.
[5] Cic. *ad Fam.* iii. 8, 6. [6] Cic. *ad Att.* v. 20, 1; *ad Fam.* iii. 8, 4 and 5.
[7] Cic. *ad Att.* v. 21, 9. [8] Cic. *ad Q. Fr.* i. 1, 7, 20.

BOOK I. had at his command a lower magistrate, the *quaestor*, and a staff of assistants known as *legati*[1].

to the quaestor or pro-quaestor; The provincial quaestors were assigned by lot, in the proportion of one to each province, although Sicily possessed two. The nomination of an official to exercise quaestorian functions could only be made by the governor when the quaestor assigned him had been removed by death or other causes. He then appointed one of his legates with the title *pro quaestore*. This magistrate or pro-magistrate, when not employed in military or financial duties, was the most obvious judicial delegate[2]; but in most provinces his avocations were too numerous to allow jurisdiction to be a regular portion of his duties, and it was only in Sicily, where the second quaestor at Lilybaeum was opportunely situated for the western circuits of the island, that quaestorian jurisdiction was a constant factor in the government of the province[3].

to the *legati*. Elsewhere the legates (*legati*) were more available. Their numbers corresponded to the necessities of the province; as a rule three were furnished to a consular and one to a praetorian command. Their names were submitted to the senate, and they were supposed to be subordinate officials of the state; although the practical influence of the governor on their appointment was very great. But the fact that he sometimes dismissed them for incompetence or maladministration was not a necessary result of this *de facto* selection, since an allotted quaestor was sometimes got rid of on similar grounds[4]. To increase

[1] Cic. *pro Flacco*, 21, 49; *ad Fam.* xii. 30, 7 (to Cornificius, governor of Africa) 'Illud non nimium probo quod scribis . . . te tuis etiam legatis lictores ademisse.'

[2] Cf. Suet. *Caes.* 7.

[3] Cf. Cic. *Div. in Caec.* 17, 56; the *sortitio* by the quaestor (*in Verr.* ii. 18, 44 'ceteras dicas omnes illo foro M. Postumius quaestor sortitus est: hanc solam tu illo conventu reperiere sortitus') does not necessarily show his jurisdiction.

[4] Cic. *in Verr.* iii. 58, 134 'Quaestores, legatos . . . multi missos fecerunt et de provincia decedere iusserunt, quod illorum culpa se minus commode audire arbitrarentur aut quod peccare ipsos aliqua in re iudicarent.'

their importance in the eyes of the natives during the exercise of their jurisdiction lictors were sometimes assigned them; but they had no right to the use of such attendants, and the permission to employ them might be withdrawn by the governor[1].

Appeal from the delegates to the governor.

Delegated is by its very nature not independent jurisdiction; and the relation of these *legati* to the governor was wholly unlike that of any two magistrates of Rome to one another. A right of hearing appeals and of reversing the sentences of his subordinate was possessed by the proconsul or pro-praetor[2]; but the very fact that the legate's jurisdiction was not independent, and was not therefore criticized on its own merits, entailed an anxious responsibility on the governor for the conduct and character of his subordinates[3].

Jurisdiction of the *interim* governor of a province.

If it was necessary for the governor to quit his province before his time of office had expired or a successor had arrived, jurisdiction with every other function of administration had to be delegated to an *interim* commander. The most obvious delegate was the quaestor, who as the holder of a provisional *imperium* now took the title *pro praetore*. It was only in the case of the quaestor's youth or obvious unfitness for the post, perhaps also in the case of the governor's retinue containing a man of higher magisterial rank and greater experience, that the temporary command was entrusted to a legate[4]. In this case again we have the theory of delegated command, but it is questionable whether in the Ciceronian period its consequences were effective. In the early Republic, when the consul might leave his province and return to it

[1] Cic. *ad Fam.* xii. 30, 7. quoted p. 130, note 1.

[2] See the section dealing with the appeal.

[3] Cic. *ad Q. Fr.* i. 1, 7, 20 'Sed tamen parvi refert abs te ipso ius dici aequabiliter et diligenter, nisi idem ab iis fiet quibus tu eius muneris aliquam partem concesseris.'

[4] Cic. *ad Fam.* ii. 15, 4 'Ego de provincia decedens quaestorem Caelium praeposui provinciae. "Puerum," inquis. At quaestorem, at nobilem adulescentem, at omnium fere exemplo; neque erat superiore honore usus quem praeficerem.'

BOOK I.

again, a supervision of the jurisdiction of the *interim* commander was possible. In the later Republic a temporary absence from a province was impossible, and we cannot conceive the governor on his way to Rome exercising a control over his delegate's proceedings, while the jurisdiction of the new governor did not commence until his entry into the province. The singular position of Pompeius in 52 B.C., when he governed Spain by means of his *legati*, undoubtedly rendered possible an appeal on judicial matters to the absent proconsul, but we are not informed of any instance in which resort was had to this right.

Ius and *iudicium* in the provinces.

After the description which we have given of the provincial edict it is hardly necessary to add that the two-fold character of civic jurisdiction was fully preserved in the province. The judicial functions of the governor or his delegate are concerned with *ius* and *iudicium*[1], or, as it is elsewhere expressed, with *lis atque iudicium*[2]. The *iudicium* itself, comprising the *formula* and the granting of *iudex* or *recuperatores*, is said to be given in accordance with the edict (*ex edicto*)[3]. The right of executing the sentence, even by means of *missio in possessionem* belongs to the delegate (e.g. the quaestor of Lilybaeum) as well as to the governor[4].

§ 3. *The Action.*

(a) *Preliminaries to Action.*

Publicity of legal procedure; external appliances at Rome;

Publicity had always been a leading characteristic of the Roman judicial system; the civic struggle was fought out in some open space, where the magistrate's ruling could

[1] Cic. *in Verr.* v. 13, 31.

[2] *ib.* iii. 13, 32.

[3] *ib.* iii. 11, 28; 12, 29; 13, 33.

[4] Cic. *Div. in Caec.* 17, 56 'Iste (Caecilius, quaestor of Libybaeum) in possessionem bonorum mulieris mittit (*al.* intrat.) . . . deinde bona vendit, pecuniam redigit.'

be heard by any auditor and the voice of the advocate could reach the assembled crowd. At the time of the Twelve Tables the Comitium, and the Forum that stretched below it, had been the seats of justice[1]: it is possible that the first witnessed the magistrate's cognizance, the second the decisions of the *iudices*. In the Ciceronian period the Forum seems to have served for both[2], and it is probable that at this time the open-air hearings had been abandoned and a protection for court and litigants sought in the great Basilicae, half markets and half porticoes, which were raised in imitation of the royal colonnades of the Graecized cities of the East. But the halls were large enough to accommodate an ample gathering of spectators, and through their open spaces the voice of the orator might be heard by the throng outside. Whether the sitting took place in the open or under the roof of one of these great halls, the general features of the arrangement of the court always remained the same. The Bench was a raised *tribunal*[3], which was occupied in turn by magistrate and *iudex*, and was sufficiently large to accommodate the assessors of both[4], and even the great panels of *iudices*. The size of the tribunal must have varied with the needs of the trial; those used by the urban and foreign praetors were small and transportable. The necessity for the latter quality was due to the fact that the praetor, in order to exercise an effective veto on his colleague, must be present in his court; but so essential was the *tribunal* to jurisdiction that his own functions would have been interrupted

[1] *Auct. ad Herenn.* ii. 13, 20.

[2] Bethmann-Hollweg, ii. p. 162. The Comitium and Forum are no longer distinguished (Cic. *Brut.* 84, 289 'in comitium veniant, ad stantem iudicem dicant'). The *stans iudex* here can only be the spectator in the *corona*, but Cicero is evidently speaking of the procedure in the *iudicium*.

[3] Cic. *de Orat.* i. 37, 168.

[4] For the assessors (*consilium* or *qui in consilio sunt*) invited by the *iudex* to assist him see Cic. *pro Rosc. com.* 4, 12; *pro Quinct.* 2, 5; 10, 36; 30, 91; for the assessors of the praetor see p. 134, note 2.

BOOK I. had he not brought his platform with him[1]. On the tribunal was planted the curule chair (*sella curulis*), a seat occupied only by the magistrate; his assessors[2] and the *iudex* or *recuperatores* who took his place were provided with benches (*subsellia*) of a more humble kind. Before the tribunal were the parties and their advocates, who rose to make formal requests of the praetor or to address the court, but during the rest of the proceedings sat on benches (*subsellia*)[3] which they were compelled to hire from some *entrepreneur*, if they had not brought their own. Behind and forming a semi-circle round them stood the ring (*corona*) of auditors whose interest in the case had brought them to the court.

in the municipal towns; Municipal jurisdiction was furnished with precisely the same appliances; the Forum and the tribunal, even at times the curule chair, were to be found in the country towns of Italy[4].

in the provinces. The wielder of the *imperium* in the provinces naturally carried the Roman customs with him. Publicity was the rule even here[5] and secret hearings in the governor's palace, although they had become common even in the early Principate, were discountenanced during the Republic[6]. It is probable that the governor, in the exercise of civil jurisdiction, always laid aside the scarlet *paluda-*

[1] Caes. *B. C.* iii. 20 (Caelius Rufus in 48 B. C.) 'tribunal suum iuxta C. Treboni praetoris urbani sellam collocavit et, si quis appellavisset, . . . fore auxilio pollicebatur.'

[2] *consilium*, see Cic. *de Orat.* i. 37, 168 'nobis in tribunali Q. Pompei, praetoris urbani familiaris nostri, sedentibus.'

[3] Cic. *Brut.* 84, 289. Cf. 84, 290; but the description in this latter passage would apply equally well to a criminal trial before a *iudex quaestionis*. The full *subsellia*, the crowded *tribunal*, the 'gratiosi scribae,' the 'corona multiplex,' the 'iudex erectus' are common to civil and criminal process.

[4] For the Basilica at Pompeii with its tribunal at the end see Overbeck, *Pompeii*, p. 122. For the *sella curulis* see Mommsen, *Inscr. Neap.* n. 2096.

[5] Cf. *in Verr.* ii. 38, 94 'palam de sella ac tribunali pronuntiat.'

[6] *ib.* v. 11, 27 'lectica usque in cubiculum deferebatur. Eo veniebant Siculorum magistratus, veniebant equites Romani: id quod ex multis iuratis audistis; controversiae secreto deferebantur, paulo post palam decreta auferebantur.'

mentum which he was entitled to wear outside the walls of Rome, and appeared in the scarlet-striped toga, the civic garb of peace.

PART II.

Judicial activity *pro tribunali* and *de plano*.

In the legal writers of the imperial period there is a distinction drawn between the magistrate's activity on his elevated seat (*pro tribunali*) and on the level ground (*de plano*)[1], the latter expression signifying any situation whatever in which he was not occupying the Bench, but was yet accessible to the public. Although the magistrate carried the *imperium* everywhere with him, yet judicial cognizance and judicial decisions (*decreta*) required his presence on the tribunal; much, however, that was of a merely formal and preparatory nature could be performed *de plano*. The distinction was not unknown to Cicero, and he uses the expressions in a non-juristic context in the respective senses of 'public' and 'unofficial[2].' But in Cicero's time the spoken word was more important in the preliminaries of an action than it had become in the time of the Empire, when written documents tended to take their place, and the frequency of proceedings *pro tribunali* was proportionately greater. The magistrate could have done little *de plano* in the exercise of contentious jurisdiction; in carrying out the legal forms (*legis actio*) of so-called 'voluntary' jurisdiction he must always have been unfettered; adoption, manumission, the granting of a guardian might be effected 'while the praetor or the proconsul was going to the bath or to the theatre[3].'

Times of jurisdiction;

The questions connected with the times of jurisdiction may be divided into three heads. They involve an inquiry

[1] Seneca, *de Clem.* i. 5 'in tribunali . . . in plano.' Suet. *Tib.* 33 'e plano . . . e tribunali.' Paulus in Dig. 48, 18, 18, 10 'pro tribunali . . . de plano.'

[2] Cic. *ad Fam.* iii. 8, 2 (from Cilicia, to Appius the late governor) 'Nihil enim habent quod aut definitum sit aut certum nisi me vultu et taciturnitate significasse tibi non esse amicum; idque pro tribunali, cum aliquid ageretur, et non nullis in conviviis intelligi potuisse . . . Illud quidem scio, meos multos et illustres et ex superiore et ex aequo loco sermones habitos cum tua summa laude . . . ad te vere potuisse deferri.'

[3] Gaius, i. 20.

BOOK I.

proceedings *in iure.*

into (1) the days on which a court could not be held; (2) the days on which a court must be held; (3) the length of time allowed for any particular trial.

Dies nefasti.

1. The *dies nefasti* had always invalidated the *legis actio*[1], and as this mode of procedure still possessed considerable vitality in the age of Cicero, they would still have impeded a good deal of judicial business. But the newer formulary system, fully established by the side of the *legis actio* in Cicero's time, offered no escape from the ban of the holy day. We shall see that when the law permitted the *formula* to be applied to cases which had been formerly regulated by the *legis actio*, the result was a *iudicium* described as *legitimum*, this epithet perpetuating the name, memory and conditions of the *legis actio*. It is practically certain that the legal preliminaries of no *iudicium legitimum* could be held on a *dies nefastus*, and the maintenance of a scruple connected with such days in the Ciceronian epoch is proved by the researches of Varro[2], the opinion of Trebatius[3], and the care taken by Caesar to make the days which he added to the calendar *dies fasti*[4]. But it is not certain whether the scruple extended further than the confines of the *legis actio* itself. The jurisdiction based on the edict of the praetor urbanus—technically known as jurisdiction *imperio continens*—and the whole of that of the praetor peregrinus had no connexion with the original forms of action, and it might therefore be expected that their validity would not be impaired by their exercise

[1] Cic. *ad Att.* vi. 1, 8 'Quid ergo profecit (Cn. Flavius, see p. 27) quod protulit fastos? Occultatam putant quodam tempore istam tabulam, ut dies agendi peterentur a paucis.'

[2] Varro, *L. L.* vi. 4, 30 'nefasti, per quos dies nefas fari praetorem: do, dico, addico.' Cf. Ov. *Fast.* i. 47 'Ille nefastus erit, per quem tria verba silentur.'

[3] Macrob. i. 16, 28 'Trebatius . . . ait nundinis magistratum posse manu mittere iudiciaque addicere' (as a proof that the *nundinae* were not sacred days).

[4] *ib.* i. 14, 12 'adiectosque omnes a se dies fastos notavit (Caesar), ut maiorem daret actionibus libertatem.'

on a holy day. But the language of Varro and of Ovid, who speak of the days in which the *tria verba* are unheard, is as applicable to the jurisdiction based on the *imperium* as to that based on *lex*. Both praetors, in all their jurisdiction, must utter one of the three formal words *do, dico, addico*, and the prohibition held, if the *edictal* utterance of these words was placed on the same level as their *verbal* utterance, and we do not press the literal interpretation of the prohibition of the praetor's speech (*fari*). PART II.

If we suppose that jurisdiction was as a rule confined to *dies fasti*, the number of days on which the praetor could with certainty be approached was particularly small, not more than about forty-five in the whole year[1]; and from these must be further subtracted the number of the moveable festivals (*feriae conceptivae*) and of those ordained by a magistrate (*imperativae*). All *lites* and *iurgia* which might interrupt the peace of the festival were on such days forbidden[2]. But a small number of court-days, when fairly distributed over the year, were probably sufficient as long as Rome maintained any resemblance to the ancient city state; the business in *iure*, especially after the formulary procedure had been introduced, was very rapidly transacted, and the business *in iudicio*, the really lengthy portion of the process, was not interrupted on *dies nefasti*. Yet, unless jurisdiction was very frequent on comitial days, it is not easy to see how this limitation of the praetor's jurisdiction was consistent with the extension of the Roman franchise to Italy, *Dies fasti.* *Dies comitiales.*

[1] Mommsen in *C. I. L.* i. p. 373; courts might be held on any of the *dies comitiales*, which Mommsen reckons at 194 in the year; [Macrob. i. 16, 14 'Comitialibus utrumque potest (cum populo agi et lege agi)']; but jurisdiction on these days was uncertain; the court could only be held if no *comitia* were announced.

[2] Cic. *de Div.* i. 45, 102 'inque feriis imperandis ut litibus et iurgiis se abstinerent (imperabatur).' If a contrast is here implied between *lites* and *iurgia* the latter may be equivalent to *arbitria*; cf. *de Leg.* ii. 8, 19; 12, 29.

BOOK I.

and the far greater amount of judicial business that this extension brought to the praetorian courts[1].

Proceedings *in iudicio; ludi.*

The procedure of the *iudices*, although happily not interrupted by the regular holy days or even perhaps necessarily by the *feriae*, was not possible on the days on which public games (*ludi*) had been ordained. On these the judges were freed from their public burden (*munus*), and the increasing number of such days, due to national wealth and leisure or to private ambition, was a great hindrance to jurisdiction, large portions of the spring and autumn being rendered unavailable for the business of the courts. But, in spite of this hindrance, the circumstance that at Rome the *iudex* was not subject to the continued control of a magistrate rendered the sittings of the *iudices* more frequent than those of a modern civil jury.

The legal Term.

2. The extremely small number of days on which a magistrate's court could with certainty be held makes it extremely probable that on these days a court *must* be held. As regards the sittings of the *iudices*, nothing resembling the fixed Court Term or Pleading Time (*actus rerum*), as it was called, of the Augustan epoch is known for the Republic; but the object of Augustus seems mainly to have been to increase the time available for judicial business, and the two Terms—Winter and Summer—into which we find the year divided after his organization, seem practically to have existed during the Republic; the respective vacations[2] being marked by the series of games in the spring and autumn.

[1] The comitial days, for which no *comitia* was announced, would be known in ample time at Rome; it is more difficult to see how such knowledge would penetrate to the municipal towns. As we cannot tell whether the praetor felt himself bound to hold a court on such days, the facilities for even urban jurisdiction on *dies comitiales* are unknown. The same difficulty applies to the days marked EN, which were partly Fasti. Mr. Fowler suggests (*Roman Festivals*, p. 9, note 6) that even the days of the post-Julian era marked NP might have been partly open for legal business.

[2] For the Republican vacation (*res prolatae*) see Plaut. *Capt.* i. 1, 10; Cic. *pro Mur.* 13, 28.

Municipal jurisdiction was probably regulated by the same respect for days and festivals; but, even after the extension of the *civitas*, the observances must have been local and not regulated by the practice at Rome.

Times of municipal and provincial juris-diction.

In the provinces the various local festivals must have been observed by the governor and had to be considered in fixing the dates of his *conventus*. The *iudices* of a circuit were selected for service at the beginning of the assize, but they might go on sitting long after the governor had quitted this *conventus* for another.

Length of a court-day.

3. The length of a court-day had, according to the Twelve Tables, been from forenoon to sunset. The hour of commencement was probably the third; by midday the absent litigant might be condemned[1]; were both parties present the court broke up at the setting of the sun, and a *lex Plaetoria* made it obligatory that the praetor urbanus should continue his jurisdiction until this *suprema tempestas*[2]. In the Ciceronian period the courts still began their sitting at the second or third hour of the forenoon[3]; the tenth hour of the evening was the time at which the undefended litigant could be condemned, and marked the usual close of the day's proceedings. No attempt could be made to fix the length of a trial, and the number of adjournments (*comperendinationes*) at intervals of ten or thirty days depended on the nature of the case and the discretion of the *iudex*.

Adjourn-ment.

[1] ANTE MERIDIEM CAUSAM COICITO (*Auct. ad Herenn.* ii. 13, 20).

[2] Censorinus, *de Die Nat.* 24, 3 (cited p. 31, note 2).

[3] Hor. *Sat.* ii. 6, 35:—

'ante secundam
'Roscius orabat sibi adesses ad Puteal cras.'

Martial, iv. 8, 2 'Exercet raucos tertia causidicos.'

The earliest time in the Ciceronian period is perhaps reflected in *pro Quinct.* 6, 25 ('Naevius . . . suos necessarios . . . corrogat ut ad tabulam Sextiam sibi adsint hora secunda postridie. Veniunt frequentes. Testificatur iste P. Quinctium non stitisse'). This is an appearance for an affidavit, not before a court, and it is not clear that the affidavit was made on the very day on which the case was called.

BOOK I.

Limit of pendency in an action;

in *legis actiones* and *iudicia legitima*;

The time during which a single action might last without requiring renewal *ab initio*—generally known as its 'limit of pendency'—depended on the source from which the action proceeded. In the case of the *legis actiones*, and the *iudicia legitima* developed from them by the application of the *formula*, the action was as eternal as the law itself; for the limit of eighteen months which Gaius assigns to such trials was the creation of the Julian legislation[1]. The case in which Cicero was engaged for Quinctius had lasted two years at the time when his final pleadings were delivered[2]; he reckons the duration of the process from the time at which the parties had first agreed to appear before a magistrate; but the case as it finally developed is no true instance of the duration of a *legitimum iudicium*. Its original promise was to be an action for adjusting the affairs of a partnership or for determining the claim to a debt; its final issue at the stage of which we possess the record was to discover whether a praetorian declaration of bankruptcy against Quinctius was valid or not[3]. It, therefore, really belonged to the class of actions *quae imperio continentur*, which were conditioned by time. The limit of pendency in these actions is the obvious one of the duration of the office of the magistrate who has granted them[4]. They must be finished within this year of office or else renewed. The case of Quinctius is not an exceptional instance of the duration of one of these *iudicia*, without renewal, beyond the term of the magistracy which has granted it; it is in the nature of an appeal to a court established by praetorian authority to determine whether the act of a former praetor had been valid, according to the *ius honorarium* itself, and had been actually carried into effect. It is a preliminary —a *praeiudicium*—to a trial at law, to determine the

in *iudicia quae imperio continentur*.

[1] Gaius, iv. 104.

[2] Cic. *pro Quinct.* 12, 40; 13, 42.

[3] See Appendix on the *pro Quinctio*.

[4] Gaius, iv. 105 'Ideo autem imperio contineri iudicia dicuntur, quia tamdiu valent quamdiu is qui ea praecepit imperium habebit.'

conditions under which this trial is to be fought out; the preliminaries of this trial reached back, as Cicero says, to a date preceding this *praeiudicium* by two years.

PART II.

Effect of the necessity of renewing praetorian actions.

It is probable that the necessity for the renewal of praetorian actions did not seriously affect their continuity. The same *formula* would in most cases be sought from the incoming praetor, and he might give the same *iudex*, familiar with the facts elicited at the previous hearings[1]. It need scarcely in practice have been a greater 'renewal' than that brought about by every adjournment of a case.

(*b*) *The Summons.*

In ius vocatio.

The first step in a process was naturally the service of a summons on the future defendant, which, in the Roman procedure, was accompanied by an attempt to enforce his presence before the praetor. It is true that the magistrate had theoretically the right of compelling the latter to appear before him; but both in the earlier and later period of Roman process, the effective summons of the defendant was regarded as the private business of the plaintiff. The older law allowed him to call on his opponent, in whatever place he might meet him, to follow him to the court; resistance was followed by force; with a solemn appeal to the by-standers (*antestatio*) the plaintiff laid hands on his adversary; any reasonable amount of violence could be used to effect the transference of the unwilling litigant, although inexpensive modes of locomotion had to be provided for those who were suffering from age or illness[2].

[1] The *exceptio rei in iudicium deductae* (Gaius, iv. 106) could never have been intended to stop such a renewal. On its meaning see the section on the *litis contestatio*.

[2] The Twelve Tables enacted 'Si in ius vocat, ni it, antestamino. Si calvitur (i. e. moratur) pedemve struit (i. e. fugit) manum endo iacito. Si morbus aevitasve vitium escit, iumentum dato. Si nolet, arceram (i.e. plaustrum) ne sternito' (Festus, p. 313; Gell. xx. 1, 25). For the *antestatio* see Hor. *Sat.* i. 9, 76 and cf. Plaut. *Pers.* iv. 9, 8 *Sat.* 'Age, ambula in ius, leno.' *Dord.* 'Quid me in ius vocas?' *Sat.* 'Illic apud praetorem dicam: sed ego in ius voco.' *Dord.* 'Nonne antestaris?'

BOOK I.

Vadimonium.

This mode of summons was still theoretically existent in Cicero's day, but it was seldom resorted to. A gentler but equally effective means had been developed in the form of the *vadimonium*. This device had been originally adopted to obviate the necessity of a second summons in cases where the trial had been adjourned. At the close of the first hearing the praetor bound the defendant to appear before him on a certain day by means of a stipulation which the latter was made to enter into with the plaintiff. The defendant promised a certain sum in the event of his non-appearance, the amount of the caution-money varying with the nature of the action; in certain cases it attained the full value of the object in dispute; in the others the plaintiff might assess it to the height of half that value or to the maximum of 100,000 sesterces[1]. The promise (*vadimonium promittere*) might remain unsanctioned (in which case it was said to be made *pure*), or it might be strengthened by security (*cum satisdatione*), or by an oath (*iureiurando*), or finally by the immediate appointment of *recuperatores* who were to condemn the defendant in case his promise was not observed[2].

It soon became apparent that the mode which effected the second appearance of a defendant might be applied to effect his first. This *vadimonium*, which replaced the primary *in ius vocatio*, was of course not enforced by the praetor, but was a voluntary stipulation entered into by the parties before their appearance in court. By this stipulation the party summoned (*vocatus*) bound himself under a penalty to present himself before the praetor by a certain day[3]. It is not known whether security, personal

[1] Gaius, iv. 186.

[2] Gaius, iv. 185.

[3] Cic. *pro Quinct.* 19, 61 'Vadari vis: promittit. In ius vocas: sequitur. Iudicium postulas: non recusat.' *Vadari* is to accept the security, *vadimonium promittere*, to offer it, *vadimonia differe*, to agree to an adjournment (*ib.* 5, 22 and 6, 23), *venire ad vadimonium*, to appear to one's bail, *vadimonium deserere*, to be *absens* and undefended (*ib.* 5, 22; 21, 67; 28, 86); *res est in vadimonium* is said of the condition of things between the security and the appearance in court (*ib.* 5, 22).

or real, had to be given by the defendant; but the terms of the agreement no doubt depended on the will of the parties. This second mode of procedure, besides being a convenient substitute for the old compulsory summons, had another signal advantage. The defendant was now given notice of the claim against him before his appearance in court; greater progress could, therefore, be made in the first hearing before the praetor, while under the old system the announcement of the action (*editio actionis*) by the plaintiff, followed by an adjournment to enable the defendant to think out his plea, must have been all that was possible in the first day's proceedings.

Arrangements in municipalities for cases to be tried at Rome.

Hitherto we have been considering the *in ius vocatio* or the giving of *vadimonium* for appearance in a court competent to try the case. But it was possible for a summons to be made to a local court, which had some jurisdiction over the parties summoned, when the case was ultimately to be tried elsewhere. We have already seen this illustrated in municipal jurisdiction after the incorporation of Italy[1]. The presence of the defendant before the local magistrate was effected, whether by *in ius vocatio* or by a first *vadimonium*, and then, if the case transcended the competence of this official, he forced the defendant to enter into a *vadimonium* to appear before the court of the praetor in Rome.

Summons in the provinces.

In the province the summons or bail was made for a defendant's appearance at a particular *conventus*, and in Sicily, as we have seen, no member of a *civitas* which was included in a particular *conventus* could be forced to give bail for his appearance in any other circuit[2]. It could not have been easy, however, for the member of one *civitas* to issue an effective summons to, or to make a *vadimonium* with, the member of another far-distant community. It has been supposed that, to remedy this defect, a process,

[1] pp. 102 and 108.

[2] p. 116.

for which some slight evidence exists, was adopted, by which the plaintiff issued to the defendant, always perhaps in writing, a statement of claim as well as a summons to appear[1]; but no trace of this procedure appears in Cicero's references to provincial jurisdiction.

Magisterial *in ius vocatio.*

Possibly the latent power of the governor to effect a summons on his own authority was employed in such cases. There is, indeed, no evidence for the magisterial power of *in ius vocatio* having been employed by the governor in any purely private suit. But it asserts itself, as a right both of the pro-magistrate and of his delegate, in the civil procedure meant to enforce public claims or to punish delicts against the state. Caecilius, the quaestor of Lilybaeum in Sicily, once had a woman summoned before his court to test the truth of a claim, which she had urged against the appropriation of some of her slaves to state purposes, that she and all her property had been consecrated to the service of Venus Erycina[2]. She was, in fact, a freedwoman of the goddess, with property of her own, which might in whole or in part have reverted to the temple in case of her decease. The pretext of 'consecration,' which she employed to shield her chattels from the aggression of Roman officials, proved her ruin; for the *recuperatores* empanelled by Caecilius pronounced that she herself was the property of the goddess; the quaestor adjudged her a slave of Venus, and, as a slave could hold no property, issued a writ of *possessio* against her goods. We find Verres himself using this right of summons against an agent of a state, charged with having taken money from an association of its citizens to press a public

[1] *Litis denuntiatio*; see Rudorff, *Rechtsgesch.* ii. § 65, note 2 'die *Denuntiatio* hat anscheinend von dem *dicam scribere* des griechischen Provinzialrechts (z. B. Donat. *ad Ter. Phorm.* i. 2, 77 "et scribam tibi dicam" a denuntiatione in personam, ne diceret "non mihi denuntiasti") und in den *iudicia ordinaria* ihren Ausgang genommen.'

[2] Cic. *Div. in Caec.* 17, 56 (Caecilius) 'vocari ad se Agonidem iubet: iudicium dat statim: SI PARET EAM SE ET SUA VENERIS ESSE DIXISSE.'

claim[1]; the agent appeared and the money was refunded; in the event of denial a *iudicium*, probably before *recuperatores*, would have resulted, in which the case would have been decided on a *formula* submitted to them. In both these instances we have indeed the summons of the governor leading up to a civil action; but in neither case are private interests in question. The cases in which Cicero, as a collector of evidence against Verres, employed the *in ius vocatio* for the purpose of procuring the production of documents[2], were the result of a right given by the criminal procedure of the time; but his summons would have been ineffectual had not his inquiries been supported by the then governor of Sicily.

(c) *Proceedings in iure.*

Chief objects of proceedings *in iure*, instruction of a *iudex*, and establishment of a *iudicium*.

The fulfilment of the summons to appear was followed by the commencement of proceedings in the praetor's court (*in iure*). The main object of these proceedings was to induce the praetor to instruct a *iudex* and to establish an appropriate *iudicium* (*iudicium ordinare*). The main events of the proceedings *in iure* were, therefore, a plaint by the plaintiff, an answer by the defendant, and the establishment of a *iudicium* by the praetor, which was instructed in accordance with these rival assertions. So far as the *legis actio* still existed, the claim and denial were verbally asserted, and the instruction to the 'iudex' *may* even now have been given verbally by the praetor; but the prevailing custom was to commit an outline of the case to writing; the *formula* so furnished always contained the statement of claim, sometimes indirectly a counter-statement of the defendant, always the issue to be decided, and sometimes the partial grounds of the decision.

[1] Cic. *in Verr.* ii. 23, 56 'Verres . . . ait se velle . . . cognoscere . . . Volcatium vocat: pecuniam referri iubet.'

[2] Cic. *in Verr.* ii. 76, 187 'in ius ad Metellum (Verres' successor), Carpinatium voco tabulasque societatis in forum defero.' Cf. iv. 66, 148.

BOOK I.

Postulatio.

Representation in postulation.

One of the forms of *legis actio* had, from its leading characteristic, borne the name of a request (*postulatio*) to the praetor for a *iudex* or an *arbiter*[1]. As the essence of the formulary system was the establishment of a *iudicium* of some kind, it is not surprising that the first stage of the proceedings *in iure* came to bear the general name of *postulatio*. It is defined from the plaintiff's point of view as 'the exposition before a judicial magistrate of one's own wants or those of one's friend,' and from the defendant's as the 'contradiction to another's demand[2].' The first part of the definition shows that representation of the interests of another was contemplated as a possibility. This representation was, in fact, a fully acknowledged feature of the formulary system, as an element in which it assumed two forms; (i) the full representation of the personality of another. Representation of this kind by means of a *cognitor* or *procurator* is perfect agency, and the person represented does not intervene at all; (ii) the mode of imperfect representation by means of pleaders (*patroni*) which is a regular feature of all developed iudicature. In this case the litigant is himself regarded as the active agent; if he is not present he is regarded as undefended, for the *patronus* cannot take his place; the latter is only an able interpreter, intervening for the purpose of illustrating the law and marshalling the proofs in his client's interests. When it is said that representation was unknown in the *legis actiones*[3], it is the first kind that is chiefly meant; that of the second kind would not indeed have been possible when the formal words of the action required utterance; but it is difficult to see how, in the discussion of evidence before the magistrate or the

[1] p. 63.

[2] Ulpian in Dig. 3, 1, 1, 2 'Postulare autem est desiderium suum vel amici sui in iure apud eum, qui iurisdictioni praeest, exponere: vel alterius desiderio contradicere.'

[3] Gaius, iv. 82.

iudex, the activity of the *patronus* could even at this time have been disallowed.

Rules made by the praetor with regard to postulation.

The praetor was careful about the dignity of his court, and indiscriminate approach to the sanctity of the *imperium* was not allowed. Perfectly free access was permitted only to an *integra persona*, who, as the phrase ran, was allowed by the edict to postulate (*cui per edictum postulare licet*)[1]. For the purpose of keeping away people who might voluntarily or involuntarily infringe the dignity of the court, the praetor framed three rules expressed in three *edicta* and posted up on his *album*. These edicts referred to three classes of individuals. The first class was composed of those to whom postulation of every kind was denied. Under it fell boys under seventeen (the Roman age of manhood with respect to the exercise of public rights), and those persons who were so deaf as to be unable to hear the praetor's rulings. If such persons had no representative of their own, the praetor assigned them an advocate[2]. The second class consisted of people to whom postulation was allowed only in their own interest: they could never act as representatives. This partial disqualification was based on sex, physical infirmity or gross immorality: it included women, blind persons and a class of individuals branded in later times as *in turpitudine notabiles*: and it was clearly based, even in the first two cases, on a desire to protect the dignity of the praetor's court. The rule that women should not appear for others was, indeed, introduced during Cicero's lifetime, in consequence of the great annoyance caused in the civil courts by the ceaseless activity of a senator's wife named Gaia Afrania[3]. The third class contained those who were allowed to postulate in all cases for them-

[1] Paulus in Dig. xlvii. 23, 4.

[2] 'Ait praetor "si non habebunt advocatum, ego dabo"' (Dig. 3, 1, 1, 4).

[3] Val. Max. viii. 3, 2; Juv. ii. 69. She was the wife of the senator Licinius Bucco, and died in 49 or 48 B. C. See Rudorff, in *Zeitschr. f. Rechtsgesch.* iv. p. 47.

selves, but only in exceptional cases for others. In this third class was included a list of persons 'who are marked by the praetor's edict as *infames*[1].' The praetor in making out this list had followed very closely the rulings of the censor; his edict merely added a new and permanent disability to disqualifications already incurred.

Representation by means of a *patronus*.

The other kind of representation, by means of a *patronus*, although far more frequent than the first, was not regulated by any such rigorous rules. When the Bar had become a profession we find that the praetor or provincial governor could suspend a particular advocate from practice in his court either temporarily or permanently[2]; but it had not yet reached this stage in Cicero's time, and, although the praetor could undoubtedly exclude every one, except the parties directly interested, from his court, we know of no general rules which gave or refused permission to advocacy. The assistance rendered to litigants by this semi-professional class was of two kinds. Eloquence and deep knowledge of the law were not always united in the same individuals; while the possessors of the first gift appeared as pleaders (*patroni*), those who had the second assisted with their advice on legal points (*advocati*)[3]: although the 'advocates' in the strict sense were sometimes merely influential men who gave weight to the litigant's case by their presence on his side.

Advocati.

Objects sought by the parties in postulation; discretionary power of the praetor.

Postulation, except it was simplified by a previous agreement between the parties, might be a lengthy and controversial business. The disputed points which might arise at this stage can only be discussed when we have considered the nature of the *formula*. It is sufficient to remark here that much depended upon the discretion of

[1] 'Omnes qui edicto praetoris ut infames notantur' (Dig. 3, 1, 1, 8).

[2] Bethmann-Hollweg, ii. p. 206.

[3] Cic. *pro Cluent.* 40, 110 'quis eum unquam non modo in patroni, sed in laudatoris aut advocati loco viderat?' Ps. Asc. p. 104 'patronus dicitur si orator est . . . advocatus si aut ius suggerit aut praesentiam suam commodat amico.'

the praetor: and to move him to take a different view of the law or to adopt a more equitable frame of mind were the objects of the patron's pleadings *in iure.* The complaints were sometimes long and querulous; but the praetor had good reasons for declining to listen to pleadings beyond a certain length. On the comparatively few court days the number of postulants was great, and the praetor could not dwell at length on one particular request. Complaints of his rulings were sometimes answered by the summary removal of the advocate from his court, and Cicero's client Quinctius had once seen his protesting friends hurried away from their place before the *tribunal* to give room to the next postulant[1].

Points of law reserved by the praetor for cognizance or for a *praeiudicium.*

Yet some of the questions raised by the lawyers could not be dismissed in this summary manner. For these the praetor had a remedy which did not interfere with his activity in granting cases. He either reserved the point of law for his own *cognitio* or framed it as a *formula* to be settled as a *praeiudicium* by a *iudex.* A case of the latter kind is the one on which Cicero engaged in Quinctius' behalf. It is in the nature of a wager (*sponsio*) to determine whether the *possessio* claimed by the plaintiff against Quinctius' goods is valid or not[2].

His rulings not always final.

But even when the praetor had given a ruling and refused both cognizance and a case, this ruling was not final. It might be indefinitely suspended by the veto of his colleague or of a higher magistrate: and the invalidation of his decree *might* lead him to alter his mind[3]. Finally, if within the limits of time which he allowed to each case he professed himself uncertain of its merits, he might compel the litigants to conclude a *vadimonium* to appear before him at some other time.

[1] Cic. *pro Quinct.* 8, 30–31 'A Cn. Dolabella ... praetore postulat ut sibi Quinctius iudicatum solvi satisdet ... Dolabella ... aut satisdare aut sponsionem iubet facere, et interea recusantes nostros advocatos acerrime submoveri.'

[2] See Appendix on the *pro Quinctio.*

[3] See the section on the appeal.

(d) *The formula.*

The *formula* a conditional judgement.

The *formula* was a written statement of a case meant to be presented to a *iudex*; it was supposed to be an expression of the law applicable to this particular case and contained in a conditional form a judgement which the finding of the *iudex* was to make absolute. It was therefore expressed in the form of a conditional sentence, beginning with the words 'if it appears or should appear' and ending with the words 'give judgement in favour of A. against B.' The *iudex* by pronouncing 'it does' or 'does not appear' either condemns or acquits. But it is a mistake to regard the function of the *iudex* as confined to the decision of what we should call 'a point of fact.' The *formula* only states the law for the particular case, it does not state the law requisite for the very condition of the *formula* (the SI PARET) to be fulfilled. The legal validity of a stipulation, an obligation, a loan might lurk in those words; they might involve the raising of the whole question what was legal proof and what was not. By the formulary system the praetor removed quite half the burden of decisions in law from his own shoulders and laid them on those of the *iudex*; the latter must be, not a man of average enlightenment with a commonsense estimate of evidence, but a juristically trained man with a capacity for dealing with subtle points of law put before him by the pleaders. Cicero's pleadings for Quinctius, Caecina, Roscius and Tullius alone furnish sufficient proof of the amount of legal appreciation required of a judge; and additional evidence of the same fact is furnished by the practice of inviting trained jurists as assessors to the Bench[1].

But the finding of the *iudex* not confined to 'fact.'

Analysis of the *formula*.

But the relation between the facts and the law can best be estimated by glancing at the juristic analysis of the

[1] Cic. *pro Quinct.* 2, 5; 10, 36; *pro Rosc. com.* 4, 12; 5, 15; 8, 22.

formula. Its structure differed so much with the different kinds of action that there was no such thing as a permanent type; yet the more constant materials out of which *formulae* were built, as opposed to the more accidental elements which might be embedded in them, might be tabulated and defined. The more essential parts were four in number:— PART II.

1. The *Demonstratio.* This was a preliminary statement of the matter in dispute; it by no means assumed the existence of the fact, but simply asserted the ground of action, as stated by the plaintiff, by its technical name, if it possessed one; if on the other hand the contractual relation was not technically recognized by the law but this nameless contract[1] was yet made the source of a *iudicium* by the praetor, the place of the *demonstratio* was taken by a similar short preface (*praescripta verba*) of the ground of action. Gaius[2] takes as instances of the *demonstratio* cases arising from the contracts of sale and deposit. In the first instance it might run:— *Demonstratio.*

QUOD AULUS AGERIUS NUMERIO NEGIDIO HOMINEM VENDIDIT;

in the second:—

QUOD AULUS AGERIUS APUD NUMERIUM NEGIDIUM HOMINEM DEPOSUIT.

A similar statement might appear at the head of *formulae* which embraced compensation for a delict, e.g. when the ground of action was an assault by a box on the ear, the *demonstratio* might run:—

QUOD AULI AGERII PUGNO A NUMERIO NEGIDIO MALA PERCUSSA EST[3].

The *demonstratio*, whether applied to contracts or delicts, states an assumed fact which is the basis of a claim and

[1] 'Contractus . . . quorum appellationes nullae iure civili proditae sunt' (Dig. 19, 5, 2).

[2] iv. 40.

[3] Collatio, ii. 6, 4; or with Lenel (*Edictum Perpetuum*, p. 321), QUOD DOLO MALO NUMERII NEGIDII AULO AGERIO PUGNO MALA PERCUSSA EST.'

not the claim itself. It is in fact meant to lead the mind of the *iudex* up to the claim, and this demand of the plaintiff is something that is to be estimated either by the praetor or the *iudex*. The *demonstratio*, in fact, appears only in a *formula* which embodies a claim to an *incertum*.

Intentio.

2. The *intentio* is the essential and integral part of every *formula*, for it embodies the claim of the plaintiff[1]. It is this that expresses the conditional fact which the voice of the *iudex* is to render absolute. If the recovery of an *incertum* is the issue of the proof of the fact it contains, it is preceded, as we have seen, by the *demonstratio*; if a *certum*, it stands alone—e.g. if we take the claim to an *incertum* based on the *bona fide* contract of lease (*locatio*), we should have:—

(*Demonstratio*) QUOD AULUS AGERIUS NUMERIO NEGIDIO FUNDUM CORNELIANUM IN AGRO SABINO LOCAVIT.

(*Intentio*) QUIDQUID OB EAM REM NUMERIUM NEGIDIUM AULO AGERIO DARE FACERE OPORTET EX FIDE BONA, or QUIDQUID PARET . . . OPORTERE.

The *intentio* for the recovery of a *certum*, on the other hand, requires no introduction: e.g.

SI PARET NUMERIUM NEGIDIUM AULO AGERIO SESTERTIUM X MILIA DARE OPORTERE.

While the above-mentioned parts of the *formula* embody the ground of claim and the demand of the plaintiff, the two latter portions express the ruling of the magistrate on these claims, in vague or definite terms according to the amount of discretion which must be left to the *iudex*.

Adiudicatio.

3. The *Adiudicatio* is a form of sentence only applying to certain special cases. It was employed when the *iudex* had to effect a division of property or rights in property

[1] Gaius, iv. 41 'Intentio est ea pars formulae qua actor desiderium suum concludit.'

between several litigants[1] whether heirs (by the action *familiae herciscundae*) or partners (by the action *communi dividundo*) or neighbours engaged in boundary disputes (by the action *finium regundorum*). The bare outline of the sentence in this case is given as:— PART II.

QUANTUM ADIUDICARI OPORTET, IUDEX TITIO ADIUDICATO;

but, though these words must have been found in every *formula* of the kind, a statement signifying a pecuniary condemnation of one or both or all of the litigants probably appeared in some words following *adiudicari* and *adiudicato*[2].

4. The sentence of the praetor in matters other than those contemplated in this particular case, was known as the *condemnatio*, although its function, like its wording, was absolutory as well as condemnatory[3]. In the case of a claim to a *certum* or even to something which was in law an *incertum*, but which had become definite by the damages being fixed by the praetor, it ran:— *Condemnatio.*

IUDEX NUMERIUM NEGIDIUM AULO AGERIO SESTERTIUM X MILIA CONDEMNA; SI NON PARET, ABSOLVE.

When the claim was to an *incertum* to be fixed by the *iudex*, if the condemnation sprang from a *bona fide* contract it might run:—

ID (i. e. *quidquid ... dare facere oportet ex fide bona*) IUDEX NUMERIUM NEGIDIUM AULO AGERIO CONDEMNATO; SI NON PARET ABSOLVITO;

If it arose from a claim to a thing;

QUANTI EA RES ERIT, TANTAM PECUNIAM IUDEX NUMERIUM NEGIDIUM AULO AGERIO CONDEMNA: SI NON PARET, ABSOLVE.

[1] Gaius, iv. 42 'Adiudicatio est ea pars formulae qua permittitur iudici rem alicui ex litigatoribus adiudicare.'

[2] e. g. Keller, *Civilprocess*, note 458 'quantum paret alteri ab altero adiudicari alterumve alteri condemnari oportere, tantum iudex alteri ab altero adiudicato tantique alterum alteri condemnato.' Cf. Rudorff, *Rechtsgesch.* ii. p. 97.

[3] Gaius, iv. 43 'Condemnatio est ea pars formulae qua iudici condemnandi absolvendive potestas permittitur.'

BOOK I.

Meaning of the command for acquittal.

It will be seen that the form of the *condemnatio* contains an alternative command—'condemn' or 'acquit.' The necessity for the latter injunction is not at first sight obvious, for an absence of condemnation might be taken to mean acquittal. Its insertion may have been due to the fact that the judgement without it may have appeared to be merely a verdict of 'not proven,' which would not have absolved the defendant from the suggestion of possible indebtedness; but the necessity for its presence is probably deeper and intimately connected with the history of the *formula*. If the latter was originally a mode of extra-legal assistance not recognized by the *ius civile* it is probable that the mere fulfilment of the action based on it did not (as in the case of the *legis actio*) *ipso iure* extinguish the claim and prevent a renewal of the case. Hence the magistrate must specifically enjoin, and the *iudex* as explicitly declare, an acquittal in each case where the claim of the plaintiff was not proved[1]. This acquittal was itself a *res iudicata* and could be raised as a counter-plea (*exceptio*) by the defendant in case an attempt were made to renew the action.

Essential and occasional parts of the *formula*.

We have seen that *all* the different parts of the *formula* did not necessarily exist together. A complete union of the four elements was, in fact, found only in actions for the division of property (*iudicia divisoria*); the other actions which had an *incertum* as their object, possessed three parts, the *demonstratio* (or *praescripta verba*), the *intentio* and the *condemnatio*; the actions whose object was a *certum* (and which, therefore, did not require demonstration) only two, the *intentio* and the *condemnatio*. The *intentio* is the only part of the *formula* which could stand quite alone[2]; it occupied this solitary position when a question was to be answered by the *iudex*, the reply to

[1] Eisele, *Beiträge*, p. 13 ff.

[2] Gaius, iv. 44 'Certe intentio aliquando sola invenitur . . . Demonstratio autem et adiudicatio et condemnatio nunquam solae inveniuntur.'

which entailed no penalty or condemnation. This was the case in incidental or preliminary decisions (*praeiudicia*), to the proof of the truth or falsehood of which no forfeit money was attached. A question of *status*, e.g.

SI PARET HOMINEM STICHUM AULI AGERII LIBERTUM ESSE,

was answered in this way, or a question as to the amount of a dowry and many others of the kind.

But, apart from these exceptional cases, the *intentio* and *condemnatio* are true correlatives of one another; they are also the most essential parts of the *formula*, and the elements whose structure determines the nature of the *iudicium*.

The *intentio*, besides the various forms which it assumed according as a *certum* or *incertum* was the object of pursuit, also differed according as it was framed with reference to the law or with reference to the circumstances (*in ius, in factum concepta*). This distinction is nothing short of the fundamental one between civil and praetorian law. 'The *formulae in ius conceptae* are typified by those in which we urge that something is ours *ex iure Quiritium* or that something *should* be presented to us (*nobis dare oportere*), or seek satisfaction for a delict, e.g. urge that some satisfaction *should* be made to us for theft (*pro fure damnum decidi oportere*); in such *formulae* the *intentio* is one of civil law (*iuris civilis*[1]).'

Formulae in ius conceptae.

In the above-mentioned claims, which are stated in the language of the praetor's court, *oportere* (connected with *dare, facere, decidere* &c.) signifies a 'should' or an 'ought' based on *ius strictum* or (to adopt a phrase which is generally confined to ownership) springing *ex iure Quiritium*. The word *oportere* appeared in certain praetorian actions, but only in those which by a fiction the praetor represented to be actions of the civil law. This mode of advance beyond the limits of the *ius civile* was doubtless

[1] Gaius, iv. 45.

BOOK I.

Actiones fictitiae.

the earliest which the praetor employed. The *legis actio* itself might be manipulated in this way, and *actiones fictitiae* were probably invented by jurists as well as by magistrates. The revolution in some departments of substantive law (e.g. rights connected with property and inheritances) were amply supported by the employment of fictitious actions as early as the Ciceronian period, and, although the student of Cicero's writings is not intimately concerned with them[1], a consideration of the law of the period would be incomplete without some notice of the mode in which the *fictio* was applied.

The man who succeeds to an inheritance by praetorian law, and not by a claim recognized in the civil law (*legitimo iure*) had no legal claim to debts owed to the estate. But a fiction of heirship can be supplied him in the following form[2]:—

SI AULUS AGERIUS LUCIO TITIO HERES ESSET, TUM SI PARERET NUMERIUM NEGIDIUM AULO AGERIO SESTERTIUM X MILIA DARE OPORTERE, IUDEX NUMERIUM NEGIDIUM AULO AGERIO SESTERTIUM X MILIA CONDEMNA: SI NON PARET, ABSOLVE.

Or, to take the case of a delict, the action for theft was possible only against Roman citizens; had a foreigner stolen something he must be fictitiously represented by the praetor peregrinus as a Roman citizen, e.g.:—

SI PARET OPE CONSILIOVE DIONIS HERMAEI FILII FURTUM FACTUM ESSE AULO AGERIO PATERAE AUREAE, QUAM OB REM EUM, SI CIVIS ROMANUS ESSET[3], PRO FURE DAMNUM DECIDERE OPORTERET, QUANTI EA RES FUIT, CUM FURTUM FACTUM EST[4], TANTAE PECUNIAE DUPLUM IUDEX DIONEM HERMAEI FILIUM AULO AGERIO CONDEMNA, SI NON PARET ABSOLVE[5].

[1] See, however, Cic. *in Verr.* ii. 12, 31 (cited note 3).

[2] Gaius, iv. 34.

[3] Some of Verres' *formulae* assumed a fiction of this kind. Cic. *in Verr.* ii. 12, 31 'Iudicia eiusmodi "qui cives Romani erant, si Siculi essent, cum Siculos eorum legibus dari oporteret; qui Siculi, si cives Romani essent."' By this means he transferred the regulations of the *lex provinciae* from one class to the other.

[4] Or with Bethmann-Hollweg (ii. p. 301), QUANTI PARET EAM REM FUISSE.

[5] Gaius, iv. 37; Lenel, *Edictum Perpetuum*, p. 263.

But the support of praetorian law could not always be effected by this easy transference. A circumstance had sometimes to be made the basis of an independent action, to which the language of the civil law would not apply: and the constantly recurring or predicted circumstance gave rise to an appropriate *formula in factum*, which found its permanent place in the praetor's *album*. 'In these there is no such *intentio* as appears in the *formulae* of the civil law. The *factum* is first set forth and then are added the words in which the edict gives the *iudex* the power of condemnation or acquittal[1].' Gaius cites as instances the actions by which the praetor protected his own rules regulating the right of summons. Against the freedman, who contrary to the orders of the edict had summoned his *patronus* into court, the following recuperatorial *iudicium* was given:—

Formulae in factum conceptae.

RECUPERATORES SUNTO. SI PARET ILLUM PATRONUM AB ILLO LIBERTO CONTRA EDICTUM ILLIUS PRAETORIS IN IUS VOCATUM ESSE, RECUPERATORES, ILLUM LIBERTUM ILLI PATRONO SESTERTIUM X MILIA CONDEMNATE; SI NON PARET, ABSOLVITE.

Or it may be illustrated by the praetorian action of deposit.

IUDEX ESTO. SI PARET AULUM AGERIUM APUD NUMERIUM NEGIDIUM MENSAM ARGENTEAM DEPOSUISSE, EAMQUE DOLO MALO NUMERII NEGIDII AULO AGERIO REDDITAM NON ESSE, QUANTI EA RES ERIT, TANTAM PECUNIAM IUDEX NUMERIUM NEGIDIUM AULO AGERIO CONDEMNATO: SI NON PARET, ABSOLVITO[2].

In the wording of neither of these *formulae* is there any suggestion of a legal obligation; the action does not spring from any relations recognized by the civil law but simply from the praetor's promise that, under such and such circumstances, he would grant an action (*actionem dabo*).

When we turn from the *intentio* to the *condemnatio*,

[1] Gaius, iv. 46. [2] Gaius, iv. 47.

The condemnation of the *formula* always pecuniary.

the leading fact observable throughout all its manifestations is that it is always expressed in terms of money[1]. That the formula could only condemn in pecuniary damages was perhaps the universal rule at Rome even in Cicero's day; it can hardly be said to be shaken by the instance with which he presents us of a *formula* given in Sicilian jurisdiction which condemns the defendant in corn[2]. That action was based on the administrative portion of the pro-praetor's edict, and, since the revenue was paid in corn, there is nothing singular in a judicial fine having been estimated in this commodity.

Hence estimation by the *iudex* necessary.

It follows from this peculiarity of the *formula* that, in a personal action, no *certa res* or *corpus* could appear in the condemnation[3]. The *legis actio* had allowed recovery of the thing, but now the *iudex* must estimate its value (*rem* or *litem aestimare*) and return that value in terms of money. The praetor's instruction in the *condemnatio*, therefore, takes the form QUANTI EA RES EST or ERIT, as in the praetorian action for deposit which we have cited.

Claims for *certa pecunia*;

All claims being pecuniary, they may be either for a fixed amount of money (*certa pecunia*) or for an unfixed amount (*incerta*). In the former case (in which the ground of action is a definite pecuniary contract) the condemnation is of the simple kind:—

IUDEX NUMERIUM NEGIDIUM AULO AGERIO SESTERTIUM X MILIA CONDEMNA; SI NON PARET, ABSOLVE[4].

for *incerta*.

For this there is but one form; but the condemnation to *incerta pecunia* admits of two. Sometimes the praetor[5]

[1] Gaius, iv. 48 'Omnium autem formularum, quae condemnationem habent, ad pecuniariam aestimationem condemnatio concepta est.'

[2] Cic. *in Verr.* iii. 21, 54; see p. 124.

[3] Gaius, iv. 48 'etsi corpus aliquod petamus . . . iudex non ipsam rem condemnat eum cum quo actum est, sicut olim fieri solebat, sed aestimata re pecuniam eum condemnat.'

[4] Gaius, iv. 50.

[5] Sometimes at the request of the plaintiff (Cic. *pro Tull.* 3, 7 'Eius rei taxationem nos fecimus').

fixed an upward limit (*taxatio*), beyond which the sentence of the *iudex* could not go, as exhibited in the following *condemnatio*:—

IUDEX NUMERIUM NEGIDIUM AULO AGERIO DUMTAXAT SESTERTIUM X MILIA CONDEMNA: SI NON PARET, ABSOLVE[1].

In all other cases the amount of the condemnation is indefinite and left to the discretion of the *iudex*. To these cases apply the QUANTI EA RES ERIT . . . TANTAM PECUNIAM of the praetorian action of deposit; and a similar condemnation is found in all *actiones in rem*, and in actions employed to support certain of the interdicts, where the amount of the condemnation is proportionate to the interest the plaintiff has in the praetor's order being obeyed.

But condemnation by the *iudex* is always to *certa pecunia*.

But, whether the condemnation ordered by the praetor was to a certain or an uncertain amount, as pronounced by the iudex it is always to *certa pecunia*. His discretion varied with the structure of the *condemnatio*. In one that specified *certa pecunia*, he could not condemn to more or less than the sum stated; in one for *incerta pecunia*, if it was *cum taxatione* he could not condemn to more than the maximum, but he might to less[2]: if it was indefinite (*infinita*), he might use his own discretion.

Condemnation in *actiones in rem*; its alternative 'restitution.'

The last mentioned form of condemnation was the one applicable to *actiones in rem*. A man who brings such an action usually aims at the recovery of the thing; but specific recovery could not be effected by the formulary system—at least, directly. Indirectly the *formula* might enforce recovery by condemning to a pecuniary estimate of the thing only in the case of non-restitution. With the instruction to pecuniary condemnation are coupled the words NISI RESTITUAT. The pecuniary estimate of the *iudex* was supposed to be higher than the actual value of the things whose recovery was sought and was (perhaps in Cicero's time as later) based on the sworn declaration of the plaintiff (*ius iurandum in litem*); it,

[1] Gaius, iv. 51.

[2] Gaius, iv. 52.

BOOK I. therefore, contained a penal element, which was meant to be effective in enforcing restitution. The function of the *iudex* in estimating the value and suggesting an alternative gives him something of the character of an arbitrator, and actions of this kind are known as *actiones* or *formulae arbitrariae*. A change of a name in a consciously absurd parody of a *formula* given by Cicero presents us with the *intentio* and part of the *condemnatio* of such an action:—

Formula arbitraria.

L. OCTAVIUS IUDEX ESTO; SI PARET FUNDUM CAPENATEM, QUO DE AGITUR, EX IURE QUIRITIUM P. SERVILII ESSE, NEQUE IS FUNDUS P. SERVILIO RESTITUETUR &c.[1]

Rigidity of the formula.

Except in the matter of pecuniary arbitration of this kind, the *formula*, taken by itself and without reference to the ultimate grounds in law and fact for the assertion of the PARET, leaves little to the discretion of the *iudex*. While the formulary system is liberal and expansive, on account of the creative power on which it was based, the particular *formula* might be rigidity itself; and this very power of creating a rigid rule of law, by which the *iudex* was absolutely bound, might seem to give the magistrate the power of making any verdict which he pleased inevitable, while devolving on the *iudex* the seeming responsibility of pronouncing on the question of fact. The modes by which this danger was averted at Rome have already been noticed and are to be found in the facts that the praetor was bound by his own *edicta* and, therefore, probably by his *formulae*, that any *edictum* might be vetoed by an equal or higher magistrate, and that a similar veto could be pronounced against a *formula* which did not correspond to an *edictum* appropriate to the case.

[1] Cic. *in Verr.* ii. 12, 31. The parody of the *formula* lies in inserting another name, 'Catulo' for 'Servilio.' Cicero employs the names of two of the jurors who were trying Verres (*in Verr.* iii. 90, 211; iv. 31, 69; 38, 82). The remainder of the *condemnatio* would run QUANTI EA RES ERIT, TANTAM PECUNIAM IUDEX, . . . CONDEMNA; S. N. P. A.

But Cicero says that the danger was realized in provincial jurisdiction: and, since these safeguards were not present there, the possibility of its existence must be allowed. He is, however, able to quote no *formula* actually given by Verres which illustrates the point. The parody of the *formula arbitraria*, which we have noticed, belongs to urban jurisdiction, and is merely a burlesque illustration of the fact that a bad praetor might tie the hands of a good *iudex*.

(e) *The Formula and the Legis Actio.*

Introduction of the *formula*; the *legis actio* still survived in the Ciceronian period.

The history of the introduction into the civil courts of Rome of the formulary system, which we have described, demands some investigation from a student of Ciceronian law; for Cicero's writings show that he stands, in a sense, at a meeting of the ways, and that during his active forensic life and that of his recent predecessors at the bar, which he occasionally recalls, the *formula* had not entirely displaced the *legis actio*. The evidence with which Cicero furnishes us on this point is often explicit. Sometimes he speaks definitely of a form of *legis actio* as in vogue, at other moments he only offers a hint, often in a non-juristic context (for he is fond of toying with legal phraseology), that some form of words or of proceeding, which it is difficult to reconcile with our knowledge of the formulary system, still survived. But even the words which Cicero uses to describe the general fact of urging a legal claim have been tested to discover whether any implication of the mode in which the claim is urged is contained in the words themselves. The merely negative result yielded by such inquiries may be illustrated first by his use of the word *actio*. In his historical reminiscences he uses it, as one would expect, for *legis actio*[1]. On one occasion, when he is speaking of the procedure of his own day and criticizing, for the benefit of his case, its unnecessarily trivial and

Cicero's use of the words *actio* and *agere*;

[1] Cic. *ad Att.* vi. 1, 8; *de Orat.* i. 41, 186.

BOOK I.

captious character, he speaks of the lawyer's life as concerned with *formulae atque actiones*[1]; but it is questionable whether a contrast between the formulary system and that of the *legis actio* is here implied: the distinction may rather be between the privately-drawn *formulae* of business proceedings and public activity in the courts. Elsewhere *actio* is used by him (as by succeeding lawyers to the latest times) in the general sense of the enforcement of a claim by any procedure whatever, whether from the point of view of the plaintiff who urges the claim[2], or of the *patronus* who pleads it[3]. At times he employs the word distinctly of the formulary process; it is applied to an action under the *Lex Aquilia* for *damnum iniuria datum*[4], and to the formulary procedure which followed the granting of a praetorian action or an interdict[5]. Nay, the word *actio* can actually be used of the *formula* itself. The most common equivalent for the latter in Cicero's pleadings is *iudicium*, for it is to the establishment of a court so described that the *formula* is directed; but looked at from the point of view of the proceedings *in iure*—the *postulatio*—or even from the point of view of the plaintiff's pleadings *in iudicio*, *actio* might be used without any difference of connotation[6]. The word *agere* yields the same negative results; it is used for any kind of procedure[7], amongst others for the formulary process[8]; it is only in the phrase

Of *lege agere*.

lege agere that we get a higher approach to definiteness.

[1] Cic. *pro Mur.* 13, 29.

[2] Cic. *Div. in Caecil.* 5, 18; *pro Caec.* 13, 37, where *actio* is the form arising from *experiundi ius*; cf. *pro Caec.* 11, 32 *ius actionemque*; *ib.* 14, 40 'actionem . . . quae . . . causam et rationem iuris amplecteretur.' The plaintiff is said 'habere actionem' (*pro Caec.* 12, 34).

[3] Cic. *pro Tull.* 2, 5.

[4] Cic. *pro Rosc. com.* 12, 35; 18, 55.

[5] Cic. *pro Tull.* 13, 33; *pro Caec.* 11, 32; 12, 34; 14, 40.

[6] Cic. *pro Caec.* 3, 8 'Potuisti enim leviore actione confligere: potuisti ad tuum ius faciliore et commodiore iudicio pervenire.'

[7] Cic. *l. c.* 12, 34 'nam quid agas mecum ex iure civili ac praetorio non habes.'

[8] Cic. *pro Tull.* 24, 54 'Verum, ut esses durissimus, agi quidem usitato iure et cotidiana actione potuit' (i. e. by the *lex Aquilia de damno*).

It cannot refer to the praetor's 'honorary' jurisdiction; it must refer to jurisdiction based on a *lex* or its equivalent, the *ius civile*, which is a recognized interpretation of this law; but it may be questioned whether, even in the famous passage of the *pro Murena*, the reference is wholly to the *legis actio*. That such forms of action are mainly in his mind is shown by his criticism of the importance laid on *singulae literae, interpunctiones verborum*, the careful preparation of the written model to be learnt by heart and reproduced by the litigants in verbal utterance, with the correct interval between the clauses that showed their interdependence; and this reference to the vigorous survival of the *legis actio* throws a valuable light on the mixed procedure of his time[1]. But the civil *formulae* of the *album*, still in process of formation and ever encroaching on the older actions, may also be included.

Cicero's references to the *legis actiones*.

When we turn from these verbal usages, from which little is to be gained, to passages which speak clearly of the *legis actiones*, we find that many of their applications had become extinct, but that many had survived. The historical inquiry into kinds of actions expressed in antique phraseology, and forming part of the mirror of antiquity, is to him one of the functions of a scientific and systematized jurisprudence[2]; but many passages, in which he touches on forms of legal procedure either in a literal or a figurative sense, show that many of the old systems

[1] Cic. *pro Mur.* 11, 25 'Primum dignitas in tam tenui scientia non potest esse. Res enim sunt parvae, prope in singulis literis atque interpunctionibus verborum occupatae. Deinde, etiamsi quid apud maiores nostros fuit in isto studio admirationis, id, enuntiatis vestris mysteriis, totum est contemptum et abiectum. Posset agi lege necne, pauci quondam sciebant: fastos enim vulgo non habebant.' He then relates the revelations of Cn. Flavius by which these possibilities were revealed. The *notae* of this passage are probably the abbreviated alphabetical signs of the formulae of the *legis actio* (cf. Isidorus, i. 23, 1). They were used by the lawyers in their commentaries for the sake of brevity; Cicero attributes their origin to the interested desire for professional obscurity.

[2] Cic. *de Orat.* i. 43, 193.

of procedure still had a vigorous life. Of the five forms of action, there is but one—that *per condictionem*—which cannot be illustrated for the Ciceronian period. It is by no means certain that the forms which we do find survived in their integrity, but each had left its trace in some department of procedure. Of these the *legis actio sacramento* did survive in *all* its old vigour[1], for it was still the mode of procedure in the decemviral and centumviral courts; that *per iudicis postulationem* was still extant in so far as a formal *verbal* request for a *iudex* or *arbiter* was even now made to the praetor[2]; it is difficult to say whether this is identical with the ordinary *postulatio* for a *formula* as made to the praetor in Cicero's time: it may have been, for the *iudicis datio* of the praetor is in itself a development of this form of action. The action *per pignoris capionem* is found, in some shape, or other employed by *publicani* in the provinces[3]; at least some part of the action *per manus iniectionem* survives in the municipal law of Urso[4]. But, so far as the complete forms are concerned, it is only the *actio sacramento* which we can assert with confidence was maintained in all its former integrity.

Traces of four of the chief *legis actiones* in the Ciceronian period.

When we turn to the *applications* of the forms to spheres of jurisdiction or to the use of solemn formal utterances, inconsistent with what we know of the later

Use of formal utterances in the courts of Cicero's time.

[1] Cic. *de Orat.* i. 10, 41, 42; *pro Mil.* 27, 74; *pro Mur.* 12, 26; *ad Fam.* vii. 32, 2; *pro Caec.* 33, 97; *pro Domo,* 29, 78.

[2] Cic. *pro Mur.* 12, 27 'illud mihi quidem mirum videri solet tot homines . . . etiam nunc statuere non potuisse utrum . . . iudicem an arbitrum . . . dici oporteret.'

[3] Cic. *in Verr.* iii. 11, 27 'Cum omnibus in aliis vectigalibus (of the provinces and Italy) . . . publicanus petitor ac pignerator, non ereptor neque possessor soleat esse: tu . . . de aratoribus (Siciliae) ea iura constituebas quae omnibus aliis essent contraria?'

[4] Lex Ursonensis, c. lxi. ['*Cui quis ita ma*]num inicere iussus erit, iudicati iure manus iniectio esto . . . Ni vindicem dabit iudicatumve faciet, secum ducito. Iure civili vinctum habeto.' Imprisonment by the creditor is also contemplated in the Lex Rubria, c. xxi.

character of the formulary system, the references are again numerous. The words with which the *auctor* was addressed (a side issue of the *actio sacramento in rem*),

QUANDOQUE TE IN IURE CONSPICIO,

were still in use in Cicero's day[1]; the utterance of the plaintiff in the *actio furti nec manifesti*,

OPE CONSILIOQUE TUO FURTUM AIO FACTUM ESSE,

seems still to have been made[2]. It is possible that a story which Cicero has to tell of the complaisant ignorance of two rival *patroni* at a time not long preceding his own has reference to the *legis actio* by which a ward exacted accounts from his guardian, technically known as the *actio rationibus distrahendis*[3]: although the use of the words *lege agendo* in this passage by no means proves the fact, for they would be equally applicable to formulary procedure based on the law of the Twelve Tables. In the action for the division of an inheritance (*familiae herciscundae*[4]), a formal phrase which seems to have contained the words HERCTUM CIERE was still employed; and it is possible that we have a reference to the ancient form of action for the delimitation of property (*finium regundorum*[5]). A curious phrase, which seems to have created

[1] Cic. *pro Caec.* 19, 54; *pro Mur.* 12, 26. Cf. p. 60.

[2] Cic. *de Nat. Deor.* iii. 30, 74 'inde illa actio *ope consilioque tuo furtum aio factum esse*; inde tot iudicia de fide mala, tutelae, mandati, pro socio, fiduciae.' It is possible that *actio* is here used for the spoken, *iudicium* for the written, formula.

[3] Cic. *de Orat.* i. 36, 166, 167 'alter plus lege agendo petebat quam quantum lex in XII tabulis permiserat: quod, cum impetrasset, causa caderet; alter iniquum putabat plus secum agi quam quod erat in actione, neque intelligebat, si ita esset actum, litem adversarium perditurum' (§ 167).

[4] Cic. *de Orat.* i. 56, 237 'nec . . . idcirco qui, quibus verbis herctum cieri oporteat, nesciat, idem herciscundae familiae causam agere non possit.' Cf. Gell. i, 9, 12, and see p. 65.

[5] Cic. *pro Mur.* 9, 22 'ille exercitatus est in propagandis finibus, tu in regendis.' A trace of the action for damage done by animals (*actio de pauperie*) has been found by some in the words of Q. Mucius in Dig. 9, 1,

BOOK I. an impression on Cicero's mind and is found in many contexts,

DE EADEM RE ALIO MODO[1],

was probably borrowed from the procedure of the *legis actio*. It was apparently a kind of introductory sentence (such as in later times might have been called a *prescriptio*) uttered by the parties for the purpose of safe-guarding their future right of action by means of a new procedure, if the one adopted failed and some other could be found applicable to the facts; the phrase seems to mean 'by this, or whatever other mode of action is open to me, I assert my claim.'

The prevalence of the formulary system in Cicero's day.

Against this evidence for the survival of the *legis actio* must be set that for the prevalence of the formulary system in Cicero's day. We have, first, the strongest assertion on the part of the orator, not only of the frequent use of the *formulae*, but of their almost universal providence for every case that could arise. 'There are legal principles, there are *formulae* to fit every case; it is almost impossible to go wrong. The praetor has moulded and published *formulae* to express every material loss or disadvantage, every injury to the feelings or misfortune that can befall any one. To these *formulae* the legal claims of the individual are accurately adjusted[2].' The intimate connexion of these *formulae* with the *iudicia* which they established leads to a close association of the words in Cicero's phraseology. The expression *iudiciorum formulae* is met with more than once; in one passage the infinity of their developments is dwelt on, and they are treated as a subject almost too vast for exhaustive classification[3]:

I, II. But the word *actio* used in this context may refer to either form of procedure.

[1] Cic. *ad Fam.* xiii. 27, 1; *de Prov. Cons.* 19, 46; *de Fin.* v. 29, 88.

[2] Cic. *pro Rosc. com.* 8, 24 'Sunt iura, sunt formulae de omnibus rebus constitutae, ne quis aut in genere iniuriae aut ratione actionis errare possit. Expressae sunt enim ex unius cuiusque damno, dolore, incommodo, calamitate, iniuria publicae a praetore formulae, ad quas privata lis accommodatur.'

[3] Cic. *Top.* 8, 33 'Partitione tum sic utendum est, nullam ut partem relin-

in another their composition is spoken of as a task for the jurist[1]. As the parties to a case had nothing to do with the structure of a *formula*, and the *advocatus* could at most advise about its choice, or the *patronus* at his advice urge the praetor to insert a qualifying word or two, we must probably understand by this passage the structure of *formulae* either by a magistrate exercising jurisdiction or by jurisconsults who advised him.

actio and *iudicium* in Cicero's writings.

The association of the two words *actio* and *iudicium* might lead to a contrast of *iudicium*, as the essence of the formulary process, to *actio* in the sense of *legis actio*; for, although the *legis actio* might lead to a *iudicium*, the contrast between the spoken form of words and the permanent written *formula* might in this way be implicitly expressed. This seems to be the case in one passage where the *actio* for *furtum nec manifestum* is mentioned side by side with a series of *bonae fidei iudicia*[2]; in another, the implied contrast is more doubtful; to frame actions, to accept and submit to *iudicia* are represented as proceedings *in iure* as opposed to those in *iudicio*[3]: but here again, if the expressions do not represent the same proceedings from slightly different points of view, the distinction between the spoken *actio* and the written *formula* may be implied. Elsewhere, however, *actio* is equivalent to *iudicium*, as it is so often in the praetor's edict; they only differ slightly in connotation as the proceeding of the plaintiff differs from the ruling of the praetor[4]; or

quas . . . At si stipulationum aut iudiciorum formulas partiare, non est vitiosum in re infinita praetermittere aliquid.'

[1] Cic. *de Leg.* i. 4, 14 'Quam ob rem quo me vocas? . . . ut stipulationum et iudiciorum formulas componam? quae et conscripta a multis sunt diligenter et sunt humiliora quam illa quae a nobis exspectari puto.'

[2] Cic. *de Nat. Deor.* iii. 30, 74; see p. 165, note a.

[3] Cic. *Part. Orat.* 28, 100 'Quare de constituendis actionibus, accipiendis subeundisque iudiciis, de excipienda iniquitate actionis . . . paulum ea separo a iudiciis, tempore magis agendi quam dissimilitudine generis.'

[4] Cic. *pro Caec.* 3, 8 'si praetor is, qui iudicia dat, nunquam petitori praestituit, qua actione illum uti velit.'

BOOK I.

again, in another passage, as the right of proceeding *in iure* towards a *iudicium* differs from this *iudicium* itself[1].

Cicero's use of *iudicium*.

In Cicero's speeches, it is true that *iudicium* and *formula* are so closely connected that the one might in every instance be written for the other. To say, however, that this proves *iudicium* to be *the* equivalent of *formula* is to ignore the fact that every one of Cicero's pleadings which have been preserved are based either on the civil *formula*, e.g. the *condictio certi* of the case in which he pleaded for Roscius, or on elements of praetorian law, such as the honorary *formula* of the *pro Tullio*, the *sponsio* of the *pro Quinctio*, the interdict of the *pro Caecina*. We know nothing about his choice of words when he pleaded the case of the woman of Arretium before the decemvirs in accordance with the *legis actio sacramento*[2]. The *legis actio* may in this case, for all we know, have been spoken of as a *iudicium* at every turn.

Mode in which the *formula* was regarded in respect of

But, although Cicero's usage of the term *iudicium* is by itself no index of the universality of the formulary process, the contexts in which he employs it are too valuable to be neglected. They furnish proof, which can be given by nothing else, of the way in which the *formula* was regarded: as a mode of creating the settlement of a claim by handing it on to a *iudex*, as an adjustment of the circumstances to the law and a compression of both in the framework of an absolute ruling, as something to which both parties must submit, once it has been given and accepted, and by which the losing party is absolutely bound.

The *iudicium* may be spoken of from the point of view of the party, the praetor and the case.

The party to the action is said to accept (*accipere*), to

[1] Cic. *Part. Orat.* 28, 99 'Atque etiam ante iudicium de constituendo ipso iudicio solet esse contentio cum . . . sitne actio illi qui agit . . . quaeritur.'

[2] Cic. *pro Caec.* 33, 97.

PART II. refuse (*recusare*), to suffer (*pati*), to elicit and proclaim (*edere*) a *iudicium*[1]; here the acceptance, refusal, and *editio* of the *formula* are meant: the defendant who falls under a case predicated in the *formula* is said 'to come under the *iudicium*' (*in iudicium venire*[2]).

the party, the magistrate, The praetor is said to grant (*dare*) a *iudicium*[3]; the establishment of a *iudicium* by means of a *formula* is described as the granting it with reference to certain words (*in verba iudicium dare*[4]); as the terms under which he establishes the court are suggested by the litigants, the *verba* of this phrase may refer to the *postulatio* of plaintiff and defendant[5]. The praetor who frames a new *formula* to meet a new circumstance is said *componere* or *constituere iudicium*[6].

and the case. The case is said to come under the *iudicium* (*in iudicium venire*[7]), the issue to be contained in it (*in iudicio agi*[8]); a phrase or clause, which, inserted by the praetor at the request of one of the parties, might make all the difference to the merits of the suit, is said to be added in or to the *iudicium* (*in iudicio, in iudicium additur*[9]). A circumstance or series of facts, to which the *formula* directly applies, is said to be shut up in the *iudicium* (*in iudicium concludi*[10]). Lastly, *iudicium* might be used, like *formula*, with the specification of the case, as in the phrases *iudicium iniuriarum, iudicium in quadruplum*[11].

Probable relation of the *formula* to the *legis actio* in Cicero's day. But, although such passages may prove the deep root that the *iudicia ordinaria* had taken in the legal mind, and an already-cited passage of Cicero shows the generality of the *formulae*, as their basis[12], none of these do much

[1] Cic. *pro Quinct.* 20, 62, 63. [2] Cic. *pro Tull.* 13, 32.
[3] Cic. *pro Caec.* 3, 8; *in Verr.* iii. 65, 152; *pro Tull.* 5, 10.
[4] Cic. *in Verr.* ii. 12, 31. [5] Cic. *pro Tull.* 17, 41.
[6] Cic. *l. c.* 4, 8. [7] Cic. *pro Caec.* 36, 104; *pro Tull.* 5, 12.
[8] Cic. *pro Tull.* 18, 42.
[9] Cic. *pro Tull.* 10, 26; 16, 38. [10] Cic. *l. c.* 11, 27.
[11] Cic. *in Verr.* ii. 27, 66; *pro Tull.* 3, 7. [12] p. 166, note 2.

BOOK I. to relieve the difficulties of the question, 'What was the precise relation of this *formula* to the *legis actio*?' For an approximate, although it must be confessed unsatisfactory, answer to this question we must turn to the account of the legislation which put the old form of procedure out of vogue. We are told of but one Republican law which aimed at abolishing the monopoly which the *legis actio* had of the civil courts. This was a *lex Aebutia* of unknown date, which, according to Gaius, 'swept away' or 'suspended' the actions of law and 'created litigation by means of *concepta verba*, that is, of *formulae*[1].' A literal interpretation of the passage would make it impossible to conceive that the *lex Aebutia* was prior to Cicero's time; but a literal interpretation is unnecessary, for Gaius uses precisely the same language about two *leges Iuliae* of the Augustan period. We have, therefore, to deal with a gradual supersession of one type of procedure by another, either commanded or permitted by a law, and, as the encroachment of the *formula* on the *legis actio* is already a marked feature of the Ciceronian epoch, we may assume that the *lex Aebutia* had given the permit or the order some time before Cicero's day. We have now to ask, 'How could a partial change of this kind be effected by legal enactment?' (1) It is possible to conceive a law declaring that certain spheres of *civil* jurisdiction—the domain of the *legis actio*—should be regulated by a procedure which had hitherto applied only to *honorary* jurisdiction, but that certain other spheres should still be controlled by the older system; (2) one may even imagine a universal choice given to the parties between the two modes of procedure; (3) it is possible to conceive legislation which permitted the praetor to substitute, where *he* pleased, the *formula* for the *legis actio* in that

Reform effected by the *lex Aebutia.*

[1] Gaius, iv. 30 'per legem Aebutiam et duas Iulias sublatae sunt istae legis actiones; effectumque est ut per concepta verba, id est, per formulas litigaremus.'

part of his *album* which contained the civil law; (4) and finally, there is the possibility of an actual mixture of the two modes of procedure in civil cases, the law permitting the written *formula* as a supplement to the spoken *legis actio*. The first of these alternatives is rendered somewhat improbable by the language of Gellius, who speaks of the 'antique law of the Twelve Tables as having been buried in oblivion' by this legislation[1]; he seems to be thinking of the gradual decline of the actions, not of their complete and sudden disappearance from certain spheres. The second of the alternatives—the choice of procedure by the party—was actually realized in the one or two cases where the *legis actio* is known to have survived in its entirety; a claim to an inheritance or to ownership might, in Cicero's time, be made by the *legis actio sacramento* before the centumviral court or by a *formula* before a *iudex*. Such a duality of procedure, extending through the whole sphere of jurisdiction, would be cumbrous if it were effective; but its ineffectiveness would have been almost certain. Once give the parties the power of asking for the *formula* in place of the action, and few would be found to decline the simpler, less captious, and more expeditious procedure. The same result would in all probability follow from the realization of the third suggestion of a praetorian power of substitution: for it is in the highest degree unlikely that the praetor would have preferred a procedure which lengthened the business of his court to one whose rapidity, brevity, and effectiveness has, perhaps, never been equalled. The fourth alternative, which introduces the *formula* as a supplement to the action, may contain this element of truth:—that the formulary procedure had not been thoroughly simplified by Cicero's time, that before the praetor gave the *formula* the parties

[1] Gell. xvi. 10, 8 'cum ... omnis ... illa duodecim tabularum antiquitas nisi in legis actionibus centumviralium causarum lege Aebutia lata consopita sit.'

made solemn and formal verbal requests, which were echoes of the preliminaries of the appropriate *legis actio*. These various suggestions may not be true alternatives after all. The law may—nay, it must—have exempted certain kinds of jurisdiction from the *formula*, e.g. that of the centumviral and decemviral courts; it may have given the praetor the power of substitution, and where, after the substitution had been effected, the praetor still allowed the *legis actio* and the *formula* to appear side by side in his *album*, it may have given the parties the alternative of action; while, lastly, custom may have maintained the fragments of some of the old *formulae* in the language of the court.

Reasons for the introduction of the formulary process.

The permission accorded by the *lex Aebutia* was probably due to the feeling that the procedure of the civil law was far behind that of honorary jurisdiction. It is probable that the *formula* had first been used in cases in which the interests of *peregrini* were concerned, that from the foreign it had crept into the urban *album*, to be employed by the praetor urbanus, as the expression of the jurisdiction which rested on his *imperium*. Hence the *formula* would long have been the mark of every *iudicium* based on the *imperium* (*quod imperio continetur*), the *legis actio* the mark of every court based directly or indirectly on a *lex* (*iudicium legitimum*).

Change in the conception of a *iudicium legitimum*; its new definition.

But, when the *formula* had been applied to the sphere of 'legitimate' jurisdiction, a new definition of *iudicium legitimum* was required. It was defined no longer in terms of the *legis actio*, but in terms of the conditions of the application of the *legis actio*, which were transferred to the *formula* in this sphere. A 'legitimate' court had the three main characteristics of the action at law[1].

[1] Gaius, iv. 103–104 'Omnia autem iudicia aut legitimo iure consistunt aut imperio continentur. Legitima sunt iudicia quae in urbe Roma vel intra primum urbis Romae miliarium inter omnes cives Romanos sub uno iudice accipiuntur.' Cf. Cic. *pro Rosc. com.* 5, 15 'omnia iudicia legitima, omnia arbitria honoraria.'

It was confined within the limits of the first milestone beyond Rome. Beyond this radius the true *legis actio*, as distinguished from reflexions of it which might be seen in the provinces, had never been applied[1], except in Italian municipal jurisdiction; but jurisdiction between *cives* in the *coloniae* and *municipia* had always been regarded as a part of jurisdiction within the central state. All civil justice exercised beyond this limit—a limit marked after the social war by the bounds of Italy itself—rested on the *imperium*. Such was the civil jurisdiction of the governor over Romans and natives in the provinces, and of the general over the soldiers in his camp.

(2) It was established for the settlement of claims only between Roman citizens. The *legis actio* had never been extended to the foreigner, and the intervention of a *peregrini persona* as a litigant necessitated the establishment of a *iudicium* resting on the *imperium*. No court, therefore, organized by the praetor peregrinus, so long as he exercised his appropriate functions, could ever be *legitimum*.

(3) The *iudicium* must be represented by the *unus iudex* who is a Roman citizen. It may seem strange that this third part of the definition takes no account of the *collegia* of the *centumviri* and *decemviri*, for their jurisdiction was most certainly 'legitimate.' But *iudicium legitimum* is being defined in terms of the *formula*, not of the *legis actio*, which was the mode of procedure in those courts. The condition of the *unus iudex* is meant to exclude all recuperatorial *iudicia*; for the granting of

[1] A passage in the *pro Murena* seems to contain an implication that the *actiones* were purely Roman. Cicero says (13, 28) 'Sapiens existimari nemo potest in ea prudentia (i.e. chiefly knowledge of the forms of action) quae neque extra Romam usquam neque Romae, rebus prolatis, quicquam valet.' The proof of this fact, however, rests partly on the *a priori* ground given by Gaius' definition of a *legitimum iudicium*, partly on the empirical ground that there is no clear case of a *legis actio* applied to *peregrini*. For the *legis actio sacramento* in the early criminal procedure for extortion (*repetundarum*) see Part II.

BOOK I.

recuperatores was, in its later history as in its origin, a function of the *imperium* [1].

Every *iudicium* which did not fulfil each of these three conditions was a *iudicium quod imperio continetur*.

Reasons for the maintenance of this conception.

There were two reasons why, in spite of the almost universal application of the *formula*, it was important to preserve the definition of the *iudicium legitimum*. One was the absolute finality of the judgement of such a court. In accordance with the traditions of the *legis actio*, an *actio in personam* under the formulary system, if 'legitimate,' was *ipso iure* extinctive of the claim that had been urged: that is, the suit, if it had passed a certain stage, could not by any possibility be renewed [2]. On the other hand, the renewal of an action which rested on the *imperium* could only be met by a plea in bar of suit to the effect that the case had already been adjudged or had entered on the stage of the *iudicium* (*exceptio rei iudicatae vel in iudicium deductae* [3]).

A second reason was the different limits of pendency of the two kinds of actions. While a *iudicium legitimum* might last for ever, one resting on the *imperium* required to be renewed when the particular *imperium* which created it had become extinct [4].

But it scarcely required a definition, even one based

[1] Gaius, iv. 105 'Imperio vero continentur recuperatoria (iudicia) et quae sub uno iudice accipiuntur interveniente peregrini persona iudicis aut litigatoris. In eadem causa sunt quaecumque extra primum urbis Romae miliarium tam inter cives Romanos quam inter peregrinos accipiuntur.' So *recuperatores* are given in the action for *vis* created by the praetor Lucullus (Cic. *pro Tull.* 10, 26).

[2] Gaius, iv. 107 'At vero si legitimo iudicio in personam actum sit ea formula quae iuris civilis habet intentionem, postea ipso iure de eadem re agi non potest et ob id exceptio supervacua est.'

[3] Gaius, iv. 106 'Et si quidem imperio continenti iudicio peractum fuerit, sive in rem, sive in personam . . . postea nihilominus ipso iure de eadem re agi potest, et ideo necessaria est exceptio rei iudicatae vel in iudicium deductae.'

[4] Gaius, iv. 105 'Ideo autem imperio contineri iudicia dicuntur, quia tamdiu valent quamdiu is qui ea praecepit imperium habebit.' Cf. p. 140.

on such important consequences, to show to the Roman world of Cicero's day what was a *iudicium legitimum* and what was not. If we are right in our view as to the structure of the praetor's *album*, and the separation in that document of the civil from the honorary *formulae*, the parties must have been fully aware when they were pursuing their rights *iure civili* and when by the assistance of the *imperium*.

(*f*) *Dangers of the formulary system.*

One of the reasons assigned for the introduction of the formulary procedure into the domain of the civil law was the extreme danger of involuntary error threatened by the *legis actio*. As in the case of all systems that have grown up without the help of writing, verbal and even mechanical accuracy in every detail was necessary to the successful conduct of a case[1]. But a written system may have similar danger for the litigant, and the rigidity of the *formula* was often a source of injustice to the plaintiff and an undue restraint upon the judge. The danger might arise from undue specification of the facts or from an exaggerated statement of the claim. The first was sometimes guarded against by the repeated insertion in the endless parentheses of certain *formulae* of the phrase *qua de re agitur* in substitution for a renewed and accurate specification of the ground of the claim[2]. Apart from verbal complications, the material specification of the facts, where necessary, resided in the *demonstratio* of the *formula*: the statement of the claim in the *intentio*. These were the only two ordinary parts of the *formula* for which the plaintiff was responsible; but an error in each led to very different results.

Precision of the *formula* its chief danger.

[1] Gaius, iv. 30 'istae omnes legis actiones paulatim in odium venerunt; namque ex nimia subtilitate veterum qui tunc iura condiderunt, eo res perducta est ut vel qui minimum errasset litem perderet. Itaque . . . effectum . . . est ut per concepta verba, id est per formulas, litigaremus.'

[2] Cic. *Brut.* 79, 275; cf. *pro Mur.* 13, 28; *Top.* 25, 95.

BOOK I.

Result of error in the *demonstratio*;

It is stated as a principle by Gaius that a false demonstration does not extinguish the plaintiff's claim, whether the falsity consists in stating too large or too small a ground for action [1], or we may conclude, in stating the wholly wrong ground. The loss of the claim in this particular case was, of course, necessary; but the action could immediately be renewed with an emended *formula*. There is no reason for doubting the application of this principle to Cicero's time, perhaps with a qualification mentioned by Gaius, which was expressed in the opinion of Labeo, a jurist of the next generation. Labeo held the possibility of the pursuit of too small a claim expressed in the *demonstratio*, the remainder of it to be pursued in another suit [2]. The view was also held that in the case of actions which produced *infamia* on the condemned, an exaggerated *demonstratio* by the plaintiff, which in this case was calculated to injure the reputation of the defendant, should be punished by the loss of the case [3].

in the *intentio*.

The *intentio* might also contain a statement of fact in the form of a specification of the thing in dispute. A misstatement in this connexion, the putting of one thing for another (*aliud pro alio*) was followed by the same consequences as a wrong demonstration. The immediate case was lost, but the action could be renewed [4]. It was different if the defendant, whether in a claim to a thing or to money, had misstated the quantity of the amount which was owed. To demand too much (*plus petere*) was for ever fatal to the claim. This was the case in the *legis actio*, if this was the sphere of a scene described by Cicero,

Plus petere.

[1] Gaius, iv. 58 'Si in demonstratione plus aut minus positum sit, nihil in iudicium deducitur, et ideo res in integro manet; et hoc est quod dicitur falsa demonstratione rem non perimi.'

[2] Gaius, iv. 59 'Sed sunt qui putant minus (i. e. less than the full claim) recte comprehendi, nam qui forte Stichum et Erotem emerit, recte videtur ita demonstrare QUOD EGO DE TE HOMINEM EROTEM EMI, et, si velit, de Sticho alia formula idem agat; quia verum est eum, qui duos emerit, singulos quoque emisse; idque ita maxime Labeoni visum est.'

[3] Gaius, iv. 60.

[4] Gaius, iv. 55.

in which the defendant's counsel protests vigorously against the plaintiff's claim, but does not see that the plaintiff had already lost his case[1]. In the formulary system the judex was bound rigidly by the praetor's command as expressed in the *intentio*; if 20,000 sesterces appeared in the latter, he could not condemn to a debt of 10,000, however clearly proved. In the pursuit of pecuniary claims Cicero points out the danger of the *iudicium* based on a *condictio certae pecuniae* as compared with an *arbitrium* whose object is *incerta pecunia*[2].

Minus petere.

To demand less than the amount due (*minus petere*), on the other hand, did not imperil the plaintiff's full claim. He gained at once the amount which he had mentioned in the *intentio*, and the remainder arising from the same obligation could be pursued in a later action. But the praetor objected to such manifold developments of the same process, and punished the plaintiff guilty of dividing his claim by granting to the defendant an *exceptio* known as *litis dividuae*, which withheld the plaintiff from prosecuting the remainder of the claim within the term of the same praetorship[3]. The other difficulties that beset the plaintiff and defendant in the formulary system can be best estimated by observing their proceedings in court.

Exceptio litis dividuae.

[1] Cic. *de Orat.* i. 36, 166, 167. See p. 165, note 3. In the sphere of the formulary system we also find (*ib.* i. 37, 168) a criticism of a barrister who, for the defence, asked for the exceptio 'CUIUS PECUNIAE DIES FUISSET,' i.e. that the claim should be limited to the amount due at the time when it was pressed. His true course would have been to invalidate the claim, if extended beyond its due limit, by the plea of *plus petitio*. The plaintiff's action would thus have been lost and could not have been renewed, on the ground *ne bis in idem*.

[2] Cic. *pro Rosc. com.* 4, 11 'Quid est in iudicio? directum, asperum, simplex: SI PARET HS 1000 DARI [OPORTERE]. Hic, nisi planum facit HS 1000 ad libellam sibi deberi, causam perdit. Quid est in arbitrio? mite, moderatum: QUANTUM AEQUIUS ET MELIUS SIT, DARI.'

[3] Gaius, iv. 56 'plus quidem intendere . . . periculosum est; minus autem intendere licet: sed de reliquo intra eiusdem praeturam agere non permittitur; nam qui ita agit per exceptionem excluditur, quae exceptio appellatur litis dividuae.'

BOOK I.

(g) 'Actionis' or 'formulae editio.' Discussions connected with the 'postulatio.'

Editio formulae.

After the summons had been effectively issued and obeyed, the first step necessary in the proceedings *in iure*[1] was for the plaintiff[2] to inform the defendant of the nature of the claim that was to be urged against him. The claim was embodied in a *formula* which the plaintiff had chosen, and all that was necessary was to lay this before the eyes of the defendant[3]. This might be done by dictation, by handing over a copy, even (in the time of Labeo and, therefore, presumably of Cicero) by leading one's opponent up to the *album* and pointing out the clause that one had chosen[4]. It is not improbable that the choice and production of civil actions during the Ciceronian period were accompanied by some formal words appropriate to the case[5]. At the same time, if the claim rested on a document, such as a written bond, a copy of such a document must be furnished by the plaintiff to the defendant (*editio instrumentorum*). In later times the defendant who had not received a copy of the necessary 'instruments' was freed from the action by raising an *exceptio doli*. The conception of *dolus*, which had been introduced into procedure by the Ciceronian period[6], may even at that

Editio instrumentorum.

[1] Cic. *de Inv.* ii. 19, 58 'in iure . . . agendi potestas datur et omnis conceptio privatorum iudiciorum (i. e. formularum) constituitur'; cf. *Part. Orat.* 28, 100.

[2] He is the party 'qui agit'; the defendant is one 'quicum agitur' (Cic. *pro Tull.* 10, 26; cf. 17, 41).

[3] 'Iudicium (i. e. formulam) edere' (Cic. *pro Quinct.* 21, 66; cf. 20, 63).

[4] Ulpian in Dig. 2, 13, 1, 1 'Edere est etiam copiam describendi facere, vel in libello complecti et dare, vel dictare. Eum quoque edere Labeo ait, qui producat adversarium suum ad album et demonstret quod dictaturus est, vel id dicendo (indicando *Momms.*) quo uti velit.'

[5] Cic. *pro Quinct.* 20, 63 'iudicium quin acciperet in ea ipsa *verba*, quae Naevius edebat, non recusasse'; cf. 20, 64: *in Verr.* ii. 12, 31.

[6] For the 'iudicium de dolo malo,' the 'everriculum malitiarum omnium' introduced by C. Aquilius, see Cic. *de Nat. Deor.* iii. 30, 74; *de Off.* iii. 14, 60. The parent of the conception held that it was present

time have been so applied. The defendant, although not under the necessity of producing documents to support his counter-claim, could be subjected to a series of questions (*interrogatio in iure*) as to the grounds on which he contested the action. If he appeared in a certain character, this character had to be explained: if, for instance, he was being actioned as the heir to an inheritance, he must supply information as to the circumstances under which he had become the heir, and as to the share of the property which he had inherited. Refusal to answer the question was contempt of court, and was punished by satisfaction of the plaintiff's claim through a *formula* framed to that effect; while the admission might form a new and wider ground of action for the plaintiff, which in later times was admitted into the *intentio*. An action based on such *formulae* was known as *actio interrogatoria*[1]. The framing of such a *formula* perhaps marks a more refined stage of procedure than that reached in Cicero's day; and it was by no means necessary for the purpose of emending the claim; for the *editio* and *interrogatio* did not make the choice of the original action absolute. Right up to the point known as the *litis contestatio*, when the issue was supposed to be finally joined by the close of the proceedings *in iure* and the acceptance of a *iudex*, the plaintiff might withdraw or emend his action.

Interrogatio in iure.

Armed with the *formula* which he had finally chosen, the plaintiff then approached the praetor and asked him to grant an action of the type proposed (*actionis postulatio*[2]). Here we have the intervention of pure magisterial

Postulatio.

'cum aliud sit simulatum, aliud actum,' and this characteristic would have suggested its early employment in the form of an exception.

[1] Bethmann-Hollweg, ii. p. 214. For attempts at reconstructing the *formula* of this action see Rudorff, *Rechtsgesch.* ii. p. 277; Lenel, *Ed. Perp.* p. 114 ff.

[2] Cic. *pro Quinct.* 20, 64 'omnia iudicia . . . quae quisque in verba postularit'; cf. *in Verr.* iii. 65, 152.

BOOK I.

power; for the praetor had now to decide, on certain formal legal grounds, whether he should grant or refuse the request[1]. The consent of the defendant to accept the action did not influence his judgement, if its unsuitability or illegality were manifest. Grounds for refusal were the obvious unsuitability of the *formula* demanded to the facts adduced by the plaintiff; the *ipso iure* unactionableness, either on moral or legal grounds, of the obligation on which the claim was based; or the facts that the granting of an action would raise again the validity of the final judgement of a court (*res iudicata*); that its fulfilment would mean the pre-judging of a criminal case to which a capital penalty was attached[2]; or that the plaintiff had not fulfilled a legal obligation essential to the action which he had brought, such as the security which the law sometimes compelled the *procurator* to furnish[3].

Grounds for refusal of action.

Did no legal ground of this kind conflict with the granting of the action, the counter-plea of the defendant was then heard. If the latter accepted the *formula*[4] there was no further question in dispute for the praetor to decide; but he might resist it, or express his willingness to accept it only in an emended form. The defendant

Protests of the defendant.

[1] Cic. *Part. Orat.* 28, 99 'Atque etiam ante iudicium de constituendo ipso iudicio solet esse contentio, cum aut sitne actio illi qui agit aut iamne sit aut num iam esse desierit aut illane lege, hisne verbis sit actio quaeritur.'

[2] Cic. *de Inv.* ii. 20, 59 'Agit is, cui manus praecisa est, iniuriarum; postulat is, quicum agitur, a praetore exceptionem EXTRA QUAM IN REUM CAPITIS PRAEIUDICIUM FIAT'; *in Verr.* iii. 65, 152 'cum hoc diceret Metellus praeiudicium a se de capite C. Verris per hoc iudicium nolle fieri.' The civil action thus refused was against Apronius, but it might have involved an implicit condemnation of Verres.

[3] Refusal on such grounds does not really invalidate the rule that 'praetor is, qui iudicia dat, nunquam petitori praestituit qua actione illum uti velit' (Cic. *pro Caec.* 3, 8). So, too, Cicero says (*l. c.*) that, if the facts fit the formula, the *iudex* is morally bound to give a judgement, however much he may disapprove the particular form of action employed.

[4] 'Iudicium accipere, pati' (Cic. *pro Quinct.* 20, 62 and 63; 21, 66).

might protest against the introduction of his name into the *formula* at all by asserting the liability of another, or urge that the action should be suspended until a pending *iudicium* had been completed, or admit a liability, but deny that it was covered by the formulary words[1]. He might admit his acceptance of the *formula* as a whole, but request that it should be modified by the insertion of some word or clause which altered the character of the plea and facilitated his defence[2]; or he might accept the existing form of the *intentio*, but urge the praetor's acceptance of a counter-plea (*exceptio*) to be inserted in the *formula*[3]. The structure of the *condemnatio*, the question, for instance, whether the praetor should fix a maximum limit by *taxatio* or not[4], would also be one of the questions on which the praetor must decide according to the merits of the case as they were presented by either party *in iure*. The praetor had facilitated procedure for the litigant by the introduction of the *formula*, but it may be questioned whether he had lightened the duties of his court. The rapidity of his procedure is attested; but the quickness of his decisions, even as exhibited in the framing of new *formulae in factum* to meet special claims, must have demanded an extraordinary capacity, and one tested to the utmost by the ever-growing use and increasingly professional character of the *advocati* and *patroni*.

[1] Cic. *Part. Orat.* 28, 99 'non fuit tua petitio, non a me, non hac lege, non his verbis, non hoc iudicio.'

[2] Cic. *pro Tull.* 16, 38 'quid attinuit te (the defendant) tam multis verbis a praetore postulare ut adderet in iudicium INIURIA.'

[3] Cic. *de Inv.* ii. 19, 58 'Ibi enim (i. e. 'in iure') exceptiones postulantur.' Cf. *ad Herenn.* i. 12, 22, and *Part. Orat.* 28, 100 'de excipienda iniquitate actionis.'

[4] i. e. admit it into the formula; see Cic. *pro Tull.* 3, 7 'Eius rei taxationem nos facimus, aestimatio vestra (i. e. recuperatorum) est.'

§ 4. *The Different Kinds of Action.*

(a) *In rem actiones.*

In rem actiones. (i) *Legis actio sacramento* before the *centumviri.*

The first form of the *in rem actio* which prevailed in Cicero's day was the old *legis actio sacramento*. It was practised before the centumviral court, of whose competence in the matter of these real actions at the close of the Republic we are furnished with a fairly full description and some vivid illustrations. The centumvirs still retained their character of a court whose functions were concerned with property assessable at the census: although, now that personal property of all kinds was included in the assessment, and there were other means of enforcing claims to real property, its connexion with registration was not so intimate as it had been, and its jurisdiction was something of a survival. From Cicero's description of the questions agitated in this court[1] we gather that it was concerned with:—

Functions of the centumviral court in Cicero's day.

1. The rights of property; the legality of transfer by means of *mancipatio* or any other mode of transfer recognized by the civil law; the assertion of ownership by means of prescription (*usucapio*), and the changes in ownership that might be effected by workings of nature such as the encroachments of water on land.

2. The rights or burdens that might accompany ownership, such as servitudes of various kinds.

3. The rights of inheritance by which ownership was created and of guardianship by which it was preserved;

[1] Cic. *de Orat.* i. 38, 173 'iactare se in causis centumviralibus, in quibus usucapionum, tutelarum, gentilitatum, agnationum, alluvionum, circumluvionum, nexorum, mancipiorum, parietum, luminum, stillicidiorum, testamentorum ruptorum aut ratorum, ceterarumque rerum innumerabilium iura versentur, cum omnino quid suum, quid alienum, quare denique civis aut peregrinus, servus aut liber quispiam sit ignoret, insignis est impudentiae.' Cf. *de Leg. Agr.* ii. 17, 44 'populi Romani hereditatem decemviri (i. e. those created under Rullus' law) iudicent, cum vos volueritis de privatis hereditatibus centumviros iudicare?'

the intricate questions of testate and intestate succession; of the validity of wills and, where no will had been made, of the right to succeed based on bonds of kinship real or fictitious, such as *agnatio* and *gentilitas*.

4. Questions of *status*; the conditions which made a man a citizen or left him a *peregrinus*, which asserted his liberty or condemned him to slavery[1]. The connexion of this last department with the others is at first sight not very obvious; and we shall find that as a fact questions of *status*, considered purely as such, were decided, not by the centumviral, but by the decemviral court. Their consideration by the *centumviri* could only have been incidental to judgements as to rights in property. Ownership did not belong to the foreigner and the slave, while the testamentary disposition of the freedman was limited. The question of *status* would, therefore, often crop up as a *praeiudicium* which required settlement before the main issue was decided.

Instances of centumviral jurisdiction.

The instances which Cicero gives of centumviral jurisdiction, although they introduce questions of substantive law, furnish too clear a picture of a part of the jurisdiction of this court to be neglected in a treatise on the procedure of his time. The *causes celèbres* seem mainly to have been concerned with questions of inheritance and of *status*. We hear of the soldier, believed to have been slain in battle, whose father had made another his heir, without of course disinheriting by name the son whom he believed to be no more. The law required disinheritance, but it was a nice point for the judgement of the centumvirs whether the sufficient grounds which the testator possessed for believing it to be unnecessary did not validate the claim of the instituted heir, although this institution was itself contrary to his manifest wishes and intentions[2].

[1] e. g. the case of Mancinus, who had been *deditus* to the Numantines (Cic. *de Orat.* i. 40, 181; 56, 238).

[2] Cic. *de Orat.* i. 38, 175; cf. i. 57, 245.

Again, there was the case of the testator who, with excessive caution, had instituted an heir in remainder to a possible posthumous son who should be born and die before he became his own master. No child was born, and it was for the centumvirs to decide whether Scaevola was right in insisting on the written words of the testament or Crassus, who upheld its clearly defined intentions in favour of his client Curius[1].

A case argued before the *centumviri* on an insignificant issue once raised the question of the legal *status* of one of the greatest families of Rome. A son of a freedman of the plebeian branch of the Claudian name, the Claudii Marcelli, had died intestate, and the family claimed the gentile rights. But the patrician Claudii urged that the plebeian house that bore their name was, in virtue of some prehistoric relation of clientship to themselves signified by their bearing the patrician name, no true self-existent clan (*gens*), and could not therefore exercise the rights of *gentilitas*, which belonged to themselves alone[2].

A case in which the interest and *status* of the foreigner were concerned may close this category. A man had been domiciled in Rome through availing himself of the clause in the treaty which his city had with that state, permitting the citizens of either community to renounce their native rights and by voluntary exile become *cives* of the other. But this man had voluntarily become the client of a Roman citizen, and this citizen attempted to exercise the patron's rights over the intestate inheritance left by his client. The claim was resisted, and the issue for the *centumviri* to decide was the abstract point of constitutional law, whether it was necessary, or indeed possible, for one who exercised in his own right the full powers

[1] Cic. *de Orat.* i. 39, 180; cf. i. 57, 242–244: *pro Caec.* 18, 53; 24, 67–69.

[2] Cic. *de Orat.* i. 39, 176 'nonne in ea causa fuit oratoribus de toto stirpis et gentilitatis iure dicendum?'

of a Roman citizen to make *applicatio* to a *patronus* and enter into a true relation of clientship with him[1].

Procedure before the centumviral court.

The process of the *legis actio sacramento*, by which these cases were decided before the centumvirs, was conducted with the later modifications which we have described[2]; the fictitious combat (*manus conserere*) took place in court, even over immoveables, a fragment of which had been brought into its precincts by the parties who had already visited the field or dwelling in dispute; and it is possible that on this visit a pretended struggle may have taken place between the parties, for the purpose of arranging a *vadimonium* for the first appearance before the praetor: for bail may here, as elsewhere, have replaced the older *in ius vocatio*. This extra-jural struggle is rendered possible by the fact that, as a preparation for the *vadimonium*, it plays a part in the procedure *per sponsionem praeiudicialem*, which, as we shall see, was clearly a development of the sacramental process. The praetor still gave *interim* possession to one of the parties (*vindicias dicere secundum alterum eorum*); and the dialogue of the action proceeded as before[3]. The *sacramentum* had now lost all religious associations, and was considered as a mere wager to be forfeited to the treasury by the loser of the case; securities (*praedes*) being given by both parties for its ultimate payment in case of failure to support their claims. Securities were also furnished by the *interim* possessor for the restoration of the thing and its fruits (*praedes litis et vindiciarum*) to his opponent in case of the latter's success. Little had changed but the value of the *sacramentum* itself; this in the imperial (and probably in the Ciceronian) period was always 1,000 asses (125 sesterces)[4].

[1] Cic. *de Orat.* i. 39, 177 'nonne in ea causa ius applicationis, obscurum sane et ignotum, patefactum in iudicio atque illustratum est a patrono?'

[2] p. 56.

[3] Cic. *pro Mur.* 12, 26; see p. 58.

[4] Gaius, iv. 95.

BOOK I.

(ii) Procedure *per sponsionem praeiudicialem.*

The next stage in the history of real actions, the fulfilment of which was seen in Cicero's time, introduces us to the *formula* and the *iudex*, but the shadow of the centumviral system lies behind. The essence of this system is also a wager, and one that is a pre-judgement of the main issue in dispute, but the wager is decided in the manner that had formerly been peculiar to pecuniary claims, and the obligation on the loser to pay it is expressed in the *dare oportere* embedded in the *formula*.

Identification and production of the object.

The first stage of this process was, as in the *legis actio*, a real or pretended identification and production of the object in dispute. Moveables were probably produced in court, their possessor being forced to this production by a praetorian interdict *ad exhibendum*. Immoveables were visited by the parties, and there a pretended struggle took place, which too often degenerated into real violence. It was supposed that one of the litigants should play the part of the ejector, the other of the ejected; the respective rôles were settled by agreement, but it is extremely probable that the actual possessor usually took the part of the ejected, the non-possessing claimant of the ejector; consequently the distribution of the rôles might be used as presumptive evidence for one or the other being actually in possession at the time, and as such it is rightly employed by Cicero in support of the claim of his client Caecina[1].

Vis moribus facta.

When this conventional violence or ejection (*vis ex conventu, vis moribus facta, deductio moribus*)[2] had taken place, *vadimonium* was agreed on for appearance before the praetor, the party ejected being the one who gave the *vadimonium*.

The next important question was to determine which

[1] Cic. *pro Caec.* 32, 95 'cur tu, Aebuti, de isto potius fundo quam de alio, si quem habes, Caecinae denuntiabas, si Caecina non possidebat? Ipse porro Caecina cur se moribus deduci volebat idque tibi de amicorum, in his de C. Aquilii, sententia responderat?'

[2] Cic. *ib.* cf. 7, 20; 8, 22.

PART II.

Determination of *interim* possession.

of the two parties was to have *interim* possession of the object in dispute. It seems clear that this could never have been determined by the *deductio*. The parts taken in this rested on the will of the parties, but *interim* possession is a matter for a court, mutual agreement by the litigants on such a question being almost inconceivable. Furthermore, the assignment of possession had an additional meaning now. In the *legis actio* both parties were in a sense at once plaintiffs and defendants; but it is fairly certain that under the new procedure the *interim* possessor was the defendant, the non-possessor the plaintiff, the two rôles being sharply distinguished in the formulary system and in the *sponsio* which in this case preceded it.

It is possible that, on the first introduction of this procedure, the praetor may have continued his function in the *legis actio* of assigning *interim* possession to one or other of the parties; but probably before the Ciceronian period (although even the case of Caecina does not enable us to determine with certainty the system that prevailed then), a practice was adopted which had better have been left alone, for it represents the lengthiest and most clumsy procedure that ever found its way into Roman law. This mode of determining *interim* possession was based on the use of what were known as the 'possessory' interdicts, that is, the commands of the praetor by which he protected that imperfect form of ownership known as *possessio*. The possessory interdicts will be considered when we are dealing with the interdictal procedure as a whole; it is sufficient to remark here that they had no original connexion whatever with *in rem actiones*[1], but simply, by forming the basis of a *iudicium*, determined the question of possession as such. They were a possible,

Use of the 'possessory' interdicts for this purpose.

[1] The account of Gaius (iv. 148 'Retinendae possessionis causa solet interdictum reddi, cum ab utraque parte de proprietate alicuius rei controversia est, et ante quaeritur uter ex litigatoribus possidere et uter petere debeat: cuius rei gratia comparata sunt UTI POSSIDETIS et UTRUBI') is probably a deduction drawn from the later use of these interdicts.

though lengthy means, of determining the question of *interim* possession, and hence their use in real actions. The praetor protected the proper possession of immoveables by the prohibitory interdict:—

The interdict *uti possidetis.*

UTI NUNC POSSIDETIS EUM FUNDUM, QUO DE AGITUR, QUOD NEC VI NEC CLAM NEC PRECARIO ALTER AB ALTERO POSSIDETIS, ITA POSSIDEATIS. ADVERSUS EA VIM FIERI VETO[1],

which was known, from its leading words, as the interdict UTI POSSIDETIS; and the *bona fide* possession of immoveables by the command:—

The interdict *utrubi.*

UTRUBI HIC HOMO, QUO DE AGITUR, MAIORE PARTE HUIUSCE ANNI NEC VI NEC CLAM NEC PRECARIO AB ALTERO FUIT, QUOMINUS IS EUM DUCAT VIM FIERI VETO[2],

which was known as the interdict UTRUBI.

Both interdicts gave rise to a *iudicium* in a manner which we shall subsequently describe. This *iudicium* settled the question as to which of the parties was the true *possessor*; it did not pre-judge the question of ownership.

Hereditatis petitio made *per sponsionem*; *interim* possession.

The claim to an inheritance (*hereditatis petitio*), as a form of real action, could be made by means of the procedure *per sponsionem*; but here there was something like an already existent legal pre-judgement as to who was to be the *interim* possessor. The individual so favoured was to be the person who, according to the rules of praetorian law, would be called to the possession of the inheritance (*bonorum possessio*). This is the basis of Cicero's criticism of an urban edict of Verres', which began:—

Si de hereditate ambigitur, . . . si possessor sponsionem non faciet.

Cicero, thinking that Verres assumes the *de facto* detainer to have the right of *interim* possession, insists

[1] Festus, p. 233.

[2] Lenel, *Ed. Perp.* p. 391 (from Gaius, iv. 160 and 150 and Dig. 43, 31).

that the very question at issue is 'who is *to be* possessor?'[1]. PART II.
We cannot estimate the justice of the criticism, because we do not know what Verres intended by the word; he might have meant the man actually in possession or he might have meant the future possessor under praetorian law. This rule of *interim* possession seems a good and practicable one to apply to intestate succession; but its application is more doubtful to cases of testate succession, when the inheritance was actually in the possession of the designated heir.

The final stage *in iure*; the *sponsio*.

Interim possession having been arranged, the case might move to its final stage *in iure*. This stage is fulfilled by two stipulations, in which the plaintiff (the non-possessor) is the challenger and asker of the question (*stipulator*), the defendant (who is also the possessor) the promiser and respondent (*promissor*). The first *sponsio*, enjoined by the praetor, was of the following form:—

Plaintiff. SI HOMO, QUO DE AGITUR, EX IURE QUIRITIUM MEUS EST, SESTERTIOS XXV NUMMOS DARE SPONDES[2]?

Defendant. SPONDEO.

The sum stipulated was insignificant, and could not even be exacted by the successful litigant; it was not therefore regarded as a penalty on his adversary, but merely as the opportunity for a *praeiudicium*; the *summa sponsionis* was not *poenalis*, but merely *praeiudicialis*, and hence there was no counter-stipulation (*restipulatio*) by the defendant[3].

The decision as to the fact contained in this first stipulation was then entrusted to a *iudex* in a *formula*, which, besides containing the usual SI PARET DARE OPORTERE, may have expressed the ground of the obligation, e. g.:—

SI PARET NUMERIUM NEGIDIUM AULO AGERIO, EX SPONSIONE:

[1] Cic. *in Verr.* i. 45, 116. (After quoting the words of the edict, he adds) 'quid ad praetorem uter possessor sit? Nonne id quaeri oportet utrum possessorem esse oporteat? Ergo, quia possessor est, non moves possessione: si possessor non esset, non dares?' Cf. *Part. Orat.* 28, 98 'Cum hereditatis sine lege aut sine testamento petitur possessio: in quibus causis quid aequius aequissimumve sit quaeritur.'

[2] Gaius, iv. 93.

[3] Gaius, iv. 94.

BOOK I.

The case as it went before the *iudex*.

NI HOMO, QUO DE AGITUR, EX IURE QUIRITIUM AULO AGERIO ESSET, SESTERTIOS XXV NUMMOS DARE OPORTERE, IUDEX NUMERIUM NEGIDIUM AULO AGERIO SESTERTIOS XXV NUMMOS CONDEMNA, SI NON PARET ABSOLVE[1].

Stipulatio pro praede litis et vindiciarum.

The second stipulation entered into between the parties had the very necessary object of guaranteeing the restoration of the property by the *interim* possessor in case of his defeat in the *sponsio*. This promise by the defendant, which was based on security, as it took the place of the *praedes* of the *legis actio sacramento in rem*, and guaranteed, as they did, the restoration of the thing and of its fruits, was known as a *stipulatio pro praede litis et vindiciarum*[2].

The decision of the *sponsio* was, therefore, quite sufficient to satisfy the claim of either successful litigant. If it was in favour of the defendant, he was already the possessor; if of the plaintiff, the defendant's promise guaranteed him full restitution or full compensation from the defendant's securities.

This action *per sponsionem praeiudicialem* before the single *iudex* was probably a real alternative to the *legis actio* before the centumvirs; that is, the plaintiff had the choice between the two. This explanation of the duality stated by Cicero[3] is more probable than the view that an appeal to the centumviral court by the defendant excluded the jurisdiction of the *unus iudex*.

(iii) The *formula petitoria*.

A third and still simpler application of the *formula* to real actions had been long in use by Cicero's day. This was the action by the *formula petitoria*, which was doubtless introduced by the praetor, but was not an *in factum actio*, for by it ownership was claimed *ex iure Quiritium*. It

[1] Rudorff, *Rechtsgesch.* ii. p. 134.

[2] Gaius, iv. 94. Cf. Cic. *in Verr.* i. 45, 115.

[3] The duality is found in the *hereditatis petitio*; 'si quis testamento se heredem esse arbitraretur, quod tum non exstaret, lege ageret in hereditatem, aut, pro praede litis vindiciarum cum satis accepisset, sponsionem faceret: ita de hereditate certaret' (*in Verr.* i. 45, 115). A similar duality is probable in cases of servitudes; see p. 194.

belonged, therefore, like the action *per sponsionem*, to the civil law portion of the *album*, and was prefaced by no edict.

Simplicity of this action.

In the preliminaries of this action the last traces of the *legis actio* had disappeared. We have no means of determining whether they had ever existed, or, if so, whether they had vanished by Cicero's time; but, in the accounts of the action which we possess, there is no trace of any such symbolic performance as the *deductio moribus*. There seems to have been no means by which plaintiff and defendant could agree as to the actual immovable in dispute; its identification must have depended wholly on the plaintiff's statement and on the evidence which he furnished; movables might have been produced in court by a praetorian order.

Nor is there any trace of *interim* possession being regulated by the clumsy use of the interdicts, although the question of possession was as important for this action as for the last that we discussed, since on it depended the rôles which the litigants were to play. The possessor was always defendant, the non-possessor plaintiff; but the possession taken account of by this action was not that imperfect kind of ownership known as juristic possession, but simple detention of the object, which resists the claim of ownership and contains in itself the faculty for restitution. It was only when the question of juristic possession was also at issue between the parties that this was determined by the application of the interdicts *uti possidetis* and *utrubi*, and the declaration of this full possession would naturally supplant mere detention as determining the respective parts which the litigants were to play.

The main action was simplicity itself; it contained no preliminaries leading up to the *iudicium*, such as the *sacramentum* or the *sponsio*, and the *iudicium* itself was concerned, not with a pre-judgement as in those cases, but with the main issue. The *formula* contains, in its *intentio*

BOOK I.

The *formula* (*arbitraria*); condemnation in default of restitution.

a simple statement of claim based on the *ius civile*, in its *condemnatio* a command to the *iudex* to condemn in the value of the thing, on proof of the claim, in default of restitution by the defendant:—

SI PARET FUNDUM CORNELIANUM (HOMINEM STICHUM), QUO DE AGITUR, EX IURE QUIRITIUM AULI AGERII ESSE, NEQUE (NISI) IS FUNDUS (HOMO) AULO AGERIO ARBITRATU TUO RESTITUETUR, QUANTI EA RES ERIT, TANTAM PECUNIAM, IUDEX NUMERIUM NEGIDIUM AULO AGERIO CONDEMNA; SI NON PARET ABSOLVE[1].

The claim expressed in the *formula* is a conditioned reassertion of the old one of the *legis actio*, HANC EGO REM EX IURE QUIRITIUM MEUM ESSE AIO; the judgement of the *condemnatio*, unlike that either of the *legis actio* or of the *sponsio*, imposes two distinct duties on the *iudex*: first, a pronouncement (*pronuntiatio*), as to the fact of ownership; secondly, an estimate of compensation in the case of the main judgement being in the affirmative and the alternative of restitution not being complied with. The simplicity and comprehensiveness of the action are due to its being a *iudicium* and *arbitrium* in one, a characteristic which caused the *formula* that expressed it to be known as *arbitraria*. The original judgement enabled the victorious plaintiff to take possession of the property now recognized as his: if no opposition was offered by the defendant to this exercise of ownership, the latter had 'restored' within the meaning of the *formula*, and it is possible that a formal acquittal of the penalty for non-restitution was then entered by the *iudex* in the defendant's favour, although the *formula* makes no verbal provision for such

[1] It is on this formula that Cicero's travesty of Verres' rulings is based (*in Verr.* ii. 12, 31). He constructs the following impossible scheme which enjoins restitution to the non-owner:—'L. OCTAVIUS IUDEX ESTO: SI PARET FUNDUM CAPENATEM, QUO DE AGITUR, EX IURE QUIRITIUM P. SERVILII ESSE, NEQUE IS FUNDUS Q. CATULO RESTITUETUR.' The formula is a conscious burlesque, meant to show the dependence of the *iudex* on the praetor's rulings. See pp. 160–161.

a judgement. Resistance to the plaintiff's right was not met by administrative assistance offered by the state to support his claim; it was overcome merely by the defendant being forced to purchase his estate or goods at a fancy price; for the *arbitrium* of the *iudex*, in case of non-restitution, was probably always based on a sworn estimate by the plaintiff.

Satisdatio iudicatum solvi.

If restitution were declined, perhaps on the ground of its impossibility, and the alternative damages awarded by the *iudex* were not paid, the plaintiff still had redress. This was afforded by the security which every one who appeared as a defendant in an *actio in rem* was bound to furnish for the restoration of the value of the thing. The value here, both of the thing itself and of its fruits, is fixed by the sentence *(iudicatum)*, and the security imposed on the defendant was known as *satisdatio iudicatum solvi*[1]. This entitled the plaintiff to an action against the defendant and his sureties if he refused to restore or to satisfy the *litis aestimatio*.

The *formula petitoria* not applied to inheritances in Cicero's time.

The *formula petitoria* was not of universal application in Cicero's time; had it covered the whole sphere proper to real actions, it would have included claims to inheritances. This inclusion was ultimately reached and the action known as *hereditatis petitio* was only a special application of this type of *formula*; but this development had not been attained at the period of which we are treating, and Cicero knows of but two modes of claiming an inheritance, *per legis actionem* and *per sponsionem praeiudicialem*[2].

[1] Gaius, iv. 89 'si . . . in rem tecum agam, satis mihi dare debes: aequum enim visum est te ideo quod interea tibi rem, quae an ad te pertineat dubium est, possidere conceditur, cum satisdatione mihi cavere, ut, si victus sis nec rem ipsam restituas nec litis aestimationem sufferas, sit mihi potestas aut tecum agendi aut cum sponsoribus tuis.'

[2] Cic. *in Verr.* i. 45, 115 'si quis testamento se heredem esse arbitraretur . . . lege ageret in hereditatem aut, pro praede litis vindiciarum cum satis accepisset, sponsionem faceret; ita de hereditate certaret.'

BOOK I.

Concurrence of these three forms of real action.

But for claims to 'things' in the narrower sense three alternative modes of procedure were, as we have seen, available in the Ciceronian period, and all three were probably in the strictest sense concurrent actions, that is, the choice between them lay in the discretion of the plaintiff. As many modes doubtless existed for the assertion and denial of servitudes. We have seen that this was within the competence of the centumviral court[1], but *stillicidia* are also in Cicero's time a matter for the decision of the *unus iudex*[2]. Such questions might have been settled by the *sponsio praeiudicialis*, but in the later period it was by an application of the *formula petitoria* that servitudes were most commonly asserted or denied.

Decisions on questions of *status*, pronounced by the decemviral court, through the *legis actio sacramento*.

Questions of *status*, involving the assertion or denial of liberty, belong to the category of *actiones in rem*, for the right to the slave is asserted against the world, and its denial by the *adsertor in libertatem* is the maintenance of an absolute claim. Such questions were still in the Ciceronian period treated as vindications and decided by the *legis actio sacramento*. Their proper sphere was the decemviral court, which pronounced the respective *sacramenta* as 'just' or 'injust.' It was here that Cicero pleaded the cause of a woman of Arretium and gained it by the maintenance of the general principle that the gift of citizenship, once possessed, could never be withdrawn, and by a particular application of this principle to Sulla's wholesale confiscation of the rights of certain Italian towns, on which the issue turned[3]. The question as to whether an individual was a Roman *civis*, as opposed to a *peregrinus*, could not have been of itself a question for the decemviral

[1] p. 182.

[2] Cic. *Orator*, 21, 72 'indecorum est, de stillicidiis cum apud unum iudicem dicas, amplissimis verbis et locis uti communibus.'

[3] Cic. *pro Caec.* 33, 97 'Cum Arretinae mulieris libertatem defenderem et Cottā decemviris religionem iniecisset non posse nostrum sacramentum iustum iudicari, quod Arretinis adempta civitas esset, et ego vehementius contendissem civitatem adimi non potuisse.'

court, which seems to have been, in this capacity, concerned only with vindications for and against *libertas*. But the proof of citizenship was a necessary corollary to such a case, for disproof of servitude was attained, if the civic attachment of the person, whose liberty was impugned, to a community recognized by Rome could be demonstrated[1]. On the other hand the question whether a person was a *civis* or *peregrinus*, like the question whether he was bond or free, must have been decided on its own merits in the centumviral court; for here it often formed the subject of a *praeiudicium*, whose decision was essential to the main issue of the question, whether of property or of inheritance, that was under consideration[2].

We do not know whether the *sponsio* was applied during this period to the settlement of such questions; later they were expressed in the only portion of the *formula petitoria* which they required; they belonged, as we have seen, to the *formulae preiudiciales* which, as they involved no condemnation, possessed only an *intentio*[3].

(b) *In personam actiones.*

Characteristics of *in personam actiones.*

An action against a person is one springing out of an obligation, by which an individual has bound himself to give, do or furnish something to another. It is the breach of the obligation which causes the indebtedness that is the ground of the action. A specific person and specific indebtedness are its characteristics; the ultimate ground

[1] On proof of the *civitas* of a man attached to the community of Rome, his *libertas* was proved *ipso iure*, and Cicero's language where this point is illustrated (*pro Caec.* 33, 96) seems to show that the idea of '*maxima* capitis deminutio' (i. e. one caused by loss of *libertas*) had not been developed in his day. A voluntary loss of citizenship (by change of *civitas*) entails the *capitis deminutio* known in later times as *media* or *minor* (Gaius, i. 159, 161), but the *involuntary* loss of *civitas*, which entails servitude ('si semel civitas adimi potest, retineri libertas non potest'), and which Cicero pronounces legally impossible, would have been placed on the same level.

[2] See p. 183.

[3] See p. 155.

of the debt, that is the original obligation, is comparatively a matter of indifference, and, though it must be adduced in proof, need not appear in the statement, of the claim.

Differences in the obligations on which they are based.

But the character of the original obligation may make a great difference to the nature of the claim. There are obligations which can be reduced to a few, simple, formal rules; there are others for which even the law cannot profess to furnish a single archetype, their particular manifestations are so varied and the claims which arise from them so complex and so freely distributed between the contracting parties. From the first type of obligation will spring a *iudicium* that is *directum, asperum, simplex*: from the latter a *iudicium liberum*—one, that is, which demands that the merits of the respective claims shall be carefully weighed by a deliberative intelligence[1]. The fundamental distinction between the obligations which give rise to personal actions, is expressed in the contrast between strict law (*ius strictum*) and equity (*aequitas*)[2]; if expressed in terms of the actions to which they give birth it is approximately, although as we shall see not exactly, the distinction between a *condictio* and a *bona fide* action. The difference between the two spheres is by no means that between civil and praetorian law. The law of the praetor showed a great capacity for developing purely equitable considerations; but the civil law, too, had its equity, and the actions of good faith were recognized under the rule of the *legis actio*[3].

Obligations of strict law and of equity.

[1] Cic. *pro Rosc. com.* 4, 11 'Quid est in iudicio? directum, asperum, simplex . . . Quid est in arbitrio? mite, moderatum.' Cf. *Part. Orat.* 28, 100 'omnia quae de iure civili aut de aequo et bono disceptantur.' Yet *iudicium* is sometimes used for *arbitrium* (Cic. *de Off.* iii. 15, 61; *Top.* 17, 66).

[2] Cic. *Part. Orat.* 37, 130 'Aequitatis autem vis est duplex: cuius altera . . . aequi et boni ratione defenditur.' For the contrast between equity and *summum ius* see Cic. *pro Caec.* 23, 65 'Si contra verbis et literis et (ut dici solet) summo iure contenditur, solent eiusmodi iniquitati aequi et boni nomen dignitatemque opponere.' Cf. *Top.* 5, 28.

[3] e. g. the *actio finium regundorum* (Cic. *de Leg.* i. 21, 55).

The actions of strict law; their one-sided character.

The chief characteristic of the actions of strict law is their thoroughly one-sided character. The plaintiff is conceived as wholly a creditor, the defendant as wholly a debtor; the plaintiff has by some act of his created an obligation, e.g. by a loan of money or by the presentation of something for which he has stipulated a return, and this obligation the defendant has not fulfilled; the plaintiff has made a gift for a consideration (*datum ob causam*), and this consideration has been neglected by the recipient who is now his debtor. There is an absolute indebtedness on the part of the defendant, and no considerations but those expressed or most obviously implied in the contract, which forms the basis of the action, are taken into account; there can, for instance, be no modification of the debt on the grounds of equity, and no counterclaims on the part of the defendant are expressed or implied in the action itself. As a proof of the gradual growth of civil law and a proof that praetorian *ius* did not have a monopoly of development, we may remark that the obligations which give rise to this rigorous type of action had by no means always been recognized in their entirety by the Roman jurisprudence. The contractual relations from which the action for a *certum* arose in Cicero's time were the stipulation, the informal loan (*mutuum*) and the literal contract (*expensi latio*), that is, a contract created by the mutual entry of a debt in the registers of the debtor and creditor[1]. But only the first of these had been concluded by what were originally the forms of strict law; the *procedure* of *ius strictum* had been extended to obligations which in their character approximated to

[1] Cic. *pro Rosc. com.* 4, 10 and 13 'Pecunia tibi debebatur certa, quae nunc petitur per iudicem . . . adnumerasse sese negat: expensum tulisse non dicit, cum tabulas non recitat. Reliquum est ut stipulatum se esse dicat. Praeterea enim quem ad modum certam pecuniam petere possit non reperio.' Cf. 5, 14 'Haec pecunia necesse est aut data aut expensa lata aut stipulata sit.'

BOOK I.

the *stipulatio.* This procedure had before the Ciceronian period come to be known as a *condictio*[1].

The *condictio.*

The name was derived from the *legis actio per condictionem* introduced by the *lex Silia* for *certa pecunia* and by the *lex Calpurnia* for *omnis certa res.* The name for the action was preserved when the *formula* was applied for the recovery of a fixed sum of money[2] or a definite thing (*certa res*), although the leading feature of the action at law which gave it its title—the challenge by the plaintiff to appear before a *iudex* within thirty days—disappeared when the formulary procedure was adopted. The leading characteristics of the action were its statement of a definite legal obligation (*dare oportere*) and of a *certum*, whether thing or money, as the object of this claim; it is distinguished by the strictness and directness of the *intentio* (SI PARET DARE OPORTERE), which professes to cover the obligation exactly and an overstatement in which (*plus petere*) is fatal to the plaintiff's claim[3]; it gives rise to a *iudicium* in the strict sense as opposed to an *arbitrium.*

The claim for *certa pecunia.*

The absolutism of the *formula* is most marked where the claim is for *certa pecunia*, or, to employ the careful legal designations, *pecunia certa credita*, an expression which

[1] Plautus refers, in connexion with *pecunia credita*, to the *iusiurandum in iure delatum* (*Curcul.* iv. 2, 10; *Rudens, prol.* 14 'quique in iure abiurant pecuniam'; l. 17 'Qui hic litem adipisci postulant periurio'), and this oath was originally one of the accompaniments only of the *condictio* (Rudorff, *Rechtsgesch.* ii. p. 83; Bethmann-Hollweg, i. p. 152; Jobbé-Duval, *Études*, i. p. 71; Lenel, *Ed. Perp.* p. 188).

[2] *pecunia certa credita* (*Lex Rubria*, c. 21 'a quoquomque pec nia certa credita signata forma publica populei Romanei . . . petetur.' *Lex Iulia Municipalis*, l. 45 'iudicem iudiciumve ita dato utei de pecunia credita [*iudicem*] iudiciumve dari oporteret').

[3] Cic. *pro Rosc. com.* 4, 10 and 11 'Pecunia tibi debebatur certa, quae nunc petitur per iudicem . . . Hic tu si amplius HS. nummo petisti, quam tibi debitum est, causam perdidisti . . . Quid est in iudicio? . . . SI PARET . . . DARI [OPORTERE]. Hic, nisi planum facit . . . ad libellam sibi deberi, causam perdit.'

shows the basis of the claim, *pecunia numerata et signata*[1], one which emphasizes its character as currency on a Roman standard. This is *par excellence* the *condictio certi*; in the *formula* adapted to this claim a definite statement appears both in the *intentio* and the *condemnatio*, and the *iudex* is more strictly bound by the latter than the plaintiff is by the former, for he cannot condemn to less or more. The statement of the ultimate cause of the debt (*causa debendi*) need not be included in the *intentio*, but it might be, and was when the plaintiff wished to leave open for himself a further ground for prosecuting the same claim in case the ground alleged had been proved to be mistaken; for a wrong statement of the *causa debendi* did no injury to his future action[2], while an *intentio* without it, which could not be supported by the facts adduced, would have been fatal to his claim. The contracts which gave rise to the *causa debendi* in Cicero's time have already been described[3].

Sponsio tertiae partis and restipulatio.

This action was not approached without peril either by plaintiff or defendant. Perhaps in accordance with the forms of the *legis actio* and the terms of the *lex Silia*, a necessary preliminary was a *sponsio* and *restipulatio* made by both parties to one another for the payment of one-third of the sum in question ($33\frac{1}{3}$ per cent.) by the loser to his victorious adversary (*sponsio tertiae partis*[4]. This *sponsio* was not treated as a *praeiudicium*,

[1] See p. 198 note 2 and cf. Gell. xiv. 24 'Petebatur apud me pecunia, quae dicebatur data numerataque.'

[2] Gaius, iv. 55 'si quis aliud pro alio intenderit, nihil eum periclitari eumque ex integro agere posse . . . velut . . . si quis ex testamento dari sibi oportere intenderit, cui ex stipulatu debebatur.' Lenel, however, suggests doubts as to whether this passage justifies the conclusion that the *intentio* of an *actio certae creditae pecuniae* (in the case in question, of an *actio ex stipulatu*) could contain the *causa debendi* (*Ed. Perp.* p. 187).

[3] p. 197.

[4] Gaius, iv. 171 'ex quibusdam causis sponsionem facere permittitur, velut de pecunia certa credita . . . tertiae partis'; c. 13 'periculosa est actio certae creditae pecuniae propter sponsionem, qua periclitatur reus si temere neget, et restipulationem, qua periclitatur actor si non debitum

BOOK I.

The *formula.*

as it might have been even though it was penal; it may have been in some manner embedded in the *formula*, e.g.

SI PARET NUMERIUM NEGIDIUM AULO AGERIO SESTERTIUM X MILIA DARE OPORTERE, IUDEX NUMERIUM NEGIDIUM AULO AGERIO SESTERTIUM X MILIA CUM TERTIA PARTE CONDEMNATO; SI NON PARET ABSOLVITO ET AULUM AGERIUM NUMERIO NEGIDIO TERTIAM (EANDEM) PARTEM CONDEMNATO[1];

or it may have been determined simply by the result of the main issue—i.e. the *formula* may have contained no reference to the *poena*, and the latter may have been paid, in accordance with the terms of the *sponsio*[2], to the victor in the *condictio.*

The claim for a *certa res.*

In the *condictio* for the recovery of a *certa res*, the claim stated in the *intentio* is a claim to a *certum*, but, in accordance with the general character of the formulary system, the condemnation is pecuniary. The value, however, of the *certa res* could not be fixed by the litigants, and it was no part of the praetor's duty to form estimates of the kind. Hence the condemnation could not be expressed in terms of *certa pecunia*; the pecuniary estimate must be left to the judex, and the *formula* would assume somewhat of the following shape:—

Estimate by the *iudex.*

SI PARET NUMERIUM NEGIDIUM AULO AGERIO CENTUM MODIOS TRITICI AFRICI OPTIMI DARE OPORTERE, QUANTI EA RES EST[3], TANTAM PECUNIAM IUDEX NUMERIUM NEGIDIUM AULO AGERIO CONDEMNA, SI NON PARET ABSOLVE.

The *iudex* performs the functions of an *arbiter* in his estimate of the value, and can take every circumstance, which may mitigate or enhance the normal value of the

petat.' Cf. Cic. *pro Rosc. com.* 5, 14 ('pecunia petita est certa, cuius (*for* cum) tertia parte sponsio facta est'); 4, 10 ('legitimae partis sponsio facta est'); *lex Rubria*, c. 21.

[1] Following Rudorff, *Rechtsgesch.* ii. p. 142. Some such reconstruction is possible whether we read *cum* or *cuius* in Cic. *pro Rosc. com.* 5, 14. See the preceding note.

[2] e. g. 'si secundum me iudicatum erit' (cf. Cic. *pro Rosc. com.* 5, 14 and 15) is suggested by Lenel (*Ed. Perp.* p. 188).

[3] Cf. Gaius in Dig. 13, 3, 4 'quanti tunc cum iudicium acciperetur'; Lenel, p. 191.

thing, into consideration in forming his judgement. It was just because the *pecunia* was *incerta* that this action, although a *condictio*, could not be spoken of as a *condictio certi*. The old name, the 'corn' *condictio* (*triticaria*), which it gained from the staple article with whose recovery it was concerned, still clung to it in its later history. It had its origin, like the action for *certa pecunia*, in similar obligations of strict law, stipulation and loan; but, unlike that action, was not burdened by the *sponsio tertiae partis*.

Condictio triticaria.

But it was possible for an obligation of strict law to contain the promise of something that was neither *certa pecunia* nor a *certa res*. A stipulation, for instance, might promise something uncertain (*incertum*), not clearly definable, or distinguishable by its qualities from other things of a similar kind, such as quantities of an article without specification of its qualities, an estate whose locality and extent were indeterminate, even such intangible realities as the doing (*facere*) or permitting (*sinere*) of a thing. An action to exact an *incertum* of this kind was not a *condictio*, for it had neither an historical nor a logical justification to the name. But it also differed from the *bonae fidei* actions, which we shall soon discuss, in two respects: in the fact that it had its basis in an obligation of strict law, and in the consequent one-sidedness, shown by the statement of an absolute claim on the side of the plaintiff, of an absolute indebtedness on that of the defendant. The *actio incerti* stands somewhere between the two.

Action for an ***incertum.***

In the *formula* prepared for this action a *demonstratio* was necessary to state the ground of the debt. The *intentio* states the obligation as something uncertain which requires determination by the *iudex*; the condemnation is left to his discretion, and he can take all modifying circumstances into consideration, e. g.

Demonstratio **and estimate by the** ***iudex.***

QUOD AULUS AGERIUS DE NUMERIO NEGIDIO INCERTUM STIPULATUS EST.

QUIDQUID OB EAM REM NUMERIUM NEGIDIUM AULO AGERIO DARE FACERE OPORTET[1], EIUS IUDEX NUMERIUM NEGIDIUM AULO AGERIO CONDEMNA; SI NON PARET ABSOLVE.

Bonae fidei actiones. Their ground in equity.

The action of good faith (*bonae fidei actio*) introduces more distinctly the idea of equity, the modification by ethical considerations of the hard, strict outline of the facts, which is all that the law can be. The aim of equity is to transcend the abstract relation expressed in *ius* and to view the interconnexions between two parties from the assumed standpoint of their higher personality. The law takes the standard of their honourable and scrupulous treatment of one another's claims, of the *fides Romana* which should animate certain relations of life, as its own, and boldly expresses it in the action; by so doing it hopes to fill up the gaps or to smooth away the projections which the circlet of a legal definition always leaves in the ethical relations which it professes to enclose.

The recognition of this dualism is an old one. We have found it in the prehistoric distinction between the *iudex* and the *arbiter*[2], and the idea of equitable adjustment found its concrete expression in the procedure of the *legis actio per arbitri postulationem*[3]. The idea of the *arbitrium* as opposed to the *iudicium*, which has already presented itself in many departments of the formulary system, is most fully realized in these actions of good faith, and with it the idea of the pecuniary condemnation being left to the discretion of the *iudex*[4]. Here, however, it is not merely the uncertainty of the thing promised, nor merely the necessity of enforcing restitution that introduces the element of doubt; it is the characteristic uncertainty attending the determination of contractual relations in which equitable considerations should play a part.

They are *arbitria.*

The *bonae fidei* contracts, from which these actions

[1] Gaius, iv. 136.

[2] p. 39.

[3] p. 65.

[4] Cic. *pro Rosc. com.* 4, 11; *de Off.* iii. 15, 61.

The *bonae fidei* contracts from which these actions spring.

spring, do not necessarily differ from those of strict law in respect of the informality of their creation. It is sufficiently probable that hardly one of these contracts was valid or judicially enforceable in accordance with the early law of Rome[1]; but this was also the case with the informal loan and with the literal contract, which, as we have seen, were obligations of strict law. No doubt the very absence of actionableness may have given them something of their sanctity; what could not be protected by law must be guarded by honour, and, even after their legal enforcement, the censor still continued to defend them by his moral animadversions. But this protection was not extended to all contracts that were originally informal: and the moral atmosphere in which they move is due to their essential nature.

The essence of such contracts is the mutual trust (*bona fides*) which the contracting parties must repose in one another: and, as something must be left to purely moral feelings in their fulfilment, equity (*aequum ius*) must be regarded in their settlement. The phrase occurring in the old action springing from the obligation of Trust (*Fiducia*) 'in accord with the honest action of honest men' (*ut inter bonos bene agier oportet*)[2] is a good expression of this two-fold necessity. The chief of the other obligations in which *bona fides* was a leading principle were the consensual contracts of purchase and sale (*emptio, venditio*), lease and hire (*locatio, conductio*), partnership (*societas*), and mandate (*mandatum*)[3], the real contracts of the loan

[1] Cf. Cic. *de Off. l. c.* 'dolus malus et legibus erat vindicatus ut tutela xii tabulis . . . et sine lege iudiciis, in quibus additur EX FIDE BONA.'

[2] Cic. *ad Fam.* vii. 12, 2; *de Off.* iii. 17, 70.

[3] Cic. *l. c.* 'Scaevola . . . "summam vim esse," dicebat, "in omnibus iis arbitriis in quibus adderetur EX FIDE BONA: fideique bonae nomen," existimabat, "manare latissime, idque versari in tutelis, societatibus, fiduciis mandatis, rebus emptis venditis, conductis locatis, quibus vitae societas contineretur: in iis magni esse iudicis statuere (praesertim cum in plerisque essent iudicia contraria) quid quemque cuique praestare oporteret."' Cf. *de Nat. Deor.* iii. 30, 74; *Top.* 17, 66; *de Orat.* i. 36, 166

BOOK I.

which required the return of the actual thing lent (*commodatum*) and deposit (*depositum*) which consisted in the entrusting of an article by one person to the unrewarded care of another. Other actions of this type were concerned with the division of property such as the *actiones familiae herciscundae* and *communi dividundo*[1].

Characteristics of *bonae fidei* actions; their two-sidedness.

The first characteristic which we may observe in the actions springing from such contracts or relations is their two-sidedness. The action expresses a mutual obligation implied in the contractual relation, and therefore recognizes counter-claims on the part of the defendant. In some of these relations each of the contracting parties has a direct action (*actio directa*) against the other; thus the action *ex empto* is the correlative of that *ex vendito*, and *ex locato* of *ex conducto*, while the conflicting actions of two partners, who necessarily stand on the same general footing of debtor and creditor to one another, are indifferently called *pro socio*. Elsewhere, the general features of the contract make one party primarily the creditor, the other the debtor, as in the obligations of mandate, loan and deposit; but here the debtor—mandatary, commodatory and depositary—is furnished with a counter-action (*actio contraria*[2]) by which he may seek indemnification for expenses incurred in connexion with his gratuitous or interested labour. The double nature of the actions for division, in which both parties are plaintiffs and defendants and which give rise to *iudicia duplicia*, is of itself obvious. It was not necessary, however, that any correlative or contrary action should be actually raised to give a two-sided character to a *bonae fidei* action; the sense of the possibility of counter-claims underlies the *formula* in any given case.

(*tutela*); *pro Rosc. Amer.* 39, 114 (*mandatum*); *pro Quinct.* 3, 13; *pro Rosc. com.* 9, 25 (*pro socio*); *de Off.* iii. 16, 66 (*emptio, venditio* with *damni praestatio* by the seller).

[1] Cic. *ad Fam.* vii. 12, 2.

[2] Cic. *de Off.* iii. 17, 70, quoted p. 203, note 3.

Ethical considerations underlying the fulfilment of the obligation.

The mode in which the claim has been or has to be satisfied is also, in the interest of both parties, subjected to a scrutiny to which no claim of strict law is exposed. A mere literal fulfilment or non-fulfilment of the obligation is not enough; ethical, which are (in the highest sense) 'business' considerations, must be taken into account, such as the amount of interest, care, attention required by the obligation and felt or expended by the defendant. The degrees required naturally differed with the contract. Of the depositary, who is a benefactor, *diligentia* is not expected; he is only responsible for fraud, gross neglect, and omission of precautions which he would have taken with his own affairs; the mandatary is responsible for *culpa* of every kind, for, though he is performing a gratuitous work, his position shows that he has tacitly promised diligent attention; the partner, on the other hand, is only liable for a carelessness greater than that which he shows in the management of his own private business.

The object of the action must be an *incertum*.

It follows naturally from the fact that such considerations were taken into account that the thing whose restoration was aimed at, however definite it might be in origin, could not remain a fixed quantity. Such accretions as its *fructus*, or the interest which it might have borne if employed productively, were considered by the *iudex* and made a factor in his arbitrament.

Form of the *demonstratio*.

The *formulae* in which these actions were expressed were necessarily *incertae* both in intention and condemnation, and as such were headed by a *demonstratio*. The *intentio* was, in Cicero's time, expressed in various modes, all of which rang the changes on 'good faith'; QUANTUM AEQUIUS MELIUS, and UT INTER BONOS BENE AGIER were variants of the EX FIDE BONA, which is the phrase finally found qualifying the QUIDQUID . . . DARE FACERE OPORTET[1].

[1] EX FIDE BONA; UT INTER BONOS BENE AGIER; QUID MELIUS AEQUIUS (Cic. *de Off.* iii. 15, 61; *Top.* 17, 66; *ad Fam.* vii. 12, 2); QUANTUM AEQUIUS ET

BOOK I.

The *formulae* for *depositum* and *societas*.

The formula *in ius concepta* for *depositum* ran:—

QUOD AULUS AGERIUS APUD NUMERIUM NEGIDIUM MENSAM ARGENTEAM DEPOSUIT, QUA DE RE AGITUR, QUIDQUID OB EAM REM NUMERIUM NEGIDIUM AULO AGERIO DARE FACERE OPORTET EX FIDE BONA, EIUS IUDEX NUMERIUM NEGIDIUM AULO AGERIO CONDEMNATO[1], SI NON PARET ABSOLVITO[2];

while that for partnership may have been expressed in the following terms:—

QUOD AULUS AGERIUS CUM NUMERIO NEGIDIO SOCIETATEM OMNIUM BONORUM COIIT, QUIDQUID OB EAM REM NUMERIUM NEGIDIUM AULO AGERIO (ALTERUM ALTERI) PRO SOCIO DARE FACERE PRAESTARE OPORTET EX FIDE BONA, DUMTAXAT QUOD NUMERIUS NEGIDIUS FACERE POTEST, EIUS IUDEX NUMERIUM NEGIDIUM AULO AGERIO CONDEMNATO; SI NON PARET ABSOLVITO[3].

The structure of all *bonae fidei* actions, apart from variants characteristic of special claims which were probably survivals of the *legis actio* or echoes of customary words used in concluding the covenant, was of this constant type, so far as they were actions of the civil law. All the contracts that we have mentioned doubtless reposed on this basis, which was marked by the *dare oportere*. The praetor could form parallel actions in which the presence of *bona fides* was implied; but this form of equity had been engrafted on the *ius civile* without the aid of the praetorian edict.

(c) *Actiones Poenales.*

A penalty as the object of an action.

The end of an action is not merely the recovery of a right or a thing; it may have the object, more directly appropriate to criminal law, of exacting a penalty (*poena*)

MELIUS SIT, DARI (Cic. *pro Rosc. com.* 4, 10); QUIDQUID SIBI DARE FACERE OPORTET EX FIDE BONA (Cic. *de Off.* iii. 16, 66).

[1] Here Lenel (*Ed. Perp.* p. 230) would insert NISI RESTITUET for the *n. r.* of the MS. of Gaius (iv. 47).

[2] Gaius, iv. 47. For the *actio depositi in factum concepta*, see p. 157.

[3] Lenel, *Ed. Perp.* p. 237.

as compensation for the violation of a right. In these penal actions the monetary penalty is sometimes the only compensation won by the injured plaintiff; but in others recovery of an object is aimed at, as well as compensation for the injury suffered by its loss. This difference in aim is the source of the distinction between simple actions of this type and 'mixed actions.' Like many similar distinctions in Roman law, it is of a somewhat superficial character; in both cases compensation is exacted for the wrong (*delictum*), but in some cases only can the object destroyed, as a tangible thing capable of valuation, be included in the estimate of the damage.

Penal actions as simple or 'mixed.'

Actions of the simpler type are typified by those springing from wrongs done to the person, whether by physical assault or verbal injury. The principles of the Twelve Tables, which had enjoined physical retribution by the sufferer for grave bodily injuries and an increasingly inadequate fine of twenty-five asses for lesser hurts[1], had long been abandoned; and as little respect could be paid to the savage penalty of death which had been inflicted for libel and slander[2]. In their place the praetor gave a *formula*[3] in which the penalty for such *iniuriae* varied according to the features of the case:—the amount of the wrong, the aggravating circumstances of its committal and the position of the litigants. The penalty of the transmitted *formula* was thus an uncertain amount of pecuniary damages (*pecunia incerta*), and the estimate of the amount fixed by the plaintiff was left to the

Actio iniuriarum.

[1] Gell. xx. 1, 31–33; Gaius, iii. 223.

[2] Cic. *de Rep.* iv. 10, 12 'duodecim tabulae, cum perpaucas res capite sanxissent, in his hanc quoque sanciendam putaverunt, si quis occentavisset sive carmen condidisset, quod infamiam faceret flagitiumve alteri.' Cf. *Tusc. Disp.* iv. 2, 4.

[3] Cf. Collatio, ii. 6, 4 'sicut formula proposita est QUOD AULI AGERII PUGNO MALA PERCUSSA EST.' See p. 151. In Plautus we find perhaps the earliest reference to the *formula* of this praetorian action (*Asinar.* ii. 2, 104 'pugno malam si tibi percussero'). See Lenel, *Ed. Perp.* p. 321.

BOOK I. equitable feelings of the *iudex*[1]. Other personal damages were estimated by the edict of the curule aediles in their police jurisdiction[2]; and, before the Ciceronian period, even the statute-law had supplemented the purely edictal jurisdiction of aedile and praetor. The primary object of the *Lex Cornelia* (Sullae) *de iniuriis* was a criminal prosecution for assault; but by usage a civil action was developed under its terms, which was concurrent with that contained in the praetorian promise[3].

Actio furti. Theft was reckoned by the jurists as one of those actions in which the subjective elements of vengeance and the desire for punishment (*ultio, vindicta*) are the grounds of the penalty. This classification was historically justifiable, for in the *actio furti* considered by itself and apart from a subsequent possible action to recover the value of the thing, a *poena* alone was exacted, although in the law of the Ciceronian period the value of the thing is uniformly made the basis of the penalty, and the *poena* contains implicitly the recovery of the stolen object. The penalty enjoined by the Twelve Tables for *furtum nec manifestum*, of two-fold the value of the thing, was retained; but a praetorian action *in quadruplum* had taken the place of the scourging and bond-service (*addictio*) with which the Twelve Tables had threatened the author of a manifest theft[4]. While the one was a 'civil' action, the other was an outcome of 'honorary' law; but both are *stricti iuris actiones* and little is left for the *arbitrium* of the *iudex*.

[1] 'aestimatio vestra est' (i. e. of the 'recuperatores') (Cic. *pro Tull.* 3, 7). Cf. Gell. xx. 1, 13 'praetores postea . . . iniuriis . . . aestimandis recuperatores se daturos edixerunt.' Gaius, iii. 224 'permittitur . . . nobis a praetore ipsis iniuriam aestimare, et iudex vel tanti condemnat quanti nos aestimaverimus, vel minoris, prout ei visum fuerit.'

[2] See p. 31.

[3] Dig. 47, 10, 37, 1 'Etiam ex lege Cornelia iniuriarum actio civiliter moveri potest condemnatione aestimatione iudicis facienda.' We cannot tell whether this development had been reached by Cicero's day.

[4] Gell. xx. 1, 7; Gaius, iii. 189. Cf. Cic. *pro Tull.* 21, 50.

PART II.

Actio damni iniuria dati; the lex Aquilia.

In an action for damage to property the estimate of the loss incurred enters more directly into the value of the compensation, although this compensation may yet be regarded primarily as a *poena*. The actions furnished by the Twelve Tables for such damage, generally called *noxia* but in later times termed *damnum iniuria datum*, were numerous and specific; but they had become well-nigh extinct even by Cicero's time. The reason for their disuse was the dominance attained by the *Lex Aquilia*, a *plebiscitum* perhaps of the year 287 B.C., which juristic interpretation had made the prevalent and almost the only means of seeking compensation for such loss[1]. It enacted that, in the case of the unlawful destruction of the slave or quadruped of another, the slayer should pay to its owner the highest value borne by the creature within the previous year: that, in the case of the unlawful 'burning, crushing or breaking' of any property besides that specified above, the destroyer should be liable for the value (i.e. as it was interpreted, the highest value) borne by the property within the last thirty days: and perhaps the very words of the law,

QUANTI ID IN EO ANNO PLURIMI FUIT,
QUANTI EA RES IN DIEBUS XXX PROXIMIS (FUIT)[2],

formed part of the *condemnatio* of the *formula* by which it was enforced.

Actio damni dati vi hominibus armatis.

But this civil guardianship of property was found to be insufficient. The revolutionary era was marked by crimes of violence which required a more summary treatment and a severer punishment: and the remedy was, in accordance with the tendencies of the time, supplied by the praetor. M. Lucullus, in 76 B.C., framed and

[1] Cf. Cic. *Brut.* 34, 131 'eōdem tempore accusator de plebe L. Caesulenus fuit, quem ego audivi iam senem, cum ab L. Sabellio multam lege Aquilia . . . petivisset.' The word *multa* is here used somewhat improperly for damages in a civil action.

[2] Gaius, iii. 210 214; Dig. 9, 2, 2; 9, 2, 27, 5.

BOOK I. introduced an action for *damnum datum vi hominibus armatis*[1]. Its chief aim was the repression of damage done by bands of armed slaves who were kept by unscrupulous masters for the violent enforcement of their private ends. The action was for four-fold the damage done (*in quadruplum*)[2]; the fixing of the maximum penalty (*taxatio*) was the work of the plaintiff, and the final estimate rested with the *recuperatores* who in this action took the place of the *iudex*[3]. The formula for the action ran:—

QUANTAE PECUNIAE PARET DOLO MALO FAMILIAE P. FABII VI HOMINIBUS ARMATIS COACTISVE DAMNUM DATUM ESSE M. TULLIO[4], TANTAE PECUNIAE QUADRUPLUM (or IN QUADRUPLUM), RECUPERATORES, FABIUM TULLIO CONDEMNATE; SI NON PARET, ABSOLVITE.

§ 5. *The Interdict.*

The interdict as the basis of an action. The magisterial utterances known as interdicts had had a long history by Cicero's time. He speaks of the praetor as engaged for 'whole days' in issuing such injunctions[5]: and yet, in spite of their having become quite an ordinary branch of procedure, as usual a means of aiding the litigant as the praetorian action itself, they never lost their original character of exceptional commands springing from the *imperium*. While the praetorian action is due only to interpretative power and on its creation loses its character of a magisterial promise or command and becomes a right of the plaintiff, it was always felt that the interdict was an exercise of pure magisterial authority (*auctoritas*). This authority came more and more to be interposed,

[1] Cic. *pro Tull.* 4, 8.

[2] For further peculiarities of this action see Appendix on the *pro Tullio.*

[3] *Ib.* 3, 7.

[4] Cic. *pro Tull.* 3, 7; cf. 13, 31.

[5] Cic. *pro Caec.* 13, 36 'Praetor . . . qui dies totos aut vim fieri vetat, aut restitui factam iubet, qui de fossis, de cloacis, de minimis aquarum itinerumque controversiis interdicit.'

not for the sake of guarding the public, but for the purpose of protecting certain otherwise unprotected individual rights: since, however, a summary command can take little cognizance of the merits of a claim before the injunction is interposed, the true cognizance and the final pronouncement on the disputed right follows the interdict. This is equivalent to saying that the interdict is made the basis of an action. The probable causes which led to this form of its employment have been already explained[1]. We have now to consider the nature of these injunctions and the procedure consequent on them in their developed form.

The interdicts are commands, individual in form but universal in character.

The interdict is, in form and in spirit, a command operating in the present. The praetor says 'I forbid' (*veto*) or 'you must restore' (*restituas*), and, although he may condition his prohibition or demand for restoration, if these conditions are fulfilled, the command is supposed to operate at once. This form of the interdict betrays its origin: it is the survival of a command based on magisterial cognizance of a breach of the law, and the form is preserved even when the violation of right has yet to be proved. These commands are not of a general character and, formally at least, state no principle applicable to the world at large; they still maintain their appearance of interlocutions addressed to individuals; they appeal, and refer to, the parties involved in the singular number; the praetor, addressing the party complained against, says 'restore' or 'produce,' or 'I forbid you using violence to prevent him from cutting down that tree.' But, in spite of the particular application expressed in its form, the universality of the utterance is fully manifested in other ways. With the progress of years the injunction has become stereotyped, so fixed and definite that, like the action, it appears in the edict as the outline of a case,

[1] p. 78.

BOOK I.

a *formula*[1] which, to be complete, only needs to be filled in with the name of the litigants.

They are elicited at the request of a party. Their purely provisional character.

This form of magisterial command had, perhaps, always awaited the complaint of an individual as the representative of his and the public's violated interests. Now that the interdict is almost wholly the basis of an action, the proposal of a party is essential to its being elicited. In the days when the command was final, the praetor must have weighed the merits of the application. Such an estimate of the rights of the case is no longer necessary for the granting of the interdict. Now that it is employed to start an action, as the very first stage towards the settlement of a controversy, the very presumption of an interdict is that the facts are doubtful. So far from presupposing a judgement on the elements of the controversy, the most essential fact of the interdict may itself be the subject of the most serious doubt. The basis of the case which Cicero pleaded for Caecina was an interdict of the praetor ordering restitution by his opponent in consequence of the latter's use of armed force (*vis armata*) to acquire possession; but the interdict was of a purely provisional character: one of the main questions which the *recuperatores* had to determine was whether Aebutius had employed the force contemplated in this injunction[2].

They create personal and conditioned obligations.

The interdict, like every command which must be obeyed, creates an obligation; it is a personal obligation imposed on an individual to do or to refrain from doing. But the command, as given by the praetor, is conditioned: it is only operative if the facts are true: 'from whence you have expelled him by violence[3], you must restore him,' is the utterance of the praetor: and the condition

[1] Cic. *pro Tull.* 12, 29 'Videtis praetores per hos annos intercedere hoc interdicto velut inter me et M. Claudium: UNDE DOLO MALO TUO, M. TULLI, M. CLAUDIUS AUT FAMILIA AUT PROCURATOR EIUS VI DETRUSUS EST; cetera ex formula.'

[2] See Appendix on the *pro Caecina*.

[3] Cic. *l. c.*

of expulsion by violence has to be proved for the command for restoration to become operative. The obligation like the command is therefore conditioned, and the proof of the condition is, like the fulfilment of the obligation, one of the main questions raised in the action which is started by the interdict. In this action the two great issues raised are (i) whether the condition exists, i.e. whether the command should be obeyed, (ii) on proof of the existence of the condition, whether the command has been obeyed. In the case of Caecina we find both issues fought out, for Aebutius maintained, not only that his action was not characterized by the violence contemplated in the interdict, but that he had 'restored[1].' These questions, whether a command should be or had been obeyed, are questions of law and fact for the *iudex* or *recuperatores*. The interdictal process, perhaps more than any other, left the main question of law for the *iudicium*, and this may account for the fact that of all Cicero's speeches that for Caecina shows the closest legal argument.

Their three-fold object.

The aim of these conditioned commands of the praetor was three-fold. (i) They might order the restitution of something; (ii) they might command the production of something; (iii) they might prohibit the doing of something.

The restitutory interdicts.

(i) The scope of the restitutory interdicts turns on the meaning of restitution as employed by the praetor. The command *restituas*, in the sense which has most interest to a student of Ciceronian law, means 'restore a given thing to a given person.' This meaning may be illustrated from interdicts which served very various purposes.

Interdictum quorum bonorum.

The interdict which guarded the transmission of praetorian inheritances (*bonorum possessio*), known from its initial words as the interdict *quorum bonorum*, ran as follows:—

QUORUM BONORUM EX EDICTO MEO ILLI POSSESSIO DATA EST,

[1] Cic. *pro Caec.* 8, 23 'Restituisse se dixit.'

BOOK I. QUOD DE HIS BONIS PRO HEREDE AUT PRO POSSESSORE POSSIDES POSSIDERESVE, SI NIHIL USUCAPTUM ESSET, QUODQUE DOLO MALO FECISTI UTI DESINERES POSSIDERE, ID ILLI RESTITUAS[1].

The interdict which protected the owner of a thing against a possessor who held it on sufferance was thus worded:—

Interdictum de precario. QUOD PRECARIO AB ILLO HABES AUT DOLO MALO FECISTI UT DESINERES HABERE, QUA DE RE AGITUR, ID ILLI RESTITUAS.

The interdicts which commanded restitution in the case of violent expulsion differed in their wording and therefore in their conditions of law and fact, according as the violence was of an ordinary kind or was asserted by armed force.

The more general interdict, known from part of its wording as *unde vi*, was, in Cicero's time, constructed as follows:—

Interdictum unde vi. UNDE TU AUT FAMILIA AUT PROCURATOR TUUS ILLUM AUT FAMILIAM AUT PROCURATOREM ILLIUS IN HOC ANNO VI DEIECISTI, CUM ILLE POSSIDERET, QUOD NEC VI NEC CLAM NEC PRECARIO A TE[2] POSSIDERET, EO ILLUM RESTITUAS[3].

[1] The *sponsio* from this interdict is mentioned by Cicero (*ad Fam.* vii. 21) 'SI BONORUM TURPILIAE POSSESSIONEM Q. CAEPIO PRAETOR EX EDICTO SUO MIHI DEDIT.' The name of the praetor who had granted *bonorum possessio*, therefore, appeared in the *sponsio*, and probably in the interdict granted by a successor; see Bethmann-Hollweg, p. 360. This interdict is, perhaps, referred to in Cic. *Top.* 4, 18 ('Si ea mulier testamentum fecit, quae se capite nunquam deminuit, non videtur ex edicto praetoris secundum eas tabulas possessio dari,' i. e. the succession here is by civil, not by praetorian, law).

[2] Lenel, *Ed. Perp.* p. 371.

[3] Cic. *pro Tull.* 19, 44. Cf. *Lex Agraria* (*circa* 111 B.C.), l. 18 ['*Sei quis eorum quorum age*]r supra scriptus est, ex possessione vi eiectus est, quod eius is quei eiectus est possederit, quod neque vi neque clam neque precario possederit ab eo, quei eum ea possessione vi eiec[*erit*].' In his interpretation of these restitutory interdicts, Cicero interprets *unde* and *restituas* in a wide sense as implying general means of access to a thing (Cic. *pro Caec.* 31, 89; 29, 82), e. g. ejection from a road is ejection from the farm to which it leads, although the farm, not the road, is the object of restitution; cf. *pro Caec.* 16, 46 'Omnis enim vis est quae periculo aut decedere nos alicunde cogit aut prohibet accedere.' *Procurator*, says Cicero (*pro Caec.* 20, 57), may, in this interdict and in that *unde vi et armis*, mean any agent whatsoever, not merely a duly accredited representative of the *dominus* (*procurator omnium rerum*).

This interdict is limited in many ways; its operation is restricted to violence done within the year, and it thus creates a temporal limitation on the right of action of the *deiectus*: its use assumes possession by the dispossessed plaintiff which has not been vitiated by the modes of its assertion: it must neither be consciously held on sufferance nor have been acquired by force or stealth: it thus opens a technical counter-plea to the defendant that the possession by the plaintiff now lost had originally been so acquired (*exceptio vitiosae possessionis*)[1]. PART II.

Interdictum de vi armata.

The praetor is much more severe in restraining usurpation by armed violence[2]. The limitation to the year is dropped[3], he does not demand explicitly the proof of possession by the plaintiff (although it may have been assumed[4]), and the *exceptio vitiosae possessionis* can no longer be urged by the defendant. The interdict over which the case for Caecina was fought ran as follows:—

UNDE TU AUT FAMILIA AUT PROCURATOR TUUS ILLUM VI HOMINIBUS COACTIS ARMATISVE DEIECISTI, EO RESTITUAS[5].

Meanings of 'restitution.'

Restitution in the above cases does not necessarily imply the formal restoration of a thing to its original possessor, but simply the removal of impediments to his holding it. Thus when, in the case of Caecina, Aebutius made the answer

[1] For this exception, based on *vis*, see Cic. *ad Fam.* vii. 13, 2 'QUOD TU PRIOR VI HOMINIBUS ARMATIS [NON] VENERIS'; cf. *pro Caec.* 32, 92 'is, qui se restituisse dixit, magna voce saepe confiteri solet se vi deiecisse, verum illud addit "non possidebat."'

[2] Cic. *pro Caec.* 11, 32 'coactis hominibus et armatis.'

[3] Cic. *ad Fam.* xv. 16, 3 'In hoc interdicto non solet addi IN HOC ANNO.'

[4] Cic. *pro Caec.* 31, 91; 32, 92. For this legal question see Appendix on the *pro Caecina*.

[5] *Ib.* 8, 23. *Dolo malo* might be added, and the names of the parties were, of course, given in the complete interdict, as in the formula mentioned by Cicero (*pro Tull.* 12, 29) 'UNDE DOLO MALO TUO, M. TULLI, M. CLAUDIUS AUT FAMILIA AUT PROCURATOR EIUS VI DETRUSUS EST.' I cite the passage here, and not in connexion with the simpler inderdict *unde vi*, because *dolus malus* seems to belong peculiarly to *vis armata* (see the whole speech *pro Tullio*). Cicero's words here are only paradeigmatic and, perhaps, some of the formula is omitted.

restitui[1], this was merely a formal mode of asserting that he had never disturbed the plaintiff in his possession. But in some of these interdicts restitution does not even imply that the litigant who asks for and obtains the order has ever had possession of the thing that he now desires to see restored; these interdicts are, in fact, a mode of acquiring as well as of recovering possession (*tam recuperandae quam apiscendae possessionis*[2]). For example, no previous ownership or possession, but simply a previous potential right, is implied in the interdict *quorum bonorum*.

Restitution is also employed in interdicts of this class without any reference to a person who benefits by the restoration; in this sense it is applied to immoveables, generally to public property (*publicae res*), and implies the restoration of a thing to some original condition which has been disturbed by the person against whom the order is issued. It was in this way that a public road, river or sewer was protected:—

QUOD IN VIA PUBLICA (IN FLUMINE PUBLICO, CLOACA PUBLICA) FACTUM IMMISSUM HABES . . . RESTITUAS.

The restitution here may simply mean permission to remove the obstacle.

Duties implied in 'restitution.'

We cannot determine for the Ciceronian period the extent of the duty implied in restitution. Later jurisprudence interpreted the word as including compensation for damages consequent on the disturbance, perhaps also on the removal of the impediment[3]. Possibly this was and always had been a universal principle in all restitutory interdicts. In later times (and we may be sure at all times) the products or fruits of a thing were also included in the duty of restitution. The date from which the debt of the *fructus* was reckoned was that of the issue of the interdict, for it was this date that created the obligation.

[1] Cic. *pro Caec.* 8, 23.

[2] Paulus in Dig. 43, 1, 2, 3; Schmidt, *Interdictenverfahren der Römer*, p. 33.

[3] Schmidt, pp. 38, 39.

The interdict *unde vi* (perhaps too the interdict *quod vi aut clam*[1]) were in later law exceptions to this rule. Here the obligation to restore the fruits was reckoned from the date of the violent dejection or of the occupation by force or fraud[2].

The exhibitory interdicts.

(ii) The exhibitory interdicts are of a simpler character; they demand the production of a person or a thing[3], and close with the command 'exhibeas,' as in the interdict which required the presentation of a testament:—

QUAS TABULAS LUCIUS TITIUS AD CAUSAM TESTAMENTI SUI PERTINENTES RELIQUISSE DICETUR . . . EAS ILLI EXHIBEAS.

The prohibitory interdicts.

(iii) The prohibitory interdicts take the form of an injunction *not* to do something. They are expressed in various ways according to the nature of the injunction. Sometimes this is an absolute command against the doing of a thing, and this is expressed by *ne . . . fiat*, or *veto*, e.g.

NE QUID IN LOCO SACRO FIAT.

IN VIA PUBLICA ITINEREVE PUBLICO FACERE IMMITTERE QUID, QUO EA VIA IDVE ITER DETERIUS SIT FIAT, VETO.

But more frequently they are commands not to hinder the doings of some one else, and their general character is a prohibition of violence being used against some one who is presumed to be doing something legal. The prohibition is expressed in the words *vim fieri veto*. As instances of the structure of such rulings we may take two interdicts which will soon engage our attention: one known as *Uti possidetis* which protected possession in immoveables, the other known as *utrubi* which guaranteed it in the case of moveables:—

Interdicta uti possidetis and *utrubi*.

UTI NUNC POSSIDETIS EUM FUNDUM, QUO DE AGITUR, QUOD NEC VI NEC CLAM NEC PRECARIO ALTER AB ALTERO POSSIDETIS, ITA POSSIDEATIS. ADVERSUS EA VIM FIERI VETO[4].

[1] QUOD VI AUT CLAM FACTUM EST, QUA DE RE AGITUR, ID . . . RESTITUAS.

[2] Schmidt, pp. 41, 43.

[3] For the meaning of 'exhibition' as defined by Labeo see Dig. 50, 16, 246 'Apud Labeonem Pithanon ita scriptum est: exhibet qui praestat eius, de quo agitur, praesentiam.'

[4] Cf. Cic. *de Rep.* i. 13, 20 (quoted p. 76, note 1).

BOOK I.

UTRUBI HIC HOMO, QUO DE AGITUR, MAIORE PARTE HUIUSCE ANNI NEC VI NEC CLAM NEC PRECARIO AB ALTERO FUIT, QUOMINUS IS EUM DUCAT, VIM FIERI VETO.

The prohibition of disturbance, contained in these interdicts, refers of necessity to the future, not to the past; they would otherwise have encroached on the sphere of the restitutory interdicts. The disturbance need not be one that has commenced after the issue of the prohibition: it may be antecedent to it, but, if it continues after the interdict has been elicited, it comes within its terms. In later (and perhaps in earlier) law damages done by the disturbance after the issue of the interdict were held to be included in the prohibition[1], and might be estimated in the action of which the interdict forms the ground.

The 'possessory' interdicts.

The most important of the interdicts in history, in civil procedure and in the study of Ciceronian law, are those denominated 'possessory,' from their protecting that imperfect form of ownership which the Romans knew as *possessio*. Of the three interdicts of this type which we shall consider, two—*uti possidetis* and *utrubi*—are prohibitory, one—*unde vi*—restitutory. The reason for treating the last mentioned in detail in a work on Ciceronian procedure is obvious; it forms the subject of one of his most finished speeches. The two others are unconnected (or at least but remotely connected) with his writings, but they formed such an integral part of the procedure of his time that it is impossible to ignore them even in a work which professes to give but an outline of that procedure.

As the whole theory of *possessio* is known to us only in its later developments, when it had become complicated by historical accidents, praetorian rulings and juristic interpretation, it is impossible to determine the original significance of this form of tenure. In its final shape it is the detention of an object with the *animus* of ownership, and, although sharply distinguished from ownership

[1] Schmidt, p. 62.

Meaning and origin of possessio.

(*dominium*) itself, is protected by the law unless the title to the object is obviously bad: so defective, in fact, that the possessor could not conceivably regard himself as having that sole and exclusive right to the detention and use of the object which is of the essence of ownership. Possibly this conception is not very far removed from the original idea of possession. It may date from the time when the only *dominium* was that of the *dominus* or head of the clan, when only clan-ownership was recognized, and when the first tentative efforts at private property were unprotected by law and could be defended only by custom or by force. When private ownership was recognized, the theory of possession as a right to property had become fixed and it must have gathered further strength with the expansion of Roman dominion in Italy. Land, it is true, was assigned in Quiritarian ownership to the poorer citizens, but who could account for the accretions made to the estates of their rich and noble leaders? All of these could not have been due to occupation of public land; they usurped domains in the conquered districts and held them against the world, and by the time of the Twelve Tables this adverse possession, if persisted in successfully for two years, constituted ownership of land. The Roman state always tended to recognize a *de facto* as a *de iure* right; it was the more tempted to do so in this case as the burden of taxation and of military service fell chiefly on land, and it was important to be able to point to specific owners in the enjoyment of full *dominium*. The idea of *possessio* is probably one that was originated and matured in relation to land; there is nothing surprising in its transference to moveables, and the shorter term of prescription required for the ownership of these reflects at once the greater difficulty of proving an original claim and the smaller value attached to them by the Roman state.

Precarious possession.

By the side of possession that might ripen into *dominium* had grown up a possession that never could be ownership.

BOOK I.

It has been conjectured with great plausibility that the idea of holding a thing on sufferance (*precario*) from a *dominus* originated in the relations between a Roman client and his lord[1]. The *cliens* originally could not be a landholder *ex iure Quiritium*, for he had no personality in private law, but his *patronus* may have allowed him to occupy a portion of his land, perhaps on payment of a rent, and this occupation was said to be *precario*. The convenience of the tenure may have led to its use between free men, and its adoption by the state has a history rendered too familiar by the agrarian troubles of Rome to need recapitulation here.

It is probably the latter that the possessory interdicts were meant originally to protect.

It is not known whether any legal protection was offered in early Rome to possession of the first kind—that possession, namely, which may become but is not yet ownership. But to the second type, as represented by the enormous domains of the state (*ager publicus*) occupied by wealthy families who alone were able to protect their rights in these distant regions, legal guarantees had to be accorded. Although the squatters possessed *precario* and could not be protected against their *dominus*, the state, yet legal intervention was necessary to guard their rights against third parties. It is such legal intervention that is probably typified in the possessory interdicts[2]. While the interdict

[1] Savigny, *Recht des Besitzes*, p. 202 (7th ed.).

[2] For the close connexion of the interdicts with *possessio* of land see Cic. *de Leg. Agr.* iii. 3, 11 'Nam attendite, quantas concessiones agrorum hic noster obiurgator uno verbo facere conetur "quae data, donata, concessa, vendita." Patior, audio; quid deinde? "possessa." Hoc tribunus plebis promulgare ausus est, ut quod quisque post Marium et Carbonem consules possidet id eo iure teneret quo quod optimo privatum est. Etiamne si vi eiecit? Etiamne si clam, si precario venit in possessionem? Ergo hac lege ius civile, causae possessionum, praetorum interdicta tollentur.' Hence the interdict is represented as the alternative of the *vindicatio* (Cic. *de Orat.* i. 10, 41 'qui aut interdicto tecum contenderent aut te ex iure manum consertum vocarent, quod in alienas possessiones tam temere irruisses'). The possessory interdicts are chiefly glanced at in *ad Fam.* vii. 32, 1 ('Urbanitatis possessionem, amabo, quibusvis interdictis defendamus'), but the restitutory interdicts may be implied as well.

unde vi is the mode of recovery on ejectment, that *uti possidetis* is the means of vindication.

It is true that this view of the interdict *uti possidetis* is not that given by the Roman jurists. The sole use which they assign to it is that of determining the rôle of the parties and *interim* possession in real actions[1]. But an examination of the character of the interdictal procedure makes it difficult to believe that this could have been other than a late and very partial application of a process that was once meant to serve more extended objects. Complexity is noted as a characteristic of interdictal procedure in general[2], but the extraordinarily cumbrous action springing from *uti possidetis* could never have been devised by the praetor as a means of deciding an incident in a trial. The process, too, is a very close parallel to the *vindicatio*: it imitates it in its salient points as though its deviser was anxious to raise the question of possession to as near a level as possible to that of property. *Praetorum interdicta* and *causae possessionum* are mentioned by Cicero in close connexion with one another[3], and this connexion is probably historic so far as the possessory interdicts are concerned. The following description of the procedure of the interdict *uti possidetis*, which is derived from Gaius[4], has, therefore, a double interest. It not only fills up the gap that we have left in our account of the real action by the *sponsio praeiudicialis*, but it shows the Republican mode of vindication in the case of possession applied to land.

The procedure under the interdict *uti possidetis*.

The first stage is marked by the statement of the parties and the granting of the interdict by the praetor. This

Granting of the interdict.

[1] Gaius, iv. 148 (cited p. 187, note); Ulpian in Dig. 43, 17, 1, 3. See Dernburg, *Entwicklung und Begriff des juristischen Besitzes des römischen Rechts*, p. 14.

[2] Frontinus, *de controv.* i, 'magna . . . alea est litem ad interdictum deducere, cuius est executio perplexissima.'

[3] Cic. *de Leg. Agr.* iii. 3, 11 (cited p. 220, note 2).

[4] Gaius, iv. 166–169; Dernburg, *op. cit.* pp. 17 ff.

interdict is one of those called double (*duplicia*), for neither party is preeminently plaintiff or defendant; each is both. The praetor, as the wording of the interdict shows, uses the same language to either litigant: 'As you now possess, so may you possess.' It is thus probable that each party makes the same claim, that each urges that he is the *possessor*.

Symbolic violence.

This first stage is followed by a formal exhibition of violence by the parties (*vim facere*), this struggle being an imitation of the mock-fight of the *vindicatio*; possibly in this interdictal process, as in the *sacramenti actio*, the litigants joined hands (*manum conserere*).

Interim possession.

Interim possession is then given to one of the two parties and security for its restoration is given by the *interim* possessor. The mode of granting this possession is, however, quite different from that practised in the *vindicatio*. It is here decided by an auction which is called an auction of the fruits (*fructus licitatio*). The thing with its fruits is the object put up, and the parties are the bidders. That one of the litigants who offers the higher sum in case of failure to establish the main issue—possession—has now the *interim* tenure of the disputed land and of its products. He promises this money, that he has bid, to his opponent, the non-possessor, in case of the latter's victory, by means of a stipulation (*fructuaria stipulatio*) strengthened by securities. This price that he has paid at auction for the possession is, in case of his defeat, to be forfeited as a penalty (*poenae nomine*) to his opponent. The fruits gained in the meanwhile during the *interim* possession are also to be surrendered to the non-possessor, if he is victorious. By this means a guarantee is at least secured that the *interim* possessor is the man 'who risks the higher penalty in the event of his defeat, who thinks himself surer of his case and has, therefore, presumably the better claim[1].'

[1] Dernburg, p. 19.

All this is merely preliminary. Now comes the central point of the action. It is based, as in the *vindicatio*, on the procedure by wager. There is a mutual *sponsio* by the parties and a mutual *restipulatio* by each. In the *vindicatio* the *sacramentum* had been based on the ground '*Iniuria vindicavisti*'; here the *sponsio* is based on the ground:—

Sponsio.

VIM FECISTI ADVERSUS EDICTUM PRAETORIS[1].

So far there is a similarity: but the ultimate destiny of the sum of the *sponsio* is not that of the sum of the *sacramentum*; the former, in case of the defeat of the wagerer, falls not to the state but to the victorious opponent. We are not told how the *summa sponsionis* on either side was settled; but it is a probable conjecture that either party could, according to his pleasure, decide the amount that he would wager with the proviso that the sum should not surpass the maximum value of the disputed object of the possession[2]. A guarantee that neither party should make an exorbitant sum the sanction of the *sponsio* was found in the fact that each proposer had to 'restipulate' to the same amount.

The iudicium.

Then followed the *iudicium*. This was an action springing from the main fact—the *sponsio*—and it centred entirely round the sums expressed in the sponsions and restipulations. It was a *praeiudicium* which decided the main issue—the question of *vis* and, therefore, the question of possession. It was the close of the case for the non-possessor if he was condemned, and for the possessor if he was condemned and *restored to his opponent the possession, the fruits and the poena*.

[1] Gaius, iv. 166 'postea alter alterum sponsione provocat, quod adversus edictum praetoris possidenti sibi vis facta sit, et invicem ambo restipulantur adversus sponsionem.' Cicero gives, as the form of *restipulatio* by the defendant in this or in a somewhat similar case, NI ADVERSUS EDICTUM PRAETORIS VIS FACTA ESSET (Cic. *pro Caec.* 16, 45).

[2] Lenel, *Ed. Perp.* p. 379.

BOOK I.

The *iudicium secutorium.*

But, if he did not restore them, a further stage was necessary. This new action is called by Gaius the *iudicium Cascellianum* or *secutorium*. The reason for its necessity was that condemnation under the formulary system was pecuniary; if, therefore, the defeated possessor would not restore, a pecuniary estimate of the possession had to be given for the benefit of the victorious non-possessor. But the latter has another right as well, the claim for the *poena* consequent on the *fructuaria stipulatio*. It is true that this, if it stood alone, might have been made the ground for a *condictio certi* and have been decided by the *unus iudex*. But it did not stand alone: it was associated with the question of recovery of possession (*de possessione reciperanda*) in a pecuniary sense: and, to avoid two new processes, the *poena* and the estimate of the unrestored possession are both made to come before *arbitri* for decision.

Alternative to this last stage.

Gaius mentions an alternative to this last stage in the procedure[1]; the non-possessing plaintiff, who has been victorious in the *sponsio*, might drop the action for the *poena* based on the *fructuaria stipulatio* and action directly for the fruits, after receiving security from the defendant *iudicatum solvi*. This procedure might have been adopted in cases where the *poena* was insignificant and where the *fructus*, in consequence of long *interim* possession, were of far greater value. This too was called a *iudicium secutorium*, as following victory in the *sponsio*, but it did not bear the name *Cascellianum*. It was probably, like the Cascellian action, an *arbitrium*, and the value of the possession was doubtless estimated with that of the fruits and by the same *arbitri*.

[1] Gaius, iv. 169 'Admonendi tamen sumus liberum esse ei qui fructus licitatione victus erit, omissa fructuaria stipulatione, sicut Cascelliano sive secutorio iudicio de possessione reciperanda experitur, ita similiter de fructus licitatione agere: in quam rem proprium iudicium comparatum est, quod appellatur fructuarium, quo nomine actor iudicatum solvi satis accipiet. Dicitur autem et hoc iudicium secutorium, quod sequitur sponsionis victoriam, sed non aeque Cascellianum vocatur.'

The *iudicium secutorium* obviously belongs to this interdict as a means of determining possession, not *interim* possession. When the interdict was used by the praetor for the latter purpose [1], the proceedings must (at least generally) have stopped with the victory in the *sponsio*; for no defeated litigant would have cared to risk pecuniary restitution in addition to the *poena* in place of the surrender of the mere temporary enjoyment of the thing.

The interdict *utrubi*.

The interdict *utrubi*, like that *uti possidetis*, aims at the retention of possession (*retinendae possessionis causa*), and both came equally to be used for the determination of *interim* tenure in a real action by the *sponsio praeiudicialis*. Like *uti possidetis* it is one of the *duplicia interdicta*, and the exception of *vitiosa possessio* appears in both. But, besides the fact that it applied to moveables, the interdict *utrubi* raised a different issue to that implied in *uti possidetis*. The question it raises is not which of the two parties is the present possessor, but which of the two parties has held the thing, without vicious possession, during the greater portion of the last year. The party who can be proved to have done so 'may take the thing with him [2].' Does this mean that he is to be the possessor or the owner? When this interdict was employed as a means of determining *interim* possession, the victor is of course only the provisional possessor. But there may have been a time when he was the true possessor, perhaps the owner. Amongst the many theories that have been put forward as to the origin of the interdict *utrubi*, not the least probable is the view that it was the mode accorded to the *peregrini*, who could not vindicate, of asserting and recovering ownership of their moveable property [3].

Its probable origin.

The interdicts *unde vi* and *de vi armata*.

The interdict *unde vi* aims at the restoration of an ejected possessor, and was doubtless developed for the purpose of protecting the legally unguarded rights of the

[1] p. 188. [2] 'Quominus is eum ducat, vim fieri veto.' See p. 218.
[3] Dernburg, p. 57.

BOOK I. occupants of the public domain; the interdict *unde vi hominibus armatis coactisve* is only an intensified form of the same action: and the procedure in both cases is in all essential features the same. According to Gaius' description, either of two methods could be adopted on the issue of such a restitutory interdict: these were the *formula arbitraria* and the *sponsio*, and the choice between them lay with the defendant[1]. If he pursued the first course, he asked the praetor for an *arbiter* and a *formula arbitraria*, i.e. one ordaining either restitution or pecuniary condemnation. If he was condemned under this *formula*, he had either to restore or, in default of restitution, to give to the plaintiff compensation to the full value of the thing (*quanti ea res est*); but he paid no further penalty (*poena*) to his victorious adversary. This procedure had the merit of effecting a complete settlement of the case in a single *iudicium*. But if the defendant, after the preliminaries of the action, leaves the court without asking for an *arbiter*, he has committed himself to the second mode of procedure[2]. This is, to use Gaius' expression, a 'perilous' mode (*cum periculo*[3]), for condemnation now involves a *poena* as well as simple restitution and compensation. This *poena* is the result of a wager. The plaintiff challenges the defendant by a *sponsio*:

Two methods of procedure: (i) by the *formula arbitraria*.

(ii) by the *sponsio*, which is both *poenalis* and *praeiudicialis*.

SI CONTRA EDICTUM PRAETORIS NON RESTITUERIT[4].

The defendant then restipulates:—

NI CONTRA EDICTUM PRAETORIS, ETC.

A *formula* is then framed containing the *sponsio* and

[1] Gaius, iv. 163.

[2] *ib.* 164 'Observare debet is qui vult arbitrum petere ut statim petat, antequam ex iure exeat, id est, antequam a praetore discedat; sero enim petentibus non indulgetur.'

[3] *ib.* 165 'Itaque si arbitrum non petierit, sed tacitus de iure exierit, cum periculo res ad exitum perducitur.'

[4] *ib.*, or perhaps in Cicero's time, VIS FACTA SIT. I am by no means sure that the *formula* given in Cic. *pro Caec.* 16, 45 (see p. 223, note 1) might not be used in the interdict *unde vi* as well as in that *uti possidetis*.

restipulatio. If the defendant is condemned under this *formula* he pays the *summa sponsionis* to his adversary as a *poena.* But the decision is only a *praeiudicium*; the main issue, the restoration of the possession or its equivalent, has not yet been effected. For this a consequent action (*iudicium secutorium*) is required[1]. When the plaintiff elicited his *formula* expressing the *sponsio*, he obtained another of a different import, to be used if he was victorious in the wager. This second *formula* was *arbitraria*: it enjoined restoration of the thing or payment of its full value.

Iudicium secutorium.

Since both these forms of procedure certainly existed at the time when Cicero pleaded the case for Caecina[2], the latter's adversary, Aebutius, had declined to adopt the first course and ask for an *arbiter*; this course, although the less perilous, admitted a weakness in the defendant's case, for the request for an *arbiter* was sometimes interpreted as an admission by the defendant that he ought to restore (*restituere se debere*), as a surrender, in fact, of the main issue and a descent to the subordinate question of 'restitution or damages[3].' Aebutius having adopted the heroic course, Caecina made a challenge to a *sponsio*, and it is to the third hearing of the case arising out of the *sponsio* that Cicero's speech belongs.

§ 6. *Defence; Exceptio; Praescriptio.*

We have now considered the main forms of action, whether guaranteed by law or by the praetor, which are of importance to a student of Ciceronian procedure. We

The main course of the trial.

[1] Gaius, iv. 165 'Sed actor sponsionis formulae subicit et aliud iudicium de re restituenda . . . ut, si sponsione vicerit, nisi ei res . . . restituatur, [*adversarius quanti ea res sit condemnetur.*']

[2] Cic. *pro Tull.* 23. 53 'Ego ipse tecto illo disturbato si hodie postulem, quod vi aut clam factum sit, tu aut per arbitrum restituas aut sponsione condemneris necesse est.'

[3] Gaius, iv. 163.

BOOK I. may now follow the course of the trial in its wider and more general aspects, such as the defence of the litigant, the representation of the parties, that dividing line between *ius* and *iudicium* known as the *litis contestatio*, the various modes in which a trial could be concluded without a full hearing, the qualifications of the *iudex* and the procedure in the *iudicium* itself, the modes of executing the sentence and the possibility of its reversal.

Defence; its character and result negative,

The defence pervades both stages of a Roman trial, that *in iure* and that *in iudicio*, and in both spheres it has a wholly negative object. In the proceedings before the praetor the right to bring the action at all can be contested by the defendant on technical grounds, and he can urge the magistrate to deny the *legis actio* or the *formula* (*denegatio actionis*[1]); if this attempt is ineffective and the case reaches the stage of the *iudicium*, the object of the defence is wholly to secure acquittal (*absolutio*) by the *iudex*. The acquittal of the defendant by no means implies the condemnation of the plaintiff, and so far has no positive effect; its usual result is the purely negative one of the maintenance of an already existing right. It is only in certain exceptional cases that the acquittal of one party necessarily implies some kind of condemnation of the other. This takes place when reciprocal or counter-claims are urged on either side. The *interdicta duplicia* such as those referring to *possessio*, the *iudicia duplicia* e.g. the actions for the division of an inheritance (*familiae herciscundae*) or for the demarcation of property (*finium regundorum*), perhaps certain suits in partnership (*pro socio*)—in all of which the litigants are at once plaintiffs and defendants—necessitate condemnation of some kind as a consequence of acquittal; and to a less extent the same might be true of those *bonae fidei iudicia* which raise an *actio contraria*[2].

except when counter-claims are urged.

[1] *Auct. ad Herenn.* ii. 12, 18 (cited p. 229, note 3). [2] p. 204.

The defence at both stages of the process may assume two forms; it may be (i) direct and (ii) indirect.

Direct defence—the denial of the *intentio*.

(i) A direct defence is the denial of the *intentio* of the *formula*, the attempted change of SI PARET into NON PARET. If the facts, on which the supposed right of the plaintiff is based, are successfully rebutted, the right itself is destroyed. The principle of Roman, as of every developed system of law, was to make the task of the defence as light as possible[1]. The burden of proof lies on the plaintiff, the *onus petitoris* is contrasted with the *commodum possessoris*[2], and all that is required for a successful defence of the direct kind is that the person actioned should show that the facts adduced by the plaintiff in support of his right do not continue to exist at the moment when the claim is urged.

Indirect defence—by *exceptio* or *praescriptio*.

(ii) The more indirect method of defence, that expressed in the *exceptio* or *praescriptio*, takes the form of a special plea by the defendant in bar of the plaintiff's suit. This method of defence attempts to show that, on certain special and sometimes technical grounds, the facts adduced by the plaintiff, although they might hold good in certain cases, do not apply to this particular case[3]. It is impossible, on purely logical grounds, to draw a distinction between this indirect method of defence and the direct method already considered: for the claim that 'the facts do not apply here' is the ground of every denial of an

[1] Cic. *Part. Orat.* 30, 104 'Nemo . . . eius, quod negat factum, potest, aut debet, aut solet reddere rationem.' Cf. Paulus in Dig. 22, 3, 2 'Ei incumbit probatio, qui dicit, non qui negat.'

[2] Ulpian in Dig. 43, 17, 1, 3.

[3] *Auct. ad Herenn.* ii. 12, 18 'Quaeritur in translationibus, primum, num aliquis eius rei actionem, petitionem aut persecutionem habeat . . . num alio modo, tempore, loco; num alia lege, num alio quaerente aut agente.' Savigny (*System*, v. p. 176) would confine the terms *translatio* and *translativa constitutio* (cf. *de Inv.* i. 8, 10; ii. 19, 20; *Auct. ad Herenn.* i. 12, 22) chiefly to the *exceptio* as embedded in the *formula* and as argued before a *iudex*. But the expressions as used by Cicero, and which belong perhaps to the technology of rhetoric rather than of law, seem to be equally applicable to pleas held valid by the praetor.

intentio. But there were reasons, historical and legal, why certain pleas in defence could be separated and classified apart from others. The philosophy of law, rightly or wrongly, professes to distinguish between the essence of a claim—that which is good in the majority of cases—and its incidental infringement in particular instances. The *exceptio* is an exposition of this second element, the accidental and the personal. Again, there are a certain number of objections, in the way of counter- or modifying claims, that can be definitely formulated as juristic objections *always* recognized by a court. Such pleas were formulated as exceptions by the praetor in his edict. Lastly, such modifications are often equitable infringements of a rule of strict law[1]; as such they often have a later historical origin than the *ius* which they impugn, and hence often seem to be something different from *ius*[2]. In Roman procedure the exceptions are praetorian modifications of civil or praetorian law.

Exceptiones a part of the formulary system.

The history of the exception only begins with the introduction of the formulary system; we are told by Gaius that the *legis actio* found no room for their employment[3]. There were, however, from very early times legal objections to claims, some of which were expressed in the *exceptiones* of later times. Thus the *lex Cincia* which limited the right of gift, and possibly the *lex Plaetoria* which protected minors who had been induced by fraud to enter

[1] Cic. *Part. Orat.* 28, 100 'de constituendis actionibus, accipiendis subeundisque iudiciis, de excipienda iniquitate actionis'; 29, 101 'quoniam semper is, qui defendit . . . resistat oportet . . . aut infitiando aut definiendo aut aequitate opponenda.'

[2] Gaius, iv. 116 'Comparatae sunt autem exceptiones defendendorum eorum gratia cum quibus agitur. Saepe enim accidit ut quis iure civili teneatur sed iniquum sit eum iudicio condemnari.' Hence the distinction between a *iudicium purum* and one with an *exceptio* added in Cic. *de Inv.* ii. 20, 60 ('is qui agit iudicium purum postulat; ille quicum agitur exceptionem addi ait oportere').

[3] Gaius, iv. 108 'Nec omnino ita, ut nunc, usus erat illis temporibus exceptionum.'

into a contract, might have been employed as a bar to an action even before the use of the *formula* was fully established. But it has been thought that in the old procedure such objections may have been considered either as *praeiudicia* to the main issue or as a ground for a *contravindicatio*. However considered, they were practically exceptions or praescriptions, although they may not have been called by either of these names.

Some appeared in the *album*, others were unwritten.

When writing became the main vehicle of civil procedure, they naturally took their place in the *formula*, for they were part of the complete statement of a case. The praetor's *album* was the first public document in which they made their appearance as exceptions [1]: but even this record gave no complete enumeration of the pleas of this kind which the praetor was willing to grant. Only some appeared in the *album* [2], but amongst these were probably all which were based on statute-law or its equivalent; others belonged to the category of what Cicero calls the ἄγραφον part of the edict [3]. They were granted by the praetor on the merits of the case: the grant was based on principles keenly felt by the judicial mind but much too vague to be stereotyped in writing. In so far as the *formula* was the praetor's own creation, all exceptions may be said to be a product of praetorian law, but not all were strictly parts of the *ius honorarium*; while some flowed from *lex* or other sources of the *ius civile*, the majority could trace their origin to the praetor's jurisdiction. Types of the first have already been furnished in the counter-pleas that were derived from the *lex Cincia* and the *lex Plaetoria*; it is possible that the Voconian law, whose

They spring both from the *ius civile* and from the *ius honorarium*.

[1] 'Praetoriae exceptiones' (*Auct. ad Herenn.* i. 12, 22; Cic. *de Inv.* ii. 19, 57).

[2] Gaius, iv. 118 'Exceptiones autem alias in edicto praetor habet propositas, alias causa cognita accommodat: quae omnes vel ex legibus, vel ex his quae legis vicem obtinent, substantiam capiunt, vel ex iurisdictione praetoris proditae sunt.'

[3] p. 122, note 2.

BOOK I.

provisions we have already considered[1], may have been similarly used as a bar to a claim for an inheritance which that law pronounced illegal. One of the meanings of Verres' decree[2] may have been to invite its use in this way: although its employment by a party as an exception would certainly not have been essential to its work. Even were the inheritance not contested, the praetor might have refused to grant it to the unqualified person on the ground of the prohibition of the law. Typical instances of the second kind of exception—those based on the jurisdiction of the praetor—are the pleas against fraud (*dolus*), intimidation (*metus*), and the constant exception which asserts the finality of a *iudicium* based on the *imperium* of the praetor (*exceptio rei iudicatae vel in iudicium deductae*[3]).

Form of the exception.

The exception is always a sentence that conditions the condemnation, but the form in which it is expressed is very varied. It may commence with the words *extra quam si* or *praeter quam si, si non, quod non*, &c. The insertion or refusal of such a saving clause was often of such vital importance to the merits of a case that no contest in the proceedings before the praetor was more ardent than that which centred round the granting of an exception[4], and a higher authority was sometimes called in to veto the *formula* in which the praetor would not permit the desired clause to appear[5]. The usual place of the *exceptio* in the *formula* is just before the *condemnatio* which it conditions, e.g. the *exceptio pacti conventi*, by which a legal claim was disallowed in consequence of an agreement between

Its place in the *formula*.

[1] p. 95.

[2] Cic. *in Verr.* i. 44, 113. See p. 96.

[3] Gaius, iv. 107. Cf. Cic. *de Orat.* i. 37, 168, 'quod ea res in indicium antea venisset.' See p. 247, note 1.

[4] Cic. *de Inv.* ii. 20, 60. See p. 230, note 2.

[5] Cic. *Acad. Prior.* ii. 30, 97 'postulant ut excipiantur haec inexplicabilia. Tribunum aliquem censeo adeant (*al.* videant): a me istam exceptionem nunquam impetrabunt.'

the parties, would appear in this manner in the *formula* of the *condictio certi.*

SI PARET NUMERIUM NEGIDIUM AULO AGERIO CENTUM DARE OPORTERE,

SI INTER AULUM AGERIUM ET NUMERIUM NEGIDIUM NON CONVENIT NE EA PECUNIA PETERETUR,

IUDEX, NUMERIUM NEGIDIUM AULO AGERIO IN CENTUM CONDEMNA, SI NON PARET ABSOLVE.

The *praescriptio.*

But what was practically an exception might appear before the *intentio,* in which case the qualifying clause was known as a *praescriptio.* This was perhaps the normal place for the exception in the early history of the *formula,* reflecting as it did the *praeiudicium* to which such objections may have led in the time of the *legis actio.* The place of the praescription in the *formula*[1] seems to show that it was considered by the *iudex* first; if he decided in favour of the party who urged it, there would be no further cognizance of the case. It is true that the exceptions gradually developed by the praetor were too intimately connected with the facts of the case itself to be separated from them; hence their insertion in the body of the *formula*; but those of early times were often of a far-reaching character which might be decided separately as praescriptions. Such were those which provided that a chief and more important issue should be decided before a subordinate issue: an application of this principle was the rule that a civil action should not prejudice a capital case, e.g. that a civil action for the recovery of extorted money should not precede the criminal *quaestio repetundarum,* or that an *actio iniuriarum* should not lead to a sentence which might be interpreted as a *praeiudicium* on an impending criminal trial for *vis.* Yet some such provisos, which may have been praescriptions in early times, had by Cicero's day followed the analogy of the

[1] Gaius, iv. 132 'Praescriptiones sic appellatas esse ab eo quod ante formulas praescribuntur, plus quam manifestum est.'

BOOK I. ordinary praetorian exceptions and taken their place before the *condemnatio* of the *formula*. As an exception Cicero quotes the ruling:—

EXTRA QUAM IN REUM CAPITIS PRAEIUDICIUM FIAT[1].

Peremptory and dilatory exceptions.

Later jurisprudence divides exceptions into those which are peremptory and those which are dilatory (*peremptoriae, dilatoriae*). The first for ever exclude the success of an action against which they are urged; such are those of *metus, dolus, res iudicata*, or one based on an agreement (*pactum*) between the parties that the recovery of a certain sum of money should never be sought. The second are those which injure the plaintiff's case only for a time, e.g. one based on an agreement between the parties that the recovery of a certain sum of money should not be sought for five years[2]. This distinction is of the utmost importance for the use of the exception in any given case; but of greater import, perhaps, for its theory is the distinction between exceptions based on matter and those based on form. To the former belongs such an exception as that based on the *pactum de non petendo*; it is grounded on a fact intimately connected with the case itself and may be perpetual or temporal in its working; those based on form, i.e. far-reaching technical objections, are by their very nature perpetual[3]. Such are the *exceptio praeiudicii* mentioned by Cicero[4], and the *exceptiones cognitoriae*[5], which are aimed against improper representation on the part of the adversary according to the rules which we shall soon describe. It is these technical objections that cause the shifting of a case from one

[1] Cic. *de Inv.* ii. 20, 59. See p. 180.

[2] Gaius, iv. 120–122.

[3] i.e. they are perpetual as long as the improper course against which they are aimed is persisted in. In so far as the course can be remedied they may be *dilatoriae exceptiones*; e.g. suppose a man to whom the edict does not permit representation gives a *cognitor* 'si obiiciatur exceptio cognitoria, si ipse talis erit ut ei non liceat cognitorem dare, ipse agere potest' (Gaius, iv. 124).

[4] note 1.

[5] Gaius, l. c.

jurisdiction, from one *formula* and from one time to another. Hence the name *translationes* given to them in the technology of rhetoric by writers such as Cicero and Quintilian[1].

Translationes.

All exceptions, if held by the court to be valid, produce the same effect, i.e. the acquittal of the defendant. And this acquittal is not merely operative for this particular *iudicium*, but holds good for any other in which the same issue is raised. The finality of the valid exception is due to the finality of the sentence of a *iudex*, for the merits of the exception included in the *formula* are decided after the *litis contestatio* and in the *iudicium*.

Exceptions, if valid, produce acquittal.

§ 7. *Representation.*

Representation in process was, as we have seen[2], held to have been unknown in the system of the *legis actio* except in certain special cases. But the principle that every litigant must appear personally in court to urge or defend his rights was one that could not possibly be maintained as Rome became first Italy and then a large portion of the world and Romans intent on trade penetrated beyond the limits of their own empire. It has been thought, however, that the first relaxation of the rigour of the older rule proceeded not from the necessities of business but from consideration for age or infirmity. We hear of an equitable rule, expressed in technical language, which may be the fragment of a law:—

Gradual recognition of the principle of representation.

UT MAIOR ANNIS LX. ET CUI MORBUS CAUSA EST, COGNITOREM DET[3].

But a more general extension of the system was essential, and this found expression in the praetor's edict and accompanied the formulary procedure. The praetor's rules specifying the qualifications of such representatives and

[1] See p. 229, note 2; and cf. Quint. *Inst. Or.* iii. 6, 46; 52; 60; 68–72.

[2] pp. 59 and 146.

[3] *Auct. ad Herenn.* ii. 13, 20. See Bethmann-Hollweg, ii. p. 417.

BOOK I.

expressed in the edict *de postulando* have already been mentioned[1]. It remains to consider the forms which this representation took and the principles by which it was regulated.

The *cognitor*.

The most purely judicial representative at Rome was the *cognitor*[2], for he was appointed for a special case and with certain formalities. The litigant gave him his mandate in the presence of the adversary, to whom he uttered certain formal words. But this *formula* need not contain a specification of the case, need not even declare whether it was a personal or a real action. According to Gaius, when the *cognitor* was given by the plaintiff the words

QUOD EGO TECUM AGERE VOLO, IN EAM REM COGNITOREM DO,

were sufficient. When he was presented by the defendant the equally simple phrase

QUIA TU MECUM AGERE VIS, IN EAM REM COGNITOREM DO,

was all that was required[3]. It is not known whether a minuter specification of the issue was needed in the Ciceronian period. The presence of the *cognitor* himself was not required when this announcement was made; but he did not become a representative until he had heard of the mandate and taken the first step in the execution of his office[4]. Any objection which the adversary may have to his assumption of these duties need not be stated at once; there was, in fact, no ground for such a statement, for the *status* and personality of the absent *cognitor* might be wholly unknown at the moment of his appointment. But the adversary's tacit consent to this appointment did not hinder him from subsequently urging objections,

[1] p. 147.

[2] For the ultimate meaning 'one who knows, is informed or is instructed,' see Cic. *Div. in Caec.* 4, 11 ('Siculi universi . . . me cognitorem iuris sui . . . esse voluerunt'), Hor. *Sat.* ii. 5, 34 ('Ius anceps novi, causas defendere possum'), Bethmann-Hollweg, ii. p. 419.

[3] Gaius, iv. 83.

[4] *ib.* 'Nec interest praesens an absens cognitor detur; sed, si absens datus fuerit, cognitor ita erit si cognoverit et susceperit officium cognitoris.'

expressed in an *exceptio cognitoria*, against the propriety of this particular individual claiming, in violation of the praetorian rulings, to be the accredited representative of another.

The principle underlying the office of *cognitor* is that of occasional delegation. But the varying interests which centred in the capital of the world and had their ramifications in every province, the growing complexity of business even more than the increasing subtlety of the law, rendered it essential that a class of men should spring up, alert, quick-witted and versed in the practice of the courts, who should treat the office in a professional spirit and live on its emoluments. The *cognitor* bears a much greater resemblance to the modern attorney than the unpaid and powerful *advocatus* who, for political or social reasons, treats a favoured party to his advice. Honesty and efficiency were doubtless as essential to success in this as in any other business; but the Dodson and Fogg of the profession are alone known to us from Ciceronian literature. What Aebutius might have been, had he been Cicero's client, we cannot say; as Caecina's opponent he figures as 'a hanger on of women, a widow's attorney, a pettifogging defender in the courts ever ready for a legal squabble, a person whom men think dull and stupid but women imagine to be a learned and brilliant lawyer[1].'

The procurator.

A much more informal representative was the *procurator*. The word itself simply means 'agent,' and a wealthy Roman might have many procurators governing his numerous estates. As a local or occasional agent he was often a slave and might be sold with the estate which he administered. But by the Ciceronian period the word had come to be peculiarly applied to the general agent (*procurator omnium rerum*) whom the Roman left behind when he quitted the limits of Italy on business or on the

[1] Cic. *pro Caec.* 5, 14.

service of the state[1]. It was important that this general agent should be a free or at least a freed man, for otherwise he could not undertake the representation of his *dominus* in a court of law. The mandate that this representative has is general and does not require any official expression in a particular case. It is enough for him to represent himself as the general agent of another to be admitted as a litigant; but his mandate is by no means so definite as that of the *cognitor*. He is treated by the praetor as a far more independent personality and has to undertake graver responsibilities.

In the time of Gaius there was a third type of representative in the person of the *procurator* other than the general agent, who was appointed or presented himself for service in a special case, the so-called *procurator litis*[2]. But this mode of representation seems to have been unknown in Cicero's time; from a passage in his speech for Roscius the actor, he appears to know of no mode of special representation other than that by the *cognitor*[3].

Problem of representation, to secure the effective fulfilment of the judgement.

The great problem of representation at Rome was to secure unity of responsibility for the carrying-out of the judgement. The responsibility must rest either on the representer or the represented. The praetor's object was to make it rest on the one or the other, and he secured it, as we shall see, in a different way for the *cognitor* and the *procurator*. For the carrying out of the judgement at all, it must be accepted as final; there must be no renewal

[1] Cic. *pro Caec.* 20, 57 'qui legitime procurator dicitur omnium rerum eius, qui in Italia non sit absitve rei publicae causa, quasi quidam paene dominus, hoc est, alieni iuris vicarius.' Cf. *pro Quinct.* 19, 62 'At quis erat procurator?... Eques Romanus locuples, sui negotii bene gerens: denique is quem, quotiens Naevius in Galliam profectus est, procuratorem Romae reliquit.'

[2] Gaius, iv. 84.

[3] Cic. *pro Rosc. com.* 18, 53 'Quid interest inter eum, qui per se litigat, et eum, qui cognitor est datus? Qui per se litem contestatur, sibi soli petit: alteri nemo potest nisi qui cognitor est factus.' So the *procurator* of *ad Fam.* vii. 32, 1 (p. 59, note 2) must be one *omnium rerum*.

of the action by the *dominus* after the right of action by his representative has been consumed by the case having once entered the stage of the *iudicium*.

Finality of the judgement secured by the structure of the *formula*.

Effective provision was made for the observance of this second principle by the structure of the *formula*. The *intentio* refers to the *dominus*,—the only possibly correct mode of reference, for it is the *dominus* who *ex hypothesi* has incurred, or is to benefit by, the obligation,—but the *condemnatio* always contains the name of the representative, of the man who has accepted the *iudicium*[1]. To quote the instance supplied by Gaius:—If Lucius Titius has appeared as representative of the plaintiff, the *formula* will run,

SI PARET NUMERIUM NEGIDIUM PUBLIO MAEVIO SESTERTIUM X MILLIA DARE OPORTERE, IUDEX NUMERIUM NEGIDIUM LUCIO TITIO SESTERTIUM X MILLIA CONDEMNA; SI NON PARET, ABSOLVE[2].

Conversely, if Lucius Titius appears as representative of the defendant, the *formula* will be,

SI PARET NUMERIUM NEGIDIUM PUBLIO MAEVIO SESTERTIUM X MILLIA DARE OPORTERE, IUDEX LUCIUM TITIUM PUBLIO MAEVIO SESTERTIUM X MILLIA CONDEMNA; SI NON PARET, ABSOLVE.

The obligation in both cases has been transferred from the represented to the representative; but it is the same obligation, renewed but not changed. Like the simple obligation of the *dominus* it is, therefore, utterly destroyed by passing the stage of the *litis contestatio*, and cannot be revived. The consequences of this consumption of the action are naturally different in the case of the plaintiff and the defendant.

Effects of the consumption of the action,

(i) If we take first the case in which the plaintiff is represented, we must draw a distinction between the more perfect mode of representation by the *cognitor* and that, resting on a less perfect mandate, which is characteristic of the *procurator omnium rerum*. When the *cognitor*

in the case of the *cognitor*,

[1] 'qui iudicem accepit' (Gaius, iv. 87).

[2] Gaius, iv. 86.

has been appointed and has represented, the right of action is entirely lost by the *dominus*—in the case of a civil action, *ipso iure*; in the case of a praetorian by the exception *rei iudicatae* or *in iudicium deductae.* No extraordinary security for the satisfaction of the judgement need, therefore, be demanded from the representative or the person represented. On the other hand, when representation takes the less perfect and specific form of that exercised by the *procurator*, the right of action by the *dominus* is not held to be consumed; the danger that he may raise the same issue again in another *iudicium* can only be met by the *procurator* being made, when he undertakes the case, to give security *ratam rem dominum habiturum*[1], or, as the phrase sometimes ran in Cicero's time, *amplius eo nomine neminem, cuius petitio sit, petiturum*[2]. This security (*cautio*) is, in fact, the substitute for the consumption of the right of action, and the necessity for furnishing it shows how little the *procurator* is regarded as a true delegate, fully recognized as such by the court. Circumstances forced the praetor to accept him as a representative, and rules were framed in the edict to make him as truly a representative, as nearly a delegate as possible. A later form of this ruling was probably as follows:—

in that of the *procurator*. Security required from the latter that the action will not be renewed.

The praetor's ruling on this point.

Cuius nomine quis actionem dari sibi postulabit, is eum viri boni arbitratu defendat: et ei, quocum aget, quo nomine aget id ratum habere eum ad quem ea res pertinet, boni viri arbitratu satisdet[3].

The first clause enacts that any one who, as a *procurator*, represents another as plaintiff shall also represent him as defendant; it is a rule framed mainly in the interest

[1] Gaius, iv. 98 'Procurator vero si agat, satisdare iubetur ratam rem dominum habiturum; periculum enim est ne iterum dominus de eadem re experiatur; quod periculum non intervenit si per cognitorem actum fuit, quia, de qua re quisque per cognitorem egerit, de ea non magis amplius actionem habet quam si ipse egerit.'

[2] Cic. *Brut.* 5, 18 (cited p. 241, note 1).

[3] Lenel, *Ed. Perp.* p. 81.

of the absent *dominus*, but it also assists the possible plaintiff by preventing the delay in the prosecution of his rights which might result from the absence of the defendant. The latter clause is wholly in the interest of the adversary; it enacts that the *procurator* should furnish the security, of which we have spoken, that the person represented should hold his acts good.

In representation for the defence, guarantee required that the obligation will be fulfilled.

(ii) In the case of a representative's appearing for the defence, the result of the consumption of the action, whether it go well or ill, is inevitably the complete liberation of the represented debtor and his securities (*sponsores*), if he have any, from all obligation to pay to the plaintiff; for the *condemnatio*, which has now become valid by the sentence of a *iudex*, has transferred the obligation of paying the debt entirely to the *cognitor* or *procurator*. The question is, 'how shall these representatives be bound to fulfil the obligation which has been transferred to them?' Here again the solution is different in the case of the *cognitor* and the *procurator*.

Satisdatio iudicatum solvi.

In both cases the guarantee for the fulfilment of the contract is the security which, in cases of representation, must be furnished that the judgement debt will be paid (*satisdatio iudicatum solvi*). But while, in the case of the *cognitor*, the *dominus* who formally appoints him furnishes this security, in the case of procuratorial representation it is the *procurator*—the representative of an absent man—who must give it[1].

Passages in Cicero illustrating these principles.

There are some interesting passages of Cicero which throw light on some of the above-mentioned points in the procuratorial representation of his time. He desires

[1] Gaius, iv. 101; cf. Cic. *Brut.* 4, 17, and 5, 18. Here Brutus has metaphorically declared himself the procurator of another seeking a promised discussion. The answer is, 'At . . . tibi ego, Brute, non solvam nisi prius a te cavero amplius eo nomine neminem, cuius petitio sit, petiturum.' The passage illustrates the individual responsibility of the *procurator*, although the *cautio de rato* here mentioned was no doubt extra-judicial. For a similar use of the formula AMPLIUS [A SE] NEMINEM PETITURUM, see *pro Rosc. com.* 12, 35.

on one occasion to enforce a claim against P. Cornelius Dolabella, his son-in-law, and reach his sureties (*sponsores*) in the background[1]. But the man whose sureties had been successfully sued, and who had paid up for him, was *infamis*: and this consequence Cicero wishes to avoid. It could be avoided by introducing *procuratores* for the defence. The procurators of the individual sureties would now be condemned in their own name, and the sureties are liberated by the fact of *their* not having entered in their own names on the *litis contestatio*. The procurators must, of course, look to be recouped by Dolabella himself; they are practically his own agents, though technically the representatives of the sureties. The primary motive of this procedure is to prevent the sureties appearing as defendants in their own name; by this means the *ignominia* that would fall on the main debtor for whom his sureties had paid (an ignominy comparable to that consequent on bankruptcy) would be avoided.

In one of the early stages of the case which Cicero pleaded for Quinctius we find an instance of a disputed obligation of a *procurator* which could hardly have arisen in the procedure of later times. After the *missio in possessionem* against Quinctius had been granted Alfenus suddenly appears as his defender and is ready to contest the validity of the writ. The demand is made that he should give *satisdatio iudicatum solvi*, and is met by the singular reply that, if the principal need not give it, it need not be furnished by the *procurator*[2]. If the

[1] Cic. *ad Att.* xvi. 15, 2 'Possumus enim, ut sponsores (of Dolabella) appellemus, procuratorem (*al.* procuratores) introducere (for the defence). Neque enim illi (the sureties) litem contestabuntur: quo facto non sum nescius sponsores liberari. Sed et illi turpe arbitror eo nomine, quod satisdato debeat, procuratores eius non dissolvere, et nostrae gravitatis ius nostrum sine summa illius ignominia persequi.'

[2] Cic. *pro Quinct.* 7, 29 'Negat Alfenus aequum esse procuratorem satisdare quod reus satisdare non deberet.'

satisdatio in question is the one that was customary in the representation of later times; if it was asked for in the name of Alfenus, not in that of Quinctius; if its ground was that Quinctius was being represented, not that Quinctius had been declared a bankrupt—the only possible conclusion is that in Cicero's time the necessity for security in representation was still a disputed principle.

§ 8. *The litis contestatio.*

Reference has already been made on several occasions to that stage in the process of a Roman civil trial which was known as the *litis contestatio,* and some of its occasional effects have already been described. It now remains to examine more closely into the nature and consequences of this dividing line between the proceedings *in iure* and those *in iudicio.*

Essential feature and origin of the *litis contestatio*.

Its essential feature was the acceptance of and submission to a *iudicium* on the part of both plaintiff and defendant[1]: and in early times this acceptance was marked by a solemn formal act, which gave its name to this stage in the procedure. When the *iudicium* had been ordained, each party called on witnesses (presumably on some or on all of those whom he had summoned to give evidence in his cause) and bade them take cognizance of the fact that a *iudex* had been proposed and accepted. The *formula* in which they made this appeal commenced with the words TESTES ESTOTE[2]. This procedure evidently

[1] Cic. *pro Rosc. com.* 11, 32 'Lite contestata, iudicio damni iniuria constituto'; 12, 35 'iste cum eo litem contestatam habebat.' *ad Att.* xvi. 15, 2 (quoted p. 242, note 1). Cf. *Lex Rubria,* c. 20 'nisei iei, quos inter id iudicium accipietur leisve contestabitur'; Festus, p. 273 'Gallus Aelius . . . ait: Reus est qui cum altero litem contestatam habet, sive is egit, sive cum eo actum est.'

[2] Festus, p. 38 'Contestari est cum uterque reus dicit *testes estote*'; p. 57 'Contestari litem dicuntur duo aut plures adversarii, quod ordinato iudicio utraque pars dicere solet *testes estote*.'

BOOK I. dates from the days of the *legis actio*, but we have no warrant for believing that it was a characteristic of that procedure as such. The *legis actio* must in the earliest times have sometimes been completed without the intervention of any *iudex* or *iudices*; but the *litis contestatio* was, so far as we know, always associated with the ordinance of a *iudicium*. It was probably an inevitable accompaniment of any *legis actio* that led to a *iudicium*—its employment being due to the fact that, before writing was applied to procedure, it was important to secure personal evidence to the break in the continuity of the trial, to the fact that the case had now been taken out of the hands of a magistrate and transferred to those of a *iudex* or a college of judges. It is very probable that, as the formulary procedure developed, this ceremonial was still for a time employed, and it may have been used in the transitional period of Cicero's day; like other verbal utterances, it may have survived as an echo of the *legis actio*. Under the increased influence of written procedure it finally disappeared, but the transition from *ius* to *iudicium* was still known as *litis contestatio*, and was followed by very important consequences.

Its consequence; impossibility of the renewal of the action.

The most vital consequence is that the trial has now reached a stage at which recall by the parties with a view to a subsequent renewal of the case, under the same or some other form, becomes impossible; once let the case enter the hands of a *iudex* and it is as unalterable as the *res iudicata* itself, unless, indeed, magisterial authority intervenes and takes the case from the *iudex* before the sentence is pronounced. Unless this extraordinary procedure is adopted, his cognizance and his sentence are final.

Theory of the finality of a judgement.

The finality to the parties of the *litis contestatio* (i. e. of submission to a *iudicium*) seems to be a somewhat illogical reflex of the finality of a *res iudicata*, but no satisfactory theory (other than that of mere convenience) has ever been assigned for this Roman principle of the finality of a judgement, which has had such an immense influence on the procedure of the modern world. It dates from the time of the *legis actio*, for Gaius tells us that in those days no case once decided could possibly be renewed[1]. We should like to know whether Gaius is speaking of the *legis actio* simply or of the *legis actio* which leads to a *iudicium*. In the former case it might be a matter of pure law (*ius*), in the latter it might be due to the introduction of the popular element, the presence of a *iudex* or *iudices*. It is hard to base this unalterability on a principle of law, for the ruling of a magistrate may be upset at any moment by the use of the intercession. If it only existed when the *iudex* was present, it might give some support to the theory that reference to the *iudex* is in the nature of an appeal to the people and, like the *provocatio* in criminal jurisdiction, unalterable. But the principle is perhaps a convention (which may or may not have been expressed in statute law) due to the sense of the utter confusion and uncertainty that would have resulted if it had been possible for a case, after a decision or at *any* stage in the decision, to have been raised again or to have been withdrawn and renewed. But the idea of a mere convention, even when based on obvious grounds of public utility, could not satisfy the scientific thought of Rome. The only thing that should be finally and absolutely binding was an obligation between the parties, and, probably at an early date, there was developed the fiction that with the *litis contestatio* there took place a renewal (*novatio*) of the original obligation, and that, with the pronouncement of the sentence, a second novation occurred. The contract had from the debtor's standpoint originally been one *dare oportere*, after the *litis contestatio* it becomes one *condemnari oportere*, after the sentence it takes the third form of

Idea of the *litis contestatio* being the renewal of an obligation.

[1] Gaius, iv. 108 'qua de re actum semel erat, de ea postea ipso iure agi non poterat.'

BOOK I.

iudicatum facere oportere[1]. All these obligations are, of course, conditional, for even the *iudicatum facere oportere* may still be contested by the condemned person in an *actio iudicati*.

The ground for finality differs with the source of the action.

We have already seen how the finality of this renewed obligation varied according to the nature of the *iudicium*[2], whether this nature were determined by the authority which constituted the court or by the class of objects with which it dealt. The variation is one of the expressions of the difference between a *iudicium legitimum*, which is *ipso iure* extinctive of a claim, and the *iudicium quod imperio continetur*, which can only become extinctive through the use of the exception *rei iudicatae vel in iudicium deductae*[3]. With the latter class of *iudicia* are associated, from this point of view, all *actiones in rem*[4]. They are not *ipso iure* extinctive, but can only be made so by the use of one of these two parts of the exception. No historical reason can be assigned for this classification; it is not, however, anomalous, because it clearly expresses the theory of novation as expounded by Gaius, this theory being strictly appropriate only to personal actions, which begin with the idea of a *debitum*. The classification must be at least as old as the *formula*, and seems to hint at the great antiquity of the theory of novation as employed to explain the finality of a judgement.

Actions based on the *imperium* and real actions must be barred by the exception *rei iudicatae vel in iudicium deductae*.

Of the two clauses of the exception, which enforce finality

[1] Gaius, iii. 180 'Tollitur adhuc obligatio litis contestatione, si modo legitimo iudicio fuerit actum. Nam tunc obligatio quidem principalis dissolvitur, incipit autem teneri reus litis contestatione: sed, si condemnatus sit, sublata litis contestatione, incipit ex causa iudicati teneri. Et hoc est quod apud veteres scriptum est: ante litem contestatam dare debitorem oportere; post litem contestatam condemnari oportere; post condemnationem iudicatum facere oportere.'

[2] p. 140.

[3] Lenel (*Ed. Perp.* p. 404) shows ground for believing that the 'exceptio rei iudicatae vel in iudicium deductae' (Gaius, iii. 181; iv. 106, 107, 121) formed but a single exception, both clauses being employed even when a *res iudicata* had not been reached.

[4] Gaius, iv. 107.

when it is not a consequence of the law, the first is obviously intended to apply when a trial has run its full course and attained the desired end of a *iudicatum*. The second, which Cicero expresses in the form *Quod ea res in iudicium antea venisset*[1], assumes that the trial has stopped short at some point before its normal close. It was employed when the sentence had not been, or could not be, pronounced. In the first case it implies that the *litis contestatio* is over, that the *iudicium* has been constituted but has not yet pronounced, that the suit is pending; in the second it implies, not only that the *litis contestatio* is over, but that the *iudicium* is dead. The plaintiff has in some way neglected to pursue his right of action and the time of pendency has expired. A limit of pendency was, in the Republic, fixed only for praetorian actions; the suit expired with the magistracy of the praetor who had given the *iudicium*[2].

Renewed action forbidden *de eadem re*.

Whether the renewal of an action was averted *ipso iure* or by the employment of this exception, the effect of *litis contestatio* was the same. With the passage of this stage in the procedure a principle became operative which is expressed in the maxim *bis de eadem re agere non licere*, i.e. that 'the same thing' (*eadem res*) could not again be brought into court. It was of the utmost importance for praetor and *iudex* to determine when a subject was 'the same'; but no complete definition of the identity of a claim appears in juristic writings; no such definition, applicable at once to real and personal actions, could probably be framed. The specifications in the *intentio* of the *formula* were too vague to make them always a determinant, to

Grounds of the identity of a claim.

[1] Cic. *de Orat.* i. 37, 168 'ne exceptione excluderetur, quod ea res in iudicium antea venisset.' Lenel (l. c.) thinks that the words here are not formal and simply state the ground of the exception.

[2] Gaius, iv. 105 'tamdiu valent, quamdiu is qui ea praecepit imperium habebit.' The *lex Iulia iudiciaria* first fixed a limit of pendency (eighteen months) for *iudicia legitima* (Gaius, iv. 104). See p. 141 and the probable limitation to the employment of this *exceptio* noted there.

make it possible to say that a case is renewed simply because it rests on an old *intentio*. For instance, in real actions, ownership alone is stated as the *causa petendi*, but ownership alone does not show the mode of acquisition, which is the decisive point: in personal actions the special cause of the debt (*causa debendi*) need not be mentioned at all in the *formula*, and the *debitum* which is mentioned may arise from many different causes, each of which is, from a juristic point of view, the basis of a different claim. Speaking generally, we may say that, besides the obvious necessity for the identity of the persons or their representatives, for *in rem actiones* the identity of the thing and that of the particular claim at law were decisive, for personal actions the ground of the obligation (*causa debendi*) was the determinant. The formal failures in the statement of an action, which might lead to its consumption, have already been stated in the discussion of the technical dangers which beset the formulary system [1].

Effects of *litis contestatio* for plaintiff and defendant.

The effect of the *litis contestatio* is, for the plaintiff, that he cannot renew the action, for the defendant, that, if condemned, he must satisfy the judgement. As a rule, no antecedent measures are taken to assist in the fulfilment of these results; but in certain exceptional cases regulations of a penalizing character were framed to bind either plaintiff or defendant to these engagements. The means adopted of securing obedience to the contractual relation implied in the *litis contestatio* take the form of forcing one of the parties to furnish security (*satisdare*) by means of a *stipulatio* that the action will not be renewed or that the result of the judgement will be fulfilled. These agreements were published by the praetor in his edict and were granted on the request of a party when the occasions for their adoption arose and the special grounds for enforcing them were present (*praetoriae stipulationes*).

These obligations sometimes strengthened by security.

We have already seen such a stipulation applied in

[1] pp. 175–177.

certain cases of representation; it must be made by the *procurator* to render improbable a renewal of the action by the *dominus*. The security here given is to the effect *amplius eo nomine neminem petiturum*[1]. The amount of the *cautio* was generally fixed at the full value of the suit as determined by the *condemnatio* or the *iudex* (*quanti interest, quanti ea res erit*).

Security required from the plaintiff;

The defendant is only in exceptional circumstances bound by a stipulation that he would carry out the judgement. It is employed in cases where, without this sanction, a fulfilment of the *iudicatum* might be doubtful and is, in this connexion, known as *satisdatio iudicatum solvi*. The requirement of this security may depend either on the nature of the case or on the personality of the defendant.

from the defendant: *satisdatio iudicatum solvi*.

In all *in rem actiones* such a security had always been demanded from the *interim* possessor of the object in dispute, the ground for it being that, if the possessor was vanquished and would neither restore the thing itself nor submit to the *litis aestimatio*, the winner of the case should have the privilege of a renewed action with him or with his sureties (*sponsores*) on the ground of the security. In the *legis actio* such caution had been represented by the *praedes litis et vindiciarum*[2]; in the action *per sponsionem praeiudicialem* by the *stipulatio pro praede litis et vindiciarum*[3], and in the *formula petitoria* by the *satisdatio*

In real actions security demanded of the *interim* possessor.

[1] Cic. *Brut.* 5, 18 (see p. 241, note). A similar security is given by a partner representing a firm, when he accepts satisfaction on behalf of all its members. He gives a guarantee that no further action will lie. See Cic. *pro Rosc. com.* 12, 35 'Nam ego Roscium, si quid communi nomine tetigit, confiteor praestare debere societati. Societatis, non suas lites redemit, cum fundum a Flavio accepit. Quid ita satis non dedit *amplius* [*a se*] *neminem petiturum*? (the *a se* of the *formula*, if genuine here, refers, of course, to the debtor of the estate). Qui de sua parte decidit, reliquis integram relinquit actionem: qui pro sociis transigit, satisdat neminem eorum postea petiturum.' Cicero mentions a stipulation of the kind in the case of a claim for an inheritance brought by a corporation against an individual (Cic. *in Verr.* ii. 23, 55 'rogant eum . . . ab sese caveat (take security) . . . de illa hereditate . . . neminem esse acturum.'

[2] pp. 57 and 185. [3] p. 190.

BOOK I.

iudicatum solvi[1]. In the *interdictum uti possidetis* the place of this security is taken by the *stipulatio fructuaria*[2].

Cases in which it is demanded of defendants in personal actions.

In *in personam actiones*, when the defendant appears in person, such security is required in cases where the defendant's position or personality can fairly be viewed with suspicion. This suspicion may be aroused by the kind of action in which he is now engaged or by some conduct of his in the past[3].

When a debtor contests the claims of his own *sponsores* in an *actio depensi*, or a sentence that has already been pronounced (*actio iudicati*), he can do so only by furnishing security *iudicatum solvi*. In early times such debtors had been subject to summary arrest and imprisonment and were only permitted defence through a *vindex*[4], and the later *satisdatio* here replaces the earlier subjection to the *manus iniectio*.

Previous conduct in business and in the courts might also render a defendant suspect (*suspecta persona*). A bankrupt (*decoctor*), however innocent his failure may have been, had to furnish this security on his defence; and the same compulsion was imposed on a defendant who, like Cicero's client Quinctius, had had his goods possessed for thirty days and put up for sale by the praetor's order on the ground that he had been undefended (*indefensus*) in an action brought against him[5].

But it is generally representation that calls forth such security from the defence. It is demanded by a universal principle when a *defensor* appears for a defendant, on the ground that the actual debtor is, through representation,

[1] p. 193. [2] p. 222.

[3] Gaius, iv. 102 'satisdationum duplex causa est; nam aut propter genus actionis satisdatur, aut propter personam, quia suspecta sit: propter genus actionis, velut iudicati depensive; . . . propter personam, velut si cum eo agitur qui decoxerit, cuiusve bona a creditoribus possessa proscriptave sunt.'

[4] Gaius, iv. 25 'iudicatus et is pro quo depensum est . . . vindicem dare debebant, et, nisi darent, domum ducebantur.'

[5] Cic. *pro Quinct.* 8, 30; 27, 84.

freed from responsibility for the debt. But the mode of defence makes, as we have seen, a difference to the incidence of the security[1]. The *dominus* gives it for the *cognitor*, but the *procurator* furnishes it himself. PART II.

In these instances of *satisdatio iudicatum solvi* furnished by the defence the amount of caution is the *quanti interest* of the plaintiff—i. e. the sum fixed in the condemnation, or, when this is uncertain, the amount decided by the *iudex*.

§ 9. *Confession.*

The three modes in which a trial can be brought to a conclusion without a thorough hearing and a careful estimate of evidence are the confession of the defendant, his neglect of a proper defence, and the taking by either party of an oath which refers to the matter in dispute and has been proffered by the adversary.

Confessio in iure. The nature of confession in court (*confessio in iure*) is known to us for the Ciceronian period by the happy preservation of certain clauses of the *lex Rubria* referring to jurisdiction in Cisalpine Gaul. From the careful wording of one of these clauses we gather that a person is *confessus* when he personally admits in court (*in iure*) before the competent magistrate (*quei ibei iure deicundo praerit*) to the plaintiff or his representative (*ei quei eam petet aut iei quoius nomine ab eo petetur*) everything that the plaintiff maintains as the ground of his action. The ground may be that of an *in rem actio*, and here the defendant admits that the thing is the property of the plaintiff (*eius eam rem esse*); in a personal action he confesses *dare, facere, praestare restituereve oportere*: in the case of a penal action that he has been guilty of the delict or is bound to repair the damage (*se fecisse obligatumve se eius rei noxsiaeve esse*[2]).

[1] p. 241.

[2] *Lex Rubria*, c. 22. The separate clauses are not strictly relative to personal and real actions respectively; *praestare restituereve* may refer to

The *confessus* is *pro iudicato*. Effects of confession in the *legis actio* probably final.

The general principle which determines the consequences of such statements is that confession counts as condemnation in a *iudicium*; the *confessus* is *pro iudicato*.

It is probable that in early times a very literal interpretation was given to this rule. In the *in rem actio*, as both parties were plaintiffs, a refusal to adopt the *contravindicatio* was regarded as a confession of the adversary's claim, and the *addictio* of the thing to the adversary was an immediate consequence of this refusal [1]. In personal actions the *aeris confessi* are put side by side with the *iudicati* as subject to execution by the *manus iniectio*, and the first class may designate, not nexal debtors, but those who have confessed to a debt in court [2]. This principle, as applied to real actions, must have survived in the Ciceronian period; a refusal to contravindicate must have been followed by loss of one's case in the centumviral court, although it is doubtful whether we should treat this refusal as a confession or as an absence of defence. Whether the result of confession in a *legis actio in personam* could lead to immediate condemnation in the Ciceronian period is rendered extremely doubtful by the uncertainty whether such an action survived in its pure form at this time.

Doubt as to its effects under the formulary system. Evidence of the *lex Rubria*.

The great doubt suggested by the wording of the *lex Rubria* is whether confession in court under the *formulary* procedure of this period led to immediate condemnation. The passages which speak of the consequences of confession are expressed in the following way [3]:—

'Sei is eam pecuniam in iure apud eum, quei ibei iure deicundo praerit, ei quei eam petet, aut ei quoius nomine ab eo petetur, dare oportere debereve se confessus erit, *neque* id quod confessus erit solvet satisve faciet *aut* se sponsione

both. The terms of the confession hint at the wording of the *condemnatio* (e. g. 'restituere') as well as of the *intentio*.

[1] Gaius, ii. 24 'praetor interrogat eum qui cedit an contra vindicet; quo negante aut tacente tunc ei qui vindicaverit eam rem addicit.'

[2] See p. 72, note 3.

[3] *Lex Rubria*, cc. 21 and 22.

iudicioque utei oportebit non defendet, *seive* is ibei de ea re in iure non responderit, neque de ea re sponsionem faciet neque iudicio utei oportebit se defendet: tum de eo . . . siremps res lex ius caussaque . . . esto atque utei esset . . . sei is . . . iure lege damnatus esset.'

'Sei is eam rem, quae ita ab eo petetur deve ea [? qua] re cum eo agetur, ei quei eam rem petet deve ea re aget, aut iei quoius nomine ab eo petetur quomve eo agetur in iure apud eum, quei ibei iure deicundo praerit, dare facere praestare restituereve oportere aut se debere, eiusve eam rem esse aut se eam habere, eamve rem de qua arguetur se fecisse obligatumve se eius rei noxsiaeve esse confessus erit deixseritve *neque* de ea re satis utei oportebit faciet aut, sei sponsionem fierei oportebit, sponsionem non faciet, aut non restituet, *neque* se iudicio utei oportebit defendet, *aut sei* de ea re in iure nihil responderit neque de ea re se iudicio utei oportebit defendet: tum de eo . . . siremps lex res ius caussaque . . . esto atque utei esset . . . sei is . . . de ieis rebus Romae apud praetorem . . . in iure confessus esset . . aut ibei . . . se non defendisset.'

Conclusions to be drawn from this evidence.

These passages describe two attitudes on the part of a defendant which might lead ultimately to condemnation. One is confession, the other is neglect of defence; and the two are connected by the disjunctives *seive, aut sei*, which in the above-cited passages have been italicized. The question is whether a greater number of wholly distinct alternatives are implied throughout or whether the *neque . . . neque . . . aut* (also italicized) simply mark off subordinate alternatives consequent on confession and show successive stages in the process which it originates. So far as the structure and obvious meaning of the sentence are concerned this is far the more probable view: and, if we accept it, we must agree with Bethmann-Hollweg[1] that *confessio in iure* did not, under the formulary system, necessarily put a summary stop to the case. The defendant, after confession, may

[1] *Civilprozess*, ii. p. 543.

Probable conclusion that the *confessio in iure* might be recalled.

adopt either one of two courses. He may (i) act up to his statement in court by making full satisfaction to the plaintiff, by declaring himself ready to meet the demands which have just been admitted by himself; or (ii) he might withdraw his confession and enter on the *litis contestatio*, with or without a *sponsio* or other formalities appropriate to that particular *iudicium*. This *iudicium* then proceeds on its ordinary course to a *res iudicata*; how much the previous *confessio in iure* prejudices the defendant's case will rest entirely on the discretion of the *iudex*: it is part of the subjective impression which leads him to his judgement. It is only when the defendant does not adopt either of these courses—satisfaction of the plaintiff's claim or reception of a *iudicium*—that he is held *pro damnato*. In this case he is subjected to execution of the usual kind, the process of which we shall soon consider. He may suffer the imprisonment ordained by the law and by the praetor who *duci iubet*; he may experience the *missio in possessionem* with the proscription of his goods. But even now he is not cut off from ultimate defence. The *confessus* is placed on a line with the *indefensus*, and how the man who has suffered *bonorum proscriptio* though offering no defence may resume his claim we know from the case of Cicero's client Quinctius. Up to the time of the sale of the goods (*bonorum venditio*) the defence may be resumed, but under harder conditions. The defendant must now offer *satisdatio iudicatum solvi*[1].

If this account of the later procedure is correct, the change in the consequences of confession shows a remarkable development of the theory that the *iudicium* is of the essence of a case, that no statement of fact before the praetor is final, and that everything is revocable which takes place before the *litis contestatio*.

[1] Cic. *pro Quinct.* 8, 30 'a Cn. Dolabella denique praetore postulat (Naevius) ut sibi Quinctius iudicatum solvi satisdet. . . . Non recusabat Quinctius quin ita satisdare iuberet, si bona possessa essent ex edicto.'

§ 10. *Neglect of Defence.*

Modes in which defence may be neglected.

Defence may be neglected in two ways. (i) The party may be present in the court but refuse to answer to the charge; (ii) he may keep away from the precincts of the court and thus make it impossible for the plaintiff to prove the charge by the usual judicial means. We have already seen that, in the *legis actio*, the defendant, who is present in court and offers no defence, counts as one who has been condemned (*iudicatus*) and is subject to the processes of execution[1]. The thing that he once professed to own goes, by *addictio*, to his adversary; his person may be seized by the formalities of the *manus iniectio*. The old legal system, on the other hand, had practically no remedies against a defendant who declined to present himself in court. The only effective measures against the defaulting litigant that we know of were developed by the praetor in his edict.

The general principle regulating the failure of defence at the time when the formulary system was fully developed, was that the *indefensus*, like the *confessus*, was *pro damnato*. His assimilation to the condemned has, as its natural consequence, the process of execution over his person and his goods.

(i) Refusal to plead.

The first kind of failure in defence—the refusal of the defendant who is present in court to avail himself of the ordinary means of rebutting the claim made against him (*qui in iure non responderit*)—is known to us, for the Ciceronian period, only from the already-cited clauses of the *lex Rubria*[2]. Although Cicero in his speech for Quinctius quotes most of the praetor's rulings on the subject of the *indefensus*, he does not cite this, for it has no bearing on his client's case. All the clauses of the edict which he reproduces refer to the condition in which

[1] Gaius, ii. 24; see p. 252, note 2.

[2] p. 253.

BOOK I.

Quinctius had been, that of absence from the precincts of the court. The consequence of the refusal to plead is condemnation by the magistrate and execution both personal and real. The defence can be resumed before the sale of the goods, but only on the condition of *satisdatio iudicatum solvi*.

(ii) Refusal to appear.

The praetor's list of *indefensi*.

In the second case, that of the non-appearance of the defendant in the proper court, the praetor in his edict distinguishes between the grounds for the absence. The separate *edicta* were doubtless framed to meet special cases as they arose; but the effect of their association was to give an exhaustive classification of the different forms which neglect of defence might assume. There is the case of the man who, there is reason to believe, is not really out of Italy, but is simply keeping out of the way with the fraudulent design of escaping his creditors; there is the case in which a man may be absent from Rome or Italy on genuine business, but has left no *procurator* to represent him; there is the case in which a man has made a voluntary *vadimonium* to appear in court, but has not kept to his bail. This third ground appeared in that part of the edict which dealt with the *in ius vocatio*; the two others in a much later portion of the edict which treated of *missio in possessionem*. The order would be—

Qui vindicem dedit, si neque potestatem sui faciet neque defendetur.

Qui absens iudicio defensus non fuerit[1].

Qui fraudationis causa latitaverit[2].

[1] For the possible presence of this clause in Cic. *pro Quinct.* 19, 60 see Keller, *Semestria*, i. p. 61; Bethmann-Hollweg, ii. p. 560. On the meaning of *absens* see Ulpian in Dig. 50, 16, 199 'Absentem accipere debemus eum qui non est eo loci, in quo [loco] petitur: non enim trans mare absentem desideramus: et si forte extra continentia urbis sit, abest. Ceterum usque ad continentia non abesse videbitur, si non latitet.'

[2] Cic. *pro Quinct.* 19, 60. Cf. *in Verr.* ii. 24, 59 'Adeunt Bidini, petunt hereditatem. . . . Insimulant hominem fraudandi causa discessisse: postulant ut bona possidere liceat.'

PART II.

It is difficult to say to which of these rulings the professed creditor of Quinctius applied when he asked for the *missio in possessionem*. The first or second seems more applicable to the facts of the case than the third. To these were added other cases where the absence of defence was unavoidable, e. g. those of an unrepresented estate, or of a man who had lost his personality in Roman law by going into voluntary exile and assuming the citizenship of some other state:—

cui heres non exstabit [1].
qui exilii causa solum verterit [2].

An exception to this severe ruling was made in the case of justifiable absence, e. g. that of one who was away from Italy on the service of the state:—

qui rei publicae causa abest neque dolo malo fecit quo magis rei publicae causa abesset [3].

In such a case the praetor does not permit the sale of the property; the *missio* here is only a provisional measure meant to secure efficient representation.

General consequence of neglect of defence is *missio in possessionem*.

In all the other cases the praetor grants *missio in possessionem* with ultimate *bonorum venditio*. Personal arrest, such as affected the *confessus* and the man who will not defend himself in court, is here by the nature of the case impracticable. It could doubtless be granted, if asked for, but could very rarely have been demanded.

Principles on which the *missio* was granted.

This magisterial right of *missio in possessionem* against the undefended was one of the most delicate which the praetor exercised. There was always the danger of its being put into force by some malignant creditor who,

[1] In this case a *tempus deliberandi* is given to the heir; it was only when it expired without result that the creditor was granted the *missio in bona* and the *bonorum venditio* (Gaius, ii. 167).

[2] Cic. *pro Quinct.* 19, 60.

[3] *Lex Iulia Munic.* ll. 116 sq. The edict may, however, at this time have contained the simpler form *qui rei publicae causa sine dolo malo afuit.* See Lenel, *Ed. Perp.* p. 334.

watching for the unavoidable absence of his debtor, availed himself of this extreme legal remedy, for the purpose of shattering the credit and good fame of the man whom he declared a bankrupt. It was naturally regarded as an extreme resource for a plaintiff[1] and as a power to be very cautiously exercised by the magistrate[2]. The praetor must attempt to inform himself of the bare facts of the case before he grants the writ; but this information is difficult, for not only is one of the parties absent, but *ex hypothesi* he is not represented. By the circumstances of the case no definite cognizance was possible, and the writ was granted chiefly on presumption, the praetor assuming that the one of the clauses under which it was granted would prove to hold good in this particular case. It is true that the validity of the writ might be contested at any moment, but only under serious conditions. The defendant must give *satisdatio iudicatum solvi*, and in the alternative *sponsio* by which the writ was contested[3] the praetor might, as in the case of Quinctius, so arrange the rôles of the parties that the defendant becomes practically a plaintiff and has to argue down a case that he has never heard[4].

The *missio* might under certain conditions be contested.

[1] Cic. *pro Quinct.* 6, 25; 15, 49; 16, 51 (see next note); 17, 54.

[2] Cic. *l. c.* 16, 51 'Itaque maiores nostri raro id accidere voluerunt; praetores, ut considerate fieret, comparaverunt; viri boni, cum palam fraudantur, cum experiundi potestas non est, timide tamen et pedetemptim istuc descendunt, vi ac necessitate coacti, inviti, multis vadimoniis desertis saepe illusi ac destituti. Considerant enim quid et quantum sit alterius bona proscribere. Iugulare civem ne iure quidem quisquam bonus vult.'

[3] Cic. *l. c.* 8, 31 'Dolabella . . . aut satisdare aut sponsionem iubet facere.'

[4] Cic. *l. c.* 'Clamabat porro ipse Quinctius . . . sponsionem porro si istius modi faceret, se (id quod nunc evenit) de capite suo priore loco causam esse dicturum'; 9, 32 'Conturbatus sane discedit Quinctius: neque mirum, cui haec optio tam misera tamque iniqua daretur, ut aut ipse se capitis damnaret, si satis dedisset, aut causam capitis, si sponsionem fecisset, priore loco diceret.'

§ 10. *The oath.*

Although the oath as an alternative to evidence in jurisdiction plays no part in Cicero's writings, yet a description of the procedure of his time would be very incomplete which ignored this remarkable survival of a period when religious sanctions were more effective than any that could be devised by the secular arm. The curious dualism of the Roman mind, which represents human and divine agencies as working side by side for the same end, is strikingly apparent in procedure by oath. We can point to no time when the oath had the unique supremacy which it possessed in Teutonic law or when it was regarded as a perpetual substitute for other kinds of proof. But we may imagine that in earlier days the appeal to this religious mode of settlement was more universal in theory and more unlimited in practice than it continued to be in the last century of the Republic. Its survival in and long after this period shows how little ground there is for the supposition sometimes entertained of the prevalence of a widespread scepticism, and that the confidence in *Fides Romana* was even now not misplaced; for the oath could never have maintained its ground in the courts had faith been weak or perjury usual. But as the *auspicia* stand to the *imperium*, so the oath stands to evidence; it is a resort, not a prime agency; it is appealed to, when the appeal is thought to be safe, owing to the personality of the swearer, and is not rendered invidious to the magistrate and *iudex* by the circumstances of the suit; it is an occasional assistance, not a leading factor, in civil procedure.

The oath as a ground of acquittal a constant but not a leading factor in Roman procedure.

Of the limitations imposed on the oath when employed in civil matters, one was legal, the other a result of practice. The legal limitation was that the *iusiurandum*—whether taken by plaintiff or defendant—should be *delatum*, i.e. taken only on the proposal of the adversary; no litigant can swear on his own initiative; the oath must be tendered

Limitations on the right to take the oath.

BOOK I.

to him[1]. The limitation of practice was that the oath should be proposed for acceptance only on the failure of other evidence[2]; but this was a maxim for the courts, above all for the practising lawyer anxious to secure the benefit of his client and to give no mode of escape to his opponent, and cannot be treated as a legal restriction.

Ius-iurandum voluntarium.

The oath which settles a civil dispute may be proffered and taken before the case is brought into court at all. This *iusiurandum voluntarium*, which cannot be enforced because there is no magisterial authority to compel it, raises the party who takes it to the position of judge in his own cause[3]. It was probably very effective in the business life of early Rome, and was the means of preventing many relations of life from being exposed to the scrutiny and publicity of the courts. And it acquired in time legal recognition by the praetor; if the oath had been proffered and sworn out of court, he would give to the party who had taken it an *exceptio iurisiurandi*, as a ground of defence to a subsequent action[4].

Ius-iurandum necessarium.

It is questionable whether any form of the enforced or necessary oath in court (*iusiurandum necessarium*), which resembled the later type in its form and its consequences, existed in very early Roman procedure. Here we find the *sacramentum*, which is an oath, but not one of the later type. It is not tendered by one party to the other, but is sworn voluntarily by each litigant and is practically compulsory on both. Nor does it obviate the

[1] Ulpian in Dig. 12, 2, 3 'Ait praetor "Si is cum quo agetur condicione delata iuraverit." . . . nec frustra adicitur "condicione delata": nam si reus iuravit nemine ei iusiurandum deferente, praetor id iusiurandum non tuebitur.'

[2] Paulus in Dig. 12, 2, 35 'Tutor pupilli omnibus probationibus aliis deficientibus iusiurandum deferens audiendus est.'

[3] Quintil. *Inst. Or.* v. 6, 4 'At is, qui defert, alioqui agere modeste videtur, cum litis adversarium iudicem faciat.' Quintilian, however, means here to include the oath *in iure* and *in iudicio*, as is shown by the words which follow:—'et eum, cuius cognitio est, onere liberat, qui profecto alieno iureiurando stari quam suo mavult.'

[4] Lenel, *Ed. Perp.* p. 406.

necessity for further evidence, for a patient investigation ensues as to whether the oath is grounded on fact or not, and whether, therefore, the *piaculum* for the false oath shall be forfeited[1]. It cannot be proved that the *ius-iurandum necessarium* of later law did not exist by the side of the *sacramentum*, but there is no trace of its existence. The first clear evidence for it is in connexion with the *condictio*—the mode of recovering, first *certa pecunia*, and then *omnis certa res*. The close connexion of the oath with this procedure remained stamped on the praetor's edict by the strange fact that the obligation for taking the oath was enjoined immediately after the rules for the recovery of a *certum*:

Its original connexion with the *condictio*.

Si certum petetur . . . eum a quo iusiurandum petetur, solvere aut iurare cogam . . . Sacerdotem Vestalem et flaminem Dialem in omni mea iurisdictione iurare non cogam[2].

Its appearance in the edict would seem to show that it was of praetorian creation, and not enjoined by the laws (the *lex Silia* and the *lex Calpurnia*) which created the procedure *per condictionem*[3]. But, however this may be, the praetor subsequently widened the practice; he extended it to all cases, and the oath became a substitute for evidence *in iure* throughout the whole domain of civil jurisdiction.

Widening of the practice: the oath as a substitute for evidence *in iure* effects a final settlement of the case.

It might be tendered by either litigant to the other; the matter of the oath rested with the profferer, and the thing which was to be sworn to might be coincident with the whole, or only with a part, of the case. The profferer, too, dictated the form of words (*concepta verba*) which expressed the religious sanction.

The taking of such a proffered oath *in iure* meant victory for the swearer; his refusal to take it meant defeat. Both consent and refusal destroyed any further

[1] p. 53.

[2] Dig. 12, 1 (*rubric*); 12, 2, 34, 6; Gell. x. 15, 31.

[3] p. 66.

right of action; for an obligatory relation, like that of the *res iudicata*, was created[1].

Question whether the oath produced the same effect *in iudicio*.

It is rather more doubtful what was the effect of the oath, when it had been proffered and accepted, not before the praetor but before the *iudex*. Quintilian's treatment of the *iusiurandum* would seem to show that protests against it were possible on the part of the litigant to whom it was tendered[2]. The whole discussion proves that it was in the discretion of the *iudex* (for it is of him rather than of the praetor that Quintilian appears to be speaking) to permit or to disallow the *delatio* of the oath, to regard it as compulsory or not on the litigant to whom it was proffered[3]. But it does not prove that, if it was taken, it was not binding on the *iudex*, but was only regarded by him as a portion of the evidence on which his pronouncement would be based. The relief of a *iudex* at finding the burden of forming a judgement thus suddenly lifted from his shoulders is dwelt on[4]; and the mode in which the offer and acceptance were acclaimed by the bench is illustrated, together with the extreme danger of a rash proposal, by a story which dates from a period not far removed from the Ciceronian[5]. C. Albucius Silus, a famous advocate of the Augustan period, when pleading before the centumvirs, contemptuously rejected a suggestion coming from the opposite side that an oath might be a satisfactory mode of settling the present issue. His contempt took the form of injudicious sarcasm. 'You wish the matter settled by an oath,' he said; 'swear if you will, but I will give you the form: swear by your father's ashes, which are still

[1] The effect of the tender of the oath is compared to novation. See Paulus in Dig. 12, 2, 26, 2 'Iurisiurandi condicio ex numero esse potest videri novandi delegandive, quia proficiscitur ex conventione, quamvis habeat et instar iudicii.'

[2] Quintil. *Inst. Or.* v. 6, 3 'Qui non recipiet, et iniquam condicionem et a multis contemni iurisiurandi metum dicet.'

[3] Cf. Savigny, *System*, vii. p. 81.

[4] Quintil. *Inst. Or.* v. 6, 4 (quoted p. 260, note 3).

[5] Senec. *Controv.* vii, *praef.* 6 & 7; cf. Quintil. *Inst. Or.* ix. 2, 95.

unburied; swear by your father's memory,' and he continued in this strain. When his speech was ended, L. Arruntius, the opponent's counsel, arose: 'We accept the condition; my client will take the oath.' In vain Albucius protested that what he had uttered was a mere form of words, that tropes and metaphors would be banished from the world if such things were to be taken seriously. The centumvirs were with Arruntius' client; they announced that they would give a verdict in his favour if he would take the oath. The oath was taken, and the case was over.

§ 11. *The Iudex and the Iudicium.*

Before considering the ordinary course of a *iudicium*, uninterrupted by the strange methods of conclusion which we have described, we must glance at the qualifications and mode of appointment of the groups or individuals who governed this second department of a Roman civil trial.

The *decemviri.*

The *Decemviri* of the Ciceronian period were, as we have seen, *iudices* in the *iudicium libertatis*[1]; but the general description of their functions which is found in Cicero, combined with their official title (*decemviri slitibus iudicandis*[2]), seems to show a more extended judicial competence in civil matters, which is to us unknown. Their employment as *iudices* is in itself remarkable, for their mode of appointment in the later Republic gives them a quasi-magisterial position. We do not know the original manner in which they were created[3]. While they were simply *iudices* they may have been named by the urban

[1] p. 194.

[2] C. I. L. i. n. 38 'Cn. Cornelius Cn. f. Scipio Hispanus pr. (139 B.C.) . . . Xvir sl(itibus) iudik(andis).' Cf. Cic. *Orator*, 46, 156.

[3] See p. 43. Even if we take the view that they were once purely plebeian officials, it is more probable that they were nominated by a magistrate with civil jurisdiction than by the tribunes.

BOOK I.

praetor for his year of office; but in the Ciceronian period it is almost certain that they were elected[1], like other minor magistrates, such as certain of the *praefecti iuri dicundo* and of the *tribuni militum*, by the *comitia tributa populi* under the presidency of the urban praetor. The plebeian qualification, if it ever existed, had vanished at least as early as the year 139 B.C.[2]; patricians were freely admitted, but, after the decemvirate had become a magistracy, its place in the *cursus honorum* would practically have excluded senators from the post.

The *centumviri*.

In the case of the *centumviri* also there is no trace of the plebeian qualification, if it existed in early times, having been preserved. In the Ciceronian period they were perhaps elected, not only from, but by the thirty-five tribes assembled in the *comitia tributa populi*. Yet they have no magisterial position whatever, no right of giving *ius*. The *legis actio*, the presidency of which is an outcome of the *imperium*, is fulfilled before the praetor; the case is then sent on to the centumvirs, who act simply as *iudices*, and it seems that the only point in which their procedure differs from that of the ordinary *iudex* is that, in the early stages of the *iudicium*, when the preliminaries are being arranged and before the trial actually begins, the praetor sits with them[3]. In the Ciceronian period the number of this board seems to have been the later

[1] Cic. *de Leg.* iii. 3, 6 'Minores magistratus, partiti iuris, ploeres in ploera sunto . . . (amongst them) litis contractas iudicanto.' *Orator*, 46, 156 'Planeque duorum virorum iudicium aut trium virorum capitalium aut decem virorum stlitibus iudicandis dico nunquam.'

[2] Scipio (p. 263, note 2) belongs to a patrician family. Cf. C. I. L. i. p. 278, where C. Julius Caesar, father of the dictator, appears with this office, and see Mommsen, *Staatsr.* ii. p. 605.

[3] This is probable, although it is impossible to say how much of the *legis actio* took place before the centumvirs themselves. If any, the praetor must have been with them. In the Ciceronian period the supervisor of the whole trial before this body seems to have been an ex-quaestor (Suet. *Aug.* 36 '(Augustus) auctor . . . fuit . . . ut centumviralem hastam, quam quaestura functi consuerant cogere, decemviri cogerent').

Republican one, 105, which may have originated after the creation of the thirty-five tribes. It was probably not until the Principate and the reconstitution of the board by Augustus that the number was increased[1].

In the case of these two colleges the litigant has little chance of determining who his judges should be, although in the case of both there was probably a limited right of challenging (*reiectio*), for it is improbable that the whole body either of decemvirs or centumvirs ever sat to hear a case.

The *unus iudex*. His qualification and mode of appointment.

On the other hand the whole theory of the *unus iudex* is that his appointment is based on the consent of the parties[2]. This consent was doubtless limited by *de facto* qualifications; in the middle Republic it was the custom to choose senators only, but there is no evidence that the civil courts were ever regulated by a *lex iudiciaria*, or that the praetor ever asserted that non-senatorial *iudices*, if proposed by the parties, should be disallowed. But it was not unnatural that the *album iudicum* for criminal cases should exercise its influence on the choice of *iudices* for the civil courts. After the Gracchan law we find an *eques* as a *iudex* in a civil case, yet senators are still not excluded. The Cluvius of Cicero's *pro Roscio comoedo* is a knight[3], and C. Aquilius Gallus in 81 B.C., when he sat to hear the case in which Quinctius was involved, may also have been still of equestrian

[1] Pliny (*Ep.* vi. 33, 3) tells us that in his time 180 *centumviri* sat to hear a single case. The number was composed of four ordinary *consilia*.

[2] Cic. *pro Rosc. com.* 4, 12 'Eundemne tu arbitrum et iudicem sumebas?' *pro Cluent.* 43, 120 'Neminem voluerunt maiores nostri non modo de existimatione cuiusquam, sed ne pecuniaria quidem de re minima esse iudicem nisi qui inter adversarios convenisset.' This theory finds expression, as regards provincial jurisdiction, in the choice by lot (*sortitio*), which is followed by the challenging (*reiectio*) of iudices and recuperatores. For *iudices* see Cic. *in Verr.* ii. 13, 32 and 34; 16, 39, 17, 42; for *recuperatores ib.* iii. 11, 28; 13, 32; 59, 136; 60, 139 and 140.

[3] Cic. *pro Rosc. com.* 14, 42.

BOOK I.

rank. But it cannot be supposed that senators were at this time excluded from the civil bench[1].

The choice of the *iudex* rested in the first instance with the plaintiff; it was his right to propose a *iudex* (*iudicem ferre*[2]) to the defendant *in iure*; the individual proposed could be rejected by the defendant on oath as not likely to prove a suitable or impartial arbitrator on the case (*eiurare, iniquum eiurare*[3]); no ground for the rejection need be given; but that organized public opinion which was expressed through the censor seems to have visited with ignominy a persistent refusal to accept a *iudicium* which was obviously based on dishonest motives[4], and it is a probable conjecture that the praetor might treat as *indefensus* a litigant who unduly delayed the plaintiff's rights by misusing this power of challenge[5]. If the defendant made no protest against the proffered *iudex*, both parties are said equally to take him (*iudicem sumere*[6]).

The *recuperatores*. Their qualification.

The *recuperatores* seem, like the *iudices*, to have been subject to no special legal qualification. We are not even told of those employed for ordinary civil procedure, as we

[1] A consular, who was therefore a senator, is found as a *iudex* subsequently to the *lex Sempronia* and before the *lex Aurelia* (Cic. *de Off.* iii. 19, 77); but it is questionable whether the case in which he took part was more than a private arbitration. See p. 54, note 1.

[2] Cic. *pro Rosc. com.* 15, 45; *de Orat.* ii. 65, 263; 70, 285. In the last passage (quoted in the next note) the word is not used of a strict trial; it records a case of political arbitration—a mild subsitute for a criminal prosecution.

[3] Cic. *de Orat.* ii. 70, 285 'Cum ei (P. Scipioni) M. Flaccus multis probris obiectis P. Mucium iudicem tulisset, *eiero*, inquit, *iniquus est.* Cum esset admurmuratum *A* inquit, *P. C., non ego mihi illum iniquum eiero, verum omnibus.*' See last note. Cf. *in Verr.* iii. 60, 137.

[4] Asc. *in Or. in Tog. cand.* p. 84 'Antonium Gellius et Lentulus censores . . . senatu moverunt causasque subscripserunt . . . quod iudicium recusarit, &c.' Antonius had refused a *iudicium* ('forum eiurare'), not a particular *iudex*, by an appeal to the tribunes.

[5] Keller, *Civilprocess*, p. 43.

[6] Cic. *pro Flacco*, 21, 50; *pro Rosc. com.* 4, 12; 14, 42. In both the latter passages the expression is used of the plaintiff.

PART II.

are of the *iudices*, that they were at one time chosen usually from the senators. The only instance in which a qualification for the recuperatorial bench appears before us is a monetary one. According to the *lex agraria* of 111 B.C.[1] a suit between *publicani* and *possessores* arising out of that law is to be tried by *recuperatores* belonging to the first class in the reformed Servian census, i.e. possessing probably 400,000 sesterces. But this law doubtless makes special qualifications for its judges; in ordinary cases it is probable that there was no fixed qualification for such a board, but that it was chosen generally from responsible citizens[2], senators, or knights, according to their availability or the proposals of the parties.

Principles that determined the giving of *recuperatores*.

The granting of *recuperatores* is, as we saw, an outcome of the *imperium*, whether of the praetor urbanus in the exercise of his honorary jurisdiction, as when he grants the interdict[3], or of the praetor peregrinus, or of the provincial governor. But the gift of *recuperatores* is not the invariable accompaniment of a *iudicium quod imperio continetur*; the praetor peregrinus at Rome and the governor of a province sometimes give *singuli iudices*[4]. We cannot say definitely what considerations dictated the choice between the *iudex* and the *recuperatores*; but the granting of the latter in place of the former must have depended to a large extent on the nature of the case. The civil trials in which they are known chiefly to have been employed are those of a breach of the peace or of aggravated assault (*vis, iniuria atrox*[5]); they are cases where quick restitution or compensation is required —cases too in which a prolongation of the settlement or of

[1] *Lex Agraria*, ll. 36 and 38.

[2] Cf. *tales viri* of Cic. *pro Tull.* 18, 43.

[3] Gaius, iv. 141.

[4] See p. 265, note 2.

[5] Cic. *de Inv.* ii. 20, 60 'Non . . . oportet in recuperatorio iudicio eius maleficii, de quo inter sicarios quaeritur, praeiudicium fieri . . . Eiusmodi sunt iniuriae ut de iis indignum sit non primo quoque tempore iudicari'; so a charge of exaction *per vim aut metum* should be brought before *recuperatores* (Cic. *in Verr.* iii. 65, 152, 153); cf. Gell. xx. 1, 3.

the proceedings is likely to lead to a still more serious disturbance of public order. They are cases, in short, in which a very speedy settlement is eminently desirable: and this rapidity of judgement seems to have been more easily attained in the recuperatorial than in the ordinary *iudicia*[1]. This rapidity may have been due partly to peculiarities in the procedure, partly to the ease with which the court was constituted.

Peculiarities of the procedure before *recuperatores*.

We have every reason to believe that the procedure before *recuperatores* was, in spite of the long and complicated pleadings on behalf of Caecina and Tullius, simpler, directer and more summary than that before a *iudex*; cases involving subtle questions of law, *formulae* in which an *exceptio* would almost of necessity appear, were avoided[2]. Complex questions could not be hindered from making their appearance during the trial; but they were not of the essence of cases in which it was to be decided whether *vis* had been used, whether *iniuria* had been committed. Another reason for the greater speediness of recuperatorial *iudicia* has been sought in the possible limitation of the number of witnesses to ten[3]. The court may also have been capable of more rapid constitution than that formed by a single *iudex*. It has been surmised that recuperatorial

[1] See Eisele, *Beiträge*, p. 59.

[2] Cic. *pro Tull.* 17, 41; 18, 42.

[3] Cic. *pro Caec.* 10, 28 'Decimo vero loco testis exspectatus et ad extremum reservatus dixit.' Cf. *Edictum Venafri*, l. 66 'iudicium reciperatorium in singulas res HS. $\bar{X}$ reddere, testibusque dumtaxat X denuntiand[*o qu*]aeri placet.' *Lex Mamilia* K. L. V. 'Iuris dictio reciperatorumque datio addictio esto . . . inque eam rem is, qui hac lege iudicium dederit, testibus publice dumtaxat in res singulas X denuntiandi potestatem facito.' In the two latter cases we are dealing with administrative law, and the limit is that of the *compulsory* witnesses, those to whom *denuntiatio* has been made. But compulsory witnesses are unknown to civil law, and the limitation hinted at in the *pro Caecina* can hardly be explained on this hypothesis, unless we consider that actions springing from the interdict *unde vi* were (as connected with breaches of the peace) treated from the point of view of police law. Mommsen (*Zeitschr. f. Alterthumsw.*, 1844, p. 457 ff.) seems to think that no limit was ever imposed to the number of *testes voluntarii*.

iudicia could be furnished at any time, and need not follow the order of the assize (*actus rerum*), where such existed, or, where it did not exist, that they at least took precedence of other courts [1]. As public prosecutions for *vis* were heard before other criminal cases [2], so it is possible that civil actions turning on similar issues may have been tried before ordinary suits.

Choice between the *iudex* and *recuperatores*.

But, although a general principle can be faintly discerned, we have no evidence for solving the problem, 'What authority decided in any given case when a *iudex* and when *recuperatores* should be employed?' Possibly the mode of determination was different in each of the three possible contingencies:—

1. Where no definite promise of either kind was made in the edict, the choice between *iudex* and *recuperatores* may in certain cases have been left to the parties [3]. The choice would in the first instance be that of the plaintiff; if the defendant would not accept *recuperatores*, the plaintiff may have been bound to propose a *iudex*, or the praetor may have interposed.

2. Where a *iudicium recuperatorium* alone was promised in the edict, the praetor (at least after the *lex Cornelia* of 67 B.C.) must have been bound to grant *recuperatores* [4].

3. Where laws ordained *iudicis recuperatorum datio*, the choice would probably have rested with the magistrate [5].

[1] Cic. *pro Tull.* 5, 10 'recuperatores dare ut quam primum res iudicaretur.' See Eisele, *Beiträge*, p. 59.

[2] See Book ii.

[3] A *iudex* might perhaps have been employed in the *actio vi bonorum raptorum* (cf. Gaius, iv. 46), although, as we know from Cicero's speech for Tullius (17, 41), *recuperatores* were more usual here. In the clause of Verres' edict which referred to controversies between *aratores* and *decumani* (*in Verr.* iii. 14, 35 'SI UTER VOLET, RECUPERATORES DABO') it is barely possible that the choice between *iudex* and *recuperatores* is implied; in such a matter of administrative law the latter would more naturally have been chosen. In another passage (*in Verr.* iii. 58, 135 'Coepit Scandilius recuperatores aut iudicem postulare') the choice is mentioned, but it is doubtful whether it lay with the plaintiff.

[4] Eisele, *Beiträge*, p. 58.

[5] *ib.* p. 61.

BOOK I.

Early stages of the iudicium.

The first stage of the *iudicium* was marked by certain formal preliminaries to the action. The *iudex* was on an appointed day approached by the parties in the Forum. His first act was, perhaps, to take the oath[1], and then he was made aware of the outlines of the case, chiefly by the *formula* being presented to him[2], perhaps also by a short discourse with the parties or their counsel. This brief verbal explanation of the facts (*causae collectio, coniectio*) had existed in the time of the *legis actio*[3], and, though less essential in the days of written procedure, its convenience must have dictated its maintenance. It was now that any rulings by the praetor about the conduct of the case were made known to the parties. Once the *iudex* had appeared, it seems that communications on such subjects to the praetor must be made through him. Aquilius, who was *iudex* in the case of Quinctius, successfully resisted an attempt made by the opposite party to induce the praetor to limit the duration of the pleadings[4]. During these preliminary proceedings the *iudex* or *recuperatores* sat alone; it was only in the centumviral court that the praetor assisted at this stage.

The patroni.

The trial was a public event, and here the *patroni* had the first real chance for the display of their gifts of eloquence. The *advocatus*, of first importance in the praetor's court, now gives way to the *patronus*[5], and this was the stage at which a jurist like Aquilius would say that 'Cicero should be consulted[6].' The rabid eloquence

[1] Cf. Cic. *de Off.* iii. 10, 44. It is in consequence of the oath that the litigant, in making requests of the *iudex*, uses the careful formula 'quae salva fide facere posset' (Cic. *l. c.*).

[2] Gaius, iv. 141 ('editis formulis').

[3] *ib.* 15, cf. Gell. v. 10, 9 and Sabinus cited by Paulus in Dig. 50, 17, 1.

[4] Cic. *pro Quinct.* 9, 33. Cf. Cic. *de Off.* iii. 10, 43 'Tantum (iudex) dabit amicitiae . . . ut orandae litis tempus quoad per leges liceat accommodet.'

[5] Cf. Cic. *pro Cluent.* 40, 110.

[6] 'Nihil hoc ad ius; ad Ciceronem' (Cic. *Top.* 12, 51).

(*canina eloquentia*) of the Republic[1] was more fittingly exercised in public prosecution or the conduct of criminal cases, but instances of what (for Cicero) is moderated invective can be found in his private speeches. His characterization of Fannius, the man with the 'cropped head, whose whole person from his toe-nails to his crown breathes of fraud, treachery, and lies[2]'; of Naevius, the ex-auctioneer who 'had sold his voice for hire[3]'; of Aebutius, the lawyer of women, the jest of men[4]; of the witnesses of the latter, one of whom had made a ready admission that he might be in the unfamiliar position 'of getting his word believed in at least one trial[5],' are typical instances of the lengths to which Ciceronian oratory could go. Elsewhere he restrains himself with difficulty; he could speak if he would, but he prefers to be moderate and conduct the case in a gentlemanly and friendly fashion[6]. There is, however, one opponent who is always spared; good taste, good policy, and reverence for the Bar always protect from vituperation the eminent counsel on the other side[7].

The length of the trial was not prescribed; the old rule of the Twelve Tables that the trial should last one day and the judgement be given on that same day[8] was evidently meant to secure that the verdict should be based on freshly heard and well-remembered evidence. It is difficult to believe that this rule could ever have been practicable, but it had one interesting result, which lasted down to Cicero's day, and that is, that with every adjournment the whole case is put again before the *iudex*. In Cicero's time the adjournment of the case on the ground of a

Adjournment.

[1] Quintil. *Inst. Or.* xii. 9, 9.
[2] Cic. *pro Rosc. com.* 7, 20.
[3] Cic. *pro Quinct.* 3, 11.
[4] Cic. *pro Caec.* 5, 14.
[5] *ib.* 10, 27.
[6] Cic. *pro Tull.* 2, 5 'Tametsi postulat causa, tamen, nisi plane cogit ingratiis, ad male dicendum non soleo descendere.'
[7] *ib.*; cf. Quintil. *Inst. Or.* xii. 9, 11.
[8] *Lex XII Tab.* in Gell. xvii. 2, 10 'Si ambo praesentes, solis occasus suprema tempestas esto.'

BOOK I. verdict that the jury was not satisfied (*sibi non liquere*)[1] appears to have been the rule rather than the exception. Such adjournments precede Cicero's pleadings for Caecina, for Tullius and for Quinctius; nor did the same advocates always appear at the different hearings. But on each occasion the whole narrative of the facts (*narratio*) is resumed again[2], and the renewed arguments cover the whole of the ground. In a single hearing (*actio*) but one speech seems to have been delivered on either side; that for the plaintiff came first: then followed the argument for the defence, and this usual order is the ground (though not the justification) for Cicero's frequent complaint in the *pro Quinctio*, that, though his client is practically on the defence, he has to occupy the position of a plaintiff in the order of debate[3]. The length of the speeches was not prescribed, and the device of staving off an immediate verdict, which would be given under circumstances unfavourable to his client, by wasting the day in oratory (*dicendo diem eximere*), was known to the Roman lawyer. On this point Cicero naturally adopts the point of view dictated by circumstances. In the speech for Quinctius there is a warm protest against any attempt to limit the pleadings[4]; in that for Tullius there is an entreaty that the other side should not abuse its privilege of speech[5].

Order of the speeches.

Length of the speeches.

Evidence (i) from witnesses.

The evidence from witnesses seems to have been taken after the case had been opened and answered by the *patroni*[6]; comments on their evidence were possible in the examination and cross-examination (*testium interrogatio*) which followed its delivery; but, if the *actio*

[1] Cic. *pro Caec.* 11, 31.

[2] Cic. *pro Quinct.* 3 ff.; *pro Tull.* 6 ff.; *pro Caec.* 4 ff.

[3] Cic. *pro Quinct.* 2, 8; 22, 71; see p. 258, note 4.

[4] Cic. *l. c.* 9, 33; 10, 34; 22, 71.

[5] Cic. *pro Tull.* 3, 6 'Unum hoc abs te, L. Quincti, pervelim impetrare ... ut ita tibi multum temporis ad dicendum sumas ut his aliquid ad iudicandum relinquas. Namque antea non defensionis tuae modus sed nox tibi finem dicendi fecit.'

[6] Titius in Macrob. iii. 16, 16.

lasted only one day, there was no possibility of treating the evidence as a whole or presenting it to the *iudex* in connexion with the arguments for the case, for it was taken after counsel's speeches had been delivered. But a single hearing must have been very exceptional in an important case, and, if a second *actio* followed, there was ample opportunity for dealing with the evidence heard on the first occasion: an opportunity which Cicero seizes in his speeches for Caecina and for Tullius [1].

Their evidence voluntary.

The evidence of witnesses was given voluntarily, and no compulsion for their appearance seems to have been exercised by the court except in certain cases. By an enactment of the Twelve Tables the witnesses to a *mancipatio* were bound to appear to testify to its conclusion [2], and, in a trial based on administrative law but conducted according to the forms of civil procedure, the magistrate who gave the *iudicium* was allowed the right of commanding by summons (*denuntiatio*) the presence of a certain number of witnesses [3]. The number that might be produced by either party in an ordinary civil suit was unlimited, and only in recuperatorial *iudicia* is there the possibility of its having been limited by law and by the edict [4]. The sole qualification for a witness in civil procedure was that he should be a free man [5].

Oath.

The witnesses were heard only on oath [6]; but the scrupu-

[1] For reflections by the *patronus* on the credibility of the evidence see Cic. *pro Quinct.* cc. 18, 23, 28; *pro Caec.* cc. 9 and 10; *pro Tull.*, cc. 1 and 10.

[2] Gell. xv. 13, 11. Mommsen regards the permit of the XII Tables 'CUI TESTIMONIUM DEFUERIT, IS TERTIIS DIEBUS OB PORTUM OBVAGULATUM ITO' (Fest. pp. 233 and 375), not as a summons to evidence but as a public proclamation of the *intestabilitas* of the man who had failed as a mancipation witness (*Zeitschr. f. Alterthumsw.* 1844, p. 457 ff.).

[3] See p. 268, note 3.

[4] p. 268.

[5] In post-Republican law the torture of slaves, and, therefore, their whole evidence so far as civil procedure was concerned, was permitted only in cases of *hereditas* and *tutela* (Paul. *Sent.* v. 15, 6; 16, 2).

[6] Cic. *pro Rosc. com.* 15, 44 and 45; *pro Caec.* 10, 28.

BOOK I.

lousness of the Roman character is shown in the form in which their evidence was tendered. Even when they stated what they had seen or heard, they expressed it in the form that 'they thought' (*se arbitrari*) the facts which they adduced to have occurred [1]. If we may judge from Cicero's treatment of second-hand evidence, there could have been no rules against its admissibility [2]; indeed such rules, although they may be necessary to protect an ignorant jury with whom impressions are stronger than the degrees of probability on which they are based, were hardly required for a Roman *iudex* or *recuperatores*. It was better that they should hear all, even the reported statement of an unsworn man, and draw their own conclusions. The weakness of such evidence might of course be dwelt on by the opponent: an attack which Cicero can only meet by the sophistic argument that lying and perjury are the same [3]. Written evidence taken out of court, and presumably in most cases based on oath, was produced and read; in an instance of evidence of this kind which we find employed by Cicero, the witnesses, whose depositions are produced in writing, report a conversation with some one who is the ultimate source of the testimony [4], and the force of such attenuated evidence could hardly have exercised a powerful influence on the court.

Second-hand evidence.

(ii) Written documents.

Written documents (*scripta, tabulae, instrumenta*) were

[1] Cic. *Acad. Prior.* ii. 47, 146 '(maiores) quemque voluerunt . . . qui testimonium diceret ut *arbitrari* se diceret etiam quod ipse vidisset.' Cf. *pro Font.* 13, 29 'illud verbum . . . *arbitror*, quo nos etiam tunc utimur cum ea dicimus iurati quae comperta habemus, quae ipsi vidimus.'

[2] Cic. *pro Rosc. com.* 15, 43. On such *testes de auditu* cf. Quintil. *Inst. Or.* v. 7, 5.

[3] Cic. *l. c.* 15, 44; 16, 46 'At quid interest inter periurum et mendacem? Qui mentiri solet, peierare consuevit.'

[4] Cic. *l. c.* 14, 43 ff. Mommsen (*l. c.*) bases these *testimonia per tabulas data* on the voluntary nature of Roman evidence. As a man could not be forced to attend, his written evidence was attested and presented; but it is evident that the attestation is no substitute for the oath; it only guarantees the accuracy of the statement of the original witness.

abundantly cited as proof: and, if there were any doubt about their genuineness, or their contents demanded closer investigation, were passed on to the *iudex* [1]. Of these some were public—laws, decrees of the senate, clauses of the edict and the like—others of a private character such as wills, account-books, stipulations and written compacts of a more informal character [2]. A *stipulatio* is put in during the case of Roscius [3], and account-books figure largely in the same suit. The evidence from these was irresistible, if the *tabulae* or *codices accepti et expensi* of the plaintiff and defendant agreed, an entry in the credit account of one being balanced by a similar entry in the debit account of the other; it was weaker when the entry was found only in one, and very weak indeed when it could be discovered only in the waxen *adversaria* of some time back and had not been entered in the permanent parchment *codex* [4]. But that such evidence could be produced and ruled admissible is only another illustration of the healthy principle of admitting everything to the cognizance of the court. A purely private memorandum, such as the diary (*ephemeris*) which Quinctius put in [5], might be entered to support a statement on a given point such as the date of an occurrence.

Consideration of the verdict.

After the cognizance (*causae cognitio*) was over, the *iudex* with his assessors [6], or the *recuperatores*, retired to

[1] For their inspection by the *iudex* see Titius in Macrob. iii. 16, 16 'tabulas poscit, literas inspicit.'

[2] Cic. *Part. Orat.* 37, 130 'Scriptorum autem privatum aliud est, publicum aliud; publicum lex, senatus consultum, foedus: privatum tabulae, pactum, conventum, stipulatio.'

[3] Cic. *pro Rosc. com.* 13, 37; cf. *pro Caec.* 25, 71.

[4] Cic. *pro Rosc. com.* 2, 5 'Suum codicem testis loco recitare arrogantiae est. Suarum perscriptionum et liturarum adversaria proferre non amentia est? . . . (§ 7) adversaria in iudicium protulit nemo: codicem protulit, tabulas recitavit.' For such evidence cf. *in Verr.* ii. 76 ff.; *pro Flacco*, 20, 48; and see Gasquey, *Cicéron Iurisconsulte*, p. 151.

[5] Cic. *pro Quinct.* 18, 57, 58.

[6] For these assessors (*consilium* or *advocati* of the iudex) see Cic. *pro Rosc. com.* 4, 12; 5, 15; 8, 22; *pro Quinct.* 2, 5; 10, 36.

BOOK I.

Grounds of the decision of the *iudex*.

consider the verdict in secret (*in consilium ire*)[1]. In coming to a decision they were not bound by any strict mechanical rules of evidence. According to the principle laid down by Cicero, which was the principle of Roman criminal as well as civil process, the general subjective impression derived by the judge from the proceedings must decide his verdict[2], the only modifying rule being the obvious one that, with certain exceptions[3], the burden of proof lies on the plaintiff[4]; this rule underlies the maxim formulated by the elder Cato that when evidence fails and the decision turns on character, the defendant's character must be considered first[5].

Form of the sentence.

There were no fixed terms in which the sentence was delivered; the cautiousness of the Roman character was betrayed in the fact that the *iudex* gave his binding judgement as an opinion (*videri*)[6], generally with the hesitating addition *si quid mei iudicii est*[7].

The *res iudicata*.

But this tentative statement expressed the unalterable fact of a *res iudicata* and created, according to the scientific analysis of the lawyer, the new obligation *iudicatum facere oportere*[8].

Enforcement of the sentence.

This contract we should expect to be enforced purely by the executive arm; but such had not been the tradition of Roman law. It is true that the *legis actio per manus iniectionem* was a mode of execution, but it was also an action, which might under certain conditions be contested by its victim. Something resembling a new process had always resulted as the consequence of a judgement.

We cannot say in what form this *legis actio* maintained

[1] Cic. *pro Quinct.* 10, 34. Cf. Titius in *Macrob. l. c.*

[2] Cic. *de Rep.* i. 38, 59 'apud me, ut apud bonum iudicem, argumenta plus quam testes valent.'

[3] For these exceptions see Bethmann-Hollweg, ii. p. 611.

[4] Cic. *Part. Orat.* 30, 104 'Nemo enim eius, quod negat factum, potest aut debet aut solet reddere rationem.' Cf. p. 229.

[5] Gell. xiv. 2, 26.

[6] Cic. *Acad. Prior.* ii. 47, 146.

[7] Cic. *de Fin.* ii. 12, 36.

[8] Gaius, iii. 180. See p. 246.

itself in Cicero's day. It has been conjectured with great probability that, even after the introduction of the formulary process, it may have been adapted to the *formula*, and, in the shape of an 'action accommodated to the *legis actio* [1],' have survived for a considerable time as the mode of enforcing the consequences of a *iudicium legitimum*. But the praetor not unnaturally adopts a similar process, tentative and favourable to the defendant, for carrying out the judgements that were the result of his own honorary actions. This is the *actio iudicati* of praetorian law, which finally becomes the universal mode of exacting the fulfilment of the judicial obligation.

The *actio iudicati*.

The object of this action is the pecuniary condemnation effected by the original trial. It could be brought if the amount of money fixed in the condemnation was not paid by the defendant within a given time (*tempus iudicati*), these days of grace being fixed sometimes by the Twelve Tables, sometimes by the edict [2]. It belongs to the party in whose favour the condemnation has been pronounced, and is given against the party who has been condemned.

Condemnation *in duplum* and *satisdatio iudicatum solvi*.

The condemnation in this action was to double the amount of the *iudicatum* (*in duplum*). We have no positive evidence for the existence of this *poena dupli* in Cicero's time: but its existence is rendered very probable, not only by the fact that the *poena* obviously follows the analogy of the action *per manus iniectionem*, but by the circumstance that a very similar action existing in Cicero's day, by which the defendant raised the question whether there has been a *iudicatum* or not, was accompanied by a similar *poena* [3]. For contesting the *actio iudicati*, *satisdatio iudicatum solvi* by the defendant was also necessary [4].

[1] 'Actio ad legis actionem expressa' (cf. Gaius, iv. 10). The conjecture is that of Bethmann-Hollweg (ii. p. 634).

[2] Gaius, iii. 78.

[3] Cic. *pro Flacco*, 21, 49; see p. 294.

[4] Gaius, iv. 25 and 102.

BOOK I.

§ 12. *Execution.*

Execution.

If the *manus iniectio* continued during the Ciceronian period, even in a modified form, we should expect the process of execution in *legitima iudicia* to be not very different to what it had been in the earlier period. And the evidence furnished by our authorities shows this to be the case. Personal imprisonment still continues, but perhaps with a slightly different significance to that which it had had in earlier times. It is not, perhaps, at this period so much the assertion of an absolute right to the person of the debtor as a precautionary means of securing the payment of his debt by limiting his liberty: in other words, this procedure is less closely modelled on that by which the *nexus* became a bondman. This result is natural when we consider that the old harsh law of *nexum* had received considerable modifications as early as the year 313 B.C.: and, although it is by no means certain that the *lex Poetilia*, which achieved this result[1], had any direct reference to judgement-debts, yet the humanizing influences which secured a modification of *nexum* and the growth of the new theory that the goods, not the person, of the debtor were the proper object of seizure, must have exercised their influence on the procedure by which the successful plaintiff, at the bidding of the court, exacted his obligations. But we cannot say in what the change consisted; we only know that, in the interval between the *lex Poetilia* and the Ciceronian period, the debtor was still *addictus* to his creditor, that he might be seen being led through the streets to his gaoler's home and that the pitying or inquiring by-stander might ask the debt, and, after learning it, ransom him on the spot or express inability or unwillingness to satisfy the claim[2].

(i) Personal execution; imprisonment.

[1] See p. 74.

[2] Cic. *de Orat.* ii. 63, 255 'Apud Naevium (*al.* Novium) . . . misericors ille, qui iudicatum duci videt; percontatur ita *Quanti addictus? Mille*

This tradition of imprisonment for debt in default of payment was too strong even for the praetor. In the execution of the results of his own *iudicia* he retains it, and it appears as one of the two normal modes of enforcing a claim in Sallust [1], in Cicero [2], and in the *lex Rubria* [3].

PART II. Imprisonment survives into the Ciceronian period

The praetorian rules of imprisonment replaced the element of arrest in the *manus iniectio*, as the praetorian *actio iudicati* represented the contentious element in that procedure [4]. The imprisonment, in fact, was not an essential part of the *actio iudicati*, but a consequence of not defending that action. When the *iudicatus* had not paid within the legal term, and, when summoned to the praetor's court, had not contested the *actio iudicati*, the plaintiff could ask the praetor for his *addictio*. We have seen that the same power could be employed against the defendant who was *confessus* or *indefensus* in the primary action, and it has already been noticed that, as the *lex Rubria* shows, even the municipal magistrate could give this permit for personal execution [5].

as a consequence of not contesting the *actio iudicati*.

The permit takes the form of a command issued by the magistrate that the creditor may take the debtor home (*duci iubere*) [6]; this debtor is now his *addictus* [7]. The

Duci iubere; addictio.

nummum . . . addidit *Nihil addo, ducas licet;*' cf. Liv. xxiii. 14 (216 B.C.) and Val. Max. vii. 6, 1.

[1] *Cat.* 33 (from the letter of C. Manlius to Marcius Rex) 'neque cuiquam nostrum licuit more maiorum lege uti neque amisso patrimonio liberum corpus habere; tanta saevitia foeneratorum atque praetoris fuit.' *Lex* here perhaps does not refer to any particular enactment, but is used in a loose sense for praetorian assistance, i. e. the general legal procedure of *bonorum possessio.*

[2] Cic. *pro Flacco*, 20, 48; *pro Rosc. com.* 14, 41; *in Pis.* 35, 86. Here the *addictio* is mentioned; Cicero says of Catiline's following (*in Cat.* ii. 3, 5) 'quibus ego non modo si aciem exercitus nostri, verum etiam si edictum praetoris ostendero, concident.' The *edictum* here is probably that having reference to personal seizure.

[3] cc. 21 and 22.

[4] Gaius, iv. 25.

[5] p. 107.

[6] *Lex Rubria*, c. 21, l. 19; cf. Paul. *Sent.* v. 26, 2.

[7] See references on p. 278, note 2, and in note 2 of this page.

creditor may keep him in his private prison (*carcer*) and even put him in bonds: but he must supply him with the necessaries of life. It is uncertain whether he could make his prisoner labour for his benefit[1]; but it is possible that the fruits of any work done by the *addictus*, over and above what was deducted for the expenses of his livelihood, went towards the solution of his debt.

Legal condition of the debtor.

The debtor is, like the *nexus* of olden times, not a slave; he is said *servire* but not to be a *servus*. He retains both his private and his public rights[2]. In his maintenance of the first he preserves the *patria potestas* over his children and the theoretical right of administering his property; for without the latter he could not conceivably satisfy the object of imprisonment by the payment of his debt. With respect to public rights, he retains his Roman nomenclature and his tribe, and, when he recovers his liberty, he is not a *libertus* but an *ingenuus*; nor does he even lose his civil honour, for he appears in none of the lists of the *infames* which we possess.

Modes of avoiding imprisonment.

Even in default of the satisfaction of the whole debt, this imprisonment might, in the Ciceronian period, be avoided by an arrangement with the creditor. The *lex Iulia Municipalis* contemplates the case of a man who has sworn that he has some (though not the full) means of meeting his engagements and has made an arrangement with his creditors to satisfy their claims in part. Such a man, although he escapes imprisonment, is yet included in the list of the *infames*[3].

It is questionable whether this imprisonment ordained by the praetor could ever have been permanent in theory: for the validity of praetorian acts is generally conditioned

[1] Rudorff (*Rechtsgesch.* ii. § 90) thinks that he could, Bethmann-Hollweg (ii. p. 665) that he could not.

[2] Quintil. *Inst. Or.* v. 10, 60; vii. 3, 26; *Declam.* 311.

[3] *Lex Iul. Munic.* l. 113; cf. Cic. *ad Fam.* ix. 16, 7, and see Greenidge *Infamia in Roman Law*, pp. 206 ff., where these passages and the expression *bonam copiam iurare* are discussed.

by the annual tenure of the *imperium*[1]. But this does not imply that the prisoner was freed on the expiry of the year of office of the praetor who had granted his *addictio*. The magistrate's successor in the curule chair might renew the rule and the imprisonment thus become practically perpetual.

But the unconditioned liberation of the prisoner was a consequence of the satisfaction of the debt, whether this was due to the debtor himself[2] or to some friend[3]. A successful defence in the originally neglected *actio iudicati* also secured the same result[4].

(ii) Execution on property.

But the praetor, consistently with the analogies before him, has more than one means of securing obedience to the orders of his court. As the *manus iniectio* had suggested imprisonment for debt, so there were many precedents which urged the praetor to enforce bankruptcy proceedings on the vanquished defendant for the satisfaction of the plaintiff's claim.

Precedents for it in early history and in public law.

One precedent was to be found in the *lex Poetilia* itself. Even supposing that law to have referred to the *nexus* only and not to the *iudicatus*, yet the principle of the seizure of the goods in place of the person of the debtor was of importance for the procedure of the courts[5]: for it showed that the two could be separated. And its results were also of value; for when, on the application of the *lex Poetilia*, there were more creditors than one, the goods must have been divided and something like bankruptcy proceedings must have been revealed.

A similar principle had been suggested from early times by public law. In certain cases, as a consequence of extraordinary penalties proposed by a magistrate and pronounced by the people, the goods of the condemned

[1] Huschke (*Nexum*, p. 181) thinks that the imprisonment expired with the *imperium* which had ordered it.

[2] Cic. *pro Flacco*, 21, 49; *missus* in this passage means 'released.'

[3] Cic. *de Orat.* ii. 63, 255; see p. 278, note 2.

[4] Cf. Ulp. in Dig. 4, 6, 23.

[5] p. 278.

BOOK I.

man were confiscated to the state and sold by public authority[1]. In other cases the act of confiscation, and the subsequent sale, were carried out for the purpose of exacting the value of a fine (*multa*) imposed by the magistrate and sanctioned by the people[2]. In both these cases the possessor of the *imperium* who had brought about the condemnation, put the quaestor into possession of the goods and the latter then sold them by auction to the highest bidder[3]: in Ciceronian times generally, although perhaps not universally, to a single bidder, who offered himself as purchaser of the whole estate and who made his profits as *sector*[4] by separate sales of its several portions.

Use made of it by the praetor. The *missio in possessionem.*

Such proceedings, it has been thought[5], may have suggested to the praetor a mode of meeting one of the difficulties of his own court which had not been provided for by law. The Twelve Tables, in their rules about execution, had contemplated only the two cases of the *confessus* and the *iudicatus*: they had taken no account of the absconding debtor, who had incurred his obligation as the result of the sentence of a court. The praetor may have employed the *missio in possessionem* first against such an absconder; he may then have used it to meet the cases of the *indefensus* and the *confessus*, and lastly have extended it to the ordinary *iudicatus*. This stage was not reached until a late period of Roman history. The *missio* is said to have been introduced by a praetor P. Rutilius[6], perhaps at a time not far removed from the date of Cicero's birth.

[1] Liv. iii. 58; iv. 15; xxv. 4.

[2] Ib. xxxviii. 60; *Lex Tab. Bant.* l. 11 (whoever is condemned must either give *praedes* to the urban quaestor) 'aut bona eius poplice possideantur facito.' For a similar mode of execution following the *litis aestimatio* in cases of extortion see Cic. *in Verr.* i. 20, 52; 23, 61; *pro Rab. Post.* 4, 8; 13, 37.

[3] Cic. *Phil.* ii. 26, 64.

[4] 'Sector . . . emptor atque possessor' (Cic. *pro Rosc. Amer.* 36, 103).

[5] Huschke, *Nexum*, p. 169; Keller, *Civilprocess*, note 1031.

[6] Gaius, iv. 35. Keller, Rudorff and others consider him to be the

The conditions of its exercise are precisely those which we have examined in connexion with personal arrest. It is employed against any one who is *iudicatus*[1], who has not paid within the time allowed by law or by the praetor and who has not defended the *actio iudicati*, i.e. against one who is practically undefended. Although a comparatively new institution in the Ciceronian period, its use is not confined to praetorian actions. It is granted as a supplement to such traces of the *manus iniectio* as may have survived as well as to the imprisonment ordered by the praetor.

Conditions of the *missio*.

What its precise relation was to this latter mode of coercion is not known. The *lex Rubria* mentions them both in a single breathless clause[2], but it is by no means certain that it intends them to be concurrent. The complaint that comes from a penniless soldier, who had thrown in his lot with the Catilinarian movement, shows that both arms of the law could be employed in 63 B.C., and his grievance seems to be that the *missio* had not abolished imprisonment for debt[3]; but the passage is too general to prove that a man's goods could be sold and his body then be doomed to imprisonment. Doubtless the creditor might ask and obtain, not merely either mode of coercion, but both together. We must believe, however, that the completion at least of the *bonorum venditio* would have released the debtor from imprisonment; it is even questionable whether the commencement of the proceedings, the grant of the *missio*, would not have had this effect.

Its relation to personal execution.

great jurist, who was consul in 105 B.C. The *bonorum emptor* is mentioned in the *lex agraria* of 111 B.C. (l. 56).

[1] Gaius, iii. 78. The passage of the Edict referring to the *iudicatus* is not given in Cic. *pro Quinct.* c. 19, because it is not applicable to the process.

[2] *Lex Rubr.* c. 22, l. 47 'eosque duci bona eorum possideri proscreibeive veneireque iubeto.' Cf. l. 51.

[3] Sall. *Cat.* 33; see p. 279, note 1.

The *missio* could be originated by a single creditor.

The process of the *missio* could be set in motion by a single creditor. On his *postulatio*, if on the summary cognizance of the praetor it was held to be well grounded, a decree was issued giving him power to possess, to give notice of and (provisionally) to sell the goods of the defaulting creditor (*bona possideri proscribive venireque iubet*[1]). In certain cases, such e.g. as that of the creditor who was *rei publicae causa absens*, the writ only empowered possession, not proscription for sale[2].

Rights of the creditor who has obtained the *missio*.

The creditor who is in the enjoyment of this writ, does not possess ownership or even juristic possession of the goods. He is said to be in possession (*in possessione esse*) primarily for the purpose of administration and guardianship; and the praetor in his edict frames strict rules to protect the creditor against the abuse of these powers of administration:—

Qui ex edicto meo in possessionem venerint, eos ita videtur in possessione esse oportere. Quod ibidem recte custodire poterunt, id ibidem custodiant. Quod non poterunt, id auferre et abducere licebit. Dominum invitum detrudere non placet[3].

Bonorum proscriptio, venditio.

The public notice of the possession (*bonorum proscriptio*) was made immediately by the admitted creditor[4]; it was probably issued even in those cases where no sale was to follow within a given time; for, though it served the purpose of inviting purchasers to the *venditio*, its primary object was to warn the other creditors interested, that

[1] Cic. *pro Quinct.* 6, 25; 19, 60. It is done *ex edicto*, both at Rome (*pro Quinct.* 6, 25; 8, 30; 19, 60; *Lex Iul. Mun.* l. 116) and in the provinces (Cic. *ad Att.* vi. 1, 15). For the extent of the *causae cognitio* required for the writ see p. 258, on the *indefensus*.

[2] *Lex Iul. Munic.* l. 116. The *pupillus* and the *rei publicae causa absens* are here exempted from the *venditio*. In these cases the proscription was only meant to secure efficient representation. Cf. p. 257.

[3] Cic. *pro Quinct.* 27, 84. The decree was merely provisional and, as such, was to be issued *considerate* (Cic. *pro Quinct.* 16, 51).

[4] Gaius, iii. 220. It was effected by means of *libelli* posted up in the most frequented places (Cic. *pro Quinct.* 6, 27; 15, 50; 19, 61; 20, 63).

they too might enter on possession[1]. It also served the secondary purpose of inviting defence of the debtor[2]. The immediate result of this proscription was that all others who had claims against the debtor now entered with the original creditor on co-possession of the estate.

The time that must elapse between the proscription and the sale was, in the time of Gaius, thirty days if the goods of a living creditor were concerned, fifteen if they belonged to one who was deceased[3]. After the lapse of this limit the praetor orders an assembly of the creditors and bids them choose a president of the auction (*magister*) from their number[4]. This meeting also settled the conditions of the sale (*lex venditionis*)[5], the most important item of which was the percentage of the debt which the creditors were to receive; this percentage was doubtless fixed at as low a rate as possible: it would be hoped that competition at the auction might raise it to a higher level: but it marked the minimum or reserve price which the creditors were prepared to accept from a buyer. The definite day for the auction was perhaps fixed now and not at the time when the goods had been 'proscribed': but, even after it had been fixed, it was sometimes found necessary to adjourn it[6]. By praetorian rules the *bonorum venditio*

[1] For these other creditors see Cic. *pro Quinct.* 23, 73 'cur ceteri sponsores et creditores non convenerint.'

[2] For immediate resistance by the *procurator* of the debtor, on the ground of the invalidity of the writ, see Cic. *ib.* 6, 27; 19, 61.

[3] Gaius, iii. 78. For the thirty days' limit in Cicero's time see the form of the *sponsio* which the praetor ordered Quinctius to make (*pro Quinct.* 8, 30) 'SI BONA SUA EX EDICTO P. BURRIENI PRAETORIS DIES XXX POSSESSA [NON] ESSENT.' In the case of the living debtor, *infamia* follows the expiry of the thirty days' possession: i.e. it begins at the moment when the *bonorum venditio*, whether fulfilled or not, *can* become operative. The *Lex Iul. Munic.* l. 116 attaches it to the *bon. possessio et proscriptio*; cf. Cic. *pro Quinct.* 8, 30.

[4] Cic. *pro Quinct.* 15, 50; *ad Att.* i. 1, 3; vi. 1, 15; *ad Fam.* xii. 30, 5.

[5] Cic. *pro Quinct.* 15, 50.

[6] Cic. *ad Fam.* xii. 30, 5 'a magistris cum contenderem de proferendo die, probaverunt mihi sese, quo minus id facerent, et compromisso et iureiurando impediri.'

had itself to be completed in thirty or fifteen days, according as the creditor was living or dead[1].

Sale of the goods.

The sale itself was effected by public auction[2], and in Cicero's time the humane practice existed of admitting the debtor himself as a bidder[3], his offers being presumably accepted only if he presented very good security. The goods were bought at the highest proportion of their original value which was offered[4]—the proportion accepted being probably anything up to or above the percentage of the debts which the creditors had agreed to accept. The purchaser (*bonorum emptor*) might increase his profits by selling the different articles individually at his discretion[5].

The *bonorum emptor*.

The civil law, in its efforts to secure unity of responsibility in the exercise of rights and the fulfilment of obligations, regards the *bonorum emptio* as a case of universal succession[6] and by a fiction represents the *emptor* as the heir of the debtor. The praetor, therefore, gives actions both to and against him[7]. But his practice of dissipating the estate by renewed sale made it impossible for pontifical law to take the same view. Its object was to attach the *sacra* to some responsible perpetuator, and this it did by affixing them to that one of the creditors who had received the largest amount of the value of the debtor's estate[8].

[1] Gaius, iii. 79.

[2] Cic. *pro Quinct.* 15, 50.

[3] Cic. *in Verr.* i. 54, 142 'Ubi illa consuetudo in bonis, praedibus praediisque vendundis . . . ut optima conditione sit is, cuia res sit, cuium periculum? Excludit (Verres) eum solum cui—prope dicam soli potestatem factam esse oportebat.' The case in question was a renewed *locatio* for *sarta tecta* put up by Verres as praetor; but Cicero seems to make the rule apply to all cases of *bonorum venditio*.

[4] *pro portione* (Gaius, ii. 155).

[5] Cic. *pro Quinct.* 15, 50.

[6] Gaius, ii. 98; iii. 77.

[7] Gaius, iii. 81; cf. iv. 35 and 68.

[8] Cic. *de Leg.* ii. 19, 48 'Quarto (loco), qui, si nemo sit qui ullam rem ceperit, de creditoribus eius plurimum servet (astringitur sacris).'—The conclusion that has been sometimes drawn from this passage, that in Cicero's time there might be bankruptcy proceedings without universal possession (see Keller, *Civilprocess*, p. 423) is unnecessary. Yet it is quite possible that the theory of universal possession was not quite developed in Cicero's day.

§ 13. *Appeal and reversal of sentences.*

The two methods of interference with a judicial decree.

Every *iudicium* being set in motion by magisterial authority, its existence may be imperilled by the limitations which beset that authority itself. The greatest of these limitations are to be found in the graduation of power which is observed in the magistracy as a whole and in the conflict of authority which exists between the members of each magisterial college. These are expressed in two powers: (1) that possessed by the higher magistrates of prohibiting the actions of lower officials: (2) that possessed, not only by higher magistrates, but by those of equal power, of rendering invalid actions already performed by magistrates of lower or equal authority. The second is the *intercessio* proper; the first, though it sometimes bears this name, differs from the true intercession both in its conditions and its effects.

(i) The right of prohibition. Its extreme form the *iustitium*.

The right of prohibition employed by a magistrate with *maius imperium* or *maior potestas* against an inferior led, in the most extreme instances of its use, to the suspension of all civil justice (*iustitium*): for the ordinary judicial magistrate, the praetor, ranks below the dictator, consul and tribune, the three exponents of this power, and, once his *iurisdictio* has been forbidden, *iudicia* can no longer exist. Such an extreme exercise of authority was, according to constitutional precedent, regulated by the senate and dictated by special necessities of the state which were supposed to demand a suspension of public business; it is only in exceptional cases that it becomes the ultimate weapon in the hand of a revolutionist in authority[1]. But it might be employed, in exceptional cases, as a constitutional check on a reckless exercise of jurisdiction. It was apparently by an employment of this

[1] e. g. in that of Tiberius Gracchus (Plut. *Ti. Gracch.* 10).

power, sanctioned by the senate, that the consul Servilius Isauricus practically suspended the revolutionary praetor Caelius Rufus from his jurisdiction in 48 B.C.[1] Yet it must not be supposed that this prohibition renders the acts of the praetor invalid; on the contrary, the *ius* that he delivers is perfectly good, even after the prohibition has been made known to him. The prohibition is only effective in so far as it is actually enforced by magisterial coercion (*coercitio*); if the praetor chooses to pay his fine, to submit to the possibility of summary arrest, or to stand on his tribunal after his curule chair has been broken by an angry consul, he can utter *ius* which is unimpeachable and found *iudicia* whose verdicts no one can impugn.

(ii) The right of veto (*intercessio*).

Very different is the right possessed by colleagues as well as superiors, by the *par* as well as the *maior potestas*, to render ineffective the completed actions of equals or inferiors; this use of the intercession entails the complete invalidity of the act against which it is levelled. The intercession originated with the principle of colleagueship, and, except in the case of the tribune whose veto was all-embracing, was usually kept within these bounds. The praetor is thus subject to his equal colleague, another praetor, but also to his greater colleague, the consul; the curule aedile to his fellow in office and also possibly to the consul; in theory the aedile must also have been subject to the praetor, although no instance of praetorian veto over aedilician jurisdiction appears to be known.

Principles regulating the veto.

A power such as this of paralyzing activities, which are an outcome of the ordinary machinery of the state, must be regulated by certain principles if it is not to become chaotic. Such principles were formed, some as the result of practice, others as a consequence of the legal theory of the intercession. In practice the veto is regarded as a mode of supervision, exercised by closely related magistrates over one another and rendered necessary by

[1] Dio Cass. xlii. 23.

the theoretical irresponsibility of the officials against whom it is directed; it is meant to prevent illegal or inequitable actions, and thus to be called into force only when the written or unwritten law of the community has been violated. Legally, the *intercessio* in any given case is final, and the veto cannot be itself vetoed: and the whole theory of this power demands that magisterial acts only shall be affected by its exercise. The decision of a *iudex* or of jurors is thus exempt from the veto.

The *intercessio* outside Rome.

A more difficult question is whether the veto could be legally exercised in jurisdiction resting on the *imperium* outside Rome. Generally speaking, it was excluded from the military domain, and did not hamper the operations of a general in the field; it was thus excluded from what may be called camp-jurisdiction, whether civil or criminal [1]. But this does not prove it to have been necessarily inoperative in ordinary provincial jurisdiction. The practical exemption of the provincial governor from this check, which is dwelt on by Cicero, was a result of his having as a rule no colleague or superior in the province [2]; he has, however, an inferior in the shape of the quaestor, and intercession was doubtless possible in this case, although here the phenomenon of delegated jurisdiction and of control based on a different theory is also present. Accidentally it might happen that a praetor and consul, or praetor and proconsul, were commanding in the same province: here the veto may have been theoretically possible, but the case was so exceptional that it offered no regular guarantee of security to the provincials or to the Roman citizens in the district.

The *intercessio* rests on *appellatio*.

The intercession against the edict or decree, which is the only aspect of the power that we need consider here, rests on *appellatio*, the request for help (*auxilium*) which is

[1] Cf. Cic. *de Leg.* iii. 3, 6.

[2] Cic. *in Verr.* ii. 12, 30; *ad Q. fr.* i. 1, 7, 22. See p. 110, note.

BOOK I.

Principles regulating the appeal.

made by the individual who appeals against the ordinance by which he thinks himself injured. This *appellatio* must be made personally to the magistrate; and the exercise of the veto must be also personal. Thus the praetor peregrinus pulls up his chair next to that of his urban colleague and waits for appeals from the latter's decisions [1]. We must suppose that he only appeared in this way when he had reason to know that his services might be required or when a would-be appellant had dispatched a message to his court; otherwise the interceding magistrate must have got sadly in arrears with his own judicial business. The usual appeals seem to have been from one home praetor to another, although they might possess different *provinciae*. Thus, apart from the case of Caelius, we find that Verres as praetor urbanus had his decisions vetoed wholesale by his colleague Piso, who was probably praetor peregrinus, in cases where Verres had decided contrary to his own edict [2]; but we have already remarked the probably unusual instance of the consul, possessing no active jurisdiction, who yet vetoes a decision of the praetor urbanus in a case of *bonorum possessio* [3]. The great exception to the rule that the veto is kept within the limits of competence is found in tribunician intercession. The fact that appeals to the college of tribunes play a part in two of Cicero's speeches on private causes (those for Quinctius and for Tullius) [4] shows how frequent such requests for *auxilium* in civil jurisdiction must have been. The result of such an appeal, if made to the whole college and not to a single one of its members, might result in a quasi-judicial process. The case is heard before the benches of the tribunes (*ad subsellia tribunorum*); they take cognizance of the facts and the college gives its

Tribunician intercession.

[1] Caes. *B. C.* iii. 20 (Caelius Rufus in 48 B. C.) 'tribunal suum iuxta C. Treboni praetoris urbani sellam collocavit et si quis appellavisset . . . fore auxilio pollicebatur.'

[2] Cic. *in Verr.* i. 46, 119.

[3] p. 29.

[4] Cic. *pro Quinct.* 7, 29; *pro Tull.* 16, 38, 39.

verdict[1], sometimes with the grounds of its decision[2]. It is possible that in such cases it may have found by a majority of votes, although if one colleague persisted in the intercession he might overrule the adverse decision of the others.

Could the appeal be made by *peregrini?*

The *auxilium* sought by the *appellatio* appears rather as a magisterial power than a popular right; hence it is possible that the possession of civic qualifications by the appellant was not a necessary condition of its exercise. We know that Caius Gracchus offered his *auxilium* to *peregrini*[3]; and, if the foreign sojourner at Rome had not possessed the right of appeal, the limitations on the jurisdiction of the praetor peregrinus must have been singularly one-sided.

Effect of the veto.

The veto might be pronounced at any point of the proceedings *in iure* and effectively stop all further procedure, until it was amended in accordance with the interceder's wishes. Its primary function is simply to invalidate, and it is not the outcome of a true theory of appeal as conceived in modern times, because the higher court, not possessing jurisdiction in this matter, cannot substitute a new ruling for the one that has been quashed.

Its reformatory character.

Yet indirectly the compulsion may be so great as to compel the lower court to substitute a new ruling for the old: and in this sense the *appellatio* might lead to the actual *reform* of a sentence. It was used, for instance, against the *denial* of an exception to an action[4]; it was employed to prevent the formula being framed without a saving clause which would make the issue different[5]. But the

[1] Liv. xlii. 33. [2] Asc. *in Milonian.* p. 47. [3] Plut. *C. Gracch.* 12.

[4] Cic. *Acad. Prior.* ii. 30, 97 (speaking of the lying fallacy with a metaphorical appeal to legal procedure) 'Sed hoc extremum eorum est: postulant ut excipiantur haec inexplicabilia. Tribunum aliquem censeo adeant [*al.* videant]: a me istam exceptionem nunquam impetrabunt.'

[5] Cic. *pro Tull.* 16, 38 'quid attinuit te tam multis verbis a praetore postulare ut adderet in iudicium INIURIA, et, quia non impetrasses, tribunos plebis appellare et hic in iudicio queri praetoris iniquitatem quod de iniuria non addiderit?'

BOOK I.

compulsion on the praetor was only practical; if the case was to be tried at all it must be tried in this amended way; but no veto could compel him to act contrary to his judgement.

Change of venue.

Another mode of interference with jurisdiction is that effected by a change of venue. We are not here concerned with the shifting of a case from an incompetent to a competent court; that was amply provided for by law or by decree of the magistrate. It is rather where two courts are competent but where one is for certain reasons preferred that the right is made manifest. As we might expect, it is a right of the parties, and its sphere is provincial jurisdiction. The plaintiff or defendant in a civil suit which had commenced in the provinces could, if he was a Roman citizen, ask that the case should be transferred from the court of the governor to a competent civil court at Rome (*Romam revocatio*)[1]. If one of the parties to the suit was a senator it was within the privilege of the governor to transfer the case to the capital, even, as it seems, without a formal request from either litigant[2]. Both these items of procedure are clearly an outcome of customary law; no legal right to the change of court was possessed by the parties, and no compulsion could be placed on the governor[3]. The custom may have been in part a concession to the privilege of the Roman and the senator, but it may also have sprung from the desire of obviating the undue influence possessed by the ruling classes in the provinces.

Romam revocatio.

[1] Cic. *in Verr.* iii. 60, 138 'Scandilius . . . postulat a te ut Romam rem reiicias.'

[2] Cic. *ad Fam.* xiii. 26, 3 (to Servius Sulpicius, governor of Achaea in 46 B.C.) 'Illud praeterea . . . feceris mihi pergratum, si qui difficiliores erunt, ut rem sine controversia confici nolint, si eos, quoniam cum senatore res est, Romam reieceris.'

[3] *Cf.* the *Fragmentum Atestinum* (perhaps a part of the *lex Rubria*), l. 10 ff. Here the jurisdiction of the local magistrate in the *municipium, colonia, praefectura* is guarded against this practice as a right of the party; 'eius rei pequn(*iaeve*) quo magis privato Romae revocatio sit (*ex hac lege nihilum rogatur*).'

Hitherto we have been considering the interference which was possible with the legal ruling of a magistrate; but this modification of *ius* might seriously affect the *iudicium* as well. The very constitution of the court, whether formed by *iudex* or *recuperatores*, might be impugned, the *formula* might be altered in consequence of a persistent veto, and, if we may argue from Imperial to Republican law, up to the very moment when the verdict was pronounced, the *iudicium* might be dissolved either by the magistrate who had constituted it or by the interference of an equal or superior power[1]. But the *res iudicata* closes the sphere of magisterial interference; the sentence is unassailable, and it is only when execution, which is set on foot by purely magisterial authority, commences, that the veto is again possible.

Interference with the *iudicium*,

and with the *res iudicata*. Renewal of a case.

But modifications of this rigid rule are apparent even in the Ciceronian period. The cases before us do not make it possible to trace the principles of revision which were valid at this time; but they prove that it was known both in the Roman and the provincial courts. The instance which comes from Rome concerns the decemviral court, where it is manifest that the importance of the question of civic freedom had led to the adoption of rules of revision which were not applied to ordinary judicial business. Cicero speaks of cases in which the Ten had declared the *sacramentum* of the vindicator of liberty to be unjust, but had subsequently, on further investigation, reversed their judgement[2]. The trial may have been

[1] Paulus *ad Sabinum* in Dig. 5, 1, 58 'Iudicium solvitur vetante eo qui iudicare iusserat vel etiam eo qui maius imperium in eadem iurisdictione habet.' The *par potestas* is here omitted on account of the disappearance of the veto in virtue of it in the time of Paulus. See Merkel, *Gesch. der Klassischen Appellation*, ii. p. 19.

[2] Cic. *pro Domo*, 29, 77, and 78 'ius a maioribus nostris . . . ita comparatum est ut civis Romanus libertatem nemo possit invitus amittere. Quin etiam, si decemviri sacramentum in libertatem iniustum iudicassent, tamen, quotienscumque vellet quis, hoc in genere solo rem iudicatam referri posse voluerunt.' *pro Caec.* 33, 97 'Cum Arretinae mulieris liber-

BOOK I.

renewed before the same judges; and the renewal was probably effected by an appeal either to the magistrate who had constituted the court or to a colleague or superior of this official. There were doubtless fixed conditions for its acceptance, amongst which the proof of false evidence in the first trial or the acquisition of new evidence for the second have been conjectured [1].

Provincial jurisdiction. Power of the governor to renew a trial. Rulings of Q. Cicero.

In provincial jurisdiction the governor had the power of ordering a new trial without invalidating his own legal ruling or that of his predecessor. Q. Cicero, when propraetor of Asia, was approached by a litigant with the complaint that a bench of *recuperatores* had been coerced by his predecessor into returning a false judgement against their will. The remedy suggested by the governor was twofold, and was contained in the decree that the appellant

Si iudicatum negaret, in duplum iret: si metu coactos diceret, haberet eosdem recuperatores [2].

The drift of the first of these rulings is obscure; it suggests at first sight a raising of the merely formal question whether a verdict on the particular issue had been returned or not *(quaestio iudicatum sit necne)*; but, in raising this question, the propriety of the former verdict, its freedom from technical or real defects, would necessarily be determined as well. It can be moved by the condemned, as the *actio iudicati* is brought by the victorious party. In form it was perhaps a *praeiudicium* with a *sponsio poenalis* [3]: and the words *in duplum ire* probably imply the further danger of the loss of double the value of the matter at stake to the appellant who attempts and loses the process. The pursuit of this action could not of itself have led to a new positive judgement in favour of the plaintiff's main claim. It could only end in a confirmation

tatem defenderem ... decemviri prima actione non iudicaverunt: postea, re quaesita et deliberata, sacramentum nostrum iustum iudicaverunt.'

[1] Merkel, *op. cit.* p. 25.

[2] Cic. *pro Flacco*, 21, 49.

[3] Lenel, *Ed. Perp.* p. 356.

or denial of the validity of the *iudicium* appealed against; if the plaintiff was defeated and the decision of the new court was *iudicatum est*, the case was over; but, if he was successful, a third trial must have resulted, for the *poena* to which the unsuccessful defendant was now liable could in no way have represented the value of the matter in dispute.

The second ruling of Q. Cicero is based on the mere fact of the jury having decided against their will. A simple renewal is, therefore, ordained: the same jury is to be appealed to: and the equitable principle is adopted of putting the complaint of undue influence to its extremest test by asking a jury, now that the compulsion has been removed, to reverse its former judgement.

In delegated jurisdiction the mandator can rescind the rulings of his delegate.

A further interference, whether apparent or real, with a *res iudicata* in the provincial courts is based on the principle of delegated jurisdiction. The mandator can by the nature of the case rescind the rulings of his delegate: and it is not surprising to find that the proconsul or propraetor can quash the rulings *in iure* that are given by his quaestor or legate. Verres, when he reversed the action of his quaestor in the case of a woman of Lilybaeum whose claim to be the property of Venus had been proved before a bench of *recuperatores*, when he forced his subordinate to restore to the woman her confiscated goods, may have been vetoing his delegate's decree of execution, and not impugning the sentence of the court; but his edicts on other occasions seem to show a more definite design of revising the decisions of the *iudicia* of his province that rested on his own or on delegated jurisdiction. An edict is quoted to the effect that

Si qui perperam iudicasset, se cogniturum; cum cognosset, animadversurum [1].

The edict itself does not directly threaten an annulling

[1] Cic. *in Verr.* ii. 13, 33; cf. 23, 57.

of the sentence; it only promises renewed cognizance of some kind by the governor and the punishment of the guilty judges. But it implies reversal, which could be easily effected by vetoing the decree of execution. The doubtful point is whether reversal went further than this, whether the cognizance promised is an entire rehearing of the case by the governor, followed by the grant of a new *formula*. There is nothing improbable in such a practice of *in integrum restitutio* where the verdict was glaringly false[1]; but the words of the edict do not necessarily imply a rehearing by the magistrate[2]; the cognizance threatened may have had as its object merely the settlement of the question whether or not there had been a miscarriage of justice. Had this been proved, the case would probably have been sent under the same formula to another *iudex*.

Rescission of a *iudicium* (*in integrum restitutio*).

Actual rescission of a *iudicium* was, indeed, possible in provincial jurisdiction of this period, but it was based on the assumption that the law on which the *iudicium* rested was utterly bad, that there had, in fact, been no trial at all, because the court had been improperly constituted or instructed. Of such a character were the wholesale restitutions effected by Metellus, the successor of Verres, of his predecessor's acts in Sicily[3].

[1] Cf. Cic. *in Verr.* ii. 27, 66 'quodque iudicium . . . factum erat . . . id irritum iussit esse eumque iudicem falso iudicasse iudicavit.'

[2] So the second passage of Cicero (*l. c.* 23, 57) contains only a reference to the punishment in the words 'Tu qui institueras in eos animadvertere qui perperam iudicassent' (Merkel, *op. cit.* p. 33).

[3] Cic. *l. c.* 25, 62 'Metellus, simul ac venit Syracusas, utrumque rescidit, et de Epicrate (cf. 25, 61) et de Heraclio' (cf. 18, 45); 26, 63 'Alia iudicia Lilybaei, alia Agrigenti, alia Panormi restituta sunt.' Cf. *pro Flacco*, 32, 79.

BOOK II

CRIMINAL PROCEDURE

§ 1. *The criminal procedure of the earliest times.*

BOOK II. — Views of crime taken by primitive societies.

PRIMITIVE societies, in their attitude towards crime, look for punishment sometimes to the individual, sometimes to the gods, rarely to the corporate life of the commonwealth. They treat the offence as a ground for private revenge, either for a simple, equivalent vengeance, such as that of retaliation (*talio*), or for the more remunerative compensation of oxen, sheep, or metal. But a vague identification of the individual with the common weal leads them also to look on crime as a sin against the tribal gods, to be paid for by penalties which represent atonement to the divine being who has been injured or angered.

When the idea of the state has been gradually unfolded from its theocratic shroud, a crime is an offence against the commonwealth itself; but even now the relation of the violated right to the state may be a nearer or more distant one. The wrong may be regarded as a blow struck directly against the public security or inflicted on the state through the persons of its injured magistrates, or, as exemplified in the more common forms of criminal activity, it may be held to be an indirect injury to the welfare of society through the harm which has been inflicted on one of its individual members. In the latter case the state has taken up the burden of the individual; it is he that

BOOK II. is the main object of protection. The idea of retribution for a personal wrong has by no means disappeared, but the political society has identified itself with its members, and a wrong done to one of these is pre-eminently a matter for the commonwealth.

Conception of crime in early Roman law,

The earliest glimpse which we get of Roman history shows us a strong military monarchy which has succeeded a quasi-theocratic rule. The stage of a national conscience which forces a government to punish crime as a secular offence has on the whole been reached; yet there are very distinct survivals of the earlier conceptions of private vengeance and of sin. Vengeance is shown in the terms which still continue to denote punishment, such as *poena* (ποινή) and *multa*, the Sabine or Oscan word which originally perhaps signified compensation in cattle and was retained with the signification of a pecuniary penalty (*poena pecuniaria*)[1]. The right of *talio* in the form of 'a broken limb for a broken limb' still survived in the Twelve Tables[2]. It is probable that the right to kill, possessed over the nocturnal thief[3] and the adulterer caught in the act, is a survival of primitive vengeance, and the latest Roman law gives a prior right of prosecution to the injured person.

(i) As a ground for vengeance.

(ii) As a sin.

The religious idea that crime is sin left a still deeper mark on Roman jurisprudence. It is manifested in the names that survived for secular penalties, in survivals of primitive modes of inflicting punishment, and in the fact that, through the disappearance of purely religious sanctions, breaches of obligations which the modern world regards as crimes remained unpunished by the secular arm. *Supplicium*, the word which denotes the severest, and usually a capital penalty[4], was in early days a 'sin-

[1] Gell. xi. 1, 5; Festus, p. 142.
[2] Gell. xx. 1, 14 'Si membrum rupit, ni cum e pacto, talio esto.'
[3] Cic. *pro Mil.* 3, 9; cf. *pro Tull.* 20, 47.
[4] Cic. *in Verr.* ii. 37, 91; *pro Leg. Man.* 5, 11; *de Nat. Deor.* iii. 33, 81.

offering[1].' In its harshest form it originally necessitated the dedication of a sinner and his goods to some unappeased divinity. *Castigatio*[2] (*castus agere*) conveys the notion of purification through atonement.

The expiation for sin.

For sin to be done away the gods must be appeased by some form of expiation, and it is this *piaculum* which, in its character and amount, was adjudged with the minutest certainty by the chief pontiff, the head of the Roman religion. Even by the close of the monarchical period classes of offences had been drawn up showing the expiation which was the exact equivalent of each. A general sense of sin might demand a recurring expiation to avert the anger of the gods from the whole community; thus the secret sins of the people were atoned for by the lustral sacrifice which closed the census. Similar atonement was demanded for individual acts which were certainly misdeeds in the eye of heaven, but which, as not positively injurious to the human race, would have fallen short of the later conception of crime[3]. A mild instance was the touching of the altar of Juno by a concubine[4]; a graver infraction of religious law might be found in a homicide for which, through mitigating circumstances that had saved the slayer, the gods had never been appeased. When Horatius had been pardoned for the murder of his sister, the sin was yet expiated at the public expense, and the youth with veiled head passed under the beam that his father had been bidden to erect[5]. In some cases the pontifical law had reached the stage of refinement of making

Intentional and unintentional sin.

[1] Festus, p. 308 'supplicia veteres quaedam sacrificia a supplicando vocabant.' The sense of sin-offering, found in Plautus (*Rudens, prol.* 25), is still preserved in the Ciceronian period (Sall. *Cat.* 9, 2; Varro, *R. R.* ii. 5, 10).

[2] Cic. *de Off.* i. 25, 88.

[3] Cic. *de Leg.* ii. 9, 22 'Sacrum commissum, quod neque expiari poterit, impie commissum esto: quod expiari poterit, publici sacerdotes expianto.'

[4] Gell. iv. 3, 3; Festus, p. 222.

[5] Liv. i. 26; Dionys. iii. 22; Festus, pp. 297 and 307. For the *piaculum* following on incest 'according to the laws of King Tullus' see Tac. *Ann.* xii. 8, 2.

intent the determinant of the act and its atonement, for classes of sins were developed in which expiation was only accepted where the offence had been involuntary[1]. The man who had sinned of full consciousness (*prudens*) could not be expiated[2], a doom which overhung the perjurer, the man who had done injury to a god by taking his name in vain[3]. For intentional perjury (*conceptis verbis peierare*) no atonement could be accepted; nothing short of the life of the perjurer could expiate this deadly wrong. When the capital penalties of the pontifical college had sunk into desuetude, there was no secular punishment for this crime[4]. Perjury in Cicero's time is but a *dedecus*, not to be visited by the criminal law, but to be swept from the state by the censors as the guardians of its moral life[5].

Deadly sin punished by the *consecratio capitis*.

But apart from the consideration of the consciousness of the agent, to which a primitive society can attach little weight except when it is glaringly present or absent, there was a fixed class of deadly sins for which the gods would accept no atonement but the life and goods of the sinner himself. This *consecratio capitis* was the penalty for the wrong done to a client by his patron[6], for the ill-treatment of elders by their children[7], and for the injury inflicted on a neighbour, whether by the removal of his boundary stone[8] or the destruction of his corn by night[9]. Incest, too, in its graver forms belonged even in the late Republic to the class of offences for which no expiation but the immolation of the sinner could atone[10].

This *ius divinum* of the pontiffs, which was to a great

[1] The practice of strange, immoral, and superstitious rites could thus be expiated (Cic. *de Leg.* ii. 15, 37).

[2] Macrob. i. 16, 10; Varro, *L. L.* vi. 30.

[3] Cic. *de Leg.* ii. 9, 22 'Periurii poena divina exitium, humana dedecus.'

[4] Cf. the statement of the principle 'deorum iniurias dis curae' by the Emperor Tiberius in 15 A.D. (Tac. *Ann.* i. 73, 5).

[5] Cic. *de Off.* i. 13, 40; iii. 31, 111.

[6] Dionys. ii. 10; Serv. *ad Verg. Aen.* vi. 609.

[7] Festus, p. 230.

[8] Dionys. ii. 74.

[9] Plin. *H. N.* xviii. 3, 12.

[10] Cic. *de Leg.* ii. 9, 22 'Incestum pontifices supremo supplicio sanciunto.'

extent family law, covered the most simple needs of a primitive community, and perhaps went back to a time when such obligations were enforced by family councils before the growth of a central government. They were taken up by the king as the religious head of the community, and judgement and execution rested with him and his council of pontiffs. The extreme penalty which they might inflict, the *consecratio*, was doubtless in origin an actual sacrifice of the victim's life on the altar of a god, his property falling to the divinity as well. In most cases the deity so appeased was the one whom he had specially offended [1]. The perjurer was devoted to the god forsworn, the son to the *manes* of his parent, the remover of boundaries to Jupiter Terminus, the corn-thief to Ceres. But in some cases there was no god peculiarly concerned, and at times we find that the head and the goods of the criminal are dedicated to different divinities. 'The persons are generally adjudged to Jupiter, dispenser of life; the landed property to the gods who nourish the human race, Ceres and Liber [2].' This was, in fact, the form taken by the *lex sacrata* of 449 B.C. [3]

Later conception of *sacratio*; excommunication and outlawry.

But the custom of consecration had lost its rigidity, perhaps before the close of the monarchy, certainly in the early days of the Republic. A man might still be declared *sacer*, but immolation is no longer his fate. The word implies no more than excommunication or outlawry. The person banned is cut off from all divine and all human assistance. He is separated from the fire and the water of his tribe (*aqua et igni interdictus*), and any one may slay him with impunity [4]. In the earliest *leges sacratae*

[1] See Rein, *Criminalrecht*, p. 30. [2] Bouché-Leclerq, *Les Pontifs*, p. 196.

[3] Liv. iii. 55 'Ut qui tribunis plebis, aedilibus, iudicibus, decemviris nocuisset, eius caput Iovi sacrum esset, familia ad aedem Cereris Liberi Liberaeque venum iret.'

[4] Festus, p. 318 'At homo sacer is est quem populus iudicavit ob maleficium; neque fas est eum immolari, sed qui occidit parricidi non damnatur.' Cf. Dionys. ii. 10 and 74.

BOOK II.

of the Republic[1] the only immediate prize that the gods now gain is the property, not the life, of the victim. This theory of a man's being cut off from the community while his life was yet spared was of the utmost importance in the history of Roman criminal procedure. It familiarized the Romans with the idea that the severest penalty did not require the sacrifice of life, and as a form of exile it survived in that 'interdiction from fire and water' to which Cicero himself fell a victim.

The secular conception of crime. Punishment through the *imperium*.

When the political society of Rome is first revealed to us, relics of the theocratic organization, which we have sketched, are found to be embedded in a strong military monarchy. A secular conception of crime as an offence against the welfare of the state has arisen, and the king is the supreme criminal judge, mainly in virtue of his *imperium*. Tradition believed not only in a criminal jurisdiction independent of that of the pontifical college, but in one of such an extended kind that the Roman monarch was forced to choose delegates for his assistance. It was believed that the more important cases were tried by the king in person, the less serious transmitted to judges chosen from the senate[2]. The germ of this distinction was sought in an arrangement attributed to Servius Tullius. That reforming monarch is said to have kept for his own court all crimes affecting the public welfare, while wrongs done to private individuals he entrusted to private judges, giving as the *formulae* for their judgement the laws which he had himself ordained[3]. The nature of this trust is susceptible of a twofold interpretation. It may suggest the delegation of criminal cases to officials who, like the king, are true criminal judges; but the more probable implication is that those offences which in later times were known by the name of private delicts were now sent before a *iudex*. It need not be held that Servius' reform

[1] Liv. ii. 8; iii. 55.

[2] Dionys. ii. 14.

[3] *ὅρους καὶ κανόνας αὐτοῖς τάξας οὓς αὐτὸς ἔγραψε νόμους* (Dionys. iv. 25).

introduced the first separation between criminal and civil procedure, or that Servius was the founder of an independent criminal law; but the arrangement does seem to imply the commencement of a differentiation between the modes in which the state and the individual should protect their rights.

Perduellio and *parricidium.*

The sphere of the secular law administered by the king must not be measured by the meagreness of its nomenclature. The leading conceptions are *perduellio* and *parricidium*, but these terms included many offences that were not properly either treason or murder. *Perduellio* included any hostile attempt to injure the state by an attack against the whole body politic or against a magistrate or even against a simple citizen when the assailant adopted the attitude of a public enemy[1]. This was pre-eminently the sphere for the exercise of the criminal powers of the king regarded as the military head of the community. His jurisdiction in treason springs from the protection which he guarantees the state against internal enemies and from his position as maintainer of discipline over the members of his army. But, as the Roman people is an army even inside the walls, discipline within the city is an elastic conception. How widely it might be extended is shown by the tradition that the murder of a sister by the soldier Horatius was treated as *perduellio*. *Parricidium*, whatever may be its true derivation or original meaning, came at an early period to imply the slaying of a free citizen who was uncondemned; but it is not improbable that other capital offences, which could not be interpreted either as acts of treason or as breaches of religious law, may have been called by this name as falling under the cognizance of the regal delegates known as *quaestores parricidii*[2].

[1] Ulpian in Dig. 48, 4, 11 'perduellionis reus est hostili animo adversus rem publicam vel principem animatus,' a late reflection of an early truth.

[2] Festus, p. 221. Parricide as the murder of a relative would probably

BOOK II.

Criminal jurisdiction in the regal period.

So far as domestic jurisdiction, the absolute control of the household by the father, was excluded, either by the nature of the guilty parties or by the character of the crime, the king in the exercise of his military, civil, and religious power was the sole exponent of violated right. He had, perhaps, little control over the penalty. It was, indeed, enjoined in his rulings and carried out by his lictors; but in its various forms, death by the *arbor infelix*, by scourging, by drowning, or by hurling from the Tarpeian rock, it was fixed by the *mos maiorum*, if not by statute law. The trial was a personal investigation (*quaestio*) undertaken by the king with the assistance of a chosen body of advisers (*consilium*)[1], and the monarch might conduct the whole process and give sentence in person. But sometimes he uttered a merely conditional judgement. He specified the charge under which the accused was to be tried and the penalty to be inflicted, but he left the finding on the facts to delegates. Two such classes of representatives are attributed to the regal period; they are the *duumviri perduellionis* and the *quaestores parricidii*.

The *duumviri perduellionis* and the *quaestores parricidii*.

The offices specified by these names seem both to have been occasional in so far as the king could grant or refuse delegates at his pleasure; but, while the *duumviri* of the monarchy were in all probability, like those of the Republic, merely created to meet special emergencies, there is much to show that the quaestorship was even from monarchical times practically a standing office. The history of these latter functionaries is a strange one. Criminal assistants during the monarchy they become

have come under the cognizance of the domestic tribunal; cf. the words of Horatius' father (Liv. i. 26), 'se filiam iure caesam iudicare. Ni ita esset, patrio iure in filium animadversurum fuisse.' As a murder of a father it might require the cognizance of the king.

[1] Compare the charge brought by Livy (i. 49) against Tarquinius Superbus, 'cognitiones capitalium rerum sine consiliis per se solus exercebat.'

financial delegates early in the Republic; but even now, as subordinates to the consuls, they are at times entrusted with criminal investigations[1]. If the quaestorship was from the earliest times a more stable office than the duumvirate, this fact might show that the king was more personally concerned with jurisdiction in treason than with that exercised in connexion with other serious crimes[2]. In all cases there may have been an appeal from the delegates to the king, but tradition does not credit the monarch with any power of pardon.

The *provocatio*.

Whether this sovereign prerogative resided anywhere in the community depends to a large extent on our interpretation of the references to the trial of Horatius, perhaps a grand juristic fiction, but one none the less valuable as embodying a legal belief as to the archetype of the *provocatio*. In this story, as well as in other statements, we find the Roman conviction that the appeal to the people existed during the regal period[3]; but this belief is accompanied by the view that the citizens had no standing right of appeal against the king such as that secured against Republican magistrates by the first Valerian law. King Tullus in the trial of Horatius merely permits the appeal[4]; this power of refusing the right of *provocatio*

[1] For the monarchical origin of the *quaestores* see Tac. *Ann.* xi. 22; Ulp. in Dig. i. 13. Zonaras (vii. 13), who attributes the institution of the financial quaestors to Publicola, identifies them with the *quaestores parricidii* (cf. Varro, *L. L.* v. 81). The name is a true index of the origin of the office, *quaestor* bearing the same relation to *quaesitor* as *sartor* to *sarcitor* (Mommsen, *Staatsr.* ii. p. 537; cf. pp. 523 and 539). For a more artificial view which seeks to reconcile the conflicting accounts of our various authorities see Zumpt, *Criminalrecht*, i. p. 77.

[2] Yet the comparative infrequency of the offence of *perduellio* might account for the occasional character of the duumvirate.

[3] Festus, p. 297; Cic. *pro Mil.* 3, 7; *de Rep.* ii. 31, 54 'Provocationem autem etiam a regibus fuisse declarant pontificii libri; significant nostri etiam augurales.' Zumpt (i. p. 80) suggests that the pontifical books treated the appeal in connexion with jurisdiction, the augural in connexion with the auspices of the popular assembly to which the appeal came.

[4] Liv. i. 26 '"Si a duumviris provocarit provocatione certato" . . . auctore Tullo . . . "provoco" inquit.'

BOOK II.

was a characteristic of the early dictatorship, and on one occasion a dictator was entreated to look to the precedent of Horatius and to follow the king's example in allowing this reference to the people [1].

Probability of a popular jurisdiction independent of the will of the king.

But such instances do not prove that in every sphere of criminal jurisdiction the people could intervene only on the consent of the king. The power of the dictatorship, from which the story of Horatius was possibly reconstructed, expresses a revival of the military aspect of the monarchy and the martial jurisdiction which the king exercised in cases of *perduellio*. It is at least possible that before the close of the monarchy custom had established different spheres of criminal jurisdiction for the people and the king respectively [2], that it had determined those in which the king might, if he chose, be absolute, and those in which the people had a standing right to be the judge in the last resort. The true point of the story of Horatius may be that the appeal had been allowed even within the admitted sphere of regal jurisdiction. This interpretation seems to be in consonance with the meaning of the word *provocatio*. *Provocare* in its primary, and sometimes in its judicial meaning is 'to challenge [3].' *Provocatio* in the domain of criminal law might be a challenge by an accused to a magistrate to appear before another tribunal on the ground that he is not acting within his own right. If the appeal of the regal period was always a voluntary 'remit' by the king, it is difficult to see why it should have been called by a name which suggests the ideas of challenge and defence. And, if it is a request for pardon, the 'citation' of the magistrate, although this might be a necessary incident in the procedure, would not be its leading idea. For a challenge to be effective

[1] The request is made to the dictator Papirius by the father of the disobedient Fabius (Liv. viii. 33, 326 B.C.).

[2] See Ihering, *Geist des römischen Rechts*, i. p. 257.

[3] Cf. Gaius, iv. 93 (of the *actio per sponsionem*) 'Provocamus adversarium tali sponsione.'

there must be a right behind it; it was only in cases where the magistrate could judge alone that the *provocatio* was an act of grace.

But the right of *provocatio* exceedingly limited during the monarchy.

But the right of challenge possessed by the individual citizen could not have been a very wide one. If we consider the extent of the military and religious jurisdiction of the king, both of which excluded the appeal, the competence of the people, so far as the sphere of their permanent jurisdiction was concerned, must have been extremely small, and 'in this conflict of competence the position of the king was far more favourable than that of the people, since the people could be summoned only by the king. Hence the popular share in criminal jurisdiction was reduced to a minimum[1].' We have no means of determining whether this popular jurisdiction grew out of an earlier clan jurisdiction, or whether Rome was originally governed by religious and military law and the *provocatio* was an aftergrowth, the result of custom and of a custom chiefly due in origin to the voluntary waiving of his rights by the king.

§ 2. *The Criminal Procedure of the Early Republic.*

Republican laws of *provocatio*.

The abolition of the monarchy was soon followed by a limitation of the military jurisdiction of the magistrates who replaced the king. P. Valerius, one of the first consuls, is said to have introduced a law allowing an appeal to the people in their centuries against every sentence of a magistrate which was pronounced against the life of a Roman citizen. This *lex Valeria* (509 B.C.) completed the popular jurisdiction which had been growing up during the monarchy so far as capital and corporal sentences were concerned, and from this time no power but the people has the right to sanction finally the death penalty and scourging

The first *lex Valeria*.

[1] Ihering, *Geist*, i. p. 258.

BOOK II.

within the walls[1]. When Cicero speaks of the expulsion of the kings having been followed by 'the right of appeal on all matters[2],' he cannot mean that every sentence, pecuniary or otherwise, which was pronounced by a magistrate, could be appealed against; for this was never the case. His meaning may be that the sphere of the appeal was now made universal in so far as it extended to military jurisdiction within the ring-wall of the city. Outside this circle martial law could still be asserted by the magistrate with *imperium*, and one of the most important distinctions between the *imperium* at home (*domi*) and abroad (*militiae*) was the untrammeled character of the latter with reference to the appeal. The limit between the spheres was originally the *pomerium*, later it became the first mile-stone outside the walls[3]. Beyond this limit the axes were borne within the *fasces*, within it they were laid aside.

The *quaestores parricidii* of the Republic.

The consuls were the supreme judges; but the principle of delegation[4] was continued and seemingly in a more permanent form. The consuls were given two assistants for general purposes, the annually appointed *quaestores* whom they nominated: and the new constitution of 509 seems to have made them more permanent and essential than those of the monarchy. Then they had been regular vicegerents of the king, but had been nominated only for a given time; now they become an annual element in the constitution. Their functions are as unlimited as those of

[1] Cic. *de Rep.* ii. 31, 53 'ne quis magistratus civem Romanum adversus provocationem necaret neve verberaret'; cf. Liv. ii. 8. Dionysius (v. 19) adds ζημιοῦν εἰς χρήματα to ἀποκτείνειν ἢ μαστιγοῦν, and Plutarch (*Publ.* 11) seems to give the law the same wide scope. He also thinks (*l. c.*) that Valerius fixed the highest fine which the consul might impose (*multa suprema*, see § 4).

[2] 'Provocationes omnium rerum' (Cic. *de Rep.* i. 40, 62).

[3] Livy (iii. 20) carries this expression back to the middle of the fifth century B.C. But the question between the *pomerium* and the first milestone was a disputed one as late as 215 B.C. (Liv. xxiv. 9).

[4] See p. 304.

their masters, the consuls: but amongst them two duties stand out prominently, criminal jurisdiction and finance. The city quaestors (*quaestores urbani*), as they were subsequently called to distinguish them from their provincial colleagues, were known as *quaestores parricidii* and *quaestores aerarii*[1]. In both capacities they were permanent delegates of the consuls, but it cannot be supposed that these magistrates needed to employ them invariably for purposes of appellate jurisdiction. The consul could in all cases give sentence himself and appear to defend it before the people. But possibly regard for his dignity, and certainly respect for his time would lead him to choose the more indirect manner of communicating with the comitia. Although the designation *parricidii* rather tends to show that the chief judicial employment of the quaestors was intended to be ordinary capital cases, the trial, that is, of crimes that did not directly affect the welfare of the state[2], yet tradition does not regard them as having confined their activity to this class of cases. Some of the conflicting traditions concerning the trials of Sp. Cassius and of Camillus represent the quaestors as having been employed in these two trials for treason[3]. By their side we still find the *duumviri perduellionis* reappearing at intervals during the Republic. Before the revival of the office for the trial of C. Rabirius in 63 B.C., its existence is suggested for one famous trial of earlier times, that of M. Manlius in 384 B.C.[4].

The tendency of the Republic was to substitute popular

[1] The *quaestores parricidii* and *aerarii* are identified by Zonaras (vii. 13), following Dio Cassius, and by Varro (*L. L.* v. 81). This identity is denied by Pomponius (in Dig. i. 2, 2, 22, 23); but his denial seems to amount only to the belief that both kinds of *quaestores* existed side by side, without their functions being interchangeable; those, e.g., employed for finance would not have been employed for jurisdiction, and *vice versa*.

[2] Hence their supposed employment in the trial of M. Volscius for false evidence (459 B.C., Liv. iii. 24).

[3] Cic. *de Rep.* ii. 35, 60; Plin. *H. N.* xxxiv. 4, 13.

[4] Liv. vi. 20.

BOOK II.

Election of the quaestors after 447 B.C.

election for nomination, and after 447 B.C. the quaestors were elected by the *comitia tributa*[1]. Those employed for criminal purposes were chosen now from elected magistrates, but the theory of special consular delegation in each given case remained unimpaired. It is quite possible that the duumvirate, too, became a magistracy in the sense of owing its existence to the people, but it was a magistracy of an occasional and extraordinary character. The decision as to whether *duumviri* should be appointed in any given case would doubtless rest ultimately with the comitia[2], but the assembly may have chosen, according to circumstances, a more or less direct method of creation. It may at times have given them a *formula* contained in the *lex* which created them, and in this case the appeal or its equivalent, the popular jurisdiction consequent on the necessity of allowing the appeal, would perhaps have been excluded. The duumvirs may have decided independently and without appeal as special commissioners having a full mandate from the assembly. Another method of appointment—one that was apparently employed for the trial of Rabirius in 63 B.C.—was effected by the people giving the magistrate power to nominate duumvirs[3]. The comitia in this case neither created the delegates nor gave them instructions, and here the formalities of condemnation by the magistrate and appeal to the people were probably always preserved.

Mode of appointment of the *duumviri perduellionis.*

Presidency of the assembly by these delegates.

With respect to the control of the assembly which these two classes of delegates might be called on to consult, there is positive evidence that the quaestor, although a magistrate without the *ius agendi cum populo*, summoned and presided over the assembly himself[4]. The auspices necessary for the purpose were gained from a superior magistrate[5].

[1] Tac. *Ann.* xi. 22. [2] Dio Cass. xxxvii. 27; Cic. *pro Rab.* 4, 12; cf. 5, 17.

[3] Mommsen, *Staatsr.* ii. 1, p. 617.

[4] See Livy's account (iii. 24) of the trial of M. Volscius; 'tribuni . . . comitia quaestores habere de reo . . . passuros negabant,' and the quaestorian formula in Varro, *L. L.* vi. 91.

[5] Varro, *l. c.*; cf. Mommsen, *Staatsr.* i. pp. 93, 195.

In the same way the duumvirs may have had the summons and guidance of the *comitia centuriata*.

Ineffectiveness of the *provocatio* through the absence of an adequate sanction

Legislation had now secured appeal against execution and perhaps against corporal punishment in political as well as non-political jurisdiction. But the guarantee was merely a promise, rendered ineffective by the absence of an adequate sanction. Before the full development of the power of veto possessed by the tribunes, the only weapon within the reach of the would-be appellant was offered by the publicity of the proceedings. He would throw himself on the mercy of the crowd, and trust that their shouts or murmurs would bend the magistrate to respect the law. *Quiritare* was the name given to this informal request for help from the Quirites gathered near the tribunal or the scene of the levy [1], and tradition spoke of Publilius Volero and Sp. Maelius as having employed this last means of defence [2]. Even after the institution of the tribunate, it still had its uses, for the tribune might shrink from the exercise of his power until he was helped or goaded on by the public opinion which he was supposed to voice. But such a casual sanction would have been fatal to any right, and it was the work of later laws such as the third Valerian and the Porcian, to supply means for the enforcement of rights already gained.

This sanction eventually supplied and the *provocatio* tends to disappear.

Finally circumstances combined to render the *act* of *provocatio* almost unnecessary. Customary law dictated that the magistrate should not pronounce a sentence which he knew must lead to the appeal, and, consequently, when he held that the crime deserved such a sentence, he made no provisional pronouncement of his own but went directly to the people. Secondly, there was the practice, to which certain breaches of military or civic duty furnished a few exceptions, of permitting the accused who had been brought before the

[1] Varro, *L. L.* vi. 68 'quiritare dicitur is qui Quiritum fidem clamans implorat.' Cf. Cic. *ad Fam.* x. 32, 3.

[2] Liv. ii. 55; iv. 14; cf. ii. 27.

BOOK II.

magistrate and who mistrusted his chances of acquittal to avoid final condemnation by voluntary exile.

The Twelve Tables; their ordinances.

In following the history of criminal procedure we next arrive at the great epoch of codification. The Twelve Tables introduced no radical changes; they contented themselves with upholding the principles which had rested on isolated statutes or on custom. Three of their ordinances might be cited in later times as giving a new foundation to certain civic liberties.

(i) on the *provocatio.*

(i) We are told by Cicero that they granted the *provocatio* 'from every kind of court and punishment[1].'

A literal interpretation of these words would lead us to the conclusion that the system of appeal was extended and that every sentence pronounced by any magistrate might be questioned. But this was not the case. The law of the Twelve Tables did not deal with the *provocatio* as such nor make it the subject of any one special enactment. It dealt with it only in connexion with the crimes and punishments mentioned in its separate clauses. The liberty to appeal was thus often repeated in the code[2], and hence it might be said, with an approximation to truth but with some degree of inaccuracy, that the charter permitted the appeal from every kind of *iudicium* and *poena.*

(ii) against *privilegia.*

(ii) It was declared, in accordance with previous custom and perhaps enactment, that no law or criminal sentence of the people (and the sentence too took the form of a *lex*) should be directed against a private individual[3].

The essential features of a *privilegium.*

The essence of the *privilegium* thus forbidden may be summed up in five points:—

[1] Cic. *de Rep.* ii. 31, 54 'ab omni iudicio poenaque provocari licere indicant XII Tabulae compluribus legibus.' *Lex* here means a subdivision of a table as in Festus, p. 273.

[2] Cf. Zumpt, *Criminalrecht*, i. p. 361 'In the laws (of the Twelve Tables) through which a special penalty was pronounced for an offence, the *provocatio* was mentioned at the end, either immediately or at least mediately in that, according to the fashion of Roman laws, the *lex Valeria* was declared to be unrepealed.'

[3] Cic. *de Leg.* iii. 19, 44; cf. 4, 11; *pro Domo*, 17, 43.

(*a*) It must have reference to a special person or special persons[1], but it must not be in their favour. An enactment conveying special powers, such as those given to Pompeius, or conferring a gift such as citizenship, was not an act of privilege[2].

(*b*) It must, therefore, be directed against an individual or individuals and inflict pains and penalties or disabilities on him or them.

(*c*) The individuals must be designated by name or by some indications which show that a definite class is intended.

(*d*) The law must be retrospective[3], not prospective. Even when it threatens penalties prospectively without the formality of a trial it could not be regarded as a *privilegium*. Thus the *lex sacrata* which made the tribune's person sacrosanct, and threatened any one who injured him with outlawry, was never regarded in this light[4].

(*e*) According to a mode of statement common in Cicero's time, the force of which we shall examine later, the law must pronounce a sentence not preceded by a *iudicium*.

Question whether the proscriptions come under the head of *privilegia*.

No acts of state would seem to be exposed to such wholesale condemnation on these grounds as the proscriptions set on foot by Sulla and the Triumvirs. Cicero sees their essential connexion with the *privilegium*[5], but, perhaps with good reason, does not cite the Sullan *régime* as an instance of this form of illegality. However iniqui-

[1] Cic. *de Leg.* iii. 19, 44 'In privatos homines leges ferri noluerunt: id est enim privilegium . . . cum legis haec vis sit ut sit scitum et iussum in omnes.'

[2] Zumpt, i. p. 367.

[3] Retrospective, i. e. with reference to the facts on which the disability is based. Sulla's disqualifications of the descendants of the proscribed were, from this point of view, retrospective.

[4] Zumpt, i. p. 368.

[5] Cic. *pro Domo*, 17, 43 'Proscriptionis miserrimum nomen . . . quid habet quod maxime sit insigne ad memoriam crudelitatis? Opinor, poenam in cives Romanos nominatim sine iudicio constitutam.'

BOOK II. tous the Sullan proscription might be, it would have been within the letter of the law, had Sulla been appointed dictator before it commenced. For the creation of a dictator *optima lege* was a suspension of the constitution, and he could exercise his inappellable military jurisdiction over those whom he adjudged traitors to the state. Our authorities, however, are agreed that the proscription list was published before the dictatorial authority was conferred[1], and that, when it was conferred, a retrospective sanction was given to the dictator's acts and a special clause of the enactment granted him the power of adjudicating on the lives and property of the citizens[2]. The *lex Valeria* which conferred these powers[3] was as wholly the work of Sulla as a Cornelian law, which also had reference to the proscription[4]: and it is impossible for us to distinguish between the provisions of the two enactments. The disabilities imposed on the children of the proscribed—a more glaring instance of a *privilegium* even than the execution of their parents—still remained in force in Cicero's day and was the one point in his legislation which neither the democratic nor the moderately aristocratic party ventured to assail. The legality of Sulla's regulations was, in fact, never questioned, and Cicero, while affirming their injustice, never doubts their legal validity[5].

The second proscription was, in its form, more legal than the first; for it did not definitely commence until the triumvirs had been invested with their extraordinary powers *reipublicae constituendae*[6], and when, therefore, all the ordinary guarantees of the constitution had been sus-

[1] Plut. *Sulla*, 32; App. *B. C.* i. 97.

[2] Plut. *l. c.*; cf. Cic. *de Leg. Agr.* iii. 2, 8.

[3] It was the work of the interrex L. Valerius Flaccus (App. *B. C.* i. 98).

[4] Cic. *pro Rosc. Amer.* 43, 125; *in Verr.* i. 47, 123; Cic. *ap. Quintil.* xi. 1, 85.

[5] Cic. *l. c.*; cf. *de Leg.* i. 15, 42.

[6] Liv. *Ep.* cxx; App. *B. C.* iv. 7.

pended. But Cicero's death was not due to an indirect order given formally by the people. A preliminary proscription of sixteen persons, amongst whom was the orator himself, had already been carried out by the consul Pedius on the mere mandate of the triumvirs.

Political crises, such as those which lead to proscription and the extirpation of a hostile party, sweep away all ordinary guarantees, and the death-dealing ordinances which they bring stand on a plane different from that of the ordinary *privilegium*. In the first place, they are formally the result of unlimited military jurisdiction over *hostes* and, in the second, they might, as in the case of the Sullan proscriptions, obtain retrospective validity. The Roman people could grant indemnity for any act; the Twelve Tables guaranteed the sovereignty of the popular assembly by declaring that its last enactment should be final without setting limits to the sphere of its legislative activity, and the Tables themselves were not guarded against repeal either temporary or permanent.

The prohibition of *privilegia* was therefore, in the ultimate theory of the constitution, nugatory. But there can be no question of its force as a working principle under ordinary circumstances. If we omit for a moment the last and least certain condition of a *privilegium*—the absence of judicial investigation—the prohibition seems to inhibit the possibility of special impeachments in either of the two forms which they can assume. An impeachment may be special either as applying a new procedure and perhaps new penalties to an act which the law already regards as a crime, or as making an act not already provided for by the criminal law into a crime. There were thinkers who attacked both these methods as violating the provision of the Twelve Tables. An instance of the first kind is furnished by the trial of Milo in 52 B.C. In this case both a new procedure and a new penalty were contemplated for offences already provided for by law, and

Are special impeachments instances of *privilegia*?

BOOK II. the enactments creating this procedure and penalty were ineffectually denounced as *privilegia*[1]. As an instance of the second kind we may cite the expansiveness of the conception of *perduellio* in tribunician prosecutions. Treason was ever embracing fresh spheres of conduct and the prosecution of Serv. Sulpicius Galba in 149 B.C. for his treachery to the Lusitanians was denounced as resembling an act of privilege[2]. The prosecution of Clodius in 61 B.C. for *incestum*, which was not incest according to the current law, was a still more glaring instance of this kind of impeachment.

But such interpretations would have struck at the root of all the special commissions established at Rome. Their frequency shows how little they could have offended the juristic sense of Romans in spite of occasional attacks by constitutional purists[3]. Doubtless the renewed definition of a crime was considered more of a *privilegium* than a mere change in procedure; but the later Republican view seems to have been to restrict the idea of privilege to sentences pronounced against an individual or group of individuals which were unproceeded by trial[4]. This is one of the grounds of Cicero's criticism of the measure of Clodius which kept him in exile[5]. We shall see, however, that this second law of Clodius was not a bill of banishment but a formal bill of outlawry enacted against one who had evaded trial by voluntary exile. The type of a pure unadulterated *privilegium* is well imagined by Cicero:—

Conception of a *privilegium* in the later Republic.

[1] Asc. *in Milon.* p. 37.

[2] Cic. *Brut.* 23, 89 'L. Libone tribuno plebis populum incitante et rogationem in Galbam privilegii similem ferente'; cf. *de Orat.* i. 53, 227 ('quaestionem ... ferente') and *pro Mur.* 28, 59. From the vague accounts it may, perhaps, be gathered that L. Scribonius Libo proposed a special commission.

[3] Tac. *Ann.* iii. 27, 5 'Iamque non modo in commune sed in singulos homines latae quaestiones.'

[4] 'poenam ... nominatim sine iudicio constitutam' (Cic. *pro Domo*, 17, 43).

[5] Cic. *de Leg.* iii. 19, 45; *pro Sest.* 30, 65; 34, 73; *ad Att.* iii. 15, 5; *pro Domo*, 10, 26; 16, 43; 17, 43; *post Red. in Sen.* 4, 8.

Velitis iubeatis ut M. Tullius in civitate ne sit bonaque eius ut mea sint[1].

But Clodius had carefully guarded against this form. Following the outline of the tralaticiary bills of outlawry introduced by the tribunes against those who had sought voluntary exile to escape trial or condemnation[2], he assumed the exile to have already commenced and framed the command of interdiction in the past tense[3].

(iii) Capital sentences can only be pronounced by the *comitia centuriata*.

(iii) A third provision of the Twelve Tables was that no capital sentence could be passed except by the greatest of the comitia[4].

The greatest of the comitia was the centuriate assembly[5], and this ordinance certainly denies capital jurisdiction to the *comitia tributa populi*, an assembly which had been formed in imitation of the *concilium plebis*, probably not long before the epoch of the decemviral legislation[6]. But later interpretation held that this clause struck a blow at the capital jurisdiction of the *concilium plebis* itself. It is, however, doubtful how far the extraordinary jurisdiction of this body, resting on a religious sanction, could

[1] Cic. *pro Domo*, 17, 44.

[2] Cic. *in Verr.* ii. 41, 100 'Nuntiabatur illi ... me ipsum apud hoc collegium tribunorum plebis, cum eorum omnium edicto non liceret Romae quemquam esse qui rei capitalis condemnatus esset, egisse causam Sthenii.' The *confessus* must in this respect have been placed on a level with the *condemnatus*, and under *confessi* may have been reckoned those who went into voluntary exile to escape prosecution.

[3] Cic. *pro Domo*, 18, 47, see § 7.

[4] Cic. *de Leg.* iii. 4, 11 'de capite civis nisi per maximum comitiatum ollosque quos censores in partibus populi locassint, ne ferunto.' Cf. 19, 44 and 45; *pro Sestio*, 30, 65; *de Rep.* ii. 36, 61.

[5] Zumpt (i. p. 365) thinks that *maximus* not only expresses the greater dignity of this assembly but the fact of its being actually the largest in size. It would have been the largest, not only because it was attended in greater numbers by the upper classes, but because the consuls had the legal power to enforce attendance at it. The fact of its being the *exercitus* would distinguish it in this respect even from the *comitia tributa populi*.

[6] It exists five years after this legislation (447 B.C.) for the election of quaestors (Tac. *Ann.* xi. 22).

BOOK II.

have come within the intention of a law such as that of the Twelve Tables, which never treated the *plebs* as a political corporation at all. We shall discuss the question later whether the provision, even as so interpreted, remained intact down to Cicero's day. Whether it remained or not, this exclusive capital jurisdiction of the *comitia centuriata* had, as we shall see, no connexion with the merits of Cicero's exile. He was never tried before the *concilium plebis*, nor did the act of outlawry pronounced against him by that body ever claim to be a judicial sentence.

For many years after the decemviral legislation no advance was made in the theory of the appeal, whether in the way of extending it or of supplying it with a more adequate sanction. Yet its perpetuity, except in the gravest crises, was assured by one of the Valerio-Horatian laws of 449 B.C., which enacted that 'no one should in future create a magistrate from whom there was no appeal, and that any one guilty of such a creation should be protected by no law sacred or profane, but might be slain with impunity[1].' This law was evidently invoked by the unlimited power of the decemvirate which had been just abolished. It rendered the creation of an absolute judicial power by the *rogatio* of a magistrate a capital offence on the part of the proposer, even when the proposal had been accepted by the people. But the scope of the *provocatio* was not extended. The 'creation' of a magistrate referred to election sanctioned by the people and did not, therefore, affect the right of the consul to nominate a dictator from whom there was no appeal. Nor did it extend the limits of the appeal beyond the original boundaries, the *pomerium* or, at the utmost, the first milestone from the city. This second extension was never reached at all except by a fiction applicable to the Roman colonies and *municipia*, while the first limitation was probably effected more than a century

Further laws of appeal; the Valerio-Horatian laws.

[1] Liv. iii. 55; cf. Cic. *de Rep.* ii. 31, 54 'ne qui magistratus sine provocatione crearetur.'

later. It was perhaps the third *lex Valeria* of 300 B.C. which introduced an important modification into the powers of the dictator. He was made subject to the *provocatio*[1] within the city, a change which, while not hampering the power of this magistracy in the field, prevented its use for ruthlessly crushing a so-called sedition in Rome.

Legislation on the *provocatio* has from this point onwards two objects. The first was to secure an adequate sanction for the rules already established, and this was effected by the third Valerian and the Porcian laws. The second, which was aimed at in a much later period of Republican history, was to limit the right claimed by the senate to establish martial law and to permit the trial and execution of citizens without appeal.

The third lex Valeria.

The third *lex Valeria* (300 B.C.) allowed the appeal from a threat of death by the axe and by the rod or from simple scourging[2]. It did not forbid the imposition of these penalties, but, like the other laws of *provocatio*, the execution after the appeal had been made[3]. The novel element in the law was the attempt to fix a sanction; it declared its violator guilty of an *improbe factum*. Nothing more than moral reprehension seems at first sight to be conveyed by this sanction; but even moral censure might be followed by almost penal consequences, since the magistrate who incurred it might be excluded from the senate at the *lectio senatus*, which some twelve years before the passing of this law was already in the hands of the censors. It is possible, however, to give the threat a more definite meaning by supposing that

[1] Festus, p. 198.

[2] Liv. x. 9 'M. Valerius consul de provocatione legem tulit diligentius sanctam . . . Valeria lex, cum eum qui provocasset virgis caedi securique necari vetuisset, si quis adversus ea fecisset, nihil ultra quam improbe factum adiecit.' This law is not mentioned by Cicero in his summary of the laws of appeal (*de Rep.* ii. 31, 54), probably on the ground implied by Livy (*l. c.*) that it was taken up into the Porcian legislation.

[3] This is the meaning of 'qui provocasset' (Liv. *l. c.*), cf. 'adversus provocationem' in Cicero's account of the first Valerian law (Cic. *l. c.* § 53).

BOOK II. the transgressor was made *improbus intestabilisque*, 'incapable of being a witness to and so proving a mancipation[1].'

The Porcian laws.

The object of the Porcian laws was to supply a still more effective sanction for the prohibition of execution and scourging. Three enactments, of unknown date and probably differing in detail, went by this name; but all three seem to have possessed a unity of purpose which is reflected in the frequent mention of a single *lex Porcia* as though it embodied the whole spirit of the Porcian legislation. Three chief characteristics are attributed to these laws.

(i) At a first glance they seem to have extended the theory and practice of *exilium*. Even in the time of Polybius voluntary exile to escape the infliction of a penalty was apparently only possible *before* condemnation had been pronounced by the people[2]. But two passages in the *Catiline* of Sallust, which reflect the law of the Ciceronian period, seem to assert that a *lex Porcia* made exile possible *after* condemnation and that in this effect it was supported by other enactments[3]. Probably, however, this is but a careless and indirect reference to a law bearing on the *provocatio*; for an enactment allowing the appeal and, therefore, permitting voluntary exile while it is being heard, might easily be said to grant exile to the condemned. It might be said to do so in a still more literal sense if, with Mommsen, we take the 'condemnation' here to refer to the sentence of the magistrate against which the appeal is lodged[4].

[1] Gell. xv. 13, 11.

[2] Polyb. vi. 14.

[3] In the debate on the execution of the Catilinarian conspirators Caesar is represented as saying (Sall. *Cat.* 51, 21) 'Sed, per deos immortales, quam ob rem in sententiam non addidisti uti prius verberibus in eos animadverteretur? An quia lex Porcia vetat? At aliae leges item condemnatis civibus non animam eripi sed exilium permitti iubent.' Cf. 51, 40 'tum lex Porcia aliaeque leges paratae sunt, quibus legibus exilium damnatis permissum est.'

[4] Mommsen in *Neue Jenaische Litteraturzeitung*, 1844, p. 258.

They were laws of appeal, and first attached an adequate sanction to the *provocatio.*

(ii) *Leges Porciae* attached an adequate sanction to laws enjoining the *provocatio*[1]. A comparison of the passages in which this aspect of the legislation is described seems to yield the result that no Porcian law made the execution of a citizen by the axe or rod or his submission to scourging *ipso iure* illegal, but merely submitted the threat of such punishment to appeal. From Cicero's statements we gather that in his own day scourging was still, as it had always been, formally a part of the *coercitio* of a Roman magistrate, and that the *leges Porciae* or the *lex Porcia* (if it was only one of these laws that protected the back of the citizen) merely added a sanction to a provision which already allowed an appeal from a threat of *verbera*[2]. The passage of Livy, which makes the *lex Porcia* a complement to the third *lex Valeria* with respect to the sanction imposed, is still more explicit[3]. The two laws had the same scope; they took cognizance of death by the axe and by the rod, death, that is, as inflicted by the *fasces*. Since, therefore, the Porcian laws were laws of appeal, and the third *lex Valeria* completed by the *lex Porcia* had the same character, the effect of the Porcian legislation must have been still further to enforce the appeal in cases where it had already been permitted[4].

(iii) Consequently the passages which seem to speak of scourging or death by scourging as having been abolished by Porcian laws[5] must be interpreted in this modified sense. The passages do not imply an absolute prohibition

[1] Cic. *de Rep.* ii. 31, 54; Liv. x. 9.

[2] Cic. *de Leg.* iii. 3, 6 'magistratus nec oboedientem et noxium civem multa, vinculis, verberibus coerceto, ni par maiorve potestas populusve prohibessit, ad quos provocatio esto'; *de Rep.* ii. 31, 54 'neque vero leges Porciae, quae tres sunt trium Porciorum, ut scitis, quidquam praeter sanctionem attulerunt novi.'

[3] Liv. x. 9, see p. 319, note 2. The protection of the citizen's back is the protection against the death penalty of scourging (the execution *more maiorum*, Suet. *Ner.* 49) as well as against flagellation as a punishment.

[4] From this point of view the Porcian law is called by Cicero the *principium iustissimae libertatis* (Cic. ap. Asc. *in Cornelian.* p. 77).

[5] Cic. *pro Rab.* 3, 8; 4, 12.

BOOK II. of the rod, and we know that the execution *more maiorum* was never abolished in Roman law. Its infliction on one who was declared a *hostis* means that it could be inflicted wherever there was held to be no appeal. The same implication is visible in Caesar's speech on the execution of the Catilinarian conspirators. 'Why not add scourging to your death penalty?' he argues; 'Because you are afraid of violating the *provocatio* permitted by the Porcian law. But you are violating it in putting these citizens to death by the administrative decree of the magistrate[1].' There is no evidence that the Roman citizen was ever freed from the penalty of scourging, whether as a result of magisterial coercion or of the laws[2]; the *leges Porciae* were framed on the analogy of the older laws dealing with the *provocatio*, and followed the usual principles of Roman protective legislation. 'These principles were the limitation of the power of the magistrate without the limitation of that of the people, and the security for the authority of the people and for the occasional imposition of a justifiably severe penalty by taking from the magistrate the right to execute and not the power to sentence[3].'

Yet the delay consequent on an appeal to the people and the difficulty of eliciting a decree sanctioning an odious and degrading punishment might have led to the practical disappearance of scourging as a means of magisterial coercion. Where scourging was enjoined by the laws, exile would have assisted the accused, and the door of banish-

[1] Sall. *Cat.* 51, 21 and 40, quoted p. 320, note 3. A reminiscence of the Porcian laws, as laws permitting the appeal, appears on a *denarius* of P. Laeca (Babelon, *Monnaies de la République Romaine*, ii. p. 369). The scene represented by the type is apparently an appeal against scourging in the military levy (*Classical Review*, xi. p. 440). For instances of the infliction of such a punishment on those who refused to serve, see Liv. ii. 55; vii. 4.

[2] An instance of scourging at Rome occurs as late as 138 B.C. A deserter 'damnatus . . . sub furca diu virgis caesus est et sestertio nummo veniit' (Liv. *Ep.* lv). For laws inflicting scourging as a *poena*, see Festus, p. 234.

[3] *Classical Review*, xi. p. 440.

ment stood open to one who would otherwise have been condemned to death by the rod[1]. BOOK II.

Their sanction.

The sanction of the Porcian laws probably consisted in making an offence against them equivalent to the crime of treason (*perduellio*). This consequence seems to be implied in Cicero's threat to prosecute Verres before a *iudicium populi*, for it was with the charge of treason that the undefined jurisdiction of the *comitia* was chiefly concerned in the orator's day. The offence complained of was the execution of a Roman citizen in a province, which Cicero appears to interpret as a violation of the spirit if not of the letter of the Porcian laws[2].

Future protective legislation aims at the abolition of martial law. The *lex Sempronia*.

Here with the interposition of an effective sanction the series of laws on the *provocatio* proper comes to an end. Future legislation aimed only at emphasizing it in a sphere within which its application was questioned. This was the sphere of martial law, which the senate of the later Republic claimed the right to create. The aim of the *lex Sempronia* of C. Gracchus (123 B.C.) was to prevent the declaration by a magistrate, on the advice of the senate, that a Roman had forfeited his civic rights and was, therefore, a *hostis*[3]; and, since a consequence of such a declaration was that a military *iudicium* was set on foot by the magistrate, it asserted the principle that no *iudicium* should be established on the *caput* of a Roman citizen except by command of the people[4]. This second clause

[1] For other views that have been held about the Porcian laws, see Zumpt, i. 2, p. 68; Lange, *Commentatio de legibus Porciis*.

[2] Cic. *in Verr.* i. 5, 12 and 14; cf. *pro Mil.* 14, 36 (ironically of Clodius' threatened procedure against himself), 'Diem mihi, credo, dixerat, multam irrogarat, actionem perduellionis intenderat.'

[3] Plut. *C. Gracch.* 4 τὸν δὲ (νόμον εἰσέφερε), εἴ τις ἄρχων ἄκριτον ἐκκεκήρυχοι πολίτην, κατ' αὐτοῦ διδόντα κρίσιν τῷ δήμῳ. ἐκκεκήρυχοι here means 'proclaim as a *hostis*.' It is not exactly equivalent to *aqua et igni interdicere* as taken by Zumpt (i. 2, p. 71). The latter declaration could be made only by the people; but the practical effects of both would be the same, so far as unconditional submission to the *imperium* in Rome was concerned.

[4] Cic. *pro Rab.* 4, 12 'C. Gracchus legem tulit ne de capite civium Romanorum iniussu vestro iudicaretur.' Cf. *in Cat.* iv. 5, 10.

BOOK II.

went further than the case of the declaration of martial law. It rendered legally impossible those special commissions with capital jurisdiction on ordinary crimes which had, as we shall see, from time to time been established by the senate. The magistrate was inevitably the object aimed at directly by the bill, but the responsibility of senators for their share in the forbidden proceedings seems also to have been recognized[1]. The sanction was at the least the declaration that the act was treason (*perduellio*); but perhaps it was even simpler than this. It is possible that on the proof of the act before the people, outlawry (*aquae et ignis interdictio*) was to follow.

Its sanction.

Its probable recognition of the *concilium plebis* as a competent court.

We are not told what popular court was intended to enforce this sanction. Since the penalty was a capital one, enforcement would be the privilege of the *comitia centuriata*, unless there was express legislation to the contrary. But there is a strong probability that such legislation was forthcoming, and that Gracchus widened the power of the people and the magistrates by giving to the *plebs*, as well as to the *populus*, capital jurisdiction in this particular case[2]. In the first place it is somewhat unlikely that the man who meant to make the tribunate the central power in the state should have been content to rest the sanction of his great *plebiscitum* on the jurisdiction of the *comitia centuriata*, which the tribune could not summon. Again the combination of two constitutional analogies might be thought to give justification for the change. The Valerio-Horatian laws had threatened outlawry against any one who created a magistrate without

[1] Schol. Ambros. p. 370 'Quia sententiam (wrongly for 'legem,' see Zumpt 1, 2, p. 73) tulerat Gracchus ne quis in civem Romanum capitalem sententiam diceret.' That this is true seems shown by Cic. *pro Sest.* 28, 61 and Dio Cass. xxxviii. 14. Senators were sometimes regarded as responsible officials. They are in the *Lex Tabulae Bantinae* (l. 7), and probably in the sanctions to the second law of Clodius by which Cicero was outlawed (Cic. *ad Att.* iii. 12, 1; 15, 6).

[2] δῆμος in Plutarch (*C. Gracch.* 4) may refer to either or both.

appeal. This seemed to make *aquae et ignis interdictio* an appropriate remedy here. But the *plebs* had never ceased to pronounce on bills of outlawry, for the formal acts of interdiction against exiles were, as we have seen[1], within tribunician competence. Thirdly, Gracchus as tribune put his own law into force against Popilius[2], and we may conclude without hesitation that for this purpose he approached the assembly of the *plebs*. Lastly the steps taken by Clodius in his attack on Cicero seem to show that he contemplated a prosecution before the tribes. The resolution which he elicited from the *concilium plebis* seems to have been preparatory to a trial before that body[3].

If these considerations justify the view that Gracchus contemplated the cognizance of the *plebs*, the clause of the Twelve Tables which claimed capital causes for the centuries was obrogated so far as this particular jurisdiction was concerned. But the conservative lawyers whom Cicero quotes seem not to have admitted the obrogation, and still appeal to the clause of the Tables as stating a fundamental principle of the constitution[4].

Effects of the laws of appeal.

If, in conclusion, we ask what general results were reached by the history of the *provocatio*, we shall find that the real difficulty of forming a conclusion as to the scope of the laws enjoining it lies in getting at their starting point. If *iudicia populi* existed in the earliest times for ordinary crimes, then the laws of appeal refer exclusively to political jurisdiction and the *coercitio* of the magistrate. But, if they created the *iudicia populi*, they must have covered the whole field of jurisdiction. The difficulty of the latter hypothesis is that the best authorities do not connect these laws with any limitation on pecuniary penalties, and that Plutarch and perhaps Dionysius[5], when

[1] p. 317.

[2] Cic. *pro Dom.* 31, 82 'Ubi enim tuleras ut mihi aqua et igni interdiceretur? quod C. Gracchus de P. Popilio . . . tulit?' Cf. *pro Cluent.* 35, 95; *de Leg.* iii. 11, 26; *de Rep.* i. 3, 6; *post Red. in Sen.* 15, 37.

[3] Rein, p. 497.

[4] Cic. *de Leg.* iii. 19, 45.

[5] See p. 308, note 1.

BOOK II. they do mention such penalties, mean only those imposed by a magistrate in order to secure obedience to his commands[1]. Perhaps pecuniary penalties as such were unknown as fixed methods of punishment, except in the case of delicts such as *furtum* and *iniuriae* which belonged to civil, or the *consecratio bonorum* which belonged to religious law. The pecuniary, as an alternative to the capital, penalty may have been imposed at the discretion of the magistrate, and may hence have been always regarded as a mode of *coercitio*. As such it would soon have fallen under the law of appeal; for we shall see, in discussing the modes of magisterial coercion, that as early as the fifth century B.C. a limit was fixed to the *multa* which the magistrate could impose on his own authority. So far, therefore, as the scope of the *provocatio* was concerned, every capital and corporal penalty and every severe money penalty had eventually to come before the judgement of the people[2]. Except in supplying additional guarantees and a more effective sanction, no advance was made by the later laws of appeal. Their limitation to the *pomerium* or the first milestone was, as we shall see, maintained in theory if not in practice.

Practical disappearance of the *provocatio*. But the growing observance of these laws caused the *provocatio* as such to disappear. They never in theory limited judgement but only execution; practically, however, observance made them a limitation of the judgement. The magistrate, when he proposes an appellable penalty, goes direct to the people. The popular jurisdiction thus embraces almost the whole sphere of criminal law, until in time it is delegated to special courts.

[1] Confiscation of goods was employed against those who evaded military service (Dionys. xi. 22); but this was, perhaps, a means of *coercitio*.

[2] The private execution of the judgement debtor by his creditors probably did not come under the *provocatio*. The *addictio* of the *fur manifestus* could not have done so, since it was neither a capital nor a pecuniary penalty. Neither of these cases have any significance for the Ciceronian period.

§ 3. *The jurisdiction of the Tribune and of the Plebs.*

Tribunician jurisdiction originally intended to enforce the tribune's decrees.

The anomalous character of the tribunate which is not a magistracy, and rules a people that is not the community, is reflected in its jurisdiction, which, like the office itself, was first an eccentric adjunct and then a most vital support to the state's machinery. The tribune was originally supposed to exercise a merely negative control over the regular magistracies of the community; but this control would have been ineffective had there been no means of enforcing it. Resort was not had to the device of judicial prosecution before the regular courts of the community; for this system was inconsistent with the Roman conception of the magistracy. Each magistrate had in some degree the power of enforcing his own decrees (*coercitio*), a power that was limited only by the right of appeal or the veto of his colleague, and this authority could not be denied to the tribune. All the weapons of coercion—arrest, imprisonment, fines, stripes and death—were at his disposal against the magistrate as against the private individual. *Coercitio* implies summary jurisdiction; and the infliction of death and scourging and of fines beyond a certain limit subjected a magistrate to the *provocatio*, and made him a partner in a trial before a popular assembly. Verbally the tribune could not have been bound by the early laws of appeal, and the only known enactment that classes him with the other magistrates in this respect merely indulges and limits him in the power of fining[1]. But it was inevitable that his procedure should follow the analogy of that of the other officials, and hence spring his judicial dealings with the people. When the office was created this consequence was not foreseen. When it was found to be a necessary consequence of the tribunician power, tradition tells us that

[1] The *lex Aternia Tarpeia* of 454 B.C. (Cic. *de Rep.* ii. 35, 60; Dionys. x. 50), see p. 335.

it was questioned by the patricians[1]. But the protest was idle, for the right of assistance (*auxilium*) could not exist without the right of punishment on its violators. The jurisdiction of the tribune and the *plebs* was thus primarily a mode of avenging the violation of plebeian rights, and stories of capital jurisdiction with this purpose, such as the trials of Coriolanus in 491 and of Kaeso Quinctius in 461[2], date from a period anterior to the Twelve Tables. But the rapid growth of this jurisdiction beyond its original limits is shown by the fact that the tribunes are represented as bringing capital cases of *perduellio*, which have no connexion with plebeian interests, before the *plebs* at a period immediately subsequent to the decemviral legislation[3]. Dionysius attempts to evolve a principle for such cases. In speaking of the conflict between the *plebs* and patricians over the trial of Coriolanus, he speaks of a compromise which allowed the *plebs* to exercise capital jurisdiction if sanctioned by the senate[4]. That such a formal compromise was ever arrived at is improbable, and perhaps the story merely reflects the truth that capital prosecutions by the tribunes were generally undertaken with the sanction of that body. As late as the third century B.C. the tribune still hears charges of treason (*perduellio*) before his own peculiar assembly. In the year 212 M. Postumius Pyrgensis, a dishonest *publicanus*, was accused by two tribunes of defrauding the state. A fine was proposed, but the disorderly conduct of his brother contractors rendered it impossible to secure a verdict of the *plebs*. The consuls referred the question of the disturbance of the assembly

But extended beyond its original limits.

Recognized power of the tribunes to pass bills of outlawry.

[1] Coriolanus is represented as saying 'auxilii non poenae ius datum illi potestati, plebisque non patrum tribunos esse' (Liv. ii. 35); cf. Liv. ii. 56 (on the tribune seizing some *nobiles* who would not yield to his *viator*), 'consul Appius negare ius esse in quemquam nisi in plebeium.'

[2] Liv. iii. 11–13.

[3] e. g. of the deposed decemvirs App. Claudius and Sp. Oppius, in 449 B.C. (Liv. iii. 56–58).

[4] Dionys. vii. 38 and 39.

to the senate, and that body strengthened the tribunes' hands by a severe expression of opinion. These then changed the pecuniary into a capital penalty. Postumius gave bail for his appearance, but dared not face his judges. The *plebs* thereupon decreed that it considered him in exile, and passed a sentence of *aquae et ignis interdictio* to prohibit his return[1].

Whatever may have been the legal controversy connected with the right of capital accusation before the *plebs*, such a resolution as that passed against Postumius seems to have been regarded as within its competence. So much was this the case that, when voluntary exile had become the almost invariable means of avoiding condemnation, it was the tribunes who were chosen to introduce to the *plebs* the formal bill of outlawry which interdicted the fugitive's return to Rome[2].

Principles which finally regulated prosecution by the tribunes on a capital charge.

But the principle which ultimately prevailed with respect to capital prosecution was that, even if undertaken by the tribune, it should be conducted before the centuries. In the middle Republic the tribunes were regarded by the government, that is, by the senate, as the fittest public prosecutors for political crimes. They formulated a penalty and brought it before the people; if it was pecuniary, it might be introduced into their own plebeian assembly of the tribes, but, if it was capital, it should go before the *comitia centuriata*. A good illustration of the principle may be found in a single case. Cn. Fulvius, an ex-praetor, was in 211 B.C. accused by a tribune of mismanagement and cowardice in the conduct of a campaign. He was first prosecuted with a pecuniary penalty before the tribes; then, on a manifestation of the gravity of the offence, the

[1] Liv. xxv. 4 'Postumius vadibus datis non adfuit. Tribuni plebem rogaverunt plebesque ita scivit 'Si M. Postumius ante K. Maias non prodisset citatusque eo die non respondisset neque excusatus esset, videri eum in exilio esse, bonaque eius venire, ipsi aqua et igni placere interdici.' Cf. Liv. xxvi. 3.

[2] Cic. *in Verr.* ii. 41, 100, quoted p. 317, note 2.

BOOK II. tribunes were urged by the clamours of the surrounding crowd to substitute a capital punishment, and the jurisdiction of the *comitia centuriata* was immediately sought. Fulvius went into voluntary exile; and the *plebs* pronounced his retirement to be true *exilium*, and doubtless passed the formal bill of outlawry[1]. In this, as in other similar cases, the tribune approaches the centuries through the praetor, whom he asks for a day on which he may appear as accuser[2]. The praetor, if he grants it, summons the assembly, but, after the summons, the tribune probably acts as president during the trial[3]. In spite of the guarantees for magisterial responsibility furnished by the standing courts of the later Republic, this function of political prosecution[4] continued to be exercised by the tribune down to Cicero's day.

Possible extension of their capital jurisdiction by C. Gracchus.

We have already suggested the possibility of a form of tribunician jurisdiction before the *plebs* having been restored by C. Gracchus. His own impeachment of Popilius may have taken place before this body, and perhaps the colleague of the latter, Rupilius, equally guilty of the cruel persecution of the adherents of Ti. Gracchus, may have been exiled by a *plebiscitum*[5]. P. Scipio Serapio was another

[1] Liv. xxvi. 3. After 'tanta ira accensa est ut capite anquirendum contio subclamaret' Sempronius the tribune 'perduellionis se iudicare Cn. Fulvio dixit diemque comitiis a C. Calpurnio praetore urbis petit . . . postquam dies comitiorum aderat, Cn. Fulvius exulatum Tarquinios abiit. Id ei iustum exilium esse scivit plebs.'

[2] Cf. Cic. *de Har. Resp.* 4, 7 'diem dixisset (Clodius), ut iecerat; fecissem ut ei statim tertius a praetore dies diceretur.'

[3] Mommsen (*Staatsr.* i. p. 195) thinks that this is implied in the procedure adopted in 169 B.C., when, after the prosecution of the censors Ti. Sempronius Gracchus and C. Claudius for *perduellio* by the tribune, P. Rutilius 'absoluto Claudio tribunus plebis negavit se Gracchum morari' (Liv. xliii. 16).

[4] From the words of Cicero (*in Verr.* Act. i. 13, 38) 'iudiciis ad senatorium ordinem translatis sublataque populi Romani in unum quemque vestrum potestate,' Mommsen concludes that Sulla had probably taken away the tribunician right of accusation (*Staatsr.* ii. p. 326).

[5] Vell. ii. 7 'eadem Rupilium Popiliumque, qui consules asperrime in Ti. Gracchi amicos saevierant, postea iudiciorum publicorum merito

anti-Gracchan accused and banished by some undefined process[1], and L. Opimius, who had crushed the movement set on foot by C. Gracchus, was acquitted after a trial before 'the people[2].'

§ 4. *Magisterial Coercitio.*

Relation of coercion to criminal jurisdiction.

It is impossible to form an adequate conception of the extent and limitations of criminal jurisdiction in the later Republic without touching on the question of magisterial coercion (*coercitio*), that power which compelled obedience to the commands of magistrates or secured the performance of public obligations which it was their duty to enforce. Coercive power, within its own unfettered sphere, is certainly not the same as criminal jurisdiction, but it is too closely in touch with it at every point to be ignored. It differs from ordinary jurisdiction in its scope; for *coercitio* was not directed to the enforcement of the permanent obligations between man and man, nor even to the punishment of ordinary and classifiable political crimes, but rather to the repression of exceptional courses of action which were directed against the state as a whole or affected it through its magistrates. It differs again in method; for coercion is not regarded as the result of judicial cognizance, nor is there any constitutional theory that it should be shared with the people. It was only in so far as certain modes of executing coercion were by the laws of *provocatio* forbidden to the magistrate on his own authority that this magisterial power led to a *iudicium*. Apart from these laws of appeal, the magistrate's powers of coercion were in theory unlimited. Even in Cicero's time he might employ

Extent and limitation of magisterial coercion.

oppressit invidia.' The mention of Popilius shows that *iudicium publicum* must here be used for a trial before the people. It is generally the equivalent of *quaestio perpetua*.

[1] Cic. *Brut.* 28, 107; *de Orat.* ii. 70, 285; *pro Flacco*, 31, 75.

[2] Liv. *Ep.* lxi; Cic. *Brut.* 34, 128; cf. Cic. *Part. Orat.* 30, 106; *de Orat.* ii. 39, 165.

BOOK II.

fines, bonds and scourging to enforce obedience to his will[1]. But the fine beyond a certain limit and the scourging necessitated the appeal, and in these cases popular jurisdiction sprang from the attempted exercise of the power. The individuals who were subjected to this authority did not belong to any special class. It could be directed, not only against private citizens, but against senators and *iudices*, and could be exercised by any superior over any inferior magistrate, to compel his respect or to force him to a performance of his duties. Its means of enforcement were:—

Modes of coercion; (i) death.

(i) Death, the infliction of which, originally inherent in the *imperium*, was, as we have seen, rendered impossible for the civic sphere by the Valerian and Porcian laws. At the close of the Republic a violation of the *provocatio* in this particular entailed a capital penalty on the offending magistrate. The capital coercion of the tribunes remained an exception to this rule. It did indeed follow the analogy of that of the other magistrates, in so far as the tribunes' tacit recognition of the appeal gave rise to their capital jurisdiction. But in theory their coercive power, when used in defence of the sanctity of their own persons, was not subject to appeal[2]. Here the old religious penalties remained in force, and a period as late as the year 131 B.C. witnessed the spectacle of the tribune C. Atinius Labeo carrying the author of his degradation from the senate, the censor Metellus, off to the Tarpeian rock with intent to hurl him down—a fate from which Metellus was saved only by the veto of the tribune's colleagues. Labeo had to be content with consecrating the censor's property to the gods[3].

[1] Cic. *de Leg.* iii. 3, 6, quoted p. 321, note 2.

[2] The *tribunicia potestas* gave the princeps the power, *κἂν ἄρα τι καὶ τὸ βραχύτατον μὴ ὅτι ἔργῳ ἀλλὰ καὶ λόγῳ ἀδικεῖσθαι δόξωσι, καὶ ἄκριτον τὸν ποιήσαντα αὐτὸ ὡς καὶ ἐναγῆ ἀπολλύναι* (Dio Cass. liii. 17).

[3] Plin. *H. N.* vii. 44; Liv. *Ep.* 59. Another capital penalty, the selling of a person into slavery, was inflicted on those who did not present themselves for the levy, and Mommsen (*Staatsr.* i. p. 152) counts it an

(ii) Imprisonment (*abductio in carcerem, in vincula*), although not recognized as a penalty in Roman law, plays a double part in the *coercitio*. It was, in the first place, one of the modes by which the magistrates defended their dignity and secured obedience, not merely from private citizens, but from lower magistrates and senators; and, secondly, it was adopted as a precautionary measure to secure the appearance on trial of one whom they accused.

(ii) Imprisonment,

As a punishment for contumacy on members of the official class, its use by any power but the tribunate is rare. Yet the Ciceronian period furnishes instances of its employment by a praetor and consul. Caesar, when praetor in 62 B.C., threw into prison the president (*quaesitor*) of a criminal court and the informer Vettius, both of whom had attempted to bring him before it[1], and as consul in 59 ordered the same penalty for M. Cato, when the business of the senate was impeded by the latter's obstructive oratory[2]. It is, however, the tribunician annals that boast most exploits of this kind, and the temporary imprisonment of a consul becomes a familiar feature of party strife in the closing years of the Republic, as a summary mode of silencing the opposition of a too zealous optimate. The *cause celèbre* was that of Q. Metellus Celer, consul in 60 B.C. His opposition to the agrarian law of Flavius was answered by imprisonment, and this tribune blocked the door with his bench when the consul attempted to summon the senate to

as a punishment.

instance of magisterial coercion. But it rather resembles the carrying out of a law; cf. Cic. *pro Caec.* 34, 99 'Iam populus cum eum vendit qui miles factus non est, non adimit ei libertatem sed iudicat non esse eum liberum qui, ut liber sit, adire periculum nolit.' It, however, resembles coercion in so far as the *provocatio* does not seem to have been extended to this sphere, and there was, therefore, no popular *iudicium*.

[1] Suet. *Caes.* 17 'Vettium pignoribus captis et direpta supellectile . . . coniecit in carcerem; eodem Novium quaestorem quod compellari apud se maiorem potestatem passus esset.'

[2] Capito *ap. Gell.* iv. 10 'Caesar consul viatorem vocavit eumque (Catonem) cum finem non faceret (of speaking in the senate) prendi loquentem et in carcerem duci iussit'; cf. Suet. *Caes.* 20.

BOOK II.

his cell. A breach was then made in the wall for the fathers to enter, and the absurd situation was only saved by the intervention of Pompeius[1]. The veto of the tribune's colleague was the only legal means of releasing the imprisoned magistrate. It was thus that M. Bibulus was saved from attempted incarceration by Vatinius[2], and that M. Crassus in 54 B.C. escaped the clutches of Ateius and started on his disastrous campaign in the East[3].

As a preventive measure.

Preventive imprisonment, for the purpose of securing the appearance of an accused at trial, was not common at Rome, for the custom of giving securities or bail (*vades, vadimonium*) was early recognized[4]. It rested entirely with the magistrate whether he should accept bail or not, although the veto of a colleague, by forbidding the arrest of the accused, could enforce its acceptance. We shall see later how this preventive imprisonment could in the Ciceronian period be employed as an actual means of punishment.

(iii) Relegation.

(iii) Relegation from Rome, although often practised against non-citizens, was directed against a burgess only once in Republican history, and that in the Ciceronian period. Cicero pronounces the action to have been wholly unprecedented. It was done by decree of A. Gabinius, consul in 58 B.C., who ordered a certain distinguished knight, L. Lamia—a disorderly citizen, but one fighting in what Cicero considered the cause of order—not to dwell within two hundred miles of Rome[5].

(iv) Fines.

(iv) The imposition of a fine (*multa*) was the commonest

[1] Dio Cass. xxxvii. 50; cf. Cic. *ad Att.* ii. 1, 8.

[2] Cic. *in Vat.* 9, 21; cf. Dio Cass. xxxviii. 6.

[3] Dio Cass. xxxix. 39.

[4] Bail is introduced into the trial of Kaeso Quinctius in 461 B.C. (Liv. iii. 13 'Hic primus vades publicos dedit').

[5] Cic. *pro Sest.* 12, 29 'L. Lamiam . . . in contione relegavit, edixitque ut ab urbe abesset milia passuum ducenta'; *ad Fam.* xi. 16, 2 'Clodianis temporibus, cum equestris ordinis princeps esset proque mea salute acerrime propugnaret, a Gabinio consule relegatus est: quod ante id tempus civi Romano contigit nemini'; cf. *post Red. in Sen.* 5, 12; *in Pis.* 10, 23.

of the modes of enforcing obedience, and was possessed by all magistrates with the possible exception of the quaestor[1]. As early as 454 B.C. the power of fining (*ius multae dictionis*), which had hitherto belonged to the consuls alone, was conferred on all the magistrates, including the tribunes and plebeian aediles, by the *lex Aternia Tarpeia* passed in the comitia of the centuries[2]. The *lex Menenia Sestia* of 452 B.C. fixed the highest fine that could be imposed by a magistrate (*multa suprema*) at two sheep or thirty oxen—the former the limit for the poor man, the latter for the rich[3]. After coined money, or at least metal by weight, had come into vogue in the decemviral period, a *lex Iulia Papiria* ('de multarum aestimatione') fixed the limit in specie. This limit was probably three thousand libral asses, the value of thirty oxen[4]. Any fine greater than this *multa suprema* could not be pronounced by the magistrate (*dicta*) but had to be proposed to the people (*irrogata*). The case was heard by a tribal assembly either of the *populus* or *plebs* according as the fines were imposed by a patrician or plebeian magistrate. Even the amount that could be proposed to the people might be limited by law; for certain enactments still fixed an absolute limit to their own penalties. This was generally less than half of the property of the accused[5].

The *multa suprema*.

But here, as in capital jurisdiction, the tribune stood

[1] Mommsen holds (*Staatsr.* i. p. 143 n. 1) that the quaestor had no power of *coercitio* through *multa* and *pignus*. For an opposite view, see Karlowa, *R. G.* i. p. 171, and Huschke, *Multa*, p. 36.

[2] Cic. *de Rep.* ii. 35, 60.

[3] Festus, p. 237; Gell. xi. 1. If we may trust Plutarch (*Public.* 11), in the very earliest times of the Republic the *multa suprema* of the consuls had been two sheep or five oxen.

[4] Cic. *de Rep.* ii. 35, 60; Liv. iv. 30. The sum was not 3,020 asses, as it is often stated. The twenty asses would be the value of the two sheep, but these were in early times an alternative to the thirty oxen. (Festus, p. 237 'cautum est ut bos centusibus, ovis decusibus aestimaretur.')

[5] Festus, p. 246; *Lex Tabulae Bantinae*, l. 12 'Sei quis mag(istratus) multam inrogare volet [*quei volet, dum minoris*] partus familias taxsat, liceto.'

BOOK II.

The tribunician *consecratio bonorum.*

apart. His power of imposing money penalties extended far beyond the limits of that of the other magistrates. His right to confiscate all the goods of an individual by consecrating them to a god (*consecratio bonorum*) was, like the execution from the Tarpeian rock, a relic of the old religious jurisdiction, and as little subject to the appeal. It was the favourite weapon of the tribune against the censor. We find it pronounced against Ti. Gracchus in 169 B.C. for continued resistance to the veto[1], against Q. Metellus in 131 as an answer to the censor's stigma[2], and against Cn. Lentulus in 70[3]. Like other vanished relics of antiquity, it was revived during the party struggles of the close of the Republic, and the year 58 B.C. witnessed an extraordinary scene. The tribune Clodius, standing with veiled head before a burning altar, consecrated all the goods of the consul Gabinius to the temple of Ceres[4]. But the weapon was turned against the dedicator; the sham was re-enacted by one of his colleagues, and the goods of Clodius were in the same year legally forfeit to the goddess[5].

(v) *Pignoris capio.*

(v) Another mode of coercion, specially used against magistrates and the official class, was the seizing of articles of their property as pledges (*pignoris capio*)[6]. This was employed not as a security for good behaviour but as a punishment. Hence the pledge was often destroyed (*pignora caedere, concidere*)[7] and the destruction was performed as an example 'in conspectu populi Romani.' The power had been exerted in 91 B.C. by the consul Philippus against a senator who inveighed against him[8]; and as

[1] Liv. xliii. 16.

[2] Plin. *H. N.* vii. 44; Cic. *pro Domo*, 47, 123; cf. p. 332.

[3] Cic. *pro Domo*, 47. 124.

[4] Cic. *l. c.*

[5] Cic. *pro Domo*, 48. 125 'exemplo tuo bona tua nonne L. Ninnius ... consecravit? ... tua domus certe et quidquid habes aliud Cereri est consecratum.'

[6] Cf. *Lex Quinctia de aquaeductibus*, l. 20 'tum is praetor ... multa pignoribus cogito coercito.'

[7] Cic. *de Orat.* iii. 1, 4.

[8] Cic. *l. c.*

a senator, who declined to perform his duties, Cicero exposed himself to the wrath of Antonius in 44 B.C. The consul in this case was not exceeding his legal powers in threatening the demolition of Cicero's doors, but the courtesy of official relations should have made him content with a security smaller and less violently exacted[1]. The use of this legal violence against a magistrate is illustrated by the relations of the consul P. Servilius Isauricus to the praetor M. Caelius Rufus in 48 B.C. The consul was not content with impeding the praetor's revolutionary designs by suspending him from his office, excluding him from the senate and dragging him from the Rostra, but broke his curule chair into fragments as a visible sign of displeasure that would impress the crowd[2]. A private individual who had infringed the magistrate's dignity was equally exposed to this form of coercion. Caesar as praetor in 62 B.C., when imprisoning Vettius, seized and destroyed some furniture of the would-be informer[3].

The *pignoris capio* of the *publicani* which we have discussed in connexion with civil law was perhaps this right granted in a modified form by the praetor to the State-contractors[4]. In this case, however, the pledge could not be destroyed but was detained as security for the debt.

Differences between the magistracies with respect to the exercise of coercion.

Although, after the *provocatio* had limited the right to inflict death and scourging, the means of coercion which we have enumerated belonged, generally speaking, to the magistracy as a whole; yet a formal difference existed between the higher and the lower magistrates and between the magistrates with *imperium* and the tribunes in the manner in which they put these methods into force. The

[1] Cic. *Phil.* i. 5, 12 'ille (Antonius) . . . cum fabris se domum meam venturum esse dixit. . . . Quis autem umquam tanto damno senatorem coegit? Aut quid est ultra pignus aut multam?'

[2] Dio Cass. xlii. 23; Quinctil. *Inst. Or.* vi. 3, 25.

[3] Suet. *Caes.* 17 'pignoribus captis et direpta supellectile.' See p. 333, note 1.

[4] Mommsen, *Staatsr.* i. p. 161.

BOOK II.

consuls and other magistrates with *imperium* had the right of summoning delinquents before their tribunal (*vocatio*) as well as of summarily arresting them in person (*prensio*). The quaestors and all lower officials had neither of these rights, and the theory of the tribune's being an exceptional magistrate who should render assistance in person was so far preserved that he had only the right of arrest[1]. We sometimes meet with tribunes who carried out their mandates with their own hands; but their presence alone was sufficient for the *prensio* to be effective. In early times they employed their *aediles* for the act of force, in later their *viatores*[2]. By the close of the Republic this distinction had become obliterated and the tribunes, without formal right, summoned individuals before them. But there was a protest even in the Ciceronian period. Varro's respect for constitutional antiquity led him to decline to obey such a summons on the ground of its illegality, and, when tribune, he never exercised his right of *vocatio*, and interposed his veto when such an exercise was attempted by his colleague[3].

Vocatio and prensio.

§ 5. *The jurisdiction of the different magistrates and the separate comitia. The Triumviri Capitales.*

Principles regulating the judicial spheres of the magistrates and the *comitia*.

The two fundamental principles regulating the relations of magistrates to people in criminal jurisdiction were (1) that capital cases should be reserved for the centuries and (2) that a case stated by a magistrate should be tried in that assembly which the magistrate could approach—that the magistrates of the people should appeal to the

[1] Varro, *ap. Gell.* xiii. 12.

[2] Aediles were believed to have been used in the trial of Coriolanus (Dionys. vii. 26). Ti. Gracchus sent one of his *viatores* to drag his colleague Octavius from the Rostra (Plut. *Ti. Gracch.* 12); cf. Liv. xxv. 4 (in the case of Postumius mentioned on p. 328) 'tribuni . . . ni vades daret, prehendi a viatore . . . iusserunt.'

[3] Varro, *ap. Gell.* xiii. 12, 6.

comitia, the plebeian magistrates, where possible, to the *plebs*. An exception to the first principle is furnished by the special capital jurisdiction of the *concilium plebis*, and exceptions to the second are found in the facts that the consular delegates, the quaestors, although possessing in their own right no *ius agendi cum populo*, yet guided the assemblies in which an appeal from their decision was considered, and that the tribune, when bound by the provision of the Twelve Tables, approached and probably had the presidency of the *comitia centuriata*.

But, generally speaking, the directing magistrate and the penalty which he proposes are true indices of the popular court which tries the case. A capital penalty, with certain exceptions in favour of the tribunes of the *plebs*, comes before the centuries; a monetary penalty proposed by a magistrate of the people is brought before the *comitia tributa populi*, a similar penalty proposed by a plebeian magistrate before the *concilium plebis*. It is from this point of view that we shall specify the various forms of popular jurisdiction that were still legally possible and still sometimes employed in Cicero's day.

Criminal jurisdiction (i) of the consul;

(i) The criminal jurisdiction of the consul was expressed in three ways.

It had been, in the first place, exercised through the quaestor, as the regular capital jurisdiction for ordinary as opposed to political crimes, but this jurisdiction had become extinct through the growth of the *quaestiones perpetuae*. Secondly, it might be asserted as part of his coercive power with or without appeal according to the nature of the sentence imposed. But the very existence of the laws of appeal led to the consuls never exceeding their inappellable *coercitio*. Thirdly, it might be jurisdiction without appeal delegated by the people. We shall trace elsewhere the growth of a custom by which the comitia assigned jurisdiction on certain crimes to special commissioners. The people, acting in this delegation on

BOOK II. the advice of the senate, generally left the appointment of the commission to that body, and the senate often selected either a consul or a praetor. But the growth of the standing courts rendered these special commissions more and more unnecessary. There is, in fact, practically no consular jurisdiction in criminal matters during the Ciceronian period.

(ii) of the praetor;

(ii) The praetors were potentially as fully criminal judges as the consuls, and there may have been a time when a portion of criminal jurisdiction was actually in their hands[1]. To them, too, as to the consuls special judicial commissions might be entrusted by the people. But their attention was mainly devoted to civil jurisdiction and provincial government until the establishment of the standing criminal courts claimed their attention.

(iii) of the curule and plebeian aediles;

(iii) The aediles, both curule and plebeian, are sometimes found exercising functions of criminal jurisdiction, all of which cannot be brought into close connexion with their special duties—the care of the archives, the market and the games—and cannot, therefore, be explained as the result of their coercive power. This criminal jurisdiction was, like the civil jurisdiction of the curule aediles, an anomaly, for these magistrates did not possess the *imperium*. It is to be explained partly as a survival (for some jurisdiction of the kind had in early times been exercised by the plebeian aediles) and partly as dictated by considerations of convenience. Before the institution of the *quaestiones perpetuae* the lack of criminal courts at Rome must have been sorely felt. The quaestors were at hand for the trial of ordinary capital crimes and the tribunes for political jurisdiction; but what was needed was a magistracy that would bring lesser crimes involving a mere money penalty before the people. This was discovered in the aedileship, and we find these magistrates prosecuting for *stuprum*[2], for usury[3], for speculation in

[1] Zumpt, i. 2, pp. 105–106. [2] Liv. xxv. 2. [3] Liv. xxxv. 41.

corn prohibited by the laws[1] and for exceeding the permitted amount of domain land[2]. A prosecution by the aedile in defence of his own dignity or person[3] may be interpreted as a result of his *coercitio*. It is true, however, that the aediles were not prohibited from undertaking the prosecution of political crimes, if these could be met by a fine—such crimes as the mild treason committed by Claudia in 246 B.C., when, jostled in the streets, she uttered a wish that her brother Pulcher were still alive to lose another naval battle and thin the ranks of the Roman rabble[4]. But Cicero's threat to prosecute Verres on graver charges of treason[5] would, if carried out, have been an unusual proceeding on the part of a curule aedile. The trial must have been conducted before the *comitia tributa populi*, and the condemnation could only have been pecuniary. Impeachments for the bribery of a bench of *iudices* and for breaches of the peace (*vis*) were more strictly in harmony with the police duties of these magistrates. A threat of the first kind of prosecution is made by Cicero as one of the first-fruits of his aedileship[6]; the second may be illustrated by the impeachment of Milo for *vis* by Clodius in 56 B.C. This trial took place in the Forum, and, as Clodius was curule aedile at the time, must have been held before the *comitia tributa populi*[7]. In fact, the aediles as the initiators of jurisdiction always approached the tribes. The curule aediles as *magistratus*

[1] Liv. xxxviii. 35. [2] Liv. x. 13. [3] Gell. iv. 14.

[4] She was prosecuted in 246 B.C. by two plebeian aediles (Gell. x. 6; Suet. *Tib.* 2).

[5] Cic. *in Verr.* i. 5, 12 and 14; v. 67, 173.

[6] Cicero (*in Verr.* Act. i. 12. 36) threatens to prosecute those 'qui aut deponere aut recipere aut accipere aut polliceri aut sequestres aut interpretes corrumpendi iudicii solent esse.'

[7] Cic. *pro Sest.* 44, 95 'Nam quid ego de aedile ipso loquar, qui etiam diem dixit et accusavit de vi Milonem?'; *pro Mil.* 15, 40 'privato Milone et reo ad populum accusante P. Clodio.' The scene in the Forum is described in Cic. *ad Q. fr.* ii. 3. Other references to the prosecution are to be found in Cic. *in Vat.* 17, 41; Ascon. *in Milon.* p. 49; Dio Cass. xxxix. 18.

BOOK II. *populi* would have brought their case before the *comitia tributa populi*; the plebeian aediles, who as magistrates of the *plebs* had no right of summoning the people, would have appeared before the *concilium plebis*.

(iv) of the tribunes.

(iv) We have already described the characteristics of the jurisdiction of the tribunes. Where it was capital, it might in certain exceptional cases be conducted before the *concilium plebis*, but usually its destination was the *comitia centuriata*. Where it was pecuniary, the tribune would invariably have employed his right of bringing the matter before the assembly of the *plebs*[1].

Functions of the *triumviri capitales*,

In the list of the magistrates we have yet found none who fills the position of a prefect of police or even that of an ordinary justice of the peace exercising summary jurisdiction and preserving public order. This deficiency was partly supplied by the *triumviri capitales* or *tresviri nocturni*[2]. The office was introduced as a standing institution about the year 289 B.C.[3] Between 242 and 124 the appointment was transferred to the people—doubtless the *comitia tributa populi*, under presidency of the praetor—and the triumvirate became a magistracy[4]. The number three continued during the greater part of the Ciceronian period, but Caesar raised the number to four[5], a change which was not permanent[6]. Their general position was that of subordinate assistants to the other

[1] An instance of both kinds of procedure is furnished by the case of Cn. Fulvius in 211 B.C. (Liv. xxvi. 3, quoted p. 330, note 1).

[2] The latter name was probably derived from their duty of extinguishing fires (Paulus in Dig. 1, 15, 1). They were the officials mainly responsible for calling out the public fire-brigade (*familia publica*).

[3] 'Triumviri capitales tum primum creati sunt' (Liv. *Ep.* xi). *Creati* may mean 'elected by the people' (see Zumpt, i. 2, p. 122); but the analogy of the appointment of the other lower magistrates and the evidence of Festus (p. 347) point to a later date (see Mommsen, *Staatsr.* ii. p. 595). *Triumviri nocturni* were believed to have existed before 289 (Liv. ix. 46).

[4] Festus, p. 347; Mommsen, *l. c.*

[5] Suet. *Caes.* 41; *C. I. L.* ix. n. 2845.

[6] The original number was restored by Augustus.

magistrates in their criminal jurisdiction. As such their functions were twofold.

in carrying out a sentence;

(i) Their name *capitales* was derived from the duties which devolved on them after the sentence had been pronounced[1]. It was they who guarded the condemned prisoners and supervised the closing scene. Nay, if the order was death by strangling, they must fulfil it with their own hands; and it was they who in the Tullianum adjusted the noose to the necks of Lentulus and his comrades in Catiline's conspiracy[2]. When death was effected by other modes they merely saw to the carrying out of the decree[3].

in conducting the preliminarie of a trial;

(ii) On the triumvirs devolved duties preliminary to a criminal trial such as preventive imprisonment, and the first inquiry into the charge made after the prisoner's arrest[4]. Cicero in his speech for Cluentius presents us with a picture of Avilius arrested for a murder, brought before the triumvirs and confessing his guilt[5]; but, if these magistrates decided that there was no evidence against the prisoner, he was immediately discharged[6].

as police magistrates.

But the triumvirs were also justices of the peace. They heard ordinary police-court charges, such as those of vagrancy or nocturnal disturbance; and 'a man found sleeping in a tavern and thought to be a runaway slave' was immediately brought before their tribunal[7]. Their

[1] Cic. *de Leg.* iii. 3, 6 'Vincla sontium servanto, capitalia vindicanto': cf. Sall. *Cat.* 55 'vindices rerum capitalium.'

[2] Sall. *l.c.*; strangling is pre-eminently *triumvirale supplicium* (Tac. *Ann.* v. 9 [vi. 4]).

[3] Val. Max. viii. 4, 2.

[4] Cf. Varro on the *quaestores parricidii* (*L. L.* v. 81 'quaestores a quaerendo, qui conquirerent . . . maleficia, quae triumviri capitales nunc conquirunt').

[5] Cic. *pro Cluent.* 13, 38. Avilius is said to have been set 'ante pedes Q. Manli qui tum erat triumvir.' The triumvirs sat, therefore, on some kind of tribunal or raised platform. Zumpt (i. 2, p. 128) thinks that they had three tribunals in the Basilica at the Columna Maenia.

[6] *ib.* 13, 39.

[7] In 52 B.C. between the proposal and the passing of the special law against Milo 'Munatius et Pompeius tribuni plebis in rostra produxerant

BOOK II.

office was at the Columna Maenia in the Forum. Here practised an inferior class of criminal barristers, on whom Cicero professes to look down with contempt[1]. But the triumvirs were heads of the police as well as justices. They had the patrolling of the town and the preservation of order in the streets. In the pursuit of these duties they imprisoned vagabond slaves and foreigners and could even scourge them[2]. There is, however, no trace of their possessing any criminal jurisdiction over citizens or any of those higher powers of cognizance which would bring them into contact with the popular assembly.

§ 6. *The procedure of a iudicium populi and of the provocatio.*

The *iudicium populi* not based on the *provocatio*. They are distinct methods of procedure.

We have already mentioned the view that the *iudicia populi* were historically independent of the *provocatio*, and that the latter was merely a denial of the competence of a magistrate. This view presumes the original existence of popular courts with fully admitted spheres of jurisdiction, and it necessarily asserts that the procedure of the *provocatio* was in the main identical with that of a *iudicium populi*. The only difference is in the beginning of the action. In the one case the word *provoco* must be employed by the accused in order to set the trial in motion, in the other it need not be used, the magistrate who recognizes his limitations himself starting the mechanism of the trial before the people. In both courts the magis-

triumvirum capitalem eumque interrogaverant an Galatam Milonis servum caedes facientem deprehendisset. Ille dormientem in taberna pro fugitivo prehensum et ad se perductum esse responderat' (Ascon. *in Milon.* p. 38).

[1] Cic. *Div. in Caec.* 16, 50; Ps. Asc. p. 121; cf. Cic. *pro Cluent.* 13, 39.

[2] Hor. *Epod.* 4, 11

'Sectus flagellis hic triumviralibus
Praeconis ad fastidium.'

Cf. Plaut. *Amph.* i. 1, 3.

trate presides, but the one is a court of first instance, the other a court of appeal[1].

But the same result may be reached even if we disbelieve in a self-existent popular jurisdiction of early days. Even if the *iudicia populi* had grown out of the *provocatio*, yet an obvious motive for the distinction between the two modes of procedure would have been that, while a trial before the people was set on foot by a magistrate as the result of his realizing the limitations on his power, the *provocatio*, when required to start the same procedure, was the consequence of his not realizing these limitations. Nor need the view that the *iudicia populi* were an outgrowth of the *provocatio* lead us to the improbable conclusion that the popular courts of Rome always continued to be formally courts of appeal, that in every case the magistrate pronounced a sentence which he knew that he had no power to execute, and that the activity of the *iudicia populi* could only be aroused by those sentences coming on appeal to the people[2].

The procedure of the *iudicium populi* consisted of two stages.

Procedure in a *iudicium populi*. The *anquisitio*.

(i) The magistrate who means to impose a sentence which he knows will subject him to the *provocatio*, holds a preliminary investigation (*anquisitio*) before an informal assembly (*contio*) which he has summoned[3]. This in-

[1] On the conditions of the appeal and the supposed disability of *confessi* and of criminals caught in the act, see Appendix.

[2] This is not necessarily implied in the words of Cicero (*de Leg.* iii. 12, 27) 'omnibus magistratibus . . . iudicia dantur . . . ut esset populi potestas ad quam provocaretur.' He need not mean that the *populi potestas* to assert itself presupposes a temporary condemnation (Mommsen in *Neue Jenaische Litteraturzeitung* for 1844, p. 258). What is stated is that all magistrates are recognized as judges in order to ensure the working of the popular courts. The *provocatio* was the *ultimate* basis for much, perhaps for all, of the authority of these courts, and jurisdiction was necessary for the magistrate at Rome, to ensure a trial before the people.

[3] *Anquisitio* perhaps means an inquiry 'on both sides,' i.e. through accusation and defence (Lange, *Röm. Alt.* ii. p. 470); cf. Festus, p. 22

BOOK II. vestigation lasts for three days and is followed by a judgement or proposal as to the penalty either in the original shape put forward at the beginning of the inquiry or in an amended form. The proposals made by the magistrate at these three *contiones* are spoken of as 'accusations'; he is represented as a prosecutor and his final accusation is embodied in a bill.

Proceedings in the *comitia*.

(ii) The scene now shifts to the assembly. After the legal interval of three market days the proposal is brought by the magistrate before the *comitia* and is either accepted or rejected by the assembled people. This *comitia* was, as in the case of legislative assemblies, preceded by a *contio*. The magistrate's final exposition of his proposal before this *contio* is spoken of as his 'fourth accusation' (*quarta accusatio*)[1]. The proposal itself is always a 'bill directed against a person' (*inrogatio*)[2], although by a curious restriction of technical nomenclature the word *inrogare* seems to be used only of varying fines (*multae*) and not of fixed penalties (*poenae*). The usual expression for the pronouncement of the latter is *iudicare*, a word which in this context means 'adjudge the penalty,' that,

'anquirere est circum quaerere.' It represents a process in which the magistrate and the accused produce evidence on either side.

[1] Cic. *pro Domo*, 17, 45 'cum tam moderata iudicia populi sint a maioribus constituta . . . ne inprodicta die quis accusetur, ut ter ante magistratus accuset intermissa die quam multam inroget aut iudicet (i.e. leaving an interval during which he should propose a fine or adjudge the penalty by framing a *rogatio*) quarta sit accusatio trinum nundinum prodicta die, quo die iudicium sit futurum'; cf. App. *B. C.* i. 74 (of the trial of Merula and Catulus in 87 B.C.) *τετράκις δὲ ἐχρῆν κηρυττομένους ἐν ὡρισμένοις ὡρῶν διαστήμασιν ἁλῶναι.* A good example of the three *contiones* and the *quarta accusatio* is furnished by Clodius' prosecution of Milo for *vis* (p. 341). The first *contio* was on Feb. 2, the second on Feb. 6, the third on Feb. 17 (Cic. *ad Q. fr.* ii. 3, 1, 2 and 3), the *quarta accusatio* on May 7 (*ad Q. fr.* ii. 7). These days are in the Calendar marked respectively N, N, NP and F or N. Yet it was held that *contiones* were not possible on *dies nefasti* (Macrob. i, 16, 29), and we should certainly have expected the final hearing to be on a comitial day.

[2] *Lex Tabulae Bantinae*, l. 12, see p. 13, note 1, and cf. Cic. *pro Domo*, 17, 43 'leges privatis hominibus inrogari.'

namely, which is embodied in the *rogatio* as the result of the magisterial inquiry[1]. The rogation as a bill, brought before a sovereign assembly exercising legislative power, could not be amended after promulgation; and if by any accident the bill was not carried through the comitia[2], a fresh promulgation with a new interval of three market days was necessary for a renewal of the prosecution[3]. This made the revival of an impeachment by the same magistrate on the same charge extremely infrequent.

Possibility of altering the original proposal.

But it was not inevitable that the penalty 'adjudged' by the magistrate at one of the first three 'accusations' was the one which he ultimately embodied in the *rogatio* and expounded at the *quarta accusatio.* He might be influenced to amend his judgement, even to the extent of turning a pecuniary into a capital accusation[4]. 'The irregular shouts of a *contio,* perhaps also definite alternatives presented by the advocates of the accused and supported by the acclamations of the crowd, might lead the magistrate, during his own preliminary investigation, to alter his own original judgement before its close and to formulate a *rogatio* in accordance with this amended estimate of the punishment adequate to the offence[5].' But amendment must have been impossible at the *quarta accusatio,* for that *followed* the promulgation, and even at the earlier stages it seems to have been unusual. Such reformation, however, must have been almost a necessity in

[1] Cic. *de Leg.* iii. 3, 6 'cum magistratus iudicassit inrogassitve, per populum multae poenae certatio esto'; cf. *pro Domo,* 17, 45, quoted p. 346, note 1. This is the sense of *iudicare* when used of tribunician prosecutions, e. g. 'perduellionis se iudicare . . . dixit' (Liv. xxvi. 3), 'perduellionem se iudicare pronunciavit' (Liv. xliii. 16).

[2] e. g. by disturbance through the auspices (Cic. *de Div.* ii. 35, 74).

[3] Cic. *pro Domo,* 17, 45 'si qua res illum diem aut auspiciis aut excusatione sustulit, tota causa iudiciumque sublatum sit.'

[4] Instances are furnished by the trial of Menenius in 476 B.C. (Liv. ii. 52 [The tribunes] 'cum capitis anquisissent, duo milia aeris damnato multam dixerunt') and by the trial of Fulvius in 211 B.C. (Liv. xxvi. 3, see p. 330, note 1).

[5] *Classical Review,* 1895, p. 4.

BOOK II.

the cases where fresh evidence came to light after the first private investigation by the magistrate and during the *anquisitio*[1].

The procedure of the *provocatio*.

Hitherto we have been treating the simple case of a magistrate recognizing the limitations on his power and going directly to the people. But we must consider the possibility of a magistrate not recognizing these limitations—an attitude which rendered the *provocatio* the only means of securing a popular trial. The case was unusual, but not hypothetical, as the process of C. Rabirius proves, and we can see from this trial that the delegated jurisdiction of the *duumviri* was (at least occasionally) so ordered as to make an appeal from their decision an integral part of the procedure.

The appeal necessitates the pronouncement of a sentence, and the sentence must have been preceded by a cognizance, however informal, of the magistrate appealed against. Yet we must suppose that, when the case went on appeal to the people, the magisterial cognizance was renewed; for the *anquisitio* could not be dispensed with. It was the only mode in which the people could inform themselves of the facts, and it is difficult to believe that a case ever came before the comitia without this preliminary investigation. We have, therefore, in the *provocatio* two stages of magisterial cognizance; the first leads to a sentence, the second to a proposal. And different stages of investigation might be represented by different magistrates. This must have happened when criminal cases were sent from the provinces to Rome. There is, indeed, reason for believing that the *provocatio* was never extended by statute law to Roman citizens abroad; but customary law seems to have dictated that a capital

[1] The separate items of evidence were probably taken at the *anquisitio*, the collected proofs being developed by the magistrate at the *quarta accusatio*. At this last stage the witnesses were still produced; see the account of the trial of Postumius (Liv. xxv. 3).

sentence should not be executed on a Roman citizen by a provincial governor. The governor might pronounce the sentence and challenge the appeal; but few were likely to put themselves into the undignified position of giving a verdict which they were unable to carry into effect. The restriction on execution, abroad as at home, must have acted as a check on jurisdiction. But the governor who, after an examination which showed him that a capital sentence was desirable, sent the case at once to Rome could not continue its investigation there. The *anquisitio* which preceded the judgement of the *comitia* must have been conducted by another magistrate.

§ 7. *Survivals of popular jurisdiction in Cicero's day.*

Jurisdiction of the people in Cicero's day.

The frequency and variety of trials before the people even during the last century of the Republic may be illustrated by a sketch of the leading cases that occurred during Cicero's lifetime, to most of which frequent reference can be found in his writings. A closer attention will be given to those in which the orator was himself concerned and about which, therefore, fuller details have been preserved.

The very year of Cicero's birth saw the commencement of a remarkable crop of tribunician prosecutions directed against unsuccessful generals.

Trials of C. Popilius Laenas;

In 106 B.C. C. Popilius Laenas was impeached. During the preceding year he had been legate of the consul L. Cassius Longinus, who had been defeated and slain by the Tigurini in Gaul. Laenas had attempted to save the remains of the army by a disgraceful treaty[1], and, after his return to Rome, was impeached by the tribune C. Caelius Caldus. Caelius, to facilitate the prosecution,

[1] *Auct. ad Herenn.* i. 15, 25; cf. iv. 24, 34.

introduced secret voting in cases of *perduellio*[1]. Popilius was condemned, and in his exile sought the shelter of Nuceria[2].

of Q. Servilius Caepio;

In 105 L. Servilius Caepio, the consul of the previous year, after plundering the temple treasures in Tolosa, brought a crushing disaster on the Roman arms in a fight with the Cimbri at Arausio[3]. Two tribunes set themselves to the work of impeachment, and their extraordinary methods could only have prevailed at a moment of national panic. C. Norbanus proposed that the *imperium* of the proconsul should be abrogated[4], L. Cassius Longinus that every one deposed from office by the people should lose his senatorial rank[5]. Caepio unsuccessfully defended his defeat[6]; he was deposed and the deposition was aggravated by the Cassian law. Nor was this all. A legal investigation followed about the robbery of the temple treasures, in which many besides Caepio were involved[7]. It is possible that this investigation was conducted before a special commission, not before the people; but, whatever the method, Caepio was condemned and became a citizen of Smyrna[8]. It is by no means certain that he was ever convicted or even tried for the defeat at Arausio[9].

[1] Cic. *de Leg.* iii. 16, 36; the offence is here called *perduellio*, in *ad Herenn.* i. 15, 25, it is described as *maiestas*.

[2] Cic. *pro Balbo*, 11, 28; cf. *de Rep.* i. 3, 6.

[3] Dio Cass. *fr.* 98 and 99; cf. Sall. *Iug.* 114.

[4] Cic. *de Orat.* ii. 28, 124; 47, 197; Liv. *Ep.* lxvii 'primo . . . post regem Tarquinium imperium ei abrogatum.'

[5] Asc. *in Cornel.* p. 78.

[6] *Auct. ad Herenn.* i. 14, 24; cf. Cic. *Part. Orat.* 30, 104.

[7] Dio Cass. *fr.* 97; cf. Cic. *de Nat. Deor.* iii. 30, 74.

[8] Cic. *pro Balbo*, 11, 28.

[9] Zumpt (i. 2, p. 351) thinks that the sacrilege may have been the sole charge on which Caepio was condemned; but he may have been convicted, on *maiestas* or *perduellio*, for the loss of the army as well. Other traditions represent Caepio as having been placed in prison (Val. Max. iv. 7, 3), and even as having died in prison (Val. Max. vi. 9, 13; cf. Gell. iii. 9, 7). The imprisonment was of course preventive, but the latter tradition, if it refers to this Caepio, must be false. A second process (supposed as a possibility by Zumpt, *l. c.*) is impossible, as a citizen of Smyrna could not be summoned to stand his trial at Rome.

BOOK II.

In 104 M. Junius Silanus was put on his trial for a five-year-old defeat. As consul in 109 he had fought unsuccessfully with the Cimbri. The tribune Cn. Domitius, who owed the ex-consul a personal grudge, was the prosecutor[1], but the accused was gloriously acquitted, only two tribes voting for his condemnation[2]. of M. Junius Silanus;

Internal troubles claimed the next victims. In 100 Q. Metellus Numidicus was prosecuted by the tribune L. Appuleius Saturninus. The penalty on senators who had not sworn to the new agrarian law—expulsion from the senate and a fine of twenty talents[3]—had been imposed; but this was not enough for the enemies of Metellus. Saturninus brought a charge against him before the people[4]; as he associated himself with the praetor Glaucia, they doubtless approached the *comitia centuriata*. The bill contained the unusual provision that the consuls should pronounce the measure of outlawry[5]. Metellus retired into voluntary exile at Rhodes[6]; but in the following year, after the suppression of the revolution, he was recalled by means of a bill proposed by the tribune Q. Calidius[7]. of Q. Metellus Numidicus;

In 98, P. Furius, who had opposed the recall of Metellus, was, after he had quitted the tribunate, accused by C. Appuleius Decianus before the people. Decianus was tribune and the place of trial was the Forum[8]; the case, therefore, must have come before the *plebs*. The accused was acquitted by the tribes, but torn in pieces by the mob[9]. of P. Furius;

[1] Asc. *in Cornel.* p. 80; Cic. *Div. in Caec.* 20, 67; *in Verr.* ii. 47, 118.
[2] Asc. *l. c.*
[3] App. *B. C.* i. 29.
[4] Liv. *Ep.* lxix.
[5] App. *B. C.* i. 31; cf. Cic. *pro Domo*, 31, 82.
[6] Liv. *l. c.*; Val. Max. iv. 1, 13.
[7] Cic. *pro Planc.* 28, 69; App. *B. C.* i. 33. Minor references to Metellus' trial and exile are frequent in Cicero. See *pro Sest.* 16, 37; 47, 101; 62, 130; *de Off.* iii. 20, 79; *pro Domo*, 32, 87; *pro Cluent.* 35, 95; *in Pis.* 9, 20; *pro Planc.* 36, 89; *de Rep.* i. 3, 6.
[8] Val. Max. viii. 1, 2; the trial took place *pro rostris*.
[9] Dio Cass. *fr.* 105; Appian's statement (*B. C.* i. 33) that Canuleius was the prosecuting tribune is a mistake.

BOOK II.

The prosecutor in his speech had spoken some words in praise of Saturninus[1]. For this he was condemned later, perhaps by *iudices*, and sought a home in Pontus[2]. The year 86 witnessed an instance of audacity that long lingered in the memory of men. C. Fimbria had caused Q. Scaevola to be wounded at the funeral of Marius. When it was found that the wound would not prove fatal, Fimbria prosecuted his victim. We know nothing of the issue of the trial[3]. In the Marian reign of terror (87 B.C.) judicial prosecutions followed the first indiscriminate massacre. Two of the most distinguished members of the optimate party, L. Cornelius Merula, who had been named successor to Cinna in the consulship, and Q. Lutatius Catulus, formerly colleague of Marius, were chosen as the objects of attack. Prosecutors were appointed, doubtless from the tribunician college, and the accused, though not imprisoned, were kept under surveillance. The legal formalities of trial, including the three *contiones*, were observed[4], but the accused did not await the certain verdict. Merula slew himself in the temple of Jupiter (he was Flamen Dialis), and Catulus, after vainly entreating the liberty of exile[5], committed suicide in his own house[6]. To this epoch perhaps belongs the condemnation of App. Claudius, the father of Cicero's enemy. During the Cinnan disturbances he was impeached by a tribune; but he sought voluntary exile and lost only the *imperium* which as propraetor he was exercising in Italy[7].

of Q. Scaevola; of L. Cornelius Merula and Q. Lutatius Catulus; of App. Claudius;

Prosecution of Cn. Papirius Carbo.

In 84 B.C. Cn. Papirius Carbo was the object of a tribunician movement which may be interpreted as the

[1] Cic. *pro Rab.* 9, 24; Val. Max. viii. 1, 2.

[2] Schol. Bob. p. 230.

[3] Cic. *pro Rosc. Amer.* 12, 33; Val. Max. ix. 11, 2.

[4] App. (*B. C.* i. 74) speaks of them as φυλασσόμενα ἀφανῶς; for the *contiones* see p. 346, note 1.

[5] Cic. *de Orat.* iii. 3, 9; *Tusc. Disp.* v. 19, 56; Val. Max. ix. 12, 4.

[6] Merula open his veins 'in Iovis sacrario' (Val. Max. ix. 12, 5; cf. Vell. ii. 22; App. *l. c.*); Catulus sought death by suffocation.

[7] Cic. *pro Domo*, 31, 83; see Zumpt, i. 2, p. 355.

threat of a prosecution. After Cinna had been murdered by his soldiers, his colleague Carbo refused to return to Rome to enable a new consul to be elected by the people. The tribunes threatened 'to make him a private individual,' i.e. perhaps to introduce a bill, similar to that aimed at Caepio in 105, which would abrogate his *imperium*. Carbo yielded to the threat and made a show of obedience to the college'[1].

Trial of M. Lucullus.

In the year 66 C. Memmius as tribune of the *plebs* prosecuted M. Lucullus for acts which many years before he had, as quaestor, committed at Sulla's command. The accused was acquitted[2].

Prosecution of Caesar.

In 58 B.C. C. Julius Caesar, on quitting Rome for his province of Gaul, was impeached by the tribune L. Antistius. A successful appeal was made to the tribune's colleagues that the accused should be exempted from appearing, on the ground that he was absent on the service of the state[3].

Trial of Milo.

In 56 B.C. P. Clodius as curule aedile accused T. Annius Milo before the *comitia tributa populi* for breaches of the peace (*vis*). The charge was based on the possession, and probably the use, of bands of gladiators. The three *contiones* and the date for the fourth are mentioned, and we hear of advocates and witnesses. But we know of no issue to the trial[4].

Tribunician prosecutions of 45 B.C.

Even under the dictator's rule tribunician prosecution was in theory unhampered. In 45 B.C. two tribunes impeached the man who had first greeted Caesar with the title of king[5].

We have kept to the last the trial of Rabirius and the

[1] App. *B. C.* i. 78 τῶν δημάρχων αὐτὸν καλούντων ἐπὶ συνάρχου χειροτονίαν. ἀπειλησάντων δὲ ἰδιώτην ἀποφανεῖν, ἐπανῆλθε μὲν καὶ χειροτονίαν προὔθηκεν ὑπάτου. The explanation adopted in the text is that of Zumpt (i. 2, p. 355). The only other possible interpretation of the words is that the tribunes threatened a *iustitium* which would incapacitate the consul for the performance of any magisterial functions.

[2] Plut. *Lucull.* 37.

[3] Suet. *Caes.* 23.

[4] For references to this trial see p. 341, note 7, and p. 346, note 1.

[5] Dio Cass. xliv. 10.

BOOK II. impeachment of Cicero, both of which demand a more detailed investigation.

Trial of C. Rabirius in 63 B.C. Origin of the charge.

The trial of C. Rabirius for *perduellio* (63 B.C.) was the revival of a very distant event but a very present question. In the year 100 occurred the revolutionary movement led by L. Appuleius Saturninus, who had eventually occupied the Capitol with an armed band. The senate declared Saturninus and his supporters public enemies[1], and the consul C. Marius armed a number of citizens willing to support the government and forced the rioters to surrender. They were imprisoned in the Curia Hostilia and there murdered by the people. The motive for inquiring into the manner of Saturninus' death thirty-seven years after the event was undoubtedly purely political[2]. It was, as Cicero says, not so much the aged senator Rabirius who was on his trial as the authority of the senate and the *imperium* of the consul[3]. The whole question of the validity of martial law was supposed to be represented in the person of the elderly prisoner who was accused of killing Saturninus; the liberty of the citizen and the sanctity of the tribunate in the person of T. Labienus, the tribune whom C. Caesar had incited to conduct the prosecution[4]. The facts of the case were in themselves doubtful. The defence admitted that Rabirius had taken a personal share in the suppression of the revolution[5]; but the general complicity of all classes in this suppression was equally clear[6], and, in particular, the murder of the tribune had been publicly recognized as the work of a slave named Scaeva, who had been given freedom on his profession of the deed[7].

[1] Cic. *pro Rab.* 7, 20. [2] Dio Cass. xxxvii. 26.

[3] Cic. *l. c.* 1, 2 'ut illud summum auxilium maiestatis atque imperii, quod nobis a maioribus est traditum, de re publica tolleretur, ut nihil posthac auctoritas senatus, nihil consulare imperium, nihil consensio bonorum contra pestem ac perniciem civitatis valeret': cf. *in Pis.* 2, 4.

[4] Suet. *Caes.* 12.

[5] Cic. *pro Rab.* 6, 19 'Confiteor interficiendi Saturnini causa C. Rabirium arma cepisse.' [6] Cic. *l. c.* 11, 31. [7] Cic. *l. c.*

Method adopted by the prosecution.

The methods open to the prosecution, if they wished an expression of popular judgement, were an ordinary tribunician impeachment for treason or the old method of judgement by the *duumviri perduellionis*. It is not clear why the latter method was preferred. Perhaps the solemnity and antiquity of the procedure were meant to impress popular imagination. It was mentally associated with the veiled head, the unlucky tree, the stake and the lictor, with a terrible execution and not with banishment, and it had the advantage of eliciting a twofold expression of the people's will. They first met to sanction the appointment of duumvirs, and then might come together to listen to the appeal from their decision. But it was a clumsy method of judicial warfare. It seems that the revival of this procedure required a special bill, and the terms of this enactment were the subject of fierce struggles in the senate and the assembly[1]. Labienus, who had charge of the measure, wished all the terms of the *horrendum carmen* of King Tullus to be maintained[2]; but Cicero struggled with success against this grotesque revival, and the penalty, although a capital one, contained no reference to crosses or lictors[3]. As finally fixed it was probably *aquae et ignis interdictio*[4] combined with the confiscation of the property of the condemned[5].

[1] Dio Cass. xxxvii. 27 *σπουδαί τε οὖν ταραχώδεις καὶ φιλονεικίαι ἀφ' ἑκατέρων περὶ . . . τοῦ δικαστηρίου.* When this had been agreed on *περὶ . . . τῆς κρίσεως αὖθις συνέβησαν.*

[2] Cic. *pro Rab.* 3, 10; 4, 11; 5, 15; 4, 13. In the last passage Cicero speaks of 'haec tua . . . I LICTOR, COLLIGA MANUS . . . CAPUT OBNUBITO, ARBORI INFELICI SUSPENDITO.' In 10, 28 he says 'si C. Rabirio . . . crucem T. Labienus in campo Martio defigendam putavit.'

[3] Cic. *pro Rab.* 5, 17 'Quam ob rem fateor atque etiam, T. Labiene, profiteor et prae me fero te ex illa crudeli, importuna, non tribunicia actione sed regia, meo consilio, virtute, auctoritate esse depulsum.' The same claim is made in 3, 10; 4, 11; 5, 15.

[4] In the speech *vita* (2, 5) and *caput* (1, 1; 1, 2; 2, 5) are said to be at stake.

[5] It is probably this aspect of the condemnation that is described as *multae irrogatio* in *pro Rab.* 3, 8. Yet certain passages of the Digest (50, 16,

BOOK II.

Appointment of the *duumviri perduellionis.*

The method of the appointment of the duumvirs was no doubt also fixed by this measure. The system of direct popular election of these officials with a mandate was not adopted; for, according to the legal notions which had long prevailed, the election of a commission by the people excluded the appeal, and to force the matter to appeal was the great object of the present performance. Resort was, therefore, had to the regal principle of nomination[1]. They were to be chosen by a praetor[2] through the lot[3]. Perhaps the praetor urbanus was specified, and the holder of the office may have been that Q. Metellus Celer who finally succeeded in getting the proceedings stopped. We do not know how the choice by the praetor was combined with selection by lot; possibly he was to nominate a certain number of candidates from whom selection would be made; for, unless the *sortitio* was tampered with, the choice of C. Caesar seems to show that the class of eligible candidates was a very narrow one. Besides C. Caesar, who was praetor elect, the choice fell on L. Caesar, who had been consul during the preceding year[4].

Rules of procedure adopted.

The bill may also have specified certain rules of procedure for the whole trial. After the case had gone on appeal to the people Cicero complains that only half an hour was allowed for the defence[5]. This restriction he attributes to Labienus, and it may have been a provision contained in the measure. Otherwise it could only have been a

244; 50, 16, 131, 1) seem to show that *multa* could be used of any penalty not fixed by law. But I know of no such Ciceronian usage.

[1] Liv. i. 26 'Rex . . . concilio populi advocato (i. e. probably *not* the comitia) "duumviros" inquit, "qui Horatio perduellionem iudicent secundum legem facio" . . . Hac lege (i. e. the formula given by the king, *not a lex rogata*) duumviri creati.'

[2] Dio Cass. xxxvii. 27; cf. Cic. *pro Rab.* 4, 12.

[3] Suet. *Caes.* 12.

[4] Dio Cass. *l. c.*; Suet. *l. c.* Possibly those who had been *iudices quaestionis* were alone eligible; C. Caesar had been in the previous year president of the court *de sicariis* (Suet. *Caes.* 11). But perhaps there was no condition of eligibility. The praetor may have nominated a fixed number of candidates who then cast lots.

[5] Cic. *pro Rab.* 2, 6; 3, 9; cf. 13, 38.

proposal of the prosecutor, accepted either by the general guide of the proceedings, the praetor, or the actual president of the *comitia*, who was in this case probably one of the *duumviri*[1].

The prosecution.

A *iudicium populi*, whether based on the *provocatio* or not, did not require a prosecutor. If there were two instances, the first was an inquiry (*quaestio*) which might be undertaken independently by the magistrate; in the second the presiding magistrate is also in a sense the accuser. But there was nothing to prevent the admission of a prosecutor, and if Rabirius was confronted with one this must have been Labienus himself; Cicero, at least, speaks of no one else as the *accusator*[2].

Condemnation by the duumvirs and appeal to the people.

When the case came to its first instance the prosecution was keenly pressed and the duumvirs condemned with a suspicious alacrity[3]. Against the sentence Rabirius lodged an appeal to the *comitia centuriata*. We must presume a considerable interval between the sentence of the duumvirs and the trial before the people. Their sentence must have been followed by the usual *anquisitio* in the three *contiones*, the judgement must have been promulgated in the form of a *rogatio*, and three market days must have elapsed before the case came to trial[4]. We are not told who presided at the assembly; analogies would seem to show that it was one of the *duumviri*[5]. The defence was first conducted by Q. Hortensius, who exhibited the baselessness of the charge on the ground of fact[6]. Cicero followed, but, in spite of his eloquence and his influence as consul, condemnation was seen to be

[1] As a trial lasted only a single day, the presiding magistrate must always have had some power of fixing the length of the pleadings. But no earlier instance of such a limitation appears to be known.

[2] Cic. *pro Rab.* 2, 6: cf. 2, 4 'rem . . . a tribuno plebis susceptam . . . a consule defensam.'

[3] Suet. *Caes.* 12 'sorte iudex in reum ductus tam cupide condemnavit ut ad populum provocanti nihil aeque ac iudicis acerbitas profuerit.'

[4] See p. 346. [5] See p. 311. [6] Cic. *pro Rab.* 6, 18.

Dissolution of the assembly.

certain. The praetor Q. Metellus adopted the last method of dissolving the assembly[1]. When the army met by centuries in the Campus, a guard was left at the Janiculum and a standard flew from the tower. When the assembly dissolved, the guard dispersed and the flag was hauled down. The lowered flag was thus a sign that the Janiculum was unguarded[2]. Metellus now seized on this antique custom; he hurried to the fort and hauled down the red ensign, with the result that the *exercitus* had to leave its station in the Campus Martius.

The prosecution not renewed. Principles regulating renewal.

Labienus did not renew the prosecution, although legally a renewal was not impossible[3]. The revival of the charge would, however, have necessitated a fresh *rogatio* and a fresh *trinundinum*. Only the trial before the duumvirs which gave rise to the appeal would have remained of the former process. But even a new trial on the same charge was not encouraged in Roman procedure. An early precedent for dropping or altering a prosecution when the original trial had not been completed was to be found in 248 B.C., when P. Claudius Pulcher, the consul of the preceding year, who had fought in violation of the auspices and had been defeated by the Carthaginians, was accused for *perduellio* by two tribunes of the *plebs*. On the final day of trial, when condemnation seemed certain, stormy weather dissolved the assembly and brought the proceedings to a close. The prosecutors wished to renew the charge with a similar penalty, but the other tribunes declared against it[4]. They would admit only a pecuniary prosecution and Claudius was condemned to a fine of 120,000 asses. The adoption of such a procedure does not seem to be in conflict with the legal principle stated by Cicero 'that a capital should never be united with a

[1] Dio Cass. xxxvii. 27.

[2] *l. c.* c. 28; cf. Laelius Felix, *ap. Gell.* xv. 27, 5.

[3] Dio Cass. *l. c.*

[4] Schol. Bob. p. 337 'tr. pl. intercesserunt ne idem homines in eodem magistratu perduellionis bis eundem accusarent'; cf. Val. Max. viii. 1, 4.

monetary penalty[1].' This cannot, indeed, mean that a pecuniary penalty should not be joined in the same sentence with a capital one: for capital penalties were often accompanied by confiscation of goods. It must mean 'that no one, for one and the same offence, should be accused in a capital process before the centuries and in a pecuniary process before the tribes[2].' But, if this be the sense of the words, the maxim must imply that the charges are concurrent or that both trials have a normal ending; otherwise the renewal of the prosecution of Claudius, a renewal that some have suspected in the case of Rabirius[3], would have been illegal. If we consider it an absolute prohibition of action before the centuries and the tribes on the same charge, then, when such a solution as that attempted in the case of Claudius was adopted, the second charge must have been based on a different technical ground from the first. *Maiestas*, for instance, must have been made to replace *perduellio*.

Prosecution of Cicero in 58 B.C. The first bill of Clodius.

The leading political motive which animated the trial of Rabirius appears again in the attempted prosecution and the banishment of Cicero which was effected by the tribune Clodius in 58 B.C. Clodius approached the *plebs* with a resolution that 'any one who shall put to death or has put to death a citizen without condemnation by the people[4] shall be debarred fire and water[5].' The terms of the bill seem to have included senators as well as magistrates, i.e. those who advised as well as those who executed the decree[6]; in this respect it followed the wording of its model, the Sempronian law[7]. Although

[1] Cic. *pro Domo*, 17, 45 'cum tam moderata iudicia populi sint a maioribus constituta ... ut ne poena capitis cum pecunia coniungatur (concessum sit).'

[2] Zumpt, i. 1, p. 366.

[3] e. g. Mommsen, *Staatsr.* ii. p. 298, n. 3 and *Strafr.* p. 590, n. 1; Heitland on Cic. *pro Rab.* p. 33.

[4] Dio Cass. xxxviii. 14. Cf. Liv. *Ep.* ciii.

[5] Vell. ii. 45.

[6] Dio Cass. *l. c.* ἔφερε μὲν γὰρ καὶ ἐπὶ πᾶσαν τὴν βουλήν.

[7] See p. 324.

BOOK II.

Cicero was not named, the application of this renewal of an already existing legal principle was obvious and was made more so by the fact that, when Clodius held a *contio* on the subject of his bill in the Flaminian Circus, Caesar dwelt with severe strictures on the execution of the Catilinarian conspirators[1]. As a resolution renewing a former enactment the bill of Clodius seemed to be the preliminary threat of a prosecution under that law[2], and, while it created no new crime, its wording showed a retrospective application[3]. This was the point in the bill, which, we are told, was deprecated by Caesar[4].

Reasons for Clodius' procedure.

It is not difficult to see why this method of re-enactment was adopted. The *lex Sempronia* seemed shattered by the procedure with reference to the Catilinarians; for, if this procedure represented valid constitutional custom, the Sempronian law was no more. Clodius wished both to elicit the temper of the people on the situation before he prosecuted Cicero, and to gain the adherence of all classes and all representative men to a principle. If it was gained, and expressed by their support of the bill, they could not consistently protect the man who had done the Catilinarians to death, for it could be shown that the principle of the bill was no new one. Cicero himself admits that the Clodian law had many 'popular' elements[5]; it was passed enthusiastically with the support even of the orator's friends[6], and after the reaction and Cicero's return from exile, its validity was never assailed.

Voluntary exile of Cicero.

Cicero had early recognized the significance of the measure. After trying in vain to elicit popular sympathy and to secure the support of influential men[7], he quitted

[1] Dio Cass. xxxviii. 17; Plut. *Cic.* 30. For the *contio* cf. Cic. *post Red. in Sen.* 7, 17.

[2] This aspect of the bill accounts for Appian's description of it (*B. C.* ii. 15), Κικέρωνα δὲ γράφεται Κλώδιος παρανόμων ὅτι πρὸ δικαστηρίου τοὺς ἀμφὶ Λέντλον καὶ Κέθηγον ἀνέλοι.

[3] Dio Cass. xxxviii. 14.

[4] *l. c.* c. 17.

[5] Cic. *ad Att.* iii. 15, 5 '(lex), in qua popularia multa sunt.'

[6] Dio Cass. *l. c.*

[7] Cic. *ad Att.* iii. 15, 4 and 5; x. 4, 3; *in Pis.* 31, 77.

Rome before it became law[1]. Clodius did not follow up the attack by citing Cicero before a popular court. His voluntary exile was taken as a proof of guilt; it was held to be a means adopted to escape prosecution; and Clodius contented himself with passing a formal bill of outlawry[2] to the effect that Cicero *had been* interdicted fire and water. This bill was, like the former, a *plebiscitum.* It is, as we saw, possible that for the offence with which Cicero was charged C. Gracchus had himself prescribed a trial before the *plebs*[3]; but, even apart from this possibility, Clodius had precedents enough for the power of the *plebs* to pass a bill of outlawry against one who had evaded trial by exile. There was the case of Postumius in 212 B.C. and that of Fulvius in 211, and it had become a developed function of the tribunes to utter the ban of interdiction against all who had sought escape by voluntary banishment, and were, therefore, held to be self-condemned[4].

Clodius passes a bill of outlawry.

Cicero's objections to the legality of this procedure[5] are based on the fact that he will not recognize it as a formal bill of outlawry, but regards it as a definite judgement of the people which was invalid on two chief and many subordinate grounds. His criticisms may be tabulated as follows:

Grounds advanced by Cicero for the illegality of the procedure.

(i) It was a *privilegium*[6].

(ii) It was a capital sentence passed, not by the centuries, but by the *concilium plebis*[7].

(iii) There had been no prosecution and no trial. Hence

[1] Dio Cass. *l. c.*

[2] Plut. *Cic.* 32.

[3] See p. 324.

[4] See pp. 317, 329 and 330.

[5] Apart from his general contention of the invalidity of the acts of Clodius' tribunate—an invalidity based chiefly on the illegality of his adoption by Fonteius (Cic. *pro Domo,* 13, 35; Plut. *Cato Min.* 40; Dio Cass. xxxix. 21).

[6] Cic. *de Leg.* iii. 19, 45; *pro Sest.* 30, 65: 34, 73; *ad Att.* iii. 15, 5; *pro Domo,* 10, 26; 16, 43; 17, 43; 26, 68; *post Red. in Sen.* 4, 8. See p. 316.

[7] Cic. *de Leg.* iii. 19, 45; *pro Sest.* 30, 65.

BOOK II. this second measure could not be a formal bill of outlawry. If it was not, it must be a *privilegium* [1].

(iv) The past tense in which the form of the interdiction was passed (*ut interdictum sit*) was ridiculous, if there had been no prosecution and no trial [2].

On these four grounds, and especially on the first two, we know that the actual *nullity* of Clodius' law was maintained by eminent jurists such as L. Cotta [3]. It was only on grounds of public expediency that the desirability of its formal repeal was finally admitted by Cicero's friends [4].

(v) A technical objection was urged, which did not affect the bill itself but only its execution, viz. that Clodius, by carrying out the provisions of his law, had undertaken a *curatio* created by his own enactment—a proceeding forbidden by a Licinian law [5].

Validity of Cicero's objections. In estimating the validity of Cicero's first four objections, the only doubtful element, which may be interpreted in his favour, is contained in the contention that there had been no prosecution and no trial. There was, indeed, one particular in which Cicero's case differed from those of

[1] Cic. *pro Domo*, 10, 26; 24, 62; 29, 77 'quis me umquam ulla lege interrogavit? quis postulavit? quis diem dixit'; cf. *pro Sest.* 34, 73; *pro Mil.* 14, 36, quoted p. 323, note 2.

[2] Cic. *pro Domo*, 18, 47 'At quid tulit legum scriptor peritus et callidus? VELITIS IUBEATIS UT M. TULLIO AQUA ET IGNI INTERDICATUR? Crudele, nefarium, ne in sceleratissimo quidem civi sine iudicio ferundum! Non tulit UT INTERDICATUR. Quid ergo? UT INTERDICTUM SIT. (31, 82) Ubi enim tuleras ut mihi aqua et igni interdiceretur? quod Gracchus de P. Popilio, Saturninus de Metello tulit . . . non ut esset interdictum, quod ferri non poterat, tulerunt, sed ut interdiceretur.'

[3] Cic. *de Leg.* iii. 19, 45; *pro Domo*, 26, 68; *pro Sest.* 34, 74; *pro Domo*, 27, 71 'senatus quidem . . . quotienscumque de me consultus est, toties eam nullam esse iudicavit.'

[4] Cic. *ad Att.* iii. 15, 5; *pro Domo*, 26, 69 'prospexistis ne qua popularis in nos aliquando invidia redundaret, si sine populi iudicio restituti videremur.'

[5] Cic. *pro Domo*, 20, 51 (on Clodius' administration of Cicero's property) 'ne id quidem per legem Liciniam, ut ipse tibi curationem ferres, facere potuisti.' This *lex Licinia* is of unknown date; it contained provisions similar to those of a *lex Aebutia* (Cic. *de Leg. Agr.* ii. 8, 21).

Postumius and of Fulvius[1]. In these two cases the accused were prosecuted; a definite limit of time was fixed for their appearance, and, when they did not appear to stand their trial, it was decreed, in the case of Postumius, that, if he did not present himself by a given day, he should be held to be in exile; in the case of Fulvius, on his not presenting himself on the given day, that he was in exile[2]. This was not the case with Cicero. He maintains that he was not accused and that no day was fixed for his appearance.

On the other hand, Clodius had his excuse. It was generally known that Cicero had gone into exile to escape prosecution, that he had fled to escape the incidence of the first law. On this ground Clodius adopted the simple, and, as he held, tralaticiary plan of recognizing Cicero's exile by a formal bill of outlawry. The question, therefore, is the technical one whether—supposing a man had gone into exile to escape prosecution, but had never been formally prosecuted—the bill of outlawry might be passed against him. It is one that we have no means of deciding; but it is at least possible that the annual bill passed by the tribunes[3] covered the cases of men who had obviously sought exile for the purpose of avoiding prosecution.

Cicero's objection to the form in which the interdiction was expressed is obviously connected with the question which we have just discussed; but the meaning of the past tense employed by Clodius demands further investigation. The expression is clearly modelled on precedents such as that of the case of Fulvius, where the form of outlawry ran *id ei iustum exilium esse.* But the phrasing does not seem justified unless a limit of time was fixed in the bill of outlawry after which the outlawry should become effective, unless, for instance, it contained the clause 'If Cicero does not return to stand his trial by a certain date, he shall

[1] Zumpt, i. 2, p. 422. [2] See pp. 329, 330. [3] See pp. 317, 329.

BOOK II. have been outlawed.' It has, indeed, been supposed that this was the case, that the bill did contain this clause[1]; and, if this conjecture is correct, the legal situation was as follows. Cicero had not been prosecuted before his exile, but before the actual outlawry there was the equivalent of a prosecution, that is, a declaration that the bill would not be effective if Cicero returned before a certain date. If Cicero proves to be wrong in his interpretation of the form of the interdiction, there is little weight in his contention that he had been neither tried nor prosecuted.

But the assumption of the existence of this qualifying clause makes Cicero guilty of a very serious *suppressio veri*. It cannot be proved correct, and we may give him the benefit of the doubt. Clodius' *ut interdictum sit*, although modelled on precedents, appeared somewhat meaningless because preceded by no protasis such as 'if he does not return.' The great point which Cicero scores is that there had been no prosecution and no fixing of a date.

Cicero's final objection, that Clodius in executing the law (by the demolition, for instance, of Cicero's house), filled an office which he had created, is easily answered. The *rogator* of a law was necessarily mainly responsible for its being carried out. Just as the tribunes had thrown prisoners from the Tarpeian rock[2], so Clodius took over the administration of Cicero's confiscated property[3]. Such

[1] This is the interpretation given by Zumpt (l. c., p. 425) to the words of Cicero (*ad Att.* iii. 4): 'Statim iter Brundisium versus contuli ante diem rogationis.' He interprets 'diem rogationis' as 'the day fixed by the law'—after which the interdiction should become effective. But perhaps the words mean 'the day on which the *rogatio* should become a *lex*.' Cicero has received an *amended* copy of the *rogatio* (*l. c.* 'Allata est enim nobis rogatio de pernicie mea: in qua quod correctum esse audieramus'), and the amendment must, of course, have been made before the final promulgation; it was not, therefore, a *lex* when he received it. Cf. *ad Att.* iii. 1.

[2] Liv. vi. 20.

[3] As a rule the confiscation was effected by the quaestors, but at the bidding of a higher magistrate (Liv. iv. 15; xxxviii. 60; *Lex Tab. Bant.*

execution could not be regarded in the light of a separate *curatio*.

Provisions of Clodius' bill of outlawry.

Clodius' bill was very carefully drawn. Its terms were amended after the first promulgation [1] and it contained many clauses. From the date of Cicero's interdiction it forbade any one to harbour him within the limits of his exile, and declared a penalty against all who should afford him shelter [2]. His property was confiscated to the State, his house levelled to the ground and its site dedicated to a temple of Liberty. A feature, perhaps a peculiarity, of the measure was that it assigned a geographical limit to Cicero's exile [3]. Cicero gives this limit as 400 miles [4], Plutarch as 500, Dio Cassius as 3,750 stadia [5], that is, rather more than 468 miles. Plutarch's and Dio's accounts are reconcilable on the supposition that Plutarch gives a round, Dio an accurate number, but the discrepancy between Cicero and Dio leads us to think of different enactments. The distance was reckoned from Rome, and its object was to keep Cicero from Italy. He had intended to go to Sicily [6], but we find a sudden change of plan. From Vibo he turned in the direction of Brundisium [7], and the ground for the change of route was Clodius' enactment. The 400 miles had been suddenly changed to 468, the distance from Rome to Leucopetra. Italy was thus interdicted, and even Sicily seemed too near; for the amended enactment forbade him this island by name [8], and Malta, which belonged to the Sicilian province, could not afford

Meaning of the limit assigned to Cicero's exile.

l. 11); but execution of this kind, although not as a rule effected by the tribunes, was certainly not regarded as a separate office created by law.

[1] See p. 364, note 1.

[2] Cic. *pro Domo*, 19, 51; Plut. *Cic.* 32; Dio Cass. xxxviii. 17.

[3] The discrepancies connected with the accounts of these limits have been admirably explained by Zumpt (i. 2, p. 427 ff.). His conclusions are here summarized.

[4] *ad Att.* iii. 4.

[5] Plut. *l. c.*; Dio Cass. *l. c.*

[6] Plut. *l. c.*

[7] Cic. *ad Att.* iii. 3 and 4.

[8] Dio Cass. *l. c.*; cf. Cic. *pro Plancio*, 40, 96 'praetor ille (Vergilius) .. me in Siciliam venire noluit.'

BOOK II.

him shelter[1]. It is possible that, in addition to Sicily, other provinces near Rome, such as Sardinia, were forbidden. Cicero even writes that he fears the law may be so interpreted as to exclude him from Athens[2]; but perhaps this is the utterance of despair.

Prohibition of repeal.

The final feature of Clodius' law was the not unusual but always fruitless prohibition of repeal which it contained[3]. It fenced itself round with elaborate safeguards. No repeal was to be moved in the senate or the popular assembly; and the clause of the bill forbidding its discussion by senators[4] was set up on the door of the curia[5]. The preliminary steps towards Cicero's restoration were, therefore, difficult. Magistrates and senators shrank from incurring the pains and penalties[6], and it may have been felt that the declaration of the nullity of the law would be easier than its repeal[7]. But the danger only lasted as long as the discussion, for when the law was abrogated its sanction fell with it[8].

[1] Cic. *ad Att.* iii. 4 'Melitae esse non licebat.'

[2] Cic. *l. c.* 7, 1 'veremur ne interpretentur illud quoque oppidum (Athenas) ab Italia non satis abesse.'

[3] Cic. *l. c.* 23, 2.

[4] NE QUIS AD SENATUM (in Cicero 'vos') REFERRET, NE QUIS DECERNERET, NE DISPUTARET, NE LOQUERETUR, NE PEDIBUS IRET, NE SCRIBENDO ADESSET (Cic. *post Red. in Sen.* 4, 8); cf. *ad Att.* iii. 12, 1.

[5] Cic. *ad Att.* iii. 15, 6.

[6] Cic. *in Pis.* 13, 29; *post Red. in Sen.* 2, 4.

[7] See p. 362.

[8] Cic. *ad Att.* iii. 23, 2. Nevertheless in the bill for his recall proposed by the eight tribunes of the *plebs* in 58 B. C. the following safeguarding clause was inserted (*l. c.*): 'In so far as the provisions of this law conflict with the prohibitions of abrogation contained in other laws ('these others,' says Cicero, 'must include Clodius' law') or expose the promulgator or abrogater to penalty or fine, this law is so far void.' On which Cicero makes the comment (§ 4): 'Atque hoc in illis tribunis plebis non laedebat. Lege enim collegae sui (or 'collegii sui') non tenebantur'—i. e. the wording of Clodius' bill only bound future colleges of tribunes; he had relied on his veto to control his own college.

§ 8. *Domestic Jurisdiction.*

An account of Roman criminal procedure would be singularly incomplete which did not take account of the Domestic Tribunal. The juristic self-existence of the family, which survived the Republic, took many a burden from the shoulders of the State, and the small number of criminal judges in the capital was rendered possible by the wide jurisdiction of the *iudex domesticus*. The son, the wife and the dependent, whether slave or freedman, were all subjects of this survival of patriarchal rule.

Domestic jurisdiction:

(i) over the son,

The power over the son was so ancient that it was held to be given by one of the royal laws (*leges regiae*)[1] and so absolute that no age or dignity exempted from it[2]. Its only legal limit was that it should not come into conflict with the *ius publicum*, and the son who was a magistrate need not obey the father who was a private citizen in all things. Death, scourging, bonds and villainage on the family estate were said to have been inflicted in early times by the paternal power, and the traditional execution of the sons of Brutus and (according to one version) that of Sp. Cassius showed how it might be used to check the designs of a revolutionary[3]. The infliction of the death penalty by a father who was in a private station seems to have been unusual during the later Republic[4]; but there are instances of capital trial and condemnation both during and after the Ciceronian period. L. Gellius, the consul of 72 and the censor of 70 B.C., tried his son for illicit intercourse with his stepmother and attempted parricide[5]. He summoned almost the whole senate as his

[1] Collatio 4, 8. [2] Dionys. ii. 26. [3] Plut. *Publ.* 6; Dionys. viii. 79.

[4] Dio Cassius (xxxvii. 36), in discussing the execution of A. Fulvius by his father in 63 B.C., adds οὔτι γε καὶ μόνος (ὥς γέ τισι δοκεῖ) τοῦτ' ἐν ἰδιωτείᾳ ποιήσας. But that such an opinion could have been held shows the infrequency of the act.

[5] Val. Max. v. 9, 1.

BOOK II.

council of advice, and the son was acquitted. In 63 B.C. A. Fulvius, a senator's son and himself a senator, had attached himself to Catiline's following and was journeying to his camp. The father brought him back, condemned him and put him to death[1]. With respect to the paternal power, adopted were in the same position as natural children, and even the father of a family who had been adrogated was, by the formula of the act, subject to the 'power of life and death' of his new parent[2]. In the adoption of a son already under power no such specific declaration seems to have been necessary, for the child transferred by mancipation became the property of his last owner. History has preserved no instance of jurisdiction over adoptive children.

and the adopted son.

The punishments found inflicted by the paternal power are death and exile[3]. There is no instance of a fine, but such a penalty was not impossible since it might be exacted from the *peculium*. To give weight to the father's judgement a council of advisers (*consilium*) was essential[4]. There were no fixed rules for its constitution, and, as it was chosen by the father himself, his chief object would naturally have been to make it as weighty and representative as possible. Near relatives would be chosen as a matter of course, mere blood-relations or cognates as well as agnates, those related in the male line. But relations by marriage and family friends might be invited too[5] and a semi-public character

The domestic *consilium*.

[1] Sall. *Cat.* 39, 5; Dio Cass. xxxvii, 36; Val. Max. v. 8, 5.

[2] The *rogatio* ran: 'Velitis, iubeatis uti L. Valerius L. Titio tam iure legeque filius siet quam si ex eo patre matreque familias eius natus esset, utque ei vitae necisque in eum potestas siet, uti patri endo filio est' (Gell. v. 19, 9). Cf. Cic. *pro Domo*, 29, 77 (of Clodius' adoption by Fonteius), 'credo enim, quamquam in illa adoptione legitime factum est nihil, tamen te esse interrogatum "auctorne esses ut in te P. Fonteius vitae necisque potestatem haberet, ut in filio."'

[3] The latter appears in a case of the Augustan age related by Seneca (*de Clem.* i. 15).

[4] Dionys. viii. 79.

[5] Val. Max. v. 8, 2 'adhibito propinquorum et amicorum consilio.'

might be given to the proceedings by calling in the assistance of distinguished public men. L. Gellius, although the issue was a private one, summoned the majority of senators[1], an effective means of proving to the leaders of society the baselessness of a scandal, and in an equally private case under the early Principate Augustus himself was summoned to the board[2]. This jurisdiction was never interfered with by the criminal legislation of the later Republic, but it is uncertain how far the judgement of the family court was binding on the community. We hear of no law which made it necessary that the state should rest content with the judgements of such a court; and, although in the case of condemnation the matter probably ended there, in the case of acquittal the father's sentence perhaps formed only a kind of *praeiudicium* 'of the greatest influence on the judgements of magistrate and people, but which did not legally exclude them[3].' We have no certain instance of a public following on a family court, although the legendary case of Horatius shows something equivalent to acquittal by the father being succeeded by a public prosecution[4].

Continuance of this jurisdiction: its relation to public criminal jurisdiction.

(ii) Over the wife or married daughter.

The jurisdiction over the wife was, in the old form of marriage which conferred *manus*, similar to that over the daughter, whose position she held in the household[5]. In the later marriage by *consensus*, where no *potestas* could be asserted by the husband over the woman, and where, from a juristic point of view, she never quitted her father's family, it has naturally been supposed that the father remained the judge[6]. But the elder Cato still speaks of a very extended marital jurisdiction at a time when the freer form of marriage was beginning to prevail[7], and it is possible that some coercive power was still possessed

[1] Val. Max. v. 9, 1, see p. 367.
[2] Seneca, *de Clem.* i. 15.
[3] Zumpt, i. p. 354.
[4] Liv. i. 26: see p. 303, note a.
[5] Dionys. ii. 25.
[6] Geib, *Criminalprocess*, p. 87.
[7] Cato, *ap. Gell.* x. 23 'Vir . . . imperium, quod videtur, habet, si quid perverse taetreque factum est a muliere.'

BOOK II.

by the husband[1], although whether it was he or the father who set in motion a trial on a serious charge before the relatives (*propinqui*) of the woman must remain uncertain. One right still given to the husband even by this weaker marriage-tie, that of slaying the wife taken in adultery, lasts through the Ciceronian period and into the Empire[2].

Reasons for the persistence of this jurisdiction,

The reasons for the persistence of this jurisdiction were manifold. Even the emancipating tendencies of the later Republic did not lead the Romans to modify their view of the closeness of the family as a self-existent corporation, for the conduct of whose members the head was wholly responsible[3]. An early disability, too, made women seem peculiarly liable to the courts of the household. If the *provocatio* was limited to those possessed of membership of the *comitia* (*communio comitiorum*), it could not have belonged originally to women, for they had not this communion[4]. This disability was removed later and a woman is found arraigned before a *iudicium populi* which sprang from the coercive power of a magistrate[5]. But by this time the custom of domestic jurisdiction had been fixed, and it was perhaps chiefly women of the lower classes, freedwomen and *meretrices* who had no proper guardians, that were subject to a public trial. An unwillingness to allow the public execution of women, exemplified in the fact that down to 31 A.D. no virgin had ever been put to death *triumvirali supplicio*[6], may

[1] Cf. Rossbach, *Römische Ehe*, p. 52.

[2] Cato, *ap. Gell.* x. 23 'In adulterio uxorem tuam si prehendisses, sine iudicio impune necares.' Cf. Hor. *Sat.* ii. 7. 61

'Estne marito
Matronae peccantis in ambo iusta potestas?
In corruptorem vel iustior.'

[3] Cato, *l. c.* and Livy (xxxiv. 1) speak of the *imperium* of the husband.

[4] Gell. v. 19 (A woman who is not in her parents' power can not be adrogated) 'quoniam et cum feminis nulla comitiorum communio est.'

[5] Gell. iv. 14 'Aulus Hostilius Mancinus aedilis curulis fuit. Is Maniliae meretrici diem ad populum dixit.' For other aedilician prosecutions of women cf. Gell. x. 6 (p. 341); Liv. xxv. 2 (p. 340).

[6] Tac. *Ann.* v. 9 [vi. 4].

also have contributed to the maintenance of the family court. The best Republican instance of the execution of punishment for a public crime being left to domestic authority is furnished by the case of the women implicated in the Bacchanalian conspiracy of 186 B.C.[1]

The *consilium*.

Whether the court was set on foot by father or husband or was a joint-board composed of both with their respective relatives, the most essential feature of these trials was the *consilium* composed of blood relatives on both sides and even of relations by marriage (*cognati* and *propinqui*)[2]. We hear of the death penalty, and perhaps of fines being inflicted[3]. The 'capital' punishment of the Principate[4] was perhaps deportation, or the expression may be used loosely for simple relegation[5]; but neither of these punishments belongs to the Ciceronian period. Perhaps in Cicero's time purely domestic offences even of a serious kind were not brought before a family tribunal but were visited only by repudiation. At this time divorce certainly required no formal trial, although in early times repudiation by the husband, in spite of its being not strictly a punishment, could only be properly effected with the help of a *consilium* of advisers[6].

(iii) Over slaves.

Slaves could be punished by their masters without even the pretence of a formal trial[7]: the punishments were arbitrary, and we find the death penalty inflicted for an

[1] Liv. xxxix. 18 : see p. 383, note 1.

[2] For *cognati* see Liv. xxxix. 18 and *Ep.* xlviii; for *propinqui*, Tac. *Ann.* xiii. 32; Suet. *Tib.* 35. This council is sometimes spoken of as though it were the court (Liv., Suet., *ll. cc.*). In a *consilium* assembled for purposes of divorce we hear of *amici* (Val. Max. ii. 9, 2).

[3] 'Multitatur, si vinum bibit' (Cato, *l. c.*), but it is questionable whether this word is to be taken strictly.

[4] Tac. *Ann.* xiii. 32 (A. D. 57). A. Plautius here decides *de capite* of his wife Pomponia Graecina.

[5] The punishment inflicted by Augustus on the two Juliae (Suet. *Aug.* 65).

[6] Val. Max. ii. 9, 2.

[7] The earliest remedial legislation belongs to the Empire, and the essence of the *dominica potestas* was first destroyed by Hadrian (*Vita Hadr.* 18 'servos a dominis occidi vetuit eosque iussit damnari per iudices, si digni essent').

BOOK II. offence against the honour of the household[1]. For crimes against others than the members of the family the slave was tried by the ordinary process of criminal law[2], which was perhaps a concession to society rather than to the wrongdoer. The execution of the penalty seems, however, to have been at times committed to his master[3]. The slaveholder's sense of insecurity led to the legal provision that the murder of a Roman in his own house by whatever hand should be avenged by the death of the whole *familia* that was sleeping beneath the roof at the moment of the commission of the crime[4].

(iv) Over freedmen.

More remarkable than the domestic jurisdiction over the slave is that over the freedman. It extended even to the death penalty and continued down to the Ciceronian period; for Caesar, a stern ruler in his own household, is said to have put to death a favourite freedman for adultery with the wife of a Roman knight[5]. Although the freedman continues in more than one respect to be attached to the *familia* of his patron[6], yet it is hardly possible that the right of life and death could have been exercised by the former master over freedmen of the best right (*iusti liberti*), who were voting citizens—over those, that is, who had been emancipated by the forms of *vindicta*, census or testament[7]. But it may have affected the slave who had gained his freedom informally by announcement before friends (*inter amicos*) or through a letter (*per epistolam*)

[1] Val. Max. vi. 1, 3. The daughter of Pontius Aufidianus had been seduced by her slave-tutor. Both slave and daughter were put to death.

[2] Val. Max. viii. 4, 2 'servus . . . a iudicibus damnatus.'

[3] Plut. *Cato Mai.* 21.

[4] Cic. *ad Fam.* iv. 12, 3 (Servius Sulpicius on the murder of M. Marcellus in 45 B. C.) 'reliquos (servos) aiebant profugisse, metu perterritos, quod dominus eorum ante tabernaculum interfectus esset.'

[5] Suet. *Caes.* 48; cf. Val. Max. vi. 1, 4.

[6] He owed *obsequium* and certain personal duties (*operae*) to his former master: he could not prosecute or witness against him in a criminal court, and required the praetor's permission to make him the object of a civil action.

[7] See Willems, *Le Droit Public*, i. p. 125, n. 8.

or by an invitation to dine as a free man at his master's table (*per mensam*)—methods of enfranchisement which were protected by the civil courts but conferred no political rights.

§ 9. *Religious Jurisdiction.*

Survival of the jurisdiction of the pontifical court.

Religious jurisdiction—that of the highest of the sacred guilds, the pontifex maximus with his *consilium* of pontifices—was the survival of a very wide jurisdiction of the king and his council of spiritual advisers. It survived in so far as a sphere of law could be imagined which was still pre-eminently *ius sacrum*. This sacred law was a part of *ius publicum* [1], but the two were administered by different classes of officials. They might, indeed, be guided by the same individuals; the chief pontiff might fill the consulship; but the individual works in the two spheres in different capacities. In spite of the secularization of law both criminal and civil, there still continued to be a State Church with its own *ius*. There was, therefore, an ecclesiastical jurisdiction, whose sphere, as well as its partition or conflict with that of the state, we may now attempt to determine.

Ecclesiastical jurisdiction over priests.

(i) Ecclesiastical jurisdiction of the head of the state religion over the priesthood is easily intelligible, especially when, as at Rome, it never extended to secular offences committed by members of the orders but only to religious lapses or to controverted matters of ritual. No conflict is created with the secular power unless the duty imposed on the man *qua* priest is in conflict with his duty in some civil capacity. But so inextricably were the priestly and official hierarchies interwoven at Rome that opportunity was not lacking for such a controversy. Of the three instances that appear in Roman history [2] we may cite

Conflict with the secular arm.

[1] Rudorff, *Rechtsgesch.* i. p. 6.

[2] They belong to the years 189 (Liv. xxxvii. 51), 180 (Liv. xl. 42) and 131 B.C. (Cic. *Phil.* xi. 8, 18).

BOOK II. the one nearest to the Ciceronian epoch as an example. In 131 B.C. the people were asked to appoint a commander for the war against Aristonicus. Crassus, consul and pontifex maximus, declared a fine against his colleague L. Valerius Flaccus, who was flamen of Mars as well as consul, if the latter abandoned his *sacra*. The people remitted the fine but bade the flamen obey the pontifex. In all three cases the conflict is adjusted in the same peculiar way. A fine is imposed by the pontifex maximus, and an appeal is made from it to the people. The *multa* is intended merely for the purpose of producing a *certatio*, a test question, and for eliciting a decision of the sovereign as to the limits of spiritual allegiance. In all the cases the people bid the recalcitrant priest obey the pontifex but remits the fine. In another case which exhibits the conflict between two religious obligations the people appear more distinctly as the supreme interpreters of ecclesiastical law. The presence of an augur was necessary for the performance of the pontifical function of inauguration. An augur had excused himself on the ground that his attention was required to the *sacra* of his family. The pontifex maximus interpreted the controversy in his own favour and, when his interpretation was not accepted, imposed a fine to enforce obedience[1]. The fine was appealed from, but the people's decision is unknown.

Jurisdiction over vestals.

Disciplinary power is also exercised over the college of vestals. The pontifex maximus flogs the vestal virgin when she permits the sacred fire to go out[2]. She is juristically, like the flaminica, the pontiff's daughter as the flamen is his son[3], and this jurisdiction over her might be explained as parental. But this interpretation is by no means necessary; the jurisdiction can be explained as ecclesiastical. There is, however, no appeal by the vestal from her punishment, probably because there is here no possibility of conflict between the religious and the civil power.

[1] Festus, p. 343. [2] Festus, p. 106. [3] Gell. i. 12.

Pontifical jurisdiction over laymen.

(ii) But the pontiff's jurisdiction must have been more than ecclesiastical; it must in some departments have extended beyond the limits of the priestly colleges to the laity and the magistrates. A fine could be imposed on any citizen for the violation of certain festivals by the performance of a secular task; the priests themselves, the rex sacrorum and the flamens, at times announced the prohibition. This fine (*multa*) was a punishment and distinct from the expiatory offering (*piaculum*), and since it was announced by a priestly edict [1] it is natural to suppose that it was exacted by the pontifex maximus. The magistrates' doings were also beset with religious pitfalls; expiatory victims (*piaculares hostiae*) were due from those who had been created on a *dies nefastus* and had then performed their magisterial functions or from those who on such ill-omened days had uttered the three judicial words of style *do, dico, addico* [2]. Varro in giving these rules is stating the law of the Ciceronian period, and Trebatius, one of Cicero's friends, wrote a book which dealt with such subjects [3]. It is difficult to see why an eminent jurist should have treated these rules, unless they were capable of enforcement: and, although it is possible that obedience to them may have been secured by the secular courts or the *coercitio* of a higher magistrate, they may have been the subjects of pontifical jurisdiction. A dim record has been preserved of a struggle between a tribune of the *plebs* and a pontifex maximus, which ended in the tribune being fined [4]. It is probable, though not certain, that it was the pontifex who pronounced the *multa*.

[1] Macrob. i. 16, 9 and 10 'praeterea regem sacrorum flaminesque non licebat videre feriis opus fieri et ideo per praeconem denuntiabant nequid tale ageretur et praecepti negligens multabatur. Praeter multam vero adfirmabatur eum . . . piaculum dare debere.'

[2] Varro, *L. L.* vi. 4, 30; cf. 7, 53.

[3] It was a work *de Religionibus* (Macrob. i. 16, 28; Gell. vii. [vi.] 12).

[4] Liv. *Ep.* xlvii 'Cn. Tremellio tribuno plebis multa dicta est, quod cum M. Aemilio Lepido pontifice maximo iniuriose contenderat: sacrorumque

BOOK II.

In the infliction of these mild ecclesiastical or religious punishments it is possible that the pontifex maximus acted without assessors[1]. He might at his discretion summon his *consilium* of pontifices, but it was only a severe sentence inflicted without its summons that was considered *durum et iniquum*[2].

(iii) We next come to a class of offences which are crimes as well as sins and which may be committed by any member of the community.

Religious crimes tried by the secular courts.

Religious offences of a general kind and committed by ordinary persons fell within the competence of the regular courts. Such outrages as the plundering of the temple of Proserpine at Locri, or of that of Juno in Brutii[3], or outbreaks like the Bacchanalian conspiracy[4] were dealt with by the secular arm. *Piacularia* might be offered by decree of the senate on the advice of the pontifices, but this is the only trace of religious interference. In doubtful offences, which bordered on the category which we are about to discuss, the pontifical college might be asked, before the establishment of a secular court, whether the deed committed was a sin. This procedure was adopted in the impeachment of Clodius for the violation of the rites of the Bona Dea[5].

Incestum.

But a class of offences stands apart, which may be generally summarized under the word 'Incest.' *Incestum* was applied to actions which religion or natural morality, which had a religious sanction, forbade, and their heinousness was not due merely to a sense of sin in the individual but to a consciousness of the divine vengeance which their

quam magistratuum ius potentius fuit.' Mommsen, on the other hand, thinks (*Staatsr.* ii. p. 58) that the pontifical jurisdiction as a whole only extended over those priests whom the pontifex maximus nominated (flamens, vestals, rex sacrorum) and that there is no certain instance of the right of *multa* against colleagues, other priests, magistrates or private individuals.

[1] Geib, *Criminalprocess*, p. 76.

[2] Cic. *de Har. Resp.* 7, 13.

[3] Liv. xxix. 20; xlii. 3.

[4] Liv. xxxix. 8–19.

[5] Cic. *ad Att.* i. 13, 3.

committal might bring on the whole community. Such a name was given to sexual relations established between individuals within certain degrees of consanguinity and to certain breaches of religious obligation such as the unchastity of a vestal. It is to offences of the first kind that the term incest more peculiarly applies in Roman law, and their punishment probably continued to be a part of purely pontifical jurisdiction longer than that of other crimes which had once been treated as sins. This seems shown by the religious penalty of death from the Tarpeian rock which reappears even under the Principate[1] and by the expiatory rites which followed condemnation on the charge[2]. The procedure in eliciting evidence also continued to be exceptional, the torture of slaves against their masters being always permitted[3]. But, in spite of these survivals, incest of this ordinary kind was a matter for the civil power. That it might be a subject for a *iudicium populi* is shown by a story illustrative of a change in the marriage law of Rome. A test case came before the people through a man being accused of an intention to marry his cousin. The people dismissed the charge, and from henceforth such marriages were permitted[4]. There was no legislation on incest of this kind in the later Republic, and it did not form the subject, or a part of the subject, of any of the *quaestiones perpetuae*. Hence, if incest was not a dead letter in the Ciceronian period, it could have been met only in one of two ways, either by a *iudicium populi* or by the establishment of a special commission.

Some cases of incest come before the secular courts.

But there was one branch of *incestum* which always remained the subject of pontifical jurisdiction; this was the unchastity of a vestal. The accused was tried before

One remains the subject of pontifical jurisdiction.

[1] Tac. *Ann.* vi. 19 (A. D. 33).

[2] *ib.* xii. 8 (A. D. 49).

[3] Cic. *pro Mil.* 22, 59 'De servis nulla lege quaestio est in dominum nisi de incestu' (in *Part. Orat.* 34, 118 he adds *coniuratio* to incest); cf. Marcian in Dig. 48, 18, 5.

[4] Plut. *Qu. Rom.* 6.

BOOK II.

Trial of a vestal and her paramour.

the high pontiff with his *consilium* of pontifices[1]. The full college of Cicero's day numbered fifteen, and although on ceremonial questions a decision agreed on by three was considered as carrying due weight, a much larger attendance was thought desirable for capital jurisdiction[2]. The proceedings seem to have been public and advocates to have been admitted[3]. Evidence might be wrung from the vestal's slaves by torture[4]; and if she was found guilty, she was led through the Forum and buried alive in the Campus Sceleratus near the Colline gate[5]; her paramour was scourged to death[6]. Here again it has been held that we are dealing with the family jurisdiction of the pontiff over his adopted daughter[7]. The explanation might be appropriate were it not for the capital sentence pronounced on the seducer. The paramour of a daughter who was on her trial could only have been condemned by a mixed court composed of his relatives as well as hers; but in the pontifical proceedings there is no trace of this mixed representation. They are far more likely to be the survival of a spiritual jurisdiction maintained in this instance by the purely religious character of the crime and the horror which it inspired. The sex of the vestals and their complete emancipation from the paternal power may have contributed somewhat to its maintenance.

But at the close of the second century B.C. we meet with

[1] Cic. *de Leg.* ii. 9, 22 'incestum pontifices supremo supplicio sanciunto.'

[2] Cic. *de Har. Resp.* 6, 12; 7, 13; cf. Asc. *in Milon.* p. 46.

[3] These facts we may perhaps gather from Cicero's account of the pontifical decision about his house in 57 B.C. (Cic. *de Har. Resp.* 6, 12). Although this was not properly a *iudicium* of the college (Mommsen, *Staatsr.* ii. p. 49) the proceedings usual in jurisdiction were probably followed.

[4] The accused vestal was required 'familiam in potestate habere' (Liv. viii. 15), i.e. she was prevented from manumitting her slaves and so escaping the evidence which might be wrung from them by torture. Cf. Cic. *pro Mil.* 22, 59; Val. Max. vi. 8, 1.

[5] Dionys. viii. 89; ix. 40; Liv. viii. 15; xxii. 57; Juv. iv. 10; Festus, p. 333.

[6] Liv. xxii. 57; Festus, p. 241.

[7] Mommsen, *Staatsr.* ii. p. 55.

Interference of the civil power with this jurisdiction in 114 B.C.

a striking interference of the civil power even with this religious jurisdiction. In 114 three vestals, Aemilia, Licinia and Marcia, were accused of unchastity on the information of a slave. Feeling ran strong in Rome, and the belief that this unwonted impurity would bring some terrible evil on the state[1] no doubt prompted the extraordinary proceedings which followed. At first the question was investigated by the chief pontiff L. Metellus with the assistance of his college. They condemned Aemilia, but Licinia and Marcia were acquitted. But the pontiff was suspected of too great leniency; the tribune Sex. Peducaeus took the matter up and induced the people to establish a commission by law, with L. Cassius as president, for the purpose of renewing the inquiry. The commission condemned the two acquitted vestals[2]. Apart from the facts that the torture of slaves was employed at this trial and that one authority speaks of *iudices*[3], we know nothing of the procedure adopted. It is possible that the judges were Roman knights after the model of the Gracchan jurors, and the forms of procedure may have been those of other standing *quaestiones* of the time. If this was the case, a precise parallel would be found in the later trial of Clodius. We are also ignorant of the punishment inflicted, for it has been questioned whether vestals acquitted by the pontifices could have been buried alive. It has even been suggested that this secularization of the procedure was not unique, but that it marked a permanent change, that the old harsh methods of execution were given up and that 'the old spiritual procedure before the pontifices was not abolished

[1] Dio Cass. *frgt.* 91 and 92.

[2] Asc. *in Milon.* p. 46 (comment to Cic. *pro Mil.* 12, 32); cf. Cic. *de Nat. Deor.* iii. 30, 74. Asconius says that Cassius the *quaesitor* 'utrasque eas et praeterea complures alias nimia etiam, ut existimatio est, asperitate usus damnavit.' 'Complures alias' cannot refer to vestals. The college consisted of but six; and Dio Cassius (*l. c.*, cf. Liv. *Ep.* lxiii) speaks of but three as condemned. The reference may be to intermediaries.

[3] Val. Max. vi. 8, 1.

BOOK II.

Later cases of incest.

but practically suspended[1].' It is a question that cannot be satisfactorily answered. There are, indeed, several cases of incest after this. Ser. Fulvius was defended by the elder C. Scribonius Curio in a speech that became famous[2]: M. Licinius Crassus, the subsequent triumvir, was accused but acquitted of intercourse with a vestal Licinia[3]; and Cicero's sister-in-law Fabia, one of the virgins, was also acquitted on the charge of an intrigue with Catiline[4]. But in none of these cases do we learn anything of the procedure employed or the punishment contemplated. In this connexion, however, it is worth noting that the revival of the pontifical jurisdiction by Domitian was not looked on with favour[5] and that the emperor himself admitted two methods of punishment, the one secular, the other religious[6].

§ 10. *Special Commissions.*

Early date assigned to special commissions. The three types.

If we may trust tradition, it was at a very early period that Rome first felt the difficulty of using her cumbrous criminal machinery to meet special emergencies. The annalists carry back the institution of special commissions to the fourth and even to the fifth century B.C. From the year 413 to the year 110 two types are represented: those established by the senate and people, and those set up by the senate alone. The last mentioned year, which ushers in a revolutionary movement, shows a commission established solely by the people[7]. So legendary and imperfect are the accounts, that the vital question whether

[1] Zumpt, i. p. 117.

[2] Cic. *Brut.* 32, 122; *de Inv.* i. 43, 80; *Auct. ad Herenn.* ii. 20, 33.

[3] Plutarch, in his account of this case (*Crass.* 1), speaks of δικασταί.

[4] Asc. *in or. in Tog. Cand.* p. 93; Sall. *Cat.* 15, 1.

[5] Plin. *Ep.* iv. 11; Dio Cass. lxvii. 3.

[6] Suet. *Dom.* 8 'Incesta vestalium virginum, a patre quoque suo et fratre neglecta, varie ac severe coercuit: priora capitali supplicio, posteriora more veteri.'

[7] The *quaestio Mamilia* described on the next page.

these commissions (especially those established by the senate) excluded appeal to the people, cannot always be determined; but a brief survey of this history of judicial delegation may be of use as showing some of the traditions on the subject which were handed down to Cicero's generation. Of four commissions established by the senate and people two were entrusted to consuls and two to praetors[1]. In the case of two which completed their work[2] there is no mention of the *provocatio*. The two others had no issue, one from the expiry of the commissioner's term of office and therefore of his mandate, the other from the voluntary exile of the accused; but in neither of these cases is there any mention of the possibility of appeal.

Commissions established (i) by senate and people;

A type of commission established by the people alone, when sovereignty was falling from the weak hands of the senate, is furnished by the *quaestio Mamilia* established in 110 B.C. The tribune C. Mamilius introduced a bill by which three commissioners (*quaesitores*) should be appointed to institute an inquiry with regard to those who had, directly or indirectly, supported Jugurtha in his conflict with Rome[3]. This commission was not chosen from the magistracy; amongst its members was M. Scaurus, at that time of consular rank. We are not told the method adopted by the three in the performance of their functions, but it is not improbable that each *quaesitor* was the president of a separate court, and it is certain that each had with him a panel of *iudices*. The equites as established by the Gracchan law were the jurymen in this commission[4]. The investigation unquestionably excluded any further appeal

(ii) by the people alone. *Quaestio Mamilia*;

[1] Commissions of 413 and 141 B.C. to consuls (Liv. iv. 51; Cic. *de Fin.* ii. 16, 54), of 187 and 172 to praetors (Liv. xxxviii. 54–60; xlii. 21 and 22).

[2] Those of 413 and 187 B.C.

[3] Sall. *Iug.* 40 'uti quaereretur in eos, quorum consilio Iugurtha senati decreta neglegisset; quique ab eo in legationibus aut imperiis pecunias accepissent; qui elephantos, quique perfugas tradidissent; item qui de pace aut bello cum hostibus pactiones fecissent.'

[4] Cic. *Brut.* 34, 128 'Nam invidiosa lege [Mamilia quaestio] C. Galbam sacerdotem et quattuor consulares L. Bestiam, C. Catonem, Sp. Albinum

BOOK II.

to the people. The mere fact of the employment of *iudices* would seem to point to this result, if even analogies from other instances of popular delegation were lacking.

There is nothing surprising in such popular delegation excluding the appeal, for the sovereign may will away his rights. It is a much more startling constitutional phenomenon to find inappellable courts established by the senate: and yet there are six cases of special *provinciae* assigned by this body for the purpose of criminal investigation in which there is no mention of a *lex* or *plebiscitum*, and no reference to the appeal[1]. Four of these commissions were given to consuls and two to praetors. Some of them are merely legendary, but even legendary jurisdiction reflects constitutional usage, and it is difficult to determine whether the silence of the historian on the subject of the appeal is the result of accident or intention. A typical instance of this doubt is furnished by the history of the best known of these commissions, that for the suppression of the Bacchanalian worship in 186 B.C.[2] Livy, after telling us how information was brought to one of the consuls, how he laid the matter before the senate, and how the senate entrusted the inquiry to him and to his colleague, proceeds to give a summary of the results. But he draws no distinction between citizens and non-citizens; he tells us that of the men accused some were left in bonds; to the crimes of others, whose guilt was more manifest, 'a capital *penalty* was attached[3].' His

(iii) by the senate alone.

The *quaestio* established for the suppression of the Bacchanalian worship.

civemque praestantissimum L. Opimium Gracchi interfectorem. . . Gracchani iudices sustulerunt'; cf. 33, 127, and Schol. Bob. p. 311.

[1] Such courts are mentioned in B.C. 331 (Liv. viii. 18; Val. Max. ii. 5, 3), 314 (Liv. ix. 26), 186 (Liv. xxxix. 8–19), 184 (Liv. xxxix. 41), 180 (Liv. xl. 37) and 132 (Plut. *Ti. Gracch.* 20; see page 384, note 1).

[2] Liv. xxxix. 8–19.

[3] Liv. xxxix. 18: Those who had only been initiated and had not been guilty of any crime 'in vinculis relinquebant: qui stupris aut caedibus violati erant, qui falsis testimoniis, signis adulterinis, subiectione testamentorum, fraudibus aliis contaminati, eos capitali poena adficiebant. Plures necati quam in vincula coiecti sunt.'

only detailed reference to execution is in speaking of the women held to be guilty, whose sex perhaps excluded them from the appeal. Those, for whom no relatives could be trusted to execute in private the sentence of the court, suffered death in public[1]. An existing inscription preserves a letter from the consuls to some unknown magistrates of the *ager Teuranus* in Brutii, enclosing a decree of the senate which had been issued against further Bacchanalian worship. The only part of this document which is of importance from the point of view of the procedure employed is wholly indeterminate in its wording. It contains a clause which interprets the senate's attitude to certain actions, and probably means 'that such actions should be held to be capital[2].'

Quaestio for trial of adherents of Ti. Gracchus.

A far clearer instance of a commission established by the senate, which was manifestly intended to exclude the appeal, is furnished by a *quaestio* of the year 132 B.C. The consuls of the year following the tribunate of Ti. Gracchus were empowered to commence judicial investigations against the friends and supporters of the murdered tribune[3]. Although the *ultimum senatus consultum* had never been passed against Ti. Gracchus, this commission may be regarded as, in spirit, a continuation of a state of martial law. The appeal was excluded as the subsequent prosecution of the consuls under the *lex Sempronia* of C. Gracchus proves[4], and capital sentences of every kind were pronounced and executed by the two commissioners. The consuls sat with a *consilium* composed of distinguished senators[5], and this board pronounced sentences of outlawry

[1] Liv. *l. c.* 'Mulieres damnatas cognatis, aut in quorum manu essent, tradebant, ut ipsi in privato animadverterent in eas. Si nemo erat idoneus supplicii exactor, in publico animadvertebatur.'

[2] *C. I. L.* n. 196, l. 24 'eorum (i. e. the senate) sententia ita fuit: "sei ques esent, quei avorsum ead fecisent, quam suprad scriptum est, eeis rem caputalem faciendam censuere."'

[3] Vell. ii. 7; Val. Max. iv. 7, 1. [4] See p. 330.

[5] Cic. *de Am.* 11. 37 'quod (Laelius) aderam Laenati et Rupilio consulibus in consilio'; cf. Val. Max. *l. c.*

BOOK II.

and of death, both on citizens and non-citizens. Amongst other capital penalties the prehistoric punishment for *parricidium* was inflicted on a *civis*[1].

Special commissions of later date; influenced by the *quaestiones perpetuae*.

The establishment of the *quaestiones perpetuae* did not obviate the necessity for special commissions, or at any rate it did not prevent their reappearance. They were still established in political crises, such as those which evoked the Varian commission and the courts created by Pompeius in 52 B.C., and in cases where the permanent courts which existed were not empowered to take cognizance of an offence. The secular revision of the trial of the Vestals in 114 and the impeachment of Clodius in 61 were results of this lack of competence. But the example of the standing *quaestiones* did produce a marked modification in the structure of the new special commissions. They were no longer represented by a magistrate or magistrates sitting alone, but were courts each of which was composed of a judge and jury (*quaesitor* and *iudices*) It is probable that in the trial of the vestals of 114 Cassius the *quaesitor* was assisted by a panel of *iudices*, and the same practice was adopted in the Mamilian *quaestio* of 110[2]. But the most striking instance of the new procedure was furnished by the Varian commission of 90 B.C.

The Varian commission of 90 B.C.

This commission was the revenge of the knights on the nobility. Its occasion was the outbreak of the social war and its pretext the negotiations with the allies, which, it was pretended, had been conducted by a party at Rome and had led inevitably to the struggle. The war seemed the failure of a policy; a natural reaction set in, and the men who had followed Drusus were to be attacked. But the attack was only a ruse employed for an onslaught

[1] Plut. *Ti. Gracch.* 20 τῶν φίλων αὐτοῦ τοὺς μὲν ἐξεκήρυττον ἀκρίτους τοὺς δὲ συλλαμβάνοντες ἀπεκτίννυσαν. Amongst those put to death was Diophanes of Mitylene, a non-citizen. Blossius of Cumae, a citizen, fled to Aristonicus, and, on the ruin of his cause, put himself to death. On C. Villius the parricide's penalty of the sack was inflicted.

[2] pp. 379 and 381.

on the nobility as a whole. The equites succeeded in inducing the tribune Q. Varius to propose a *plebiscitum* on the subject of constructive treason (*maiestas*), which should establish a commission for its execution[1]. It has been suspected that this *lex Varia de maiestate* had a wider scope than the immediate object which the commission was intended to secure: that it was, in fact, to some extent a general law of treason. The chief ground for this belief is the circumstance that Varius was condemned under the provisions of his own measure[2], but the immediate objects formed the chief purport of the law, its tenor being 'to inquire into the conduct of those by whose help or advice the allies had taken up arms against the Roman people[3].' The president of the court is unknown, the *iudices* were drawn from the equestrian order. All other courts of justice were suspended, and the commission sat alone to do its gloomy work[4]. The work was only too well done, and brought about the inevitable reaction. In the second year of the war (89 B.C.) the tribune M. Plautius Silvanus, with the support of the nobility, elicited a *plebiscitum* which gave to the people the nomination of the *iudices*. Each tribe was in each year to elect fifteen persons, whether senators, knights or commoners (for there was no condition of eligibility), and from these 525 the judges for a single *quaestio* were to be chosen[5]. In these popularly elected courts senatorial influence must have preponderated, as is shown by the condemnation (probably in 88 B.C.) of

Lex Varia de maiestate.

Lex Plautia.

[1] App. *B. C.* i. 37 *οἱ ἱππεῖς . . . δήμαρχον ἔπεισαν ἐσηγήσασθαι κρίσεις εἶναι κ.τ.λ.*; Asc. *in Cornelian.* p. 73; *in Scaurian.* p. 22; Cic. *Tusc. Disp.* ii. 24, 57.

[2] Cic. *Brut.* 89, 305; Val. Max. viii. 6, 4. Varius is said to have carried his law 'adversus intercessionem collegarum' (Val. Max. *l. c.*).

[3] 'Ut quaereretur de iis, quorum ope consiliove socii contra populum Romanum arma sumpsissent' (Asc. *in Scaurian.* p. 22).

[4] Cic. *Brut.* 89, 304; Asc. *in Cornelian.* p. 73.

[5] Asc. *in Cornelian.* p. 79. The words of Cicero, on which Asconius comments, are 'Memoria teneo, cum primum senatores cum equitibus Romanis lege Plotia iudicarent, hominem dis ac nobilitati perinvisum Cn. Pompeium causam lege Varia de maiestate dixisse.'

BOOK II.

Cn. Pompeius, 'the enemy of heaven and the nobility[1].' It is not likely that these *iudices*—whether the list was first made out in 89 or 88 B.C.—had control of any other *quaestio* than that for *maiestas*; and even this they must soon have lost, for Cicero speaks as though the equites had had a continuous tenure of power from the time of C. Gracchus down to that of Sulla[2].

Impeachment of Clodius in 61 B.C.

In 61 B.C. an impeachment was directed against P. Clodius Pulcher for the violation of the rites of the Bona Dea. The outrage itself had taken place at the end of the previous year[3], when the festival of the goddess was being celebrated at the house of C. Julius Caesar, praetor and pontifex maximus. It was a woman's festival at which no man might be present; but Clodius, the admirer of Caesar's wife Pompeia, disguised himself as a female lute-player and, guided by a slave-girl, slipped into the throng of assembled women. Here he was engaged in conversation by a servant of Caesar's mother Aurelia, who soon realized by the tones of his voice that she was talking to a man. The alarm was given; there was a flutter amongst the women, a hurried search for the delinquent, and an end to the ceremonial. Clodius had fled to the room of the girl who had been his guide, and with her help he escaped[4]. No one had recognized him with certainty, it was known only that it was a man[5], but there was a strong suspicion of Clodius' guilt[6]

[1] Cic. *ap. Asc.* l. c.

[2] Cic. *in Verr.* Act. i. 13, 38.

[3] Cic. *ad Att.* i. 12, 3. The date of the women's sacrifice was one of the early days of December (Fowler, *The Roman Festivals*, p. 255).

[4] Plut. *Caes.* 10; *Cic.* 28.

[5] Cic. *ad Att.* i. 13, 3 'Credo enim te audisse, cum apud Caesarem pro populo fieret, venisse eo muliebri vestitu virum.' Here Cicero represents the official view of the case. In *ad Att.* i. 12, 3 he represents the personal and names Clodius.

[6] Suet. *Caes.* 6 '(P. Clodium) inter publicas caerimonias penetrasse ad eam (Pompeiam) muliebri veste tam constans fama erat ut senatus quaestionem de pollutis sacris decreverit.'

and he was charged[1]. There was evidently no standing court that could take cognizance of this kind of *incestum*, nor was it one that came within the pontifical cognizance. If attention was paid to the crime, it would have to be by means of a special commission. Q. Cornificius, an ex-praetor, but holding no office at the time, raised the question in the senate. The first step taken was to elicit a declaration from the official heads of religion that the act was a sin (*nefas*). The pontiffs declared that it was[2], and the senate decreed that a *rogatio* should be prepared for the people. Both consuls, Piso and Messala, were entrusted with the duty of seeing it through. The bill which they prepared dealt only with the special case of Clodius, and contained a proposal that a praetor should be appointed (perhaps by lot[3]) to preside at the *quaestio*, and that this praetor should select from the then existing *album iudicum* the jury to try the case[4]. The object in proposing this mode of selection was clearly to ensure a conviction on the pretence of securing the purity of the court. As such it was rightly resisted; but there is no proof that the measure meant to take all right of challenging from the defendant. When the measure came before the people, strong forces were seen to be working against it. Clodius' young friends besought the voters to throw it out; Piso its proposer could find hardly a word to say in its favour, and the *comitia* was dismissed. It was in vain that the senate, by a large majority, passed a resolution 'that the consuls should exhort the people to accept the bill[5].' A modified plan was finally adopted as

Establishment of the court.

Controversy as to the selection of *iudices*.

[1] Dio Cassius (xxxvii. 46) is wrong in saying that other charges were combined with this, e.g. Clodius' incest with his sister. He also misunderstands the main charge (*κατηγορήθη μὲν τῆς τε μοιχείας, καίπερ τοῦ Καίσαρος σιωπῶντος*).

[2] Cic. *ad Att.* i. 13, 3.

[3] Zumpt, ii. 2, p. 270.

[4] Cic. *ad Att.* i. 14, 1; the plan was 'iudices a praetore legi, quo consilio idem praetor uteretur.'

[5] Cic. *ad Att.* i. 13, 3; i. 14, 5.

BOOK II.

likely to be more successful. Hortensius accepted, and persuaded the senate to accept, the compromise that a tribunician measure should be brought before the *plebs*, differing from the consular *rogatio* only in the mode in which it proposed that the *iudices* should be chosen[1]. The jury was no longer to be selected by the presiding praetor, but was to be taken in the ordinary manner from the *album*[2]. It was before a court so constituted that the trial took place. The prosecutor[3], L. Cornelius Lentulus Crus[4], who was supported by subordinate accusers (*subscriptores*) was perhaps appointed or accepted by the senate, for this was in a sense a government prosecution. The challenging of the *iudices* is described and the manner in which, according to Cicero's view, all respectable citizens were eliminated from the representatives of the three orders[5]. The prosecutor, following the principle admitted in cases of incest, called for certain slaves of Clodius to be put to the torture; but all, whose evidence would have been most damaging to the accused, had already been sent away from Rome. The female slaves of Pompeia were also submitted to the rack[6].

The course of the trial.

Clodius was acquitted; and, from Cicero's statement that the votes were thirty-one to twenty-five[7], it would seem that the number of *iudices* who tried the case was fifty-six.

[1] Cic. *ad Att.* i. 16, 2. This was not, as Zumpt thought (*l. c.* p. 271), a general law concerning all such religious offences. The words *de religione*, by which it is described (*ad Att.* i. 16, 2), are equivalent to the *de religione* (*ad Att.* i. 13, 3) and the *de Clodiana religione* (*ad Att.* i. 14, 1) of the consular *rogatio*. Cicero, too, says (*ad Att.* i. 16, 2) that the *iudicum genus* was the only point in which the new law differed from the old. Plutarch's mode of statement, that Clodius was the victim of a tribunician prosecution (*Caes.* 10 ἐγράψατο . . . εἷς τῶν δημάρχων ἀσεβείας), is, however wrong, also against Zumpt's view.

[2] i. e. selected by lot from *decuriae* of the three orders, presented by the praetor urbanus according to a mechanical system of rotation.

[3] Cic. *ad Att.* i. 16, 4.

[4] Schol. Bob. p. 329.

[5] Cic. *l. c.* § 3 'maculosi senatores, nudi equites, tribuni non tam aerati quam, ut appellantur, aerarii.'

[6] Schol. Bob. p. 338.

[7] Cic. *ad Att.* i. 16, 5; i. 16, 10.

Plutarch, however, has preserved a tradition that most of the jurors gave no vote at all, their suspension of judgement being signified by their rubbing out both the letters A(bsolvo) and C(ondemno), which were on either side of their waxen tablets[1]. If the number of the jury was fifty-six, the spoilt votes must have counted for acquittal, but in this case Plutarch must be wrong in saying that the majority compromised in this way[2]. If the majority did act as he presumes, the jury must have been very much larger than fifty-six; but Cicero's statements are decidedly against this view[3].

BOOK II.

Commissions of 52 B.C. Reasons for their creation. Anarchy in the capital.

The suppression of anarchy in the capital was the motive for the last series of special commissions seen by the Republic[4]. The candidature for the consulship, which was to be held in 52 B.C., was the source of endless disorder and corruption. The rivals were T. Annius Milo, P. Plautius Hypsaeus and Q. Metellus Scipio. Clodius, himself a candidate for the praetorship, and for this reason amongst many others unwilling to see Milo elected consul, supported his two competitors, and the rival factions met almost daily in deadly conflicts in the streets. The elections dragged on, and on January 1 Rome had neither consuls nor praetors[5]. An interrex would in the ordinary course of things have been appointed, but this was rendered impossible by the obstructive tactics of Pompeius, who supported his father-in-law Scipio, and of one of the

[1] Plut. *Caes.* 10; *Cic.* 29 *τὰς δέλτους οἱ πλεῖστοι συγκεχυμένοις τοῖς γράμμασιν ἤνεγκαν.*

[2] 29 being the majority of 56, this would leave only two votes for clear acquittal.

[3] Zumpt (ii. 2, p. 274) gives a strained explanation of the discrepancy. Starting from the assumption that the number of a jury as fixed by the *lex Aurelia* was 75, he thinks that perhaps 40 had spoilt their votes. But only in 19 of these cases was this done so completely that no vote was held to be registered; in 21 the votes were declared registered.

[4] The narrative is given by Asconius *in Milonianam*, pp. 31–55. The references which I shall give from other writers are merely supplementary to this main source.

[5] Dio Cass. xl. 46; Plut. *Pomp.* 54.

BOOK II.

tribunes, T. Munatius Plancus. The deadlock continued until a chance event, which turned the situation into open anarchy, occurred. On January 20 Clodius was killed by the supporters, if not by the orders, of Milo on the Appian Way and his body was taken to Rome. The tribunes were now the only magistrates in the state, and two members of the college, Munatius Plancus and Pompeius Rufus, thought fit to carry the body to the Forum and place it on the Rostra for the purpose of exciting odium against Milo. The mob under the leadership of Sex. Clodius took the body into the Curia and burnt it by means of such furniture as they could collect. The result was that the senate-house was soon in flames, and the Porcian Basilica which stood near it was also consumed. An interrex had by this time been appointed[1], but the rabble attacked his house and that of Milo who was absent. Repulsed with showers of arrows, they seized the *fasces* and offered them first to Hypsaeus, then to Scipio; finally they went to the gardens of Pompeius proclaiming him now consul, now dictator.

Death of Clodius.

Burning of the Curia.

The burning of the Curia had aroused far more indignation than the murder of Clodius. Hence it was that Milo, who was thought to have gone into voluntary exile for the purpose of escaping trial, took heart to return to Rome on the very night which witnessed the destruction of the senate-house[2]. He continued his candidature for the consulship, which would now bring the additional advantage of exemption from prosecution. A series of interreges now held office without producing the desired result, for riots still prevented the consular *comitia* being held. Finally resort was had to martial law; the safety of the state was entrusted to the interrex, the tribunes, and Pompeius as proconsul[3]. The last, who was also given power to raise levies throughout the whole of Italy,

Declaration of martial law.

[1] Dio Cass. xl. 49.

[2] Dio Cass. xl. 49 and 50; Cic. *l. c.*

[3] Cic. *pro Mil.* 23, 61.

was looked on as the real head of the government, and various demands were made before him by the heads of the respective factions. Some urged him to enforce the production of Milo's slaves, others demanded those of Clodius, for evidence, for punishment, or for both[1]. Meanwhile the question of the murder of Clodius was raised by Scipio in the senate; but it was felt that little could be done until some more satisfactory executive power than that created by martial law was established. The idea of a dictatorship, which had been long in the air[2], was abandoned, and in accordance with a decree of the senate moved by Bibulus and supported by Cato, Pompeius was created sole consul by the interrex and immediately entered on his office[3]. Three days later he referred to the senate on the question of new criminal legislation, and two laws were promulgated on its decree[4]. One dealt with breaches of the peace (*vis*) and referred by name to the recent disorders, the killing of Clodius[5], the burning of the Curia, the attack on the house of the interrex. The other referred to corrupt practices in elections (*ambitus*)[6]; both laws sharpened the penalties and abbreviated the trials for these crimes. The new penalty was apparently *aquae et ignis interdictio*; that confiscation was joined

Pompeius appointed sole consul. The *leges Pompeiae.*

[1] It is difficult to see how the demand for Milo's slaves could have had anything to do with the impending prosecution; for the examination of his slaves against him would have been illegal; see p. 394, note 1.

[2] Asc. p. 37 'cum crebesceret rumor Cn. Pompeium creari dictatorem oportere neque aliter mala civitatis sedari posse.'

[3] Liv. *Ep.* cvii; Plut. *Pomp.* 54; *Cato Min.* 47; *Caes.* 28; App. *B. C.* ii. 23; Dio Cass. xl. 50. On the subject of Pompeius' constitutional position at Rome during this year see Appendix.

[4] Asc. p. 37 'duas (leges) ex s. c. promulgavit.' Zumpt (*l. c.* p. 420 ff.) takes *leges* here to have its not unfrequent meaning of clauses of a law. One law, he thinks, included *ambitus* and *vis* with a common procedure. But separate *quaestiones* were established with separate presidents, and it is more in accordance with the general character of this type of legislation to suppose distinct laws for the two offences, the procedure being mentioned in both.

[5] Cic. *pro Mil.* 6, 15.

[6] App. *B. C.* ii. 23; Dio Cass. xl. 52.

BOOK II.

to it is by no means proved by the subsequent sale of Milo's goods. The law of *ambitus* was given a retrospective character[1], but the validity of both *quaestiones* was probably to expire with the end of the current year. The brevity of the proceedings consisted chiefly in the rules that the witnesses should be heard first and that the subsequent pleadings should occupy but a single day, two hours being granted to the prosecution and three to the defence. Other clauses, or perhaps other laws, which were apparently meant to apply to all criminal courts, limited the number of advocates (*patroni*) on either side and prohibited the appearance of witnesses to character (*laudatores*)[2], who had been a fruitful source of undue influence with juries. These last ordinances were, perhaps, meant to be permanent, but they did not survive the epoch of the civil wars and the triumph of Caesar[3]. Finally, rewards were offered for the successful prosecution of bribery, and amongst others immunity to the accuser for his own similar offences in the past[4]. The laws were opposed, chiefly on the ground that they were *privilegia*, but were finally carried, and the courts which they provided for were then constituted. The court *de vi* was to have as its president a consular created by popular suffrage[5]; for that *de ambitu* no exceptional provision seems to have been made, and its president, A. Torquatus, may have been an ordinary praetor. For the panels a number of special *iudices* was selected by Pompeius, doubtless under the provisions of his laws, from the three orders of the *lex Aurelia*. But it was a smaller and more select body than

Presidents and *iudices* of the courts *de vi* and *de ambitu*.

[1] Plut. *Cato Min.* 48; App. *B. C.* ii. 23.

[2] Dio Cass. xl. 52; Tac. *Dial. de Orat.* 38 'primus haec tertio consulatu Cn. Pompeius adstrinxit imposuitque veluti frenos eloquentiae.'

[3] Asc. *in Scaurian.* p. 20 'Defenderunt Scaurum (54 B. C.) sex patroni, cum ad id tempus raro quisquam pluribus quam quatuor uteretur: at post bella civilia ante legem Iuliam ad duodenos patronos est perventum.'

[4] Dio Cass. xl. 52.

[5] L. Domitius Ahenobarbus was chosen *quaesitor*; his reputation for impartiality is dwelt on by Cicero (*pro Mil.* 8, 22).

that presented by the ordinary *album* and numbered 360 in all[1]. The list may have been made up by the equal choice of 120 from each of the classes of senators, equites, and tribuni aerarii; for, although in the separate panels which gave judgement the numbers of the separate orders are found to be unequal, this inequality may have been the result of the first *sortitio*.

Prosecutions of Milo.

Four prosecutions were immediately entered against Milo. Under the new legislation he was accused of *vis* and *ambitus*, while under the already existing and permanent laws a renewed charge of *vis* was joined with one of forming illegal associations (*de sodaliciis*). The trials *de vi* and *de ambitu* under the special legislation were to take place first. The president of the first court was L. Domitius, of the second A. Torquatus; both presidents ordered Milo to be present on April 4. The accused appeared before the tribunal of Domitius, but sent his friends to that of Torquatus to ask for an adjournment. The concession was gained that the charge of *ambitus* should not be heard until the trial *de vi* had ended. At the outset of this latter trial, a preliminary question called for the decision of the *quaesitor* and his *consilium*[2]. The prosecutor demanded of the president the exhibition of fifty-four of Milo's slaves. Milo denied that they were

The trial *de vi*.

[1] Dio Cass. xl. 52; Plut. *Pomp.* 55; Asc. p. 39 'Album quoque iudicum qui de ea re iudicarent, Pompeius tale proposuit ut nunquam neque clariores viros neque sanctiores propositos esse constaret'; Cic. *pro Mil.* 8, 21 'delegit ex florentissimis ordinibus ipsa lumina.' Velleius (ii. 76) boasts that his grandfather C. Velleius was 'honoratissimo inter illos trecentos et sexaginta iudices loco a Cn. Pompeio lectus.' The 300 senators who were to be *iudices* in the year 51 B. C. (Cic. *ad Fam.* viii. 8, 5) were not identical with this list, which was meant only for the year 52. They represent the restored list which was fixed in Pompeius' second consulship. It is uncertain whether the 360 were to be used only for the special *quaestiones* or for all the processes of 52, but the former view is more probable. The words of Dio Cassius (xl. 52 πάντας τε γὰρ τοὺς ἄνδρας, ἐξ ὧν τοὺς δικάσοντας ἀποκληροῦσθαι ἔδει, αὐτὸς [Pompeius] ἐπελέγετο) by no means imply their general employment.

[2] i. e. the *consilium* of *iudices*, whom a little further on we shall find listening to the evidence.

BOOK II.

in his power. The answer given by Domitius and based on the opinion of the *iudices* appears to have been that Milo's slaves could not be tortured, but that the prosecutor could present any number he liked of those belonging to the party which he represented[1]. The procedure then followed the rules prescribed by the *lex*. First the witnesses were summoned and heard for three days before the president and the *consilium* of *iudices*, of which we have just spoken. Caesar, as a justification for the pardon which he granted to many of those exiled under Pompeius' laws, complains that different benches of *iudices* heard the evidence and pronounced the sentence[2]; that, in short, the jury of the first three days was not that of the fourth. The fact seems to have been that, as Pompeius' whole list of *iudices* was a small one, the fifty-one required for any given case could only be empanelled for a single day. The device was, therefore, adopted of having the oral evidence delivered before the quaesitor and a (probably small) *consilium*, then verified and reduced to writing and finally read out before the final jury which was to decide the

The procedure under the new laws.

[1] Asc. p. 40 'Apud Domitium autem quaesitorem maior Appius postulavit a Milone servos exhiberi numero IIII et L, et cum ille negaret eos qui nominabantur in sua potestate esse, Domitius ex sententia iudicum pronuntiavit ut ex servorum suorum numero accusator quot vellet ederet.' Zumpt (*l. c.* p. 462) reads 'eorum' for 'suorum' and interprets the ruling to mean that the prosecutor should make out a list of those slaves whose evidence he wanted, and that the judge promised his help in finding them. If the request for the torture of Milo's slaves was legal, it could only have been made so by the law establishing this special *quaestio*, for the torture of slaves against their master was as a rule permitted only in incest, and perhaps conspiracy. But there is no evidence that torture was applied to Milo's slaves, and perhaps 'suorum' means 'of their own party,' i.e. the Clodian. That Clodius' slaves were tortured we learn from Cicero (*pro Mil.* 22, 59).

[2] Caes. *B. C.* iii. 1 'Item praetoribus tribunisque plebis rogationes ad populum ferentibus nonnullos ambitus Pompeia lege damnatos illis temporibus, quibus in urbe praesidia legionum Pompeius habuerat, quae iudicia aliis audientibus iudicibus aliis sententiam ferentibus singulis diebus erant perfecta, in integrum restituit, qui se illi initio civilis belli obtulerant.'

verdict. Possibly the first bench might have been able to stop the case, like our grand jury; but, if it sent it on, the oral evidence was not repeated, and the great defect of this procedure, implicitly noticed by Caesar, was that the jury which gave the verdict had never seen the demeanour of the witnesses. On the third day a digest of the evidence which had been delivered was read over and proved by the first *consilium*[1]; it was now ready for the second jury that was to hear the pleadings and pronounce the verdict. The fourth day was devoted to an inspection by the *iudices*, plaintiff and defendant of the lots by which the *sortitio* of the second jury was to be made[2]. On the fifth day this jury was chosen by lot. It numbered eighty-one and sat in full session. Before it the speeches for the prosecution and defence, of two and three hours respectively, were delivered[3]. The close of the speeches was followed by the final challenging of the jury by prosecutor and accused. Each could reject fifteen jurors, five from each of the three orders[4], the result being that fifty-one was the number left

[1] '(lex) iubebat ut . . . dicta eorum (testium) iudices confirmarent' (Asc. p. 40). I have been unable to adopt the explanation of Mommsen (*Zeitschr. f. Alterthumswissenschaft*, 1844, p. 457, and on *C. I. L.* I. n. 198, l. 38; cf. *Strafr.* p. 422) that the words mean a permission to the *iudices* to make statements on the case. He thinks the *lex Pompeia* gave exemption from the rule 'Ioudex nei quis disputet' (*lex Acilia*, l. 39). The remarks of Cicero to individual *iudices* (*pro Mil.* 16, 44) seem to be appeals to their knowledge, not to their testimony.

[2] 'ut . . . coram accusatore ac reo pilae, in quibus nomina iudicum inscripta essent, aequarentur' (Asc. p. 40). For the expression *sortes aequare* see Cic. *de Div.* i. 18, 34; Asc. *in Cornelian.* p. 70. Zumpt (*l. c.* p. 465) thinks that there were two objects in this examination, (i) to see that the lots were all alike, (ii) to see that they contained the right names. It is difficult to assign a reason for this examination being the only incident of the fourth day. Mr. A. C. Clark (on Cic. *pro Mil.* p. 128) would shorten the whole process by a day, by reading *A. D. vii* for *A. D. vi Idus Aprilis* in Asconius, p. 41.

[3] Dio Cass. xl. 52; Cic. *de Fin.* iv. i. 1.

[4] Dio Cass. xl. 55. Cato was a terror to those accused under these laws. They did not wish to choose him, but dared not challenge him; for to challenge him was to give away their case (Plut. *Cato Min.* 48).

to give the verdict. The trial whose outline we have sketched, although stormy at times, was brought to a close within the prescribed limits, for it commenced on the fourth and ended on the eighth of April. The witnesses were cross-examined (*interrogati*) by Cicero, M. Marcellus and Milo himself, but Cicero alone spoke for the defence. Milo was convicted by thirty-eight to thirteen votes. The details of the ballot show that the numbers of the separate orders in the final panel were unequal[1].

Condemnation of Milo. He is accused and condemned on other charges.

On the very next day Milo was accused of *ambitus* under the special law. He did not present himself and was condemned in absence. Prosecutions under the ordinary laws *de vi* and *de sodaliciis* then followed with the same result. Almost before the latter were ended Milo was safely housed in Massilia. His goods were sold; but this fact does not prove that confiscation was made a definite portion of the sentence. If he was *aqua et igni interdictus* his property would have to be realized at once, for such a man ceased to be a citizen of Rome; but, in any case, the magnitude of Milo's debts would have made his condemnation the signal for his creditors to seek *bonorum possessio*.

Condemnation of others.

Condemnation was also dealt out to other disturbers of the peace, and the manifold nature of the existing jurisdiction made it difficult to run the gauntlet of the courts. Yet hatred of the Clodians saved Saufeius, the leader of the

[1] The numbers given by Asconius (*l. c.* p. 53) show eighteen senators, seventeen equites and sixteen tribuni aerarii. A similar inequality is found in the trial of Saufeius (Ascon. *l. c.* p. 55). Zumpt (*l. c.* p. 467) holds that the numerals are corrupt and that the numbers of the three orders were equal. M. Cato was amongst the *iudices* in the first trial of Milo and was believed to have given his vote for acquittal. According to Velleius (ii. 47) he either showed his tablet or let his vote be known ('palam lata absolvit sententia'), but this is implicitly denied by Asconius (*l. c.* p. 54 'scire tamen nemo umquam potuit utram sententiam tulisset'). For the possibility of some such proceeding, however, compare Cicero's account of the voting in a trial which took place in 54 B. C. (*ad Q. fr.* iii. 4, 1 'Domitius Calvinus . . . aperte absolvit, ut omnes viderent').

gang which had killed Clodius, from the penalties both of the special Pompeian and of the ordinary Plotian law *de vi*[1]. Sex. Clodius, who had been the leader in the burning of his patron's body, and many others, chiefly members of the same faction, were convicted either before the courts or in their absence.

§ 11. *Martial law.*

Summary jurisdiction on the advice of the senate.

The conception of martial law was based on the idea of possible emergencies which, it was supposed, could not be met even by the establishment of a special judicial commission by senate and people. Epidemics of crime such as poisoning, murder, arson, seemed to demand the immediate exercise of the unlimited *imperium* of the magistrate. This exercise could only be justified by the advice of the great magisterial *consilium*, the senate. Although it is true that this body by its decree did not create a new power, but merely seemed to liberate the forces latent in the *imperium*, yet its counsel to the magistrates that the time had come for an exercise of their extreme coercive power was practically a declaration of martial law. The early Republic, indeed, had deliberately provided for such a crisis by the possibility it allowed of creating a dictator, whose unlimited power might, according to the views of Cicero and the Emperor Claudius, be employed in domestic discord no less than in military emergencies[2]. Yet even in these early days tradition (perhaps by an anachronism) represents the senate as issuing the warning which in later times was supposed

[1] It is remarkable that although this second trial was before an ordinary court, the number of the *iudices* should still have been fifty-one (Ascon. *l. c.* p. 55). Is it possible that the number under Pompeius' law was borrowed from the *lex Plotia de vi*?

[2] Cic. *de Leg.* iii. 3, 9 'Ast quando duellum gravius, discordiae civium escunt, oenus, ne amplius sex menses, si senatus creverit, idem iuris quod duo consules teneto'; Imp. Claud. *Oratio* i. 28 'in asperioribus bellis aut in civili motu difficiliore.'

BOOK II.

to recognize in the consular *imperium* something equivalent to dictatorial power[1].

A substitute for the dictatorship.

The later constitution had no such regular provision for an emergency as the dictatorship, and the responsibility for meeting the crisis fell on the ordinary magistrates and the senate: that is, on a corporation and individuals incapable by constitutional law of undertaking such a task. The legality of the exercise of such summary capital jurisdiction depended on the status and the sex of the victims.

Applied in the case of ordinary crimes.

The execution of the 170 women put to death for poisoning in 331 B.C.[2]—if the *quaestio* (as seems to have been the case) was conducted by the consuls, and the women were put to death purely by magisterial decree—may have been legal, for women at this time may have possessed no right of appeal. If similar sentences were inflicted by Roman magistrates on Italian allies, as in 314 B.C.[3], and not by the local magistrates on the advice of the senate, as was perhaps the case in the suppression of the Bacchanalian conspiracy of 186[4], this was a signal violation of the treaty rights of the allies, but not a direct breach of the laws of Rome[5]. It was only the male citizen of Rome that might not be put to death without appeal. It is uncertain whether the Roman members of the Bacchanalian guild were executed in this summary fashion[6]; but, if they were, the act was unquestionably a violation of statute law, justified, if at all, only by the danger arising from the widespread nature of the association. It is unfortunate that the question cannot be settled, for, if the appeal was not permitted in this case, the execution of the

[1] e.g. in the revolution threatened by Manlius Capitolinus (384 B.C. Liv. vi. 19), the phrase 'ut videant magistratus ne quid . . . res publica detrimenti capiat,' was believed to have been employed. For a supposed earlier use of the formula in the case of an external war see Liv. iii. 4 (464 B.C.).

[2] Liv. viii. 18; Val. Max. ii. 5, 3.

[3] Liv. ix. 26.

[4] See p. 383.

[5] Except in so far as these laws guarded treaty rights.

[6] See p. 382.

Bacchanalians would furnish a tolerably early precedent for the suspension of the right of appeal in the Ciceronian period. Our ignorance is rendered of the less importance by the fact that Cicero himself does not connect his action with precedents drawn from this or similar instances; yet this jurisdiction of the ordinary magistrates with the approval of the senate, which is represented as an outcome of the guardianship of the state against conspiracies (*coniurationes*), may have been the example for the much contested power exercised by certain organs of government at the end of the Republic.

Its application to political offences. The declaration of martial law.

This was the power of declaring the existence of a state of στάσις: of specifying a portion of the body politic and its heads as enemies of the Republic (*hostes*), the government which pronounced the ban being professedly represented by the senate itself and those magistrates who were willing to obey its behests: and of advising the officials who had the right of presiding over this body, chiefly those with *imperium*, and sometimes even the pro-magistrates, to do all in their power to ward off the impending danger[1]. The formula employed was to the effect that the consuls, praetors and tribunes of the *plebs* (with the addition at times of other officials with the *imperium*) should see that the state took no harm[2]. This ultimate decree of the senate (*senatus consultum*

[1] Our authorities mention an appeal to the consul in 121, to consuls in 63, to consuls, praetors and tribunes in 100, to these and to the proconsuls in 49, to the interrex, proconsul, and all other magistrates with *imperium* in 77. See the historical instances cited on pp. 400, 401. Cicero, as a proconsul who had not yet laid down his *imperium*, says, with reference to the decree against Caesar in 49 B.C., 'non est committendum ut iis paream, quos contra me senatus, ne quid res publica detrimenti acciperet, armavit' (Cic. *ad Att.* x. 8, 8). Cf. Caes. *B. C* i. 5.

[2] e. g. 'Quoniam ⟨M.⟩ Lepidus exercitum privato consilio paratum cum pessimis et hostibus rei publicae contra huius ordinis auctoritatem ad urbem ducit, uti Appius Claudius interrex cum Q. Catulo pro consule et ceteris, quibus imperium est, urbi praesidio sint operamque dent ne quid res publica detrimenti capiat' (Speech of Philippus in 77 B.C., from Sall. *Hist.* bk. i. *frgt.* 77, § 22).

ultimum) did not, in its early applications, specify the particular individuals implicitly denounced as enemies; the interpretation of its meaning rested with the executive authority. Later[1] we find specification of the *hostes*, although the magistrates' activity was not supposed to be limited to the individuals so named[2]. After the passing of this decree the responsibility of the senate as a corporation ceased, although by the *lex Sempronia* individual senators could be held responsible for their advice[3]. The magistrates who acted did so at their own peril, and could not shift the responsibility for what statute law regarded as a judicial murder on their advising body by again consulting the senate as to the proofs of the guilt of the accused, or as to the method of execution to be employed.

Instances of the exercise of this power.

The right has no early history, and the first attempt to invoke it was a failure. In the disturbances that followed the legislation of Ti. Gracchus (133 B.C.) an effort was made to elicit such a decree. But the consul P. Scaevola was a lawyer and refused to put the question[4]. The murder was, therefore, accomplished without the senate's sanction. C. Gracchus and his adherents (121 B.C.) were the first victims to this power and Opimius the first consul who exercised it[5]. The legal question was raised immediately[6], and the acquittal of the consul[7] undoubtedly did much to strengthen the claims of this martial law to constitutional recognition. The tumult of Saturninus

[1] In the years 88, 82 and 77.

[2] Mommsen, *Staatsr.* iii. 2, p. 1245.

[3] See p. 324, and cf. Cic. *pro Sest.* 28, 61 'Consule me, cum esset designatus (Cato) tribunus plebis, obtulit in discrimen vitam suam: dixit eam sententiam cuius invidiam capitis periculo sibi praestandam videbat.'

[4] Plut. *Ti. Gracch.* 19. The consul answered *βίας μὲν οὐδεμίας ὑπάρξειν οὐδὲ ἀναιρήσειν οὐδένα τῶν πολιτῶν ἄκριτον.*

[5] Cic. *in Cat.* i. 2. 4; *Phil.* viii. 4, 14; Plut. *C. Gracch.* 14 and 18 *οὗτος μέντοι ('Οπίμιος) πρῶτος ἐξουσίᾳ δικτάτορος ἐν ὑπατείᾳ χρησάμενος.*

[6] Cic. *de Orat.* ii. 25, 106; ii. 30, 132.

[7] Cic. *Brut.* 34, 128; Liv. *Ep.* lxi.

(100 B.C.) was encountered by a decree which armed the consuls, praetors and tribunes against him[1]; weapons were distributed to all who would stand firmly by the government, and knights with members of the noblest Roman houses took part in the siege which ended finally in the death of the tribune and of his comrade Glaucia[2]. Two instances of unpunished usage seemed to have established the validity of the right; its utility was too obvious to escape the eye of the successful revolutionist. On the first Sullan restoration (88 B.C.) twelve of the opposite party, including Marius and his son, were declared *hostes* by the senate[3]. A similar use of the power was made by Carbo in 82 B.C. in the interest of the anti-Sullan party[4], and the Sullan *régime* was again defended against M. Lepidus in 77 by the employment of this weapon. On this occasion an attempt was made to name the proconsul himself as the public enemy and to arm the interrex, a proconsul and all other magistrates with *imperium* against him[5].

The revelation in 63 B.C. of a widespread movement against the government led to Cicero's receiving such discretionary power as could be conferred by the senate. The decree of October 21 was couched in general terms[6]; during the next month the two leaders of the insurgent army, Catiline and Manlius, were declared enemies by name[7]. The decree was followed by a military *iudicium* on the accomplices of the insurgents who had been seized within Rome, and in this trial Cicero employed the senate as his advising body. In the next year the disturbance raised by Q. Metellus Nepos led to a momentary employment of the decree[8], but it had no other issue than the removal of the turbulent tribune and the temporary

[1] Cic. *pro Rab.* 7, 20; cf. *in Cat.* i. 2, 4.
[2] Cic. *pro Rab.* 7, 20; *Phil.* viii. 5, 15.
[3] Liv. *Ep.* lxxvii; Val. Max. i. 5, 5; Plut. *Sulla*, 10.
[4] App. *B. C.* i. 86. [5] Sall. *Hist.* bk. i. *frgt.* 77, § 22, see p. 399, note 2.
[6] Sall. *Cat.* 29; Cic. *in Cat.* i. 2, 4. [7] Sall. *Cat.* 36.
[8] Dio Cass. xxxvii. 43.

BOOK II.

suspension of the praetor Caesar[1]. In 52 such a commission was entrusted to Pompeius before he became sole consul[2], and in 49 B.C. the ultimate decree was passed against Caesar[3]. In its death struggles the senate clung to the much-used weapon, although lately it seemed to have lost its power; in 43 B.C. a state of war was declared both generally and against special individuals; in February the proclamation was made in general terms; in March, after the fate of Trebonius, Dolabella was made a public enemy; in April, after the announcement of the engagement at Mutina, the same declaration was made against Antonius.

The state of war produced by the declaration.

The state of war produced by this decree is vividly pictured by Cicero when dwelling on the last instance of its use. Whether it be *bellum* or *tumultus* that is declared, the civil courts are closed, the raising of levies begins and the private citizen dons the military dress[4]; the senators, when they have given the fatal vote, quit the Curia and appear again in fighting garb[5]. One consequence of the state of war thus manifested was the prevalence of military jurisdiction; the enforcement of the decree was accompanied by unrestrained coercion and the arbitrary cognizance that might accompany it[6], and any punishment,

Military jurisdiction and its consequences.

[1] Suet. *Caes.* 16. (Caesar supported Metellus in carrying) 'turbulentissimas leges adversus collegarum intercessionem . . . donec ambo administratione rei publicae decreto patrum submoverentur.'

[2] See p. 390, and cf. Cic. *pro Mil.* 26, 70.

[3] Caes. *B. C.* i. 5 and 7; cf. Cic. *ad Att.* x. 8, 8.

[4] Cic. *Phil.* v. 12, 31 'censeo . . . tumultum decerni, iustitium edici, saga sumi dico oportere, dilectum haberi,' cf. vi. 1, 2. For the choice between *bellum* and *tumultus* see viii. 1, 2.

[5] Dio Cass. xli. 3 (of the declaration of war against Caesar in 49); xlvi. 29 (of that against Antonius in 43). For the military preparations generally cf. Cic. *pro Rab.* 7, 20; Sall. *Cat.* 29; and see Mommsen, *Staatsr.* iii. 2, p. 1247.

[6] Sall. *Cat.* 29 'Ea potestas per senatum more Romano magistratui maxima permittitur, exercitum parare, bellum gerere, coercere omnibus modis socios atque cives, domi militiaeque imperium atque iudicium summum habere; aliter sine populi iussu nullius earum rerum consuli ius

even the death sentence, could be imposed without appeal. The loss of life was accompanied by that of property[1], as was ever the case with *hostes*; even Caesar recognizes this in his advocacy of milder measures for the Catilinarians[2], and if gentler punishments than death and confiscation be adopted, these must be regarded as acts of grace. It was such a mitigation that Caesar suggested when, as an alternative to the death penalty which threatened Lentulus and his accomplices, he proposed the perpetuation of preventive imprisonment—an extension of such precautionary measures as had already been adopted against certain of the conspirators[3]. The chief victims of this jurisdiction were those against whom the decree had been directly levelled or those whose participation in the disturbance to be quelled gave them the appearance of open *hostes*. But others who might be found to have been participants in the movement could be tried summarily by the magistrate, and for this purpose he might summon a *consilium* of advisers[4]. Cicero's employment of the senate as his advising body was unexampled[5]. It cannot be looked on as illegal, since the consul might take advice of whom he would. But this procedure cannot be regarded as easing the magistrate of his burden; it at the best only strengthens his hands for the work which he must execute alone. The

est.' For the theory that this passage is an interpolation see Willems, *Le Sénat*, ii. p. 252 n.

[1] Plut. *C. Gracch.* 17 (of the punishments inflicted on C. Gracchus' followers) τὰς οὐσίας αὐτῶν ἀπέδοντο πρὸς τὸ δημόσιον.

[2] Sall. *Cat.* 51, 43 'Sed ita censeo, publicandas eorum pecunias, ipsos in vinculis habendos per municipia.'

[3] Sall. *Cat.* 42 'complures Q. Metellus Celer praetor ex senatus consulto causa cognita in vincula coniecerat.'

[4] Cic. *de Am.* 11, 37, see p. 383, note 5.

[5] Sallust, while not doubting the validity of the *S. C. ultimum*, dwells on the unusual nature of Cicero's action (*Cat.* 50, 3 'consul . . . convocato senatu refert, quid de eis fieri placeat, qui in custodiam traditi erant. Sed eos paulo ante frequens senatus iudicaverat contra rem publicam fecisse').

BOOK II.

examination of the conspirators and the witnesses before the senate could not be regarded as a senatorial *iudicium*[1], for the senate possessed no judicial authority: nor was it the result of a *quaestio* established by this body[2], for the power that commands a criminal investigation does not itself judge; nor, finally, could the work of judgement and execution be considered as accomplished at the bidding of the senate, for the council had not issued, and had no power to issue, an order of the kind.

Estimate of the legality of this power.

In attempting to estimate the legality of this power, one's attention naturally turns in the first place to the question of precedent, which justified so much at Rome. The case for the senate is, from this point of view, distinctly weak, for, although the *mos maiorum* was appealed to[3], there were obvious reasons which rendered it impossible to find justificatory examples in the distant past. Like the summary criminal jurisdiction of consul or praetor[4], it was a substitute for the vanished dictatorship, and subsequently to the decline of this office there was no revolution in Rome antecedent to that of the Gracchi. Nor can its validity be based on a guardianship of the state by the state; for it might happen that the opposing or anti-senatorial party might be a truer representative of the constitution in its legal sense than the senatorial government itself, as, indeed, was the case in the Gracchan movements. Every society must draw a broad line between political opposition and criminal conspiracy: but this was not drawn at Rome, and the senate by passing the ultimate decree took the first step in a revolution.

[1] This is the view of his conduct which Cicero gives in *in Pis.* 7, 14 'Crudelitatis tu . . . senatum consul in concione condemnas? Non enim me, qui senatui parui; nam relatio illa salutaris et diligens fuerat consulis, animadversio quidem et iudicium senatus.'

[2] This is the principle which Cicero states in *pro Domo*, 13, 33 'hoc esse denique (dico) proprium liberae civitatis, ut nihil de capite civis aut de bonis sine iudicio senatus aut populi aut eorum, qui de quaque re constituti iudices sint, detrahi possit.'

[3] Cic. *pro Mil.* 26, 70; Sall. *Cat.* 29.

[4] p. 381.

The question of its right is legally insoluble, and the insolubility is based on the fact that there was no permanent government in Rome except one that was accepted by custom.

Sentiment and custom, on the part of most sections of the community, declared at times that the use of this power was justified, and its justification is admitted even by anti-senatorials such as Sallust and Caesar[1]. An armed force, such as Catiline's army in Etruria, could only be opposed by exceptional measures on the part of the executive authorities. But sentiment and custom did not allow the execution without appeal of a few prisoners captured within the walls, however grave the danger. Hence the successful challenge of Cicero's action in the execution of Lentulus and his accomplices.

The power made illegal by statute. *Lex Sempronia.*

The exercise of such unprecedented power had, indeed, been challenged from the first. The *lex Sempronia* of C. Gracchus aimed directly at this prerogative of magistrates and senate and, although it made the magistrates chiefly responsible, it seems, as we have seen, to have included individual senators in its ban[2]. Henceforth there could be no question of the illegality of the consequences of the senate's ultimate decree; for Cicero's juggle—that the Gracchan law only protected the lives of *cives* and that individuals specified by the senate had been declared *hostes*[3]—is an argument in a circle. It was the very possibility of such a declaration that the Gracchan law

[1] Sall. *Cat.* 29, see p. 402, note 6. Caesar never says that its employment was justified, but, writing with studied moderation and, therefore, perhaps not expressing his real views, he dwells without protest on its use 'in ipso urbis incendio atque in desperatione omnium salutis' (*B. C.* i. 5), 'in perniciosis legibus, in vi tribunicia, in secessione populi, templis locisque editioribus occupatis' (*ib.* i. 7).

[2] See pp. 324, 400.

[3] Cic. *in Cat.* iv. 5, 10 'At vero C. Caesar intellegit legem Semproniam esse de civibus Romanis constitutam; qui autem rei publicae sit hostis, eum civem esse nullo modo posse; denique ipsum latorem Semproniae legis iniussu populi poenas rei publicae dependisse.'

BOOK II. denied. Although society may agree to treat certain overt acts of violence against it as a sign of war, no amount of treasonable design can legally make a citizen into an enemy, unless that treason has been proved in a court of law.

§ 12. *Italian and municipal jurisdiction.*

Jurisdiction over *cives* in Italy before the social war;

The full *cives* in the *coloniae* of Roman citizens before the social war, or in those municipal towns which had gained the franchise, possessed partnership in the *comitia* (*communio comitiorum*) and with it the *provocatio*; they had, therefore, a right to trial before the Roman people. For this purpose the appeal must have been extended by a fiction beyond the mile-limit of the city[1]; and the solution adopted possibly took the form of arresting and bringing within the legal sphere a resident in one of these towns who had committed a crime which would inevitably lead to the *provocatio*. Within this limit he could make the appeal and thus be tried by a *iudicium populi*. There is evidence for the employment of this procedure in the case of a crime committed by a Roman citizen in Italy during the second Punic war[2].

after the social war. Traces of municipal jurisdiction.

After the social war the centralization in criminal does not appear to have been so complete as that in civil jurisdiction. Even after Sulla's codification one of the

[1] Compare the fiction which treated civil jurisdiction in the municipal towns as a *legitimum iudicium*. See p. 109.

[2] Liv. xxix. 21 and 22. Q. Pleminius, propraetor and legatus of P. Scipio in 205 B.C. plundered the town of Locri in South Italy, and a complaint was lodged by Locrian envoys before the senate. The senate appointed a commission to investigate. This commission ('praetor et consilium') found Pleminius and his accomplices guilty ('damnaverunt') and sent them in chains to Rome. Pleminius died in prison before the close of the *iudicium populi* which was investigating his crime. The commission was not a judicial one and pronounced no sentence. It merely investigated and reported, and the preliminaries of the *iudicium* took place in Rome.

most important of the *quaestiones perpetuae*—that established by the *lex Cornelia de sicariis et veneficis*—took cognizance only of murders which had been committed in Rome and within a mile of the city[1] (the old limits of the *provocatio*), and the criminal jurisdiction of the municipal towns seems to have been of a comprehensive kind. References to it are scarce, but we may cite the investigation begun against Cluentius at Falerii[2], the brigands tried and put to death by the authorities of Minturnae[3], and the slave Strato crucified for *furtum* at Larinum[4]. Better evidence for its extent is contained in Caesar's municipal law, which makes condemnation in a *iudicium publicum* of a municipal town a disqualification for the municipal senate[5].

Cives sine suffragio.

The *cives sine suffragio*, in accordance with the general principle that *communio comitiorum* is the condition of the *provocatio*, should not have had the right of appeal and consequently the privilege of being tried in the Roman popular courts. But there is evidence that the theory was not pressed and that a protest was raised against their execution without appeal[6]. The status was wellnigh extinct in Cicero's time through the raising of the old *municipia* (his native Arpinum, for instance) to the condition of the full franchise, although in the territory of Capua, which was no township, it probably lasted on to the social war.

[1] Collatio i. 3.

[2] Cic. *pro Cluent.* 63, 176.

[3] App. *B. C.* iv. 28. The *duumvir* who arrested Marius at Minturnae (Vell. ii. 19) was simply carrying out the outlawry pronounced by the Roman senate.

[4] Cic. *l. c.* 66, 187.

[5] *Lex Iulia Munic.* l. 119 'queive in eo municipio colonia praefectura foro conciliabulo, quoius erit, iudicio publico condemnatus est erit.'

[6] When the Campanian legionaries, who had mutinied and seized on Rhegium in 281 B.C., were executed, the tribune M. Fulvius Flaccus protested 'ne in cives Romanos adversus morem maiorum (senatus) animadverteret' (Val. Max. ii. 7, 15). For a similar protest in 210 B.C. see Liv. xxvi. 33.

BOOK II.

Socii.

In the case of *liberae* and *foederatae civitates*, in Italy and the provinces before the social war, in the provinces alone after this period, there is no question of Roman jurisdiction; for the essence of *libertas* was a limited external and a complete internal sovereignty, and such states possessed the fullest control over their own courts.

Latini. *Provocatio* sometimes given to the Latins.

To this category the towns with *Latinitas* belonged; for the Latins were *foederati*[1]. But there seems always to have been a number of Latin residents domiciled in Rome (*incolae*), and it may have been for this reason that it was thought advisable to hold out the *provocatio* as a prize to the Latins. This is done by the *lex Acilia repetundarum* passed under the influence of C. Gracchus (122 B.C.) which provides that all Latins, who had not acquired the *civitas* through holding magistracies in their native towns, should, if they proved successful prosecutors under this law, acquire the *provocatio*, if they preferred it to the alternative reward of Roman citizenship[2]. One of the effects of this extension may have been that the Latins so privileged could exercise a choice of jurisdiction between Roman courts and those of their native towns. The extension can have had nothing to do with the protection of the Latin soldier against martial law in the field. Whether he was defended in this respect against his own commander depended on the law of his native state; but a proposal was made by Livius Drusus, the opponent of C. Gracchus, to give him constant protection against the Roman commander and thus to secure him a privilege which was, as we shall see, not possessed by Roman citizens during the Republic[3]. That this law was

[1] Cic. *pro Balbo*, 24, 54.

[2] *Lex Acilia*, l. 78. Such an alternative seems to have been presented by the proposal for enfranchisement made by the consul M. Fulvius Flaccus in 125 B.C. (Val. Max. ix. 5, 1 'M. Fulvius Flaccus ... cum perniciosissimas rei publicae leges introduceret de civitate Italiae danda et de provocatione ad populum eorum qui civitatem mutare noluissent').

[3] *ὅπως μηδὲ ἐπὶ στρατείας ἐξῇ τινα Λατίνων ῥάβδοις αἰκίσασθαι* (Plut. *C. Gracch.* 9).

not only proposed but passed seems proved by an incident in the Jugurthine war, which took place some fourteen or fifteen years later. An officer who had been made prefect of one of the conquered towns of Numidia garrisoned by Roman troops and was accused of betraying his post, was condemned, scourged and executed because, though a Latin by nationality, he had acquired Roman citizenship[1]. An incident of 51 B.C., discussed by Cicero, throws little light on the rights of Latins of the Ciceronian period; for, although an illegality was committed, its precise nature cannot be determined. The consul M. Marcellus scourged a magistrate of Novum Comum (one of Caesar's foundations in Cisalpine Gaul permitted by the *lex Vatinia*)[2], whom he found in Rome, probably in the attempted exercise of civic rights[3]. If Comum was a valid foundation, its citizens were Latins and its magistrates Roman citizens[4]. But the validity of the act of foundation seems to have been denied by the consul, who treated the town as having no civic life, and its magistrate as never having enjoyed office and as not, therefore, a citizen of Rome. It is questionable whether Marcellus granted the *Latinitas* of the man considered as a private individual, for in this case he was scourging the member of a nominally sovereign state; he may have dealt with him as though he were a mere provincial. Cicero, in his comment on the act[5], says that the man's Transpadane citizenship should have saved him from the outrage; but whether in virtue of

[1] 'nam is civis ex Latio erat' (Sall. *Iug.* 69). That this is the meaning of *civis ex Latio* is perhaps shown by the rank of the man. One who was of sufficient importance to be the praefect of a garrisoned town and who was in the immediate retinue of Metellus (Plut. *Mar.* 8) must have held a magistracy in his own city: and, if he belonged to one of the later Latin communities, he had by this means acquired Roman citizenship. Sallust is explaining why though a Latin by origin Turpilius was yet subject to the martial law of Rome.

[2] Suet. *Caes* 28.

[3] App. *B. C.* ii. 26; Plut. *Caes.* 29.

[4] Ascon. *in Pisonian.* p. 3.

[5] Cic. *ad Att.* v. 11, 2 'Marcellus foede in Comensi: etsi ille magistratum non gesserit, erat tamen Transpadanus.'

BOOK II. the Latin rights which it conferred, or in consequence of the shadowy claim to the Roman *civitas* made for the whole Transpadane community by the leaders of the popular party, must remain uncertain.

§ 13. *Provincial and military jurisdiction.*

Unlimited jurisdiction of the governor.

His *consilium.*

In his relations to the purely subject states of a province (*civitates stipendiariae*) the governor exercised the unlimited jurisdiction of the military *imperium*; but custom, although not law, prescribed that he should summon to his assistance a *consilium* of advisers [1], and that this board should be selected out of two elements: the *conventus civium Romanorum* belonging to the special locality in which the governor was holding his assize [2], and the aggregate of the governor's personal attendants known as the *cohors praetoria.* A board composed wholly of the latter was supposed to be packed and prejudiced [3] and was, therefore, generally avoided. Since the governor had the power of asking any one to be his adviser, it was even possible in an important prosecution to summon expert advice from another province—nay, even a neighbouring provincial governor himself, as when Cn. Cornelius Dolabella, propraetor of Cilicia in 80 B.C., was summoned by Nero, the governor of Asia, to assist at a trial in the latter province [4]. The governor, in his conduct of the procedure, might fairly elicit the opinions of the members of the simple or composite *consilium*, and might, if he pleased, abide by the decision of the majority; but both were concessions and neither a legal duty [5].

[1] Cic. *in Verr.* ii. 30, 74 and 75. [2] *ib.* i. 29, 73; ii. 29, 70.

[3] *ib.* ii. 30, 75 (of the trial of Sopater) 'hominem innocentem . . . de sententia scribae medici haruspicisque condemnat.'

[4] Cic. *in Verr.* i. 29, 72 and 73. Philodamus of Lampsacus was tried for an *émeute* provoked by Verres. The circumstances were unusual; for Verres, the legate of the governor of Cilicia, was involved, although the

Local criminal jurisdiction.

Although it is possible that the governor could usurp all criminal jurisdiction and summon any case to his own court, yet the permitted autonomy of the towns was probably considerable; and crimes of an ordinary character, committed by natives or by slaves, would probably have been tried by the local courts[1]. Conversely, when the crime took the form of a sedition or popular rising, it was thought better that the pro-magistrate should send the ringleaders to be tried at Rome. The senate was first addressed and, if the matter seemed sufficiently grave, the accused were then summoned (*evocati*) by the consuls[2]. But so little organized under the Republic was the criminal jurisdiction of the provincial world that there seems to have been no regular system of extradition from one province to another or even from Rome to the provinces. It was, as we know from Q. Cicero's attempts to 'entice' Zeuxis of Blandus back to Asia[3], extremely difficult to get at a criminal who had once slipped beyond the sphere of a governor's jurisdiction.

Cases remitted to Rome.

Unlimited jurisdiction over Roman citizens in the provinces.

The power of the governor over Roman citizens in his province was, from a legal point of view, absolute and unlimited, and even extended to the infliction of capital punishment of every kind; for to this sphere the *provocatio* was never extended by law during the Republic,

'perpaucis sententiis.' Whether this means a small majority, or a minority or a small *consilium* is uncertain. The opinion of the powerful assessor Dolabella carried great weight.

[1] An instance is furnished by the jurisdiction of the senate of Catina in Sicily in connexion with the theft of a statue of Ceres from its shrine; the accused in this case was a slave (Cic. *in Verr.* iv. 45, 100 'rem cunctus senatus Catinensium legibus iudicabat'). It is not impossible that certain kinds of criminal jurisdiction may have been guaranteed to states by the *lex provinciae*.

[2] Cic. *in Verr.* i. 33, 84 (of the rising at Lampsacus as represented by Verres) 'Non te ad senatum causam deferre, non de tam atrocibus iniuriis conqueri, non eos homines, qui populum concitarant, consulum literis evocandos curare oportuit?' An instance of the application of this procedure is given in § 85.

[3] 'elici blanditiis, ut tu scribis, ad iudicium necesse non fuit' (Cic. *ad Q. fr.* 1, 2, 5).

BOOK II. and our records, however scanty, seem to show that both the execution and the threat of capital punishment could be directed against Roman citizens. Its fulfilment is attested by the tradition which Diodorus preserves that Q. Mucius Scaevola, when governor of the province of Asia (perhaps in 98 B.C.) pronounced capital sentences on *publicani*, and the narrative seems to imply that they were carried out[1]. An instance of the threat of such a penalty was to be found in the intemperate letters of Q. Cicero, when he was propraetor of the same province. He writes to a man of equestrian census and who bears an Italian name, seemingly a Roman knight, to threaten him with death by the cross or by fire[2]: and, although the brutality of the language is censured by his brother, no hint is given of its illegality. Apart from these instances, not only is there no tradition of the *provocatio* having been extended to the provinces, but no other legal means is known by which a case could have been forced from the governor's hands and transmitted to the tribunals of Rome. Such a prerogative has been imagined for the tribunate; but it is an unlikely power for this magistracy to have possessed, since there is no other evidence of their *auxilium* having extended beyond the city walls, and the only passage which can be quoted in support of this view is so incorrect in its details that no weight can be attached to the circumstances which it describes. Plutarch tells us[3] that Caesar, in gratitude to the Greeks for the assistance which they had rendered him in his impeachment of Dolabella, aided them in their prosecution of P. Antonius

[1] Diod. xxxvii. 5, 2. For a discussion of the details of this case see *Classical Review*, x. p. 228.

[2] Cic. *ad Q. fr.* i. 2, 2, 6. The reference is to a 'homo levis ac sordidus sed tamen equestri censu Catienus.' Quintus, it seems, had already condemned his father, and says of the son 'illum crucem sibi ipsum constituere, ex qua tu (*sc.* Quintus) eum ante detraxisses; te curaturum, fumo (or 'in furno') ut combureretur, plaudente tota provincia.'

[3] *Caes.* 4.

for bribery before M. Lucullus, propraetor of Macedonia. The accused is said to have appealed to the tribunes; but the incident is almost unquestionably the same as that told of C. Antonius by Q. Cicero and by Asconius[1]—accounts which show that Antonius was defendant in an action for recovery at Rome, and that, therefore, Plutarch is mistaken, not only in the nature of the trial but in the more important detail of the locality of the court.

Yet this jurisdiction was limited by customary law.

Yet, in spite of this absence of legal checks, the criminal procedure of the provinces was, in the protection of the citizen as in other respects, closely modelled on that of Rome: and custom seems to have directed that the governor should remit capital cases of Roman citizens to the home government, and that, in the exercise of his jurisdiction, he should inflict on them no degrading punishment. This is the significance of Cicero's appeal in the famous passage of the Verrines[2]; it is an appeal to the injury done to the 'Roman name' in the eyes of the provincials by Verres' action. He cites as precedents to be followed the rules made by the protective legislation of the city, the *lex Porcia* and the *lex Sempronia*; he invokes the guarantee furnished by the restored tribunate, whose *auxilium* was not valid outside the walls; but he makes no mention of any law which extended the *provocatio* to the provinces—obviously because there was no such law to quote. The conclusion which he draws is probably a fair expression of Roman sentiment on the subject. It is a *facinus* to put a Roman citizen in bonds, a *scelus* to scourge him, *prope parricidium* to put him to death. The sentiment reflects the necessity, on which he dwells, of keeping up the dignity of the Roman name in the barbarian world; it is the immunity from capital punishment, above all from the death penalty in a degrading form[3], that enables the

[1] Q. Cicero, *de Pet. Cons.* 2, 8; Asc. *in or. in Tog. Cand.* p. 84.
[2] Cic. *in Verr.* v. 63, 163–170.
[3] Cf. Cic. *pro Rab.* 5. 16 'Mors denique si proponitur, in libertate

BOOK II.

citizen to move fearlessly amongst foreign kingdoms and peoples[1]. It was perhaps due to the fact that the citizen was protected by law at Rome, by custom in the provinces, that, while in the one case he said *provoco* against the decree of the magistrate, in the other he asserted his claim by the words *civis Romanus sum*[2].

Unlimited jurisdiction of the *imperator* in the field.

If we turn to the more purely military sphere we find that, except for the exemption of the Latins[3], the jurisdiction of the *imperator* in the field, whether over citizens or subjects, continued to be unlimited by law down to the close of the Republic. The continuance of a rigid martial law in this department is attested by Cicero[4], and it is difficult to believe that flogging in the army, which is found as late as 134 B.C.[5], was ever abolished. The exceptions made by the *lex Iulia de vi publica* (whether of Caesar or Augustus)—exceptions which provide for a moderate degree of coercion by tribunes and praefects in the restraint of military offences[6]—probably reflect the law of the later Republic. The *legatus* of the Principate had also the power of life and death over his soldiers[7], and perhaps this right was not one delegated by the princeps, but a relic of the undisputed power of the Republican commander of an army to execute capital sentences. There is abundant evidence for the infliction and the execution of such sentences during the Ciceronian period. Decimation was employed by Crassus during the war with Spartacus[8], and instances of its use are found during the civil

moriamur; carnifex vero et obductio capitis et nomen ipsum crucis absit non modo a corpore civium Romanorum, sed etiam a cogitatione, oculis, auribus.'

[1] Cic. *in Verr.* v. 64, 166 'Si tu apud Persas aut in extrema India deprensus, Verres, ad supplicium ducerere, quid aliud clamitares nisi te civem esse Romanum?'

[2] Cic. *l. c.* v. 64, 166; 66, 169; *ad Fam.* x. 32, 3.

[3] p. 408.

[4] Cic. *de Leg.* iii. 3, 6 'militiae ab eo, qui imperabit, provocatio ne esto.'

[5] Liv. *Ep.* lvii.

[6] Paul. *Sent.* v. 26, 2.

[7] Dio Cass. lii. 22, 3.

[8] Plut. *Crass.* 10; App. *B. C.* i. 118.

struggles[1], although the latter are, perhaps, not a safe index of its legality. But the severest kind of capital punishment known in the Roman army, the *fustuarium*, is mentioned by Cicero as existing in his own day[2] and was actually inflicted on a *primus pilus* by Calvinus, proconsul of Spain, in 39 B.C.[3] Its employment on this occasion is mentioned as unusual but not as illegal[4].

§ 14. *The iudicia publica or quaestiones perpetuae.*

The *iudicium publicum*; a fusion of civil with criminal procedure.

The new procedure, which sprang up a few years before the opening of the last century of the Republic, and which prevailed during the Ciceronian period, was in some sort a fusion of the processes of civil jurisdiction with those of the old criminal courts. But the civil elements preponderated, and the result was, in the main, an application of the procedure of private law, in its most salient characteristics, to criminal cases. This hybrid was called a *iudicium publicum*, a name which is found applied (perhaps improperly) to the old procedure before the people[5], but which soon became monopolized by the new development. The first instances of its appearance are in the *Lex Bantina*[6] and the *lex Acilia Repetundarum*[7], the approximate dates of which are 130 and 122 B.C.

Its resemblances to civil jurisdiction;

The resemblances to civil jurisdiction are striking. The presiding magistrate is usually the civil magistrate, the praetor, and the case is heard before a bench of *iudices*. But these civil elements have been subjected to considerable modification. It is no longer the *unus iudex* that gives

[1] It was employed by Caesar after the mutiny at Placentia (Dio Cass. xli. 35), and Suetonius says generally of the military discipline which Augustus preserved 'cohortes, si quae cessissent loco, decimatas hordeo pavit' (*Aug.* 24).

[2] Cic. *Phil.* iii. 6, 14.

[3] Vell. ii. 78; cf. Dio Cass. xlviii. 42.

[4] Vell. *l. c.*

[5] Vell. ii. 7, see p. 330, note 5.

[6] l. 2 'in poplico ioudicio.'

[7] l. 11 '*queive*] quaestione ioudicioque publico condemnatu[*s siet*'; cf. 'publica quaestio' in Cic. *pro Caec.* 10, 29.

BOOK II.

the verdict, but a panel of *iudices* larger even than that of the *recuperatores*, with which these new judges can trace an historical continuity: and the old distinction between *ius* and *iudicium* has disappeared. The magistrate now sits with the jury and pronounces the verdict—an association which, by a false constitutional analogy, originated the custom of speaking of the *iudices* as his *consilium*[1]—and it is the magistrate who is said, in the terminology of the civil law, *iudicium exercere*[2]. In its earlier stages this procedure borrowed more than its mere outline from the civil courts; for in the first of these *iudicia* which was established, that set up by the *lex Calpurnia* of 149 B.C. to hear cases of extortion, the *actio sacramento* was retained, at least as an alternative to some other form of action[3]. Such formalities were due to the genuine delictal character of the actions tried in these courts: for, when the procedure was first applied, what the accuser in every case demanded was compensation for a delict in the interest of an injured party. This characteristic was always manifested in trials for extortion and peculation, which were ever followed by an assessment of damages (*litis aestimatio*)[4]. Yet the compensation is wider than that demanded in a purely civil action. It is demanded in the interest of the state as well as of the plaintiff, and the state attaches penal or quasi-penal consequences to conviction in such trials. Although throughout this system the principle prevails that the activity of a court could not be aroused without a prosecutor[5], yet, since reparation is exacted in the public

but its chief analogies are those of criminal law.

[1] Cic. *ad Fam.* viii. 8, 3; *pro Cluent.* 30, 83. [2] *Lex Acilia*, l. 46.

[3] *ib.* l. 23 '*aut quod cum eo lege Calpu*]rnia aut lege Iunia sacramento actum siet.' The possibility of the *legis actio* in an *actio repetundarum* was (so far as the plaintiffs were concerned) due to the fact that the *patronus* was a Roman citizen (Cic. *Div. in Caec.* 20, 65); but its employment before a court not represented by the *unus iudex* and resembling that of the *recuperatores* is an anomaly. See p. 173.

[4] *Lex Acilia*, ll. 58 and 59; Cic. *pro Mur.* 20, 42; *ad Fam.* viii. 8, 3.

[5] Cic. *pro Rosc. Amer.* 20, 56 'nocens, nisi accusatus fuerit, condemnari non potest.'

interest, any member of the community may be the accuser [1]. These latter characteristics attach them to public law, and exhibit their genuinely corrective and criminal character. The names given to their presidents (*quaesitor* [2]; *qui quaeret*) [3] and to the courts themselves (*quaestiones*) also recall the old criminal jurisdiction.

Substitution of the *iudicia publica* for the *iudicia populi*.

The substitution of these *iudicia publica* for the *iudicia populi* was not effected by a sudden revolution in criminal procedure but by making the former process gradually supplant the latter. Fresh spheres of criminal law were ever being usurped by the new system, and standing courts (*quaestiones perpetuae*), modelled on this system, were gradually constituted by a succession of legal enactments. The Republic never developed anything resembling a judicature act, and each court depended on a special *lex* or *plebiscitum* for its validity and its forms. Thus a *lex maiestatis* is accompanied by a *quaestio de maiestate* [4], the *leges quaestionesque* on certain crimes are indissolubly connected, and the judge in a particular case is one *qui ex hac lege quaeret* [5]. In spite of Sulla and Caesar, no true codification of criminal law was attempted during the life of the free state, and to the last these *iudicia* bore on them the marks of their gradual growth. Not unfrequently offences practically identical were grouped under different laws, and an accuser might choose whether he would prosecute a man for *peculatus* or the *crimen repetundarum*, for the

[1] Justin. *Inst.* iv. 18. 1 'Publica autem dicta sunt, quod cuivis ex populo exsecutio eorum plerumque datur'; cf. Dig. 23, 2, 43, 10. The *crimen iniuriarum* under the *lex Cornelia* was an exception to the rule. Here only the injured party could prosecute (Dig. 3, 3, 42, 1 'ad actionem iniuriarum ex lege Cornelia procurator dari potest: nam, etsi pro publica utilitate exercetur, privata tamen est').

[2] Cic. *pro Cluent.* 20, 55; Serv. *in Aen.* vi. 432.

[3] *Lex Acilia*, l. 44.

[4] Cic. *pro Cluent.* 35, 97.

[5] *Lex Acilia*, ll. 17 and 44. The special *lex* became the special characteristic of a *iudicium publicum* in the Middle Empire, when the other distinguishing mark, the jury system, had disappeared. Then it was said 'non omnia iudicia in quibus crimen vertitur et publica sunt, sed ea tantum quae ex legibus iudiciorum publicorum veniunt' (Dig. 48, 1, 1).

BOOK II.

latter or for *maiestas*[1], for *maiestas* or for *vis*, or whether he should bring the crime of *incendium* under the law *de sicariis* or the law *de vi*[2]. It was not until the Principate that an attempt was made to determine with precision the character of the crimes included in a single *lex*, and to make it impossible to appeal to more than one law in the case of a single offence[3].

The gradual establishment of the courts.

The gradual extension of the new procedure, both before and during the Ciceronian period, can be most effectively exhibited by giving, as far as it is possible, a purely chronological account of the establishment of the standing courts. By abandoning a systematic classification we shall be able to see more clearly how tentative the successive steps were and how long the old procedure struggled with the new.

The standing courts are in origin one of the results of the reaction of the provinces on Rome[4]. It was found that no effective tribunal existed before which the complaints of Rome's subjects against the extortionate conduct of their governors could be heard; for the early procedure was occasional and unsatisfactory. The custom had, indeed, grown up of treating the offence as a civil delict, but as one of an extraordinary kind. It was felt that the regular civil court was hardly competent to deal with the question as though it were a private claim[5]: but, on the other

Early trials for extortion.

[1] Cic. *pro Cluent.* 41, 116.

[2] Rein, p. 63.

[3] Suet. *Tit.* 8 'vetuit inter cetera de eadem re pluribus legibis agi.'

[4] Cic. *Div. in Caec.* 5, 17 and 18 'Quasi vero dubium sit quin tota lex de pecuniis repetundis sociorum causa constituta sit . . . nam civibus cum sunt ereptae pecuniae, civili fere actione et privato iure repetuntur; haec lex socialis est: hoc ius nationum exterarum est'; *ib.* 20, 65 'Etenim cum lex ipsa de pecuniis repetundis sociorum atque amicorum populi Romani patrona sit'; *in Verr.* ii. 6, 15 'in hac quaestione de pecuniis repetundis, quae sociorum causa constituta est lege iudicioque sociali.'

[5] It had, however, always been possible, and still remained possible during the Ciceronian period, for the *peregrini* to bring their claim, as a simple civil law action for recovery, before the praetor peregrinus at Rome (Asc. *in Or. in Tog. Cand.* p. 84, see p. 413).

hand, as the object of the action was recovery, it was not suited to a *iudicium populi.* The senate, before whom the complaints of the provincials came in the first instance, not unnaturally thought of the old international court of *recuperatores.* To instruct a praetor to hear the action, with a bench empanelled from the senate itself, was the remedy adopted. In 171 B.C. envoys from both Spains were introduced into the senate, and there complained of the avarice and insolence of the Roman magistrates. They made out to the satisfaction of the fathers a *prima facie* case for compensation, and the praetor who had obtained Spain as his province was commissioned to choose five *recuperatores* from the senatorial order to sit in judgement on each of the accused, and to permit the latter to choose *patroni.* The Spanish envoys were also bidden to choose their patrons, and both accusers and accused had a voice in the selection of *recuperatores*[1]. This suggestive procedure seems to have been perpetuated by the earliest law that founded a permanent *quaestio*, the *lex Calpurnia repetundarum* of 149 B.C.[2] The details of its provisions are unknown, but, if we may judge from the hints given by the *lex Acilia*, it introduced no great change, so far as the forms of the trial were concerned, however novel and important the first attempt to define such a crime as extortion must have been. The praetor peregrinus was, doubtless, directed to instruct *recuperatores* who were chosen from the senate. The recovery was *in simplum* and the *actio sacramento* was, or might be, used. *Patroni* were assigned to the plaintiffs, but by what authority is unknown.

Lex Calpurnia repetundarum.

[1] Liv. xliii. 2.

[2] Cic. *Brut.* 27, 106 'Nam et quaestiones perpetuae hoc (C. Papirio Carbone cos. 120) adulescente constitutae sunt, quae antea nullae fuerunt: L. enim Piso tribunus plebis legem primus de pecuniis repetundis Censorino et Manilio consulibus tulit'; *de Off.* ii. 21, 75 (44 B.C.) 'nondum centum et decem anni sunt, cum de pecuniis repetundis a L. Pisone lata lex est, nulla antea cum fuisset'; cf. *in Verr.* iii. 84, 195, iv. 25, 56.

BOOK II.

The next court to be established was one for which a serious need must have been felt in Rome. To the middle of the second century the state seems to have dealt with murder purely through the agency of the *quaestores parricidii* and the clumsy procedure which they set in motion. But in 142 B.C. L. Tubulus incurred his great disgrace while administering, as praetor, a *quaestio inter sicarios*[1], and there is a strong probability that this court was of a permanent character[2].

Quaestio inter sicarios.

Lex Iunia repetundarum.

The court for extortion was again constituted, this time by a *lex Iunia*. Both the date and the nature of this law are unknown, and we hear of it only from a passing reference in the *lex Acilia* of 122[3].

Lex Acilia repetundarum.

This latter law was the second reconstitution of the Calpurnian court. Its main object, perhaps, was to bring the rules of procedure into harmony with the judiciary law of C. Gracchus[4]. But the *lex Acilia* did more than this. It marked an advance in the conception of the delict, which now assumes more of the nature of a crime. In place of the trial by process of civil law for simple restitution, it establishes a *iudicium* in which the *sacramentum* finds no place, which enjoins recovery *in duplum*, and in which the money is exacted from the condemned

[1] Cic. *de Fin.* ii. 16, 54 'An tu me de L. Tubulo putas dicere? qui, cum praetor quaestionem inter sicarios exercuisset, ita aperte cepit pecunias ob rem iudicandam, ut anno proximo P. Scaevola tribunus plebis ferret ad plebem vellentne de ea re quaeri. Quo plebiscito decreta a senatu est consuli quaestio Cn. Caepioni. Profectus in exilium Tubulus statim nec respondere ausus; erat enim res aperta.' References to Tubulus are also made in *de Fin.* iv. 28, 77; v. 22, 62; *de Nat. Deor.* i. 23, 63; iii. 30, 74; *ad Att.* xii. 5, 3.

[2] Zumpt (i. 2, p. 106) supposed it to be a *quaestio* conducted by the praetor alone.

[3] *Lex Acilia*, ll. 23 and 74.

[4] Cf. Cic. *in Verr.* Act. i. 17, 51, where, addressing M. Glabrio then (70 B.C.) praetor, he says 'Fac tibi paternae legis Aciliae veniat in mentem, qua lege populus Romanus de pecuniis repetundis optimis iudiciis severissimisque iudicibus usus est.' For another reference to the law see *ib.* i. 9, 26.

by an official of the state[1]. It seems also to have provided for one of the annual praetors taking this court as his allotted province; for a *praetor repetundis* is in existence before Sulla determined the functions of criminal jurisdiction connected with this magistracy[2].

Lex Sempronia against judicial corruption.

The action taken against L. Tubulus, who had been threatened with a special commission established by the people[3], shows that no standing *quaestio* for judicial corruption existed in 141 B.C. This was provided by C. Gracchus through the law sometimes briefly described as enjoining *ne quis iudicio circumveniretur*. The Gracchan law seems only to have aimed at the corrupt members of the magistracy; as re-enacted by Sulla, it was made to bind his new senatorial *iudices* as well[4]. It is probable, although not certain, that under Gracchus it had formed the ground for a separate *quaestio*. With Sulla it did not. He made the principle a part of his general law on murder by providing in his *lex de sicariis* only for those cases of judicial corruption which had capital convictions as their issue[5]. Since Sulla never contemplated the possibility of the *equites* or any lower order exercising jurisdiction, the curious anomaly resulted that, in the mixed courts introduced by the Aurelian law, the senatorial portion of each panel was alone liable to penalties

[1] See Mommsen in *C. I. L.* i. p. 65.

[2] C. Claudius Pulcher, consul in 94 B.C., is called *iudex q. veneficis, pr. repetundis* (*C. I. L.* i². p. 200). See Mommsen, *Strafr.* p. 724.

[3] See p. 420, note 1.

[4] Cic. *pro Cluent.* 55, 151 'hanc ipsam legem NE QUIS IUDICIO CIRCUMVENIRETUR C. Gracchus tulit; eam legem pro plebe, non in plebem tulit. Postea L. Sulla, . . . cum eius rei quaestionem hac ipsa lege constitueret . . ., populum Romanum . . . alligare novo quaestionis genere ausus non est,' i. e. he did not make it bind the *equites*, chiefly because he did not mean them to be *iudices*; cf. *ib.* 56, 154 'ea lege . . . quae tum erat Sempronia, nunc est Cornelia . . . intellegebant . . . ea lege equestrem ordinem non teneri.'

[5] In other cases an *actio repetundarum* could be brought against *iudices* for bribery (Cic. *pro Cluent.* 37, 104); but this too must have been only possible against senators.

BOOK II.

for corruption [1]. Exemption from such liability was, in fact, a much-prized equestrian privilege [2].

Quaestio de ambitu.

Undue influence at elections (*ambitus*), which formed with extortion and judicial corruption the great triad of evils in Roman public life, may also have been visited by the Sempronian legislation. At least in 116 B.C. a *quaestio de ambitu* seems to have existed [3].

Lex Servilia repetundarum.

The court for extortion was once again remodelled by a *lex Servilia* (*circa* 111 B.C.). It was the work of C. Servilius Glaucia and probably of his tribunate [4]. The few facts that we know about the measure show novelties sufficient to justify fresh legislation on an old subject. Glaucia introduced the custom of a dual hearing of the case in full (*comperendinatio*) [5] and he made liable to pecuniary restitution those who had illegally profited by the spoils of a provincial governor [6]. The gift of *civitas* to the Latins, as a reward for successful prosecution [7], had been anticipated by the *lex Acilia* [8].

Nearly all these tentative steps had concerned themselves with offences of a public and quasi-political character, and even now certain state offences, such as treason, still

[1] Cic. *pro Cluent.* 37, 104. A clause in the judiciary law of Livius Drusus (91 B.C.) dictated by such condemnations as that of Rutilius Rufus, had been intended to bind the *equites* retrospectively, but it was successfully resisted (Cic. *pro Rab. Post.* 7, 16 'potentissimo et nobilissimo tribuno plebis M. Druso novam in equestrem ordinem quaestionem ferenti SI QUIS OB REM IUDICANDAM PECUNIAM CEPISSET aperte equites Romani restiterunt'). The clause is mentioned by Appian (*B. C.* i. 35), but only as applying to the new *iudices*.

[2] Cic. *ad Att.* ii. 1, 8 (60 B.C.) 'Quid verius quam in iudicium venire, qui ob rem iudicandam pecuniam acceperit? Censuit hoc Cato, adsensit senatus; equites curiae bellum, non mihi; nam ego dissensi.'

[3] Marius was in this year accused in consequence of his candidature for the praetorship. Plutarch in his account of the trial (*Mar.* 5) mentions δικασταί.

[4] Cic. *Brut.* 62, 224 '(Glaucia) et plebem tenebat et equestrem ordinem beneficio legis devinxerat.' The exact date of his tenure of the tribunate is unknown.

remained in a nebulous and fluctuating form. The vast field of private wrong-doing remained wholly unexplored until Sulla, having finished his reconstitution of the Republic, set himself to his great work of codification. The main task undertaken by him and his commissioners was to fix the floating conceptions which had passed current as law, to classify offences and to give each cognate series a common name and a punishment that was only too definite and rigid. Definition of this kind is in itself creative work: but that symmetry, which was a characteristic of the undertakings of the dictator, was in this case somewhat marred by considerations of convenience. An indefinite number of High Courts, each for a special and narrow offence, was impossible; but at the same time division of labour was aimed at, with a view to expedition. Hence the device of grouping together certain offences of a somewhat similar character and placing each group under the supervision of a special court. Each group, according to the principle of criminal legislation which had now become a tradition, was the subject of a separate *lex Cornelia*, and these laws created seven branches of crime, some by re-enactment, others by applying for the first time the principle of codification. Four of these enactments dealt with the offences of public life and were concerned with extortion (*repetundarum*)[1], treason (*maiestas*)[2], peculation (*peculatus*)[3] and corrupt practices at elections (*ambitus*)[4]. Three groups, which represented the more

Quaestiones established by Sulla.

[1] Cic. *pro Rab. Post.* 4, 9. [2] Cic. *ad Fam.* iii. 11, 2; *pro Cluent.* 35, 97.

[3] Amongst the praetorian *provinciae* for 66 B.C. was that of C. Orchivius for *peculatus* (Cic. *pro Cluent.* 53, 147). In 65 B.C. S. Sulpicius Rufus was, as praetor, president of this court. In this connexion Cicero, addressing this president, uses the words 'Quid tua sors? tristis, atrox: quaestio peculatus . . . cogendi iudices inviti, retinendi contra voluntatem . . . Sullana gratificatio reprehensa . . . lites severe aestimatae' (*pro Mur.* 20, 42). The *Sullana gratificatio* perhaps refers to the fact that people who had in their hands state property given them by Sulla were now worried by actions for *peculatus*.

[4] It is probably to a law of Sulla's that Schol. Bob. p. 361 (ad Cic.

BOOK II. serious crimes of private life, comprised (1) assassination, poisoning and arson (*incendium*), summed up in the *lex de sicariis et veneficis*[1]; (2) breach of trust, crimes in matters of inheritance, forgery and coining, dealt with by a *lex de falsis, testamentaria et nummaria*[2]; and (3) *iniuriae*[3]. This last law only contemplated the worst cases of *iniuria atrox*, of which acute personal violence had been a feature. It did not, therefore, abolish or render superfluous the edict and the praetorian actions[4].

Lex Plautia de vi. To the same, or perhaps to the ante-Sullan period, belongs a *lex Plautia de vi*[5], the ruling law on the subject of breaches of the peace during the Ciceronian period[6]. Its *rogator* is unknown, but may have been the tribune who was the author of the judiciary law of 89 B.C.[7]

The next series of laws attempted to deal with an evil which reached its greatest height after the downfall of the Sullan constitution. The restored democracy sold its favours to the candidate who would buy its votes, and

pro Sulla, 5, 17) refers ('superioribus temporibus'—i.e. before the *lex Calpurnia* of 67 B.C.—'damnati lege Cornelia hoc genus poenae ferebant ut magistratuum petitione per decem annos abstinerent').

[1] Cic. *pro Cluent.* 54, 148; Dig. 48, 1, 1; Justin. *Inst.* iv. 18, 5.

[2] *de falsis, testamentaria* (Justin. *l. c.* 18, 7), *nummaria* (Cic. *in Verr.* i. 42, 108).

[3] Dig. 3, 3, 42, 1.

[4] p. 207.

[5] Sall. *Cat.* 31.

[6] Besides Catiline (Sall. *l. c.*), P. Clodius (Cic. *pro Mil.* 13, 35), M. Saufeius (Asc. *in Milon.* p. 55), M. Tuccius and App. Claudius minor (Cic. *ad Fam.* viii. 8, 1) were prosecuted under this law. The relation of this Plautian law to the *lex Lutatia* of Q. Catulus (perhaps the consul of 78 B.C.) under which M. Caelius Rufus was seemingly accused (Cic. *pro Cael.* 29, 70) is unknown. Zumpt's idea (ii. 1, p. 275) that the Plautian referred to magistrates and senators, the Lutatian to other classes, appears unfounded. It rests on no direct evidence, and there is no reason why senators should be classed with magistrates with reference to breaches of the peace. The two laws probably dealt with different classes of offences. Rein's view (p. 738) was that the Lutatian law was in some way a supplement ('ein prozessualischer Nachtrag') to the more comprehensive Plautian. Mommsen (*Strafr.* p. 654) identifies, but with some hesitation, the law of Catulus with the *lex Plautia*. He thinks that Catulus had it carried by a tribune, but admits that 'Q. Catulus ... tulit' (Cic. *pro Cael. l. c.*) hardly gives this sense.

[7] p. 385.

Laws against corrupt practices at elections.

three laws dealing with corrupt practices (*ambitus*) follow in rapid succession, each attempting to remedy the failure of its predecessor by enjoining a severer penalty. The *lex Calpurnia* (67 B.C.) expelled the offender from the senate, excluded him for ever from office and imposed a fine as well[1]. The *lex Tullia* (63 B.C.), Cicero's own offspring[2], prescribed banishment from Rome, and probably from Italy[3], for ten years[4], while the *lex Licinia de sodaliciis* (55 B.C.), which was directed more particularly against the formation of political associations (*sodalicia, sodalitates*) for corrupt practices, seems to have had interdiction as its penalty[5].

Lex Papia against the usurpation of civic rights.

The Papian law of 65 B.C. gave a more permanent character to investigations which had before been temporarily undertaken for the protection of Roman citizenship against the encroachments of foreigners. The Licinio-Mucian law of 95 B.C. had started an inquiry into claims to citizenship which is spoken of as a *quaestio* and as forming a *iudicium*[6]; but its work was merely temporary, while the court founded by the *lex Papia* was a permanent establishment with praetor and *iudices*[7], the praetor being

[1] Dio Cass. xxxvi. 21; cf. xxxvii. 25, and Asc. *in Cornelian.* p. 68; *in Or. in Tog. Cand.* p. 89; Cic. *pro Mur.* 23, 46; 32, 67.

[2] Cic. *pro Mur.* 2, 3; 3, 5; *in Vat.* 15, 37.

[3] Cic. *pro Mur.* 22, 45 ('e civitate exturbare'); 41, 89 ('quem nova poena legis et domo et parente et omnium suorum consuetudine conspectuque privat'); *pro Planc.* 34, 83 ('me . . . mea lege exilio ambitum sanxisse'). The law is also mentioned in *pro Sest.* 64, 133.

[4] Dio Cass. (xxxvii. 29) alone speaks of a ten years' exile as the penalty; and he mentions it in connexion, not with the law itself, but with the *senatus consultum* of 64 B.C. which preceded the *lex*.

[5] This law increased the penalty for corrupt practices (Dio Cass. xxxix. 37), and that it involved exile is stated by Cicero (*pro Planc.* 3, 8 'postulatur a vobis ut eius exilio qui creatus sit iudicium populi Romani reprehendatis').

[6] Cic. *pro Balbo*, 21, 48 'cum . . . acerrima de civitate quaestio Licinia et Mucia lege venisset, num quis eorum . . . in iudicium est vocatus?'

[7] Cic. *pro Arch.* 2, 3 'in quaestione legitima et in iudicio publico, cum res agatur apud praetorem populi Romani . . . et apud severissimos iudices'; cf. *pro Balbo*, 14, 32. The law is referred to in Cic. *de Off.* iii. 11, 47.

BOOK II. perhaps at times replaced by a presiding *iudex*[1]. Any one might contest the rights of an individual to Roman citizenship, apparently even a single foreigner; for the prosecutor of Balbus, who was, like the object of his attack, a native of Gades, seems himself to have failed to establish his claim to the Roman *civitas*[2]. The attack was sometimes made by the native community which desired to retain the member of its state who had lapsed into the citizen body of Rome[3]. No penalty other than the loss of the pretended citizenship seems to have been inflicted by this court[4].

Lex Fabia de plagiariis.

The embers of the social and the first civil war were seen in acts of violence and brigandage, of which the traders and capitalists of Rome were not slow to avail themselves for their own profit. Kidnapping (*plagium*) had become a favourite trade, and the evil evoked the *lex Fabia de plagiariis*, which took cognizance of the fraudulent assertion of the rights of ownership over any man. The date of the law is unknown, but we learn from a reference of Cicero that the enactment was in force in 63 B.C.[5]

[1] Cic. *pro Balbo*, 23, 52 'dabo etiam (interpretationem) iudicum qui huic quaestioni praefuerunt.'

[2] *ib.* 14, 32 'reliqueras enim civitatem tuam, neque nostras potuisti leges inspicere; ipsae enim te a cognitione sua iudicio publico reppulerunt.'

[3] *ib.* 17, 38 'Illis enim (Gaditanis) repetentibus L. Cornelium responderem'; cf. 23, 52 'iudices cum prae se ferrent palamque loquerentur quid essent lege Papia de M. Cassio Mamertinis repetentibus iudicaturi, Mamertini, publice suscepta causa, destiterunt.' In the prosecution of Balbus the accuser seems to have acted against the will of Gades, the community in question (*pro Balbo*, 17, 38 and 39).

[4] This is probably all that is implied in the *poena* of *pro Balbo*, 3, 6 and 7, 17. See Mommsen, *Strafr.* p. 859.

[5] Cic. *pro Rab.* 3, 8 'An de servis alienis contra legem Fabiam retentis... plura dicenda sunt?' There are some insecure indications that the crime of *plagium* was mentioned in a Cornelian law. Appuleius (*Metam.* viii. 24) has the words 'Quamquam enim prudens crimen Corneliae legis incurram, si civem Romanum pro servo tibi vendidero.' But, if this is not a mistake of Appuleius' (Mommsen, *Strafr.* p. 780), the crime may be that of *falsum*. The passage in Cic. *pro Cluent.* 7, 21 by no means proves that Sulla dealt with *plagium* in his *lex de sicariis*. The passage runs:

Lex Pompeia de parricidiis.

Parricidium, in its narrow sense of the murder of a relative, was made the object of special investigation by the *lex Pompeia*, which gave a careful enumeration of all the grades of relationship which could give occasion to the enforcement of the law. This *lex* was probably a product of the second consulship of Cn. Pompeius (55 B.C.). Earlier than this the crime had been embodied in the Cornelian murder law, and it was for this reason that the trial of Roscius of Ameria took place before the *quaestio de sicariis*[1].

Caesar's criminal legislation.

Caesar's consulship and dictatorship, although they visited no new crimes, introduced drastic recodifications of existing laws. To him belong *leges de repetundis*[2], *de vi* and *de maiestate*[3], and it is possible that at least one other of the *leges Iuliae*, which created or reinstituted *quaestiones*, may be due to him[4].

Incidence of these criminal laws.

During the later portion of Cicero's life the courts were supposed to have embraced all categories of crime and the Roman world to be living under an adequate penal law[5]. But this world was strictly Roman. The law and the *quaestio* were one, and the incidence of the former could not have been wider that that of the latter. Thus the *lex*,

'M. Aurius adulescentulus, bello Italico captus apud Asculum, in Q. Sergii senatoris, eius qui inter sicarios damnatus est, manus incidit et apud eum in ergastulo fuit.' It is not said here that Sergius was condemned for *plagium*. It is doubtful whether Sulla dealt with the offence at all; but, if he did, the fact throws no light on the date of the Fabian law; his legislation may have sharpened the penalty for some of the offences mentioned in it, or be a proof that no such law existed at the time.

[1] Cic. *pro Rosc. Amer.* 4, 11 'Te quoque magno opere, M. Fanni, quaeso ut, qualem te iam antea populo Romano praebuisti, cum huic eidem quaestioni iudex praeesses, talem te et nobis et rei publicae hoc tempore impertias . . (5, 11) Longo intervallo iudicium inter sicarios hoc primum committitur.'

[2] Cic. *pro Sest.* 64, 135; *pro Rab. Post.* 4, 8; *ad Fam.* viii. 8, 2.

[3] Cic. *Phil.* i. 9, 23.

[4] i.e. the Julian law of *peculatus*. It is, however, more probable that it was the work of Augustus.

[5] Cic. *pro Balbo*, 28, 65 (56 B.C.) 'cum omnium peccatorum quaestiones sint.'

like the *quaestio, de sicariis* only took cognizance of a murder committed within the capital or a radius of a mile beyond it[1]. But most of the laws and the permanent commissions which they established must have referred to Roman citizens generally and, in the case of common offences, to their slaves. After the social war they, therefore, embraced Italy. Beyond this limit we have the government of the *imperium*, not of *lex*. We have already observed the method by which this government was regulated[2]. A provincial ruler might, like Q. Cicero in the case of parricide, model his punishments on those of Rome[3]; but such a procedure was probably a rare and unwise departure from local custom. The Republic never evolved a criminal law for the empire. If such existed even under the early Principate, it must have been the result of the *leges iudiciorum publicorum* of Augustus.

§ 15. *The presidents of the quaestiones perpetuae.*

The praetors the normal presidents of these courts.

The quasi-civil character of the actions from which the *quaestiones* originated had made the praetors seem the most appropriate presidents for the guidance of these courts[4], and the increase of the commissions by Sulla went hand in hand with his strengthening of this magistracy. The *provinciae* of the six praetors available for criminal jurisdiction were possibly determined by the senate, and it is certain that they were distributed amongst the designated magistrates by the use of the lot[5]. The fullest account of the distribution of such functions amongst

[1] Collatio i. 3, 1. The murder with which Oppianicus was charged seems to have taken place at Rome (Cic. *pro Cluent.* 16), and this was certainly the case with the one for which Cluentius was prosecuted (*ib.* 62, 175).

[2] p. 410. [3] Cic. *ad Q. fr.* i. 2, 2, 5. [4] p. 415.

[5] Cic. *in Verr.* Act. i. 8, 21 'Ecce autem illis ipsis diebus cum praetores designati sortirentur et M. Metello obtigisset ut is de pecuniis repetundis quaereret'; *pro Mur.* 20, 42 'Quid tua sors? tristis, atrox; quaestio peculatus'; cf. Collatio i. 3, 1, see p. 431, note 6.

Distribution of the courts amongst the praetors.

the members of the college belongs to the year 66 B.C. C. Orchivius is found guiding the court for peculation, Cicero that for extortion, while C. Aquilius presides over *ambitus* and probably over other cognate offences as well. Q. Voconius Naso, if he was praetor, and not, as some have thought, a mere *iudex quaestionis*, is administering the law *de sicariis et veneficis*, and at the time is concerned with that branch of it which takes cognizance of poisoning[1]. P. Cassius presides over the court for *maiestas*[2]. The province of the sixth praetor is unknown, but was perhaps *falsum*[3]. The two judges, M. Plaetorius and C. Flaminius, who share with Voconius the presidency of the murder court, are doubtless *iudices quaestionis*[4].

The spheres of jurisdiction not absolutely fixed.

But the praetorian spheres of jurisdiction cannot be considered fixed, nor perhaps were they even strictly annual. The groups of *quaestiones*, or of their parts, might be readjusted every year, and the praetors must be regarded

[1] Cic. *pro Cluent.* 53, 147 'Quid M. Plaetorii et C. Flaminii inter sicarios? quid C. Orchivii peculatus? (cf. *ib.* 34, 94) quid mea de pecuniis repetundis? (cf. *pro Rab. Post.* 4, 9) quid C. Aquilii (cf. *Top.* 7, 32; *de Off.* iii. 14, 60) apud quem nunc de ambitu causa dicitur? quid reliquae quaestiones? . . . (54, 148) iubet lex ea, qua lege haec quaestio constituta est, iudicem quaestionis, hoc est Q. Voconium, cum iis iudicibus qui ei obvenerint . . . quaerere de veneno.' Mommsen (*Staatsr.* ii. p. 588, n. 2) thinks that Q. Voconius Naso was a *iudex quaestionis*. There is no positive evidence on the point, for the fact that Cicero, quoting the words of the law, calls him *iudex quaestionis* (*pro Cluent.* 54, 148) is of itself no proof. The *lex Cornelia* gave the presidency either to the praetor or to a *iudex* (Collatio i. 3, 1, see p. 431, note 6).

[2] Asc. *in Cornelian.* p. 59 'quo anno praetor Cicero fuit, reum Cornelium duo fratres Cominii lege Cornelia de maiestate fecerunt . . . et cum P. Cassius praetor . . . adesse iussisset &c.'

[3] *Falsum* was amongst 'haec quotidiana, sicae, veneni, peculatus, testamentorum etiam lege nova quaestiones' (Cic. *de Nat. Deor.* iii. 30, 74).

[4] They did not hold the aedileship before 68 or 67 (Zumpt, ii. 2, p. 164) and so could not have been praetors in 66. For several *iudices quaestionum* holding courts at the same time cf. Cicero's statement (*in Vat.* 14, 34) that when Vatinius and Clodius violently interrupted a process before the praetor Memmius in 58 B.C. 'iudices quaestionum de proximis tribunalibus esse depulsos.'

BOOK II. as a group of High Court judges who distribute the courts amongst themselves, or have them distributed by the senate, for the coming year, according to considerations of convenience. The introduction of a new court might at any time add to the work of a department. Thus when in 55 B.C. the *lex Licinia de sodaliciis* had created a new crime and a new procedure, these were, for the time being, brought under the presidency of the court for *maiestas*, as is shown by the fact that in 54 B.C. C. Alfius Flavus is praetor in the trial of A. Gabinius for *maiestas*[1] and in that of Cn. Plancius for *sodalicia*[2].

Nor could the maintenance by each praetor of a particular sphere of activity for the whole year have been as necessary in home as in provincial jurisdiction. The amount or importance of the cases which each court was to try could not be foretold, nor could it be decided at the outset to what extent the general administrative functions of the praetor would encroach on his criminal jurisdiction. Hence a readjustment of the distribution (probably with the consent of the senate) must have been possible—a possibility which may be illustrated by the fact that, after the *sortitio* of 62 B.C., the praetor Q. Metellus Celer was given the province of Cisalpine Gaul[3]. This possibility of redistribution may explain the anomalies which we sometimes find. Two trials for *vis* are known to us for the year 56 B.C.; but while in the prosecution against Caelius the praetor Cn. Domitius Calvinus was president[4], the court which tried Sestius was directed by M. Aemilius

[1] Cic. *ad Q. fr.* iii. 1, 7, 24 'Gabinius . . . cum edicto C. Alfii de maiestate eum adesse oporteret'; *ib.* iii. 3, 3 'quaesitor gravis et firmus Alfius.'

[2] Cic. *pro Planc.* 17, 43; 42, 104. Mommsen (*Staatsr.* ii. p. 201, n. 2) thinks that Alfius was not praetor, on the somewhat unsatisfactory grounds that he is called *quaesitor* and that he presides over two courts in the same year. But *quaesitor* is a generic title, and the second objection assumes that the spheres of praetorian competence were definitely fixed.

[3] Cic. *ad Fam.* v. 2, 3 and 4.

[4] Cic. *pro Cael.* 13, 32.

Scaurus[1]; Domitius, however, was also in the same year the president of a court *de ambitu*[2]. Such an anomaly in distribution as that which gave two presidents for *vis* in a single year may have been assisted by the fact that this particular offence was provided for by two different laws, the Plautian and the Lutatian; yet it seems that two trials for *vis* even under the same law (the Plautian) might have different *quaesitores*, whether these were praetors or not. Thus in 52 B.C. (a year in which ordinary arrangements must have been disturbed by the Pompeian legislation)[3] L. Fabius is the president of the court which tried Milo, Considius of that which tried Saufeius[4].

Iudices quaestionis.

But six praetors could not possibly provide for all the courts, even if we set aside their manifold subdivisions, and few (perhaps none) of the later laws establishing *quaestiones* insisted on a praetor as the president. They spoke, like the *lex Acilia repetundarum*, of a *iudex . . quei quaeret*[5], or, like the *lex Cornelia de sicariis et veneficis*, of a *iudex quaestionis*[6]. In the case of some of the courts the praetor, after conducting the preliminaries, seems to have appointed by lot from the jury a president for the further hearing of the case[7]; but the official who generally appears before us with the title *iudex quaestionis* belongs to the murder court alone. The position was occupied by

The *iudex quaestionis* of the murder court.

[1] Cic. *pro Sest.* 47, 101; 54, 116.

[2] Cic. *ad Q. fr.* ii. 3, 6.

[3] p. 392.

[4] Asc. *in Milon.* pp. 54 and 55. It is not stated, but it is probable, that Milo, like Saufeius, was condemned under the *lex Plautia*.

[5] l. 42; cf. ll. 19 and 62. The *iudex* and the praetor appear side by side in this law; the former is the more general term.

[6] Cic. *pro Cluent.* 54, 148; cf. Collatio i. 3, 1 'praetor iudexve quaestionis, cui sorte obvenerit quaestio de sicariis.' In what way sortition was applied to the *iudices quaestionis* we do not know. Perhaps they divided portions of a *quaestio* amongst themselves in this way. They were popularly known, in accordance with the older phraseology, as *quaesitores* (Schol. Bob. p. 323 'iudices quaestionum. Eosdem et quaesitores nominabant, praepositos scilicet et ipsis iudicibus').

[7] Schol. Bob. p. 323 'cum praetor C. Memmius quaesitorem sortito facere vellet.'

C. Claudius Pulcher who, between his curule aedileship (99 B.C.) and his praetorship, was *iudex quaestionis* for the trial of cases of poisoning[1]. Not long after (*circa* 82 B.C.) M. Fannius, who subsequently presided, as praetor, over the court that tried Sex. Roscius, administered as *iudex* the law *de sicariis et veneficis*[2]. C. Junius, *quaesitor* or *iudex quaestionis* of the court that condemned Oppianicus (74 B.C.), held the same position[3] and was, like Claudius, of aedilician rank[4]. C. Julius Caesar, after his aedileship, exercised the duties of the same office (64 B.C.)[5].

It was inevitable that, in a court in which so many concurrent cases would have to be tried, the praetor should have this assistance[6]. Its functions might, as in 66 B.C., be divided between a praetor and *iudices quaestionis*[7], and the praetor might take either the department *de sicariis* or that *de veneficis*, as he pleased[8]. But the quasi-magisterial position of this *iudex quaestionis* is remarkable. It is shown by the fixed qualification (for it is always an ex-aedile that is appointed)[9], and also by the fact that,

His quasi-magisterial position.

[1] 'aed. cur. iudex q. veneficis pr. repetundis' (*C. I. L.* i². p. 200), cf. p. 421.

[2] Cic. *pro Rosc. Amer.* 4, 11, see p. 427, note 1.

[3] Cic. *pro Cluent.* 33, 89 'Condemnatus est C. Iunius qui ei quaestioni praefuerat . . . tum est condemnatus cum esset iudex quaestionis'; cf. 20, 55, where he is called 'quaesitor ex lege illa Cornelia quae tum erat.'

[4] *ib.* 29, 79 'illum hominem aedilicium, iam praetorem opinionibus hominum constitutum.' For the qualification cf. Cicero's words of C. Visellius Varro (*Brut.* 76, 264 'Is cum post curulem aedilitatem iudex quaestionis esset, mortuus est').

[5] Suet. *Caes.* 11.

[6] p. 429.

[7] Similar assistance must have been required in *falsum* (Cic. *de Nat. Deor.* iii. 30, 74, see p. 429, note 3), but the president here may have been chosen from the jury.

[8] A praetor, M. Fannius, presides in the trial of Sex. Roscius for parricide, which was held before this court (Cic. *pro Rosc. Amer.* 4, 11, see p. 427, note 1); cf. M. Popilius Laenas, a praetor, in a trial for matricide (Val. Max. viii. 1 *amb.* 1).

[9] In the case of C. Octavius, father of Augustus, the post of *iudex quaestionum* is held after the plebeian aedileship (*C. I. L.* i. p. 278). In the case of P. Claudius, the son of Cicero's enemy, the office of *quaesitor* was held between the quaestorship and the praetorship (Orelli 3, 109). The aedileship, which is sometimes not held in the *cursus honorum*, may

as the magistrate takes the oath *in leges*, so this *iudex* swears to respect the special law which he is administering[1]. Like a magistrate, too, he is held responsible for an unjust judgement elicited by bribery[2]. The manner of his creation is unknown, and we cannot tell whether he was appointed by the praetor, to whom the *sors* of the particular *quaestio* had come, or by the people[3]. The first method is the less probable, since the functions of this *iudex* do not resemble those of subordinate jurisdiction. Besides conducting the trial from the *sortitio* of the *iudices*[4] onward to the finding of the sentence[5], he seems, if we may judge from Caesar's procedure, to have had the capacity of determining what cases were within the competence of the court[6].

§ 16. *The iudices of the quaestiones perpetuae and the leges iudiciariae.*

The *iudices* originally senators.

The development of the *quaestiones perpetuae* from the court for extortion and the manner in which that court was originally organized[7], prepare us for the fact that the *iudices* were originally chosen from the senate[8]. The revolutionary movement of the Gracchi was characterized

not have been essential or the *quaesitores* of different courts may not have required the same qualification.

[1] Cic. *pro Cluent.* 33, 91 'Multam petivit (Quinctius). Qua lege? Quod in legem non iurasset (Iunius).'

[2] Dig. 48, 8, 1 'cum magistratus esset publicove iudicio praeesset.'

[3] Certainly not by the senate, as has sometimes been thought. The senate might assign judicial *provinciae*, but could hardly have created a judicial magistrate. Mommsen inclines to think that the office followed as a matter of course on the aedileship (*Staatsr.* ii. p. 590).

[4] Cic. *pro Cluent.* 33, 91; *in Verr.* i. 61, 157 and 158.

[5] Cic. *pro Cluent.* 20, 55.

[6] Suet. *Caes.* 11 'in exercenda de sicariis quaestione eos quoque sicariorum numero habuit qui proscriptione ob relata civium Romanorum capita pecunias ex aerario acceperant, quamquam exceptos Corneliis legibus.' If Q. Voconius Naso was *iudex quaestionis* and not praetor in 66 B.C. (p. 429) the *iudex* exercised *coercitio* (Cic. *pro Cluent.* 53, 147 'quae vis est qua abs te hi iudices . . . coerceantur?') and had lictors (*ib.*).

[7] p. 419.

[8] Dio Cass. *frgt.* 88; Plut. *Ti. Gracch.* 16.

BOOK II.

by various attempts to weaken the authority of this body in the courts. The first proposal of C. Gracchus, perhaps modelled on one of his brother Tiberius[1], was that the *iudicia* should be given to two orders, whether by making three hundred *equites* permanently members of the senate or by creating a mixed panel of senators and three hundred *equites*[2]. The former of these two measures was the one which was probably advanced, but this proposal of his first tribunate miscarried, and the *lex iudiciaria* which he carried through during his second tenure of this magistracy transferred jurisdiction in all the existing *quaestiones* wholly to the class that was now recognized as that of the 'knights.' The *equites*, as the term was understood now and throughout the Ciceronian period, seem to have been all Roman citizens who were possessed of what had come to be considered the equestrian census (perhaps 400,000 sesterces)[3] and who were not past or present members of the senate. The Gracchan scheme also excluded men closely related to senators[4] and all ex-magistrates[5]—prohibitions which were clearly due to a desire to avoid corruption of the jurors in dealing with magisterial offences. But we do not know whether these negative conditions, or

Lex iudiciaria of C. Gracchus.

The *equites*.

[1] Plut. *Ti. Gracch.* 16.

[2] Plutarch's account (*C. Gracch.* 5, cf. *Compar.* 2) is susceptible of both interpretations, but rather leans to the second. The account of Livy (*Ep.* lx) who states the number of *equites*, probably wrongly, as six hundred, is distinctly in favour of the first.

[3] There is no authority for this census earlier than the Principate; but that the knights who sat on juries at the close of the Republic were chosen with reference to property is shown by Cicero (*Phil.* i. 8, 20 'census praefiniebatur . . . in iudice enim spectari et fortuna debet et dignitas'). The awkward gap in the *lex Acilia repetundarum* should probably be filled up by a census qualification, e.g. according to Mommsen's earlier view it ran (l. 16) 'facito utei CDL viros ita legat quei ha[ce civitate HS $\overline{\text{cccc}}$ n. plurisve census siet].'

[4] 'queive eius quei in senatu siet fueritve pater frater filiusve siet.'

[5] 'dum ne quem eorum legat, quei tr. pl., q., IIIvir cap., tr. mil. l. IIII. primis aliqua earum, triumvir a. d. a. siet fueritve.' The exclusion of ex-quaestors implies that of all magistrates with *imperium*, the aediles and the censors.

BOOK II.

even that of past membership of the senate, were maintained in the judiciary laws which made the *equites* wholly or partly the masters of the courts[1]. The Gracchan juror must also be between the ages of thirty and sixty and must dwell in Rome or within a mile of the city—provisions so desirable that their subsequent observance may be taken for granted. The universal employment of the new equestrian *iudices* is shown by the fact that their services were demanded even for special commissions such as that established by the *lex Mamilia* of 110 B.C.[2], and only once between their institution and the time of Sulla was their control of the courts called in question. The *lex Servilia* (*Caepionis*) of 106 B.C. attempted to renew the original Gracchan proposal. According to one account this law proposed that the *iudicia* should be shared between senators and equites[3]; according to another the courts were given to the senate[4]; and this latter view is supported by Cicero's statement that, before the *lex Plautia* of 89 B.C., senators and knights had never sat together in the courts[5], and by his view that the Servilian law was peculiarly favourable to the senate and unfavourable to the equestrian order[6]. The discrepancy is reconcilable on the supposition that Caepio attempted the effort made formerly by C. Gracchus and subsequently by Drusus, and proposed the reception of a certain number of knights into

Lex Servilia (Caepionis).

[1] The ex-quaestor would, of course, be excluded from the *equites* after Sulla; he became a senator. But such magistrates as the *triumviri capitales* and the military tribunes elected by the people would require special exclusion.

[2] p. 381.

[3] Iulius Obsequens c. 101 'per Caepionem cos. senatorum et equitum iudicia communicata'; Cassiodorus, *Chron.* 384 C 'his coss. (Q. Servilio et C. Atilio) per Servilium Caepionem consulem iudicia equitibus et senatoribus communicata sunt.'

[4] Tac. *Ann.* xii. 60 'cum . . . Serviliae leges senatui iudicia redderent.'

[5] Cic. *ap. Asc. in Cornelian.* p. 79, see p. 385, note 5.

[6] Cic. *de Inv.* i. 49, 92 'offensum est quod eorum qui audiunt voluntatem laedit: ut si quis apud equites Romanos cupidos iudicandi Caepionis legem iudiciariam laudet'; cf. *Brutus* 44, 164; *pro Cluent.* 51, 140.

BOOK II. the senate[1]. The law was doubtless passed, and the date of its early repeal is unknown. So short, however, was its duration that Cicero could speak of the *equites* having possessed the courts for 'a continuous term of almost fifty years' between the epochs of the Gracchan and the Sullan legislation[2]. We know that they were in possession in 100 B.C.[3], and in the years 92 and 91 B.C. two ex-consuls, P. Rutilius Rufus and M. Aemilius Scaurus, were impeached before them on charges of extortion[4].

Attempted reform of Livius Drusus.

The judicial tyranny of the order led M. Livius Drusus in 91 B.C. to try for a third time the remedy of Gracchus and of Caepio. Livius proposed to add three hundred knights to the senate and to give the courts back to the members of the council thus enlarged[5]. The law was passed but annulled on formal grounds, and the desire of so many legislators was not attained until Sulla was

Lex Cornelia of Sulla.

master of the state. In 81 B.C. the senate, thinned in numbers by massacre and war, was recruited by about three hundred members of the equestrian order, selected, or at least formally approved, by the *comitia* of the tribes[6], and the *iudices* were henceforth to be chosen

[1] Mommsen in *Zeitschr. f. Alterthumswissenschaft*, 1843, p. 812 ff.

[2] Cic. *in Verr.* Act. i. 13, 38 'Cognoscet ex me populus Romanus quid sit quam ob rem, cum equester ordo iudicaret, annos prope quinquaginta continuos . . . ne tenuissima quidem suspicio acceptae pecuniae ob rem iudicandam constituta sit.' So Velleius (ii. 32) knows of no permanent change between the ordinances of Gracchus and of Sulla.

[3] Cic. *pro Rab.* 7, 20 (amongst the classes that took arms against Saturninus was the) 'equester ordo . . . eius aetatis, quae tum magnam partem rei publicae atque omnem dignitatem iudiciorum tenebat.'

[4] Liv. *Ep.* lxx; Vell. ii. 13; Cic. *ap. Asc. in Scaurian.* p. 21.

[5] App. *B. C.* i. 35. Here, as in the accounts of the Gracchan and Servilian changes, we sometimes get the legal view that Livius gave the *iudicia* to the senate [Vell. ii. 13 '(Drusus) cum senatui priscum restituere cuperet decus et iudicia ab equitibus ad eum transferre ordinem'; Asc. *in Scaurian.* p. 21 '(Scaurus) M. quoque Drusum tribunum plebis cohortatus sit ut iudicia commutaret'], sometimes the historical view that they were shared between the senate and the equestrian order (Liv. *Ep.* lxxi 'ut aequa parte iudicia penes senatum et equestrem ordinem essent').

[6] App. *B. C.* i. 100; cf. Vell. ii. 32; Tac. *Ann.* xi. 22 'post lege Sullae viginti creati (quaestores) supplendo senatui, cui iudicia tradiderat'; Cic.

from this body. The enlarged senate may have numbered about six hundred, and this complement might have been permanently attained by the new method which was adopted of filling up its ranks annually through the quaestorship[1]. But the courts could not be supplied from the whole body of the senators. The magistrates[2], the pro-magistrates, the *legati* and all who were absent on the service of the state had to be excluded. A full house in the year 61 B.C. showed about 415 members[3], and four hundred may perhaps be taken as the approximate number of senators which was annually available for judicial duty. But the number could not be left to chance. It was imperative that each year the names of those whose position or circumstances enabled them to sit in the courts should be ascertained, and thus a special jury-list of senators, which even now may have assumed the form of a distinct register (*album iudicum*), must have been drawn up. Its custody may have been, as in later times, in the hands of the praetor urbanus, and he may have arranged for its division into the smaller units prescribed by the Cornelian law.

Division of the *iudices* into *decuriae*.

The whole body of *iudices* was divided into a number of decuries, in each of which senators of all grades were represented. These *decuriae* were as purely artificial subdivisions as the Athenian panels, of which they may have been a conscious imitation, and like them, bore no close relation to the courts whose purposes they served. To assign a particular *decuria* permanently to a particular *quaestio* would have been to invite the corruption of its members, and such an assignment was never made. But the word was not yet applied to denote whole classes

in Verr. Act. i. 13, 37 (70 B.C.) 'inter decem annos, posteaquam iudicia ad senatum tralata sunt.'

[1] Tac. *Ann.* xi. 22, see p. 436, note 6.

[2] Cic. *in Verr.* Act. i. 10, 30.

[3] Cic. *ad Att.* i. 14, 5 'homines ad quindecim Curioni nullum senatus consultum facienti adsenserunt; ex altera parte facile cccc. fuerunt.'

BOOK II.

or orders of jurymen such as those created later by the Aurelian law[1]. The decuries of Sulla were far smaller bodies, and as a rule one of these could have done little more than serve the purposes of a single jury. They were numbered according to a regular sequence; thus Verres, we are told, had belonged and, if acquitted, would belong to the second decury on the roll[2]. The praetor, we are told (and perhaps the urban praetor is meant), assigned the decury for a single case according to its precedence on the list. The *iudices* for the case were selected by lot from this division; a number somewhat exceeding that required for the trial was the result of this sortition, and the size of the panel was still further diminished by the right of challenging (*reiectio*) exercised by accuser and accused[3]. But it might happen that a decury which did not attain its full numbers, either because some of its members had already been chosen for another case or because others had entered on magistracies and had thus ceased to be qualified[4], might not supply the *iudices* required for a particular trial, and in this case a supplementary allotment (*subsortitio*) from the next decury was allowed. For the proper exercise of this power the president of the *quaestio* and the urban praetor were jointly responsible. It was the duty of the first to make the demand for this allotment

Mode of assigning *iudices* for particular cases.

Sortitio and *reiectio*.

Subsortitio.

[1] This wide sense appears in Cicero's comments on the *tertia decuria* (i. e. 'class' or 'order') which Antonius added to the jurors in 44 B.C. (*Phil.* i. 8, 19; v. 6, 15; xiii. 2, 4). For a similar use of the word in the Principate see Suet. *Aug.* 32, *Calig.* 16; Plin. *H. N.* xxxiii. 1, 30 and 31.

[2] Cic. *in Verr.* ii. 32, 79 'Hunc hominem in iudicum numero habebimus? Hic alteram decuriam senatoriam iudex obtinebit?'

[3] Schol. Gronov. p. 392 (Orell.) [comment to Cic. *in Verr.* Act. i. 6, 16] 'Nam iudices semper sortiebantur et sortitione facta non omnes iudicabant, sed electio fiebat et eiiciebantur ab utraque parte usque ad certum numerum imparem ... Per decurias erat senatus divisus; unam decuriam pr. dabat ut ex hac iudices reiicerentur.' The statement that the challenge always resulted in an uneven number of *iudices* is, as we shall see, incorrect.

[4] Cic. *in Verr.* Act. i. 10, 30 (after enumerating *iudices* that after Jan. 1 must go off the *consilium*, he adds) 'subsortiemur etiam in M. Metelli locum, quoniam is huic ipsi quaestioni praefuturus est.'

and to see that it was legally conducted, of the second to enter the names of these supplementary *iudices* on his register (*codex*). For a failure of duty in both these particulars, Junius the *quaesitor* and Verres the urban praetor were respectively fined and censured[1]. Nay, the *iudex* himself had to be sure that he was coming from the right decury and that he was not exercising his functions as a supplementary juror at too late a period in the case. Error may have been forgiven, and Fidiculanius Falcula, who was fined for appearing at the last moment in the wrong jury-box during the hearing of the case against Oppianicus, may have been convicted of guile[2].

It is evident that such subsortition might deplete the next decury on the list, and thus remove jurors from a case which was known to be impending. The accused might avail himself of such a possibility and, by collusion with the president of a court already in action, seek to remove the most obnoxious members of the decury which he knew was to sit in judgement on himself. This ruse was attempted by Verres, but successfully checkmated by Cicero[3].

[1] Cic. *pro Cluent.* 35, 96 'Ab illo enim (*sc.* Iunio) sive quod in legem non iurasset, sive quod ex lege subsortitus iudicem non esset, multa petita esse dicitur'; cf. 34, 92; 33, 91 'Multam petivit. Qua lege? ... quod C. Verres, praetor urbanus, homo sanctus et diligens, subsortitionem eius in eo codice non haberet qui tum interlitus proferebatur'; *in Verr.* Act. i. 13, 39 '(Cognoscet ex me populus Romanus) quod inventi sint senatores qui C. Verre praetore urbano sortiente exirent in eum reum quem incognita causa condemnarent'; *in Verr.* i. 61, 157 'Nam de subsortitione illa Iuniana iudicum nihil dico. Quid enim? contra tabulas, quas tu protulisti, audeam dicere? Difficile est.'

[2] Cic. *pro Cluent.* 37, 103 'Dixitne tandem causam C. Fidiculanius Falcula, qui Oppianicum condemnarat, cum praesertim . . . paucos dies ex subsortitione sedisset . . .? Uno iudicio multa est ab eo petita, sicut ab Iunio, quod non suae decuriae munere neque ex lege sedisset'; *pro Caec.* 10, 29 (of Fidiculanius Falcula) 'venisse in consilium publicae quaestionis, cum eius consilii iudex non esset, et in eo consilio, cum causam non audisset et potestas esset ampliandi, dixisse *sibi liquere*.'

[3] Cic. *in Verr.* i. 61, 158 'eius modi subsortitionem homo amentissimus suorum quoque iudicum fore putavit per sodalem suum Q. Curtium iudicem

BOOK II.

The right of challenge under the Sullan system.

Now that the *iudices* were given partly by the magistrate carrying out the law and partly by chance, the right of challenge (*reiectio*) was the sole survival of the principle that the *iudex* is a man furnished by agreement of the parties[1]. This right was, according to our sole informant, exercised first by the accuser, then by the accused[2]; but the fact that Cicero, in his prosecution of Verres, seems to have challenged a senator who had been retained by the accused, has been thought to establish the reverse practice, at least in certain *quaestiones*[3]. The power of challenge was, by the Sullan ordinances, granted on a more liberal scale to senators than to members of the general public[4]. This was but an act of justice, for the senator, although he might have more friends, would also discover more enemies in the members of his own order. The average man could reject three *iudices*[5], the senator perhaps double this number[6]. Equity would seem to dictate that, when a

quaestionis: cui nisi ego . . . restitissem, ex hac decuria vestra, cuius mihi copiam quam largissime factam oportebat, quos iste annuerat, in suum consilium sine causa subsortiebatur.'

[1] p. 265.

[2] Schol. Gronov. p. 389 (ad Cic. *in Verr.* Act. i. 3, 10) 'In reiectione autem prior accusator reiiciebat, et sic defensor vel reus.'

[3] Cic. *in Verr.* i. 7, 18 'Ita reieci iudices ut hoc constet post hunc statum rei publicae quo nunc utimur simili splendore et dignitate consilium nullum fuisse. Quam iste laudem communem sibi ait esse mecum: qui, cum P. Galbam iudicem reiecisset, M. Lucretium retinuit; et, cum eius patronus ex eo quaereret cur suos familiarissimos Sex. Peducaeum, Q. Considium, Q. Iunium reiici passus esset, respondit quod eos in iudicando nimium sui iuris sententiaeque cognosset.' As Zumpt remarks (ii. 2, p. 119), Cicero could hardly have spoken of Lucretius like this, if he was on the bench before him: and the argument is sound, for the retention of Lucretius is clearly presented from Cicero's hostile point of view, not from the self-laudatory standpoint of Verres.

[4] *ib.* ii. 31, 77 'de se homines, si qui extra istum ordinem sunt, quibus ne reiiciendi quidem amplius quam trium iudicum praeclarae leges Corneliae faciunt potestatem, hunc hominem . . . nolunt iudicare.'

[5] Cic. *l. c.*

[6] Verres is known to have rejected six: P. Galba, Sex. Peducaeus, Q. Considius, Q. Iunius (*in Verr.* i. 7, 18, see note 3), C. Cassius [*ib.* iii. 41, 97 'Hunc (C. Cassium) tu in hac causa testem, Verres, habebis, quoniam

senator was on his trial, the prosecutor, to whatever order he might belong, should also have the superior right of challenge, for it was as important to eliminate the friendly as the hostile peers of the accused; but we do not know what provision ruled the prosecutor's right of challenge in such cases. The whole ordinance that dealt with the unequal *reiectio* lasted only during the existence of a purely senatorial panel. When the three orders judged, no trace appears of a senator possessing a superior right of challenging members of the senatorial decuries. If the original provision was contained in the Cornelian laws which established each separate *quaestio*[1], this clause in each of the laws must have been obrogated by the *lex Aurelia*; if it was contained in Sulla's *lex iudiciaria*, it fell with the repeal of that law.

Strength of the juries.

The strength of the particular juries under the Sullan system, after they had been reduced by the challenge of the parties, cannot be determined, nor is it known whether the number of *iudices* was prescribed in the special enactments establishing the courts or in the general judiciary law. Sulla's legislation was such a complete whole that a close relation between the judiciary and the special criminal laws, or at least the assertion of uniform principles of procedure in the latter—neither of which as a rule existed in Roman criminal legislation—may perhaps be affirmed. The numbers may, therefore, have been regulated on some principle, but they were not the same for all cases. Thirty-two *iudices* pronounced judgement on Oppianicus in 74 B.C.[2]; but, in the case of Verres four years later, if Cicero

iudicem ne haberes providisti '] and P. Cervius (*ib.* v. 44, 114 'P. Cervium ... qui, quia legatus isto praetore in Sicilia fuit, primus ab isto iudex reiectus est ').

[1] The conclusion that it was is supported by the analogy of the *lex Acilia repetundarum*, which prescribes the mode of challenge in cases of extortion; but such a general regulation might conceivably have been a part of a iudiciary law.

[2] Cic. *pro Cluent.* 27, 74 'In consilium erant ituri iudices XXXII. Sententiis XVI absolutio confici poterat.'

BOOK II. is literally correct in saying that the transference of the trial to another year would cause the loss of 'almost the whole *consilium*' by the disappearance of eight judges, the number which pronounced the verdict must have been far smaller[1].

Choice between open and secret voting.

A further Sullan ordinance, which, on account of its transitory nature, may be mentioned here, dictated that the accused should have the privilege of deciding whether the votes should be given openly or by ballot[2]. It is not certain, although it is probable, that it applied to all the *quaestiones*, nor can its place in the Sullan legislation be determined[3]. It was doubtless intended as a mode by which responsibility could be thrown on individual *iudices*, when the accused was certain that they would be unable to defend an openly adverse sentence. But open voting had the disadvantage of giving undue weight to the verdict of those who gave their opinions first; it was important that these should not be influential men; hence provision was made that the order of voting should be determined by lot[4].

Reaction against the Sullan system.

The compromise attempted by Sulla's judiciary law had ceased to be one as soon as the *equites* drafted into the senate had identified themselves with senatorial interests. This was rapidly accomplished; the senatorial *iudicia* soon presented a united front and carried out a consistent policy of acquitting guilty members of their order. The leaders of the reaction of 70 B.C. had necessarily to deal with the question of the transference of the *iudicia*, and it

[1] Cic. *in Verr.* Act. i. 10, 30. After enumerating eight names, he adds 'Ita secundum Kal. Ian. et praetore et prope toto consilio commutato.'

[2] Cic. *pro Cluent.* 27, 75 'Consurgitur in consilium, cum sententias Oppianicus, quae tum erat potestas, palam ferri velle dixisset.' Cicero speaks of the right as a thing of the past. It had doubtless been repealed by the *lex Aurelia.*

[3] It must remain doubtful whether such general ordinances were contained in the *leges* establishing the *quaestiones* or in a judiciary law. See p. 441.

[4] Cic. *pro Cluent.* 28, 75 'Ecce tibi eiusmodi sortitio ut in primis Bulbo et Staieno et Guttae esset iudicandum.'

BOOK II.

seems that their original proposals aimed at a complete restoration of the equestrian order[1]. Fortunately, more moderate councils prevailed; the swing of the pendulum was averted, and the new device of a true *communicatio iudiciorum* was finally adopted. Three classes were to be represented in the courts, and the statements which speak of the *iudicia* having been given to the *equites*[2], or having been shared between this body and the senate[3], are due partly to a confusion between the original proposal and the final measure, partly to an identification, which we shall discuss elsewhere, of the *equites* with the third order of *tribuni aerarii*[4]. The law which was actually carried by the praetor L. Aurelius Cotta, enjoined that senators, *equites* and this third class should judge together and in equal numbers[5]. The senatorial qualification was that of the Cornelian law, the equestrian approximately at least that of the Sempronian[6]; for the second class that now possessed a third share in the juries was a moneyed one and was roughly identifiable with that of the great middle-men and contractors[7]. The inclusion of the *tribuni aerarii*

Lex Aurelia. The *iudicia* given to three orders.

The *tribuni aerarii.*

[1] Cic. *in Verr.* iii. 96, 223 'quid possumus contra illum praetorem dicere, qui quotidie templum tenet, qui rem publicam sistere negat posse nisi ad equestrem ordinem iudicia referantur?'

[2] Liv. *Ep.* xcvii 'iudicia . . . per L. Aurelium Cottam praetorem ad equites Romanos translata sunt'; cf. Plut. *Pomp.* 22; Ps. Asc. p. 127.

[3] Cic. *pro Cluent.* 47, 130 'illo ipso tempore . . . erant iudicia cum equestri ordine communicata'; Vell. ii. 32 'Per idem tempus Cotta iudicandi munus, quod C. Gracchus ereptum senatui ad equites, Sulla ab illis ad senatum transtulerant, aequaliter in utrumque ordinem partitus est'; cf. Schol. Gronov. p. 386.

[4] Cf. Schol. Bob. p. 229 'lex Aurelia iudiciaria ita cavebat ut ex parte tertia senatores iudicarent, ex partibus duabus tribuni aerarii et equites Romani, eiusdem scilicet ordinis viri.'

[5] Asc. *in Pison.* p. 16 'Legem iudiciariam . . . tulit L. Aurelius Cotta praetor, qua communicata sunt iudicia senatui et equitibus Romanis et tribunis aerariis'; cf. *in Cornelian.* pp. 67 and 78; Schol. Bob. p. 229 (see note 4).

[6] p. 435.

[7] Cic. *in Verr.* ii. 71, 174 'At quorum iudicio condemnatum? Nempe eorum quos ii, qui severiora iudicia desiderant, arbitrantur res iudicare oportere, publicanorum iudicio; quos videlicet nunc populus iudices poscit,

BOOK II.

introduced, if a popular element[1], one of an exceedingly moderate kind; for several passages of Cicero prove how difficult it was to distinguish them from members of the equestrian order[2]. There was a time when the *tribuni aerarii* were real officials of the state. As paymasters of the tribes they had perhaps collected the tribute and had certainly paid it as the wages of war (*stipendium*) to the soldiers[3]. But the Roman *tributum* had ceased to have any connexion with the Roman tribes as early as 167 B.C., the date at which direct taxation ceased in Italy. The functions of collection, if exercised by the tribunes, must then have expired, and it is probable that the business of payment, for which they had once been responsible, ceased as well. The name, however, continued; but it seems to have been retained only to denote the class in the census from which these paymasters had been chosen. The class was, perhaps, the second in the later *comitia centuriata*, that which comprised the possessors of 300,000 sesterces[4]. As owners of a moderate capital they would

de quibus, ut eos iudices habeamus, legem ab homine non nostri generis, non ex equestri loco profecto, sed nobilissimo promulgatam videmus.'

[1] According to Dio Cassius (xliii. 25) they were ἐκ τοῦ ὁμίλου.

[2] Only senators and *equites* are mentioned as *iudices* in *pro Font.* 12 [16], 36; *pro Cluent.* 43, 121; cf. *ib.* 47, 130 (p. 443, note 3); *pro Flacco*, 38, 96; Schol. Bob. p. 229 (p. 443, note 4). Cicero speaks of the *tribuni aerarii* as an *ordo* in 100 B.C. and as distinct from the *equites* (*pro Rab.* 9, 27; cf. *in Cat.* iv. 7, 15). They are represented as a body defending the state against revolution, and the *equites* and *tribuni aerarii* together constitute the middle class as opposed to the *plebs* [*pro Planc.* 8, 21 'Hi tot equites Romani, tot tribuni aerarii (nam plebem a iudicio dimisimus quae cuncta comitiis adfuit) quid roboris, quid dignitatis huius petitioni attulerunt!'].

[3] Cato. *ap Gell.* vi (vii). 10 'Pignoris capio ob aes militare, quod aes a tribuno aerario miles accipere debebat'; Varro, *L. L.* vi. 180 'quibus attributa erat pecunia, ut militi reddant, tribuni aerarii dicti'; Festus, p. 2 'Aerarii tribuni a tribuendo aere sunt appellati.'

[4] Belot, *Histoire des Chevaliers Romains*, ii. p. 291. That a census was required for the third order by the Aurelian law is shown by Cicero (*Phil.* 1, 8, 20 'census praefiniebatur . . . non centurioni quidem solum sed equiti etiam Romano. Itaque . . . qui ordines duxerunt res et iudicant et iudicaverunt'). Cicero does not say that these centurions sat for the most part among the *equites*; many may have come into the panels through the census of the *tribuni aerarii*. The principle of the census was

thus be inferior only to the knights, and the small interval that separated the qualifications of the two orders would account for their frequent identification.

Number of *iudices* under the new system.

We are nowhere told the number of names that annually appeared on the new register of judges. It is a natural supposition that the size of the whole bench was determined by the number of senators available. But we cannot say whether the *lex Aurelia* fixed a precise limit to this number and, therefore, to that of the other orders, or whether, after the urban praetor had made out his senatorial list, he then selected in the same proportions from the *equites* and the *tribuni aerarii*. The number of senators available under the *lex Cornelia* may have been approximately 400[1], and, if this proportion was observed throughout, the *album* of the *lex Aurelia* would have contained about 1,200 names; but chance references to the numbers of senators performing judicial duties show us 300 in 51 B.C.[2] and 360 in 49 B.C.[3] Perhaps the number 360 should be read in both passages; 1,080 would thus be the number of all the names on the register, a curious total to be prescribed by a law, but one perfectly explicable if the number of senators available for judicial work set the standard for the full list.

Selection by the urban praetor.

The list was made out annually by the urban praetor, who selected the *iudices* at his own discretion and on oath[4]. In the choice of the required senators he must

still adhered to when Augustus instituted a class of inferior *iudices*; they were the possessors of a property of 200,000 sesterces (Suet. *Aug.* 32).

[1] p. 437.

[2] S.C. in Cic. *ad Fam.* viii. 8, 5 'cum de ea re ad senatum referretur a consulibus, qui eorum in ccc iudicibus essent, s. f. s. (i.e. 'sine fraude sua') adducere liceret.'

[3] Cic. *ad Att.* viii. 16, 2 'Iudices de CCCLX qui praecipue Gnaeo nostro delectabantur.' Both these references are later than the judiciary law of Pompeius passed in 55 B.C.; but there is no reason for supposing that this enactment altered the size of the *album*; see p. 448.

[4] Cic. *pro Cluent.* 43, 121 'praetores urbani, qui iurati debent optimum quemque in selectos iudices referre, nunquam sibi ad eam rem censoriam ignominiam impedimento esse oportere duxerunt.'

BOOK II. have been mainly bound by circumstances: for, if even the *lex Aurelia* limited their number, this limit could never have fallen far short of the number actually available. Yet even here he need only choose 'the best' and must have been gifted, like every magistrate who exercised the right of selection, with the power of anticipating the censors' verdict by excluding palpably unworthy members from the register [1]. In his selection of the required numbers from the *equites* and the *tribuni aerarii* his choice seems to have been absolutely free [2]. In proving the census of the individuals of these two orders the assistance of the quaestors seems to have been called in [3]. The list was probably now, as it was in later times, kept in the *aerarium* [4]. Each of the three portions of the *album* seems now to have been divided into decuries. Thus in each court the members of three decuries would sit, a practice which led to the description of each *ordo* as in itself a *decuria* [5].

The *lex Aurelia* had made such an increase in the size of

[1] The converse was, of course, impossible, for the censorian *ignominia* would have already excluded a man from the senate. In the case of a senator who had been excluded and restored, the law did not require the praetor to reject him on account of his past *probrum* (see p. 445, note 4); nor did it demand the exclusion of members of the other orders on this ground (Cic. *pro Cluent.* 43, 120 'Quapropter in omnibus legibus, quibus exceptum est de quibus causis aut magistratum capere non liceat aut iudicem legi aut alterum accusare, haec ignominiae causa praetermissa est').

[2] It seems to have been limited only by disqualification from the judicial bench pronounced as a *poena* by certain criminal laws (see note 1).

[3] Dio Cass. xxxix. 7 (57 B.C.) *οἱ ταμίαι, δι' ὧν τὴν ἀποκλήρωσιν τῶν δικαστῶν γενέσθαι ἐχρῆν.* *ἀποκλήρωσις* (*sortitio*) is perhaps a mistake of Dio's. The context shows that the passage refers to the choice of *iudices* for the year. But the quaestors could not have employed the lot before the praetor exercised his right of selection. Possibly the list was divided into *decuriae* by *sortitio*.

[4] Cic. *Phil.* v. 5, 15 (of the new 'decury' instituted by Antonius in 44 B.C.) 'Hos ille demens iudices legisset, horum nomina ad aerarium detulisset?'

[5] p. 438, note 1.

Strength of individual juries.

the *album* that we should expect the individual juries to be larger than they had been under the Sullan system. This expectation is verified; but our information is so scanty that it cannot be determined whether the increase was effected by multiplying the size of the jury as fixed by individual laws, or whether the *lex Aurelia* determined a constant number for all cases. The latter hypothesis is rendered probable by the fact that in 55 B.C. Cicero, when predicting for an opponent a speedy appearance before a court of law, could threaten the verdict of seventy-five men, just as a modern orator might threaten that of twelve [1]. The numbers recorded as having actually tried cases approximate to this total [2], the slight variations being, perhaps, explicable on the ground that some of the jurors purposely spoilt their votes [3]. But it is difficult, even on this hypothesis, to explain so low a number

[1] Cic. *in Pis.* 40, 96 'An ego exspectem dum de te quinque et septuaginta tabellae diribeantur, de quo iam pridem omnes mortales omnium generum, aetatum, ordinum iudicaverunt?' Cicero is not speaking of a specific charge, but of any accusation based on political grounds (e. g. *maiestatis, repetundarum*).

[2] In 59 B.C. L. Valerius Flaccus was accused of extortion. Cicero says (*pro Flacco*, 2, 4) 'An equites Romanos (appellem)? Iudicabitis principes eius ordinis quinquaginta, quod cum omnibus senseritis.' The *tribuni aerarii* are here included in the *equites*, for he has already mentioned the senators alone (cf. *ib.* 38, 96 and see p. 444). The whole jury would thus have been seventy-five. In 54 B.C. A. Gabinius was accused of *maiestas*. Cicero says of his acquittal (*ad Att.* iv. 16, 9) 'Quo modo ergo absolutus (Gabinius)? . . . accusatorum incredibilis infantia . . . Attamen xxxii condemnarunt, xxxviii absolverunt' (cf. *ad Q. fr.* iii. 4, 1 'Gabinius absolutus est . . . qui . . . sententiis condemnatus sit xxxii cum lxx tulissent'). The total number in this case was, therefore, seventy. In the trial of M. Aemilius Scaurus, accused *repetundarum* and defended by Cicero (54 B.C.), there voted twenty-two senators, twenty-three *equites* and twenty-five *tribuni aerarii*, i. e. seventy in all (Asc. *in Scaurian.* p. 30). As the numbers of the orders are unequal, some jurors were either absent or spoilt their votes (p. 389). The total number required for this trial must have been seventy-five.

[3] For the practice see the account of the verdict on Clodius in 61 B.C. (p. 389); or the variations may be due to the non-attendance of certain *iudices* who had eluded the *coercitio* of the president. The latter hypothesis is that of Zumpt (ii. 2, p. 210).

BOOK II.

as fifty jurors, which is on one occasion presented by Cicero [1].

Lex Pompeia.

A slight modification in the mode of selecting *iudices* was introduced by Pompeius in 55 B.C., obviously for the purpose of securing the purity of the courts and of getting rid of the corrupt, or even perhaps the professional, juryman [2]. The *album* was still to be composed of the three orders, but in at least two of these, the *equites* and the *tribuni aerarii*, the minimum census of 400,000 and 300,000 sesterces was no longer to be considered a sufficient qualification. The praetor had hitherto exercised great freedom of choice and had in the main selected from those who made voluntary profession of their willingness to serve. Now he was instructed first to take those of the highest census in each class and then to choose others in a descending scale. The conception of the office of juryman as a burden (*munus*) seems to have been restored, and presumably those only who could furnish sufficient cause for exemption (*excusatio*) were released from the duty. Yet even this change was not held to have given a sufficiently aristocratic character to the jurors, and Caesar, in spite of his democratic proclivities, felt himself compelled to abolish the third order of *tribuni aerarii*,

Change introduced by Caesar.

[1] This appears in the trial of Procilius (whether for *vis* or *maiestas* is uncertain) in 54 B.C. (Cic. *ad Att.* iv. 15, 4 'Procilius condemnatus . . . Debemus patrem familias domi suae occidere nolle; neque tamen id ipsum abunde. Nam absolverunt xxii, condemnarunt xxviii'). Zumpt (ii. 2, p. 210) would read xxxii and xxxviii, making seventy in all. For the fifty-six jurors of Clodius' trial see p. 388. As this was the result of a special commission, the number of jurors may have been exceptional.

[2] Asc. *in Pison.* p. 16 'Rursus deinde Pompeius in consulatu secundo, quo haec oratio dicta est, promulgavit ut amplissimo ex censu ex centuriis aliter atque antea lecti iudices, aeque tamen ex illis tribus ordinibus, res iudicarent'; Cic. *in Pis.* 39, 94 'Ecquid vides, ecquid sentis, lege iudiciaria lata, quos posthac iudices simus habituri? Neque legetur quisquis voluerit, nec quisquis noluerit non legetur. Nulli coniicientur in illum ordinem, nulli eximentur; non ambitio ad gratiam, non iniquitas ad simulationem coniicietur. Iudices iudicabunt ii quos lex ipsa, non quos hominum libido delegerit'; cf. *Phil.* i. 8, 20, p. 434, note 3.

perhaps because he saw in them the corruptible type of professional jurymen [1]. BOOK II.

Lex Antonia.

This solution was not accepted by the dictator's professed follower, M. Antonius [2]. He introduced in 44 B.C., and actually established during the course of that year, a third *decuria*, as an order itself had now come to be called. The qualifications for this new class cannot be precisely determined, for we possess in the criticisms of Cicero a mere caricature of the conditions of admission. The class was not defined by reference to a census, and service of various kinds seems to have been the means of passing into the order. Ex-centurions were qualified by their grade [3], common soldiers probably by their length of service. Whether the same qualification admitted 'gamblers, exiles and Greeks' we cannot say [4]. Perhaps certain kinds of civil as well as military service qualified for the position; but the general result seems to have been an introduction of soldiers on a large scale to the bench, a singular consequence of the prevailing influence of militarism on politics. The men chosen may have been as honest as the average jurors; but Antonius' haste in getting the new panel to work (it was already established by November of the current year) [5] seems to show some pressing personal motive, such as that suggested by Cicero [6]. The new measure was

[1] Suet. *Caes.* 41 'Iudicia ad duo genera iudicum redegit, equestris ordinis ac senatorii: tribunos aerarios, quod erat tertium, sustulit.' The object of the change was ὅπως τὸ καθαρώτατον ὅτι μάλιστα ἀεὶ δικάζοι (Dio Cass. xliii. 25).

[2] According to Cicero, by Antonius' proposal 'omnes iudiciariae leges Caesaris dissolvuntur' (*Phil.* i. 8, 19).

[3] Cic. *Phil.* i. 8, 20 'At quae est ista tertia decuria? Centurionum, inquit. Quid? isti ordini iudicatus lege Iulia, etiam ante Pompeia, Aurelia non patebat? Census praefiniebatur, inquit.'

[4] *ib.* v. 5, 12 'Antesignanos et manipulares et Alaudas iudices se constituisse dicebat. At ille legit aleatores, legit exules, legit Graecos.' The *exules* are here exiles from their own communities.

[5] *ib.* v. 5, 15.

[6] *ib.* i. 8, 20 'Aliter enim nostri negant posse se salvos esse ... Hic enim est legis index ut ii res in tertia decuria iudicent qui libere iudicare

BOOK II.

of short duration. Antonius, it is true, during his negotiations with the senate in the following year, clung steadfastly to his bill. But by the month of March it had been repealed[1], and it was never renewed. The Triumvirate rendered protection through military jurors unnecessary; but the introduction of a third decury, based like that of the knights on a property qualification, was thought by Augustus a necessity, or at least an advantage, to the administration[2].

The other judiciary laws of the Republic dealt only with the details of procedure. The first introduced a slight change in the method of voting.

Lex Fufia on the method of voting.

Although the ballot, which prevailed universally since the *lex Aurelia*[3], effectually prevented the individual juryman from being held responsible for his vote, the mutual recriminations of the orders on a shameful acquittal or conviction suggested the desirability of securing a class responsibility by the device of having their votes taken separately. This was secured by a law of the praetor Q. Fufius Calenus, passed in 59 B.C.[4], which enacted that three urns should be placed in court and that the tablets of each order should be dropped into a separate vessel. Henceforth, as in the trials of Scaurus and Drusus in 54 B.C.[5], or in the convictions under the Pompeian laws of 52 B.C.[6], the decision arrived at by each class of jurymen was published to the world[7].

non audeant'; cf. v. 6, 15 'Scelerum magnitudo . . . hanc tertiam decuriam excogitavit.'

[1] Cic. *Phil.* xiii. 3, 5.

[2] Suet. *Aug.* 32, see p. 444, note 4.

[3] p. 442, note 2.

[4] Dio Cass. xxxviii. 8.

[5] Scaurus (Asc. *in Scaurian.* p. 30, see p. 447, note 2), Drusus (Cic. *ad Q. fr.* ii. 16, 3 'Drusus erat de praevaricatione a tribunis aerariis absolutus, in summa quattuor sententiis, cum senatores et equites damnassent').

[6] Asc. *in Milon.* pp. 53 and 54; see p. 396.

[7] If we are to believe Asconius (*in Or. in Tog. Cand.* p. 90) the votes of the orders had been taken separately as early as 65 B.C. Speaking of Catiline's acquittal, he says 'liberatus est Catilina sed ita ut eum senatorum urna damnaret, equitum et tribunorum absolveret.' Mommsen (*Strafr.* p. 445) suggests that before 59 B.C. this may have been done at the discretion of

Lex Vatinia introduces a new system of challenging.

Another reform of the same year was the introduction of a principle of challenging (*reiectio*). It was due to the initiation of the tribune P. Vatinius, and its object was to secure to the parties a wider choice of *iudices*. We learn from Cicero that its character was equitable and favourable to the accused[1], but, in his estimate, he suggests only the bare outlines of the measure, and it is almost impossible to determine the precise nature of the change introduced by the tribune. It is described indifferently as a system of challenging alternate benches (*consilia*)[2] and alternate *iudices*[3]. The latter expression may obviously be an equivalent for the first, which is the more explicit. One whole *consilium* is in some way the unit to be rejected jointly and alternately by the parties; but it is possible to imagine more ways than one in which this might have been effected. We can conceive three *consilia* put forward by the praetor, and leave given to either party to challenge one of these[4], but this would have been an ineffective mode of challenge (for there could have been little reason why one whole *consilium* should be more suspected than another) and it would have implied a great plenitude of judicial power always available, since three *consilia* would have consisted of the better part, or perhaps the whole, of nine decuries of *iudices*. Perhaps two *consilia* would have satisfied

the president. But Asconius' words may be a wholly mistaken comment on the passage of Cicero which he is annotating ('a senatoribus, qui te auctoritate sua spoliatum ornamentis vinctum paene Africanis oratoribus tradiderunt'), a passage which probably refers to the attitude of the senate before the trial.

[1] Cic. *in Vat.* 11. 27.

[2] Cic. *l. c.* 'quoniam crebro usurpas legem te de alternis consiliis reiiciendis tulisse.'

[3] Cic. *pro Planc.* 15, 36 'non intellego quam ob rem senatus . . . de ipso denique ambitu reiectionem fieri voluerit iudicum alternorum'; Schol. Bob. p. 321.

[4] Cf. Cic. *in Verr.* ii. 13, 32 (p. 115) 'Quod privatus a populo petit aut populus a privato, senatus ex aliqua civitate qui iudicet datur, cum alternae civitates reiectae sunt.'

BOOK II.

the conditions. The accuser and accused may have had the power of rejecting half of each by challenging *iudices* alternately. The remaining half of each, when joined together, would have formed the final panel. It is, indeed, possible that six complete decuries may for this purpose have been given by the praetor. After the challenge the equivalent of three decuries would have been left, and from this the *consilium* might have been selected by a resort to the ordinary right of challenge, allowed to the parties under the system prevailing before the Vatinian law[1].

Ambiguity in this law of Vatinius.

A slight ambiguity in Vatinius' law is said to have led to a controversy, in which the legislator himself was a partner. In 58 B.C. Vatinius was accused under the *lex Iunia Licinia* for irregularities in his legislation of the previous year. He appealed against the structure of the court[2], and we are told (although not on the best authority) that the appeal was based on the assumption, not admitted by the presiding praetor, that the temporary president of the court (*iudex quaestionis*) might be challenged like the other *iudices* of the *consilium*[3]. If

[1] We might imagine that the parties, not the praetor, presented the *consilia* or groups of decuries which were to be challenged; but it is difficult to believe that general judicial arrangements would have permitted of such a free choice, and Cicero distinguishes the mode of selecting a jury by the rejection of alternate *iudices* from the system of *editio iudicum*, i.e. their presentation by the parties (*pro Planc.* 15, 36). It may be remarked, however, that this contrasted *editio* is that of the *lex Licinia de sodaliciis*, which gave to the plaintiff a choice far in excess of that of the defendant.

[2] Cic. *in Vat.* 14, 33.

[3] Schol. Bob. p. 323 'cum praetor C. Memmius quaesitorem sortito facere vellet et Vatinius postularet ut ipse et accusator suus mutuas reiectiones de quaesitoribus facerent (ipsius enim Vatinii lege quam tulerat in tribunatu non satis aperte neque distincte apparebat utrum sorte quaesitor esset deligendus an vero mutua inter adversarios facienda reiectio) conspirati quidam pro ipso Vatinio immissi tribunal conscenderunt et sortes, quae intra urnam continebantur, dispergere adgressi sunt, atque ita effectum est gratiose per P. Clodium ut omnia secundum voluntatem suam Vatinius obtineret.'

the statement is correct, Vatinius' contention was that three or two *quaestiores* must be presented with the *consilia*; and, if the praetor's ruling was valid, either they need not be presented or the three or the two must, after presentation, be left untouched by the parties, for the praetor to determine which was ultimately to preside. Whatever its scope, this *lex Vatinia* must have satisfied a want and served more than a temporary purpose, for it is mentioned as still existing in 55 B.C.[1]

Choice of *iudices* under the *lex Licinia de sodaliciis*. *Iudices editicii.*

Another change in the mode of selecting *iudices*, which was introduced towards the close of the Republic, was a still further approach to the older view that the *iudex* is given by the parties (*iudicis editio*). But it was confined to a single *quaestio* and based on special grounds. The Licinian law of Crassus' second consulship (55 B.C.), which aimed at the suppression of associations (*sodalicia* or *sodalitates*) which could be used for illegal political practices, provided that the juries empanelled for the purpose should be composed of what were now called *editicii iudices*, that is, of a panel presented in the first instance by the accuser and modified by the challenge of the defendant. The principle was no new one. The *lex Acilia repetundarum* seems to have contained the provision that the prosecutor should select a hundred *iudices*, of whom the accused might challenge fifty[2]; and before the date of the *lex Licinia de sodaliciis* a proposal had been made in the senate, probably in the debate preceding the Tullian law of *ambitus*[3], that for the trial of this particular crime the accuser should select, and the accused reject, a certain number of jurymen. The scheme of the Licinian law was that the accuser should name four tribes from which the *iudices* were to be chosen[4];

[1] Cic. *pro Planc.* 15, 36.

[2] *Lex Acilia*, l. 19.

[3] Cic. *pro Planc.* 17, 41; cf. *pro Mur.* 23, 47 'Idem editicios iudices esse voluisti.'

[4] Cic. *pro Planc.* 15, 36 'Neque enim quidquam aliud in hac lege nisi editicios iudices es secutus: quod genus iudiciorum si est aequum ulla

BOOK II. of these the accused might challenge one, and the panel was then to be constituted of the remaining three. This procedure was adopted in the trials of Plancius and of Messius in 54 B.C.[1] The motive for the application of such a system to the offence of forming *sodalicia* was the desire of securing a jury cognizant of the facts. It was thought that the prosecutor would select those tribes in which illegal canvassing had been most in evidence, and that the *iudex* would thus perform his prehistoric function of a witness as well as of a judge[2]. The peculiar harshness of the ordinance, which gave far the greater power of choice to the accuser, led to the conception that *editicii iudices* were pre-eminently those put forward by a single litigant[3].

Motive of the change.

Introduction of the tribe into the jury system.

The novel introduction of the tribe into the jury system is explained by the object of the law; but its entrance into the sphere of jurisdiction must not be supposed to have excluded reference to the three orders in the choice of *iudices*. Since, however, no previous judiciary law, in its instructions for the framing of the *album*, seems to have prescribed a selection from the tribes, which in the case of the senatorial members of the register would have been obviously impossible, it is not easy to see how

in re nisi in hac tribuaria, non intellego quam ob rem senatus hoc uno in genere tribus edi voluerit ab accusatore neque eandem editionem transtulerit in ceteras causas.'

[1] Cic. *pro Planc.* 16, 38 'Tu autem, Laterensis, quas tribus edidisti? . . . Quid Plancio cum Lemonia? quid cum Ufentina? quid cum Clustumina? Nam Maeciam non quae iudicaret sed quae reiiceretur esse voluisti'; *ad Att.* iv. 15, 9 'Messius defendebatur a nobis, e legatione revocatus: nam eum Caesari legarat Appius. Servilius edixit ut adesset. Tribus habet Pomptinam, Velinam, Maeciam.'

[2] Cic. *pro Planc.* 15, 37 'Hoc igitur sensimus; cuiuscumque tribus largitor esset . . . quam quisque tribum turpi largitione corrumperet, eum maxime iis hominibus, qui eius tribus essent, esse notum. Ita putavit senatus, cum reo tribus ederentur eae quas is largitione devinctas haberet, eosdem fore testes et iudices.'

[3] Serv. *ad Verg. Eclog.* iii. 50 'editicius est iudex quem una pars eligit'; cf. Cic. *pro Planc.* 17, 41.

a tribal choice could be combined with the existing *album iudicum*. With respect to the senatorial element, it is probable that there was never any selection by the parties. In the earlier suggestion for *iudices editicii* made during the Ciceronian period 125 jurors of the equestrian order were to be chosen by the plaintiff, seventy-five rejected by the defendant and fifty left to judge[1]. The *tribuni aerarii* may be included in this category, but senators are not. The addition by some other means of twenty-five senators to a similar number from each of the other orders would have given the normal number of seventy-five[2]. Analogy, therefore, makes it probable that the *editio* of the Licinian law did not apply to the senators available for jurisdiction, and practical considerations seem to yield the same result; for, although a sufficient number of senators may have been found in three Roman tribes, there could be no guarantee that this would always be the case. It seems equally clear that, if the *album* was not drawn up *tributim*, the choice of members of the other orders could not have been made with reference to this register at all. Doubtless *equites* and *tribuni aerarii* were to constitute the remainder of the panel prescribed by the Licinian law, but these must have been chosen from the selected tribes, not from the *album*. This is implied in speaking of the choice as one made from the whole people, and not from jurors chosen for a given case (*delecti*) from the register[3]. We do not know how the required members of the two orders were chosen from the tribes. Perhaps their qualifications were proved by

[1] Cic. *pro Planc.* 17, 41 'An vero nuper clarissimi cives nomen editicii iudicis non tulerunt, cum ex CXXV iudicibus, principibus equestris ordinis, quinque et LXX reus reiiceret, L ferret, omniaque potius permiscuerunt quam ei legi conditionique parerent; nos neque ex delectis iudicibus sed ex omni populo, neque editos ad reiiciendum sed ab accusatore constitutos iudices ita feremus ut neminem reiiciamus?'

[2] p. 447.

[3] See note 1, and cf. *pro Planc.* 16, 40 'Tu deligas ex omni populo aut amicos tuos aut inimicos meos?'

BOOK II. the quaestors and their selection made by the urban praetor. There is some evidence that, after the choice from the three tribes had been made, the selection even then might not be final. We read of the challenge of five jurors permitted to the accused on the consent of the praetor and the *iudices* themselves[1]. If the trial in which this occurred was one *de sodaliciis*, as seems to have been the case, the *lex Licinia* must have given a permissive right of *reiectio*, at least to the accused, even after the court had been constituted from the three tribes which had survived his challenge[2].

§ 17. *The course of the trial in a quaestio perpetua.*

The assize. The Roman criminal assize, which commenced as soon as the list of *iudices* for the year had been prepared[3], seems to have closed with the first day of September, in the sense that the name of no accused could be presented after this date[4], although a trial once begun pursued its normal course and might even run on uninterruptedly into the following year. The primary object of this limitation was probably to secure, if possible, the termination of the case before the magistrate who had begun the hearing: since, although it was lawful, it was not expedient that the *iudicium* should be transferred to his successor[5].

[1] Cic. *pro Planc.* 16, 40 'Tu . . . ne quinque quidem reiectis, quod in proximo reo de consilii sententia constitutum est, cogas causam de fortunis omnibus dicere?'

[2] There is no real evidence that the president of the court was chosen by one party or by both. The fact that we know of two different *quaesitores* for 54 B.C., Alfius in the case of Plancius (p. 430) and Servilius in the case of Messius (p. 454, note 1), does not of itself prove the point. The arrangements for these supplementary *quaestiones* are too little known to justify such a conclusion. See p. 430.

[3] Dio Cass. xxxix. 7.

[4] Under the *lex Acilia* the prosecution must be undertaken before the kalends of September (l. 7), and a *patronus* is not to be given to one who does not make the *nominis delatio* before this date (l. 9).

[5] Cf. Cic. *in Verr.* Act. i. 10, 30, and see Mommsen in *C. I. L.* i. p. 64.

But convenience may also have dictated the rule. The close of the assize was the beginning of the autumn holiday, when judges, barristers and jury fled to the country[1]. Exceptions to the rule are found only in trials for *vis*. They might be heard at any time of the year, as is proved by the trials of M. Tuccius in the October of 51 B.C.[2] and of C. Manilius at the very close of Cicero's tenure of the praetorship (66 B.C.)[3]. A long vacation judge must thus have been left behind for the months between September and January, whether in the shape of the permanent president of that court or a substitute[4]. Cases of *vis* were heard also on *dies festi* and *ludi*, when all the other criminal courts were closed[5]. Actual festivals or games were, however, the only days between January and September on which criminal justice was suspended: for the dates of trials show that no mark in the calendar obstructs their performance. They are held indifferently on *fasti* and *nefasti dies*, on comitial days and on those marked NP[6]. With respect to the

Cases of *vis* heard *extra ordinem*.

Days on which the courts did not sit.

[1] Cic. *ad Att.* i. 1, 2 'cum Romae a iudiciis forum refrixerit, excurremus mense Septembri legati ad Pisonem, ut Ianuario revertamur.'

[2] Cic. *ad Fam.* viii. 8, 1 '(C. Sempronius Rufus) M. Tuccium accusatorem suum post ludos Romanos reum lege Plotia de vi fecit hoc consilio, quod videbat, si extraordinarius reus nemo accessisset, sibi hoc anno causam esse dicendam.' 'Extraordinarius reus' is one whose case is taken 'extra ordinem.' The *postulatio* against Rufus may have been made before Sept. 1, but a long interval may have elapsed before his trial.

[3] Plut. *Cic.* 9; Dio Cass. xxxvi. 27; Asc. *in Cornelian.* p. 60. Plutarch makes the charge one of *peculatus*; Asconius (probably rightly) represents Manilius as guilty of *vis* ('qui iudicium per operarum duces turbaverat'); cf. Q. Cic. *de Pet. Cons.* 13, 51.

[4] The court, as we have seen (p. 431), sometimes had different presidents in the same year.

[5] Cic. *pro Cael.* 1, 1 'Si quis, iudices, forte nunc adsit, ignarus legum, iudiciorum, consuetudinis nostrae, miretur profecto quae sit tanta atrocitas huiusce causae quod diebus festis ludisque publicis, omnibus forensibus negotiis intermissis, unum hoc iudicium exerceatur . . . Idem, cum audiat esse legem quae de seditiosis . . . civibus . . . quotidie quaeri iubeat' &c.

[6] The trial of Milo in 52 commenced on April 4, and ended on April 8: three of these days (5, 7, 8) were *nefasti*. We hear of trials

BOOK II.

Order of cases in the same court.

order of cases in the same court and before the same magistrate, it was determined, chiefly no doubt by the time at which the action was brought, but secondarily by the time thought necessary by the prosecutor, and granted by the president or the law, for collecting evidence. The regular order of business in a court might, however, be disturbed by various considerations. Cases were taken out of their turn (*extra ordinem*) either on account of the close connexion of their subject-matter with some other case [1], or on account of the seriousness of the offence with which they dealt [2], or because they were concerned with breaches of the peace (*vis*); for, even when heard within the limits of the calendar, the last-mentioned cases took precedence of others [3].

Place and time of trial.

The place of trial was the Forum [4]; here was planted the *tribunal*, which contained not only the praetor on his curule chair, or the *iudex quaestionis*, but the *iudices* on their benches (*subsellia*) [5]. The benches of the parties, their advocates and their witnesses [6] were on the ground in front of this raised

on July 5 (*ad Att.* iv. 15, 4) and on Feb. 13 (*ad Q. fr.* ii. 13, 2), which are NP. Other hearings are on Feb. 11 and July 3, which are N (*ad Q. fr.* ii. 3, 6; *ad Att.* iv. 16, 5), and on March 11, which is C (*ib.* ii. 4, 1). So in the valid days for Verres' trial—Aug. 5–15; Sept. 2–4, 20–29; Oct. 1–25 (Cic. *in Verr.* Act. i. 10, 31; ii. 52, 130)—days of all denominations are included. Even the granting of the case did not follow the rules of civil jurisdiction, e. g. Sestius is *postulatus* for *ambitus* on Feb. 10, which is N (*ad Q. fr.* ii. 3, 5).

[1] Cic. *pro Cluent.* 20, 56 'C. Fabricium . . . reum statim fecit, utque ei locus primus constitueretur propter causae coniunctionem impetravit.'

[2] Cic. *de Inv.* ii. 19, 58 'cum venefici cuiusdam nomen esset delatum et, quia parricidii causa subscripta esset, extra ordinem esset acceptum.'

[3] Cic. *pro Mil.* 6, 14 (of the murder of Clodius) 'Quod si per furiosum illum tribunum senatui quod sentiebat perficere licuisset, novam quaestionem nullam haberemus. Decernebat enim ut veteribus legibus tantummodo extra ordinem quaereretur.'

[4] Cic. *in Verr.* v. 55, 143 'forum plenum iudiciorum.' The Forum is mentioned in the *lex Acilia*, ll. 37, 38, 65, 66.

[5] Cic. *in Vat.* 14, 34; Asc. *in Milon.* p. 40.

[6] For the *subsellia* of accuser and accused see Cic. *pro Rosc. Amer.* 36, 104; *pro Flacco*, 10, 22; 18, 42; *ad Fam.* viii. 8, 1.

platform[1]. The case was heard only by daylight, as we may learn from the municipal law of Urso, which doubtless reflects Roman usage. It is there ordained that the *iudicium publicum* shall not begin before daybreak, nor continue beyond the eleventh hour, that is, one hour before sunset[2].

The procedure. *Postulatio.*

The first stage in the procedure was, as in a civil action, a request to the magistrate, the praetor or the *iudex quaestionis*, for permission to bring the charge (*postulatio*)[3]. It had a real meaning in so far as a successful postulation demonstrated the accuser's right to prosecute—a right which might be questioned even on grounds of character; for the law forbade *infames* of certain kinds to undertake this public duty[4] except they were directly defending their own interests[5]. At this stage, too, the oath that the prosecution was undertaken *bona fide* (*iuramentum calumniae*) was taken by the accuser[6].

Iuramentum calumniae.

Only one accuser was permitted for a single offence; hence a concurrence of would-be prosecutors required a *praeiudicium* of the court as to which was to perform this duty[7]. This preliminary trial was known as the *divinatio*[8],

Divinatio.

[1] Asc. *in Milon.* p. 41.

[2] *Lex Ursonensis*, c. 102 'ne quis . . . ante h(oram) I neve post horam XI diei quaerito neve iudicium exerceto.'

[3] The full phrase is 'delationem nominis postulare' (Cic. *Div. in Caec.* 20, 64). *Postulare* is used in a general sense for prosecute, and in this wide sense is hardly distinguishable from *nomen deferre* (Cic. *in Vat.* 14, 34; *ad Fam.* viii. 8, 2; *ad Q. fr.* ii. 3, 5; Cic. *ap. Asc. in Cornelian.* p. 62).

[4] Cic. *pro Cluent.* 43, 120 '(leges) quibus exceptum est de quibus causis . . . non liceat . . . alterum accusare.' It became a class which had no right to prosecute 'propter delictum proprium ut infames' (Macer in Dig. 48, 2, 8), and many of its components, e. g. those previously found guilty of *calumnia* and *praevaricatio* (Ulp. in Dig. 48, 2, 4), may have been disqualified in the Ciceronian period.

[5] Dig. *ib.* § 11.

[6] *Lex Acilia*, l. 19; Cic. *ad Fam.* viii. 8, 3.

[7] It took place between the *postulatio* and the *nominis delatio* (Cic. *Div. in Caec.* 19, 62; 20, 64; *ad Fam.* viii. 8, 3).

[8] Various guesses were made at the meaning of the word, which are useful as throwing a not wholly imaginary light on the procedure.

BOOK II. and the question was argued before the president and a jury, the latter not necessarily consisting of those jurors who were to try the main charge[1]. It was the interest of the state to secure an able and earnest prosecutor, to avoid both weakness and collusion[2]; and the possession both of ability and good faith was eagerly argued by the respective claimants. Their personal qualifications were dwelt on[3] and their circumstances placed in the most favourable light. An orator would represent his close connexion with a province as an overwhelming ground for allowing him to appear as its agent in a prosecution for extortion[4]; he might at the same time show that his adversary's intimate relations with the accused were a sufficient ground for disqualifying him from the position which he sought[5]. On these general grounds, and with no appeals to the details of evidence[6], the *iudices* gave their decision. In the absence of proofs the abler speaker must generally have won the day, and the procedure of the *divinatio* so far justified its existence.

Nominis or *criminis delatio.* After the *divinatio*, if this procedure had proved necessary, or, if it had not, after the *postulatio* but at

Gavius Bassus, *ap. Gell.* ii. 4 'divinatio iudicum appellatur, quoniam divinet quodammodo iudex oportet quam sententiam sese ferre par sit,' i. e. divination was required, as Gellius explains, because 'cum eligendus accusator est, parva admodum et exilia sunt quibus moveri iudex possit'; Ps. Asc. p. 99 'alii ideo putant divinationem dici quod iniurati iudices in hac causa sedeant et quod velint praesentire de utroque possint; alii quod res agatur sine testibus et sine tabulis et, his remotis, argumenta sola sequantur iudices et quasi divinent.'

[1] Cic. *in Verr.* i. 6, 15 'quo in numero e vobis complures fuerunt.'

[2] The accuser should be one 'quem minime velit is, qui eas iniurias fecisse arguatur' (*Div. in Caec.* 3, 10).

[3] Cic. *Div. in Caec.* 12, 37; 'vox, memoria, consilium, ingenium' were demanded.

[4] *ib.* cc. 4–6.

[5] e. g. the quaestor was not a proper person to prosecute his former superior (*ib.* 19, 62) on account of the peculiarly close relation between them (*ib.* 19, 61 'Sic enim a maioribus nostris accepimus praetorem quaestori suo parentis loco esse oportere').

[6] See p. 459, note 8.

some interval[1], came a more definite information as to the charge (*nominis* or *criminis delatio*)[2]. This was made before the president alone, its object being the specification of the personality of the accused and the offence alleged against him. At this stage the presence of the accused was perhaps essential[3], unless he had, after the postulation, furnished a valid excuse for absence. He might avoid the *nominis delatio* entirely by pleading the *beneficium* of being *rei publicae causa absens*. This had been made a valid excuse for not appearing in a criminal court by a *lex Memmia*, whose existence is attested for the year 114 B.C.[4] Still earlier (122 B.C.) the *lex Acilia repetundarum* had forbidden a charge of extortion against a magistrate during his term of power[5], and in the Ciceronian period we find that a political prosecution at least could be avoided through investiture with office[6].

Justifiable absence of the accused.

In the case of absence other than that which the law had made excusable, the accused was cited to appear[7]. We have no case which proves conclusively what happened

Unjustifiable absence; its consequences.

[1] Cic. *ad Fam.* viii. 6, 2 'Illud mihi occurrit quod inter postulationem et nominis delationem uxor a Dolabella discessit.'

[2] delatio nominis (Cic. *Div. in Caec.* 20, 64 ; *pro Cluent.* 8, 25 ; *ad Fam.* viii. 6, 2), deferre nomen (Cic. *Div. in Caec.* 3, 10 ; *in Verr.* i. 6, 15 ; *pro Rosc. Amer.* 3, 8 ; *pro Cluent.* 8, 23 ; 17, 49), deferre crimen (Cic. *pro Lig.* 1, 1).

[3] Geib, p. 270.

[4] Val. Max. iii. 7, 9 (of M. Antonius charged with incest in 114 B.C. see p. 379) 'quaestor proficiscens in Asiam . . . ubi literis certior incesti se postulatum apud L. Cassium praetorem . . . cum id vitare beneficio legis Memmiae liceret, quae eorum qui rei publicae causa abessent recipi nomina vetabat, in urbem tamen recurrit'; cf. Suet. *Caes.* 23 (p. 353).

[5] 'de heisce, dum mag(istratum) aut imperium habebunt, iudicium non fiet' (*Lex Acilia*, l. 8). Then follow magistrates from the dictator downwards. Perhaps the enumeration was complete, but the fragmentary nature of this portion of the inscription prevents us from determining the point.

[6] Milo had impeached Clodius for *vis* (57 B.C.). Clodius ἀγορανομίαν τε ᾔτει, ὡς καὶ τὴν δίκην τῆς βίας, ἂν ἀποδειχθῇ, διαφευξόμενος (Dio Cass. xxxix. 7). Rules of this kind were perhaps (like that of the *lex Acilia*) contained in the laws establishing special *quaestiones*.

[7] Cic. *ad Att.* iv. 15, 9 'Servilius edixit ut adesset.' For the procedure in provincial jurisdiction see *in Verr.* ii. 40, 98 (Verres in the case of Sthenius) 'citat reum ; non respondet. Citat accusatorem'; cf. v. 41, 109.

BOOK II. when he declined. The only instance from the Ciceronian period is one which is a product of provincial jurisdiction; but its merits were vigorously discussed by the authorities at home, and the conclusions represent principles of Roman procedure[1]. Unfortunately the basis of these conclusions is extremely obscure, and the pleadings of Cicero leave us in the dark as to why the proceedings of Verres against the absent Sthenius were resisted by the senate. The resistance must have been based on irregularities in Verres' proceedings or on a suspicion of unfairness. The governor had here invited prosecution of a man during his absence[2]; he had perhaps fixed an impossibly short date for his appearance, and may have taken no pains that the summons should reach him. Yet we know that, in provincial jurisdiction, the *nominis receptio* of an *absens* was not strictly illegal[3], and that a governor might by this means keep an obnoxious subject in practical exile during his whole year of office[4]. But we also know that Roman procedure had at all times a strong objection to condemnation in absence, and the action taken by Q. Cicero in the case of Zeuxis[5] shows that a governor did not like to try a man, who was for the time being beyond the limits of his province, even on the gravest crimes[6]. Yet contumacious absence[7] must have been interpreted as voluntary

[1] In the case of Sthenius (see p. 461, note 7) two resolutions were proposed in the senate: (i) 'ne absentes homines in provinciis rei fierent rerum capitalium'; (ii) 'cum Sthenius reus absens factus esset, de absente iudicium fieri nullum placere, et, si quod esset factum, id ratum esse non placere' (Cic. *in Verr.* ii. 39, 95).

[2] Cic. *in Verr.* ii. 38, 94.

[3] *ib.* ii. 41, 101 'Nam si ita defenderet "recipi nomen absentis licet: hoc fieri in provincia nulla lex vetat," mala et improba defensione verum aliqua tamen uti videretur.'

[4] As Verres did Diodorus (Cic. *in Verr.* iv. 19, 41).

[5] p. 411.

[6] Cicero in one passage treats *absentia* of the accused as a possible ground for restitution (*Phil.* ii. 23, 56 'Quam attulisti rationem populo Romano cur eum restitui oporteret? Abentem credo in reos relatum').

[7] Trajan's principle that no one should be condemned *absens* was not interpreted to cover cases of contumacious absence; but the rule was

exile; in this case it is probable that the trial could proceed and, as its issue, the condemned man might be included amongst those whose outlawry was pronounced by the annual decree of the tribunes[1]. It is possible that against *contumaces* this outlawry might be pronounced even without formal condemnation.

Interrogatio.

If the accused appeared at the *nominis delatio*, a series of questions was put to him by the prosecutor (*interrogatio*) for the purpose of making out a prima facie case to the satisfaction of the president[2]. If the prisoner admitted his guilt at this stage, the procedure of the *quaestio* offered no opportunity for a summary closing of the case. For the president who heard the preliminaries of the trial was undertaking no formal cognizance, and consequently the effects of confession *in iure*, whatever they might have been[3], could not apply here. We are, indeed, told, although not on the best authority, that where the issue was expressed in damages (*litis aestimatio*), the admission of the accused on the subject of extortion, or his mere silence when interrogated on the fact, produced an immediate estimate of the pecuniary penalty[4]. The consequences of such a trial were not strictly penal, and it is possible that even here the assessment of damages,

Confession and its consequences.

adopted that the punishments on *contumaces* should be only such as affected *existimatio*, never such as affected *caput* (Ulp. in Dig. 48, 19, 5).

[1] Sthenius, as irregularly condemned, was exempted by the tribunes from the operation of this decree (Cic. *in Verr.* ii. 41, 100 'de omnium sententia pronuntiatum esse "non videri Sthenium impediri edicto quo minus ei liceret Romae esse"').

[2] Cic. *pro Domo*, 29, 77 'quis me unquam ulla lege interrogavit? quis postulavit? quis diem dixit?' Here the *interrogatio* and *postulatio* refer to proceedings before a *quaestio*, the *diem dicere* to those before the *comitia* (Mommsen, *Strafr.* p. 388). *Interrogatus* is often used in the sense of 'prosecuted' (Sall. *Cat.* 18 and 31; Vell. ii. 13).

[3] p. 253.

[4] Ps. Asc. p. 128 'cum . . . in ius vocatus esset, dicebat accusator apud praetorem reo: "Aio te Siculos spoliasse." Si tacuisset, lis ei aestimabatur ut victo; si negasset, petebatur apud magistratum dies inquirendorum eius criminum et instituebatur accusatio.'

which was the work of the jury, was preceded by their formal pronouncement on the guilt of the accused. In cases where the consequences were more decidedly penal, we have no evidence that confession was accepted as a proof of guilt and that a verdict was given even by a jury without consideration of the evidence. A sentence by the president alone, without consultation of the *iudices*, is in these circumstances inconceivable. In the *quaestiones* his functions are merged in theirs, his guidance of the preliminaries of a case cannot be regarded as an independent trial, and we know that a formal *cognitio* was absolutely essential to a verdict[1]. The *dictum* of Quintilian and Seneca[2] *magistratus de confesso sumat supplicium*, if it have any historical validity at all[3], must apply to purely magisterial cognizance, such as that in the provinces[4] or that of the imperial court at Rome, not to the standing commissions. We are forced to argue the subject on general grounds because we possess no instance of the operation of true confession of guilt in a court of the Ciceronian period. The *confessiones* so often appealed to by Cicero are mere admissions of details which the prosecutor deems to be important[5]. Sometimes they

[1] Cic. *in Verr.* i. 9, 25 'causa cognita possunt multi absolvi, incognita quidem condemnari nemo potest.'

[2] Quint. *Decl.* 314; Seneca, *Controv.* viii. 1.

[3] Geib (p. 277) thinks it a pretended legal rule of the rhetors, most of such rules being got, as fixed traditions, from the writings of the Greeks. Such positions were valued only as themes for treatment. He adds, 'the writings of the rhetors are quite the worst and the most useless sources from an historical point of view. A position stated only by them, and resting on no other authority, may be treated as without exception incorrect and invented'; cf. Mommsen, *Strafr.* p., 438.

[4] Cato's statement (Sall. *Cat.* 52 'Quare ego ita censeo . . . de confessis sicuti de manifestis rerum capitalium more maiorum supplicium sumendum') has reference only to the military jurisdiction consequent on martial law. He means that the prisoners were confessed and manifest *hostes*.

[5] Cic. *in Verr.* iii. 95, 221 'Absolvite eum qui se fateatur maximas pecunias cum summa sociorum iniuria cepisse'; iv. 47, 104 'omnibus in rebus coarguitur a me, convincitur a testibus, urgetur confessione sua,

amount to an admission of the vital point in fact, but by no means of its interpretation in law[1]. True confession undoubtedly rendered the proceedings before the *iudicium* very summary. It was almost useless to employ the rhetorical figure of 'deprecation' before a court which was supposed to pronounce strictly on the law and could not mitigate the punishment[2], and few *patroni* would have ventured to admit the truth both of fact and motive and to rest the defence simply on the general character of the accused or on the extenuating circumstances which marked this particular case.

Inscriptio.

If the interrogation satisfied the president of the need of going further with the case, he drew up an *inscriptio* with the statement of the charge[3]. That it was signed by the prosecutor seems shown by the manner in which *subscriptio* alternates with *inscriptio* in later legal terminology[4] and by the name *subscriptores* given to the

manifestis in maleficiis tenetur'; v. 64, 166 'Hoc teneo, hic haereo, iudices, hoc sum contentus uno, omitto ac negligo cetera: sua confessione induatur ac iuguletur necesse est.'

[1] Cic. *pro Lig.* 1, 2 'Habes, igitur, Tubero, quod est accusatori maxime optandum, confitentem reum sed tamen hoc confitentem, se in ea parte fuisse qua te, Tubero, qua virum omni laude dignum patrem tuum.'

[2] Cic. *de Inv.* i. 11, 15 'Purgatio est cum factum conceditur, culpa removetur . . . Deprecatio est cum et peccasse et consulto peccasse reus se confitetur et tamen ut ignoscatur postulat: quod genus perraro potest accidere.' Cf. *Auct. ad Herenn.* i. 14, 24. For the utility of its employment see Quint. *Inst. Orat.* v. 13, 5 'Deprecatio quidem, quae est sine ulla specie defensionis, rara admodum et apud eos solos iudices qui nulla certa pronuntiandi forma tenentur'; vii. 4, 17 'ultima est deprecatio, quod genus causae plerique negarunt in iudicium unquam venire . . . (18) in senatu vero et apud populum et apud principem et ubicunque, si iuris clementia est, habet locum deprecatio'; vii. 4, 20 'Id autem, quod illi viderun, verum est, reum a iudicibus hoc defensionis modo liberari non posse.'

[3] Cic. *pro Domo*, 20, 51; a type of such a document has been preserved, which, though associatd with an offence unknown to the Republicant *quaestiones*, may reflect the Republican terminology (Paulus in Dig. 48, 2, 3 'Consul et dies. Apud illum praetorem vel proconsulem Lucius Titius professus est se Maeviam lege Iulia de adulteriis ream deferre, quod dicat eam cum Gaio Seio in civitate illa, domo illius, mense illo, consulibus illis adulterium commisisse').

[4] Dig. 47, 1, 3; 48, 2, 7.

BOOK II. subordinate accusers of the Ciceronian period. They are associated with the *nominis delatio*[1], and probably signed their names below that of the leading prosecutor. The importance of this inscription was that it definitely fixed the charge. From this point it was only the offence taken cognizance of by the particular *quaestio,* before which the case was heard, that could be considered, and no other offence proved in the course of the trial could influence the verdict or draw down the penalty[2]. Where a law establishing a court took cognizance of a group of offences, the inscription narrowed down the issue to some particular clauses of the enactment, to forgery or to coining in one *lex Cornelia,* to poisoning or to stabbing in another. But it might even happen that a single offence, such as extortion, might rest on a great many separate counts[3], and it is probable that the particular counts which were to be proved had, in quite general terms, to be specified separately in the indictment. After the *inscriptio* had been drawn up, the charge was formally admitted by the president (*nominis receptio*)[4], and the person accused now becomes technically *reus.* The president then fixed a day for the appearance of the accused before the full court. It was generally the tenth day from the *nominis receptio*[5], and a shorter interval than this was reckoned illegal[6]. Some

Nominis receptio. Interval before the trial.

[1] Asc. *in Cornelian.* p. 59 'Detulit nomen Publius, subscripsit Gaius.'

[2] Cic. *de Inv.* ii. 19, 59 'Ea igitur poena si affici reum non oporteat, damnari quoque non oportere, quoniam ea poena damnationem necessario consequatur.'

[3] Quint. *Inst. Orat.* iii. 10, 1 'Plures (controversiae) aut eiusdem generis, ut in pecuniis repetundis, aut diversi, ut si quis sacrilegii et homicidii simul accusetur. Quod nunc in publicis iudiciis non accidit, quoniam praetor certa lege sortitur.'

[4] Cic. *in Verr.* ii. 38, 94; 41, 101; iv. 19, 40; *ad Fam.* viii. 8, 2; Val. Max. iii. 7, 9.

[5] Asc. *in Cornelian.* p. 59 (of the prosecution of Cornelius for *maiestas* in 66 B.C.) 'cum P. Cassius praetor decimo die, ut mos est, adesse iussisset': cf. Cic. *ad Q. fr.* ii. 13, 2 (54 B.C.) 'Cognosce nunc Idus. Decimus erat Caelio dies. Domitius iudices ad numerum non habuit.'

[6] Cicero as praetor in 66 B.C. is said to have attempted to shorten the

criminal laws, however, fixed the interval at thirty days[1], and the *crimen repetundarum* demanded this or a far longer period for the collection of evidence which had generally to be sought beyond the seas. In the prosecution of Scaurus but thirty days were asked by his accusers[2], in that of Verres, a hundred and ten were granted but only sixty were actually employed[3]. The accused made a similar use of the time in preparing his defence, and hence the curtailing of the interval beyond the minimum of ten days was regarded as an inequitable exercise of authority on the part of the president[4]. The first part of the proceedings now close and the accused awaits his appearance before a jury. During this interval he is left free; for preventive imprisonment and the giving of bail have practically disappeared, although the former still survives in cases of emergency and is applied at least to people of the lower orders, as may be seen in the treatment of Tarquinius and Vettius, the informers[5]. But this coercive power of the magistrate (for such it always remained) was rarely employed, and the *reus*, whose guilt was clear, was encouraged by freedom to seek voluntary exile. If this was true exile, that is, acceptance of *civitas* in another community, it is questionable whether the trouble was taken to frame a formal verdict; an administrative act of interdiction would, in this case, probably have been sufficient[6]; but, on any hypothesis, the case came speedily to a close. A still speedier termination was effected by the retirement of the accuser, and there are many instances of prosecutions

Preventive imprisonment rarely resorted to.

Voluntary exile of the accused.

Retirement of the accuser.

time in the trial of Manilius for *vis*; see p. 457 (Plut. *Cic.* 9). Perhaps this shortening, which was protested against, was due to the nature of the offence.

[1] Cic. *in Vat.* 14, 33 'Quaero . . . postulatusne sis lege Licinia et Iunia? edixeritne C. Memmius praetor ex ea lege ut adesses die tricesimo?'

[2] Asc. *in Scaurian.* p. 19. [3] Ps. Asc. p. 125. [4] p. 466, note 6.

[5] Sall. *Cat.* 48; Plut. *Luc.* 42. Vettius was imprisoned while awaiting trial before a *quaestio* (Cic. *ad Att.* ii. 24, 4 'Nunc reus erat apud Crassum Divitem Vettius de vi'). Cf. p. 334.

[6] p. 317, note 2.

BOOK II.

falling through on this ground[1]. His mere non-appearance on the day fixed for the hearing before the *iudices* caused the charge to be immediately dismissed[2].

Modes in which the prosecutor might betray his trust.

This is but one of the circumstances which illustrate the dependence of the State on the *bona fides* of the prosecutor—a dependence which led to the evolution of rules intended to keep him to the strict path of duty. These rules were embodied in, and to a certain extent enforced by, law. Dereliction of duty is conceived in three ways. There is the conception of a prosecution knowingly undertaken on false grounds and, therefore, prompted by malice and conducted by fraud (*calumnia*), of collusion of the prosecutor with the accused for the purpose of securing an acquittal (*praevaricatio*), and of the complete abandonment of the accusation, not on the ground of the conviction of its baselessness, but from private and unworthy motives, which render the prosecutor false to the trust which he has undertaken for the State (*tergiversatio*[3]).

Calumnia. Earlier and later methods of dealing with this offence.

Calumnia was a special crime in the eye of the criminal law, and, as such, might be the subject of a special *iudicium*. The *lex Remmia*, which made it into an offence[4],

[1] Asc. *in Cornelian.* p. 63 'Metellus fecit reum Curionem'; (an agreement was made, part of which was that) 'neque Metellus perstaret in accusatione Curionis; eaque pactio ab utroque observata est'; Plut. *Sulla* 5 (after Sulla's propraetorship in the East, Censorinus accused him of *peculatus*) οὐ μὴν ἀπήντησεν ἐπὶ τὴν κρίσιν ἀλλ' ἀπέστη τῆς κατηγορίας; Plut. *Pomp.* 55 (prosecution of Scipio, Pompeius' father-in-law, in 52 B.C.) ὁ δὲ κατήγορος ἀπέστη τῆς δίκης; cf. App. *B. C.* ii. 24.

[2] Cic. *in Verr.* ii. 40, 99 (of the case of Sthenius, see p. 462) 'Si praesens Sthenius reus esset factus . . . tamen, cum accusator non adesset, Sthenium condemnari non oporteret . . . (of Cicero's own prosecution of Verres) omnis illa mea festinatio fuit . . . ob eam causam ne tu ex reis eximerere si ego ad diem non affuissem'; Asc. *in Cornelian.* p. 59 (prosecution of Cornelius in 66 B.C.) 'cum P. Cassius adsedisset et citati accusatores non adessent, exemptum nomen est de reis Corneli.'

[3] Marcian in Dig. 48, 16, 1, 1 'Calumniari est falsa crimina intendere, praevaricatio vera crimina abscondere, tergiversari in universum ab accusatione desistere.'

[4] Dig. 48, 16, 1, 2.

may have fixed the degrading and very un-Roman penalty of branding. The letter K was imprinted on the forehead of the condemned, and the man who dreads the Kalends might still be mentioned in Cicero's time[1]. Yet even at this period the law and the punishment, although neither were extinct, were practically in suspense, the reason probably being that the *lex Remmia* was the basis for no standing court (*quaestio perpetua*) and that the penalty could only be enforced by a *iudicium populi*. The *quaestiones* had made a wholly different provision for calumnious accusation. It appears to have been dealt with in each special law which established a court, and was decided 'in the course of the trial' (*in iudicio publico*) after the main verdict had been given[2]. When a jury had, by an enormous majority, emphatically declared its belief in the innocence of the accused, and by both verdict and proceedings had demonstrated to the public the utter baselessness of the charge, it was almost the duty of the president of the court to put the prosecutor on his trial before the same jury on the charge of *calumnia*[3]. In the only case of the kind known to us acquittal was the result, and we cannot say whether any strictly penal consequence would have followed condemnation. The only known consequence of such a conviction was that of the disqualification for various functions which the Romans described as *infamia*. The censors had probably always

[1] Cic. *pro Rosc. Amer.* 20, 57 'sed si ego hos bene novi, literam illam, cui vos usque eo inimici estis ut etiam Kalendas omnes oderitis, ita vehementer ad caput affigent ut postea neminem alium nisi fortunas vestras accusare possitis.'

[2] Cf. the praetor's third edict *de postulando* (Dig. 3, 2, 1) 'qui in iudicio publico calumniae praevaricationisve causa quid fecisse iudicatus erit.'

[3] Asc. *in Scaurian.* p. 30 (after the close of the trial against Scaurus for extortion) 'Cato praetor (who had been president during the trial) cum vellet de accusatoribus in consilium mittere multique e populo manus in accusatores intenderent, cessit imperitae multitudini ac postero die in consilium de calumnia accusatorum misit. P. Triarius nullam gravem sententiam habuit; subscriptores eius M. et Q. Pacuvii fratres denas et L. Marius tres graves habuerunt,' i. e. they were all acquitted.

BOOK II. been on the watch for the malicious prosecutor, and their animadversions were applied by the praetor for his own purpose, the rules of postulation[1], and by Caesar for his regulation of the qualification to municipal offices[2]. The calumnious accuser might also have been repelled by the presidents of the criminal courts from further activity in prosecution[3]. Such disqualifications, though resting generally on the discretion of the admitting magistrate, might be determined by law, and as such they would assume a quasi-penal character.

Iuramentum calumniae. A further guarantee against this form of abuse in prosecution was found in the oath which every accuser had to take, at the *postulatio* and before the *nominis delatio*, that he had adequate grounds for bringing the charge and was not animated by malicious motives (*iuramentum calumniae*)[4]. The man convicted of calumnious prosecution would thus, in addition to his special offence, have been a perjurer as well, and could on this ground alone have been visited with *infamia* by the censors.

Praevaricatio. *Praevaricatio* is often mentioned in the Ciceronian writings[5], but is not known to have been dealt with by any special law or to have been accompanied by an appropriate *poena*. Its treatment seems to have been confined to the particular laws establishing the *quaestiones*, and the procedure by which a conviction was enforced was the same as that in *calumnia*, the trial following the suspicious acquittal of the accused and being apparently

[1] Dig. 3, 2, 1 (p. 469, note 2).

[2] *Lex Iulia Municipalis*, l. 120 'quemve k(alumniae) praevaricationis caussa accussasse fecisseve quod iudicatum est erit.'

[3] Except in his own interest, see p. 459.

[4] *Lex Acilia*, l. 19 'in ious educito nomenque eius deferto sei deiuraverit calumniae causa non po[*stulare*'; Cic. *ad Fam.* viii. 8, 3; Asc. *in Cornelian.* p. 64. For the time at which this oath was taken see p. 459.

[5] Cic. *Part. Orat.* 36, 124 'praevaricationem . . . iudicii corruptelam ab reo': cf. *pro Cluent.* 32, 87; *Div. in Caec.* 18, 58. In *Phil.* ii. 11, 25 it is used in a transferred sense, and in *in Pis.* 10, 23 of an accepted fact of which there was no judicial proof.

heard by the same jury[1]. There is no known instance of judicial condemnation on such a charge[2], and the only consequence which we hear of as following conviction was *infamia* of various degrees. *Praevaricatio* takes its place by the side of *calumnia* in the praetor's edict and the *lex Iulia municipalis*[3]. In one case where the collusion of the prosecutor had been secured by the payment of money, an action for recovery lay against the *praevaricator*. By Caesar's law of extortion, the collusive accuser, who had been paid in stolen money by the accused, was held to have benefited by the spoils of the province and might be actioned under the clause *quo ea pecunia pervenerit*[4].

Tergiversatio.

Tergiversatio is hardly a separate offence in Ciceronian law[5]. The frequency with which prosecutions were dropped, after the postulation and even after the delation of the name[6], shows how little desistance from an accusation could have been regarded as a legal offence. Yet when such desistance was obviously due to suspicious motives, or when it took place without good grounds in the course of the trial, it was visited with ignominy[7], which could doubtless be expressed in the form of some kind of *infamia* and was probably the object of legal cognizance. As such

[1] The *lex Acilia* l. 75, although here very fragmentary, apparently provides for the trial by the same jury. For an acquittal on a charge of *praevaricatio* in 54 B. C. see Cic. *ad Q. fr.* ii. 16, 3 (p. 450, note 5).

[2] There is no proof that Clodius was ever tried for the offence, although Catiline's acquittal was held to be due to his collusion (Asc. *in Orat. in Tog. Cand.* p. 87 'Ita quidem iudicio est absolutus Catilina ut Clodius infamis fuerit praevaricatus esse'; cf. Cic. *in Pis.* 10, 23).

[3] See p. 469, note 2, p. 470, note 2; the *infamis* of Asc. *l. c.* probably refers merely to public opinion.

[4] Cic. *ad Fam.* viii. 8, 2 'quo vento proiicitur Appius minor ut indicaret pecunias ex bonis patris pervenisse ad Servilium praevaricationisque causa diceret depositum HS LXXXI.'

[5] *Tergiversari* is used in a general or metaphorical sense (*pro Flacco*, 20, 47; *pro Planc.* 19, 48).

[6] p. 467.

[7] Cic. *pro Cluent.* 31, 86 'nec sine ignominia calumniae relinquere accusationem.'

BOOK II.

it may have been assimilated to *praevaricatio* both in conception and in procedure.

Methods of the accused. Appeal to the feelings of the *iudices*.

If the prosecutor performs his duty and the accusation is pressed, the *reus* is thrown back on the somewhat primitive methods of working on the feelings of his judges which ever prevailed at Rome. He assumes the garb of mourning and the squalid disarray of grief[1]. This, it is true, is no part of the procedure, but its permission is remarkable as a sign of the recognition of the fact that emotion should enter into the verdict and that unreasoning pity is no irrelevant element in the working of justice. The sentiment finds a similar but more matured expression in the tone of the oratory of the Ciceronian period, whose function was not merely to prove, but to charm and bend[2]. The *iudices* in a *quaestio* could not escape from the trammels of the special law which they were interpreting, but they were true interpreters, not slaves of its letter, and an orator might, without awakening surprise, attempt to widen the horizon of their interpretation by treating the law as a mere imperfect support for that justice which is to be sought by an immediate conviction, based to a large extent on considerations which the law itself has purposely ignored[3].

[1] It is recorded of Rutilius Rufus (p. 436) that 'nec obsoletam vestem induit nec insignia senatoris deposuit nec supplices ad genua iudicum manus tetendit' (Val. Max. vi. 4, 4). On the change of clothing by the friends of the accused see App. *B. C.* ii. 24. Milo in 52 B. C. refused to submit to methods which he thought degrading, and this refusal was thought to have contributed to no slight extent to his condemnation (Plut. *Cic.* 35).

[2] Cic. *Orat.* 21, 69 'Erit igitur eloquens . . . is qui in foro causisque civilibus ita dicet ut probet, ut delectet, ut flectat. Probare necessitatis est, delectare suavitatis, flectere victoriae.' For instances of attempts *flectere* by an appeal to irrelevant considerations see Cic. *pro Planc.* 12, 29; 42, 104; *in Verr.* i. 58, 151–153; *pro Font.* 17 [21], 46–49; *pro Mur.* 41, 88; *pro Sulla*, 31, 88–89; *pro Flacco*, 42, 106.

[3] Cic. *pro Flacco*, 39, 98 'Semper graves et sapientes iudices in rebus iudicandis quid utilitas civitatis, quid communis salus, quid reipublicae tempora poscerent cogitaverunt'; *de Inv.* i. 38, 68 'Nemo enim leges legum causa salvas esse vult sed rei publicae, quod ex legibus omnes

BOOK II.

After the expiry of the time fixed by the president for the appearance of the parties, the procedure before the *iudices* began. The parties and the jurors were cited by the herald to appear[1], and the presence of the latter might be enforced by the *coercitio* of the president[2], or, if the latter was merely a *iudex* drawn by lot from the jury, probably of the magistrate who had conducted the preliminaries of the case. The objection to the trial of an absentee, which seems to have prevailed at the earlier stage of the *nominis delatio*[3], appears to find no place at this stage of the procedure. Whether the non-appearance of the accused be due to voluntary exile or to contumacy, the case goes on to its legitimate end. Milo and many others convicted in 52 B.C. were condemned in absence[4], and in the court established for the trial of Caesar's murderers in 43 B.C. we read of the voting of the *iudices*[5]. That this was the usual procedure in the standing courts we learn from the change subsequently introduced by Augustus, who enacted that in undefended prosecutions the voting should be open and the condemnation unanimous[6]. The proceedings in such cases were probably very summary. When the prosecutor had stated the case and exhibited a certain amount of evidence, the *iudices*, on finding that there was no defence, would have given their verdict immediately; but the fact of their voting at all shows that the fixed penalty enjoined by the law was imposed, and that mere interdiction of the

The procedure before the *iudices*. Citation to appear.

Trial of an absent *reus*.

rempublicam optime putant administrari ... (69) Ergo in hoc quoque iudicio desinite literas legis perscrutari et legem, ut aequum est, ex utilitate reipublicae considerate.'

[1] Cic. *pro Cluent.* 17, 49; 18, 50; Asc. *in Cornelian.* p. 59; in provincial jurisdiction, Cic. *in Verr.* ii. 40, 98. It is to this *citatio* probably, and not to the order to be present by a certain date, that Cicero refers in *pro Cluent.* 58, 159 ('Est enim sapientis iudicis . . . animadvertere qua lege reus citetur').

[2] Cic. *Phil.* v. 5, 14. On the probability of the case being conducted in the absence of some of the *iudices* see p. 447, note 3.

[3] p. 462.

[4] Asc. *in Milon.* pp. 54 and 55.

[5] Plut. *Brut.* 27; App. *B. C.* iii. 95; Dio Cass. xlvi. 48.

[6] Dio Cass. liv. 3.

BOOK II.

absentee was not resorted to. It is, however, possible that, in accordance with the earlier principles of criminal procedure, the exile who had sought the *civitas* of another town and had thus ceased to belong to Rome could be interdicted without the formality of condemnation.

Excusable absence followed by adjournment.

Excusable absence entailed the adjournment of the case. Its chief grounds were those which were operative at the *nominis delatio* [1], the tenure of a magistracy or *absentia rei publicae causa*. The necessity of appearing on the same day before another court was also accepted as a reason [2]. Illness, too, was a valid excuse, but one so abused that the *lex Tullia de ambitu* of 63 B. C. seems not to have admitted it or to have allowed it only under severe conditions [3].

Empanelling and swearing of the *iudices*.

The construction of the bench of *iudices* then followed in the manner which we have described [4] and the jurors were sworn [5], those who sat for the *praeiudicium* of the *divinatio* being the only exceptions to this rule [6]. It might happen that the constitution of the jury took so long a time that an adjournment was necessary before the case began. Thus several days elapsed between the formation of the panel which tried Verres and the pleading of Cicero [7].

The main procedure. The *patronus*.

With the commencement of the main procedure the *patronus* steps to the front. He is, as in civil process, distinct from the *advocatus* [8]. The latter is an adviser, but the patron is a pleader. As a rule representation

[1] p. 461.

[2] Asc. *in Milon.* p. 40, see p. 393.

[3] Cic. *pro Mur.* 23, 47 'Morbi excusationi poena addita est.' Mommsen (*Strafr.* p. 883) takes this clause as referring to the *iudices*; but Cicero, when he says (*l. c.*) 'incommodo morbi etiam ceterae vitae fructus relinquendi,' can hardly have been speaking of a fine. It is not certain that this rule did find its way into the *lex Tullia.* Cicero is speaking of the severe proposals that preceded the law.

[4] pp. 438, 451–456.

[5] Cic. *pro Rosc. Amer.* 3, 8; *in Verr.* Act. i. 10, 32; i. 4, 9; v. 8, 19; *pro Cluent.* 10, 29.

[6] p. 459, note 8.

[7] Cic. *in Verr.* Act. i. 6, 16 and 17.

[8] p. 148, and cf. Cic. *in Verr.* ii. 30, 74 and *pro Sulla,* 29, 81.

of this kind was not permitted to the prosecutor, who was obliged to conduct his case in person. But in certain trials, such as those for extortion where a community, or perhaps a whole nation, had to be represented, the *patronus* was himself the prosecutor and might be described indifferently as the *accusator* or as the agent (*actor, cognitor*) of the persons in whose interest he was bringing the charge [1]. If in ordinary cases the accuser required support, he gained it in the form of assistants to the prosecution (*subscriptores*), who were not *patroni* but *accusatores* [2] and were equally liable with their principal to be put on trial for *calumnia* [3]. The *subscriptores* were supposed to supplement the weaknesses of their chief accuser [4], whether in oratory or in knowledge of law; but they served other purposes as well. There was an idea that the subordinate accuser might be a guardian (*custos*) of the leading prosecutor [5], who might keep him to the path of duty and prevent his collusion or abandonment of the case. Certainly greater confidence was inspired by a prosecution supported by more than a single person, and it was considered unusual to enter on an accusation without a *subscriptor* [6]. Those who had been rejected in the *divinatio* as the chief accusers might

Subscriptores.

[1] For *actor* see Cic. *Div. in Caec.* 16, 54 'Nam provincia accusat, cum is agit causam quem sibi illa defensorem sui iuris, ultorem iniuriarum, actorem causae totius adoptavit'; cf. 4, 12; 5, 19; *in Verr.* Act. i. 1, 2; v. 70, 179. For *cognitor* see *Div. in Caec.* 4, 11 'Auxilium sibi per me a vobis atque a populi Romani legibus petunt . . . me cognitorem iuris sui, me actorem causae totius esse voluerunt.'

[2] Cic. *pro Mur.* 27, 56; *pro Planc.* 1, 3; *pro Cael.* 2, 3; 15, 35; *pro Mil.* 3, 7; Asc. *in Milon.* p. 42.

[3] e.g. the three accusers of Scaurus were put on their trial (Asc. *in Scaurian.* p. 30, see p. 469, note 3).

[4] Cic. *Div. in Caec.* 15, 47 'Esto; ipse nihil est, nihil potest; at venit paratus cum subscriptoribus exercitatis et disertis'; *pro Flacco*, 33, 82 'Invidisti ingenio subscriptoris tui. Quod ornabat facete locum quem prehenderat et acute testes interrogabat . . .'; cf. *ad Q. fr.* iii. 4, 1.

[5] Cic. *Div. in Caec.* 16, 50 'Custodem, inquit (Caecilius), Tullio me apponite.'

[6] Cic. *ad Fam.* viii. 8, 1 'Itaque sine ullo subscriptore descendit et Tuccium reum fecit.'

proffer a claim to be accepted in this subordinate post[1]—a claim, however, that might be rejected by the jury empanelled to try this *praeiudicium*[2]. The prosecutor was supported sometimes by one[3], sometimes by two[4], at others by (what was apparently the maximum) three *subscriptores*[5].

Number of the *patroni*.

The accused might have many *patroni*, and the antique custom of employing but one had almost died out at the time when Cicero was a leader at the bar[6]. Custom limited the number to four, but before the close of Cicero's life twelve might have been seen in a single case[7]. They were all on a nominal equality, but doubtless one was considered the leader. The duration of counsel's speeches had been limited long before this restriction was adopted by Pompeius in 52 B.C.[8] The limitations were imposed by the special laws of the *quaestiones*[9], and their character is illustrated by the municipal regulations of Urso which give the chief accuser four hours, the *subscriptor* two, but

Duration of the speeches.

[1] Cic. *Div. in Caec.* 16, 50.

[2] Cic. *in Verr.* i. 6, 15 'Quod meum factum lectissimi viri atque ornatissimi (quo in numero e vobis complures fuere) ita probarunt ut ei . . . non modo deferendi nominis sed ne subscribendi quidem, cum id postularet, facerent potestatem.'

[3] In the trials of Cornelius (Asc. *in Cornelian.* p. 59), Fonteius (Cic. *pro Font.* 12 [16], 36) and Flaccus (Cic. *pro Flacco*, 33, 82).

[4] In the trials of Gabinius (Cic. *ad Q. fr.* iii. 3, 2), Milo and Saufeius (Asc. *in Milon.* pp. 42 and 54), and P. Clodius (Val. Max. iv. 2, 5).

[5] In the trials of Scaurus (Asc. *in Scaurian.* p. 19), Murena (*pro Mur.* 27, 56), and Caelius (*pro Cael.* 11, 25-27). Three was also the number of the would-be accusers of Verres (Cic. *Div. in Caec.* 15, 47 and 48).

[6] Cic. *pro Cluent.* 70, 199 'totam hanc causam vetere instituto solus peroravi.'

[7] Asc. *in Scaurian.* p. 20. For this passage and the temporary limitation in the number of *patroni* introduced by Pompeius see p. 392.

[8] p. 392. For limitations existing in 70 and 59 B.C. see Cic. *in Verr.* Act. i. 11, 32 'Si utar ad dicendum meo legitimo tempore'; i. 9, 25 'Hic tu fortasse eris diligens ne quam ego horam de meis legitimis horis remittam'; *pro Flacco*, 33, 82 'ut duceret iudicium? cui sex horas omnino lex dedit.'

[9] In *pro Flacco*, *l. c.* the *lex* is doubtless the *Iulia repetundarum*, under which the trial was held.

permit each accuser to transfer some of his allotted time to the other. The accused is, under this municipal act, to have twice the time granted to the prosecution[1]. It is probable that the limit, as in Attic law, did not include the time occupied by the reading of documents or written evidence[2]. The close of the pleadings was marked by the herald's announcement *dixerunt*[3].

Order of the speeches. Evidence taken after their close.

In the procedure of the *quaestio* the evidence was taken after the pleadings[4], a peculiarity illustrated by Cicero's frequent references to evidence that will be adduced[5]. The case was opened by the prosecutor and answered by the counsel of the accused in set speeches (*perpetuae orationes*[6]), in which a judicious selection of the facts are given; the merits of the yet unuttered testimony are dwelt on, and the broad issues of the case are developed or combated. Then the oral testimony was appealed to. When the evidence of witnesses is treated in Cicero's speeches as a thing of the past[7], which he can now

[1] 'totidem horas et alterum tantum' (*Lex Ursonensis*, c. 102). For the limitation in comitial trials see p. 356.

[2] Geib, p. 326.

[3] Cic. *in Verr.* ii. 30, 75; Quint. *Inst. Orat.* i. 5, 43.

[4] Cic. *in Verr.* Act. i. 18, 55 'cum omnia dicta sunt, testes dantur'; cf. Quint. *Inst. Orat.* v. 7, 25.

[5] Cic. *pro Rosc. Amer.* 29, 82 'Si quid est quod ad testes reservet, ibi quoque nos, ut in ipsa causa, paratiores reperiet quam putabat'; 30, 84 'de Capitone post viderimus si, quem ad modum paratum esse audio, testis prodierit'; 36, 102 'alter . . . testimonium etiam in Sex. Roscium dicturus est'; *pro Cluent.* 6, 18 'Omnis testium copia quae futura est'; *pro Cael.* 8, 19 'Aiebant enim fore testem senatorem . . . A quo quaeram, si prodierit . . .'; 8, 20 'est enim dictum ab illis fore qui dicerent . . .'; 28, 66 'Quos quidem ego, iudices, testes non modo sine ullo timore, sed etiam cum aliqua spe delectationis exspecto.'

[6] Cic. *in Verr.* Act. i. 18, 55.

[7] Cic. *pro Font.* 9 [13], 29; *pro Flacco*, 5, 12; 15, 34; 17, 39; 19, 43; *in Verr.* v. 11, 27; *pro Scauro*, 10, 21 'est enim unum maximum totius Sardiniae frumentarium crimen de quo Triarius omnes Sardos interrogavit.' The difficulty in this case of Scaurus is that Triarius the prosecutor had, in the first *actio*, questioned only one witness (*pro Scauro*, 13, 29). Hence, with reference to the Sardinian evidence, Mommsen would prefer 'interrogabit.' 'Interrogavit,' he suggests, might refer to Triarius' preparations for the prosecution; cf. *pro Mur.* 24, 49, where preparations for

BOOK II. examine in detail, these speeches are all 'second pleadings' (*actiones secundae*) delivered after an adjournment, and the evidence taken after the first *actio* is here reviewed. These were the circumstances under which he spoke for Fonteius, for Flaccus, and for Scaurus[1]. Sometimes, however, even when there had been an adjournment (*comperendinatio*) it was thought advisable to keep some of the evidence for the end of the second *actio*[2].

Cicero's conduct of the case against Verres marks no exception to these general rules. In the first *actio*, which he meant to be decisive, the evidence was taken after the pleadings; the only change which he introduced was to make the first accusation shorter than usual. His first speech was little more than an enumeration of offences, and each point was to be immediately confirmed by the production of the appropriate witness. In his use of the *altercatio*, which, as we shall see, followed the testimony, he seems to have dwelt more than was usually the case on the evidence which had just been delivered[3]. Triarius,

evidence are mentioned. An apparent exception to the place of the evidence is found in Asc. *in Cornelian.* p. 60 ('Non poterat negare id factum esse ⟨Cicero⟩'). But here the fact on which evidence was to be given was the very basis of the charge. Hence it might have been admitted by the defendant's *patronus* before the witnesses had been questioned. On these cases see Mommsen in *Zeitschrift f. Alt. Wiss.* 1844, p. 457 ff.

[1] Cic. *pro Font.* 12 [16], 37 'Iam enim mihi videor hoc, prope causa duabus actionibus perorata, debere dicere'; 13 [17], 40 'M. Fonteius ita duabus actionibus accusatus est'; *pro Flacco*, 10, 21 'Nam antea, cum dixerat accusator acriter et vehementer cumque defensor suppliciter demisseque responderat'; *pro Scauro*, 13, 29 'primam actionem confecisti'; 14, 30 'priorem actionem totam sustulisti.'

[2] Cicero (*in Verr.* ii. 72, 177) exhibits the possibility of this. Although thisi s professedly the second action, he says, 'Producam testes'; cf. *ib.* 33, 80. The change introduced by Pompeius in 52 B.C. with respect to the position of the evidence in the trial (p. 392) was not permanent; see Quint. *Inst. Orat.* v. 7, 25.

[3] Cic. *in Verr.* Act. i. 18, 55 'Faciam hoc non novum ... ut testibus utar statim: illud a me novum, iudices, cognoscetis quod ita testes constituam ut crimen totum explicem; ubi id interrogando, argumentis atque oratione (i. e. presumably in the *altercatio*) firmavero, tum testes ad crimen accommodem.'

in his first *actio* against Scaurus, seems to have adopted a policy the very converse of Cicero's, for he appears to have shortened the hearing of the evidence considerably[1].

Close of the evidence. Reply of prosecutor. Rejoinder of accused. *Altercatio.*

The close of the evidence was followed by a reply on the part of the prosecutor and a rejoinder on that of the defendant[2]. These were not made in the form of set speeches, but in brief questions and answers by the respective *patroni* (*altercatio*). This skill in fence might make the reputation of a mediocre orator[3]. It required readiness, wit, good temper—qualities not always found in the great pleaders who, at a later date, content with the great demonstration of a set speech, were too often apt to leave the altercation to junior counsel[4]. Cicero possessed the full panoply of the perfect orator[5] and was specially renowned for his power of brisk repartee in this most trying branch of the conduct of a case[6].

Evidence.

If we turn now to evidence, we find that Cicero's definition of it as 'conviction based on externals'[7] necessarily includes confession whether voluntary or enforced.

Confession.

The Romans were not ignorant of the fact that confession was not proof; but they considered it such excellent evidence[8] that, where torture could be employed to elicit it from the accused, this device was adopted.

Torture applied to slaves.

This form of inquisition could not legally be used against free men, but was permitted for the discovery of offences supposed to have been committed by slaves. Even here it was not

[1] Cic. *pro Scauro*, 13, 29 'Tu vero comperendinasti uno teste producto.'

[2] Geib, p. 326 would place the *altercatio* after the pleadings and before the evidence. There is nothing to determine its position but probability and the 'argumentis atque oratione' of Cicero in p. 478, note 3. Quintilian says only 'est usus eius ordine ultimus' (*Inst. Orat.* vi. 4, 1).

[3] Quint. *l. c.* § 5 'nec immerito quidam quamquam in dicendo mediocres hac tamen altercandi praestantia meruerunt nomen patronorum.'

[4] Quint. *l. c.* § 6.

[5] Quint. *l. c.* § 3 'neque perfectus orator sine hac virtute dici potest.'

[6] Quint. *Inst. Orat.* vi. 3, 4.

[7] Cic. *Top.* 19, 73 'Testimonium autem nunc dicimus omne quod ab aliqua re externa sumitur ad faciendam fidem.'

[8] Cf. p. 464, note 5.

the whole of the evidence, for a negation persisted in by a slave under torture did not always save him from the cross[1]. It was probably not employed when the rest of the evidence was clear, but was regarded merely as a supplementary means of eliciting the truth, in spite of the fact that experience had often proved its valuelessness.

Method of this inquisition.

When the offence with which the slave was charged affected the state or individuals other than his owners, the torture was applied under official authority. When the offence touched the owner, the torture might be applied by him; but the *consilium* of relatives and friends should be present, and when slaves out of the power of the investigator are asked for and surrendered, the *advocati* of their master assist in the investigation. In the gruesome picture which Cicero gives of the *quaestio* undertaken by Sassia[2] a dual *consilium* supervised the process, for one of the victims belonged to the young Oppianicus, the others to herself. This council was a check on the extravagance of torture, for, when it was convinced that the eliciting of the truth could no longer be the object of the *quaestio*, it advised the cessation of the inquiry.

Tabellae quaestionis.

In such cases of domestic investigation a record of the evidence (*tabellae quaestionis*) was drawn up and attested by signatories (*obsignatores*) for the benefit of a future court of law[3]. We must assume a similar record in cases where suspected slaves had been examined by public authorities.

Torture of a whole *familia* on the murder of its master.

As a rule the inquisition was directed only against certain slaves accused of participation in a crime; but there was one occasion on which the whole *familia* of a household fell under suspicion. This was the murder of its master. The wholesale torture that followed such an event, like the universal execution of the servile members

[1] Val. Max. viii. 4, 2.

[2] Cic. *pro Cluent.* 63, 176 and 177; cf. 65, 182.

[3] *ib.* 75, 184 'Nam tabellae quaestionis plures proferuntur, quae recitatae vobisque editae sunt, illae ipsae quas tum obsignatas esse dixit'; for the *obsignator* see 66, 185; 66, 186.

of the household which we have already considered[1], was based on the idea that it was the slaves' duty to protect their lord and that it could only be through their neglect or cognizance that he had met his death. Of the two cruel regulations the first was more merciful than the second, for the inquisition might fix the guilt on a definite person and free the rest. Such a *quaestio* was regarded as the inalienable right of the head of the household who was avenging his father's murder[2].

Evidence of free witnesses. The oath.

If we turn from the confession of presumed principals and accomplices to the evidence of independent witnesses, we find again that this could not be assisted by torture in the case of free men. The rule embraced *libertini*, even when their sudden manumission aroused suspicion or had obviously been effected *in fraudem legis*[3]. The only compulsion on free witnesses was the oath[4], which, however, did not lead to an assertion of knowledge, but only of belief, expressed in the scrupulous formula 'I think' (*arbitror*)[5].

Rules of evidence.

There are few rules of evidence observable which can be considered absolutely binding, for such principles can hardly grow up in an eminently popular judicature. But it was a commonplace of the orators that the uncorroborated testimony of one witness should not be sufficient to secure

[1] p. 372.

[2] Cic. *pro Rosc. Amer.* 28, 77 'quod in tali crimine quod innocentibus saluti solet esse, ut servos in quaestionem polliceantur, id Sex. Roscio facere non licet . . . ii servi ubi sunt? Chrysogonum, iudices, sectantur . . . (78) Omnia, iudices, in hac causa sunt misera atque indigna: tamen hoc nihil neque acerbius neque iniquius proferri potest. Mortis paternae de servis paternis quaestionem habere filio non licet.' Compare the account of the investigation which followed the death of Scipio Aemilianus (App. *B. C.* i. 20 εἰσὶ δ' οἳ βασανιζομένους φασὶ θεράποντας εἰπεῖν κ.τ.λ.).

[3] Cic. *pro Cael.* 29, 68; *pro Mil.* 21, 57; cf. Asc. *in Milon.* pp. 30 and 40; see p. 492, note 2.

[4] Cic. *in Verr.* Act. i. 10, 32; ii. 33, 80; v. 11, 27; *pro Font.* 7 [11], 24; 9 [13], 29; 10 [14], 32; *pro Flacco*, 5, 12; *pro Cael.* 2, 4; 8, 20; 22, 54 and 55. The appeals in these passages are to *iusiurandum* and *religio*; the witnesses are spoken of as *iurati*.

[5] Cic. *pro Font.* 9 [13], 29; *Acad. prior.* ii. 47, 146; cf. p. 274.

BOOK II.

a conviction[1]. Other obvious commonplaces were the appeals to the life[2], position[3], wealth[4] of the witness as grounds of his credibility. His personal interest in the issue of the case might be pointed to as vitiating his testimony[5], and his demeanour before the court[6] was of course dwelt on as a sign of the trustworthiness of his statements. This last test led to far greater importance being attached to personal than to written evidence[7]. Second-hand evidence (that of *testes de auditu*) was admitted, but was impugned as of far less value than testimony as to impressions which had been derived directly through the senses[8].

Capacity for giving evidence.

The regulations as to who might or should give evidence cannot be perfectly illustrated for the Ciceronian period, and it would be rash to attribute to this epoch all the rules of the later Roman law. Women, although incapable of bearing testimony to a mancipation, were even now

[1] Plutarch (*Cato Min.* 19) says that in a case, when the prosecution had furnished but a single witness, the counsel for the defence told the jury *ὡς ἑνὶ μαρτυροῦντι προσέχειν οὐδὲ Κάτωνι καλῶς ἔχει.*

[2] Cic. *pro Flacco*, 15, 34 (Asclepiades 'damnatus turpissimis iudiciis domi, notatus literis publicis'); 18, 43 (Nicomedes 'et furti et pro socio damnatus est'). In discrediting a witness especial stress was laid on proof of former perjury (Cic. *pro Rab. Post.* 13, 36 'ubi semel quis peieraverit, ei credi postea, etiamsi per plures deos iuret, non oportet').

[3] Cic. *pro Flacco*, 18, 42 (of Heracleides of Temnos) 'Temni usque ad illam aetatem in senatum venire non potuit'; 22, 52 'Trallianos Maeandrio causam commisisse, homini egenti, sordido, sine honore, sine existimatione, sine censu.'

[4] Cic. *Top.* 19, 73; *pro Flacco*, 3, 6; 22, 52 and 53.

[5] Cic. *pro Font.* 7 [11], 23 and 24; 8 [12], 27. The theory of a conspiracy of the witnesses might be suggested, as of the Sardi in the case against Scaurus (Cic. *pro Scauro*, 17, 38; cf. Quint. *Inst. Or.* v. 7, 23). A barrister defending a case of extortion might impugn the credibility of provincial witnesses for the prosecution on the ground of their interest in the issue (Quint. *Inst. Or.* v. 7, 5 'ut in causis repetundarum, qui se reo numerasse pecunias iurant litigatorum non testium habendos loco').

[6] Cic. *pro Flacco*, 4, 10. A general summary of the grounds of credibility is given in *Part. Orat.* 14, 48; it may be refused to witnesses 'si natura vani, si leves, si cum ignominia, si spe, si metu, si iracundia, si misericordia impulsi, si praemio, si gratia adducti.'

[7] Quint. *Inst. Or.* v. 7, 1.

[8] Cic. *pro Planc.* 23, 57 'illa vox vulgaris *audivi* ne quid innocenti reo noceat oramus'; cf. § 56 and Quint. *Inst. Or.* v. 7, 5.

perfectly good witnesses in a criminal court[1]. Minors could give evidence under the *lex Cornelia repetundarum*[2], although their testimony was probably prohibited by other laws. Some of the later prohibitions may with certainty be pronounced to be already in vogue. Close family relationships—those, at least, of ascendants to descendants—rendered evidence invalid, and freedmen were not allowed to incriminate their patrons[3]. The only prohibition connected with *infamia*, which we know to have been growing up during this period, refers to condemnation in certain criminal courts. A man condemned under the *lex Iulia repetundarum* wholly lost the power of testimony in a *iudicium publicum*[4], and any one condemned in a criminal court lost the right of giving evidence in a case falling under the *lex Iulia de vi*[5]. This latter provision may have applied to certain other courts, but we cannot say how far the disqualification from evidence of the *damnatus* extended in the Ciceronian period. Different laws establishing *quaestiones* may also have contained a list of persons disqualified *propter notam et infamiam vitae* such as was found in the *lex Iulia de vi*[6], for the category is thoroughly republican, and might quite as well have been found in laws of the Ciceronian as in those of the imperial period.

[1] Cic. *in Verr.* i. 37, 93 'Malleolus a me productus est et mater eius atque avia'; cf. § 94. In the trial of Milo (52 B.C.) the *virgines Albanae* gave evidence. Fulvia, the wife of Clodius, and Sempronia his mother-in-law, were also witnesses (Asc. *in Milon.* p. 41).

[2] Cic. *in Verr.* ii. 33, 80 'dicet etiam praetextatus Sopatri filius.' The evidence of *impuberes* was excluded in cases coming under the *lex Iulia de vi* (Dig. 22, 5, 3, 5). This law may have been the work of Augustus, not of Caesar; but we can hardly conceive the former as introducing a wholly new principle of evidence.

[3] Paul. *Sent.* v. 15, 3 'adversus se invicem parentes et liberi, itemque (*patroni et*) liberti nec volentes ad testimonium admittendi sunt: quia rei verae testimonium necessitudo personarum plerumque corrumpit.'

[4] Dig. 48, 11, 6, 1; cf. 22, 5, 15.

[5] Dig. 22, 5, 3, 5.

[6] Dig. *l. c.* 'quive in vinculis custodiave publica erit, quive ad bestias ut depugnaret se locaverit, quaeve palam quaestum faciet feceritve, quive ob testimonium dicendum vel non dicendum pecuniam accepisse iudicatus vel convictus erit'; cf. Collatio, ix. 2, 2.

BOOK II.

An isolated disqualification from evidence is that of the *patronus* of the accused; he might not give testimony in the case which he was conducting [1].

Cases in which evidence could not be compelled.

There was, further, a class of people who could not be made to give evidence against their will (*inviti*). According to the *lex Iulia de vi*, and, therefore, probably according to Ciceronian law, near *cognati* and *affines* of the accused were in this category [2]. The relationship of client and patron, in the loose form in which it prevailed in Cicero's time, was also a bar to compulsory testimony. It is doubtful whether the *lex Acilia repetundarum* [3] (122 B.C.) means to make the prohibition absolute or not; somewhat later (116 B.C.), and in connexion with a different *quaestio*, it appears in the form that such evidence could not be enforced [4]. It is possible that the exemption of the *publicani* from compulsory evidence [5] existed in Cicero's day, since even at this time their position was so far privileged that their books could not be sealed and taken into court [6]. Testimony against accomplices (*indicium dare*) was perhaps permitted in the *iudicia publica*, but under certain reservations which were doubtless determined by the special laws of the *quaestiones* [7].

[1] Cic. *in Verr.* ii. 8, 24 (of Hortensius) 'Nonne te mihi testem in hoc crimine eripuit non istius innocentia sed legis exceptio.' In the *lex Acilia* only one *patronus* is exempted from evidence (l. 33 '*queive* . . . causam deicet dum taxat unum').

[2] Collatio, ix. 2, 3 'Hi homines inviti in reum testimonium ne dicunto; qui sobrinus est ei reo propiorve cognatione coniunctus quive socer, gener, vitricus privignusve eius erit.'

[3] l. 33.

[4] C. Herennius, called as a witness against Marius, when tried for *ambitus* in 116 B.C. *οὐκ ἔφη πάτριον εἶναι καταμαρτυρεῖν πελατῶν ἀλλὰ τὸν νόμον ἀφιέναι ταύτης τῆς ἀνάγκης τοὺς πάτρωνας* (Plut. *Mar.* 5).

[5] 'inviti testimonium non dicunt publicani' (Dig. 22, 5, 19); see Mommsen in *Zeitschr. f. Alt. Wiss.* l. c.

[6] Cic. *in Verr.* ii. 76, 187. See p. 494, note 9.

[7] Cic. *Div. in Caec.* 11, 34 (of Caecilius' complicity with Verres) 'Quapropter si tibi indicium postulas dari, quod tecum una feceris, concedo, si id lege permittitur.' The grant of the *fides publica* in jurisdiction by martial law was made by the senate (Sall. *Cat.* 47; Cic. *pro Rab.* 10, 28

BOOK II.

Evidence for the prosecution obligatory, for the defence voluntary.

There was a striking difference between the evidence for the prosecution and that for the defence. The former was alone obligatory, the latter was purely voluntary[1]. The accuser's compulsory evidence was gained by a formal announcement to the parties concerned, which contained a demand for their testimony. This *denuntiatio*[2] was made by the leading prosecutor himself through a mandate got from the magistrate who was carrying out the rules of the law regulating the particular *quaestio*. The law entered into details with respect to the prosecutor's mandate, and the *lex Iulia repetundarum* fixed the number of *comites* who might accompany him in his search for evidence[3]. The enforcement of the legal rules by the president of the *quaestio* was sufficient for Italy. In the province the *coercitio* came from the provincial governor[4], and it was a nice question how far the compulsion was enforceable by local or by Roman law. The two might differ on such a question as the production of documents, and Cicero had to employ all the terrors of the law to beat down the opposition of a Syracusan official who said that 'Roman enactments were nothing to him[5].' A pro-

'Ac, si fides Saturnino data est . . . C. Marius dedit . . . Quae fides, Labiene, qui potuit sine senatus consulto dari?'), and it seems as though the senate could grant it in any matter touching the public safety (Cic. *ad Att.* ii. 24, 2; cf. Liv. xxxix. 19).

[1] Quint. *Inst. Or.* v. 7, 9 'duo genera sunt testium, aut voluntariorum aut eorum quibus in iudiciis publicis lege denuntiatur, quorum altero pars utraque utitur, alterum accusatoribus tantum concessum est.'

[2] 'denuntiare' (Cic. *pro Flacco*, 15, 35); 'testimonium denuntiare' [(Cic. *pro Rosc. Amer.* 38, 110 'si accusator voluerit testimonium eis denuntiare'); *in Verr.* i. 19, 51; ii. 27, 65 ('quibus ego testimonium denuntiavi, quorum edidi nomina Metello'); *pro Flacco*, 6, 14] 'denuntiare testibus' (Cic. *in Verr.* ii. 4, 12).

[3] Cic. *pro Flacco*, 6, 13 'lege hac recenti ac nova (Iulia repetundarum) certus est inquisitioni comitum numerus constitutus.'

[4] Cic. *in Verr.* ii. 27, 65, see note 2.

[5] *ib.* iv. 66, 149 (The object was to get a copy of a decree of the Syracusan senate; the attempt was resisted by a certain Theomnastus, probably some kind of recorder; the case was heard before Metellus) 'ego legem recitare omnium mihi tabularum et literarum fieri potestatem oportere. Ille (Theomnastus) furiosus urgere nihil ad se nostras leges pertinere.'

BOOK II.

vincial governor friendly to the accused might be a great stumbling-block to the prosecutor. He was sometimes unwilling to enforce the obligation to testimony, and the recommendations of the president and the mandate of the law were sometimes of more avail than his feeble activity[1].

Number of compulsory witnesses.

The number of compulsory witnesses was, however, limited. In the trial of M. Aemilius Scaurus (54 B.C.) the law (in this case the *lex Iulia repetundarum*) fixed the maximum at 120[2], and the number doubtless differed in different enactments. But it is not likely that a limit was ever fixed to the number of voluntary witnesses[3]. The motive for the limitation was to prevent a 'superfluous multitude' of individuals being burdened with the necessity of appearing[4], but perhaps it had also the object of keeping the procedure of the court within reasonable limits. A practical limitation may sometimes have been supplied by the fact that the cost of the maintenance of witnesses seems to have fallen on the party who had summoned them[5].

[1] Cic. *in Verr.* ii. 26, 64 (of Metellus' conduct) 'a civitatibus laudationes petere, testes non solum deterrere verbis sed etiam vi retinere coepit. Quod nisi ego meo adventu illius conatus aliquantum repressissem et apud Siculos non Metelli sed Glabrionis literis ac lege pugnassem, tam multos testes huc evocare non potuissem.' Glabrio was praetor and guide of the proceedings against Verres; the law was the *lex Cornelia repetundarum* which he was administering.

[2] Val. Max. viii. 1, 10 'cum accusator diceret lege sibi centum atque xx hominibus denuntiare testimonium licere.'

[3] Dig. 22, 5, 1, 2 'Quamquam quibusdam legibus amplissimus numerus testium definitus sit, tamen ex constitutionibus principum haec licentia ad sufficientem numerum testium coartatur, ut iudices moderentur et eum solum numerum testium, quem necessarium esse putaverint, evocari patiantur.' For *evocare* in the sense of *denuntiare* see Cic. *in Verr.* ii. 26, 64; the reference throughout is probably to necessary witnesses; cf. Mommsen, *l. c.*

[4] Dig. *l. c.* 'ne effrenata potestate ad vexandos homines superflua multitudo testium protrahatur.'

[5] Cic. *pro. Flacco*, 6, 14 'adiunxit illa ut eos . . . qui domi stare non poterant, largo et liberali viatico commoveret'; cf. 17, 41 (of the death of a witness) 'edacem enim hospitem amisisti.' Cicero is speaking of the prosecutor, and the witnesses may, therefore, have been compulsory.

It is possible that, with respect to voluntary evidence, the president of the court may have had some discretion as to how much of it need be taken. He is known, at least, to have had some control over the length of the examination[1].

Examination of witnesses.

The obligatory witnesses necessarily appeared in court, as also did the voluntary ones who did not content themselves with sending written depositions. The examination was conducted by the parties, and there is no trace of questions having been put by the *quaesitor*, although, when we consider other indications of his taking an active part in the proceedings, it is not impossible to credit him with such a power[2]. The examination-in-chief was conducted by the party who had called the witness[3], and he then passed into the hands of the other party for cross-examination[4]. A summary of the evidence was committed to writing[5], primarily perhaps for use in other trials; but such a redaction might be valuable when the case did not come to an end in a single hearing, and where there was

[1] Cic. *de Orat.* ii. 60, 245 '"Licet," inquit "rogare?" Philippus. Tum quaesitor properans, "Modo breviter."' In Cicero (*de Fin.* ii. 19, 62) we find the following story 'A. Varius, qui est habitus iudex durior, dicere consessori solebat, cum, datis testibus, alii tamen citarentur, "Aut hoc testium satis est aut nescio quid satis sit."' But Varius seems to have been an ordinary *iudex*, not a *quaesitor* (Geib, p. 340).

[2] Geib, p. 340 and Mommsen (*Strafr.* p. 422) take the view that the *quaesitor* had no such power. Literature furnishes no evidence for or against it.

[3] Cic. *in Verr.* i. 11, 29; *pro Flacco*, 10, 22; Quint. *Inst. Or.* v. 7, 21.

[4] Cic. *in Verr.* Act. i. 18, 55; v. 59, 155; *pro Cael.* 8, 19; 28, 66; Asc. *in Milon.* p. 41. Both the examination and cross-examination were called *interrogatio*.

[5] Cicero used evidence in a former trial as a proof that a single issue had been before the court (*pro Cluent.* 23, 62 'numquid aliud in illis iudiciis versatum est? . . . nihil, nihil, inquam, aliud . . . exstat memoria . . . testium dicta recita'). So evidence taken in a provincial trial might be cited afterwards in a Roman court (Cic. *in Verr.* i. 31, 78 and 79; 33, 84). In the trials of 52 B.C. the redaction of the evidence was a necessity of the procedure; see p. 394, and cf. Asc. *in Milon.* p. 52 ('post audita et obsignata testium verba') and for the reading of the evidence, Cic. *pro Mil.* 17, 46 ('Legite testimonia testium vestrorum').

BOOK II.

either a renewed hearing (*ampliatio*) or an adjournment ordained by law (*comperendinatio*)[1].

Written evidence attested by *signatores*.

Written evidence (*testimonium per tabulas*) was a substitute for personal testimony and was always voluntary[2]. It proceeded either from compulsory witnesses who could not appear, and who, therefore, might have been excused by law, or from voluntary witnesses who were quite ready to give their testimony but were unwilling to take the trouble to appear. These depositions were strengthened by *signatores*[3]; but Quintilian must be wrong in saying that the attestation in writing takes the place of the oath in personal evidence[4], for it is inconceivable that the *signatores* could in every case guarantee the truth of the testimony, which the oath was supposed to do. In some cases they did, indeed, guarantee an extra-judicial fact of their own knowledge. In copies, for instance, of documents such as the account-books of the *publicani*, the *signatores* attest that the copy has the same tenor as the original[5]. But in many cases all that they could guarantee was that the deposition was the genuine statement of the deposer. This written evidence was read in court during the course of the speeches[6] and had not, like the personal testimony,

[1] For evidence quoted in second *actiones* see p. 477, and cf. Cic. *in Verr.* i. 37, 94; 49, 128.

[2] Quint. *Inst. Or.* v. 7, 2 'nemo per tabulas dat testimonium nisi sua voluntate.'

[3] *ib.* v. 7, 1.

[4] *ib.* v. 7, 32 'saepe inter se collidi solent inde testatio, hinc testes; haec enim se pars iureiurando, illa consensu signantium tuetur.'

[5] Cic. *in Verr.* ii. 77, 189 'tabulas in foro, summa hominum frequentia, exscribo: adhibentur in scribendo ex conventu viri primarii.' A similar attestation was gained by Verres with respect to the condition of the Sicilian fleet. He summoned the captains (*navarchi*) and got each to say that he had the full complement of men for his ship; then 'advocat amicos statim, quaerit ex his (*navarchis*) singillatim quot quisque nautas habuerit. Respondit unus quisque, ut erat praeceptum. Iste in tabulas refert: obsignat signis amicorum providens homo ut contra hoc crimen, si quando opus esset, hac videlicet testificatione uteretur' (*in Verr.* v. 39, 102).

[6] Cic. *pro Cael.* 22, 55 'Recita L. Lucceii testimonium'; the verbal

to be delayed until their close. A curious blending of personal and written evidence is presented by a passage in Cicero's speech for Cluentius. The testimony of an aged man about the death of his son is read in court during the speech for the defence [1], but the man who gives the evidence is himself in court and is asked to rise while the statement is being read [2]. The anomaly has been well explained as due to delicacy, regard being had to the feelings of a father who is testifying about the death of his own son [3].

Evidence of juristic persons; given through *legati*.

Individuals are not the only persons who can give evidence. *Res publicae* are juristic persons, and as such can furnish *testimonia publica*. To such bodies, however, the general principles of personal evidence would not apply. Resort was had to the method by which communities transacted international business. The states were represented by *legati*, who were given *mandata* by the proper organs of government. The information transmitted by these envoys to the court, as having been prepared *fide publica* in the community, was regarded as the evidence of the community itself (*testimonium publicum*) [4], and the verbal additions, which the *legati* made in accordance with their instructions, possessed the same weight [5]. Sometimes

testimony in this case was to be given after the *actio* (*pro Cael.* 8, 19) see p. 477.

[1] Although the verbal evidence, we know, was taken after the *actio* (Cic. *pro Cluent.* 6, 18 'omnis testium copia quae futura est'; see p. 477).

[2] Cic. *l. c.* 60, 168 'Quis huic rei testis est? Idem qui sui luctus, pater . . . is hunc suo testimonio sublevat. Quod recita. Tu autem, nisi molestum est, paullisper exsurge.'

[3] Mommsen in *Zeitschr. f. Alt. Wiss. l. c.* Geib (p. 344) explains it as a change of purpose. The witness had first deposed in writing; but afterwards (perhaps at the special request of the accused) had decided to appear personally. He would have been heard at the close of the proceedings, but his written evidence could be read during the speech for the defence.

[4] Cic. *in Verr.* iii. 31, 74; 36, 83; 37, 85; 38, 87; cf. 42, 99; 44, 106; *pro Flacco*, 17, 39; 22, 52.

[5] e. g. the evidence of Asclepiades, one of the *legati* of the Acmonenses, in the trial of Flaccus. He and his comrades had appeared for the

BOOK II. the envoys appeared with public written documents, sometimes only with instructions (*mandata*). The latter were carried out by merely verbal statements, which are found where the object of the testimony is merely evidence to character (*laudatio*). Procedure of this kind is discoverable in the trial of Cluentius [1]. The administrative bodies which framed the *testimonia publica* were of various kinds; sometimes the evidence was expressed in the ψήφισμα of a popular assembly [2], more usually it was embodied in the resolution of a local senate. There are some cases known where the senate framed its evidence on oath [3], which was regarded as a means of strengthening this kind of testimony, but not as a necessary formality. The *legati* themselves, when they added their own evidence to the written testimony, seem to have been sworn [4]. The public testimony, when on paper, might, like all other written evidence, be read during the speeches [5].

Laudationes. Testimonials to character (*laudationes*) are precisely on a level with ordinary evidence, differing from it only in purpose, not in character. Individual *laudatores* were sworn [6], and the testimonial was no doubt elicited by

accused, but his evidence turned out badly for Flaccus, and Cicero discredits it (*pro Flacco*, 15, 36). Asclepiades is here called 'auctor suae civitatis.' Two bodies of *legati* with sealed representations had appeared for the Acmonenses, one on the side of the accuser, the other on that of the accused. Cicero, to discredit the evidence of the former, throws over that of the latter (*ib.* 16, 37 and 38).

[1] Cic. *pro Cluent.* 69, 197 (*laudatio* of Cluentius by neighbouring communities) 'Age vero, vicinorum quantum studium . . . Non illi in libellis laudationum decreta miserunt, sed homines honestissimos, quos nossemus omnes, huc frequentes adesse et hunc praesentes laudare voluerunt.'

[2] Cic. *pro Flacco*, 7, 17.

[3] *Ib.* 'Ego testes a Sicilia publice deduxi. Verum erant ea testimonia non concitatae contionis sed iurati senatus'; cf. *pro Arch.* 4, 8 'Adsunt Heracleenses legati . . . huius iudicii causa cum mandatis et cum publico testimonio venerunt . . . cum habeas . . . integerrimi municipii ius iurandum fidemque.'

[4] Cic. *in Verr.* ii. 5, 13 (of a *legatio* of *laudatores* from the *civitas Mamertina*) 'eius autem legationis principem . . . iuratum dicere audistis; cf. *pro Font.* 10 [14], 32 'cum . . . M. Fonteium . . . iurati privatim et publice laudent.'

[5] Cic. *pro Cluent.* 69, 196.

[6] note 4.

a few questions. Such depositions were either public or private. The former—the recommendations of states or corporations[1]—were merely a part of the *testimonia publica* and were governed by the same rules. The latter were the statements of individuals either given personally or, in their absence, by writing[2]. Political reasons caused this kind of evidence to be given so lightly[3] that it was considered scarcely respectable to present one's self in court without ten of these witnesses to character[4]. To have no *laudator* at all might be a sign of strength; to have less than the customary number was a confession of weakness[5].

Evidence of slaves elicited under torture; limitations on the use of this evidence.

The evidence of slaves, even in matters in which they were not directly implicated, was elicited under torture. But there were very considerable limitations on the power of employing such testimony. The slave could not be examined on a matter which tended to incriminate his

[1] Cic. *pro Cluent.* 69, 197; *pro Flacco,* 15, 36; 26, 61; 40, 100; *pro Cael.* 2, 5; *pro Balbo,* 18, 41; *in Verr.* ii. 5, 13; 46, 113; iv. 7, 15; 63, 140; 64, 142; 67, 150; v. 22, 57; *pro Font.* 2 [6], 14; 16 [20], 45; *pro Sest.* 4, 10. In the last case the *laudatio* is, for greater effect, read not by the *scriba* but by the young P. Sestius.

[2] Personal *laudatio* (Cic. *ad Fam.* i. 9, 7, ['Cn. Pompeius] cum, ut laudaret P. Sestium, introisset in urbem') written (*ad Fam.* i. 9, 19); personal and written (Asc. *in Scaurian.* p. 28 'Laudaverunt Scaurum consulares novem . . . Horum magna pars per tabellas laudaverunt, quia aberant: inter quos Pompeius quoque; nam quod erat pro cos. extra urbem morabatur'). Cicero says (*ad Fam.* i. 9, 4; cf. § 19) 'Vatinium autem scire te velle ostendis quibus rebus adductus defenderim et laudarim.' He could hardly have been *defensor* and *laudator* in the same case, for the *laudator* is a witness (see p. 484); it is questionable whether *laudare* has its technical sense here.

[3] Cic. *ad Fam.* i. 9, 19 'Recordare enim quibus laudationem ex ultimis terris miseris.'

[4] Cic. *in Verr.* v. 22, 57 'in iudiciis qui decem laudatores dare non potest, honestius est ei nullum dare quam illum quasi legitimum numerum consuetudinis non explere.' Ten were furnished in the trial of Scaurus; besides the novem consulares (note 2) there was 'unus praeterea adulescens . . . frater eius, Faustus Cornelius Syllae filius' (Asc. *in Scaurian.* p. 28).

[5] For the temporary abolition of *laudationes* by Pompeius in 52 B.C. see p. 392.

BOOK II. master[1]; of the two exceptions to this rule, the case of incest was perpetually valid: that of conspiracy[2], since it is connected with the revolutionary senatorial proceedings of 63 B.C., is of very questionable legality. But even when the slaves of another person were tortured (as were those of Pompeia in the trial of Clodius)[3], it seems, if we may judge from the refusal of Chrysogonus in the case of Sex. Roscius, that this could only be done by the permission of their owner[4]. The two limitations are so great that it is impossible to conceive the evidence of slaves as having played any large part in the procedure of the *iudicia publica*.

Mode in which this evidence was taken. The torture was applied under the supervision of the *quaesitor* of the court[5], from whom permission for its use had always to be obtained[6]. But the investigation was not conducted under the eyes of the jury[7]; hence the depositions of the slaves must have been committed to writing and attested, as in the procedure of the inquisition[8]. This evidence was apparently elicited after the pleadings[9], and the depositions were probably read to the jury after the

[1] Cic. *pro Rosc. Amer.* 41, 120; *pro Deiot.* 1, 3.

[2] Cic. *pro Mil.* 22, 59 'De servis nulla lege quaestio est in dominum nisi de incestu, ut fuit in Clodium'; *Part. Orat.* 34, 118 '(nostri), cum in dominos de servis quaeri noluissent, tamen de incestu et coniuratione, quae facta me consule est, quaerendum putaverunt'; cf. *pro Sulla*, 28, 78 'Quaestiones nobis servorum accusator ac tormenta minitatur.' Nevertheless Milo in 52 B.C. thought it worth while to manumit his slaves and this act was used against him in the trial (Cic. *pro Mil.* 21, 57; 22, 58). This does not prove, however, that they might be tortured against him (see p. 394, note 1). He might have feared the result of an inquisition on the slaves who had committed the murder (see p. 479).

[3] p. 388.

[4] Cic. *pro Rosc. Amer.* 28, 77 and 78; 41, 119 and 120; 42, 122.

[5] Cic. *pro Sulla*, 28, 78 'tormenta gubernat dolor . . . regit quaesitor'; cf. *Auct. ad Herenn.* ii. 7, 10.

[6] Cic. *Part. Orat.* 34, 117 'Sin quaestiones habitae aut postulatio ut habeantur causam adiuvabunt'; Asc. *in Milon.* p. 40, see p. 393.

[7] Cic. *pro Mil.* 22, 59 'Sed quaestiones urgent Milonem quae sunt habitae nunc in atrio Libertatis.'

[8] Cic. *pro Cluent.* 65, 184; see p. 480.

[9] Hence 'minitatur' in Cic. *pro Sulla*, 28, 78; see note 2.

rest of the evidence had been given and (if there was no *comperendinatio*) just before the voting took place[1].

Documentary evidence.

Documentary evidence (*ex tabulis*) was as familiar as any other mode of proof[2]. As in civil procedure account-books (*codices, tabulae accepti et expensi*) play the largest part, and the conclusions which could be drawn from their being kept in an unsystematic fashion were as important in a criminal as in a private trial[3]. Their entire absence could, however, rouse no suspicion when the accused was under the *patria potestas*[4].

Important conclusions could be drawn from such account-books in cases of extortion, where it could be proved that objects had been acquired, but where no entry showed that they had been bought; or in charges of bribery, where an expenditure was said to have been made and yet no record of it was found. Cicero uses the first kind of argument against Verres with reference to the works of art which had come into his possession[5], he employs the second in defence of Cluentius to shield him from the charge of having corrupted a jury[6]. The alienation of the property of a ward[7], or the falsification of the official accounts of a magistracy[8], might also be suspected from

[1] In the trials of 52 B.C. the proceedings were reversed, hence 'sunt habitae' in Cic. *pro Mil.* 22, 59; see p. 492, note 7.

[2] Cic. *in Verr.* Act. i. 11, 33 'nunc hominem tabulis, testibus, privatis publicisque literis auctoritatibusque accusemus'; cf. Quint. *Inst. Or.* v. 2, 5 ('de tabulis').

[3] Cic. *in Verr.* i. 23, 60; cf. *ad Att.* xii. 5, 4.

[4] Cic. *pro Cael.* 7, 17 'Tabulas qui in patris potestate est nullas conficit.'

[5] Cic. *in Verr.* i. 23, 61 'Unum (signum) ostende in tabulis aut tuis aut patris tui emptum esse: vicisti'; iv. 16, 36 'tabulae nullum indicant emptum.'

[6] Cic. *pro Cluent.* 30, 82 'profectio ipsius pecuniae requiratur. Confecit tabulas diligentissime Cluentius. Haec autem res habet hoc certe ut nihil possit neque additum neque detractum de re familiari latere.'

[7] Cic. *in Verr.* i. 36, 92.

[8] *ib.* i. 38, 95 . . . 39, 102. These official accounts were strictly not separable from private accounts; the *rationes* were probably only copies from the general *codex*. For other investigations of *tabulae* connected with expenditure for criminal purposes see *pro Cluent.* 12, 34; 14, 40.

BOOK II.

the character of the private ledger. These documents, and others of various kinds, might be impounded through the law enforced at Rome and in the provinces[1]. Power was given to the prosecutor to demand them and to compel their delivery[2], and in case of refusal to produce them, a formal house-visitation was permitted, such as is described by Cicero in connexion with the domiciles of Verres[3], of Apronius[4] and of an ex-chairman of a company of *publicani*[5]. The documents, when found, were immediately sealed (doubtless in the presence of witnesses) to avoid all suspicion of forgery[6]. Within three days after the expiry of the time granted for the collection of the evidence, they must be in the custody of the president of the court; he immediately produced them, and had them sealed by the jurors to avoid all possibility of subsequent falsification[7]. At the time of trial these original documents were handed about amongst the jury for inspection[8].

Right of search.

Account-books of the *publicani*.

The semi-official position of the state middlemen caused an exception to be made in favour of their accounts (*tabulae publicanorum*). They need not produce originals[9], but were bound to furnish copies to the prosecutor. All

[1] p. 485.

[2] Cic. *in Verr.* i. 23, 60 (of Verres' account-books) 'cum ab eo tabulas postularemus'; cf. iv. 66, 149.

[3] *ib.* i. 19, 50 'quae signa sustulit! quae cognovi egomet apud istum in aedibus nuper, cum obsignandi gratia venissem.'

[4] *ib.* iii. 66, 154 'Haec epistola est . . . quam nos Syracusis in aedibus Apronii, cum literas conquireremus, invenimus.'

[5] *ib.* ii. 74, 182 'sane homini praeter opinionem improviso incidi. Scrutatus sum quae potui et quaesivi omnia . . . obsignavi statim.'

[6] *ib.* i. 19, 50 (note 3); ii. 74, 182 (note 5); iv. 63, 140 (of temple accounts at Syracuse, showing losses) 'quas ego literas obsignandas publico (i.e. state-Syracusan) signo deportandasque curavi'; i. 38, 98; iv. 66, 149.

[7] Cic. *pro Flacco*, 9, 20 'Triduo lex ad praetorem deferri, iudicum signis obsignari iubet . . . Ne corrumpi tabulae facile possint, idcirco lex obsignatas in publico poni voluit.'

[8] In Cic. *pro Balbo*, 5, 11 we have the story of the *iudices* refusing to look at the accounts of Q. Metellus Numidicus 'cum ipsius tabulae circumferrentur inspiciendi nominis causa'; cf. *ad Att.* i. 16, 4; Val. Max. ii. 10, 1.

[9] Cic. *in Verr.* ii. 76, 187 'Quod lege excipiuntur tabulae publicanorum quo minus Romam deportentur.'

this documentary evidence was read during the speeches, not by the pleader himself[1] but by the *scriba* of the court[2].

Functions of the *quaesitor* during the trial.

The consideration of this last item in evidence brings us to the close of that part of the proceedings which was concerned with proof. During this time the *quaesitor* had not been inactive. He was responsible for order in the court[3]; with the *consilium* he discussed any novel point that was raised about the procedure[4], and there are clear indications that he assisted the judgement of the *iudices* by occasional remarks[5]. But there is no record of anything resembling a formal summing up.

The judgement.

The close of the evidence, therefore, marked the end of the public proceedings. The judgement which had now to be delivered was determined by two main conditions, the second of which was perhaps more actual than the first. In the first place the sentence was supposed to take cognizance only of the offence stated by the special law and falling under the special court, and, secondly, it was automatic in its effect; if a definitive judgement was

[1] For the command *Recita* with which they are introduced see Cic. *in Verr.* i. 33, 83 and 84; 38, 96; ii. 74, 183; iii. 10, 26; *pro Flacco*, 32, 78.

[2] Cic. *in Verr.* iii. 10, 26 (one of Verres' Sicilian edicts) 'Da, quaeso, scribae; recitet ex codice. Recita edictum de professione.'

[3] *Auct. ad Herenn.* iv. 35, 47 'quaesitoris est unum quemque horum (accusatoris, defensoris, testis) in officio suo continere.' On disturbance from the spectators he might order the judges to disperse ('consilium dimittere,' Cic. *in Verr.* v. 63, 163) and so probably close the sitting for the day. In Plut. *Pomp.* 4 we find a praetor βραβεύοντα τὴν δίκην.

[4] For a decision given *de consilii sententia* see Cic. *pro Planc.* 16, 40 (p. 456); cf. Asc. *in Milon.* p. 40 (see p. 394) where the expression is *ex sententia iudicum*.

[5] Cic. *pro Rosc. Amer.* 30, 84 'L. Cassius ille, quem populus Romanus verissimum et sapientissimum iudicem putabat, identidem in causis quaerere solebat "cui bono fuisset."' This maxim could hardly have been uttered, or his reputation as a *iudex* gained, in any other capacity than that of a *iudex quaestionis* or *quaesitor*. This, in fact, is the interpretation given by Asconius (*in Milon.* p. 46 'quotiens quaesitor iudicii alicuius esset, in quo quaerebatur de homine occiso'). The same character seems to be implied in his designation of *scopulus reorum* (Val. Max. iii. 7, 9). He was president of the court for the trial of the vestals in 114 B.C.; see p. 379. A *quaestio inter sicarios* may have existed as early as 142 B.C. See p. 420.

BOOK II.

pronounced, it had to express unconditioned condemnation or acquittal. The penalty was fixed absolutely by the law and could not be modified by the court[1].

Preparation for the verdict; *in consilium ire.*

The *iudices* who are preparing to vote are said *in consilium ire*[2], the counsel who close the proceedings and ask the jury to consider their verdict are said *mittere in consilium*[3]. The first phrase is obviously drawn from the deliberations of the recuperatorial court, and both expressions suggest a discussion on the part of the criminal juries to which they are applied. No legal principle is in conflict with such a possibility, for the *ioudex nei quis disputet* of the *lex Acilia*[4] is almost certainly a prohibition against the *iudices* making remarks during the proceedings[5]. The only difficulties in the way of a theory of a deliberated verdict are the silence of our authorities, the size of the juries, and our ignorance of any place in the open courts of the day to which they could have retired to debate the question. But the argument from silence is always weak, and the two latter difficulties are not particularly serious; so that it must remain more of an open question than it is generally considered to be

[1] Cic. *de Inv.* ii. 19, 59 'Ea igitur poena si affici reum non oporteat, damnari quoque non oportere, quoniam ea poena damnationem necessario consequatur'; *pro Sulla*, 22, 63 'Nemo iudicium reprehendit, cum de poena queritur, sed legem. Damnatio enim est iudicum ... poena legis.'

[2] Cic. *pro Cluent.* 20, 55; 27, 74; 30, 83; 'consurgitur in consilium' (*ib.* 27, 75) expresses their rising for this purpose.

[3] Cic. *in Verr.* i. 9, 26 'Testibus editis ita mittam in consilium.' In Cic. *ad Fam.* viii. 8, 3 [(Appius minor) mittit in consilium eosdem illos qui lites aestimarant iudices] 'eosdem illos ... iudices' is a parenthetical remark of the writer. Caelius has forgotten to mention earlier that it was the same jury which had assessed the damages in the case of Appius' father. In Asc. *in Scaurian.* p. 30, the phrase is used of the president of the court.

[4] l. 39.

[5] It is not, therefore, a rule against discussion such as that observed in Greek states (Arist. *Pol.* ii. 8, 13 τῶν νομοθετῶν οἱ πολλοὶ παρασκευάζουσιν ὅπως οἱ δικασταὶ μὴ κοινολογῶνται πρὸς ἀλλήλους). Geib (p. 365) and Mommsen (*Strafr.* p. 443) take the view that the Roman criminal jury did not deliberate.

whether the Roman jury discussed the merits of the case before they pronounced their verdict.

The voting of the *iudices*. The three possible verdicts.

The *iudices* then gave their judgement by ballot, except during the period when, according to Sulla's provision, open voting was in some cases allowed[1]. The three possible verdicts were *absolvo*, *condemno* and *non liquet*. Under the procedure of the *lex Acilia*, the vote *liquet* or *non liquet* was taken first (apparently not by ballot); then voting tablets containing the letters A and C on either side were employed for the final verdict[2]. In later times the three votes were given at the same time[3], and, if the tablets still contained the letters A and C on either side, the verdict of N L must have been given by defacing the former signs and scratching these letters on the wax; for the mere defacement of the signs A and C seems to have been reckoned as no vote and not as a verdict of 'not proven'[4].

Verdict decided by a majority of votes.

The majority of votes decided the verdict[5]. An absolute majority was required for condemnation; if this was not secured, the accused was acquitted, although some of the non-condemnatory votes might have been those of *non liquet*[6]. For this last verdict a majority of votes was also required. In the earlier procedure, under which the vote of 'proven' or 'not proven' was given first, a verdict could be taken from two-thirds of the members of a jury, who had pronounced *sibi liquere*[7], and at this period it is obvious that a vote of N L by more than one-third

[1] p. 442.

[2] *Lex Acilia*, ll. 49 and 51.

[3] This is plain from Cicero's account of the voting in the trial of Oppianicus (*pro Cluent.* 28, 76).

[4] p. 447; in the *lex Acilia* (l. 54) 'ubei nihil scriptum erit' the pronouncement is 'sine suffragio.'

[5] Cic. *ad Fam.* viii. 8, 3 '(praetor Laterensis) legis (Iuliae repetundarum) . . . unum et centesimum caput legit, in quo ita erat QUOD EORUM IUDICUM MAIOR PARS IUDICARIT, ID IUS RATUMQUE ESTO'; cf. *Lex Acilia*, l. 55.

[6] Cic. *pro Caec.* 10, 29 (in the case of Oppianicus) 'si uno minus damnarent, condemnari reus non posset'; but some of the votes were *non liquet*.

[7] *Lex Acilia*, l. 49.

BOOK II.

of a jury had to be accepted. The Romans never took the precaution, adopted by Attic law, that the number of a jury should be an unequal one; hence equality of votes was possible, and this seems always to have entailed acquittal[1].

Judgement pronounced by the president.

After the voting the tablets were counted by the president (*tabellas diribere*)[2]. He then pronounced the judgement[3]. Condemnation or acquittal seems generally to have been declared by the phrases *fecisse*[4] or *non fecisse videtur*[5]; in the case of a *litis aestimatio* the president's declaration apparently took the form of *redigam* or *non redigam* ('I will' or 'will not exact restitution'[6]). When a verdict of *non liquet* had been returned by the jury[7], he uttered the word *amplius* (sc. *cognoscendum*)[8]. This last decision led to a renewal of the case (*ampliatio*)[9]. Renewals of

Ampliatio.

[1] Cic. *pro Cluent.* 27, 74 'In consilium erant ituri iudices xxxii, sententiis xvi absolutio confici poterat'; *ad Fam.* viii. 8, 3 'Cum aequo numero sententiae fuissent, Laterensis . . . pronuntiavit . . . *non redigam*'; cf. Plut. *Mar.* 5 (Marius accused of *ambitus*) ἀπέφυγεν ἴσων τῶν ψήφων γενομένων.

[2] Cic. *in Pis.* 40, 96; *ad Q. fr.* iii. 4, 1.

[3] Cic. *ad Fam.* viii. 8, 3 (note 1); cf. Plut. *Pomp.* 4 (in a judgement arising out of *peculatus* we hear of the praetor γνώμην ἀναγορεύσαντος . . . τῶν δικαστῶν).

[4] Cic. *in Verr.* ii. 38, 93, where in a charge of falsification of public documents, which was treated as a public delict, the sentence ran 'Sthenium literas publicas corrupisse videri'; cf. *ib.* v. 6, 14 (of the trial of slaves) 'fecisse videri pronuntiavit.' 'You pronounced your own condemnation' is 'tu ipse de te fecisse videri pronuntiavisti' (*in Pis.* 40, 97).

[5] Cic. *ad Att.* iv. 16, 8 [17, 5] 'Quid, quaeris, aliud? Iudicia, credo. Drusus, Scaurus non fecisse videntur.'

[6] Cic. *ad Fam.* viii. 8, 3 (note 1); cf. the use of 'redigere' in *pro Rab. Post.* 13, 37.

[7] Cic. *pro Cluent.* 28, 76.

[8] Cic. *Brut.* 22, 86 (of a special cognizance entrusted by the senate to the consuls) 'cum consules, re audita, *amplius* de consilii sententia pronuntiavissent'; Cic. *in Verr.* i. 9, 26 'etiamsi lex ampliandi faciat potestatem'; Ps. Asc. *ad loc.* (p. 164) '*amplius* pronuntiabatur, . . . cum dixissent iudices *non liquet*.' For this pronouncement in provincial jurisdiction see Cic. *in Verr.* i. 29, 74.

[9] *Auct. ad Herenn.* iv. 36, 48 'quid fuit, iudices, quare in sententiis ferendis dubitaveritis aut istum hominem nefarium ampliaveritis?'; cf. Cic. *in Verr.* i. 9, 26 (note 8).

this kind had to be repeated until the court had reached a verdict of 'guilty' or 'not guilty'; and so tempting to a jury was such an expression of doubt in certain kinds of cases that the *lex Acilia* provides against a too frequent use of this power by making the *iudices*, who give the verdict of *non liquet* and thus produce an *ampliatio* more than twice in a single case, liable to a pecuniary penalty[1]. The date for the new trial, which followed his sentence of *amplius*, was probably fixed by the president himself, and the trial involved a complete rehearing of the case *ab initio.* All the pleadings (*actiones*) were renewed, and, as in civil process, a new *patronus* might replace the old[2]. New evidence was, of course, admissible: but it is possible that the proceedings might be shortened by having the old evidence, which had been taken at the former trial, read instead of heard at its renewal[3].

Such wholesale rehearings of a case became so much less frequent towards the close of the Republic that Cicero could speak of a verdict of *non liquet* as a characteristic of 'the old school of jurisdiction'[4]. We know, in fact, of no criminal case of his time in which the *ampliatio* was resorted to, and, with the exception of the trial of Oppianicus, of not one in which a verdict of *non liquet* was returned by even a minority of the judges.

The chief reason for this disappearance of the renewed hearing was that, for the longest and most difficult processes, those for extortion, a system of compulsory adjournment (*comperendinatio*) had been devised. Under

[1] The following words can be made out (*Lex Acilia*, l. 48) '*iu*]dicare, is HS n(ummum) ccIoo, quotiens quomque amplius bis in uno iu[*dicio iudicare negarint*].'

[2] This is the case in the consular court mentioned by Cicero (*Brut.* 22, 87); cf. p. 498, note 8.

[3] p. 487.

[4] Cic. *pro Cluent.* 28, 76 'homines sapientes et ex vetere illa disciplina iudiciorum, qui neque absolvere hominem nocentissimum possent, neque eum, de quo esset orta suspicio pecunia oppugnatum, re illa incognita primo condemnare vellent, non liquere dixerunt.'

BOOK II.

Comperendinatio; a system of compulsory adjournment.

this system, which is illustrated by the cases of Verres, Fonteius, Flaccus and Scaurus[1], the whole process was divided into two parts (*actio prima, secunda*). Between the two actions a fixed interval was prescribed, which was, originally at least, the single day from which the *comperendinatio* derived its name[2]. The two portions of the trial formed a complete whole; no vote was taken after the first and the case went on continuously, the second action being regarded as the necessary complement of the first[3]. Each *actio* might last several days. As to the first, we know that had Cicero not shortened the proceedings, the *actio prima* of the Verrines would have suffered an adjournment of over forty days[4]; and, even in the ordinary course of things, since, although the pleadings were limited, the number of witnesses was not, the evidence, generally of great length in a case of extortion, could not have been exhausted in a single sitting. The second action, although its length as illustrated by the Verrines could only have existed on paper, was one in which the pleadings, as concerned with the evidence already adduced and a criticism of the arguments already advanced, were more earnest and technical even than in the first; it must, therefore, have been a process which no single day could see to its close. The first *actio* consisted of the speeches for the prosecution and defence, and the evidence which followed them; the second consisted of renewed pleadings by both counsel in the same order, the prosecutor speaking first, the accused last. Hence, in the second *actio* against Verres, Cicero pretends to

[1] For the last three cases see the evidence on p. 477 that Cicero's speeche are *actiones secundae*.

[2] Cic. *Brut.* 22, 87 'unum quasi comperendinatus medium diem fuisse.'

[3] Cic. *in Verr.* Act. i. 18, 55 'Si quis erit qui perpetuam orationem accusationemque desideret, altera actione audiet'; *in Verr.* i. 9, 26 'Adimo enim comperendinatum. Quod habet lex in se molestissimum, bis ut causa dicatur . . .'

[4] *ib.* Act. i. 18, 54.

predict the course of the arguments which will be employed by Hortensius[1]. It is uncertain whether the proceedings had to be brought to an end with the close of the second *actio*: that is, whether a verdict of *non liquet* was possible where the *comperendinatio* existed; for Cicero, although he contrasts this procedure with the simple *ampliatio*[2], nowhere says that the two were not concurrent.

Probably confined to cases of extortion.

The system of compulsory adjournment was first introduced by the *lex Servilia repetundarum*[3] (*circa* 111 B.C.), and it seems to have continued a feature of all trials of extortion, but probably only of this class of cases, down to the close of the Republic. Thus the two actions appear in the trials of Verres (70 B.C.), Fonteius (69 B.C.) under the Cornelian, and in those of Flaccus (*circa* 59 B.C.) and Scaurus (54 B.C.) under the Julian law[4]. The motive for the introduction of this system is probably to be found in the complexity of the issues raised by trials for extortion and in the enormous mass of evidence which had,

[1] Cic. *in Verr.* ii. 72, 177 'Qui id defendet Hortensius?'; iii. 88, 205 'Quid ad haec Hortensius? Falsum esse crimen? Hoc nunquam dicet'; v. 1, 2 'video ubi se iactaturus sit Hortensius: belli pericula . . . commemorabit'; v. 13, 32 'Hic scilicet est metuendum ne ad exitum defensionis tuae vetus illa Antoniana dicendi ratio atque auctoritas proferatur'; cf. i. 28, 71 'Nisi vero illud dicet, quod et in testimonio Tettii priore actione interpellavit Hortensius.' All these references prove the error of the Pseudo-Asconius in saying (p. 163) 'comperendinato iudicio dicit prior defensor et defensionem tamquam duplicem in medio positam obruit ultimus accusator.'

[2] Cic. *in Verr.* i. 9, 26 'Verum, ut opinor, Glaucia primus tulit ut comperendinaretur reus: antea vel iudicari primo poterat vel amplius pronuntiari . . . Ego tibi illam Aciliam legem restituo qua lege multi semel accusati, semel dicta causa, semel auditis testibus condemnati sunt . . . Testibus editis ita mittam in consilium ut, etiamsi lex (i. e. such as the *lex Acilia*) ampliandi faciat potestatem (i. e. in place of the necessary *comperendinatio*) tamen isti turpe sibi existiment non primo iudicare.' When Cicero reproaches a juror with the fact that 'in eo consilio, cum . . . potestas esset ampliandi, dixisse sibi liquere' (*pro Caec.* 10, 29) he does not necessarily imply that the 'potestas ampliandi' did not exist for all trials.

[3] See preceding note.

[4] pp. 478, 500.

BOOK II.

in such cases, to be examined and weighed. It was discovered that juries found it difficult to come to a decision after a single hearing; *ampliationes*, following on a verdict of *non liquet*, were so frequent that their employment had to be restrained by law[1]; and it may have been felt that one of the chief reasons for this uncertainty of jurors was that they were supplied with no comments on the evidence. A naked mass of contradiction was before them, not harmonized either for proof or disproof by the orator's skill. Such a review was now possible through the speeches in the second action of the *comperendinatio*, and these, whatever light they threw on the truth, must have increased the conviction and comfort of the *iudices*.

Recovery the object of certain criminal prosecutions. The *litis aestimatio*.

In certain cases an issue other than that of the mere guilt or innocence of the accused had to be raised: recovery was the object of certain prosecutions, and in trials for extortion (*repetundarum*)[2] and peculation (*peculatus*)[3] conviction on the main charge was followed by an assessment of damages (*litis aestimatio*)[4]. In cases of extortion this was a complicated and difficult matter, since the claim for damages might come from so many different quarters. The demands of each state had to be considered separately, and the separate claims were stated one by one in the list of damages which was committed to writing[5]. In estimating such damages juries exercised

[1] p. 499. [2] Cic. *in Verr.* Act. i. 13, 38; *pro Cluent.* 41, 116.

[3] Cic. *pro Mur.* 20, 42.

[4] When Cicero says (*pro Cluent.* 41, 116) 'maiestatis absoluti sunt permulti, quibus damnatis, de pecuniis repetundis lites [majestatis] essent aestimatae' he means that conviction for the first offence would have necessitated prosecution for the other, with an accompanying *litis aestimatio*. His point is that a jury may regard an offence lightly and yet follow it, if by any chance conviction ensues, with a heavy assessment of damages.

[5] Such a document is quoted by Cicero (*in Verr.* i. 38, 96) 'Recita. DE LITIBUS AESTIMATIS CN. DOLABELLAE PR(AETORIS) PECUNIAE REDACTAE; QUOD A COMMUNI MILYADUM'; cf. 39, 99. Whether the claims of individuals were stated separately, or grouped under those of their respective states, we cannot say

a very free discretionary power and were inclined to be generous to the plaintiffs[1]; for, once a conviction on the main charge had been secured, their sympathy with the accused had disappeared. The close connexion of the *iudicium* with the *litis aestimatio*[2] made it necessary that both should be under the control of the same jury, who performed successively the rôles of judges and of arbitrators. BOOK II.

In the laws of extortion which, like the Servilian, Cornelian, and Julian[3], enjoined the possibility of the recovery of money from any one who had shared improperly in the spoils of a provincial governor—from a prosecutor for instance, who had been bribed for purposes of collusion—the jury, which had tried the main case and assessed the damages due by the chief spoliater, was made responsible for this subordinate assessment as well; it was an appendix to the main trial and hence no new evidence was admitted[4]. In this case, too, the jury did not feel bound by the rigid rules of evidence required for conviction for a crime, and Cicero remarks that individuals already mulcted in damages on a charge of participation in the spoils of

[1] Cic. *pro Cluent.* 41, 115 and 116.

[2] The two are distinguished by Cicero, *ib.* § 116 'statuitur aestimationem litium non esse iudicium.'

[3] Cic. *pro Rab. Post.* 4, 8 and 9 'Iubet lex Iulia persequi ab iis, ad quos ea pecunia, quam is ceperit qui damnatus sit, pervenerit . . . hoc totidem verbis tralatum caput est, quot fuit non modo in Cornelia sed etiam ante in lege Servilia.'

[4] *ib.* 13, 36 'cum in his iudiciis ne locus quidem novo testi soleat esse ob eamque causam iidem iudices retineantur qui fuerint de reo, ut iis nota sint omnia neve quid fingi novi possit'; (37) 'Lites QUO EA PECUNIA PERVENERIT non suis propriis iudiciis sed in reum factis condemnari solent'; Cic. *ad Fam.* viii. 8, 2 and 3 'proiicitur Appius minor ut indicaret pecuniam ex bonis patris pervenisse ad Servilium praevaricationisque causa diceret depositum HS LXXXI . . . Mittit in consilium eosdem illos qui lites (of his father's case) aestimarant iudices.' Yet the trial does not seem to have been technically one for *praevaricatio*, as Mommsen seems to think (*Strafr.* pp. 448 and 725). It was technically *repetundarum* under the clause which enabled recovery to be made from any one to whom money had been improperly paid (*pro Rab. Post.* 13, 37; *pro Cluent.* 41, 116). In this case the money had been paid *praevaricationis causa.*

BOOK II. another, were, when accused of extortion on this amongst other grounds, sometimes acquitted by the very jury which had imposed the assessment[1].

§ 18. *Execution.*

Execution, in criminal as in civil trials, was either pecuniary or personal.

Pecuniary execution. In those trials, in which a money penalty was exacted, the accused might give securities (*praedes*) for his debt immediately after his conviction: that is, at the stage when he first became a debtor, primarily to the state and, in matters of extortion, in a secondary degree to the persons represented by his accusers. Under the procedure

Praedes or *bonorum possessio.* of the *lex Acilia*[2] the *praedes* are given or, in default, *bonorum possessio* takes place after the condemnation but before the assessment of damages, the amount of the security being fixed by a majority of the *consilium*. But this must have been a very imperfect security, because based on very intangible grounds, and passages of Cicero seem to show that in his time these proceedings might take place *after* the *litis aestimatio*[3]. Even, however, if the person convicted did not furnish security, his imprisonment, which had been sometimes employed in such trials when conducted before the people[4], does

[1] Cic. *pro Cluent.* 41, 116 'hoc quotidie fieri videmus ut, reo damnato de pecuniis repetundis, ad quos pervenisse pecunias in litibus aestimandis statutum sit, eos idem iudices absolvant.' For a case of concurrence of the charges *quo ea pecunia pervenit* and *repetundarum* see Cic. *ad Fam.* viii. 8, 3 (Servilius after being acquitted by an equality of votes of a share in the spoils of App. Claudius) 'neque absolutus neque damnatus (i.e. morally, on the ground of the equality of votes) . . . de repetundis saucius Pilio tradetur.'

[2] l. 57.

[3] *pro Rab. Post.* 4, 8 'Sunt lites aestimatae A. Gabinio, nec praedes dati, nec ex bonis populo universa pecunia exacta est'; 13, 37 'si aut praedes dedisset Gabinius aut tantum ex eius bonis, quanta summa litium fuisset, populus recepisset.'

[4] Liv. xxxviii. 58.

not seem to have been ordered by the court. In this matter the analogy of criminal rather than of civil justice was followed, and, as in the case of conviction to a definite *poena*, the debtor was free to seek a place of exile, in which he had probably already deposited the greater part of his stolen goods [1]. This was invariably the case when the assessment was, or had been predicted by the offender to be, in the phrase of the time, of 'capital' amount [2]; but, when he had given no *praedes* and his property, or any portion of it, could be realized at Rome, the state took possession of his goods by the ordinary method of *bonorum possessio* and *proscriptio* [3]. The method of satisfying the debt which is enjoined by the *lex Acilia* [4], a system probably current in Cicero's day, was the same as that following pecuniary condemnation in the earlier period [5]. The quaestor enters into possession at the bidding of the praetor or other president of the court [6], and it is his business to proscribe and sell the goods [7]. He then, whether he has got the money through *praedes* or by *bonorum venditio*, pays the damages to the successful plaintiffs, the money being no longer owed to them by the person convicted but by the state.

Personal execution. The death penalty for *parricidium*.

It is needless to remark that the severest form of personal execution, the deprivation of life, was still one of the penalties inflicted by the *iudicia populi*, and could, when pronounced by such courts, be avoided only by exile. The only crime taken cognizance of by the *iudicia publica*, for which the survival of this penalty

[1] Suet. *Caes.* 42 'cum locupletes eo facilius scelere se obligarent quod integris patrimoniis exulabant.'

[2] *lis capitis* (Cic. *pro Cluent.* 41, 116).

[3] Cic. *pro Rab. Post.* 4, 8; 13, 37; see p. 504, note 3.

[4] ll. 61–9.

[5] Liv. xxxviii. 60; see p. 282.

[6] In the case of the *iudex* chosen from the jury (p. 431), if this presidency was known in cases involving a *litis aestimatio*, bankruptcy proceedings, as a function of the *imperium*, probably belonged to the praetor.

[7] Cf. Cic. on p. 504, note 3, 'pecunia exacta est.'

BOOK II.

can be proved, is that of *parricidium*. There can be no question that, under the Cornelian law, the ancient death penalty, the punishment by the *culeus*, was retained, and all attempts to explain Cicero's language[1] in some other sense have proved fruitless. It is probable that Sulla, like Pompeius afterwards, distinguished different degrees of parricide, and that it was only the worst guilt that was visited by this prehistoric penalty; other cases were met by interdiction, the normal punishment inflicted by the Cornelian law of murder[2]. We know that, according to the *lex Pompeia*, the murder of a direct relation in the ascending line (parents and grandparents) might be visited with the old capital punishment; in all other cases the penalty was interdiction[3]. It is probable that this unique survival of the death penalty in laws establishing *quaestiones* was rendered nugatory by the provision that it should only be inflicted on the confessed parricide[4].

Punishments for other crimes; generally interdiction.

Amongst other crimes of an ordinary and non-political character, arson and murder were in imperial times punished by interdiction[5], and as the punishment was capital in the Ciceronian period[6], while there is no reference to

[1] Cic. *pro Rosc. Amer.* 11, 30 'hanc conditionem misero ferunt, ut optet utrum malit cervices Roscio dare an insutus in culeum per summum dedecus vitam amittere.' In cc. 25 and 26 he dwells on the nature of the penalty; cf. *Auct. ad Herenn.* i. 13, 23; *de Inv.* ii. 50, 149. From *ad Q. fr.* i. 2, 2, 5 we learn that the punishment was inflicted by Q. Cicero on two Mysians at Smyrna.

[2] The penalty under both laws was the same; Dig. 48, 9, 1 'Lege Pompeia de parricidiis cavetur, si quis patrem, matrem . . . occiderit . . . ut poena ea teneatur quae est legis Corneliae de sicariis.'

[3] Dig. 48, 9, 1 and 9.

[4] Suet. *Aug.* 33 'manifesti parricidii reum (ne culeo insueretur, quod non nisi confessi afficiuntur hac poena) ita fertur interrogasse: "Certe patrem tuum non occidisti?"'

[5] Collatio, xii. 5. Cf. i. 2, where deportation is the equivalent of this penalty.

[6] 'DEQUE EIUS CAPITE QUAERITO' (Cornelian law in Cic. *pro Cluent.* 54, 148). The *praeiudicium* in Cic. *de Inv.* ii. 20, 59 (see p. 180, note 2) perhaps refers to a concurrence of the *actio iniuriarum* with a prosecution for attempted murder (Mommsen, *Strafr.* p. 630) or for *vis* (see p. 233), or, perhaps, for some kind of *iniuria* which was punished capitally under the Cornelian law.

the death sentence, outlawry must also have been its penalty at this time[1]. Forgery (*falsum*) and its cognate offences were, in their more extreme forms, punished at a later period, and probably at this time, by interdiction[2]. The punishment for *iniuriae* is unknown[3], and the only penalty that we hear of in connexion with the Fabian law of *plagium* was pecuniary[4]. BOOK II.

When we turn to political crimes and offences against the public peace, we find that the penalty for *vis* earlier than the Julian law is indeed unknown, but that Cicero's references to it imply exile as its consequence[5]. It would, therefore, have been interdiction, the actual punishment inflicted by Caesar[6]. Exile, too, was, as we have seen, the consequence of the *lex Licinia de sodaliciis*[7]. The penalty of the Cornelian law of *maiestas*, although unknown, could hardly have been less serious than that for *vis*[8], and, under Caesar's law of treason, interdiction

[1] Cf. Cic. *pro Cluent.* 71, 202 'conservate A. Cluentium, restituite incolumem municipio.'

[2] Dig. 48, 10, 33 'Si quis falsis constitutionibus nullo auctore habito utitur, lege Cornelia aqua et igni ei interdicitur.' The word *constitutiones* is an imperial addition, but the punishment may be Cornelian.

[3] The words of Marcian in Dig. 47, 10, 37, 1 ('Etiam ex lege Cornelia iniuriarum actio civiliter moveri potest condemnatione aestimatione iudicis facienda') by no means proves that the penalty was merely pecuniary, but, if anything, the reverse.

[4] Dig. 48, 15, 7.

[5] Cic. *pro Sulla*, cc. 31 and 32 'Vita erepta est superiore iudicio: nunc ne corpus eiiciatur laboramus ... quod fortuna in malis reliqui fecit, ut cum parente, cum liberis ... lugere suam calamitatem liceat, id sibi ne eripiatis, vos, iudices, obtestatur ... quid est quod expetas amplius? ... An vero inimicum ut expellas?'; *pro Sest.* 69, 146 'An ego in hac urbe esse possim his pulsis ... neque eae nationes, quibus me senatus commendavit ... hunc exulem propter me sine me videbunt.'

[6] Cic. *Phil.* i. 9, 23 'Quid quod obrogatur legibus Caesaris, quae iubent ei qui de vi, itemque ei qui maiestatis damnatus sit, aqua et igni interdici.'

[7] p. 425.

[8] The passage in *Auct. ad Herenn.* iv. 8, 12 ('ut eum, qui fortunas omnium voluerit prodere, praecipitem proturbetis ex ea civitate, quam iste ... voluerit obruere') suggests interdiction.

BOOK II. was certainly the punishment[1]. Caesar is credited with a general sharpening of the penalties of the criminal courts. He is described as adding to exile confiscation of half the property of the condemned. It is of little moment whether voluntary or enforced exile is here intended, for the former was followed and the latter preceded by interdiction, and it is to the act of interdiction that this penalty was added. He is also said to have attached to condemnation for parricide (in its narrower sense) the confiscation of the whole property of the condemned[2].

Infamia. Milder chastisements took the quasi-penal form of the infliction of *infamia* of various degrees, a type of penalty which may be illustrated by the ten years' abstinence from *honores* imposed by the *lex Cornelia de ambitu*, the perpetual disqualification inflicted by the *lex Calpurnia*, the exclusion from the senate, judicial bench and witness-box of the *lex Iulia repetundarum*, and the deprivation by some law of extortion of the right to speak *in contione*[3]. There is but one law of this period known to us which introduced a moderate punishment other than that of mere disqualification for public duties. Temporary relegation. If the statement is correct that the *lex Tullia de ambitu* made the penalty for its contravention abstention from Rome, and probably from Italy, for ten years[4], the idea of temporary relegation was introduced, perhaps for the first time, into Roman jurisprudence. Relegation differs from outlawry in that it maintains civic rights intact, and the punishment of the Tullian law must have been of this nature: for the temporary loss of all rights with the certainty of their

[1] Cic. *Phil.* l. c.; cf. Paul. *Sent.* v. 29, 1 'His antea in perpetuum aqua et igni interdicebatur.'

[2] Suet. *Caes.* 42.

[3] pp. 423, note 4, 425; Dig. 48, 11, 6, 1; Suet. *Caes.* 43 'Repetundarum convictos etiam ordine senatorio movit'; *Auct. ad Herenn.* i. 12, 20 'Lex vetat eum, qui de pecuniis repetundis damnatus sit, in contione orationem habere.'

[4] p. 425.

sudden revival at the end of a given period is an idea unfamiliar to the Roman mind. BOOK II.

Restitution.

If we turn, lastly, to the offences for which restitution was demanded, we find that for *peculatus* no other penalty than the mere recovery is known[1]. In extortion also simple or double restitution[2] is, apart from certain kinds of disqualification, the sole result of conviction. Exile is, indeed, a frequent consequence of condemnation for this delict[3], but it is voluntary banishment, due to incapacity or unwillingness to pay the damages assessed, and we know from disqualifications, which during the Ciceronian period were incidental to condemnation[4], that exile could not have been its necessary consequence.

Exile the chief consequence of condemnation.

The conception of *exilium*.

Exile is clearly the leading feature of the infliction of penalties during the closing years of the Republic, and its place in the procedure of this period can only be understood by a brief review of its history; for it was this which determined the manner in which it was conceived and employed. The conception of *exilium* was based upon two ideas which were more or less common to Graeco-Italian civilization. These were (1) that no man possessed legal rights, creating a personality either in public or in private law, other than those of the *civitas* of which he was a member: (2) that it was not possible to be a citizen of two different *civitates* at the same time. The first principle was absolutely valid; the second was a rigid rule

[1] Perhaps, although there is no direct evidence from the Republican law of Rome, in some cases double, in others quadruple restitution may have been demanded (Mommsen, *Strafr.* p. 771).

[2] It was double under the Acilian, and probably the Servilian, law. Mommsen thinks (*Strafr.* p. 728) that Sulla reintroduced restitution *in simplum*. The only evidence for the view that the *lex Iulia* (of Caesar) introduced quadruple restitution is the fact that Augustus in 17 B.C. exacted fourfold from orators who had violated the *lex Cincia* (Dio Cass. liv. 18).

[3] Rutilius Rufus, after his condemnation (*circa* 91 B.C.), lives at Mitylene and Smyrna (Cic. *pro Rab. Post.* 10, 27; *pro Balbo*, 11, 28). T. Albucius, after his conviction (103 B.C.) at Athens (Cic. *Tusc. Disp.* v. 37, 108).

[4] p. 508.

BOOK II.

of Roman public law[1]; but it may also be called a part, not merely of the *ius civile* of Rome, but of the *ius gentium* of the Graeco-Italian world, for full reciprocity in civic rights (*συμπολιτεία*) was a very rare international relation[2].

One consequence of these rules was expressed in *exilium*, a term which implied the destruction of one *status* and the birth of another. A Roman who abandoned Rome, and succeeded in getting his name entered on the civic register of another city, was an *exul* from Rome; he had suffered the highest *capitis deminutio* known in Cicero's day; all the rights and obligations based on the *ius civile* had been surrendered or shaken off. Similarly, a man from another city who entered the body politic of Rome was an *exul* from his native state[3]. Whether his own city recognized the possibility of a dual citizenship was a matter of indifference. Rome in her treaties with such communities must have emphasized the principle of her own civil law, and declined to admit to her *civitas* a man who owed any kind of allegiance to another community.

International relations, which contemplated migration and exile,

From the earliest period of Roman history there existed between Rome and that class of cities which was sovereign and federate (*civitates liberae et foederatae*) international relations, embodied in a clause of the treaty (*foedus*), which dealt with the possibility of this kind of migration and exile. Such relations were apparently a characteristic not only of the *aequum foedus*, but also of the *iniqua foedera* by which suzerainty over allied communities was guaranteed to Rome[4]. Towns with such treaties were, in Italy,

[1] Cic. *pro Balbo*, 11, 28 'Duarum civitatum civis noster esse iure civili nemo potest; non esse huius civitatis, qui se alii civitati dicarit, potest'; *pro Caec.* 34, 100 'Cum ex nostro iure duarum civitatum nemo esse possit, tum amittitur haec civitas denique, cum is qui profugit receptus est in exilium, hoc est, in aliam civitatem.'

[2] Certain Greek states, however, gave their citizenship to individuals who remained full members of other communities (Cic. *pro Balbo*, 12, 30).

[3] For such *exules* living at Rome see Cic. *Phil.* v. 5, 12.

[4] Cic. *pro Balbo*, 16, 35. Cf. p. 511, note 6, and Dig 49, 15, 7, 1.

Tibur, Praeneste, Neapolis and 'the other federate towns,' as Polybius expresses it[1]. Amongst 'the others' we know Tarquinii[2] and Nuceria[3] as places of refuge. Other Italian states with peculiarly favourable treaties, which, therefore, probably possessed this right, were Heraclea[4], Petelia, Croton and Rhegium[5]. In the provinces we can point to Gades and Tarraco in Spain[6], Massilia in Gaul[7], Smyrna in Asia[8], Athens[9], Patrae[10] and other places in Greece[11].

BOOK II.

employed as a means of escaping punishment.

This international relation was employed at an early period as a means of modifying the harsher consequences of the criminal law. Rome was unwilling to execute the capital penalties enjoined by her own penal code, and a means of avoiding their execution was found in *exilium*. When a criminal was put on his trial on a capital charge, he was seldom arrested and imprisoned. As a rule he remained at large, and before the trial, if he took a hopeless view of his case[12], or just before the verdict if his expectations of acquittal were not likely to be fulfilled[13],

[1] Polyb. vi. 14, 8 ἔστι δ' ἀσφάλεια τοῖς φεύγουσιν ἔν τε τῇ Νεαπολιτῶν καὶ Πραινεστίνων ἔτι δὲ Τιβουρίνων πόλει, καὶ ταῖς ἄλλαις, πρὸς ἃς ἔχουσιν ὅρκια. For Tibur and Praeneste cf. Liv. xliii. 2.

[2] Liv. xxvi. 3. [3] Cic. *pro Balbo*, 11, 28. [4] *ib.* 8, 21.

[5] Liv. xxiii. 30. [6] Cic. *pro Balbo*, 12, 29; 11, 28. [7] Asc. *in Milon.* p. 54.

[8] Cic. *pro Balbo*, 11, 28. [9] Cic. *Tusc. Disp.* v. 37, 108.

[10] Cic. *ad Fam.* xiii. 19, 2.

[11] Cic. *ad Att.* iii. 7, 1. We cannot always conclude from the place of the exile's residence that this was a *foederata civitas*; for a man might be a citizen of one state and live in another. Thus C. Antonius Hybrida, condemned for *vis* (Dio Cass. xxxviii. 10, 3; *pro Flacco*, 2, 5; 38, 95; *pro Cael.* 31, 74), became a great power in Cephallenia (Strabo, x. 2, 13); but this is no reason for believing that he was a citizen of that state. C. Memmius Gemellus, who became a citizen of Patrae (*ad Fam.* xiii. 19, 2), is found visiting Mitylene (*ad Att.* v. 11, 6). If it is true that Decianus *circa* 97 B.C. (see p. 352) went into exile to Pontus (Schol. Bob. p. 230), this could hardly have been formal *exilium*; for it is unlikely that international relations with a *rex socius*, although in many respects the same as those with a *foederata civitas* (Festus, p. 218), guaranteed mutual rights of exile.

[12] See the cases of Milo (p. 390) and of Cicero (p. 361).

[13] Polyb. vi. 14, 7 τοῖς γὰρ θανάτου κρινομένοις, ἐπὰν καταδικάζωνται, δίδωσι τὴν ἐξουσίαν τὸ παρ' αὐτοῖς ἔθος ἀπαλλάττεσθαι φανερῶς, κἂν ἔτι μία λείπηται φυλὴ τῶν ἐπικυρουσῶν τὴν κρίσιν ἀψηφοφόρητος, ἑκούσιον ἑαυτοῦ καταγνόντα φυγαδείαν.

BOOK II.

he left Rome, journeyed to one of the federate states and became a citizen of that community. The verdict might indeed be pronounced at Rome, but it was now null and void: for no Roman assembly could condemn the citizen of another state[1].

Interdiction a means of preventing the return of the *exul.*

But the community of Rome had to be guaranteed against the chance of the condemned man's employing the right of exile a second time, and thus returning to his parent city. This guarantee was furnished by the survival of the old religious penalty, by which a man was cut off 'from the fire and water' of his tribe[2]. Each year a formal bill of outlawry *(aquae et ignis interdictio)* was passed, by which those who had sought voluntary banishment for the purpose of avoiding condemnation, or perhaps even trial[3], by the criminal courts, were for ever cut off from the community. If they returned, the law offered them no protection. They were accursed (*sacri*) and any one might slay them with impunity.

Change in the conception of interdiction; it becomes a penalty.

But with the new development of criminal jurisprudence in the last century of the Republic, there was a marked change in one of these conceptions. Exile remained what it was before, a voluntary act; it was not a punishment but an escape from punishment[4], and Cicero is probably

[1] There are traditions of attempts at *exilium* being frustrated in the case of Q. Pleminius (204 B.C.; Liv. xxix. 21 'alii, auditis quae Romae acta essent, in exilium Neapolim euntem forte in Q. Metellum . . . incidisse et ab eo Rhegium vi retractum tradunt') and in that of L. Tubulus (141 B.C.; Asc. *in Scaurian.* p. 23 'Is propter multa flagitia cum de exilio accersitus esset, ne in carcere necaretur venenum bibit'). In both these cases it is probable that the admission to the new citizenship had not been accomplished.

[2] p. 301. [3] p. 317, note 2.

[4] Cic. *pro Caec.* 34, 100 'Exilium enim non supplicium est, sed perfugium portusque supplicii. Nam qui volunt poenam aliquam subterfugere aut calamitatem, eo solum vertunt; hoc est, sedem ac locum mutant. Itaque nulla in lege nostra reperietur, ut apud ceteras civitates, maleficium ullum exilio esse multatum: sed cum homines vincula, neces ignominiasque vitant, quae sunt legibus constitutae, confugiunt quasi ad aram, in exilium. Qui si in civitate legis vim subire vellent, non prius civitatem quam vitam amitterent: quia nolunt, non adimitur iis civitas sed ab iis

correct in saying that not a single Roman law ever ordained exile as a penalty for crime. But the character of *aquae et ignis interdictio* had changed. It was no longer the precautionary measure, but in itself the penalty. The laws of Sulla and his successors, which established *quaestiones*, seem as a rule to have avoided the infliction of death, and to have made the severest punishment assume the form of interdiction. There is, therefore, only a very small and very formal degree of truth in Cicero's statement that no Roman could lose his *civitas* against his will[1]; for, though loss of citizenship was probably not mentioned in the formula of interdiction, it was the immediate result of such a declaration, since voluntary exile on the part of the condemned was the inevitable consequence of the law which ordered interdiction. The only difference between this and the earlier *exilium* was that now self-banishment was sought after, and not before, the sentence. A brief interval must have been allowed between the finding of the judgement of the court and its operation, to allow of the condemned man's seeking shelter against the ban, and it must have been possible for the outlaw to realize and transfer his property during this interval.

Imprisonment not recognized as a punishment.

Imprisonment, although playing no part in the penal legislation of the later Republic, was not unrecognized as

relinquitur atque deponitur.' Cicero's references to 'vincula' and 'neces' are fully in harmony with the comitial jurisdiction which was still in vogue. The nearest approach to *exilium* as a *poena* was made by Cicero's own *lex Tullia de ambitu* (p. 508); Cicero, it is true, once speaks of the penalty as exile (*pro Planc.* 34, 83), but elsewhere he denies it the name (Cic. *ad Att.* ix. 14, 2, where, speaking of those condemned under Pompeius' laws, he describes them as men 'quibus exilii poena superioribus legibus non fuisset'); and the denial is correct, for the penalty did not destroy *civitas* and was not, therefore, true *exilium*.

[1] Cic. *pro Domo*, 29, 77 'cum hoc iuris a maioribus proditum sit, ut nemo civis Romanus aut sui potestatem aut civitatem possit amittere, nisi ipse auctor factus sit.' In *Auct. ad Herenn.* ii. 28, 45 we find the idea of *exilium* identified with that of *aquae et ignis interdictio* ('quasi non omnes, quibus aqua et igni interdictum est, exules appellentur').

BOOK II. a form of punishment. We have considered it already as a mode of coercion and as a preventive measure[1]. In the latter, its only true judicial character, it survived in the procedure of Ciceronian times as a possibility that might under certain circumstances be resorted to, either in its pure form or, in the case of political offences and distinguished prisoners, in that of *libera custodia*, the practice by which the accused were handed over to magistrates or senators, who were in some way held responsible for their safe-keeping[2]. It was entirely alien to Roman ideas to regard imprisonment as a definite punishment for crime, and we know of no criminal law of the Republic which threatened incarceration as a penalty. But the dependence both of imprisonment and of a trial before the people on the magisterial will occasionally gave to this precautionary measure a quasi-punitive character which survived into Cicero's day. In the matter of the deprivation of personal freedom the liberties of the Roman citizen were very inadequately guarded. If a private man detained a citizen in custody, the production of the latter might be ordered by a praetorian interdict *ad exhibendum;* but no such means were available against a magistrate. In this case the only method of securing the release of the imprisoned sufferer was the *auxilium* of another magistrate of equal or higher authority. It is obvious that a conspiracy amongst the magistrates might lead to the detention of a man for an indefinite period, and this unanimity of action was sometimes enjoined by the senate, when it was held that the coercive measure might be continued to the benefit of the state. An

But preventive imprisonment is sometimes employed as a penalty.

[1] p. 333.

[2] Sall. *Cat.* 47, 3 and 4 (on the arrest of those supposed to be accomplices of Catiline) 'senatus decernit uti abdicato magistratu Lentulus itemque ceteri in liberis custodiis habeantur. Itaque Lentulus P. Lentulo Spintheri, qui tum aedilis erat, Cethegus Q. Cornificio, Statilius C. Caesari, Gabinius M. Crasso, Caeparius . . . Cn. Terentio senatori traduntur.'

early instance of the employment of imprisonment as a chastening influence may be found in the story of the detention of the poet Naevius. Imprisoned by the *triumviri capitales* for his petulant attacks on the aristocracy, he was released by the tribunes when he had expressed his penitence in poems composed during his sojourn in jail[1]. During the gloomy days of the second Punic war, a banker who had from time to time looked out of his office with a wreath of roses on his head was, on the instructions of the senate, haled off to a prison from which he was not released until the close of the struggle[2]. During the social war we find the same means employed to meet a graver offence. A citizen had cut off the fingers of his left hand to render himself incapable of service. The senate ordered the confiscation of his goods; this was a part at least of the legal punishment[3]; but it also commanded that he should be kept perpetually in bonds[4], an injunction which can only be regarded in the light of advice to the magistrates as they succeeded one another not to exercise their powers of *auxilium*. Precisely similar advice was given by Caesar in the discussion of the fate of the Catilinarian conspirators. Here, too, their property was to be confiscated, for that was part of the penalty due to the *hostis*; but, as an act of grace, in lieu of the death penalty, preventive imprisonment was to be perpetuated so as to become a punishment[5]. His *sententia* closed with the rider that no further reference to the prisoners be made at the meetings of either senate or people[6]. This, had it been adopted in a decree of the senate, would

[1] Gell. iii. 3, 15.

[2] Plin. *H. N.* xxi. 3, 8.

[3] Dionys. xi. 22, see p. 326, note 1.

[4] 'publicatis enim bonis eius ipsum aeternis vinculis puniendum censuit' (Val. Max. vi. 3, 3).

[5] p. 403.

[6] Sall. *Cat.* 51, 43 'neu quis de eis postea ad senatum referat neve cum populo agat: qui aliter fecerit, senatum existimare eum contra rem publicam et salutem omnium facturum.'

BOOK II.

have been the equivalent of their strongly-worded advice to the magistrates that the affair should be regarded as closed.

Thus it was that a part of the mere administrative machinery of the state became used for the ends of criminal justice. It was a use to which the government was sometimes forced by the decline of corporal punishment and the growth of the theory of exile; for imprisonment was almost the only method which the later Republic possessed of securing the deterrent effects of punishment without resorting to extreme measures.

§ 19. *Appeal and restitution.*

The *provocatio* and the *intercessio* employed in *iudicia populi*,

In connexion with the jurisdiction of the *iudicia populi* appeal in the form of *provocatio* has already been considered [1], and the principles regulating that by *appellatio*, which have been treated with reference to civil process [2], were equally valid for criminal jurisdiction. In this sphere, as in others, it invokes the *intercessio*, which can only be made against a magisterial act and renders that act invalid. In the *iudicia populi* the veto could thus be pronounced against the introduction of the charge (*nomen recipere, causam dicere*), the arrest of the accused, the calling together of the *comitia*, the summons to vote and, finally, the execution of the sentence [3].

not in *iudicia publica*.

The *iudicia publica*, on the other hand, were for the most part free from the trammels of the appeal. With respect to the decision of the *iudices* the analogy of the civil law was followed. As the appeal had never been allowed against the decision of a *iudex* in civil cases, so it was prohibited against that of the *iudices* in the *quaestio*. Nor could the acts of the presiding magistrate be challenged either by *provocatio* or *appellatio*, since, during the trial,

[1] p. 305 sq. [2] p. 289 sq.
[3] For instances see Mommsen, *Staatsr.* i. p. 276.

BOOK II.

his activity was merged in and undistinguishable from that of the jury.

But *appellatio* could be made against some rulings of the president of the court.

There was, however, one possible opening for the *appellatio* to the *par maiorve potestas*. The appeal in this form could be made against the act of the magistrate in granting the case, and any ruling of his could be challenged up to the point at which the *iudices* were associated with him. He could in all probability be appealed against even after the *nominis receptio*[1], and during the interval between this point and the expiry of the time which he had fixed for the commencement of the proceedings before the *iudices*[2]. With respect to presidents of these courts other than the praetors, it is probable that the *iudex quaestionis* of the *quaestio de sicariis* was, on account of his quasi-magisterial position[3], himself appealed against; in the case of the court being guided by a president whom the praetor appointed by lot from the jury, the appeal doubtless lay against the praetor himself. In the strict theory of this appeal the *par* as well as the *maior potestas* must have been recognized as competent to offer *auxilium*: but it is probable that here as elsewhere the tendency was to make the tribunate the great corrective power in the state. In 58 B.C. Vatinius, when prosecuted under the *lex Iunia Licinia*, entered a protest against the constitution of the court[4]. Here the tribunes were approached and the object of the request was the complete suspension of the process (*ne causam diceret*)[5]. The effect of such an appeal, if it

[1] p. 466. [2] *ib.* [3] p. 432. [4] p. 452.

[5] Cic. *in Vat.* 14, 33 'Quaero etiam illud ex te . . . postulatusne sis lege Licinia et Iunia? edixeritne C. Memmius praetor ex ea lege ut adesses die tricesimo? cum is dies venisset, fecerisne, quod in hac re publica non modo factum antea nunquam est sed in omni memoria est omnino inauditum, appellarisne tribunos plebi ne causam diceres?' The appeal of C. Antonius to the tribunes (Q. Cic. *de Pet. Cons.* 2, 8; Asc. *in Or. in Tog. Cand.* p. 84) was not made from the president of a *quaestio perpetua*, but from the praetor peregrinus *in iure*. The case was one of extortion; but the Greeks had, with Caesar's support, brought the case as a simple action for recovery before the competent civil court. See p. 418, note 5.

BOOK II.

Effect of such an appeal.

was allowed, was, as in civil process, purely cassatory; but it might also, as in the civil sphere, be directed with a reformatory object. The tribunes might stay proceedings until something had been done: until, for instance, the court had been constituted according to law. Their veto might, indeed, be final, for they might come to the conclusion that, even where there was no technical flaw in the proceedings or the court, the offence with which the accused was charged was not properly an object of investigation of the particular *quaestio* before which he was impeached. But the use of the *appellatio* in the *quaestiones* was so unusual [1] that we may imagine its rare employment to have been called forth almost solely by technical flaws which could be remedied.

The *provocatio* was unheard of in the procedure of the *iudicia publica*. This was an appeal against the judicial sentence of a magistrate; and here there was no sentence; for even the magisterial decisions incidental to the preliminaries were mere preparations for the judgement of a standing court, which might itself be thought to represent the people since it had been established by popular enactment. The old principle of perpetual delegation, of the surrender of the right of appeal on the appointment of a commission, might have operated here to secure the inappellability of the *iudices*, even though the *quaestiones* were established indifferently by *plebiscita* and by *leges*.

Attempt of Antonius to submit to the *provocatio* the courts which tried *vis* and *maiestas*.

Hence the proposal of Antonius in 44 B.C., that the *provocatio* should be allowed against the decision of the *iudices* in certain *quaestiones*, was looked on as a revolutionary measure. Antonius carried a law which gave an appeal to the people against the verdicts of the courts which enforced Caesar's severe laws of *vis* and *maiestas* [2].

[1] Cic. *in Vat.* 14, 33 (p. 517, note 5).

[2] Cic. *Phil.* i. 9, 21 'altera promulgata lex est ut de vi et maiestatis damnati ad populum provocent, si velint. Haec utrum tandem lex est an legum omnium dissolutio?'

He evidently did not base the principle of the appeal on the nature of the sentence, for interdiction was the punishment for other crimes as well [1]. If he gave any theoretical grounds for the change, these must have been found in the nature of the two crimes. Treason and breaches of the peace were peculiarly offences against the majesty and safety of the body politic, and the people alone were to decide in the last resort when they had been committed. But the real motive of the innovation was probably in a narrow sense political. Prosecutions for these crimes were party weapons, and the Caesarian party, which Antonius represented, relied on the masses as the Republicans did on the courts. This enactment seems to have disappeared with the other Antonian laws at the end of 44 B.C., and no attempt was made at its renewal. When its author was again in power the Republic was at an end, the verdict of the army replaced that of the courts and the people did not deserve consideration as a power.

Reversal of sentences; alien to Roman principles, but sometimes employed.

Restitution (*in integrum restitutio*) or the reversal of the sentence of a court with its effects is an idea that has never appealed strongly to the legal mind. The sanctity of the *res iudicata* was peculiarly great at Rome, and the stability of the constitution was thought to be shaken by spasmodic exercises of the power of pardon and by that reflexion on the wisdom or purity of a court which, save in unusual circumstances, was thought to be implied in the restoration of a convicted exile. Such acts were the fruits of democracy and revolution, not of the aristocratic and stable life of Rome [2]. But in a city where the criminal

[1] p. 506.

[2] Cic. *pro Sulla*, 22, 63 'status enim rei publicae maxime iudicatis rebus continetur'; *in Verr.* v. 6, 12 'Perditae civitates desperatis iam omnibus rebus hos solent exitus exitiales habere, ut damnati in integrum restituantur, vincti solvantur, exules reducantur, res iudicatae rescindantur'; *de Leg. Agr.* ii. 4, 10 'neque vero illa popularia sunt existimanda, iudiciorum perturbationes, rerum iudicatarum infirmationes, restitutio damnatorum; qui civitatum afflictarum, perditis iam rebus, extremi

BOOK II.

courts had always been used as political weapons, such procedure was inevitable, and the revision of the sentences of popular courts and of *quaestiones* can equally be illustrated from its history.

Reversal through the *comitia* (i) of a judgement of the *comitia*;

The reversal by the people through its *comitia* of a judicial sentence formerly passed by one of these assemblies, seems to be based on the simple analogy of the repeal of a law. It can scarcely be regarded as the recall by a court of its own sentence, for little effort seems to have been made to secure that the particular assembly which had pronounced the sentence should reverse it, and, although it may have eventually been considered as an exercise of a sovereign right of pardon, this conception does not seem to have been the starting-point for the power. As ancient precedents for this prerogative Cicero quotes the cases of Kaeso Quinctius, M. Furius Camillus and M. Servilius Ahala[1]. Nearer to his time was the restoration by a *plebiscitum* of Popilius, who had been banished by a tribunician enactment of C. Gracchus[2]. This was doubtless the repeal of a bill of interdiction, and the same procedure may be witnessed in the restoration of Metellus, although here the outlawry pronounced by the centuries[3] was repealed by the *rogatio* of a tribune[4]. Similarly

exitiorum solent esse exitus'; cf. 3, 8 and *pro Sest.* 30, 66. Caesar thinks it worth while to introduce a reason for his restoration of exiles (*B. C.* iii. 1), and the law of Sulpicius 'ut exules revocarentur' is one of the 'perniciosae leges' (Liv. *Ep.* lxxvii).

[1] Cic. *pro Domo*, 32, 86 'At vero . . . Kaeso ille Quinctius et M. Furius Camillus et M. Servilius Ahala . . . populi incitati vim iracundiamque subierunt, damnatique comitiis centuriatis, cum in exilium profugissent, rursus ab eodem populo placato sunt in suam pristinam dignitatem restituti.' Cicero perhaps means to represent restitution by the same assembly that had condemned them. Other traditions represent Camillus and Servilius as having fallen victims to the *plebs* (Liv. iv. 16 and 21; Val. Max. v. 3, 2). Kaeso Quinctius had gone into voluntary banishment (Liv. iii. 13); possibly interdiction had been pronounced against him by the centuries, but it was more probably the work of the *concilium plebis*.

[2] Cic. *Brut.* 34, 128; *post Red. in Sen.* 15, 38; *ad Quir. post Red.* 4, 10.

[3] p. 351.

[4] Cic. *pro Planc.* 28, 69; *post Red. in Sen.* 15, 38.

BOOK II.

Cicero himself, who had been banished by a *plebiscitum* declaring him outlawed, was, after a tribunician bill of restitution had been ineffectually tried[1], restored by a centuriate law[2].

(ii) of a judgement of a *quaestio*.

The theory that the decision of the *iudices* in a *quaestio* might be upset by the people was expressed in 88 B.C. by the tribune P. Sulpicius Rufus, when he passed a law for the restoration of the exiles who had been condemned by the Varian commission[3]. The proposal was not put forward merely as an act of pardon, but had as its professed ground some technical irregularity in the constitution of the commission. This *lex Sulpicia* was repealed with the tribune's other laws, but the example which it had set could not fail to be imitated. In 63 B.C. L. Caecilius Rufus made a proposal to diminish the penalty of the *lex Calpurnia de ambitu* from perpetual exclusion from the senate and office[4] to a temporary suspension of these rights. He was acting in the interest of two men already condemned, his half-brother P. Cornelius Sulla and P. Autronius Paetus, and his proposal to give his bill retrospective force was equivalent to one to rescind the sentence of a court. The project was abandoned, apparently through the exercise of Cicero's influence[5]. In 50 B.C. we read that C. Scribonius Curio thought of trying to obtain, doubtless by a tribunician rogation, the restoration of C. Memmius, who had been condemned by the *lex Pompeia de ambitu*

[1] p. 366, note 8.

[2] Cic. *ad Att.* iv. 1, 4 'cognovi . . . incredibili concursu Italiae legem comitiis centuriatis esse perlatam'; *pro Domo*, 27, 71 'Nam non est ita latum ut mihi Romam venire liceret sed *ut venirem*.' Cicero is proud of the expression that he 'should' (as though the Clodian bill was invalid), not that he 'might' return.

[3] *Auct. ad Herenn.* ii. 28, 45 'Sulpicius qui intercesserat ne exules, quibus causam dicere non licuisset, reducerentur, idem posterius, immutata voluntate, cum eandem legem ferret, aliam sese ferre dicebat, propter nominum commutationem: nam non exules sed vi eiectos se reducere aiebat.'

[4] p. 425.

[5] Cic. *pro Sulla*, 22, 63 and 64. It was said that Sulla himself disapproved the proposal (*ib.* 23, 65).

BOOK II. of 52 B.C.[1], and in 49 B.C. we have Caesar's restitution of persons condemned under the Pompeian laws, not by an exercise of his arbitrary authority but by praetorian and tribunician rogations[2]. With the exception of the attempted modification of the *lex Calpurnia* in 63 B.C., which did not assume the direct appearance of the rescission of a sentence, all the above instances of reversal of judgements are concerned with special commissions, and, as the latter were the products of political strife, it is not surprising that the opposite party, when in power, should upset their verdicts. But Antonius as tribune of the *plebs* is said to have restored a man condemned for an ordinary crime without even alleging any irregularity in the trial as the ground for upsetting the judgement of the court[3]. It seems clear that in the Ciceronian period the theory was fully established that the people had the power of rescinding the verdicts of juries; it is described as a *beneficium*[4] and must have been conceived as a power of pardon. Any one of the three legislative assemblies was competent for the purpose. Most of the proposals are tribunician, but the restitution granted by Caesar was effected by a praetorian law as well.

Story of a *quaestio* reversing its own sentence.

The *quaestio* which had pronounced a sentence was a transitory thing, and we should not expect it to have had

[1] Cic. *ad Att.* vi. 1, 23 (50 B.C.) 'De Memmio restituendo ut Curio cogitet te audisse puto.'

[2] Caesar, *B. C.* iii. 1 'praetoribus tribunisque plebis rogationes ad populum ferentibus . . . in integrum restituit. Statuerat enim prius hos iudicio populi debere restitui quam suo beneficio videri receptos'; cf. Suet. *Caes.* 41; Dio Cass. xliii. 27. On the grounds alleged for the restoration see p. 394.

[3] Cic. *Phil.* ii. 23, 56 'Licinium Lenticulam (or 'Denticulam') de alea condemnatum . . . restituit . . . Quam attulisti rationem populo Romano cur eum restitui oporteret?'; cf. Dio Cass. xlv. 47. Rein (p. 833) suggests that the man had been condemned under the *lex Cornelia de falsis*.

[4] 'beneficium legis' (Cic. *Phil.* ii. 23, 56); so Caesar did not wish his own restoration of exiles to seem an act of pardon ('suo beneficio' note 2).

any power of cancelling its own verdicts. Yet the remission of a penalty (*remissio poenae*) by a court which had already pronounced it, is a feature in a strange story told by Valerius Maximus. A communication of a portentous occurrence connected with a condemned woman was made by the jailer to the praetor, and by the praetor to his *consilium*, with the result that the jury altered their verdict [1]. It is difficult to estimate the value of this story, but the point which it illustrates—that a court could immediately alter its own sentence—seems to be denied by Cicero in a criticism of an act of Verres' provincial jurisdiction [2]. The criticism, however, seems directed rather against the impropriety than the illegality of the act, and it is probable that the governor had the power of pardon in his province, a power which of course carried with it the right to rescind his own sentences as well as those of his delegates.

Provincial governor's power of pardon.

Two quasi-restitutory powers remain to be considered. One is the remission of the ban of outlawry associated with martial law, the other is the declaration of amnesty. Neither power repeals a sentence, but both put the individual in a better position than he was in before from the point of view of the criminal law and exempt him from certain possible penal consequences.

The remission of outlawry was not necessary until the

[1] The incident that moved the jury was the support of a mother's life by her daughter's breast (Val. Max. v. 4, 7). Mommsen shows (*Strafr.* p. 479) that the attribution of the occurrence to a date earlier than 191 B.C. (Festus, p. 209; Plin. *H. N.* vii. 36, 121) makes its details impossible, as no such *quaestio* existed then. Its association with the temple of *Pietas* may be wrong; but this would not of itself prove the story to be false. It must have its origin in some historical fact; but, as we cannot tell whether it is ante-dated or post-dated, it is of little use to the historian.

[2] Cic. *in Verr.* v. 6, 13 (Verres had suddenly released from threatened execution and restored to their master a number of slaves convicted of crime and conspiracy) 'Hoc vero novum . . . ut ipse qui iudicarat, ut statim e medio supplicio dimiserit.'

Remission of outlawry, which has been pronounced by the senate.

epoch in the history of martial law was reached when certain individuals were named as *hostes* in the senatorial decree [1]. We might have expected the senate which named them to be the authority to recall the ban. But this is not the case; it is the people that performs this function and declares the quasi-condemnation of the magistrates and senate to be unjust. After Marius and eleven of his adherents had been named as *hostes*, Cinna attempted at the commencement of his consulship to recall them by law [2]. The attempt was ineffectual, but Marius on his triumphant entry into Rome (87 B.C.) contemptuously pretended that a law was necessary for his restoration [3]. Similarly in 43 B.C. Octavian had the outlawry of Dolabella revoked by decree of the people [4].

Amnesty.

Amnesty, on the other hand, for acts which may in the future be regarded as offences against the law, but which have not yet been the subject of judicial cognizance or a declaration of outlawry, had by the Ciceronian period become a prerogative of the senate [5]. It was this body which declared Caesar's murderers scatheless in 44 B.C. [6], a declaration which did not save them from subsequent

[1] p. 400.

[2] Dio Cass. *frgt.* 119.

[3] Plutarch (*Mar.* 43) says that the tribes were summoned, but that it was not thought worth while to carry the law through; Velleius however (ii. 21) says that the measure was carried ('prior ingressus Cinna de recipiendo Mario legem tulit') and Appian (*B. C.* i. 70) mentions a tribunician bill as being passed; (cf. Dio Cass. *frgt.* 119).

[4] App. *B. C.* iii. 95 *νόμῳ δ' ἑτέρῳ ἀπέλυε μὴ εἶναι πολέμιον Δολοβέλλαν.* The *lex Plotia de reditu Lepidanorum*, supported by Caesar (*circa* 75–70 B.C.; Suet. *Caes.* 5) may have been of the same character; those who had followed Lepidus and gone over to Sertorius being indirectly *hostes*, although they may not have been named as such.

[5] Cf. the senate's power of granting *fides publica* to individuals; p. 484, note 7.

[6] Vell. ii. 58 'consul Antonius . . . liberos suos obsides in Capitolium misit fidemque descendendi tuto interfectoribus Caesaris dedit. Et illud decreti Atheniensium celeberrimi exemplum, relatum a Cicerone (cf. Cic. *Phil.* i. 1, 1), oblivionis praeteritarum rerum decreto patrum comprobatum est'; cf. *ib.* i. 13, 31 and Plut. *Brut.* 19. According to Appian (*B. C.* iv. 94, speech of Cassius) it was an amnesty against all further prosecution for the murder (*φόνου μὴ εἶναι δίκας*).

condemnation by a court; and during the second triumvirate we find the senate giving those of its members, who had raised troops on their own account during the civil war, immunity against a charge of *latrocinium*[1] and, thereby, exempting them from prosecution under the *lex Cornelia de sicariis*[2].

[1] Dio Cass. xlix. 43 *δόγμα ἐγένετο μηδένα τῶν ἐς τὴν γερουσίαν τελούντων ἐπὶ λῃστείᾳ κρίνεσθαι.*

[2] Merkel, *Über die Begnadigungscompetenz im römischen Strafprocesse*, p. 24.

APPENDIX I

THE NEXUS AND THE VINDEX.

(Note to pp. 71 and 73.)

The attempt on p. 71 to explain the contract of *nexum* is, like all others that have been made, conjectural; but I have not adopted the usual course of explaining *nexum* by means of the *legis actio per manus iniectionem*. There is no evidence from antiquity that the *manus iniectio*, in the sense which it bore in the Twelve Tables and in conformity with the rules there laid down, ever applied to the nexal debtor. The only evidence of this which can be adduced is gained by taking *aeris confessi* in the procedure described by Gellius (xx. 1, 45 'Aeris confessi rebusque iure iudicatis triginta dies iusti sunto') as a reference to the *nexus* (Muirhead, *Hist. Intr. to Private Law of Rome*, 2nd ed. p. 192), and not, as I have done (p. 72), to the judgement debtor who confesses. The theory which I have suggested is that the contract of *nexum* is quite independent of the *legis actio per man. ini.*, and that by this contract the debtor did not become a quasi-judgement debtor, but a *mancipium* of his creditor. *Mancipium*, of course, does not imply that he is a slave, but simply that he is owned. The son under power is owned, but is not a slave.

The more general theory is that the *nexus* was *pro iudicato*, and in conformity with this view Huschke (*Nexum*, p. 56) conjectured the following formula for the contract:—

Quod ego tibi mille libras hoc aere aeneaque libra nexas dedi, eas tu mihi post annum iure nexi dare damnas esto;

the *dare damnas esto* expressing a quasi-condemnation (cf. *lex Ursoncnsis*, c. lxi 'Si quis in eo vim faciet, ast eius vincitur, dupli damnas esto').

But that the contract of servitude for debt, so widely spread in the Greek world (Diod. i. 79, 5), had at Rome this artificial and derivative origin is improbable. At Athens we can even observe the two processes—the contract and the judgement—by which servitude for debt was effected (*Ath. Pol.* c. 2); and it is unlikely that, wherever these two methods are found, the contract should be pronounced a quasi-judgement.

With respect to the *vindex* of the *leg. act. per man. ini.* (p. 73) there are three questions which must be raised. These are (1) what rôle he played, (2) what he was liable for, (3) whether his unsuccessful intervention released the debtor. There is a pretty general agreement amongst modern authorities that he was some kind of representative who took over the action, that he was liable for double the amount of the original debt [because by this intervention he had committed a delict (Huschke, *Nexum*, p. 96; Girard, *Droit Romain*, p. 959, n. 3)] and that his intervention, even when unsuccessful, liberated the chief debtor (Zimmern, *Civilprozess*, p. 132; Huschke, *Nexum*, pp. 95, 96; Puchta, *Inst.* pp. 95, 96; Keller, *Civilprocess*, § 19; Bethmann-Hollweg, *Civilprozess*, i. p. 197; Ihering, *Geist*, i. p. 153). Unger was a dissentient. In an article in the *Zeitschrift für Rechtsgeschichte* (vii. p. 192 sq.) he pointed out the emphatic nature of the statements that representation was unknown in the *legis actio* (Gaius, iv. 82; Just. *Inst.* iv. 10) and showed that the *vindex* is one who simply denies that the creditor has a right over a particular person (Festus, p. 376). Both lay hands on the debtor, and the procedure was probably a *sacramento actio.* So far Unger is undoubtedly right. The answer to question (1) is that the *vindex* may be materially, but is not formally, a *procurator* or defender; he is a man who is conducting *his own* case in the interest of another. Unger further held that the *vindex*, if unsuccessful, was only liable for the amount of the *sacramentum*—a view which is probable and consistent with the legal position of the *vindex*, unless we believe that his interference was considered delictal. Questions (2) and (3) really go together, for, if the *vindex* was only liable for the *sacramentum*, his conviction could not free the debtor whom he had championed. The latter was then liable *in duplum*, perhaps because his action in denying the debt and presenting the *vindex* ('vindicem dabat,' Gaius, iv. 21) was considered a delictal interference with the course of justice.

If, on the other hand, the *vindex* was liable for double the debt, it seems reasonable to suppose that the debtor was freed, although this is by no means certain, since the *vindex* is, as we have seen, not formally a representative, nor a defendant in an action, and does not take the *litis contestatio* with respect to the debt on himself.

In the midst of such evenly balanced probabilities it seemed safer to state the ordinary view in the text, and to suggest the modifying considerations in this note. Unger's view is the most attractive because it is the most scientific; but in dealing with these questions of early Roman procedure, we are dealing with a time when there was plenty of law but little jurisprudence. There may have been a lack of logical connexion between the position of the *vindex* and his liabilities, and unfortunately the central fact—the meaning of the *poena dupli*—is still an unfathomable mystery.

APPENDIX II

CICERO'S SPEECHES FOR QUINCTIUS, ROSCIUS THE ACTOR, TULLIUS AND CAECINA.

COMMENTARIES ON THE SPEECHES[1].

General (on some or all of the Speeches).

Hotmani (F.) *Iurisconsulti opera.* Tom. iii (Geneva, 1600).

Garatoni (G.) *M. T. Ciceronis orationes* (Naples, 1777, &c.).

Keller (F. L. von) *Semestrium ad M. Tullium Ciceronem libri tres* (Zurich, 1842).

Bethmann-Hollweg (M. A. von) *Römischer Civilprozess* (Bonn, 1865), Bd. ii. pp. 783–841 (*Anhang, drei Reden des M. Tullius Cicero in Civilsachen*).

Gasquy (A.) *Cicéron Jurisconsulte* (Paris, 1887).

On the 'pro Quinctio.'

Rau (S. J. E.) *Disputatio iuridica ad M. Tullii Ciceronis orationem pro P. Quintio* (Leyden, 1825).

Frei (J.) *Der Rechtsstreit zwischen P. Quinctius und S. Naevius; eine Einleitung zu Cicero's Rede für P. Quinctius* (Zürich, 1852).

Kübler (B.) *Der Process des Quinctius und C. Aquilius Gallus* in *Zeitschrift der Savigny-Stiftung* (1893), pp. 54 ff.

On the 'pro Roscio comoedo.'

Rovers (J. A. C.) *De Ciceronis oratione pro Roscio comoedo* (Utrecht, 1826).

Munchen (M.) *M. Tullii Ciceronis pro Q. Roscio comoedo orationem iuridice exposuit* (Köln, 1829).

Puchta in *Rheinisches Museum für Jurisprudenz*, Bd. i. (1833), p. 316 ff.

Schmidt (C. A.) *M. Tullii Ciceronis pro Q. Roscio comoedo oratio* (Leipzig, 1839).

On the 'pro Caecina.'

Cras (H. C.) *Dissertatio iuridica inauguralis qua specimen iurisprudentiae Ciceronianae exhibetur, sive Ciceronem iustam pro A. Caecina causam dixisse ostenditur* (Leyden, 1769).

On the 'pro Tullio.'

Huschke (P. E.) *Orationis pro M. Tullio quae extant cum commentariis et excursibus. Inter analecta literaria curante J. G. Huschkio* (Leipzig, 1826).

[1] The Commentaries are referred to in the following notes by the names of their authors alone.

(1) *PRO QUINCTIO.*

GELLIUS says that this was the first case pleaded by Cicero, and that he was twenty-six years old at the time[1]. The date thus assigned to it is the consulship of Tullius and Dolabella (81 B.C.), and this assignment agrees with certain notes of time given in Cicero's speech. Quinctius, we are told, left Rome in the January of the year when Scipio and Norbanus were consuls[2] (83 B.C.); he returned on the Ides of September of the same year[3]; but Naevius, his opponent, waited eighteen months before pressing his case against him[4]. Cicero also remarks that his first forensic efforts were made under the dictatorship of Sulla[5].

In his conduct of the defence Cicero succeeded M. Junius, now hampered by official business[6]. The counsel for Naevius was Q. Hortensius[7], who was assisted by L. Philippus[8], his senior at the Bar. They were furnished with advice and support by an *advocatio* of distinguished men[9].

The *iudex* in this, as in the former, hearing was C. Aquilius Gallus; and by his side there sat as assessors[10] L. Lucilius Balbus, M. Claudius Marcellus and P. Quinctilius[11].

The case had now come on for a renewed hearing after an adjournment (*ampliatio*), which was necessitated perhaps by Aquilius having declared himself not sufficiently informed by the earlier pleadings. Hortensius threw the blame for this delay on the advocates of Quinctius and attempted to get from the praetor a limit of time for the speeches on either side[12]. But Aquilius, who, as *iudex*, had now entire control of the proceedings, had scouted this claim. Yet the plaint was not without effect on Cicero; he promises to be brief, and to deal summarily with what he represents as a very lengthy controversy. It was, however, the controversy, not the case, that had been drawn out. When Cicero speaks of the proceedings as having lasted two years, he is reckoning from the Ides of September of 83, when Quinctius had concluded his final

[1] Gell. xv. 28. [2] 6, 24. [3] 7, 29. [4] 8, 30. [5] *Brutus*, 90, 311.
[6] 'nova legatione impeditus' (1, 3). [7] 2, 8; 10, 35; 24, 77.
[8] 22, 72; 24, 77; 26, 80. [9] 14, 47; 22, 72. [10] 1, 4 and 5; 16, 53.
[11] 17, 54. [12] 9, 33 and 34; 22, 71.

vadimonium, to the present date (the spring or summer of 81). But it was at this latter date that the real case, in which he pleads, was brought before the praetor, and neither the proceedings *in iure* nor those *in iudicio* appear to have been unusually long.

The facts of the case, as gathered from Cicero, are as follows:—

C. Quinctius, brother of Cicero's client P. Quinctius, was in partnership with S. Naevius. Their business lay in the territory of Narbonese Gaul[1]. It consisted in the working of cultivated land and a cattle farm, both of which were in good condition. After some years of partnership C. Quinctius died suddenly in Gaul, Naevius himself being there at the time. C. Quinctius left P. Quinctius his heir by will, and shortly afterwards the latter went to Gaul[2] to examine into his new interests in the business. He lived on the best terms with Naevius. For nearly a year they were together; they had many discussions about the partnership and the Gallic estate, and during the whole of this time no complaint was made by Naevius that the business owed him anything or that C. Quinctius had incurred any debt to him apart from the business.

But C. Quinctius had left a few other debts to Publius. These were payable at Rome, and Publius gave notice that he would sell by auction at Narbo the goods which he had just inherited. Naevius urges him, in a friendly way, not to do this; he says that he has money at Rome and that it is at Quinctius' disposal. Quinctius, therefore, abandons the auction and leaves for Rome, Naevius quitting Gaul for the same destination at the same time[3].

Caius' chief creditor had been P. Scapula, and the money was now owed to Scapula's children. The payment was submitted to arbitration and Aquilius Gallus, soon to be Quinctius' judge, was, as a friend of the Scapula family, chosen to be

[1] 2, 12; 25, 80. The site of the business was specified by Cicero, but the manuscript reading is corrupt. We find *Sebaguinos* and *Sebaginnos* in 25, 80. The reading *Segusiavi*, adopted by Orelli and some later editors, is scarcely possible; for this people was beyond the limits of the then province of Gaul (Caesar, *B. G.* i. 10; vii. 64). Hirschfeld (ad *C. I. L.* xiii. 1, p. 221) suggests that Cicero wrote *trans Alpes in Cebennas*, an equivalent to *trans Alpes ad extremos provinciae fines*.

[2] 4, 15.

[3] 4, 16.

arbitrator. The intervention of an *arbiter* was desirable, because the settlement raised a question of exchange, the debts having been incurred in Gaul and being payable at Rome[1]. Quinctius, still buoyed up by Naevius' promises, arranges to pay the Scapulae[2].

But a change had come over Naevius. He now says that he will not lend Quinctius a penny until all the accounts of the partnership have been cleared up, and it is certain that there will be no further question between them about the business[3]. Quinctius asks for a delay of this settlement and an immediate loan; but the request is refused. He succeeds, however, in getting a few days' grace from the Scapulae, sends to Gaul to sell the property he had put up for sale and liquidates his debt[4].

Quinctius then calls on Naevius to arrange the issue between them[5]. A peaceful meeting (*congressus*) and an attempt at a settlement (*constitutum*)[6] without recourse to law are the means suggested. Both parties are to be represented by friends, Quinctius by S. Alfenus, Naevius by M. Trebellius. But the meeting was in vain; no agreement (*pactum*) could be reached[7].

The only recourse was to a law-suit. Naevius was plaintiff; but the old forcible *in ius vocatio* was disappearing, and the mutual *vadimonium* was resorted to[8]. Bail was given by both parties for their presence; adjournments and rebailing followed; then Naevius appeared to his bail[9].

Cicero then glides smoothly over a most doubtful incident.

[1] 4, 17 'quod propter aerariam rationem non satis erat in tabulis inspexisse, quantum deberetur, nisi ad Castoris quaesisses, quantum solveretur.' See Lambinus, *ap. Garatonium, in loc.* 'In Gallia pecuniae dissimilis fuit ratio ac Romae, ut apparet ex oratione pro Fonteio et aliis locis... propter dissimilem pecuniae rationem non satis commode poterat inter P. Quinctium et Scapulae liberos convenire quantum solveretur. Sumptus igitur ea de re est arbiter.' 'ad Castoris,' which is probably the true reading, must refer to the banking houses near that site.

[2] 5, 18.

[3] 5, 19.

[4] 5, 20 'deteriore tempore absens auctionatur: Scapulis difficiliore conditione dissolvit.'

[5] *ib.* 'ut quam primum... res transigeretur.'

[6] Cicero in his speech for Caelius (*pro Cael.* 8, 20) attempts to disprove the assaults committed by his client 'cum sit iis confitendum nunquam se ne congressu quidem et constituto coepisse de tantis iniuriis experiri.'

[7] 5, 21 'res convenire nullo modo poterat.'

[8] 5, 22 'res esse in vadimonium coepit'; see p. 142.

[9] *ib.* 'venit ad vadimonium Naevius.'

According to his narrative, Naevius at this final meeting said that he too had held an auction in Gaul, and that he had arranged so that the partnership owed him nothing. He added that he was not inclined to accept or to give bail any longer[1]. To Cicero these words mean that Naevius is no longer a plaintiff; but, if language that could be twisted into this form had been employed, Naevius must have repudiated it. His subsequent conduct shows that he denied releasing Quinctius from his *vadimonium* and that he maintained its renewal.

But, according to the view taken by Cicero and his client, the two parties leave without any *vadimonium* for a further adjournment[2]. Quinctius stays at Rome for about thirty days. He procures an adjournment of other cases he has on hand[3], then leaves for Gaul in company with L. Albius, a witness in the subsequent case. The date of his departure became an important item in Cicero's defence; it was, according to various readings in the speech, the 29th or 31st of January[4].

Naevius hears, from a friend, L. Publicius, who had met Quinctius at Vada Volaterrana, that the latter is on his way northwards. This news decides his action. His object is now to prove that Quinctius had not stood to his bail and to ask the praetor for a writ of *bonorum possessio*[5]. He summons his friends to meet at a place named *tabula Sestia* (probably a bank) on the following day at 7 o'clock in the morning[6]. There he asserts that Quinctius has deserted his bail[7] and he draws up an affidavit (*tabulae*) to this effect, which is signed by the witnesses.

Armed with this affidavit he approaches the praetor Burrienus, and asks him for a writ of *bonorum possessio* in accordance with his edict (*ex edicto*). We have already examined the grounds on which such a writ could be granted against the *indefensus*[8]. We cannot say on what particular ground it was given in this case, or even whether Cicero has mentioned

[1] 6, 23 'se iam neque vadari amplius neque vadimonium promittere.'

[2] *ib.* 'ita sine vadimonio disceditur.'

[3] *ib.* 'cum ceteris, quae habebat, vadimonia differt.'

[4] In 6, 24 it is *ante diem* iv; in 18, 57 it is *prid. Kal. Febr.* One of the two readings must be wrong, but its falsity makes no difference to the facts of the case.

[5] See p. 255.

[6] See p. 139, note 3.

[7] 6, 25 'P. Quinctium non stitisse et se stitisse.'

[8] p. 256.

the appropriate clause. The ruling which Hotomannus and Lambinus professed to find in manuscripts of the *pro Quinctio* —*Qui absens iudicio defensus non fuerit*[1]—would have been the most appropriate[2].

In any case Burrienus granted the *missio*. It is almost impertinent to raise the question 'Was he right?' If we hold that the writ could only be issued on a *causae cognitio*, we have no proof that this did not take place. By the nature of the case the cognizance could not take account of the defendant's evidence, for that would have defeated the object of the writ. The praetor granted it on prima facie evidence that a guarantee had been given for appearance in court, that this guarantee had not been observed, and that the case was not defended by a representative. These three facts must have been made out to Burrienus' satisfaction. The procedure was necessarily one-sided and might seem harsh[3]. But then the *missio in possessionem* was not a definitive judgement; it might be contested, and it is almost certain that the civil disabilities (*infamia*) did not follow the *missio*, but the *bonorum venditio*[4]. In a sense infamy began with the *missio*, for it was a serious stain on a man's commercial reputation[5]; but the writ was not absolute until after the expiry of the thirty days.

But Quinctius finds a sudden champion. His agent, S. Alfenus, tears down the notices of sale (*libelli*) and announces that he is Quinctius' *procurator*[6]. If Naevius presses his case, he (Alfenus) will meet him in court.

It is clear that this defence did not invalidate Burrienus'

[1] See Lambinus, *ap. Garatonium, in loc., Qui absens iudicio defensus non fuerit.* 'Haec verba desiderantur in omnibus libris vulgatis; restituimus autem in manuscriptis reperta.' To which Garatoni adds 'Proferat Hotomannus, proferat Lambinus membranas, in quibus tale quid compareat: viros dixero.' A summary of the opinions held on this point by more modern jurists and scholars is to be found in Frei, pp. 10 and 11.

[2] Of the undisputed grounds mentioned by Cicero (19, 60) the nearest in appropriateness is *qui fraudationis causa latitaverit.* But it is not very suitable to the case. Even a prejudiced praetor could scarcely have regarded Quinctius as *latitans.*

[3] Cicero says (16, 51) that by custom such a writ was only granted *multis vadimoniis desertis.*

[4] See p. 285, note 3. For a summary of juristic opinions on this point see Frei, p. 15.

[5] 15, 50 'cuius bona ex edicto possidentur, huius omnis fama et existimatio cum bonis simul possidetur.'

[6] 6, 27 'denuntiat sese procuratorem esse'; see p. 237.

action. It came too late. It followed the *missio in possessionem* and, at the time of the issue of the writ, Quinctius was undefended.

Meanwhile Naevius was proceeding to carry out the writ. Quinctius was expelled from the land that he still held in common with Naevius in Gaul[1]. He took refuge with the propraetor of Gaul, C. Flaccus. The governor punished, or threatened to punish, the acts of force[2], probably on the grounds that undue violence had been used, and the *dominus* expelled *invitus*[3]. The acts of Naevius' agents were, therefore, illegal; they might have been met by an action for damages (*iniuriae*), or perhaps by the use of the *interdictum de vi*; but they have little to do with the merits of the case as Cicero had to present it.

Naevius was bound to recognize Alfenus as *procurator*; but he claims that the latter as the representative of Quinctius should 'as *procurator* give security for the liquidation of the judgement[4].' The request was perhaps made on two grounds, both good in law: (1) that Alfenus is representing a man who, if he acted on his own account, would have to give the *satisdatio*, for this was the normal mode of contesting a writ of possession: (2) that Alfenus, regarded merely as a representative, should give the usual security. Alfenus is afraid that if he consents to give security, this will be a recognition of the *missio* and will prejudice Quinctius' case[5]; he forgets that he is also a *procurator*, or, if he remembers it, his contention is, as we have remarked[6], an evidence that in Cicero's time the necessity for security in representation was still a disputed principle.

On this point Alfenus appealed to the college of tribunes[7]—a procedure which evoked a complaint from Hortensius that a dilatory method of shirking the *iudicium* was being adopted[8].

[1] 'agro communi' (6, 28). The land was still *communis* because the accounts between Quinctius and Naevius had never been squared.

[2] 7, 28 'eam rem quam vehementer vindicandam putarit, ex decretis eius poteritis cognoscere.'

[3] Cf. the words of the edict quoted in 27, 84 'dominum invitum detrudere non placet.'

[4] 7, 28 'ut procurator iudicatum solvi satisdaret.'

[5] *ib.* 'negat Alfenus aequum esse procuratorem satisdare quod reus satisdare non deberet.'

[6] p. 243. Cf. Kübler, p. 65.

[7] 7, 29.

[8] 20, 63 'non est istud iudicium pati neque iudicio defendere, cum

There was apparently a difference of opinion amongst the members of the college. All that was legally needed to stop the case was the veto of one member against the praetor's (actual or future) decree that Alfenus could only intervene by furnishing security. But it was not unusual for the tribunes to decide on such judicial appeals by a majority of votes[1]. The *intercessio*, however, was promised by one of the college, M. Brutus. He said that he would pronounce the veto unless an agreement was come to between Alfenus and Naevius[2], the suggested agreement apparently being to wait for Quinctius' return to conduct his case in person.

It is usually held that what Brutus refused to veto was the decree of the praetor ordering *satisdatio*[3]. But, if the praetor had persisted in his refusal to grant a case without *satisdatio* to Alfenus, the effect of such a veto would merely have been to inhibit Alfenus' defence. It would not have protected Quinctius against the writ of *bonorum possessio* being made absolute and the *venditio* being proceeded with.

Brutus, therefore, may have threatened to veto the writ of *bonorum possessio* until the case was defended. Hence his insistance on an arrangement which should allow Quinctius to defend the case in person. The arrangement is accepted and Alfenus promises that Quinctius shall appear in court on September 13[4].

Quinctius comes to Rome and appears to his bail[5]. But Naevius is now wholly inactive. He allows an interval of eighteen months to elapse before he takes up the matter again. Perhaps in the revolutionary confusion of this time he may have wished, as a deserter from the popular party to the conquering aristocracy, as a flatterer and witty parasite of his new protectors, to secure their help before he made a fresh attack on Quinctius[6]. The reason that might have been

auxilium a tribunis petas'; 20, 65 the 'appellatio' was made 'morae' not 'auxilii causa.'

[1] p. 291.

[2] 20, 65 'Quid? si M. Brutus intercessurum se dixit palam, nisi quid inter ipsum Alfenum et Naevium conveniret.'

[3] This is apparently the view of Bethmann-Hollweg (p. 797) and of Frei (p. 18).

[4] 7, 29.

[5] 8, 30 'vadimonium sistit.'

[6] For the change of front of Naevius, his parasitic character and his wit, see 3, 11; 17, 55; 22, 70; 30, 93. It must have been during this

furnished by Hortensius for this delay on the part of his client was, that the restored peace was the only condition of his getting a recognition of his just claims[1].

When the case is again taken up in 81 B.C., Dolabella is praetor. Naevius approaches him and asks that Quinctius should be made to give security *iudicatum solvi*, on the ground that Quinctius' goods had been possessed for thirty days in accordance with the edict of the praetor Burrienus[2]; for this edict had never been withdrawn. The advocates of Quinctius demanded that Naevius, too, against whom Quinctius intended to pursue his counter-claims[3] in the same *iudicium*, should give the same *cautio*[4], and, further, they denied that Quinctius' goods had been possessed *ex edicto*[5].

Dolabella holds that provisionally he shall consider the writ good and that, in the ordinary course of things, it can only be contested by Quinctius' giving *satisdatio iudicatum solvi*, to give which would be a recognition that the writ was valid, that it was *ex edicto*. But he allows Quinctius a loophole of escape from this admission. As an alternative he permits him to enter into a legal wager (*sponsio*) with Naevius that 'the goods had not been possessed for thirty days in accordance with the edict of P. Burrienus, the praetor[6].' The sum stipulated in such a case was insignificant, perhaps twenty-five sesterces[7], for the *sponsio* was not *poenalis*; hence there was no restipulation on the opposite side.

According to the most generally accepted reading in the *pro*

period that S. Alfenus fell victim to Sulla's proscription (81 B.C.) that Naevius as *sector* purchased his property and made Quinctius his *socius* in this business; see 22, 70; 24, 76; 29, 88. In the account of this interval I have followed the excellent description of Bethmann-Hollweg (p. 789).

[1] Bethmann-Hollweg, p. 800.

[2] 8, 30.

[3] Cf. 23, 74 'cum ipse (Naevius) ultro deberet.'

[4] 8, 30 'Recusabant qui aderant tum Quinctio: demonstrabant de re iudicium fieri oportere ut aut uterque inter se aut neuter satisdaret: non necesse esse famam alterius in iudicium venire.'

[5] *ib.* 'non recusabat Quinctius quin ita satisdare iuberet (Dolabella), si bona possessa essent ex edicto.'

[6] 8, 30 'iubet P. Quinctium sponsionem cum Sex. Naevio facere *si bona sua ex edicto P. Burrieni praetoris dies xxx possessa non essent.*' The reading *si . . . non essent* is equivalent to the reading *ni . . . essent*. Both make Quinctius *stipulator*. It is only if we read *si . . . essent* that he becomes *promissor*.

[7] Cf. Gaius, iv. 9

Quinctio, Quinctius is *stipulator*, i. e. the man who asks *spondesne?* Naevius the *promissor*, i. e. the man who says *spondeo*. The wager propounded by Quinctius may have run as follows:—

Si bona mea ex edicto P. Burrieni praetoris dies triginta possessa non sunt, sestertios viginti quinque dare spondes?

To this Naevius answered *spondeo*.

The questions concerning this procedure, which we should like to but cannot answer, are (1) Was Quinctius owing to his position necessarily *stipulator*, or was this rôle arbitrarily assigned him by the praetor? (2) Did the *stipulator* necessarily open the case, as Quinctius was forced to do, or was this position (apart from his being *stipulator*) involved in his impeachment of the writ, or was the rôle of plaintiff assigned him at praetorian discretion[1]?

It is this *praeiudicium*, raised by the *sponsio*, which is the case in which Cicero is pleading. His line of argument is as follows:—

(1) That there was no *causa* for Naevius' request for *bonorum possessio*.

(*a*) Because there was no debt at all, either *ex societatis ratione* or *privatim*[2].

The reasons adduced are somewhat weak. The first ground advanced is that, after the death of C. Quinctius, Publius had been in Gaul with Naevius for more than a year, and yet there had been no mention of the debt; the second, that Naevius brought no final action against Quinctius arising from the *societas*, which Quinctius could meet on equal terms, but seeks to ruin him through this unjustifiable claim of *missio in possessionem*[3].

(*b*) Because, so far from the *vadimonium* being *desertum*, there was no *vadimonium* at all[4].

After appealing to the general principle that the desertion of one *vadimonium* was no good ground for a request for the

[1] Gasquy (p. 81) considers that the position as plaintiff or defendant followed the part taken in the *sponsio*, but that the *sponsio* was regulated by the praetor. Bethmann-Hollweg (p. 790) holds that the burden of proof should have rested on Naevius, but when he says, 'der Prätor Cn. Dolabella aber legte *per decretum* diesem (Quinctius) die sponsion,' he seems to make Quinctius the *promissor*. His view appears to be that the *promissor* should have been plaintiff.

[2] 11, 37. [3] 11, 37; 14, 47. [4] 28, 86.

writ[1], Cicero adduces proof that this final *vadimonium* was never concluded. Naevius, to a question put to him by Quinctius, said that it had been made on February 5. But Quinctius, on referring to his diary (*ephemeris*), finds that he had left for Gaul before that date[2]. The diary was doubtless put in, and its evidence was strengthened by that of Quinctius' companion on the journey, L. Albius. Naevius, on the other hand, had put in his own *adstipulator* at the *vadimonium* to rebut this evidence[3].

(*c*) Because Quinctius was really defended[4].

It is very probable that Naevius was fully aware that Alfenus was Quinctius' permanent procurator; there is also a presumption that Naevius should have known that Alfenus served Quinctius *at Rome*[5]. But the real legal difficulty—that the defence of Alfenus came after the writ was issued—is not met by Cicero.

(2) That Naevius could not have possessed *ex edicto*, because Quinctius did not come under the conditions stated in the edict[6].

(*a*) The most vital ground adduced is that which we have just considered, viz. that Quinctius was defended.

(*b*) Because violence, forbidden in the edict, had been used in expelling Quinctius[7].

As we have seen[8], this might have been a ground of an action against Naevius, but it could hardly invalidate the writ.

(*c*) Because Quinctius, in expelling Naevius, had anticipated the writ[9].

The writ was asked for *ante Kal. V intercalares.* Quinctius is expelled from the land in Gaul *pridie Kal. intercalares.* The 700 miles from Rome to the Gallic estate had been covered in two days.

Here again was a ground for damages, but hardly for invalidation.

(3) That Naevius had never 'possessed' at all, because the only possession recognized by the edict was universal possession (*in universis*)[10]. This Naevius had never attempted to secure, for Quinctius' house and slaves at Rome, and his private landed property in Gaul, remained untouched.

[1] 14, 48; 16, 51. [2] 18, 57. [3] 18, 58. [4] 19, 60.
[5] Cf. 22, 73. [6] 28, 86 and 87; cf. 19, 60. [7] 29, 89.
[8] p. 536. [9] 25, 79 and 80. [10] 29, 89.

We have no direct knowledge of the interpretation of the praetor's ruling in this matter, which prevailed in Cicero's time; but as this occupation, probably at that time and certainly afterwards, was not regarded as true possession at all, but merely as guardianship (*custodia*) in the interest of the creditor[1], it is extremely improbable that its universal application to all the debtor's property was demanded.

The best point in Cicero's arguments, if it could be proved, is the contention that Quinctius had never deserted his *vadimonium* (1 *b*), and consequently that there was no ground whatever for Naevius' original demand for *bonorum possessio*. A weak point in Naevius' proceedings was, perhaps, his consenting to allow Quinctius to appear in person after the writ had been issued[2]; but he acted under pressure, and perhaps, when he concluded this *vadimonium* with Quinctius, he still regarded the writ as good. He may have held that Quinctius was only appearing to contest the validity of the writ. A far weaker point in his case is the strange delay which followed, and his relations with Quinctius during this interval. They are hardly those of a serious creditor who has taken the extremest measures against his debtor. The validity of Burrienus' writ could not be questioned, but it must have been a serious question for the *iudex* whether the thirty days' possession had not been broken by Naevius' conduct. On this ground Quinctius may have gained the verdict. He seems on grounds of equity to have deserved it. Burrienus may have acted in good faith; but a man like Quinctius, who had hitherto proved himself solvent, was part-owner of a Gallic estate and possessed of other property of his own, could hardly be regarded as a fraudulent absentee, and was not a proper object of a writ of *bonorum possessio*.

[1] Paulus in Dig. 41, 2, 3, 23 'Quod autem Quintus Mucius inter genera possessionum posuit, si quando iussu magistratus rei servandae causa possidemus, ineptissimum est: nam qui creditorem rei servandae causa... mittit in possessionem . . . non possessionem sed custodiam rerum et observationem concedit'; cf. Gaius, in Dig. 42, 5, 13.

[2] p. 537.

(2) *PRO ROSCIO COMOEDO.*

The date of this speech can be approximately fixed by a passage which is generally taken to refer to the counter-revolution of Sulla (81 B.C.)[1]. The interval between this time and the trial is stated; but it is questionable whether the manuscript reading descriptive of this interval is correct. It is 'abhinc annis xv[2],' for which Hotomannus suggested 'abhinc annis IV,' a suggestion which has been accepted by most editors. If we follow this view, the date would be 76 B.C., and the orator would have been in his thirty-first year at the time of the delivery of the speech.

Cicero pleaded for Roscius before C. Calpurnius Piso, who was now *iudex* and had, at a previous stage of the controversy, acted as *arbiter* either in a *compromissum* or an *actio pro socio.* He was assisted by assessors (*consilium*), one of whom was M. Perperna. The counsel for Fannius, the plaintiff, is described as that 'old hand' P. Saturius[3], a man elsewhere mentioned and praised by Cicero[4]. The specific *narratio* of the speech, if there was one, has been lost, but the facts appear to have been as follows:—

C. Fannius Chaerea had a slave named Panurgus, of whom he was the sole owner[5]. Perceiving the promise of intellectual qualities, he entrusted him to Roscius to be made an actor. A partnership (*societas*) was thus formed, Fannius contributing the capital, Roscius the labour[6]. The part-ownership was made over gratuitously by Fannius[7], and according to the ruling legal principle, all that this common slave acquired became the property of both masters according to their share

[1] 12, 33 'Tum enim (when Roscius acquired the land at Tarquinii) propter rei publicae calamitates omnium possessiones erant incertae.'

[2] 13, 37.

[3] 'veterator, ut sibi videtur' (8, 22). He is mentioned also in 1, 3; 6, 18; 10, 27.

[4] As a *iudex* in the trial of Oppianicus (Cic. *pro Cluent.* 38, 107; 65, 182).

[5] 10, 28.

[6] Fannius probably paid for his maintenance; Roscius is represented as contributing only the *disciplina* (*l.c.*).

[7] 10, 27 'questus est non leviter Saturius communem factum esse gratis cum Roscio, qui pretio proprius fuisset Fannii.'

(*pro parte*)[1]. Whether by agreement, or in consequence of the absence of a definite agreement[2], the profits were to be equally divided[3].

The partnership was successful in its object. Panurgus came on the boards and was applauded[4]; but his career was suddenly cut short. He was killed by a certain Q. Flavius of Tarquinii[5].

An action for damages was then instituted against Flavius. The action was one *damni iniuria dati* under the *lex Aquilia*. The damages to be granted in this action were regulated by the highest value which the slave had had during the past year, and these could be estimated, not by reference to his body only but to his talents or other circumstances which had determined his value to his master[6]. Roscius' training thus created a considerable increment in the valuation of Panurgus.

Two methods of bringing the action were possible in the case of such a *servus communis*[7]. Either of the partners could separately demand reparation for the share which he had in the slave[8], or the partners could bring a joint action for recovery, in which case one would naturally act for the other or others.

An action in this case is known to have been brought by Roscius, who made Fannius his *cognitor*[9]; but it was probably a joint action, Fannius suing for himself in person while he represented Roscius. The result of the action, if successful,

[1] Ulpian in Dig. 45, 3, 5 'Servus communis sic omnium est non quasi singulorum totus, sed pro partibus utique indivisis, ut intellectu magis partes habeant quam corpore: et ideo si quid stipulatur vel quaqua alia ratione adquirit, omnibus adquirit pro parte, qua dominium in eo habent.'

[2] *ib.* 17, 2, 29 'Si non fuerint partes societati adiectae, aequas eas esse constat.'

[3] 11, 32 'pro dimidia parte . . . "Magno tu tuam dimidiam partem decidisti." "Magno et tu tuam partem decide."'

[4] 10, 29.

[5] 11, 32.

[6] Gaius, iii. 212 'Nec solum corpus in actione huius legis aestimatur, sed sane si alieno servo occiso plus dominus capiat damni quam pretium servi sit, id quoque aestimatur: velut si servus meus ab aliquo heres institutus, antequam iussu meo hereditatem cerneret, occisus fuerit.'

[7] 11, 32.

[8] Ulpian in Dig. 9, 2, 19 and 20 'Sed si communem servum occiderit quis, Aquilia teneri eum Celsus ait . . . scilicet pro ea parte, pro qua dominus est qui agat.'

[9] 11, 32.

would have been that any damages recovered would have been divided equally between the two partners.

The case had proceeded some way, the formula had been given[1], the *litis contestatio* had taken place and the *iudex* had been appointed[2], when Roscius came to a private agreement with Flavius to settle the matter out of court. The compensation given by Flavius was a farm[3], which, according to Fannius, was worth 100,000 sesterces, the value which Fannius in bringing his action had attributed to Panurgus' services during the year in which he was killed[4].

The great question at issue, which was to dominate the future proceedings, was whether the *pactio* concluded by Roscius was on behalf of himself only or on behalf of the *societas*[5]. There can be no question as to Roscius' legal right to compound for himself, for a partner could alienate any share[6], and therefore any interest, that was peculiarly his own. Fannius, however, claimed that Roscius had transacted for the *societas*, that he himself had ceased to persist in his action against Flavius in consequence of this impression, and that Roscius had given him none of the compensation which he had recovered from the *pactio*.

One year later, and three years before the final case in which Cicero spoke[7], Fannius brought an action against Roscius to recover his part of the compensation. As to the nature of this action, Cicero describes it as a mere *compromissum*, i. e. an agreement of two parties under a wager (*poena compromissa*) to abide by the decision of an *arbiter*[8]. It has been held,

[1] As Flavius probably denied the debt, the formula (in accordance with the principle *lis adversus infitiantem crescit in duplum*) may have run as follows—'Si paret Flavium Fannii et Roscii servum communem iniuria occidisse, quam ob rem, quanti is servus in eo anno plurimi fuit, tantam pecuniam dare oportet, tantae pecuniae duplum iudex Flavium Fannio condemna. S. N. P. A.' See Lenel, *Ed. Perp.* p. 158.

[2] 11, 32. [3] 12, 33. [4] 10, 28.

[5] 12, 34 'Ergo huc universa causa deducitur, utrum Roscius cum Flavio de sua parte an de tota societate fecerit pactionem.'

[6] Gaius in Dig. 17, 2, 68 'Nemo ex sociis plus parte sua potest alienare, etsi totorum bonorum socii sint'; cf. Paulus in Dig. 12, 1, 16.

[7] If we consider that Roscius' pact took place four and not fifteen years before the final trial; see p. 542.

[8] 4, 12 'Quaero abs te quid ita de hac pecunia . . . de tuarum tabularum fide compromissum feceris, arbitrum sumpseris, quantum aequius et melius sit, dari repromittive, sic petieris.'

however[1], that it was really a formal *actio pro socio* ordained by the praetor. The grounds of this conclusion are (1) the qualifying words *quantum aequius melius* cited by Cicero, words which do not suit the ordinary *compromissum*, i. e. a mutual *poenae stipulatio*, by which both parties bind themselves unconditionally to the decision of the *arbiter*; (2) the choice of the *arbiter* through the plaintiff, that functionary in a *compromissum* being agreed to by both parties, and (3) the issue—the absolution in consequence of the *arbitrium*[2], for in the *compromissum* there is no formal judgement. The last two grounds of objection are not very serious, for even in a *compromissum* the *arbiter* must be selected *first* by one of the parties and 'acquittal' is present, although the term may be a transference from the language of the regular courts. It is not even certain that modifying circumstances (such as would be expressed in *quantum aequius melius*) could not be taken into account in the *stipulatio* on which the *compromissum* was based. This procedure may, in the Ciceronian period, have been more of the nature of an *arbitrium* than it afterwards became. Whatever the nature of the action, Fannius based his claim, as in the subsequent cases, on his ledgers (*tabulae*)[3], and the claim was for 50,000 sesterces, half the amount of the compensation which Roscius had derived from Flavius.

C. Piso, who was chosen as *arbiter*, suggested the following compromise. Roscius was to agree to pay 100,000 sesterces to Fannius on condition of a *restipulatio* by Fannius that, if he personally pursued and got compensation out of Flavius, he should give Roscius half of the money so recovered[4].

The sum which Roscius was to stipulate to pay is surprisingly large; for it is no less than double the compensation originally demanded by Fannius. It has, therefore, been the subject of various emendations. Manutius would reduce the 100,000 to 10,000 sesterces; Lambinus conjectured 15,000. Ernesti and Puchta make it 50,000, the share in the *societas* which had been the ground of the action. But 100,000 ses-

[1] Bethmann-Hollweg, p. 809.

[2] 9, 26 'Quaere quare sit absolutus.'

[3] 4, 12.

[4] 13, 37 and 38. Fannius could still pursue an action against Flavius in his own name, in spite of the *litis contestatio* of the former case (p. 544). For in that case he had acted *for* Roscius, or *for* the *societas*; now he could act for himself (*de sua parte*).

terces was actually the amount which Fannius entered into his *adversaria* as owed by Roscius[1]: and a fairly satisfactory explanation of the award, which is consistent with the manuscript reading, has been suggested by Bethmann-Hollweg[2]. He thinks that Fannius had, in the process before Piso, demanded 50,000 sesterces (half of what Roscius had gained from Flavius), and as much again as compensation for his trouble and expense as *cognitor* in the action. Piso recognized the claim, but only on the condition of Fannius' restipulation; and Roscius accepted the award on the advice of his lawyers, because Piso might have condemned him unconditionally to the 100,000 sesterces[3].

Fannius was still free to action Flavius, for the latter in his pact had gained no guarantee from Roscius *amplius a se neminem petiturum*[4]; and, if we are to believe Cicero, he subsequently availed himself of this liberty with success. Cicero maintains that Fannius on his own account subsequently got 100,000 sesterces as compensation out of Flavius, no portion of which did he give to Roscius[5]. But the evidence, on which this statement was based, was extremely weak. It was mere hearsay. Cluvius, who was the *iudex* in the case between Fannius and Flavius, was supposed to have made this assertion to two senators, T. Manilius and C. Luscius Ocrea. It is the testimony of the two latter that is read in court. Flavius was dead, and could not be called as a witness[6]. Why Cluvius did not appear in person is not known.

The importance of this fact, if it could be proved, would have been very great. It might have been used to show the belief of Fannius that Roscius was acting only for himself in his *pactum* with Flavius, and it relieved Roscius of the indebtedness to Fannius created by Piso's award: for Fannius had not performed the condition of the *restipulatio*.

[1] 1, 4 'Leve et tenue hoc nomen? HS ccciↃↃↃ sunt. Quomodo tibi tanta pecunia extraordinaria iacet? Quomodo HS ccciↃↃↃ in codice accepti et expensi non sunt?'

[2] p. 810.

[3] Bethmann-Hollweg (*l. c.*) held further that no formal promise was made by Roscius in the form of a stipulation, since Fannius was unable to produce proof of such an agreement. See p. 547.

[4] 12, 35. See p. 240. The fact that this guarantee was not secured by Flavius is a presumption that Roscius was acting only for himself.

[5] 14, 40 sq.

[6] 14, 42.

But Roscius was then guilty of a concession which must have prejudiced his future case. Fannius demanded out of court and actually got from Roscius half of the money which Roscius had recovered in his pact with Flavius, i. e. 50,000 sesterces[1]. What moved Roscius to this payment we do not know, but it has been suggested that 'after his former experience he might have dreaded a second trial and hoped once for all to reconcile his rancorous opponent with a payment which was inconsiderable in comparison with his splendid income as an artist[2].' But the payment of this half might be, and probably was, used by Fannius' counsel as a proof that Roscius owed the remainder.

Fannius, however, was not content with this concession. He demanded the other half of the 100,000 sesterces[3], and it is this claim which was the subject of the trial in which Cicero spoke.

This claim was expressed in the form of a *condictio certi* (i. e. *certae pecuniae*), the procedure being by the *sponsio poenalis* (*tertiae* or *legitimae partis*) and entailing the stipulation and restipulation of the parties to pay, in case of failure, the third part of the sum in dispute[4]. The obligation from which such a *condictio certi* could arise was one of three. It must be either loan (*mutuum*) or a literal contract (*expensi latio*) or a verbal contract (*stipulatio*)[5]. Fannius admitted that it was not the first; he called no witnesses to prove it was the third; he, therefore, alleged that it was the second—a book-debt. If Fannius maintained that there had been a stipulation, his contention must have been that it had been changed by novation into a literal contract. Cicero holds that it should have been a stipulation, hence his insistance on the entire absence of evidence for all trace of such an agreement[6].

The reality of a book-debt, such as this, rested on the

[1] 17, 51 'iam antea HS Iↄↄↄ dissolverat.'

[2] Bethmann-Hollweg, p. 813.

[3] 16, 48 'quoniam Fannius a me petit HS Iↄↄↄ.

[4] See p. 200 for this *sponsio* and for the suggestion of Lenel (*Ed. Perp.* p. 188) that it contained the words 'si secundum me iudicatum erit' found in 5, 14 and 15.

[5] 5, 14 'haec pecunia necesse est aut data aut expensa lata aut stipulata sit.'

[6] 5, 13 'Stipulatus es—ubi? quo die? quo tempore? quo praesente? quis spopondisse me dicit? nemo.'

assumption that Roscius had given Fannius the power to put the sum in question down under the head of *expensum*, and that it was not found under the counter-entry of *acceptum*. Its regularity would have been increased if Roscius, as debtor, had entered it under the head of *acceptum*, while it did not appear as *expensum* in his ledger. The two facts of importance for establishing such a debt were (1) a clear inscription in the creditor's *codex*: (2) evidence of the consent of the debtor, which, in default of written or oral testimony by third parties, could only be gained by an appeal to *his* ledger.

Such evidence Fannius was unable to furnish. No such entry under the head of *expensum* appeared in his regularly kept *codex*; as evidence of the obligation he could exhibit only an entry in his notes (*adversaria*)[1], the waxen tablets which formed the rough material of his ledger. The *codex* of Roscius, on the other hand, did not bear out the existence of the obligation at all. It contained no mention of the sum under the head of *acceptum*. It is not known what the conditions of evidence required for a literal contract were at this time[2]. The dual inscription would doubtless have settled the point without further evidence; but, in default of the inscription on the supposed debtor's books, it is difficult to imagine a satisfactory mode of attestation. Cicero had for some reason asked for the production of the *tabulae* of Perperna, the assessor of Piso, and of Saturius, the counsel of Fannius[3]. It is difficult to determine the motive for this request. It may have been made for the purpose of showing how *codices* should be kept, or to prove that Fannius had made regular entries of obligations to or from them which were more recent than Roscius' pretended obligation to him. Perhaps, however, the production of these ledgers had an even more intimate bearing on the case.

Cicero passes under examination the motive which led Fannius to choose a form of action—the *condictio certi*—which

[1] 2, 5.

[2] The presence of the two parties was never necessary. Gaius, iii. 138 'Sed absenti expensum ferri potest, etsi verbis obligatio cum absente contrahi non possit.' Gasquy believes (p. 150) that witnesses were necessary 'who signed at the side of the contracting parties and affixed their seals, or even inscribed on their own registers the credit and the debt.'

[3] 1, 3.

he represents as extraordinary under the circumstances. For, granting that the claim rested on a book-debt, the evidence for this was weak and the *periculum* to the plaintiff, in case of failure to support his claim, was great. It is sarcastically suggested that the choice was due to Fannius' desire not to imperil the reputation of Roscius, for the consequence of condemnation in an *arbitrium pro socio*, which he might have brought, was *infamia* of a certain kind[1]. But Fannius had probably a very good reason for his choice. An *arbitrium pro socio* would have exposed him to a cross-action and, if we believe that Fannius had really recovered from Flavius in an action at law, his *restipulatio* to pay half this compensation to Roscius might be made the ground either of a counter-claim against him or of an exception based on his judicial arrangement (*compromissum*) with Roscius (*exceptio transacti*).

Cicero's pleadings may be divided into those of law and fact.

(1) In law he argues (*a*) the point which we have just examined, i. e. that the more natural procedure would have been that by *arbitrium*[2]. It has some moral weight in answer to the general ground given by Fannius to prove the naturalness of the literal obligation, i. e. the relations of partnership between him and Roscius, and Roscius' duty to share the profits. But it was impossible to rebut the action of Fannius on this ground. The plaintiff had actually made a literal obligation the basis of the action, and this ground naturally gave rise to a *condictio certi*.

(*b*) The great point of substantive law which is raised is, whether a quondam partner could recover compensation arising from his partnership for himself only, or must recover for the *societas*. The plaintiff's counsel, Saturius, had maintained that 'quodcumque sibi petat socius, id societatis fieri[3].' Cicero, arguing to the contrary, takes the relation of *hereditas* as an analogy; the heir acquires for himself alone, not for his co-heirs[4]. The analogy is a bad one; for the essential difference between *hereditas* and *societas* is that the 'hereditas' *as possessed by the 'heredes'* has never been a unity; they have never combined for joint action as *socii* must do. The principles

[1] 9, 25. [2] 9, 25; 4, 10. [3] 18, 56.

[4] *i. e.* 'ut heres sibi soli, non coheredibus petit: sic socius sibi soli, non sociis petit.'

of the Ciceronian were probably those of the later law, and by these any acquisition made on the basis of joint capital must be shared between the partners. The communication of a profit is not conditioned by the intention of the partner who trades or by his share, but simply by the extent of the *societas*, whether it be a universal partnership (*societas omnium bonorum*)[1] or one formed for a special object (*unius negotii*)[2]. Yet, in spite of the weakness of Cicero's analogy, Roscius was right in compounding for himself. For, as we saw[3], where the shares or claims are divisible mentally or actually, any share or claim is capable of alienation by its possessor. But, so far as the present case was concerned, this point of law was also secondary. The duty of Roscius to share his compensation had only been adduced by Fannius as a proof of the reasonableness of Roscius' debt.

(2) The two important questions in the case are those of fact.

(*a*) The first and less vital of these facts is one which Cicero seeks to prove: namely, that Fannius had received from Flavius a compensation which he did not share with Roscius[4]. If proved, it would be a good point, but not a vital one. It might show that there was no ground for Roscius' debt, but it would not disprove the existence of the debt as based on the literal obligation.

(*b*) The really vital question of fact is the existence of this literal obligation. Here Cicero has an easy task. He shows, firstly, the entire absence of evidence for the grounds of the debt, if the literal contract was a novation[5], and secondly, the weakness of the evidence furnished by a note in *adversaria* as opposed to a formal entry in a *codex*[6]. To the latter point Fannius, it appears, could only make the would-be specious, but rather feeble, rejoinder that he did not enter the item in his ledger because he did not wish Roscius' indebtedness to be known to the world[7].

[1] Paulus in Dig. 17, 2, 3 'Cum specialiter omnium bonorum societas coita est, tunc et hereditas et legatum et quod donatum est aut quaqua ratione adquisitum communioni adquiretur.' Cf. Ulpian in Dig. 17, 2, 73.

[2] Dig. 17, 2, 52. The same principle applies to banking. Anything that comes *ex argentaria causa* must be shared (§ 52, 5).

[3] p. 544.

[4] 14, 40 sq.; see p. 544. [5] 4, 13 sq.; see p. 547. [6] 2, 5 sq.

[7] 3, 9 'Nolebas sciri debere tibi Roscium. Cur scribebas? Rogatus eras ne referres? Cur in adversariis scriptum habebas?'

To these arguments are added certain moral considerations, perhaps effective but of no juristic importance:—(*a*) that the chief value of the slave was the intellectual value which had been given him by Roscius [1]—an answer to the contention of Fannius' counsel that, by giving his slave gratis to Roscius, he had put more into the partnership [2]; (*b*) a comparison of the character of the litigants—a *laudatio* of Roscius [3] and some witticisms at the expense of Fannius [4].

(3) *PRO TULLIO.*

This speech was delivered in the praetorship of a Metellus [5], probably L. Metellus, who was consul in 68 and may, therefore, have been praetor in 71 B.C. Cicero pleaded in a renewed hearing of the case, which had already been before the same *recuperatores* [6]. This board of judges was rendered possible by the action being praetorian, and advisable on account of the desirability of a speedy settlement [7]. The defendant Fabius was represented by L. Quinctius, the 'popular' tribune of the *pro Cluentio* [8] and characterized by Cicero in that speech as a pleader of bad causes [9].

The facts which led up to the case were, according to Cicero's statement, as follows:—

M. Tullius had a farm, inherited from his father, in the neighbourhood of Thurii. P. Fabius became his neighbour in the following way. He had joined in partnership with one Cn. Acerronius to purchase a farm adjacent to that of Tullius [10]. The partners had given a large price for it—in fact, almost twice as much as it was worth at its best. The estate, after it was acquired, proved to be practically worthless; the land was out of cultivation and the buildings out of repair [11]. It seems, so far as can be gathered from the fragmentary

[1] 10, 28 sq. [2] 10, 27. See p. 542. [3] 6, 17. [4] 7, 20.

[5] 17, 39. On the evidences for the date see Huschke, pp. 91–93; Drumann, *Geschichte*, v. p. 258.

[6] 1, 1; 2, 5; 3, 6.

[7] 5, 10 'recuperatores dare ut quam primum res iudicaretur.'

[8] *pro Cluent.* 28, 77; 29, 79. For his popular style of oratory cf. Cic. *Brut.* 62, 223.

[9] *pro Cluent.* 39, 109. [10] 7, 16. [11] 6, 14 and 15.

character of the speech, that Fabius, disgusted with his purchase, proposed to sell his share to his partner Acerronius. The latter accepted the offer. He was under the impression that the estate was larger than it was in reality, for he had been led by Fabius to believe that it included a strip of land known as the *centuria Populiana*, which, Cicero maintains, really belonged to the neighbouring farm of Tullius[1]. This land Fabius seems to have openly included in the sale (*proscriptio*), and its inclusion seems to have met with a protest from Tullius[2].

Acerronius, the purchaser, demanded the usual *finium demonstratio*. This was completed for all but one portion of the estate, the exception being the *centuria Populiana*. Fabius could not hand it over as 'vacant' property, for it was occupied by representatives of Tullius[3]. It was clear that the sale could not be completed until the ownership of this bit of land was settled.

Tullius was now on his estate near Thurii, of which the disputed *centuria* was claimed to be an *annexe* or a part. There he is visited by Fabius, who, taking Acerronius with him, requests Tullius to enter on the preliminaries of an action as to the ownership of the *centuria*. He asks Tullius to play the part of the ejector or the ejected in the *deductio moribus*. Tullius agrees to play the part of ejector, and says that he will give security to meet Fabius before the court at Rome. Fabius accepts the conditions and they part[4].

On the next night, just before dawn, a band of armed slaves, which, according to Cicero[5], Fabius had already collected for the purpose, burst into a building erected on the *centuria*, which was inhabited by Tullius' slaves, slaughtered the occupants and ransacked the building[6]. One of the slaves, who had himself been wounded, escaped and brought the news to Tullius[7]. He summoned his friends as witnesses of the outrage, and lodged an action against Flavius before the praetor Metellus[8].

[1] 7, 16. [2] 7, 17.

[3] *l. c.* '(Fabius) fines Acerronio demonstravit neque tamen hanc centuriam Populianam vacuam tradidit.'

[4] 8, 20 'Appellat Fabius ut aut ipse Tullium deduceret aut ab eo deduceretur. Dicit deducturum se Tullius vadimonium Fabio Romam promissurum. Manet in ea condicione Fabius. Mature disceditur.'

[5] 8, 18. [6] 9, 21. [7] 9, 22. [8] 17, 39.

The formula of this action, which was one for *damnum datum vi hominibus armatis*, we have already examined[1]. The damages were fourfold (*in quadruplum*): the fixing of the maximum (*taxatio*) was the work of the plaintiff, the *aestimatio* rested with the *recuperatores*[2].

This praetorian action, first created by the praetor M. Lucullus (probably in 76 B. C.), was, as we have seen[3], introduced to meet a growing evil which was a result of the turbulence following on the first civil war. It aimed at repressing the maintenance and use of large bands of armed slaves and the enforcement of private rights by violence[4]. For injury of this kind the *lex Aquilia de damno*, with its restitution *in simplum* or, on denial, *in duplum*, was thought insufficient[5]; and even the *actio iniuriarum*, with its damages dependent on the estimation of the *iudex* (*actio aestimatoria*), was not considered appropriate, partly because there was no guarantee of the penalty being adequate and partly because injury to feelings (ὕβρις) had to be proved in such an ordinary action for damages[6].

The chief characteristics of this action for *damnum datum* were:—

(1) That it did not speak of *damnum iniuria*. The object of this reticence was 'illam latebram tollere[7].'

(2) That it made the owner of the *familia* responsible for the acts done by the *familia* as a whole or by any members of that body. Whether this responsibility might take the form of *noxae deditio* is uncertain.

(3) The act must be malicious and intentional (*dolo malo*).

But did the action mean to take account of malicious conspiracy resulting in damage, but without overt acts of violence on the part of the conspirator? Cicero maintains that it did, and that the *dolo malo* clause widened the sphere of the action[8].

[1] p. 210.

[2] 3, 7 'eius rei taxationem nos fecimus; aestimatio vestra est; iudicium datum est in quadruplum.'

[3] p. 210.

[4] 4, 8 and 5, 10.

[5] 4, 9.

[6] See Czyhlarz, *Inst.* p. 208.

[7] 5, 11.

[8] 10, 26 'At istuc totum *dolo malo* additur in hoc iudicio eius causa qui agit, non illius quicum agitur'; 11, 28 'ergo addito *dolo malo* actoris et petitoris fit causa copiosior. Utrum enim ostendere potest, sive eam ipsam familiam sibi damnum dedisse, sive consilio et opera eius familiae factum esse, vincat necesse est.'

He urges that *dolus malus* and the act (which, if of the kind imagined by the action, of itself shows *dolus malus*) are alternatives[1]. It is sufficient to prove the one or the other in order to secure a conviction.

(4) The action was directed 'in universam familiam[2].' This can only mean that it was not necessary for the *actor et petitor* to specify any particular individual as responsible for any particular part of the *damnum*. In all other senses the action was given, not against the *familia*, but against the *dominus*. The principle could only have had a deeper meaning if *noxae deditio* had been allowed. This would have been the most serious penalty of all, as implying surrender of the whole of the *familia*.

The line adopted by Cicero's opponents was that Fabius had acted in pure self-defence. Technical objection was, therefore, taken to the form of the action. It was claimed that, though there may have been violence, it was not committed of malice and premeditation (*dolo malo*). It was urged that the word *iniuria* should have been added in the formula submitted to the jury. This addition would have rendered the issue to be tried, not a question of fact merely, but a question of motive, and would have left scope for the plea of self-defence as a legitimate ground for the acts of violence, the reality of which in their essential particulars seems not to have been denied[3].

(1) As regards the representation of the facts which had occurred previously to the assault, it was urged that Tullius' slaves had established themselves in a kind of encampment on Fabius' land, and that they had burnt down a cottage erected by Fabius[4].

The justification for the act of self-defence was argued on the general principles of Roman law. The law of the Twelve Tables was quoted 'ut furem noctu liceat occidere et luci si se telo defendat,' and even the *lex sacrata* 'quae iubeat impune occidi eum qui tribunum pl. pulsaverit.' The latter enactment

[1] 13, 32 'cum consilium sine facto intellegi possit, factum sine consilio non possit.'

[2] 5, 10 'in universam familiam iudicium dare, quod a familia factum diceretur.'

[3] 1, 1 'Nunc vero posteaquam non modo confessus est vir primarius.'

[4] 23, 53; 24, 54.

was probably cited as a general instance of self-help on the part of the *plebs*.

Cicero's answer to these arguments is that killing, except in the extremest necessity, was not countenanced by the law. The thief, for instance, may not be slain unless he offers resistance with a weapon [1]. The laws have not even permitted a man to defend his life with a weapon in his own house under all circumstances [2]. He denies that there were facts which could possibly have led to a consciousness of such danger; and, if there was only a fear of an attack, it was no legal principle that a man should commit murder for fear of being subsequently murdered himself [3]. Even supposing that Tullius had erected a building on Fabius' land—a far smaller act of retaliation—the mere destruction of this building *vi aut clam* would have been visited by the laws. A restitutory interdict would have been granted against Fabius [4].

(2) As a part of the defence it was urged that the act was not done *dolo malo* [5]. There had been no premeditation or malicious intention. Cicero answers that *dolus malus* merely widens the scope of culpability to cover those who act for others [6], and that, as a matter of fact, the whole of the series of actions and each one of them was permeated with *dolus malus* [7].

Again, urged Quinctius, *dolus malus* on the part of a whole *familia* is impossible [8]. Cicero's answer to this point, so far as it has been preserved, is that this contention threatens every case that could possibly be tried under this formula [9].

(3) It was contended that the act was not done *iniuria*. Great efforts were made by Fabius to get the praetor Metellus to amend his formula by the insertion of this word. On his

[1] 21, 50 '(Fur) nisi utetur telo eo ac repugnabit, non occides; quod si repugnat, ENDO PLORATO, hoc est conclamato, ut aliqui audiant et conveniant.'

[2] 'sine testibus et arbitris ferro' (*l. c.*).

[3] 24, 56.

[4] 22, 53.

[5] 13, 33 'Nam in dolo malo volunt delitescere.'

[6] *l. c.* 'in quo, non modo cum omnia ipsi fecerunt quae fatentur, verum etiam si per alios id fecissent, haererent ac tenerentur.'

[7] 13, 31.

[8] 15, 35 'Primum enim illud iniecit, nihil posse dolo malo familiae fieri.'

[9] *l. c.* 'fecit . . . ut omnino huiusce modi iudicia dissolveret.'

refusal, an unsuccessful appeal was made to the tribunes to quash the ruling in law, if this word was not inserted[1].

The answer of praetor and tribunes was that acts such as those contemplated in the formula could not be done *iure* (so far, *iniuria* was implied), but that they would not add the qualifying word[2]. This answer was equivalent to the statement that *iniuria* in the technical sense (ὕβρις) was not implied and was not the issue, but that *iniuria*, in the untechnical sense of wrong-doing, was an element in the act of violence itself. The reasons for this answer, as given by Cicero, are (1) that the magistrates did not wish to make this action turn simply on the question of damage (*damnum*) as prevised by the *lex Aquilia*[3]; (2) that this action took account only of certain facts (*atrocia facta*) and did not allow the issue to be raised whether these had been done *iniuria*[4]. Apart from the advantage of raising a point which might be the centre of endless argument, the appeal to the tribunes may have been based on the assumption that this action was only an extension of that given by the *lex Aquilia*. The answer of these magistrates declares it to be a quite different and wholly independent action.

(4) *PRO CAECINA.*

This is, with the possible exception of the *pro Balbo*, the most juristic speech of Cicero's that has descended to us. It is more closely argued even than his defence of Balbus; for there the legal point was a comparatively simple question of constitutional law: here he had to deal with the intricacies of the interdict, and they are dealt with in a way which illustrates at once his subtlety in exegesis[5] and the uncertainties of this

[1] 16, 38; 17, 39. [2] 17, 39.

[3] 17, 41 'neque enim is, qui hoc iudicium dedit, de ceteris damnis ab lege Aquilia recedit, in quibus nihil agitur nisi damnum, qua de re praetor animum debeat advertere'; 18, 42 'non ergo praetores a lege Aquilia recesserunt, quae de damno est, sed de vi et armis severum iudicium constituerunt.'

[4] 18, 42 'et miramini satis habuisse eos, qui hoc iudicium dederunt, id quaeri utrum haec tam acerba, tam indigna, tam atrocia facta essent necne, non utrum iure facta an iniuria?'

[5] Cf. Cic. *Orator*, 29, 101, 102 'Is erit igitur eloquens . . . qui poterit parva summisse, modica temperate, magna graviter dicere. Tota mihi

particular branch of law in the Republican period. It was a speech which could not have been delivered when jurisprudence had become more definite and the *iudex* was bound to his verdict by fixed rulings[1].

The date of the speech can be fixed within certain limits. It seems to have been delivered after the death of Sulla in 78 B.C., for Cicero speaks of the reign of terror as a thing of the past[2]; and before the speech for Cluentius in 66 B.C., for in this defence of Caecina, as in the Verrines, Cicero blames C. Fidiculanius Falcula for his conduct as *iudex* in the case of Oppianicus[3], while in the *pro Cluentio* he takes back this blame[4]. The general view assigns it to 69 B.C., when Cicero was thirty-seven years old.

The present was the third hearing of the case. It had been twice before the *recuperatores* and had been twice adjourned (*ampliata*) by them on the ground *sibi non liquere*[5]. The general reasons for the giving of *recuperatores* have already been considered[6]. The possibility of their being given here rested on the fact that the interdict, on which this case turned, was a part of *ius honorarium*, and the *unus iudex* was thus not considered the normal, perhaps the necessary, judge. The chief reason for their being granted was perhaps the desire for a speedy settlement[7], on the grounds that the question turned on restitution, and that a further prolongation of the issue might provoke to a breach of the peace. Cicero appeared for the plaintiff Caecina, and C. Calpurnius Piso was counsel for Aebutius, the defendant[8].

The facts of the case, as gathered from Cicero[9], are as follows:—

M. Fulcinius, of Tarquinii, was a banker at Rome, who had married Caesennia, a woman of the same township. As administrator of his wife's dowry, he purchased with it a farm belonging to himself, at Tarquinii. The step was an ordinary

causa pro Caecina de verbis interdicti fuit: res involutas definiendo explicavimus, ius civile laudavimus, verba ambigua distinximus.'

[1] Tac. *Dial. de Orat.* 20 'Quis de exceptione et formula perpetietur illa immensa volumina, quae pro Marco Tullio aut Aulo Caecina legimus? Praecurrit hoc tempore iudex dicentem.'

[2] 33, 95.

[3] 10, 28.

[4] Cic. *pro Cluent.* 37, 104; 50, 139.

[5] 2, 6; 11, 31.

[6] p. 267.

[7] Cic. *pro Tull.* 5, 10; see p. 551.

[8] 12, 35.

[9] 4, 10 sq.

case of *mutatio dotis*[1] and its object appears simply to have been a good investment, times being bad and land cheap at the time of the purchase[2]. Caesennia thus became owner of an estate which ceased to form part of her husband's goods, instead of being merely creditor of a sum of money like her husband's other clients[3]. Some time afterwards[4], Fulcinius gave up his banking business and purchased for himself some lands adjoining his wife's farm. Subsequently he died, making M. Fulcinius, his son by Caesennia, his heir. To Caesennia herself he left the joint usufruct with his son of all his property, i.e. half the income from his estates. But a short time afterwards the young M. Fulcinius also died. He left as heir one P. Caesennius; to his own wife he bequeathed a considerable sum of money, and to his mother the larger portion of his property[5]. The estate was then put up to auction for the benefit of the joint legatees[6], and the *auctio* took place at Rome[7].

It is here that Aebutius first appears upon the scene. He had made himself extremely useful to Caesennia and was trusted by her as a business man, or, to quote Cicero's version of the relationship, he had pushed himself into a position of confidence with the widow, by which he profited[8]. He now busied himself with the accounts of the *auctio* and the division of the estate[9].

Caesennia's friends and relations[10] now advised her to purchase the land near her own farm which her husband had bought. They represented that it would be a good investment of the money coming to her by the partition of the inheritance. She determined to follow their advice and entrusted the commission to Aebutius[11]. She thus entered with him on a contract of *mandatum*.

Aebutius appeared at the auction, made a bid and secured

[1] Iulianus in Dig. 23, 4, 21 'constat posse inter uxorem et virum conveniri ut dos, quae in pecunia numerata esset, permutaretur et transferatur in corpora, cum mulieri prodest.' See Bethmann-Hollweg, p. 829.

[2] 4, 11 'temporibus illis difficillimis solutionis . . . quo mulieri esset res cautior.'

[3] Cf Gasquy, p. 189.

[4] 'aliquando post' (4, 114).

[5] 'partem maiorem bonorum' (4, 12).

[6] 'auctio hereditaria' (5, 13).

[7] 5, 15.

[8] 5, 14.

[9] 5, 13.

[10] 'amici cognatique' (5, 15).

[11] 'mandat ut fundum sibi emat' (5, 15); 'Aebutio negotium datur' (6, 16).

the property[1]. The farm was assigned to him (*addictus*) in his own name, and he promised to pay the banker who had conducted the sale. For this purpose he entered into a book-debt, thus practically borrowing the money from the bank, and this debt he satisfied, also in his own name[2]. Aebutius afterwards used these entries of *expensum* and *acceptum* in the banker's ledger as evidence that he had purchased the property for himself. If he really wished to purchase for Caesennia, he could, if she declined to pay, recover the money from her by an *actio mandati contraria*[3]; there was, therefore, no reason why he need keep the farm for himself. Cicero alleges that Caesennia actually paid the purchase-money to Aebutius. But for this fact no evidence was forthcoming. It might have been furnished, Cicero maintains, had not Aebutius made away with the widow's accounts[4]. It is obvious that Aebutius' own ledger contained no entry of *acceptum* from Caesennia.

Caesennia, however, entered on occupation of the farm, leased it out[5], and continued to maintain possession of it for four years, from the time of its sale until her death[6]. Aebutius afterwards maintained that she exercised these rights merely in accordance with the usufruct that she enjoyed under her husband's will[7]; in accordance with the terms of this will nothing but the *nuda proprietas* could pass to a purchaser during her lifetime.

Shortly after entering on possession of the farm Caesennia had married A. Caecina. On her death, about four years later, she left a will by which Caecina was made heir to 11½ twelfths (*ex deunce et semuncia*), i.e. $\frac{23}{24}$ of her property, M. Fulcinius, a freedman of her former husband, to $\frac{1}{36}$ (*ex duabus sextulis*), and Aebutius to $\frac{1}{72}$ (*sextula*)[8]. Reducing these portions to their common factor, Caecina was to have $\frac{69}{72}$, M. Fulcinius $\frac{2}{72}$, and Aebutius the mere *souvenir* of $\frac{1}{72}$ of the whole. The fact of her leaving Aebutius something *may* be an indication that she thought that the farm was hers, but is no proof of the fact. It shows only that she probably believed in Aebutius' honesty: but it is conceivable that she may not have paid him the

[1] 'fundus addicitur Aebutio' (6, 16).

[2] 6, 17 'se autem (dicit) habere argentarii tabulas, in quibus sibi expensa pecunia lata sit acceptaque relata.'

[3] See p. 204.

[4] 'quod ipse tabulas averterit' (6, 17).

[5] 'possedit locavitque' (6, 17).

[6] 7, 19.

[7] *l. c.*

[8] 6, 17.

purchase-money and may have consented to let him keep the farm.

It was at this point that Aebutius began informally to raise the plea, which was to be developed in the subsequent case, that Caecina, as a member of the degraded *civitas* of Volaterrae, was no longer a citizen of Rome. In consequence of his loss of citizenship it was maintained that he did not possess the *ius commercii* and, therefore, could not be a *heres* at all. The consequence of the maintenance of this plea would have been that the *hereditas* would have been divided between the remaining heirs. If this plea were recognized, Aebutius would have got far more than the equivalent of the farm, and would probably have taken little trouble to prove his ownership of that item of the inheritance.

Caecina, however, undeterred by Aebutius' insinuations and, according to Cicero, actually 'in possession of the goods,' demands, as heir, an arbitration for the division of the inheritance (*arbitrium familiae herciscundae*)[1]. The immediate action taken by Aebutius about the disputed farm prevented this request from being carried out, and we must assume that, at the time of the trial, no *partitio* had been carried out and that the heirs were still *consortes*. Aebutius, in fact, at once[2] made a formal declaration (*denuntiatio*) to Caecina in the Forum at Rome, that the farm was his and that he had bought it for himself. This act does not necessarily prove that Caecina was in possession. Such a declaration might be made indifferently by the possessor or the non-possessor, although certainly it would come more naturally from the latter. Primarily, it was meant to stop the appeal to the *actio familiae herciscundae*, but (if Caecina was possessor) it might be construed as an intention on the part of Aebutius to commence an *actio in rem*.

Caecina interpreted it in this sense. He fixed a day on which the symbolic violence prescribed by procedure should take place[3]. Such violence was a preliminary both of the *actio in rem* in two of its forms[4] and of the interdict *uti possidetis*[5]. Here it is more likely to have been the preliminary of the

[1] 7, 19 'In possessione bonorum cum esset (Caecina) et cum iste (Aebutius) sextulam suam nimium exaggeraret, nomine heredis arbitrum familiae herciscundae postulavit.'

[2] 'illis paucis diebus' (7, 19).

[3] 8, 22 'ex conventu vim fieri.

[4] pp. 185, 186.

[5] p. 222.

vindication determining ownership than of the interdict determining possession. In the distribution of the rôles Caecina wished to be the party ejected (*deiectus*)[1]. Cicero nowhere maintains that it was definitely arranged that his client should play this part; but Caecina's wish probably implies a claim to be in possession of the farm. The rôles were not necessarily determined by the accident of possession[2]; but it is probable that the *de facto* possessor or detainer of the object was usually the *deiectus*. The question 'whether Caecina possessed' was, as we shall see, to become one of the main issues in the case.

The first stage of the procedure was then entered on. Caecina on the appointed day came to a place called the *castellum* Axia, from which he and his friends were to proceed to the farm in dispute. Here he was informed that Aebutius had collected a large band of free men and slaves, and Aebutius himself presently came to the *castellum* and made a *denuntiatio* to Caecina that he had collected such a band, adding, according to Cicero, that he would use extreme violence if Caecina attempted to enter on the land[3]. This announcement was clearly an assertion of Aebutius' possession, and was meant to avoid a breach of the peace; but it rendered the *deductio moribus* impossible[4]. Yet Caecina determined to persevere. Aebutius had guarded all the ingresses to the disputed farm, and, Cicero says, had even placed armed men in the undisputed farm of Caecina bordering on it[5]. This was one of the ingresses, but the step, if taken, rather detracted from the professedly defensive character of Aebutius' action.

Caecina was thus barred ingress even to his own land, but he found a way to the disputed farm, and reached the olive-border that was one of its limits. Aebutius then gave orders, according to Cicero, to kill any one who passed this border. Yet Caecina persisted, and was on the point of crossing the boundary, when the combined attack by Aebutius' forces was made. Caecina and his friends were routed and retired[6], though no one seems to have been hurt.

[1] 7, 20; 32, 95.

[2] Cf. Cic. *pro Tullio*, 8, 20 'Appellat Fabius ut aut ipse Tullium deduceret aut ab eo deduceretur.'

[3] 7, 20 '(Aebutius) denuntiat Caecinae se armatos habere: abiturum eum non esse, si accessisset.'

[4] This was to be *in rem praesentem*; cf. 8, 22 'ad eum fundum . . . in quo ex conventu vim fieri oportebat.'

[5] 8, 21 'in illum proximum, de quo nihil ambigebatur.'

[6] 8, 22.

It is easy to see that these facts, gathered from Cicero's speech, might take a different colouring according to the representations of Caecina's opponents and a belief that Aebutius was the real possessor of the farm. If he was possessor, he may have maintained that Caecina, under the pretence of a *moribus deductio*, was coming to take violent occupation of the farm and that he had only taken precautionary measures to resist this attempt.

The result, however, was that an immediate *vindicatio* was rendered impossible, and Caecina, therefore, applied to the praetor P. Dolabella for an interdict to reinstate him in possession. The interdict applied for was not the ordinary one *de vi*, but the interdict *de vi hominibus armatis* or *de vi armata*[1]. This interdict, although possibly presuming *possessio* on the part of the *deiectus*, was granted without any exception being allowed to the *deiector* on the ground of vicious possession by the *deiectus*[2]. The interdict framed in these absolute terms was granted to Caecina by Dolabella[3]. The answer of the defendant was *restitui*, a formal mode of asserting that he had never disturbed Caecina in his possession[4]. Of the two modes of litigation under this interdict, which are described by Gaius[5], one had been tacitly declined. Aebutius had not asked for an *arbiter*, a request sometimes interpreted as an admission by the defendant 'restituere se debere'[6]; consequently Caecina had made a challenge to a *sponsio*; and this was the case before the *recuperatores*.

As the occasion on which Cicero delivered this speech was a renewed hearing of the case, there was ample opportunity for estimating the nature of the defence; and it is with the points in this defence that Cicero is mainly concerned in his rejoinder.

The defence was conducted mainly on legal grounds, the three first of which are very closely connected. The points which Piso had attempted to demonstrate were, briefly,

(1) That the terms of the interdict did not apply to this case.

(2) That the interdict required *possessio* on the part of the person ejected.

[1] 8, 23. See p. 215. [2] p. 215.

[3] 8, 23 'P. Dolabella praetor interdixit, ut est consuetudo, *de vi hominibus armatis*, sine ulla exceptione, tantum ut, unde deiecisset, restitueret.'

[4] p. 215. [5] iv. 163 ff. See p. 226, and cf. Cic. *pro Tullio*, 23, 53.

[6] Gaius, *l. c.*

(3) That Caecina did not 'possess.'

(4) That Caecina's 'possession' was in any case impossible, if it was based on inheritance, on account of the disabilities inflicted on his *civitas* Volaterrae, which prevented his being an heir.

(5) Facts were adduced which went to prove Aebutius' ownership.

(6) A suggestion was made, perhaps by the *recuperatores*, that some other form of action might have been brought.

With respect to the first point (1) Aebutius based his defence on the terms of the interdict because he did not deny the main facts—the assembling of armed men and the use of threats of violence to keep Caecina back (*reicere*) from the farm in dispute[1]. Admissions which proved these facts had, according to Cicero, been drawn from Aebutius' own witnesses[2]. The defence was that there was no 'dejection,' only a resistance to an attempt at forcible entry[3]. Its main contention was that *reiectio*, not *deiectio*, had taken place; it was, therefore, a claim that implied 'possession' by Aebutius. Apart from this claim it became a verbal quibble of little weight, and it is from this point of view that it is discussed by Cicero. The verbal defence also implied that the *vis* contemplated in the interdict had not been realized, for defence was no violence. It seems also to have been maintained that, as there was no actual assault, *vis* in the literal sense of the edict had not taken place[4].

These verbal arguments of his opponents led to Cicero's analysis of the meaning of the terms of the interdict[5]. The interpretation is probably correct in itself, but is not very much to the point in default of the settlement of the question of possession. As is usual in a bad case, the unessential points are dwelt on at disproportionate length. The points are:—

(*a*) That the *deicere* of the edict does not imply merely

[1] 9, 24 'ferro, inquit, ferro . . . te reieci atque perterrui.'

[2] 9, 24–30.

[3] 11, 31 'non deieci, sed obstiti'; 23, 64 'non deieci, non enim sivi accedere'; 13, 38 'reieci ego te armatis hominibus, non deieci.'

[4] 14, 41 'Tamen hoc interdicto Aebutius non tenetur. Quid ita? Quod vis Caecinae facta non est . . . Nemo, inquit, occisus est neque sauciatus.' No technical defence was adopted to the 'hominibus armatis' clause. The plea stated by Cicero (23, 64 'Non fuerunt armati, cum fustibus et cum saxis fuerunt') was an imaginary one, meant to illustrate the absurdity of the actual defence.

[5] 'voluntas et consilium et sententia interdicti' (18, 50).

dejection from the actual spot contemplated, but also includes prohibition from reaching it[1].

(*b*) That *vis* does not mean merely injury to life or limb, but includes every action that alarms the mind by inspiring it with a fear of such injury[2].

Cicero goes on to illustrate this equitable and liberal interpretation of the interdict by points which were not raised in the defence: e. g. the *familia* of the interdict would cover the case of ejection by a single slave; the *procurator* mentioned in it is not merely the agent strictly so called, but any free man acting on behalf of the principal; *hominibus coactis* covers any *multitudo* guilty of the *vis*, not merely one specially summoned for the purpose; *armatis* implies anything that can be used as a weapon of offence[3].

(2) The second contention, that the terms of the interdict required *possessio* on the part of the *deiectus*[4], is denied by Cicero. 'Possession,' he says, was required in the ordinary interdict *de vi*, but not in the interdict *de vi hominibus armatis*[5]. As regards the fact, that 'possession' was not mentioned in this second interdict, Cicero is probably right; whether it was implied is another question. It is certain that vicious possession (*vi, clam, precario*) was protected in this second interdict in the sense that no exception based on the vicious possession of the ejected was allowed to the ejector[6]. But possession (including vicious possession) may conceivably have been presumed. Savigny held that possession is implied in both these interdicts in the words *unde me deiecisti*, that the specific words *cum ego possiderem* were only added in the first interdict

[1] 12, 35; 14, 39. As a *reductio ad absurdum* Cicero says (17, 50) 'deiectus vero qui potest esse quisquam, nisi in inferiorem locum de superiore motus?'

[2] 15, 42; cf. 16, 46 'omnis enim vis est, quae periculo aut decedere nos alicunde cogit aut prohibet accedere.'

[3] 19, 55; 20, 57; 21, 59 and 60.

[4] 'illa defensio . . . qui non possideat, nullo modo posse (deici)' (31, 90).

[5] 31, 91 'cur ergo aut in illud quotidianum interdictum *unde ille me vi deiecit* additur *cum ego possiderem*, si deici nemo potest, qui non possidet; aut in hoc interdictum *de hominibus armatis* non additur, si oportet quaeri possederit necne.'

[6] Gaius, iv. 155 'Interdum tamen etsi eum vi deiecerim, qui a me vi aut clam aut precario possideret, cogor ei restituere possessionem, velut si armis eum vi deiecerim.'

on account of the exception which followed *nec vi neque clam nec precario ab illo possiderem*, and that they were only omitted in the second interdict because the exception was suppressed[1]. The objection brought by Gasquy[2] that 'the consequence of Savigny's view would be to put any one who possessed even by an act of violence in a better situation than one who did not possess at all' is specious but not fatal; for the praetor was not thinking of abstract justice in removing the exception of vicious possession, but only of getting rid of an impediment to summary jurisdiction. Yet the same author gives an able statement of the view that possession was not demanded in this second interdict, when he holds this interdict to have been a mere measure of police. If the praetor merely wished to stop armed violence, there was no need for him to raise the question of possession.

(3) Assuming that 'possession' was required by the interdict, did Caecina 'possess'? That he did not was one of the contentions raised by the defence. By the question whether Caecina 'possessed' is meant whether he had actual physical control of the land with the *animus* of ownership, and a control not vitiated by illegal methods of detention, or a detention (e.g. *precario*) which the law declared could never be a symbol of ownership.

Caecina's possession was on the face of it a continuation of Caesennia's; but it was maintained by Aebutius' counsel that Caesennia only possessed through usufruct[3]—that is, had only a *quasi-possessio*, which was perhaps at this time unprotected by praetorian actions[4]. Even if we admit that Caesennia had a quasi-possession as *usufructuaria*, she could not have transmitted this right to her heir. She had but a life interest in the property (if it is assumed that she was not also the owner), and Caecina had no claim whatever to continue this interest.

Cicero's arguments for Caecina's possession are obscure, and the passage in which they occur seems at first sight to base it on a continuation of Caesennia's usufructuary *quasi-possessio*[5].

[1] Savigny, *Recht des Besitzes*, § 14. [2] p. 236.

[3] 32, 94.

[4] Ultimately quasi-possessors were granted *actiones utiles* in contradistinction to the *actiones directae* granted only to true possessors.

[5] 32, 94 'Caesenniam possedisse propter usum fructum non negas. Qui colonus habuit conductum de Caesennia fundum, cum idem ex eadem

But it is almost impossible that he should have used such an argument, and the true method of reasoning implied in the passage appears to be as follows:—'You admit Caesennia's possession on a certain title. I assert that this possession, which you admit, was based on another and a better title. It is the possession on this better title that Caecina continued.' Mere continuance of possession was, however, according to Roman principles, not sufficient for the heir. He must in some specific way seize the possession[1]. Cicero maintains that his client had acted in a manner equivalent to the usurpation of possession; for he produces evidence of the fact that Caecina, when going round his estates, had entered on that farm and received accounts from the *colonus*[2]. As a further proof of possession he adds the fact that Caecina had put himself in the position *moribus deduci*[3]. This, however, merely expressed Caecina's wish, not the fact. An additional evidence has been found in the *denuntiatio* of Aebutius. It is interpreted as the first step in a real action for recovery, and it has been thought that, had Aebutius been in peaceful possession, he would certainly have awaited an action from Caecina[4]. But the *denuntiatio* seems to be little more than a protest against the threatened action *familiae herciscundae*[5]. It was an appeal to settle the tenure of this land before that action commenced. The best argument for the possession of Caecina is the physical act of collecting rents mentioned by Cicero.

(4) It was maintained that Caecina's possession was in any case impossible, if it was based on inheritance, since the disabilities inflicted on his native place, Volaterrae, prevented his being an heir[6].

This argument Cicero meets on two grounds: (*a*) that the deprivation of the *civitas* of the Volaterrans was itself illegal, as offending against a fundamental principle of the constitution, and that Sulla had himself employed in his law the tralaticiary clause respecting fundamental principles[7].

conductione fuerit in fundo, dubium est quin, si Caesennia tum possidebat cum erat colonus in fundo, post eius mortem heres eodem iure possederit?'

[1] Paulus in Dig. 41, 2, 30, 5 'Quod per colonum possideo, heres meus nisi ipse nactus possessionem non poterit possidere: retinere enim animo possessionem possumus, apisci non possumus.'

[2] 32, 94. [3] p. 561. [4] Bethmann-Hollweg, p. 840.

[5] p. 560. [6] 7, 18; 33, 95. [7] 33, 95. See p. 81.

The fundamental principle in question was that no one could be deprived of his *civitas* (that is, of his *libertas*) against his will[1]. The first argument on which Cicero bases this principle is that of a *praeiudicium* which he had elicited. He had argued for the *libertas* of a woman of Arretium, a town under the same disabilities as Volaterrae[2], before the *decemviri*, and they had decided the judgement in his favour[3]. He leads one to suppose that their decision had been based on the principle which he is illustrating. He then explains apparent exceptions. He proves that in the case of the *deditus* there is none; for the man so surrendered, if not accepted by the enemy, remains a citizen of Rome[4]. His exposition of the exceptions furnished by really penal measures, such as the sale of the men who shirk the levy and the census, is less happy. But, if they are exceptions, they are the only ones[5]. Lastly comes the case of *exilium*, the act by which *civitas* was lost. But this, as Cicero shows, had never been ordained by law; it had always been a voluntary escape from punishment[6].

(*b*) Next it is shown that even Sulla had left the Volaterrans a partial citizenship, and one sufficient to secure Caecina's rights. Sulla had given them *ius Ariminense* or *ius duodecim coloniarum*, the rights of Ariminum, or of the last twelve Latin colonies planted in Italy. This *ius* contained the *ius commercii* ('nexa atque hereditates') and, therefore, the right of *testamenti captio*[7].

(5) Facts, which we have already considered[8], were adduced to prove Aebutius' ownership. Against these, counter-considerations are adduced by Cicero[9].

(6) A suggestion was made, perhaps by the *recuperatores*[10], that another form of action might or should have been brought[11]. To this suggestion Cicero returns the general

[1] *civitas* and *libertas* stood or fell together, for there was no *media capitis deminutio* in Cicero's time.

[2] Cf. Cic. *ad Att.* i. 19, 4.

[3] Cf. Cic. *pro Domo*, 29, 78.

[4] Cf. Cic. *Top.* 8, 37.

[5] 34, 99 'Quod si maxime hisce rebus adimi libertas aut civitas potest, non intelligunt qui haec commemorant, si per has rationes maiores adimi posse voluerunt, alio modo noluisse?'

[6] 34, 100. See p. 512.

[7] 35, 102.

[8] p. 559.

[9] pp. 559, 566.

[10] Cf. 13, 39 'Huiusce rei vos statuetis nullam esse actionem, nullum experiundi ius constitutum, qui obstiterit armatis hominibus?'

[11] 3, 8 'Potuisti enim leviore actione confligere: potuisti ad tuum ius

answer that the choice of action rests wholly with the plaintiff; even the praetor does not prescribe the form in which he shall pursue his rights. As to the positive suggestions of an alternative which were thrown out, they were a civil *actio iniuriarum* and a criminal prosecution for *vis*. The suggestion of the *actio iniuriarum* came from one L. Calpurnius[1], who may be either one of the *recuperatores* or a legal adviser to one or the other party. To this suggestion Cicero gives the obvious answer, that what Caecina desires is restitution and that this is not given by the *actio iniuriarum*[2]. To the other suggestion of a prosecution for *vis*—perhaps Cicero's own, and not one emanating from the bench—the same answer would have been returned. The reason for the suggestion of these alternatives was, perhaps, that the court did not feel that the facts of the case fitted in with the form of the interdict. This doubt may be illustrated by Cicero's own consultation of Aquilius. At first the great jurist expressed the opinion that verbal grounds excluded Cicero's case[3]; but subsequently he modified his view, and admitted that the wording of the interdict was not unfavourable to Caecina[4].

It has generally been believed that Cicero gained his case, although there is no positive evidence of the fact. The lasting impression made by his pleading on his client's mind is, however, attested in a grateful letter written by the latter[5].

faciliore et commodiore iudicio pervenire; quare aut muta actionem aut noli mihi instare ut iudicem.' Aebutius' counsel had insisted that this was the wrong action (13, 37). Cf. 3, 9; 12, 35; 13, 39.

[1] 12, 35 'quaero si te (Piso, the defendant's counsel) hodie domum tuam redeuntem coacti homines et armati . . . prohibuerint, quid acturus sis? Monet amicus meus te L. Calpurnius ut idem dicas, quod ipse antea dixit, iniuriarum.'

[2] *l. c.* 'quid ad causam possessionis? . . . actio enim iniuriarum non ius possessionis assequitur.'

[3] 'verbo me excludi dicebat: a verbo autem posse recedi non arbitrabatur' (28, 79).

[4] 'Praetor, inquit, interdixit ut, unde deiectus esset, eo restitueretur, hoc est, quicumque is locus esset unde deiectus esset' (28, 80).

[5] 'Ubi hoc omnium patronus facit, quid me veterem tuum, nunc omnium clientem (sentire) oportet?' (*ad Fam.* vi. 7, 4). Cf. letters 5, 6, 9 of the same book, and *ad Fam.* xiii. 66. It has been questioned whether the 'Caecina quidam Volaterranus' of *ad Att.* xvi. 8, 2 is the same person.

APPENDIX III

THE CONDITIONS OF THE PROVOCATIO.

THE view which I have taken in the text is that the criminal appeal (*provocatio*) was unconditioned, except by the nature of the punishment threatened or the locality within which the appeal was made. Zumpt, in his *Criminalrecht* (i. 2, p. 170 ff.), stated two conditions which, in his opinion, excluded the appeal. These were confession and open evidence of guilt. Where these existed, the magistrate might exercise summary jurisdiction. With respect to the first condition, he held that the maxim *confessus pro iudicato est* was as valid for the criminal as for the civil law, and that evidence is found for it in the procedure consequent on the Bacchanalian conspiracy (Liv. xxxix. 17); although when a confession of the fact was accompanied by a defence on grounds of law or extenuating circumstances, a *iudicium populi* might result (Val. Max. vi. 1, 10). With respect to the second condition of open evidence of guilt, the expression *manifesta res* is found applied to a murder (Liv. iii. 33; cf. Cic. *de Rep.* ii. 36, 61)—the same epithet which appears in the distinction which the civil law established between kinds of theft (*furtum manifestum, nec manifestum*). The only passage referring to Republican history which reflects a summary treatment of a 'manifest' crime, is contained in Cato's speech on the execution of the Catilinarian conspirators (Sall. *Cat.* 52)[1].

If we examine the evidence for the two conditions separately, we find that the most important passage relative to confessions is that which concerns the punishment of the Bacchanalian conspirators (Liv. xxxix. 17 and 18). It runs as follows:—

[1] For the consequence of *confessio* in *parricidium* see p. 506. Confession here resulted in a difference of punishment, not of trial.

'(The heads of the society, high priests and founders of the rite) adducti ad consules fassique de se nullam moram iudicio fecerunt. . . . Qui tantum initiati erant . . . nec earum rerum ullam, in quas iureiurando obligati erant, in se aut alios admiserant, eos in vinculis relinquebant: qui stupris aut caedibus violati erant, qui falsis testimoniis, signis adulterinis, subiectione testamentorum, fraudibus aliis contaminati, eos capitali poena adficiebant.'

We have already dwelt on the elements of doubt involved in the interpretation of this narrative[1]. Its words may imply that those who confessed, or were manifestly guilty, were executed by the summary jurisdiction of the consuls. But the account is very compressed, and Livy's contrast may simply be between those executed after trial by the people and those for whom preventive imprisonment was used as a punishment. If, however, the first alternative—the one accepted by Zumpt—is the correct one, the circumstances of this *quaestio* are too exceptional to make it typical of regular Roman procedure.

The story quoted from Valerius Maximus (vi. 1, 10) to illustrate the conditions of the appeal furnishes an excellent instance of an abuse of procedure on which we have already dwelt[2]—the mode in which preventive imprisonment might, by a conspiracy of the magistrates, be used as a punishment. But the story proves nothing more. It runs as follows:—

'C. Pescennius IIIvir capitalis C. Cornelium . . . honore primi pili ab imperatoribus donatum, quod cum ingenuo adulescentulo stupri commercium habuisset, publicis vinculis oneravit. A quo appellati tribuni, cum de stupro nihil negaret sed sponsionem se facere paratum diceret quod adulescens ille palam atque aperte corpore quaestum factitasset, intercessionem suam interponere noluerunt. Itaque Cornelius in carcere mori coactus est.' The man asked for a trial and it was refused. But, as there was no cognizance by a higher magistrate and therefore no proposal of a penalty for *stuprum*, it was impossible to say whether it was a case for the *provocatio* or not.

If we turn to the second condition of open evidence of guilt, it must first be noticed that, even with respect to the delicts of the civil law, the distinction between *manifestum* and *nec manifestum* is one that affects punishment, not trial. The epithet 'manifest,' as applied to a crime, might, therefore,

[1] p. 382. [2] p. 514.

have no bearing on procedure. The legendary story of a 'manifest murder,' cited in this connexion, is told as follows by Cicero and Livy:—

'Quo tamen e collegio laus est illa eximia C. Iulii, qui hominem nobilem L. Sestium, cuius in cubiculo ecfossum esse se praesente mortuum diceret, cum ipse potestatem summam haberet, quod decemvirum sine provocatione esset, vades tamen poposcit: quod se legem illam praeclaram neglecturum negaret, quae de capite civis Romani nisi comitiis centuriatis statui vetaret' (Cic. *de Rep.* ii. 36, 61).

'Cum sine provocatione creati essent, defosso cadavere domi apud Sestium patriciae gentis virum invento prolatoque in contionem, in re iuxta manifesta atque atroci C. Iulius decemvir diem Sestio dixit et accusator ad populum extitit cuius rei iudex legitimus erat: decessitque ex iure suo ut demptum de vi magistratus populi libertati adiceret' (Liv. iii. 33).

The point of the story is obvious. C. Iulius, as decemvir, might have pronounced judgement himself; but he waived his rights and permitted the appeal. The narrative tends to show that, had not Rome then been governed by an inappellable magistracy, a trial before the people would have resulted from this murder, which is, strangely enough considering its circumstances, called *manifesta*.

We are left with Cato's utterance on the Catilinarians, which has already been referred to[1]:—

'Qua re ego ita censeo: cum nefario consilio sceleratorum civium res publica in maxima pericula venerit, eique indicio T. Volturci et legatorum Allobrogum convicti confessique sint caedem, incendia aliaque se foeda atque crudelia facinora in cives patriamque paravisse, de confessis sicuti de manifestis rerum capitalium more maiorum supplicium sumendum.'

It is by no means certain that the words 'manifesti rerum capitalium' need imply manifest guilt proved before a magistrate *alone*; but, apart from this doubt, the utterance cannot be held to prove any principle regulating ordinary jurisdiction. Cato's assumption is that against a manifest *hostis* the full *imperium* may be used. The conspirators are manifest *hostes*, like Catilina in the field; therefore, they may be condemned by the military *iudicium* consequent on the declaration of martial law.

[1] p. 464, n. 4.

The evidence, on the whole, does not seem to prove either of the two conditions maintained by Zumpt. It is rather stronger as regards the *confessi* than as regards the *manifesti*. Yet we can hardly believe that confession before a magistrate and his *consilium*—one not made public in a *contio*—could be accepted as a final justification for punishment[1]. It is still less likely that the magistrate could proceed on his own responsibility against a supposed *manifestus*; for such a power would have endangered all civil liberty. It is true that the tribunes might refuse their *auxilium*, and the victim of arrest might be imprisoned for life. But an appellable sentence could not be carried out by the magistrate alone. The veto is not the sole sanction of the *provocatio*; after the Porcian laws the magistrate who violates the right of appeal is guilty of *perduellio*.

[1] Even in civil procedure we have shown it to be probable that the confession *in iure* (i. e. before a magistrate) could in later times be recalled by the *confessus* (p. 253).

APPENDIX IV

ON THE POSITION OF POMPEIUS AS SOLE CONSUL IN 52 B.C.

(Note to p. 391).

ZUMPT in his *Criminalrecht* (ii. 2, p. 411 ff.) held the view that in the year 52 B.C. Pompeius was the only curule magistrate in the state. He thought that Pompeius was not elected by the people, but nominated by the *interrex*. No magistrates of the people, he said, are known to have existed for this year except the *triumviri capitales* (Asc. *in Milon.* p. 38), and he attempted to show that praetorian offices—those of the presidents of the ordinary criminal courts, whom Asconius calls *quaesitores*—were held by men who were not praetors. One of these, M. Favonius, was certainly not praetor; in the following year (51 B.C.) he vainly contested an office which was probably the praetorship (Cic. *ad Fam.* viii. 9, 5). A second, M. Considius Nonianus, was to have held Cisalpine Gaul for his province in 49 B.C. (Cic. *ad Fam.* xvi. 12, 3), and in that year commanded near Capua with the rank of propraetor (Cic. *ad Att.* viii. 11 B, 2). Zumpt thought, therefore, that Considius held the praetorship in 50 B.C. But his appointment to one of Caesar's provinces in 49 makes it more likely that he held the praetorship earlier; for the *senatus auctoritas*, that dealt with these extraordinary praetorian appointments, provided :—

'Uti quodque collegium primum praetorum fuisset neque in provincias profecti essent, ita sorte in provincias proficiscerentur' (Cic. *ad Fam.* viii. 8, 8).

As he could not be propraetor in Gaul, he not unnaturally commanded with that rank in Italy; for after 52 B.C. continuity in the *imperium* was no longer necessary. We know nothing about the position held by the other *quaesitores* mentioned by Asconius, namely, A. Manlius Torquatus and L. Fabius.

As Zumpt held that no curule magistrates were elected, he thought that the general business of the state must have been transacted by delegates appointed by Pompeius.

Against this view must be set the considerations (1) that an examination of the names of the *quaesitores* proves only that one, Favonius, was not a praetor; (2) that Pompeius himself may have been elected consul by the people, and that the other *comitia* may have followed; elections had at least been held for the office of *IIIvir capitalis*; (3) that no authority credits Pompeius with dictatorial power, and that, even if he had it, the dictatorship had never abolished the other magistracies of the people; it had only suspended their *independent* authority.

ADDITIONAL NOTES

Page 13, Note 1.

To the instances given in this note should be added *Fragmentum Tarentinum* (*L'Année Épigraphique*, 1896, pp. 30 and 31). This municipal law of Tarentum, belonging to the Ciceronian period, furnishes an admirable illustration of the dual method of prosecution in enforcing the obligations of administrative law. In the case of malversation of the public funds it is the magistrate who is to bring the action ('eiusque pequniae magistratus, queiquomque in municipio erit, petitio exactioque esto'); in the case of unauthorized destruction of buildings within the town any one may bring the action ('eiusque pequniae [que]i volet petiti[o] esto').

Page 58.

In the clause *unde tu me ex iure manum consertum vocasti, inde ibi ego te revoco* (Cic. *pro Mur.* 12, 26), *unde* and *inde* are probably to be taken in a causal sense, *ibi* alone having a local signification. The clause will then mean 'On the ground on which you have summoned me *ex iure*, on that very ground I summon you there in turn.'

Page 102.

To the evidences for a remodelling of the constitutions of particular towns should be added the *Fragmentum Tarentinum* (*L'Année Épigraphique*, 1896, pp. 30 and 31). If the view gathered from its language is correct, that it dates from a period not long after the *lex Iulia* of 90 B. C. and is, therefore, some years earlier than the *lex Iulia Municipalis* (Liebenam, *Städteverwaltung*, pp. 209, 472), the document shows that the later type of municipal constitution was fully evolved not long after the social war, although it may only have been applied in isolated cases. Tarentum under this statute has as magistrates *IIIIvirei aedilesque* elected by a *comitia curiata*, and its senators are called *decuriones*. Unfortunately, the fragment contains no direct reference to civil or criminal jurisdiction. It refers only to administrative jurisdiction consequent on the contravention of certain injunctions.

Page 115, Note 3.

It should have been stated in this note that there is a possibility of the principle recognized in this case being that the *iudex* should be of the nationality of the defendant. But had this been the case, I think that the *lex provinciae*, or Cicero, would have stated the principle more clearly—as clearly as it is stated in the passage cited on p. 116, note 1. The mention of *iudices* without any qualification certainly suggests jurors from the *conventus*.

Page 262, Note 4.

Mr. Strachan-Davidson suggests to me that the words of Quintilian 'eum, cuius cognitio est, onere liberat' suggest the *iudex extra ordinem datus* of the Principate rather than the *iudex ordinarius*, *cognitio* being generally used for magisterial or extraordinary investigation. In this case, the passage has no direct bearing on the *iudicia ordinaria* or on the Ciceronian period. Even, however, if Quintilian has a definite kind of *iudex* before his mind's eye, it is questionable whether he means to limit the principle to one kind of jurisdiction. Not much can be gathered from the principle in itself, for the relief of the *iudex* may be due to his regarding the oath as a substitute for evidence or as conclusive evidence. But, if Quintilian is thinking exclusively of extraordinary jurisdiction, he no doubt regards the oath here as a substitute for evidence (for the *iudex extra ordinem* acts *vice* the magistrate). With respect to the operation of the oath *in iudicio* in ordinary jurisdiction, we have nothing but the scene in the centumviral court, described on pp. 262, 263, on which we can base a conclusion.

Page 319, Note 2.

Mommsen (*Strafrecht*, pp. 167, 544, 632) interprets the *improbe factum* of the third Valerian law as meaning that the magistrate who violated the conditions of the *provocatio* was a common offender; that the act was not a magisterial act, to be punished as a political offence (p. 544), but one belonging to the category of ordinary crimes. In such a case 'deckt ihn dabei sein Amt nicht und wird die Handlung als die eines Privaten betrachtet, also als Mord bestraft' (p. 167).

Page 356, Note 3.

Suet. *Caes.* 12 (quoted p. 357, note 3). Mommsen, although he takes the view (*Staatsr.* ii. p. 617) that the lot was used in the appointment of the duumvirs, throws out the suggestion (*ib.* p. 618, note 1) that it may have been employed merely to determine which should pronounce the sentence. This view simplifies the procedure considerably; but, if it is correct, one can hardly imagine that Q. Metellus Celer was the nominating praetor. Metellus evidently disapproved of the whole proceedings, and would never have directly appointed Caesar, their originator, as one of the *duumviri*.

Page 363, Line 21.

'The annual bill passed by the tribunes' (cf. pp. 317, 329, 361, 363, 467, 474). Cicero (*in Verr.* ii. 41, 100) speaks of the annual interdiction of the tribunes as having been effected by an edict. I have spoken of this measure sometimes as a bill, sometimes as an administrative act; for it seems as though it must have assumed both forms. Where the *quaestiones* had condemned, interdiction had already been pronounced by the people, and the magistrates need only declare who had been interdicted. But the people had pronounced no interdiction from Rome, either in the case of a man's going into exile to avoid condemnation in a *iudicium populi*, or in the case of a capital condemnation pronounced by a governor in a province. In such cases, it seems as though some formal resolution must have been elicited from the *plebs*; for the magistrate, although he can declare interdiction, cannot interdict.

PAGE 395.

It is impossible to discuss at length the vexed, and from the point of view of procedure not very important, point of the number of days that Milo's trial actually lasted. An admirable examination of the question will be found in Mr. A. C. Clark's edition of the *pro Milone.* The view that I have stated in the text rests on the assumptions (1) that the trial began on April 4 and ended on April 8, which is stated by Asconius, if the numerals are not corrupt; (2) that when Asconius says (p. 40) 'quarta die adesse omnes in diem posterum iuberentur ac coram accusatore ac reo pilae . . . aequarentur; dein rursus postera die sortitio iudicum fieret,' he means that the *aequatio pilarum* was to take place on the fourth day, the *sortitio* on the fifth, although it is possible to translate the passage differently. The difficulty has arisen from the fact that Asconius (p. 41) seems actually to describe only four days' proceedings, and makes the *contio* of Plancus immediately follow the closing of the evidence and precede the day of the trial (cf. Cic. *pro Mil.* 2, 3, 'hesterna contione'). It is just possible that Asconius has missed out something in this summary; for a *contio* announced ('vocata contione' p. 52) and held between three o'clock in the afternoon ('circa horam decimam,' p. 41) and nightfall is, even in the Rome of this period, remarkable. If there was a blank day, following the evidence and preceding the trial, the *contio* must have been held on that day. It is difficult to account for this interval; but it must have had the advantage of enabling the speakers to prepare arguments based on the evidence which had been delivered—an advantage secured in another way by the *comperendinatio* (p. 502).

INDEX OF SUBJECTS

(The references are to the pages ; *n.* signifies the note on a page.)

Abductio in carcerem, in vincula, 333.

Absence, of defendant in civil procedure, see *Indefensus* ; of accused in criminal procedure, 461 ff., 473.

Absentia rei publicae causa, 257, 353, 461, 474.

Absolutio, 228.

Absolvo, vote of, 497.

Acceptum in literal contract, 548, 559.

Accomplices, evidence against, 484.

Account-books, see *Codex* and *Tabulae*.

Accusatio, see Prosecute ; *quarta*, 346, 347, 348 *n.* 1.

Accusator, in a comitial trial, 357 ; used of *patronus* in some cases, and of *subscriptor*, 475. See Prosecutor.

Acquittal, in civil procedure, 228, 235 ; in criminal procedure, 497, 498.

Actio, 2 *n.* 1 ; use of the word by Cicero, 161, 167 ; in the sense of a 'hearing' (in civil procedure), 272, 273 ; (in criminal procedure), 499 ; *actio prima, secunda*, 478, 500.

Actio aestimatoria, 553 ; *aquae pluviae arcendae*, 40 ; *arbitraria*, 160 ; *auctoritatis*, 60 *n.* ; *bonae fidei*, see *Fides* ; *bonorum vi raptorum*, 91 *n.* 1 ; *communi dividundo*, 153, 204 ; *per condictionem*, 65, 164 ; *confessoria*, 60 ; *contraria*, 204, 228, 559 ; *damni dati vi hominibus armatis*, 91 *n.* 1, 209, 553 ; *damni iniuria dati*, 209, 543, 553 ; *depensi*, 250 ; *depositi*, 157, 159, 206 ; *directa*, 204 ; *de dolo malo*, 178 *n.* 6 ; *empti et venditi*, 203 *n.* 3, 204 ; *in factum*, 156, 190 ; *familiae herciscundae*, 40, 45, 65, 153, 165, 204, 228, 560, 566 ; *fictitia*, 156 ; *finium regundorum*, 40 *n.* 1, 45, 153, 165, 196 *n.* 3, 228 ; *furti*, 63, 91, 165, 208 ; *hypothecaria*, 89 ; *incerti*, 201 ; *iniuriarum*, 207, 553, 568 ; *interrogatoria*, 179 ; *iudicati*, 246, 250, 277, 279, 281, 283, 294 ; *per iudicis arbitrive postulationem*, 51, 63 ff., 164, 202 ; *legis*, 5, 9, 10, 36 ; meaning of and procedure in, 50 ff. ; *locati, conducti*, 203 *n.* 3, 204 ; *mandati*, 203 *n.* 3 ; *mandati contraria*, 559 : *per manus iniectionem*, 44, 51, 68 ff., 108 *n.* 5, 164, 252, 255, 276, 277, 279, 281, 283, 527, 528 ; *negatoria*, 61 ; *de pauperie*, 165 *n.* 5 ; *in personam*, see *Persona* ; *per pignoris capionem*, 52, 67 ff., 164 ; *poenalis*, 206 ; *rationibus distrahendis*, 64, 165 ; *rei uxoriae*, 64 ; *in rem*, see *Res* ; *sacramento*, 11, 42, 44, 51, 164, 171, 182, 194, 528 ; in *lex Calpurnia repetundarum*, 416, 419 ; procedure in, 52 ff., 185 ff., 575 ; *pro socio*, 203 *n.* 3, 204, 206, 228, 542, 545, 549 ; *per sponsionem praeiudicialem*, 185, 186 ff., 193, 194, 221, 249 ; *tigni iuncti*, 55.

Actions, publication of, 27.

Actor, 49, 50, 475 ; *et petitor*, 554.

Actus rerum, 129, 138, 269.

Addico, 69, 137.

Addictio, 44, 69, 73, 208, 252, 255, 279, 281, 559.

Addictus, 73, 278, 279, 280.

Adjournment, in civil jurisdiction, 139, 270 ; in criminal jurisdiction, see *Ampliatio*.

Adiudicatio in the *formula*, 152.

Administrative jurisdiction, 12 ; in the provinces, 122 ff., 129 ; in a municipal town, 575, 576.

Adrogatio, formula of, 368 *n.* 2.

Adsertor in libertatem, 54, 61, 194.

Adstipulator, 540.

Adversaria, 275, 546, 548, 550.

Advocacy, see *Advocatus* and *Patronus*.

Advocatus, in civil procedure, 148, 167, 181, 237, 270, 531 ; in criminal

procedure, 474; in inquisition on slaves, 480.
Aediles, criminal jurisdiction of, 340 ff., 353; prosecution of women by, 370 *n.* 5; *coercitio* of, 341; curule, their jurisdiction, 31, 83, 208; of *plebs*, possess right of fining, 335; employed for arrest, 338; in the municipalities, 100, 576.
Aequatio pilarum, 578.
Aequitas, 196.
Aerarii tribuni, see *Tribuni*.
Aerarium, *album iudicum* kept in, 446.
Aes et libram, obligation *per*, 71.
Aestimatio, 553. See *Litis*.
Ager, *publicus*, 220; prosecution for excessive occupation of, 341; *Romanus*, 55.
Agere, uses of, 49, 162; *lege*, 162.
Agnati, 41.
Agnatio, 183.
Album of the praetor, 84, 87, 147, 163, 172, 175, 178, 191, 231; *iudicum*, 265, 388, 437, 445, 446, 448, 454, 455.
Allies of Rome, 32, 99; sentences of Roman magistrates on, 398.
Altercatio, 478, 479.
Ambitus, 391, 422, 429, 431, 457 *n.* 6; earliest *quaestio de ambitu*, 422; later laws on, 425.
Amnesty, 524.
Ampliatio, 488, 498, 501, 502, 531, 557.
Amplius, 498.
Anquisitio, 345 and *n.* 3, 348, 357.
Antestatio, 141.
Appeal, civil, none from the provinces to Rome, 109; in the provinces, 110; nature of in Cicero's time, 287 ff., 536; criminal, 305, 312, 318, 516 ff.; in *quaestiones perpetuae*, 452, 516 ff.
Appellatio, origin of, 25; intercession based on, 289, 291; in criminal procedure, 516 ff.
Applicatio, 185.
Aquae et ignis interdictio, see *Interdictio*.
Aratores, 116 *n.* 3, 123, 124, 129.
Arbiter, 18, 39, 62, 63, 67, 70, 200, 202, 226, 227, 533, 542, 544, 545, 562; functions of, 45.
Arbitrator, *arbiter* or *iudex* as an, 18.
Arbitria, 45.
Arbitrium, 63, 177, 192, 545, 549, 560; as opposed to *iudicium*, 64, 198, 202.
Arbor infelix, 304.
Arrest, see Imprisonment and *Manus iniectio*.
Arson, 506.
Assault, action for, 63. See *Iniuria*.
Assemblies, at Rome, jurisdiction of the different, 338 ff.; reversal of sentences by, 520 ff.; remission of outlawry by, 524; in municipal towns, 99, 103, 576; local, give evidence, 490. See *Centuriata*, *Concilium*, *Iudicium populi*, and *Tributa*.
Assessors of magistrate and *iudices*, 133, 134, 542.
Assize, criminal, at Rome, 456.
Attorney, the *cognitor* as an, 237.
Auctio hereditaria, 558 *n.* 6.
Auctor, 59, 165.
Auctoritas of the magistrate, 210.
Auspices of *quaestores parricidii*, 310.
Auspicia, necessary for intercourse with the people, 20 *n.* 8.
Auxilium, 289, 290, 291, 328, 412, 413, 514, 515, 517.

Bacilla, 105.
Bail, see *Vadari*, *Vades*, *Vadimonium*.
Ballot, introduced in comitial trials for *perduellio*, 350; voting by, in the *quaestiones*, 497; Sullan ordinance as to, 442.
Banishment, see *Exilium* and *Interdictio*.
Bankruptcy, see *Bonorum*.
Basilicae, 133, 343 *n.* 5.
Beneficium, Restitution as a, 522.
Bona Dea, violation of rites of, 386.
Bonam copiam iurare, 74 *n.* 2, 280 *n.* 3.
Bonorum possessio, in inheritance, 29, 188, 213, 290; in bankruptcy, 96, 128, 144, 534, 541; in criminal trials, 504; *proscriptio*, 128, 254; procedure in, 284; in criminal trials, 505; *venditio*, 128, 254, 257, 283, 535; procedure in, 285 ff.; in criminal trials, 505; *vi raptorum actio*, 91 *n.* 1.
Bribery, aedilician impeachment for, 341; of president of a criminal court, 433. See *Ambitus*.

Calendar, judicial, 136 ff., 457 ff.
Calumnia, 468 ff., 475; *calumniae iuramentum*, 459, 470.
Campus Sceleratus, 378.
Capitis deminutio, 195 *n.* 1, 510, 567.
Carcer, 280.
Cascellianum iudicium, 224.
Castella, 34.
Castigatio, 299.
Causae, *collectio*, *coniectio*, 270; *cognitio*, 275, 535.
Cautio, *iudicatum solvi*, 538; *de rato* or *rati*, 240, 241 *n.* Cf. *Satisdatio*.
Census, its connexion with the *centumviri*, 41, 182; with the *lex Voconia*,

95; of *Equites*, 434 *n.* 3, 448; probable, of *tribuni aerarii*, 444.
Centumviri, 16, 40, 58, 173; appointment of, 43, 264; jurisdiction of, 182 ff.
Centuriata comitia, 41, 311, 318, 324, 329, 330, 338, 339, 342, 351, 357, 361, 444.
Centurions as *iudices*, 444 *n.* 4, 449.
Certatio in pontifical jurisdiction, 374.
Cessio in iure, 75.
Challenge of *iudices*, see *Reiectio*.
Citatio, 473 *n.* 1.
Cives sine suffragio, 407.
Civis ex Latio, meaning of, 409 *n.* 1.
Civitas, as a reward to prosecutors for extortion, 422; loss of, 513, 567; *sine suffragio*, 34.
Clients, holding *precario*, 220; exempted from compulsory evidence, 484.
Codex, accepti et expensi, 275, 493, 548, 550; of urban praetor, 439.
Coercitio, 12, 94, 288, 321, 326 and *n.* 1, 327, 339, 341, 375; principles of magisterial, 331 ff.; formal differences in magisterial, 337; relation to criminal jurisdiction, 331; of president of a court, 433 *n.* 6, 447 *n.* 3, 473; in enforcement of evidence, 485.
Cognitio, 576; *extraordinaria*, 98, 149.
Cognitor, 146, 251, 475, 543, 546; appointment and functions of, in civil procedure, 236 ff.
Cohors praetoria, 410.
Colonies of Roman citizens, 34, 99, 103 *n.* 2, 173, 318, 406.
Columna Maenia, 343 *n.* 5, 344.
Comites of prosecutors in search of evidence, 485.
Comitia, in the municipalities, 99, 103, 576; at Rome, see *Centuriata*, *Tributa*.
Comitiatus maximus, 317 *nn.* 4 and 5.
Comitium, 73, 133.
Commissions, special for criminal jurisdiction, 324, 339, 340, 379; various types of, 380 ff.
Commodatum, 64, 204.
Commodum possessoris, 229.
Communi dividundo actio, 153, 204.
Communicatio iudiciorum, 443.
Communio comitiorum, as a condition of the *provocatio*, 370, 406, 407.
Comperendinatio, in civil jurisdiction, 139; in criminal jurisdiction, 422, 478, 488, 493; nature and history of, 499 ff.
Compromissum, 542, 544, 545, 549.
Concepta verba, 261, 300.
Conciliabula, 103 *n.* 2.
Concilium plebis, 317, 318, 335, 339, 342, 361.
Condemnatio of the *formula*, 153; always pecuniary, 158; *cum taxatione* or *infinita*, 159; in representation, 239.
Condemno, vote of, 497.
Condictio, 45; in the *legis actio*, 65 ff.; in the formulary system, 196, 198 ff.; its connexion with the oath, 261; *certi*, 91, 199, 224, 233, 547, 549; *certae* or *certae creditae pecuniae*, 108, 177, 547; *triticaria*, 201.
Confession, in civil procedure, 50, 251 ff.; in criminal procedure, 463 ff., 479, 569; of parricide, 506.
Confessoria actio, 60.
Confessus, in civil procedure, 72, 75, 252, 254, 279, 282; in criminal procedure, 569, 572; *aeris confessi*, 72 *n.* 3, 252, 527.
Confiscation of goods as a punishment, 326 *n.* 1, 515; accompanying interdiction, 355, 365; following comitial trials, how executed, 364 and *n.* 3; as a penalty on *hostes*, 403; added to exile and inflicted on parricides by Caesar, 508.
Congressus, 533.
Coniuratio, torture of slaves against master in, 377 *n.* 3, 492.
Coniurationes, 399.
Consecratio, capitis, 300, 301; *bonorum*, 301, 302, 326, 332, 336.
Consensus, marriage by, 369.
Consilium, of king, 304; of provincial governor, 410; in domestic jurisdiction, 368, 370, 371; in inquisition on slaves, 480; in special commissions, 383; in jurisdiction under martial law, 403; of civil *iudex*, 133 *n.* 4, 542; used for *iudices* in a *quaestio*, 387 *n.* 4, 393, 394, 395, 416, 442, 451, 495, 504, 523; *consurgere in*, 492 *n.* 2; *dimittere*, 495 *n.* 3; *ire in*, 276, 496; *mittere in*, 496 and *n.* 3.
Consortes, 560.
Constitutum, 533.
Consuetudo, 91; *certa*, 92.
Consuls, institution of, 25; survival of civil jurisdiction of, 29, 82, 290; criminal jurisdiction of, 308, 339; *coercitio* of, 333, 337.
Contio, in comitial trials, 345, 346, 347, 352, 353, 357; preceding legislation, 360; of Plancus in Milo's trial, 578.
Contracts, *bona fide*, 64; consensual, 65.
Contravindicatio, 56, 60, 231, 252.

Conventus, 114, 118, 124, 129, 139, 143; *civium Romanorum*, 410.
Corona of auditors, 134.
Corpus, as the subject of an action, 158.
Culeus, punishment of the, 506. Cf. 384 *n.* 1.
Culpa, 205.
Curatio forbidden to its creator, 362.
Curiata comitia in Tarentum, 576.
Curulis sella, 134.

Damnum, 556; *datum vi hominibus armatis*, 91 *n.* 1, 209, 553; *decidere*, 63 *n.* 3, 155; *infectum*, 108; *iniuria datum*, 209, 543, 553.
Dare, (facere) oportere, 61, 155, 198, 206, 245; *damnas esto*, 527.
Death, as a means of *coërcitio*, 332; inflicted by paternal power, 368; penalty on *hostes*, 403; in *iudicia populi*, 505; for *parricidium*, 505; sentence of, carried out by *tresviri capitales*, 343.
Decemviri stlitibus iudicandis, 16, 40, 42, 58, 173, 263, 264, 567; revision of sentences of, 293.
Decimation, 414.
Decoctor, 250.
Decumani, 117, 123, 124, 125.
Decuriae of *iudices*, 388 *n.* 2, 437, 446, 449.
Decuriones, 103, 576.
Deditus, 567.
Deductio moribus, 186, 191, 552, 561, 562, 566.
Defence in civil procedure, 227 ff.; neglect of, 255 ff., 534 ff.
Defensor, 250.
Deferre nomen, 459 *n.* 3.
Deiectio, in the interdict *unde vi*, 563.
Delatio nominis or *criminis*, 456 *n.* 4, 461, 466.
Delecti iudices, 455.
Delegation of jurisdiction, 129, 131, 295, 304, 309, 518.
Delicts, 207.
Deminutio capitis, see *Capitis*.
Demonstratio, of the *formula*, 151, 175, 201; *finium*, 552.
Denegatio actionis, 228.
Denuntiatio, in the *condictio*, 65, 66; announcing an action, 560, 566; to witnesses, 273, 485.
Deportation, 371.
Depositum, 64, 204.
Deprecatio, 465 *n.* 2.
Dicam scribere, 144 *n.* 1.
Dico, 137.
Dictator, 19, 306, 319, 397, 574; *optima lege*, 314.
Dies, comitiales, 137 *n.* 1, 138 *n.* 1; *fasti*, 137, 457; *festi*, 457; *nefasti*, 68, 136, 137, 346 *n.* 1, 375, 457.
Diligentia, 205.
Disqualification, resulting from condemnation, 508; from the senate, 508; from speaking *in contione*, 508; from the judicial bench, 446 *n.* 2; from prosecution, 459; from evidence, 483. Cf. *Infamia*.
Divinatio, 459, 474, 475.
Divisoria iudicia, 154.
Divorce, 371.
Do, 137.
Dolus malus, 178 *n.* 6, 553, 554, 555. See *Exceptio*.
Domestic jurisdiction, 304, 367 ff.
Dominium, 59, 219; *ex iure Quiritium*, 33 *n.* 1.
Dominus, 14 *n.* 1, 219; in representation, 239 ff., 251.
Dowry, action for recovery of, 64. See *Mutatio*.
Drowning, penalty of, 304. Cf. *Culeus*.
Ducere, 69, 254, 279.
Duoviri aediles, 100.
Duplum, *ire in*, 294; liability *in*, 528, 529. Cf. *Poena*.
Duumviri, as municipal magistrates, 100 *n.* 2, 104, 407 *n.* 3; *perduellionis*, 304, 309, 310, 348; in trial of Rabirius, 355 ff., 577.

Edict, of praetor, 5, 87, 89, 105; of the curule aediles, 31 *nn.* 3 and 4.
Edicta, nature of, 86; of the praetor, 88; wording of, 90; *de postulando*, 147; on neglect of defence, 256.
Edictum, *perpetuum*, 87; *de postulando*, 90; *provinciale*, 119 ff.; *Siciliense*, 119; *tralaticium*, 87, 119; *urbanum*, 119, 120.
Editicii iudices, 453 ff.
Editio, *actionis* or *formulae*, 143, 178; *instrumentorum*, 178; *iudicum*, 452 *n.* 1, 453.
Eiurare iudicem, 266.
Emancipation of slaves, modes of, 372.
Empti et venditi actio, 203 *n.* 3, 204.
Emptio, venditio, 203; *bonorum*, 286.
Emptor bonorum, 286.
Ephemeris, 275, 540.
Equites, as *iudices* in civil matters, 265; in special commissions, 379, 381, 393, 435; in *quaestiones perpetuae*, 434, 436, 443, 448, 455; not liable for corruption, 421, 422.
Equity, 202.
Error in the *formula*, result of, 176 ff

Evidence, in civil procedure, 273 ff.; in criminal procedure, 467, 477, 479 ff.
Evocare, used of summoning cases, 117, 411; of summoning witnesses, 486 *n.* 3.
Exceptio, 229 ff.; absence of, in *legis actio*, 230; form and place of, 232; *cognitoria*, 234, 237; *dilatoria*, 234; *doli*, 178, 232, 234; *iuris iurandi*, 260; *litis dividuae*, 177; *metus causa*, 232, 234; *pacti conventi*, 232; *peremptoria*, 234; *praeiudicii*, 180 *n.* 2, 234; *rei iudicatae vel in iudicium deductae*, 141 *n.* 1, 154, 174, 232, 234, 240, 246; *transacti*, 549; *vitiosae possessionis*, 215, 225, 562, 564, 565; of M. Scaevola, 120.
Excusatio, of criminal *iudices*, 448; of accused, 474 and *n.* 3.
Execution, in civil procedure, real, 69 ff., 281 ff.; personal, 278 ff.; in criminal procedure, pecuniary, 504 ff.; personal, 505 ff.; appeal against, 516.
Exilium, 312, 320, 330, 467; following convictions for extortion, 509; conception and history of, 509 ff., 567; instances of, 350, 351, 361, 509 *n.* 3, 511 *n.* 11, 512 *n.* 1; sometimes frustrated, 511 *n.* 1; local limits imposed on Cicero's exile, 365.
Expensi latio, 197, 547.
Expensum in literal contract, 548, 559.
Extinction of claim, 174, 240. See *Litis contestatio*.
Extradition in the Roman Empire, 411.
Extraordinaria cognitio, 98.
Extraordinarius reus, 457 *n.* 2.
Exul, 510; *exules*, at Rome, 449 *n.* 4.

Facere, obligation of, 62.
Falsum, 429, 432 *n.* 7, 507. See *Lex Cornelia*.
Familia, 60, 71; in the interdict *unde vi*, 564; *publica*, 342 *n.* 2.
Fas, 21, 22, 81 *n.* 1.
Fasces, 104, 105 *n.* 1, 308, 321.
Fasti, publication of, 27 *n.* 5. See *Dies*.
Fecisse, *non fecisse videtur*, 498.
Feriae, *conceptivae*, 137; *imperativae*, 137.
Festi dies, see *Dies*.
Festuca, 42, 56.
Fides, *bona*, 47, 203; *bona fide* contracts, 64, 153, 203; actions or *iudicia*, 83 *n.* 5, 196, 228; characteristics of, 202 ff.; *publica*, granted to witnesses, 484 *n.* 7, 525 *n.* 5; *fide publica*, evidence prepared, 498; *Romana*, 202, 259.
Fiducia, 45, 203.
Fines, 327; as a mode of *coercitio*, 334.
Fining, right of, given to tribune, 327; possessed by magistrates, 335.
Foederatae civitates, 32, 100, 105, 111, 407, 510; with right of *exilium*, 511.
Foedus, 111; *aequum*, *iniquum*, 510.
Fora, 34, 35 *n.* 2, 103 *n.* 2, 114.
Formula, 9, 10; prototype of the, 30; of the civil law, 83, 108, 163; praetorian, 88, 155, 157; character and structure of, 150 ff.; rigidity of, 160; its relation to the *legis actio*, 161 ff.; dangers of the, 175 ff.; in the interdict, 226, 227; given by aediles, 31; criminal, of the king, 302; *arbitraria*, 160, 192; *in factum concepta*, 155, 157, 181, 190; *in ius concepta*, 83 *n.* 5, 155; *Octaviana*, 120 *n.* 1; *petitoria*, 190 ff., 194, 195, 249; *praeiudicialis*, 155, 195; multiplicity of *formulae*, 89, 166; *formulae* in the towns of Italy, 105, 108.
Forum, at Rome, 133, 344, 378, 458; in Italian towns, 134; as a circuit, 116; *agere*, 129; *contractus*, 34, 47; *rei*, 33, 47.
Freedmen, domestic jurisdiction over, 372; duties owed by, 372 *n.* 6; limitation of evidence of, 483; could not be tortured, 481, 492 *n.* 2.
Fructuaria stipulatio, 222, 224, 250.
Fructus, estimate of, in *bona fide* actions, 205; *licitatio*, 222.
Fruits, arising from *interim* possession, 70. See *Fructus*.
Furti actio, 63, 91, 165, 208.
Furtum, 326; *manifestum*, 208, 569; *nec manifestum*, 165, 208, 569.
Fustuarium, 415.

Gentiles, 41.
Gentilitas, 183, 184.
Gentium ius, see *Ius*.
Governor of a province, carrying out praetorian injunctions, 96. See Provinces.
Guardians, action against, 64.

Hasta, 42.
Herctum ciere, 65, 165.
Hereditatis, *petitio*, 127, 188, 190 *n.* 3, 193; *possessio*, 96, 120 *n.* 3, 127; *vindicatio*, 60.
Heres, must possess *ius commercii*, 560.

Hostis, 33, 322, 515; declaration that a citizen is a, 399, 400, 403, 405, 524, 571.
Hours of jurisdiction, 139, 459.

Janiculum, flag on the, 358.
Identity of a claim, 247.
Imperator, unlimited jurisdiction of, 414.
Imperio continens, jurisdiction, 136.
Imperium, of the king, 20; of the praetor, 78; of municipal magistrates, 104; of provincial governor, 110; interpretation springing from, 94; civil jurisdiction based on, 137, 173, 289; criminal jurisdiction based on, 410, 428; grant of *recuperatores* through, 267; punishment through, 302; abrogation of, 350, 352, 353; *domi* and *militiae*, 308; *maius*, 287.
Imprisonment, in civil procedure, 254, 278 ff.; see *Manus iniectio*; in criminal procedure and as a mode of *coercitio*, 333, 343, 350 *n.* 9, 467; employed as a penalty, 403, 513 ff.
Improbe factum, 319, 577.
Improbus, 320.
Incendium, 424.
Incest, 300, 316, 387, 492; conception of and procedure in, 376 ff.
Incolae, of federate states, 100 *n.* 4; of municipal towns, 103; Latin, in Rome, 408.
Indefensi, praetor's list of, 256.
Indefensus, 250, 254, 255, 266, 279, 282, 534.
Iudicium dare, 484.
Infames, 280; of the praetor's edict, 148.
Infamia, 70, 176, 242, 285 *n.* 3, 446 *n.* 1, 459, 469, 470, 471, 483, 535, 549; as a consequence of condemnation in *quaestiones*, 508.
Iniuria, 85, 207, 268, 326, 506 *n.* 6, 536; in the *formula* for *damnum*, 554, 555, 556; *atrox*, 267, 424. See *Actio iniuriarum* and *Lex Cornelia*.
Iniuriarum crimen under *lex Cornelia*, 417 *n.* 1, 507.
Inrogatio, 346; *multae*, 355 *n.* 5.
Inscriptio, 465, 466.
Insignia of the praetor, 31.
Instrumenta, 178, 274.
Integrum, restitutio in, in civil procedure, 90, 98, 296; in criminal procedure, 519 ff.
Intentio, of the *formula*, 152, 154; in *bona fide* actions, 205; *iuris civilis*, 155, 175; in representation, 239.
Intercessio, in civil procedure, 97, 133, 287, 288 ff., 537; in criminal procedure, 334, 516.
Interdictio aquae et ignis, 301, 323 *n.* 3, 324, 325, 329, 351, 355, 361, 362, 363, 364, 391, 396, 425, 506, 507, 577; origin and early meaning of, 512; change in the conception of, *ib.*; identified with *exilium*, 513 *n.* 1. See Tribunes.
Interdicts, in earlier procedure, 75 ff.; in later procedure, 210 ff.
Interdictum, *duplex*, 222, 225, 228; *exhibitorium* or *ad exhibendum*, 186, 217, 218, 514; *possessorium*, 187; *de precario*, 214; *prohibitorium*, 217; *quorum bonorum*, 213, 216; *recuperandae possessionis*, 216, 555; *uti possidetis*, 76 *n.* 1, 188, 191, 217, 220, 250, 560; procedure in, 221; *utrubi*, 188, 191, 218, 225; *quod vi aut clam*, 217; *unde vi*, 214, 216, 220, 225, 536; *unde vi armata*, 212, 215, 226, 562.
International jurisdiction, 46.
Interrogare, in criminal procedure, 463 *n.* 2.
Interrogatio, in civil procedure, 179; in criminal procedure, 463; *testium*, 272, 487 *n.* 4.
Intestabilis, 320.
Italy, before the social war, 32 ff., 99, 406 ff.; after the social war, 100 ff., 406 ff.
Iudex and *Iudices*, subject to *coercitio*, 332; civil, 15; origin of, 16; in the monarchy, 24, 302; given by aediles, 31; qualification of, 38, 46, 265; functions of, 44, 98, 150, 270 ff., 275; in the Italian towns, 105; in the provinces, 114 ff., 132, 139, 265 *n.* 2; criminal, in special commissions, 379, 381, 384, 385, 387, 435, 473; created by *lex Plautia*, 385; by Pompeius in 52 B.C., 392; reversal of sentences of, 521; of *quaestiones perpetuae*, 433 ff.; responsibility of, 421, 439, 442; not subject to appeal, 516; reversal of sentences of, 522, 523; as president of *quaestio*, 426, 431, 473, 505 *n.* 6, 517; *domesticus*, 367; *editicii*, 453 ff.; *extra ordinem datus*, 576; *ordinarius*, 576; *quaestionis*, 356 *n.* 4, 429, 431, 432, 433, 452, 458, 459, 495 *n.* 5, 517; title applied to magistrates, 19, 25, 41; *iudicem dare*, 164; *ferre*, 266; *sumere*, 266.
Iudicare in comitial trials, 346.
Iudicati, *actio*, 246, 250, 277, 279, 281, 283; *tempus*, 277.
Iudicatum, 193.

Iudicatus, 72, 252, 255, 279, 281, 282, 283; *pro iudicato*, 252, 527, 569.
Iudicia, duplicia, 204, 228; *ordinaria*, 169; *publica*, characteristics of, 415 ff.; replace *iudicia populi*, 417.
Judicial corruption, *quaestio* for, 421.
Iudicium, civil, 16, 81, 98, 105, 108, 114, 122, 132, 192, 293, 416; uses of the word, 167 ff.; as opposed to *arbitrium*, 64, 196; procedure in, 270 ff.; criminal, 313, 331; *legitimum*, 48, 84, 108, 136, 140, 172, 174, 246; military, 323; *populi*, 9, 10, 19, 323, 325, 377, 406, 505; procedure of, 344 ff.; renewal of, 358; *appellatio* in, 516; reversal of sentence of, 520; *lex Remmia* perhaps enforced by, 469; *iudicia populi* of Cicero's time, 349 ff.; *publicum*, 10, 330 *n.* 5, 415; of a municipal town, 407, 459; *quod imperio continetur*, 140, 172, 174, 246, 267; *secutorium*, 224, 225, 227; *dare*, 169; *exercere*, 416; *ordinare*, 145.
Iure, in, cessio, 75; proceedings, 145, 178; pleadings, 149.
Iurgare, 40 *n.* 1.
Iurgia, 137 *n.* 2.
Iurisdictio, imperio continens, 136; *urbana*, 30.
Juristic persons, evidence of, 489.
Ius, 6 *n.* 1, 15, 21, 80, 81, 98, 105, 108, 114, 132, 245, 288, 416; *aequum*, 203; *Aelianum*, 28, 92 *n.* 3; *agendi cum populo*, 310; *applicationis*, 185 *n.* 1; *Ariminense*, 567; *civile*, 29, 33, 36, 84, 85, 96, 155, 163, 192, 206, 231, 510; *commercii*, 33, 560, 567; *divinum*, 8, 300; *duodecim coloniarum*, 567; *gentium*, 30, 33, 47, 92 *n.* 2, 93, 510; *honorarium*, 85, 92, 96, 105, 140, 231, 557; *praetorium*, 85 *n.* 3; *publicum*, 10, 367, 373; *Quiritium*, 33 *n.* 1, 59, 155, 190, 192, 220; *sacrum*, 373; *strictum*, 40, 45 *n.* 4, 196; actions of, 197, 208; *vocatio in*, 141 ff., 185, 256, 533.
Iusiurandum, in civil procedure, 90, 259; *delatum*, 198 *n.* 1, 259; *in litem*, 159; *necessarium*, 260, 261; *voluntarium*, 260.
Iustitium, 287, 353 *n.* 1.

King, position of the, 19 ff., 302 ff.
Knights, right of distraint possessed by, 68. See *Equites*.

Latini, 32, 33, 34, 47, 100, 105, 408.
Latrocinium, 525.
Laudatio, 490, 491.
Laudatores, 490, 491; prohibited by Pompeius, 392.
Law, relation of the magistrates to, 79; native, in the provinces, 127.
Legati, 437; in a province, 130; jurisdiction of, 131; of states giving evidence, 489.
Legis actio of voluntary jurisdiction, 135. For contentious jurisdiction see *Actio*.
Lex, meanings of, 21, 312 *n.* 1; as the basis of jurisdiction, 48, 79; as the basis of the *quaestiones*, 417, 427, 442 *n.* 3.
Lex and *Leges*, *Acilia repetundarum*, 408, 415, 419, 420, 422, 431, 434 *n.* 3, 441 *n.* 1, 453, 456 *n.* 4, 458 *n.* 4, 461, 470 *n.* 4, 484, 496, 497, 499, 501 *n.* 2, 504, 505, 509 *n.* 2; *Aebutia*, replacing *legis actio* by *formula*, 93, 170 ff.; *Aebutia*, closing offices to their creators, 362 *n.* 5; *Aemilia*, *provinciae Macedoniae*, 113; *agraria* of 111 B. C., 267; *annua*, 94; *Antonia iudiciaria*, 449; *Antonia de provocatione*, 518, 519; *Appuleia agraria*, 351; *Aquilia de damno*, 75 *n.* 3, 86, 162, 209, 543, 553, 556; *Aternia Tarpeia*, 327 *n.* 1, 335; *Aurelia iudiciaria*, 266 *n.* 1, 389 *n.* 3, 392, 438, 441, 442 *n.* 2, 443 ff., 450; *Baebia*, 36; *Bantina*, 415; *Caelia tabellaria*, 350; *Calpurnia de ambitu*, 425, 508, 521, 522; *Calpurnia de condictione*, 45, 66, 67, 198, 261; *Calpurnia repetundarum*, 416, 419; *Cassia* on loss of senatorial rank, 350; *Cincia*, 230, 231, 509 *n.* 2; *Clodia* on putting uncondemned citizens to death, 359; *coloniae Genetivae*, see *Ursonensis*; *Cornelia de ambitu*, 423, 508; *Cornelia de edictis*, 95, 97, 98, 122; *Cornelia de falsis*, 424, 507 *n.* 2, 522 *n.* 3; *Cornelia iniuriarum*, 208, 417 *n.* 1, 424, 507 *n.* 2; *Cornelia iudiciaria*, 436 ff., 441, 445; *Cornelia maiestatis*, 423, 507; *Cornelia nummaria*, 424; *Cornelia peculatus*, 423; *Cornelia de proscriptione*, 314; *Cornelia repetundarum*, 423, 483, 486 *n.* 1, 501, 503, 509 *n.* 2; *Cornelia de sicariis et veneficis*, 407, 421, 424, 426 *n.* 5, 429 *n.* 1, 431, 432, 525; *Cornelia testamentaria*, 424; *data*, 48, 111, 113; *Duodecim Tabularum*, see 51: see Twelve Tables; *Fabia de plagiariis*, 426; *Fufia iudiciaria*, 450; *Fufia de religione*, 388; *Fulvia de civitate danda*, 408 *n.* 2; *Furia de sponsu*, 75; *Hieronica*, 116,

117; *iudiciaria*, 265; *Iulia de adulteriis*, 7 *n.* 1; *Iulia de civitate*, 100, 575; *Iulia iudiciaria* (of Caesar), 448, 449 *n.* 2; (of Augustus), 247 *n.* 2; *Iulia iudiciorum publicorum*, 428; *Iulia de iure magistratuum*, 112 *n.* 3; *Iulia de maiestate*, 427, 507, 518; *Iulia municipalis*, 103, 104, 280, 407, 470 *n.* 2, 471, 575; *Iulia peculatus*, 427 *n.* 4; *Iulia repetundarum*, 112 *n.* 3, 427, 476 *n.* 9, 483, 485, 486, 497 *n.* 5, 501, 503, 508, 509 *n.* 2; *Iulia de vi*, 427, 483 and *n.* 2, 484, 507, 518; *Iulia de vi publica*, 414; *Iunia Licinia*, 452, 517; *Iunia repetundarum*, 420; *Licinia*, forbidding the holding of offices by their creators, 362; *Licinia Mucia*, 425; *Licinia de sodaliciis*, 425, 430, 452 *n.* 1, 453 ff., 507; *Livia*, granting protection to Latins, 408; *Livia iudiciaria*, 436; *Lutatia de vi*, 424 *n.* 6, 431; *Mamilia*, 435, see *quaestio*; *Memmia*, on exemption from prosecution, 461; *Menenia Sestia*, 335; *municipalis*, 102; *Papia de peregrinis*, 425; *Papiria Iulia*, 335; *Papiria Plautia*, 100; *Peducaea*, 379; *Pinaria*, 45, 62; *Plaetoria*, about minors, 230, 231; *Plaetoria*, about the praetor's jurisdiction, 139; *Plautia iudiciaria*, 385, 435; *Plautia Papiria*, 100; *Plautia de reditu Lepidanorum*, 524 *n.* 4; *Plautia de vi*, 397 *n.* 1, 424, 431; *Poetilia*, 74, 278, 281; *Pompeia de ambitu*, 391, 392, 521; *Pompeia iudiciaria*, 448; *Pompeia de parricidiis*, 427, 506; *Pompeia, provinciae Bithyniae*, 114; *Pompeia de vi*, 391, 392, 395 *n.* 1; *Porciae*, 320 ff., 413, 572; *provinciae*, 113, 128, 411 *n.* 1; *Publilia de sponsu*, 75; *regiae*, 22, 367; *Remmia*, 468; *Rubria*, 102, 105, 107, 252 ff., 255, 279, 283, 292 *n.* 3; *Rupilia*, 113, 114, 116, 117, 129; *sacrata*, 301, 313, 554; *Sempronia de capite civium Romanorum*, 323, 330, 359, 360, 383, 400, 405, 413; *Sempronia iudiciaria*, 266 *n.* 1, 434; *Sempronia, ne quis iudicio circumveniretur*, 421; *Servilia iudiciaria*, 435; *Servilia repetundarum*, 422, 501, 503, 509 *n.* 2; *Silia de condictione*, 45, 66, 198, 199, 261; *Sulpicia de reditu exulum*, 521; *Tullia de ambitu*, 425, 453, 474, 508, 512 *n.* 4; *Ursonensis*, 104 *n.* 4, 108 *n.* 5, 164, 459 *n.* 2, 476; *Valeria de proscriptione*, 314; *Valeriae de provocatione*, 307, 319, 321; *Valeriae et Horatiae*, 40, 301 *n.* 3, 318, 324; *Varia de maiestate*, 385; *Vatinia de reiectione iudicum*, 451; *Vatinia*, permitting foundations in Gaul, 409; *venditionis*, 285; *Voconia*, 95, 128, 231.

Libellus, as a notice of *proscriptio*, 284 *n.* 4, 535.

Libera custodia, 514.

Liberae civitates, 32, 99, 101, 111, 407.

Libertas, of a state, 408; of an individual, *iudicium* on, 61, 194, 567.

Liberti iusti, 372.

Libertini, see Freedmen.

Licitatio fructus, 222.

Lictors, of the praetor, 31; in the municipal towns, 104.

Liquet and *non liquet*, 272, 497, 498, 500.

Lis capitis, 505 *n.* 2.

Litigare per formulas, 170 *n.* 1.

Litis, aestimatio, in civil procedure, 62, 67, 72 *n.* 3, 158, 193, 249; in the *quaestiones*, 416, 463, 498, 504; procedure in, 502 ff.; *contestatio*, 50, 179, 235, 239, 242, 254, 529, 544, 545 *n.* 4; meaning and effects of, 243 ff.; *denuntiatio*, 144 *n.* 1.

Locatio, 65, 152; *locatio, conductio*, 203.

Lot, see *Sortitio*.

Ludi, cessation of jurisdiction during, 138, 457.

Magister, auctionis, 285; *populi*, 19.

Maiestas, 350 *n.* 9, 359, 385, 429, 430, 518.

Mancipatio, 71, 182, 273.

Mancipia, 41.

Mancipium, 71 *n.* 1, 527.

Mandata, given by states to *legati*, 489, 490.

Mandati actio, 203 *n.* 3.

Mandatum, 65, 203, 558.

'Manifest,' applied to offences, 569, 570, 571.

Manus, conferred by marriage, 369; *conserere*, 185, 222; *iniectio*, 44, 68, 108 *n.* 5, 250, 252, 255; *iniectio pro iudicato*, 75; *pura*, 75.

Martial law, 390; conception of and procedure under, 397 ff.; remission of outlawry consequent on, 524; proclamation of, forbidden, 323, 405; in the army, 414.

Matricide, 432 *n.* 8.

Mile-limit and mile-stone, see *Miliarium*.

Miliarium primum, 36, 308, 318, 406, 407.

Military jurisdiction, 410 ff., 414 ff.; consequent on martial law, 401, 402.

Minors as witnesses, 483.

Missio in possessionem, 90, 98, 99, 104,

107, 122, 132, 254, 256, 257, 282, 535; principles regulating, 257, 283 ff.
Mobilia et moventia, production of, in an action, 55.
Mos maiorum, 80, 92 *n.* 2, 304, 404; execution *more maiorum*, 322.
Multa, 13 *n.* 1, 209 *n.* 1, 282, 298, 326, 334, 346; *ius multae dictionis*, 335; *dicta* and *inrogata*, 335; limit of *multa inrogata*, 335; *multae irrogatio*, 355 *n.* 5; imposed by pontifex maximus, 374, 375; *suprema*, 335.
Municipal magistrates, 103; civil jurisdiction of, 99 ff.; criminal jurisdiction of, 406 ff.
Municipes, 103.
Municipium, 34, 35 *n.* 2, 99, 100, 103 *n.* 2, 109, 173, 318, 407.
Munus of *iudices*, 138, 448.
Murder, 506. See *Parricidium* and *Sicariis*.
Mutatio dotis, 558.
Mutuum, 45 *n.* 4, 64, 197, 547.

Narratio, 272.
Nefas, offence pronounced, 387.
Nefasti, see *Dies*.
Negatoria actio, 61.
Nexa, 41.
Nexum, 61 *n.* 1, 71, 278, 527.
Nexus, 71, 278, 280, 281, 527.
Notae, 163 *n.* 1.
Novatio, submission to a *iudicium* regarded as, 6, 245; oath compared to, 262 *n.* 1.
Noxae deditio, 553, 554.
Noxia, 45, 209.
Nuncupatio, in contract of *nexum*, 71.

Oath, as an alternative to evidence in civil procedure, 259 ff., 576; of witnesses, 273, 481; *in leges* and *in legem*, 433 and *n.* 1; taken on prosecution, 459, 470; of civil *iudex*, 270; of criminal *iudices*, 474.
Obligations that give rise to actions, 196 ff.
Obsignatores, 480.
Onus petitoris, 229.
Outlawry, see *Interdictio* and Martial law.

Pactio, 544; *pactiones* of the *publicani*, 125, 126.
Pactum, 50, 533; *de non petendo*, 234.
Paludamentum, 135.
Paramour of vestal, punishment of, 378.
Pardon, power of, 305, 522; of provincial governor, 523.
Parricidium, 303, 427, 432 *n.* 8; punishment for, 384, 506.
Partitio of an inheritance, 560.
Patronus, in civil procedure, 146, 148, 167, 181, 270, 272; in criminal procedure, 474, 476; assignment of, 456 *n.* 4; new *patronus* on *ampliatio*, 499; could not give evidence, 484, 491 *n.* 2; Pompeius limits the number of *patroni*, 392.
Peculatus, 457 *n.* 3, 498 *n.* 3, 509.
Peculium, 368.
Pecunia, *certa*, *incerta*, 39, 45, 61, 66, 67, 158, 159, 177, 200, 201, 207, 261; *certa credita*, 108, 198; *pecuniae creditae*, 113; *quo ea pervenerit*, 471, 504 *n.* 1. Cf. 503.
Pecuniary penalties, in early Roman law, 326; not to be joined with capital, 358.
Penal actions, 207.
Pendency, limit of, in an action, 140, 174, 247.
Perduellio, 8, 303, 306, 316, 323, 324, 328, 330 *n.* 3, 350 *n.* 9, 354, 359, 572. Cf. *Duumviri*.
Peregrinae civitates, 46.
Peregrini, 30, 48, 172, 225, 291, 418 *n.* 5; *iudices*, 118.
Peregrinus, 33, 173, 183, 194, 195.
Perjury, in *actio sacramento*, 53; in religious law, 300.
Perpetuae orationes, 477.
Persona, *integra*, 147; *suspecta*, 250; *actio in personam*, 55, 63, 69, 195, 250, 252.
Petere plus, *minus*, 176, 177, 198.
Piaculares hostiae, 375.
Piacularia, 376.
Piaculum, 261, 299, 375.
Piamentum, 53.
Pignus, 64; *pignora caedere*, *concidere*, 336; *pignoris capio*, 124; as a mode of *coercitio*, 336; of the *publicani*, 337; *captio*, 67.
Pilas aequare, 395 *n.* 2, 578.
Plagium, 426, 507.
Plano, *de*, functions of the magistrate, 135.
Plebs, jurisdiction of, 327 ff., 339, 361; capital jurisdiction of, 324. See *Concilium plebis*.
Poena, 298; in civil procedure, 206, 208, 209, 222, 224, 226, 295; *certa*, 124; *compromissa*, 544; *dupli*, 75, 277, 529; *pecuniaria*, 298; in criminal procedure, 346; *poenae remissio*, 523; *poenae stipulatio*, 545.
Poenalis, *actio*, 206; *sponsio*, 189, 200.
Poisoning, see *Veneficia*.
Police duties of triumvirs, 343, 344.

Pomerium, 308, 318, 326.
Pontifex Maximus, 23; jurisdiction of, 373.
Pontiffs, college of, 23; associated with civil jurisdiction, 26; with the *legis actio*, 51: *consilium* of *pontifex maximus* in jurisdiction, 373, 376, 378.
Possessio, meaning and origin of, 218ff.; in connexion with the *missio*, 284; in connexion with interdicts, 221; in the interdict *unde vi armata*, 562, 564, 565; *in universis*, 540; *interim*, in *actio sacramento*, 57, 61, 69, 185; in the procedure *per sponsionem*, 186, 189, 221, 225; in the *formula petitoria*, 191; in the interdict *uti possidetis*, 222; *in possessione esse*, 284; *missio in possessionem*, see *Missio*.
Possessores, suits between *publicani* and, 14, 267.
Postulare, in criminal procedure, 459 *n.* 3.
Postulatio, in civil procedure, 146 ff., 164, 179; for *missio in possessionem*, 284; in criminal procedure, 459.
Potestas, *dominica*, 371 *n.* 7; *maior*, 287; *par*, 288, 293 *n.* 1; *par maiorve*, 288, 517; *patria*, 60, 493; of the *addictus*, 280.
Praefectura, 35 *nn.* 2 and 3, 100, 101, 103 *n.* 2.
Praefectus, *iuri dicundo*, 35, 101, 107, 264; *urbi*, 24.
Praeiudicium, 52, 67, 140, 141, 149, 155, 183, 189, 195, 199, 223, 227, 231, 233, 294, 369, 459, 474, 476, 506 *n.* 6, 539, 567.
Praes, in *actio sacramento*, 54, 185; *praedes litis et vindiciarum*, 69, 185, 249; sale of, 69; *pro praede litis et vindiciarum*, 190, 249; *praedes* given in criminal trials, 504.
Praescripta verba, 151.
Praescriptio, 166, 229, 233.
Praetor, 19, 25; institution of a special, 28; civil jurisdiction of the, 83; his proceedings *in iure*, 149; the authority for municipal jurisdiction, 107; grants tribune access to *comitia centuriata*, 330; *coercitio* of, 333, 337; criminal jurisdiction of, 340; as president of *quaestio perpetua*, 428 ff.; peregrinus, 30, 83, 97, 137, 173, 290, 419, 517 *n.* 5; provincial, 36; *repetundis*, 421; urbanus, 30, 83, 96, 102, 122, 264, 290; regulates *album iudicum*, 437, 445, 448, cf. 456; assigns criminal *iudices*, 438.
Praetoria cohors, 410.
Praevaricatio, 468, 470, 471, 503 *n.* 4.
Precarium, 220.
Preliminary inquiries of *tresviri capitales*, 343.
Prensio, right of, 338.
Presidents of the *quaestiones perpetuae*, 428 ff.; duties of, 433, 438, 447 *n.* 3, 459, 464, 473, 487, 495, 498.
Privilegium, nature of a, 312 ff.; Clodius' bill as a, 361, 362; Pompeian laws as *privilegia*, 392.
Procare, 65 *n.* 1.
Proconsul, 37, 118.
Procurator, 146, 214, 251, 256, 535; appointment and functions of, 237 ff.; *litis*, 238; *omnium rerum*, 237; *vindex* not a, 528; in interdict *unde vi*, 564.
Professio iugerum, 124.
Promissor in a stipulation, 189, 538 *n.* 6, 539.
Promulgation at comitial trials, 347.
Propraetor, 37, 118.
Proprietas nuda, 559.
Pro quaestore, 130.
Prorogatio imperii, 37.
Proscriptio, as a notice of sale, 552. See *Bonorum*.
Proscriptions, 313 ff.
Prosecute, right to, 11, 459.
Prosecutor, duties of, 468 ff.; retirement of, 467.
Provinces, civil jurisdiction in the, 109 ff.; criminal jurisdiction in the, 323, 410 ff.
Provincia, 30, 106, 111.
Provocatio, 19, 245; meaning of, 305 ff.; laws establishing, 307 ff., 318 ff.; effects of laws of, 325, 331; execution of debtor and *addictio* not subject to, 326 *n.* 2; sale into slavery not subject to, 332 *n.* 3; in connexion with the tribunate, 327; procedure of, 344, 348; in connexion with special commissions, 381, 382, 383; from *quaestiones perpetuae*, 518 ff.; of *cives* in Italy, 406; granted to Latins, 408; not extended to provinces, 411; conditions of the, 370, 569.
Publicani, 14, 68, 119, 121, 123, 125, 129, 164, 267, 412, 488; exempted from compulsory evidence, 484; need not produce originals of accounts, 494.
Publicus ager, 220.
Punishments, of religious law, 299 ff.; in the regal period, 304; inflicted by *quaestiones*, 505 ff. See Execution.

Quaesitor, in special commissions, 381, 384, 392, 393; in *quaestiones perpetuae*, 417, 430 *n.* 2, 431 *n.* 6.
Quaestio, 304, 357; *Mamilia*, 380 *n.* 7, 381, 384; *perpetua*, 330 *n.* 5; *inter sicarios*, 420; on slaves, 480.
Quaestiones, 417; *perpetuae*, 5, 339, 340, 417, 428; characteristics of, 415 ff.; gradual creation of, 417; establishment of, 418 ff.; presidents of, 428 ff.; *iudices* of, 433 ff.; procedure in, 456 ff.; reversal of their own sentences by, 522, 523.
Quaestor, jurisdiction of, in province, 130; function of, in *bonorum possessio*, 282, 505; power of *coercitio*, 335 and *n.* 1; assists in making out *album iudicum*, 446, cf. 456.
Quaestores, *aerarii*, 309; *parricidii*, 303, 304, 308, 339, 340, 343 *n.* 4, 420; *pro praetore*, 131; *urbani*, 309.
Quattuorviri, 100 *n.* 2, 576; *aediles* or *aediliciae potestatis*, 104 *n.* 2, 106; *iuri dicundo*, 104, 106, 576; *praefecti*, 35, 101.
Quiritare, 311.
Quiritium ius, see *Ius*.

Raptorum vi bonorum, *actio*, 91 *n.* 1.
Receptio nominis, 462, 466, 516, 517.
Recovery, in cases of extortion, 419, 420, 502, 509; in cases of peculation, 502, 509.
Recuperatores, origin of, 47; qualification and appointment, 266 ff., 551, 557; to enforce *vadimonium*, 142; in action for *damnum*, 210; given by curule aediles, 31; employed in the provinces, 124, 129, 132, 145, 265 *n.* 2, 294; resemblance to *iudices* of the *quaestiones*, 416; employed in cases of extortion, 419.
Redigam, non redigam, 498.
Refusal of action, grounds for, 180.
Reiectio iudicum, in civil procedure, 265; in criminal procedure, 438, 440, 451, 456.
Reiicere ad leges suas, 115.
Relegation, 508; as a mode of *coercitio*, 334; as a punishment, 371, 508.
Religious jurisdiction, 373 ff.
Remissio poenae, 523.
Repetundarum, *quaestio*, 233; earlier and later method of dealing with this offence, 418 ff.; civil law action for, 418 *n.* 5, 517 *n.* 5; *actio*, for bribery, 421 *n.* 3.
Representation, unknown in *legis actio*, 59, 146, 235, 528; praetor's rules about, 147; under the formulary system, 235 ff.
Res, *certa*, 45, 61, 62, 66, 67, 158, 198, 200, 261; *corporalis*, 55; *eadem*, 247; *furtiva*, 55; *iudicata*, 180, 254, 276; finality of, 244 ff., 293, 519; interference with, 293 ff., 519 ff.; *publicae*, evidence of, 489; *rei vindicatio*, 55; *in rem actio*, 55, 159, 182, 194, 246, 249, 252, 560.
Restipulatio, 67, 189, 199, 223, 227, 545, 549.
Restitutio in integrum, see *Integrum*.
Restitution, in *formula arbitraria*, 159, 192; in the restitutory interdicts, 215, 562.
Reus, in civil procedure, 50; in criminal procedure, 466.
Revocatio Romam, 292.
Rex socius, relations with a, 511 *n.* 11.
Rogatio, in comitial trials, 347, 357, 358; of a bill of interdiction, 364 *n.* 1.

Sacer, 301, 512.
Sacra, attached to property, 286.
Sacramento actio, see *Actio*.
Sacramentum, 11, 185, 260, 261, 293; meaning of, 52 ff.
Sacratio, 53.
Satisdatio, *iudicatum solvi*, 193, 224, 241, 242, 249, 250, 251, 254, 256, 258, 277, 536; *ratam rem dominum habiturum* or *amplius neminem petiturum*, 240, 249, 546.
Scourging, 304, 321, 322.
Scribae, 104, 495.
Search, right of, in collecting evidence, 494.
Sector, 282, 537 *n.* 6.
Selecti iudices, 116.
Sella curulis, 134.
Senate, grants *fides publica* to witnesses, 484 *n.* 7; employed as a judicial *consilium* by Cicero, 403. See Amnesty and Martial law.
Senates, of municipal towns, 103; give evidence, 490; of provincial towns, 115, 411 *n.* 1; give evidence, 490.
Senators, criminal responsibility of, 324, 359, 400; coercion of, 333, 336, 337; privilege in criminal trials given to, by Sulla, 440; as civil *iudices*, 38, 46, 265; as criminal *iudices*, 393 and *n.* 1, 433, 437, 443, 454; liable for corruption, 421.
Senatus consultum, *de Bacchanalibus*, 383; *ultimum*, 383, 400, 403 *n.* 5.
Servitudes, processes applied in, 60, 182, 190 *n.* 3, 194.
Sicariis, *quaestio de*, 356 *n.* 4, 427, 428,

429, 432, 495 *n.* 5, 517. See *Lex Cornelia* and *Quaestio*.
Signatores, to written evidence, 488.
Slavery, for debt, 128, 528; sale into, as a punishment, 332 *n.* 3.
Slaves, evidence of in civil procedure, 273 *n.* 5; criminal jurisdiction over, 371; torture of, 388, 394 *n.* 1, 491 ff.; torture of, against master, 377, 378 and *n.* 4, 388, 391 *n.* 1, 394 and *n.* 1, 491; inquisition of, through torture, 479 ff.
Slay, right to, in adultery, 370; in self-defence, 555.
Societas, 65, 203, 542; as contrasted with *hereditas*, 549; *omnium bonorum*, 550; *unius negotii*, 550.
Socii of Rome, 32. See Allies.
Sodalicia, 425, 430, 453.
Sodaliciis, de, impeachment, 393. See *Lex Licinia*.
Sodalitates, 425, 453.
Soldiers, as criminal *iudices*, 449.
Son, jurisdiction over the, 367.
Sortes aequare, 395 *n.* 2.
Sortitio, of *iudices* in civil procedure, 265 *n.* 2; of *iudices* in criminal procedure, 393, 395, 433, 438; of *decuriae iudicum*, 446 *n.* 3; of *duumviri perduellionis*, 356, 577; of *provinciae* in criminal jurisdiction, 428, 430, 431 *n.* 6, 433.
Special commissions, see Commissions.
Speculation in corn, prosecution for, 340.
Spoilt votes, in criminal jurisdiction, 389, 447.
Spondeo, 61.
Sponsio, 52, 54 *n.* 1, 61, 67, 99, 149, 189, 195, 214 *n.* 1, 223, 226, 227, 254, 258; in *condictio*, 66; *poenalis*, 189, 200, 294, 547; *praeiudicialis*, 189, 538; *tertiae partis*, 199, 201, 547.
Sponsores, 241, 242, 249, 250.
Status, questions of, 155, 183, 194.
Stillicidia, 194.
Stipendiariae civitates, 113, 410.
Stipendium, 444.
Stipulatio, 61, 63, 197, 547; as evidence, 275; *fructuaria*, 222, 224, 250; *poenae*, 545; *pro praede*, 190; *praetoria*, 248.
Stipulator, 189, 538 *n.* 6, 539.
Strangling as a punishment, 343 and *n.* 2.
Stuprum, prosecution for, 340.
Subscriptio, 465.
Subscriptores, 465, 475, 476; in trial of Clodius, 388.
Subsellia, 134, 458; *tribunorum*, 290.
Subsortitio, 438.
Summons, in civil procedure, 141 ff.; in criminal procedure, 461, 473.
Superstites, 56.
Supplicium, 298.
Suprema tempestas, 139.
Surety, see *Praes*.
Syngraphae, 121 *n.* 1, 126.

Tabellae quaestionis, 480.
Tablets, voting, 497; in trial of Clodius, 389.
Tabulae, as evidence or as the basis of a claim, 274, 275, 493 and *n.* 8, 545, 548; *publicanorum*, 494; as an affidavit, 534; *testimonium per tabulas*, 274 *n.* 4, 488.
Talio, 44, 63, 207, 297, 298.
Tarpeian rock, death from the, 304, 332, 336, 364, 377.
Taxatio, 159, 210, 553.
Tergiversari, use of, 471 *n.* 5.
Tergiversatio, 468, 471.
Term, legal, 138, 456.
Testamenti captio, 567.
Testimonium, *per tabulas*, 488; *publicum*, 489, 490. See Evidence.
Testis, *de auditu*, 274 *n.* 2, 482; *voluntarius*, 268 *n.* 3.
Theft, action for, 63, 208. Cf. *Actio furti*.
Time, limits of, imposed on pleaders, 356, 357 *n.* 1, 476.
Times, of civil jurisdiction, 136; of criminal jurisdiction, 457.
Torture, see Slaves.
Translatio, *translativa constitutio*, 229 *n.* 3, 235.
Treason, see *Maiestas* and *Perduellio*.
Treaty, see *Foedus*.
Tresviri (or *Triumviri*) *capitales* (or *nocturni*), 43, 53, 435 *n.* 1, 515; functions of, 342 ff.; *reipublicae constituendae*, 314.
Tribe, introduction of, into the jury system, 454.
Tribunal, at Rome, 133, 458; of *triumviri capitales*, 343 *n.* 5; in the municipal towns, 104; *pro tribunali*, 135.
Tribunes of the Plebs, right of veto of, 288, 290, 517, 518, 537; appeal to, 536, 556; *coercitio* of, 327, 332, 333, 335, 336; jurisdiction of, 327 ff., 339, 340; outlawry pronounced by, 317, 329, 361, 363 577, cf. 467, 474; right of, to prosecute perhaps abolished by Sulla, 330 *n.* 4.
Tribunicia potestas, 332 *n.* 2.
Tribuni, *aerarii*, 393, 443; probable

qualifications of, 444. 448, 455; abolished, 448; *militum*, 43, 264, 435 *n.* 1; *militum consulari potestate*, 28.
Tributa, 125 *n.* 2.
Tributa comitia, 43, 264, 310, 317, 335, 339, 341, 342, 353, 436.
Tributum, 444.
Trinun nundinum, or *Trinundinum*, 347, 357, 358.
Tripertita, 27.
Triticaria condictio, 201.
Triumvirale supplicium, 343 *n.* 2, 370.
Triumviri, see *Tresviri*.
Tullianum, 343.
Tutela, 203 *n.* 3.
Twelve Tables, procedure under, 4; mark an epoch in procedure, 9; absence of details of procedure in, 26; pronounce capital penalty on a corrupt juror, 46; fix the length of a court day, 139; state rules of summons, 141 *n.* 2; *actio rationibus distrahendis* in, 165; modified by *lex Aebutia*, 171; state rules for assault, 207; for manifest theft, 208; for damage, 209; about witnesses to a mancipation, 273; about execution in civil procedure, 282; about criminal law, 312 ff.; reserve capital cases for *comitia centuriata*, 325, 339.

Ultio, 208.
Universal possession, see *Possessio*.
Usucapio, 41, 182.
Usufruct, 558, 559, 565.
Usury, prosecution for, 340.

Vacation, legal, 138, 457.
Vadari, 142 *n.* 3.
Vades in criminal trials, 334.
Vadimonium, in civil procedure, from municipal towns to Rome, 102, 108, 143; in the provinces, 143; as a means of summons, 142, 185, 186, 256, 533, 534; enforced by the praetor, 149; uses of the word, 142 *n.* 3; in criminal procedure, 334.
Venditio, 65. See *Bonorum*.
Veneficis, de, quaestio, 429, 432. See *Lex Cornelia*.
Venue, change of, 116, 292.
Verdict, form of the civil, 276; form of the criminal, 495, 497.
Vestals, pontifical jurisdiction over, 374; trial of, for incest, 377 ff.
Veto, see *Intercessio*.
Viatores, 104, 338.
Vici, 34.
Vindex, 73, 75, 164 *n.* 4, 250, 527, 528.
Vindicatio, 55, 56, 69, 75; *per formulam petitoriam*, 190 ff.; *hereditatis*, 60; *in libertatem*, 60, 61; *per sponsionem*, 185, 186 ff., 193, 194, 221.
Vindiciae, 185.
Vindicta, 208.
Vis, in civil law, 233, 267, 563, 564; in criminal law, 391, 430, 431, 457 *n.* 3, 507, 518, 568; aedilician impeachment for, 341, 353; cases of, taken *extra ordinem*, 457, 458; *ex conventu, moribus facta*, 186, 560 *n.* 3; *vim facere*, 222.
Vocatio, right of, 338; *in ius*, 141 ff., 185, 256, 533.
Voting of *iudices*, 497.

Wager, procedure by, 54 *n.* 1, 186. See *Actio sacramento*.
Wife, jurisdiction over the, 369.
Witnesses, limitation of the number of, in civil procedure, 268; in criminal procedure, 486. See Evidence.
Women, may not have possessed *provocatio*, 370, 398; tried by *iudicium populi*, 370; public execution of, avoided, *ib.*; as witnesses, 482.

INDEX TO PASSAGES IN CICERO

(The references are to the pages.)

OPERA RHETORICA

Brutus: PAGE

4, 17 241
5, 18 . . 240, 241, 249
22, 86 498
22, 87 . . . 499, 500
23, 89 316
27, 106 419
28, 107 331
32, 122 380
34, 128 . 331, 381, 400, 520
34, 131 209
44, 164 435
62, 223 551
76, 264 432
79, 275 175
84, 289 . . 133, 134
89, 304 385
89, 305 385
90, 311 531

ad Herennium:

i. 12, 20 508
i. 12, 22 . 181, 229, 231
i. 13, 23 506
i. 14, 24 . . 350, 465
i. 15, 25 . . 349, 350
ii. 7, 10 492
ii. 12, 18 . . 228, 229
ii. 13, 20 . 133, 139, 235
ii. 20, 33 380
ii. 28, 45 . . 513, 521
iv. 8, 12 507
iv. 24, 34 349
iv. 35, 47 495
iv. 36, 48 498

de Inventione:

i. 8, 10 229
i. 11, 15 465
i. 38, 68 472
i. 43, 80 380

PAGE

de Inventione (*cont.*):

i. 49, 92 435
ii. 19 229
ii. 19, 57 231
ii. 19, 58 . 178, 181, 458
ii. 19, 59 . . 466, 496
ii. 20 229
ii. 20, 59 . . 180, 506
ii. 20, 60 . 230, 232, 267
ii. 22, 67 91
ii. 50, 149 506

Orator:

21, 69 472
21, 72 194
29, 101 556
29, 102 556
46, 156 . . . 43, 263

De Oratore:

i. 10, 41 . 56, 76, 164, 220
i. 10, 42 . 55, 58, 164
i. 36, 166 . 64, 165, 177, 203
i. 36, 167 . 64, 165, 177
i. 37, 168 . 133, 134, 177, 232, 247
i. 38, 173 . . . 41, 182
i. 38, 175 183
i. 39, 176 184
i. 39, 177 185
i. 39, 180 184
i. 40, 181 183
i. 41, 186 . . . 27, 161
i. 43, 193 163
i. 53, 227 316
i. 56, 237 . . . 65, 165
i. 56, 238 183
i. 56, 240 28

De Oratore (*cont.*): PAGE

i. 57, 242–244 . . 184
i. 57, 245 183
ii. 25, 106 . . . 400
ii. 28, 124 . . . 350
ii. 30, 132 . . . 400
ii. 39, 165 . . . 331
ii. 47, 197 . . . 350
ii. 60, 245 . . . 487
ii. 63, 255 . 69, 278, 281
ii. 65, 263 . . . 266
ii. 70, 285 . . 266, 331
iii. 1, 4 336
iii. 3, 9 352
iii. 33, 134 . . . 26
iii. 40, 159 . . . 71

Partitiones Oratoriae:

14, 48 482
28, 98 189
28, 99 . . 168, 180, 181
28, 100 . 167, 181, 196, 230
29, 101 230
30, 104 . 229, 276, 350
30, 106 331
34, 117 492
34, 118 . . 377, 492
36, 124 470
37, 130 . 92, 93, 196, 275

Topica:

4, 18 . . . . 88, 214
5, 28 . 71, 80, 85, 196
7, 32 429
8, 33 . . . . 89, 166
8, 37 567
9, 39 40
12, 51 270
17, 66 . 64, 196, 203, 205
19, 73 . . . 479, 482
25, 95 . . . . 80, 175

ORATIONES

Pro Archia: PAGE
2, 3 . . . 425
4, 7 . . . 101
4, 8 . . . 490

Pro Balbo:
3, 6 . . . 426
3, 7 . . . 426
5, 11 . . . 494
8, 21 . 34, 100, 101, 511
11, 28 . 350, 509, 510, 511
12, 29 . . . 511
12, 30 . . . 510
14, 32 . . . 425, 426
15, 34 . . . 111
15, 35 . . . 81, 111
16, 35 . . . 510
17, 38 . . . 426
17, 39 . . . 426
18, 41 . . . 491
21, 48 . . . 425
23, 52 . . . 426
24, 54 . . . 408, 422
28, 65 . . . 427

Divinatio in Caecilium:
3, 10 . . . 460, 461
cc. 4–6 . . . 460
4, 11 . . . 236, 475
4, 12 . . . 475
5, 17 . . . 418
5, 18 . . . 162, 418
5, 19 . . . 475
11, 34 . . . 484
12, 37 . . . 460
15, 47 . . . 475, 476
15, 48 . . . 476
16, 50 . . 344, 475, 476
16, 54 . . . 475
17, 56 . . 130, 132, 144
18, 58 . . . 470
19, 61 . . . 460
19, 62 . . . 460
20, 64 . . . 459, 461
20, 65 . . . 416, 418
20, 67 . . . 351

Pro Caecina:
2, 6 . . . 557
3, 8 . . 2, 162, 167, 169, 180, 567
3, 9 . . . 568
4 . . . 272
4, 10 . . . 81, 557
4, 11 . . . 558
4, 12 . . . 558

Pro Caecina (*cont.*): PAGE
5, 13 . . . 558
5, 14 . . 237, 271, 558
5, 15 . . . 558
6, 16 . . . 558, 559
6, 17 . . . 559
7, 18 . . . 566
7, 19 . . 40, 559, 560
7, 20 . . . 186, 561
8, 21 . . . 561
8, 22 . . 186, 560, 561
8, 23 . . 213, 215, 562
9 . . . 273
9, 24 . . . 563
10 . . . 273
10, 27 . . . 271
10, 28 . . 268, 273, 557
10, 29 . 415, 439, 497, 501
11, 31 . . 272, 557, 563
11, 32 . 2, 80, 162, 215
12, 34 . . . 85, 162
12, 35 . . 557, 564, 568
13, 36 . . . 210
13, 37 . . 2, 162, 568
13, 38 . . . 563
13, 39 . . . 567, 568
14, 39 . . . 564
14, 40 . . . 2, 162
14, 41 . . . 563
15, 42 . . . 564
16, 45 . 87, 90, 223, 226
16, 46 . . . 214, 564
17, 50 . . . 564
18, 50 . . . 563
18, 51 . . . 90
18, 53 . . . 184
19, 54 . . . 60, 165
19, 55 . . . 564
20, 57 . . 214, 238, 564
21, 59 . . . 564
21, 60 . . . 564
23, 64 . . . 563
23, 65 . . . 196
24, 67–69 . . . 184
25, 71 . . . 275
28, 79 . . . 568
28, 80 . . . 568
29, 82 . . . 214
31, 89 . . . 214
31, 90 . . . 564
31, 91 . . . 215, 564
32, 92 . . . 215
32, 94 . . . 565, 566
32, 95 . . . 186, 561
33, 95 . . 81, 557, 566

Pro Caecina (*cont.*): PAGE
33, 96 . . . 195
33, 97 . . 58, 164, 168, 194, 293
33, 98 . . . 13
34, 99 . . . 333, 567
34, 100 . . 510, 512, 567
35, 102 . . . 567
36, 104 . . . 169

Pro Caelio:
1, 1 . . . 457
2, 3 . . . 475
2, 4 . . . 481
2, 5 . . . 491
7, 17 . . . 493
8, 19 . . 477, 487, 489
8, 20 . . 477, 481, 533
11, 25 . . . 476
11, 27 . . . 476
13, 32 . . . 430
15, 35 . . . 475
22, 54 . . . 481
22, 55 . . . 481, 488
28, 66 . . . 477, 487
29, 68 . . . 481
29, 70 . . . 424
31, 74 . . . 511

In Catilinam:
i. 2, 4 . . . 400, 401
ii. 3, 5 . . . 279
iv. 5, 10 . . . 323, 405
iv. 7, 15 . . . 444

Pro Cluentio:
6, 18 . . . 477, 489
7, 21 . . . 426
8, 23 . . . 461
8, 25 . . . 103, 461
10, 29 . . . 474
12, 34 . . . 493
13, 38 . . . 343
13, 39 . . . 343, 344
14, 40 . . . 493
16 . . . 428
17, 49 . . . 461, 473
18, 50 . . . 473
20, 55 . 417, 432, 433, 496
20, 56 . . . 458
23, 62 . . . 487
27, 74 . . 441, 496, 498
27, 75 . . . 442
28, 75 . . . 442

Pro Cluentio (*cont.*): PAGE
28, 76 . . 497, 498, 499
28, 77 . . 551
29, 79 . . 432, 551
30, 82 . . 493
30, 83 . . 416, 496
31, 86 . . 471
32, 87 . . 470
33, 89 . . 432
33, 89–91 . . 13
33, 91 . . 433, 439
34, 92 . . 439
34, 94 . . 429
35, 95 . . 325, 351
35, 96 . . 439
35, 97 . . 417, 423
37, 103 . . 13, 439
37, 104 . . 421, 422, 557
38, 107 . . 542
39, 109 . . 551
40, 110 . . 148, 270
41, 115 . . 503
41, 116 . . 418, 502, 503, 504, 505
43, 120 . . 17, 265, 446, 459
43, 121 . . 444, 445
47, 130 . . 443, 444
50, 139 . . 557
51, 140 . . 435
53, 146 . . 80
53, 147 . . 423, 429, 433
54, 148 . . 424, 429, 431, 506
55, 151 . . 421
56, 154 . . 421
58, 159 . . 473
60, 165 . . 88
60, 168 . . 489
62, 175 . . 428
63, 176 . . 407, 480
63, 177 . . 480
65, 182 . . 480, 542
65, 184 . . 492
66, 185 . . 480
66, 186 . . 480
66, 187 . . 407
69, 196 . . 490
69, 197 . . 490, 491
70, 199 . . 476
71, 202 . . 507
75, 184 . . 480

Pro Cornelio ap. Asconium:
p. 62 . . 459
p. 79 . . 385, 386, 435

Pro Deiotaro:
i. 3 . . 492

Pro Domo: PAGE
10, 26 . . 316, 361, 362
13, 33 . . 404
13, 35 . . 361
16, 43 . . 316, 361
17, 43 . . 312, 313, 316, 346, 361
17, 44 . . 317
17, 45 . . 346, 347, 359
18, 47 . . 317, 362
19, 51 . . 365
20, 51 . . 362, 465
24, 62 . . 362
26, 68 . . 361, 362
26, 69 . . 362
27, 71 . . 362, 521
29, 77 . . 293, 362, 368, 463, 513
29, 78 . . 164, 293, 567
31, 82 . . 325, 351, 362
31, 83 . . 352
32, 86 . . 520
32, 87 . . 351
40, 106 . . 81
47, 123 . . 336
47, 124 . . 336
48, 125 . . 336

Pro Flacco:
2, 4 . . 447
2, 5 . . 511
3, 6 . . 482
4, 10 . . 482
5, 12 . . 477, 481
6, 13 . . 485
6, 14 . . 485, 486
7, 17 . . 490
9, 20 . . 494
10, 21 . . 478
10, 22 . . 458, 487
14, 30 . . 478
15, 34 . . 477, 482
15, 35 . . 485
15, 36 . . 490, 491
16, 37 . . 490
16, 38 . . 490
17, 39 . . 477, 489
17, 41 . . 486
18, 42 . . 458, 482
18, 43 . . 482
19, 43 . . 477
20, 47 . . 471
20, 48 . . 275, 279
21, 49 . . 130, 277, 281, 294
21, 50 . . 266
22, 52 . . 482, 489
22, 53 . . 482
26, 61 . . 491
31, 75 . . 331
32, 78 . . 495

Pro Flacco (*cont.*): PAGE
32, 79 . . 296
33, 82 . . 475, 476
35, 88 . . 90
38, 95 . . 511
38, 96 . . 444, 447
39, 98 . . 472
40, 100 . . 491
42, 106 . . 472

Pro Fonteio:
2 (6), 14 . . 491
7 (11), 23 . . 482
7 (11), 24 . . 481, 482
8 (12), 27 . . 482
9 (13), 29 . . 477, 481
10 (14), 32 . . 481, 490
12 (16), 36 . . 444, 476
12 (16), 37 . . 478
13 (17), 29 . . 274
13 (17), 40 . . 478
16 (20), 45 . . 491
17 (21), 46–49 . . 472

De Haruspicum Responsis:
4, 7 . . 330
6, 12 . . 378
7, 13 . . 376, 378
7, 14 . . 71

De Lege Agraria:
ii. 3, 8 . . 520
ii. 4, 10 . . 519
ii. 8, 21 . . 362
ii. 13, 33 . . 13
ii. 17, 44 . . 182
ii. 34, 93 . . 31, 100, 105
iii. 2, 8 . . 314
iii. 3, 11 . . 220, 221

Pro Lege Manilia:
5, 11 . . 298

Pro Ligario:
1, 1 . . 461
1, 2 . . 465

Pro Milone:
2, 3 . . 578
3, 7 . . 305, 475
3, 9 . . 298
6, 14 . . 458
6, 15 . . 391
8, 21 . . 393
8, 22 . . 392
12, 32 . . 379
13, 35 . . 424
14, 36 . . 323, 362
15, 40 . . 341

Pro Milone (*cont.*): PAGE
16, 44 395
17, 46 487
21, 57 . . . 481, 492
22, 58 492
22, 59 . 377, 378, 492, 493, 394
23, 61 390
26, 70 . . . 402, 404
27, 74 . . 55, 58, 164

Pro Murena:
2, 3. 425
3, 5. 425
9, 22 . . . . . 40, 165
11, 25 . . 26, 27, 163
12, 26 . 56, 58, 59, 60, 164, 165, 185, 575
12, 27 . . 18, 39, 164
13, 28 . . . 173, 175
13, 29 162
20, 41 30
20, 42 . 416, 423, 428, 502
22, 45 425
23, 46 425
23, 47 . . . 453, 474
24, 49 477
27, 56 . . . 475, 476
28, 59 316
32, 67 425
41, 88 472
41, 89 425

Philippicae:
i. 1, 1 524
i. 5, 12 337
i. 8, 19 449
i. 8, 20 . 434, 444, 448, 449
i. 9, 21 518
i. 9, 23 . . 427, 507
i. 13, 31 524
ii. 11, 25 470
ii. 13, 31 31
ii. 23, 56 . . 462, 522
ii. 26, 64 282
iii. 6, 14 415
v. 5, 12 . . 449, 510
v. 5, 14 473
v. 5, 15 . . 446, 449
v. 12, 31 402
vi. 1, 2 402
viii. 5, 15 401
xi. 8, 18 373
xiii. 3, 5 450

In Pisonem:
2, 4. 354
7, 14 404
9, 20 351

In Pisonem (*cont.*): PAGE
10, 23 . . 334, 470, 471
13, 29 366
16, 37 112
22, 51 103
31, 77 369
35, 86 279
39, 94 448
40, 96 . . . 447, 498
40, 97 498

Pro Plancio:
1, 3. 475
3, 8. 425
8, 21 444
12, 29 472
15, 36 . . 451, 452, 453
15, 37 454
16, 38 454
16, 40 . . 455, 456, 495
17, 41 . . 453, 454, 455
17, 43 430
19, 48 471
23, 56 482
23, 57 482
28, 69 . . . 351, 520
34, 83 . . . 425, 513
36, 89 351
40, 96 365
42, 104 . . . 430, 472

De Provinciis consularibus:
3, 6. 112
4, 7. 113
19, 46 166

Pro Quinctio:
1, 3. 531
1, 4. 531
1, 5. 531
2, 5. . . 133, 150, 275
2, 8. . . . 272, 531
2, 12 532
3 272
3, 11 . . . . 271, 537
3, 13 204
4, 15 532
4, 16 532
4, 17 533
5, 18 533
5, 19 533
5, 20 533
5, 21 533
5, 22 . . . 142, 533
6, 23 . . . 142, 534
6, 24 . . . 531, 534
6, 25 . . 88, 139, 258, 284, 534
6, 27 . . 284, 285, 535
7, 28 . . . . 97, 536

Pro Quinctio (*cont.*): PAGE
7, 29 . . 97, 242, 290, 531, 536, 537
7, 30 97
8, 30 . 149, 250, 254, 284, 285, 531, 537, 538
8, 31 . . . 149, 258
9, 32 258
9, 33 . . 270, 272, 531
9, 34 531
10, 34 . . . 272, 276
10, 35 531
10, 36 . . 133, 150, 275
11, 37 539
12, 40 140
13, 42 140
14, 45 88
14, 47 . . . 531, 539
14, 48 540
15, 48 88
15, 49 258
15, 50 . . 88, 284, 285, 286, 535
16, 51 . 258, 284, 535, 540
16, 53 531
17, 54 . . . 258, 531
17, 55 537
18 273
18, 57 . . 275, 534, 540
18, 58 . . . 275, 540
19, 60 . 87, 88, 256, 257, 284, 540
19, 61 . . 69, 142, 284, 285
19, 62 238
20, 62 . . . 169, 180
20, 63 . 169, 178, 180, 284, 536
20, 64 . . . 178, 179
20, 65 . . . 88, 537
21, 66 . . . 178, 180
21, 67 142
22, 70 . . . 537, 538
22, 71 . . . 272, 531
22, 72 531
22, 73 . . . 88, 540
23 273
23, 73 285
23, 74 538
24, 76 . . . 88, 538
24, 77 531
25, 79 . . . 88, 540
25, 80 . . . 532, 540
26, 80 531
26, 83 88
27, 84 . . 250, 284, 536
28 273
28, 86 . . 142, 539, 540
28, 87 540
29, 88 . . . . 88, 538

PAGE
Pro Quinctio (*cont.*):
29, 89 . . 87, 88, 540
30, 91 133
30, 93 537

Apud Quintilium:
xi. 1, 85 314

Pro Rabirio:
1, 1 355
1, 2 . . . . 354, 355
2, 4 357
2, 5 355
2, 6 . . . . 356, 357
3, 8 . . . 321, 355, 426
3, 9 356
3, 10 355
4, 11 355
4, 12 . 310, 321, 323, 356
4, 13 355
5, 15 355
5, 16 413
5, 17 . . . 310, 355
6, 18 357
6, 19 354
7, 20 . 354, 401, 402, 436
9, 24 352
9, 27 444
10, 28 . . . 355, 485
11, 31 354
13, 38 356

Pro Rabirio Postumo:
4, 8 . . 282, 427, 503, 504, 505
4, 9 . 422, 423, 429, 503
7, 16 422
10, 27 509
13, 36 . . . 482, 503
13, 37 . 282, 498, 503, 504, 505

Post Reditum ad Quirites:
4, 10 520

Post Reditum in Senatu:
2, 4 366
4, 8 . . 316, 361, 366
5, 12 334
7, 17 360
15, 37 325
15, 38 520

Pro Roscio Amerino:
3, 8 . . . . 461, 474
4, 11 . . . . 427, 432
5, 11 427
11, 30 506
12, 33 352

Pro Roscio Amerino (*cont.*): PAGE
20, 56 416
20, 57 469
25 506
26 506
28, 77 . . . 481, 492
28, 78 . . . 481, 492
29, 82 477
30, 84 . . . 477, 495
36, 102 477
36, 103 282
36, 104 458
38, 110 485
39, 114 204
41, 119 492
41, 120 492
42, 122 492
43, 125 314

Pro Roscio Comoedo:
1, 3 . . . . 542, 548
1, 4 546
2, 5 . . 275, 548, 550
3, 9 550
4, 10 . 39, 64, 67, 197, 198, 200, 206, 549
4, 11 . 177, 196, 198, 202
4, 12 . 133, 150, 265, 266, 275, 544, 545
4, 13 . . . 197, 550
5, 13 547
5, 14 . . 67, 197, 200, 547
5, 15 . 150, 172, 200, 275, 547
6, 17 551
6, 18 542
7, 20 . . . . 271, 551
8, 22 . . 150, 275, 542
9, 25 . . . . 204, 549
9, 26 545
10, 27 . . . . 542, 551
10, 28 . . 542, 544, 551
10, 29 543
11, 32 . . 243, 543, 544
12, 33 . . . . 542, 544
12, 34 544
12, 35 . 162, 241, 243, 249, 546
13, 37 . . 275, 542, 545
13, 38 545
14, 40 . . . . 546, 550
14, 41 279
14, 42 . . . . 265, 266
14, 43 274
15, 43 274
15, 44 . . . . 273, 274
15, 45 . . . . 266, 273
16, 46 274

Pro Roscio Comoedo (*cont.*): PAGE
16, 48 547
17, 51 547
18, 53 238
18, 55 162
18, 56 549

Pro Scauro:
10, 21 477
13, 29 . . 477, 478, 479
14, 30 478
17, 38 482

Pro Scauro apud Asconium:
p. 21 436

Pro Sestio:
4, 10 491
12, 29 334
16, 37 351
28, 61 . . . . 324, 400
30, 65 . . 316, 317, 361
30, 66 520
34, 73 . . 80, 316, 361, 362
34, 74 362
44, 95 341
47, 101 . . . 351, 431
54, 116 431
62, 130 351
64, 133 425
64, 135 427
69, 146 507

Pro Sulla:
22, 63 . . 496, 519, 521
22, 64 521
23, 65 521
28, 78 492
29, 81 474
31 507
31, 88-89 472
32 507

Pro Tullio:
1 273
1, 1 . . . . . 551, 554
2, 5 . . . 162, 271, 551
3, 6 . . . . . 272, 551
3, 7 . 91, 158, 169, 181, 208, 210, 553
4, 8 . . . . . 210, 553
4, 9 553
5, 10 . 169, 269, 551, 553, 554, 557
5, 11 553
5, 12 169
6 272
6, 14 551
6, 15 551

Pro Tullio (*cont.*): PAGE
6, 17 . . . 551
7, 16 . . . 551, 552
7, 17 . . . 552
8, 18 . . . 552
8, 20 . . . 552, 561
9, 21 . . . 552
9, 22 . . . 552
10 . . . 273
10, 26 . 169, 174, 178, 553
11, 27 . . . 169
11, 28 . . . 553
12, 29 . . . 212, 215
13, 31 . . . 555
13, 32 . . . 169, 554
13, 33 . . . 162, 555
15, 35 . . . 555
16, 38 . 18, 169, 181, 290, 291, 556
16, 39 . . . 290
17, 39 . 551, 552, 556
17, 41 . 169, 178, 268, 556
18, 42 . 81, 169, 268, 556
18, 43 . . . 267
19, 44 . . . 214
20, 47 . . . 298
21, 50 . . . 208, 555
22, 53 . 227, 554, 555, 562
23, 53 . 227, 554, 562
24, 54 . . . 162, 554
24, 56 . . . 555

In Vatinium:
9, 21 . . . 334
11, 27 . . . 451
14, 33 . 452, 467, 517, 518
14, 34 . 429, 458, 459
15, 37 . . . 425
17, 41 . . . 341

In Verrem, actio i:
1, 2 . . . 475
3, 10 . . . 440
6, 16 . . . 438, 474
6, 17 . . . 474
8, 21 . . . 428
10, 30 . 437, 438, 442, 456
10, 31 . . . 458
10, 32 . 474, 476, 481
11, 32 . . . 476
11, 33 . . . 493
12, 36 . . . 341
13, 37 . . . 437
13, 38 . 330, 386, 436, 502

In Verrem, PAGE
actio i (*cont.*):
13, 39 . . . 439
17, 51 . . . 420
18, 54 . . . 500
18, 55 . 477, 478, 487, 500

actio ii:
i. 4, 9 . . . 474
i. 5, 12 . . . 323, 341
i. 5, 14 . . . 323, 341
i. 6, 15 . 460, 461, 476
i. 7, 18 . . . 440
i. 9, 25 . . . 464, 476
i. 9, 26 . 420, 422, 496, 498, 500, 501
i. 11, 29 . . . 487
i. 19, 50 . . . 494
i. 19, 51 . . . 485
i. 20, 52 . . . 282
i. 23, 60 . . . 493, 494
i. 23, 61 . . . 282, 493
i. 28, 71 . . . 501
i. 29, 72 . . . 410
i. 29, 73 . . . 410
i. 29, 74 . . . 498
i. 30, 75 . . . 410
i. 31, 78 . . . 487
i. 31, 79 . . . 487
i. 33, 83 . . . 495
i. 33, 84 . 411, 487, 495
i. 33, 85 . . . 411
i. 36, 92 . . . 493
i. 37, 93 . . . 483
i. 37, 94 . . . 483, 488
i. 38, 95 . . . 493
i. 38, 96 . . . 495, 502
i. 38, 98 . . . 494
i. 39, 99 . . . 502
i. 40, 106 . . . 96
i. 41, 105 . . . 87
i. 41, 106 . . . 87
i. 41, 107 . . . 95, 96
i. 42, 107 . . . 96
i. 42, 108 . . . 96, 424
i. 42, 109 . . . 94
i. 43, 110 . . . 87
i. 43, 112 . . . 87, 128
i. 44, 113 . . . 232
i. 44, 114 . . . 87, 93
i. 45, 115 . 87, 190, 193
i. 45, 116 . . . 87, 189
i. 45, 117 . . . 119, 120
i. 46, 118 . 87, 120, 128
i. 46, 119 . . . 290
i. 47, 123 . . . 314
i. 48, 125 . . . 87, 88
i. 49, 128 . . . 488
i. 58, 151–153 . . . 472
i. 60, 155 . . . 13

In Verrem, PAGE
actio ii (*cont.*):
i. 61, 157 . . . 433, 439
i. 61, 158 . . . 433, 439
ii. 4, 8 . . . 169, 485
ii. 4, 12 . . . 485
ii. 5, 13 . . . 490, 491
ii. 6, 15 . . . 418
ii. 8, 24 . . . 484
ii. 12, 30 . . . 110, 289
ii. 12, 31 . 46, 156, 160, 169, 178, 192
ii. 13, 32 . 113, 114, 115, 116, 265, 451
ii. 13, 33 . . . 87, 295
ii. 13, 34 . . . 87, 265
ii. 15, 37 . 113, 116, 129
ii. 15, 38 . . . 116
ii. 16, 39 . . . 113, 265
ii. 17, 41 . . . 129
ii. 17, 42 . . . 265
ii. 18, 44 . . . 130
ii. 18, 45 . . . 296
ii. 22, 53 . . . 127
ii. 23, 55 . . . 249
ii. 23, 56 . . . 145
ii. 23, 57 . . . 295, 296
ii. 24, 59 . 113, 115, 256
ii. 25, 60 . . . 115
ii. 25, 61 . . . 296
ii. 25, 62 . . . 296
ii. 26, 63 . . . 296
ii. 26, 64 . . . 486
ii. 27, 65 . . . 485
ii. 27, 66 . . . 169, 296
ii. 29, 70 . . . 410
ii. 30, 74 . . . 410, 474
ii. 30, 75 . . . 410, 477
ii. 31, 77 . . . 440
ii. 32, 79 . . . 438
ii. 33, 80 . . . 481, 483
ii. 37, 91 . . . 298
ii. 38, 93 . . . 498
ii. 38, 94 . 134, 462, 466
ii. 39, 95 . . . 462
ii. 40, 98 . . . 461, 473
ii. 40, 99 . . . 468
ii. 41, 100 . 317, 329, 463
ii. 41, 101 . . . 462, 466
ii. 46, 113 . . . 491
ii. 47, 118 . . . 351
ii. 49, 121 . . . 102
ii. 52, 130 . . . 458
ii. 71, 174 . . . 443
ii. 72, 177 . . . 478, 501
ii. 74, 182 . . . 494
ii. 74, 183 . . . 495
ii. 76 . . . 275
ii. 76, 187 . . . 6, 145, 484, 494

In Verrem, actio ii (*cont.*): PAGE

ii. 77, 189 . . . 488
iii. 10, 25 . 87, 90, 121
iii. 10, 26 . . . 87, 495
iii. 11, 27 . 68, 124, 164
iii. 11, 28 . 90, 132, 265
iii. 12, 29 . . . 90, 132
iii. 13, 32 . 129, 132, 265
iii. 13, 33 . . 90, 132
iii. 13, 34 123
iii. 14, 35 . 87, 123, 129, 269
iii. 15, 38 . 33, 117, 124
iii. 21, 54 . 124, 125, 158
iii. 22, 55 124
iii. 29, 70 123
iii. 31, 74 489
iii. 36, 83 489
iii. 37, 85 489
iii. 38, 87 489
iii. 41, 97 440
iii. 42, 99 489
iii. 44, 106 . . . 489
iii. 57, 132 . . . 54
iii. 58, 134 . . . 130
iii. 58, 135 . 54, 269
iii. 59, 136 . . . 265

In Verrem, actio ii (*cont.*): PAGE

iii. 60, 137 . . . 266
iii. 60, 138 . . . 292
iii. 60, 139 . . . 265
iii. 60, 140 . . . 265
iii. 65, 152 . 90, 120, 169, 180, 179, 267
iii. 65, 153 . . . 267
iii. 66, 154 . . . 494
iii. 84, 195 . . . 419
iii. 88, 205 . . . 501
iii. 89, 207 . . . 112
iii. 90, 211 . . . 160
iii. 95, 221 . . . 464
iii. 96, 223 . . . 443
iv. 7, 15 491
iv. 16, 36 493
iv. 19, 40 466
iv. 19, 41 462
iv. 25, 56 419
iv. 31, 69 160
iv. 38, 82 160
iv. 45, 100 . . . 411
iv. 47, 104 . . . 464
iv. 63, 140 . 491, 494
iv. 64, 142 . . . 491
iv. 66, 148 . . . 145

In Verrem, actio ii (*cont.*): PAGE

iv. 66, 149 . 485, 494
iv. 67, 150 . . . 491
v. 1, 2 501
v. 6, 12 519
v. 6, 13 523
v. 6, 14 498
v. 8, 19 474
v. 11, 27 . . 134, 477, 481
v. 13, 31 132
v. 13, 32 501
v. 13, 34 . . 102, 108
v. 21, 53 13
v. 22, 57 491
v. 39, 102 488
v. 41, 109 461
v. 44, 114 441
v. 54, 141 54
v. 54, 142 31
v. 55, 143 458
v. 59, 155 487
v. 63, 163 495
v. 63, 163–170 . . 413
v. 64, 166 . . 414, 465
v. 66, 169 414
v. 70, 179 475

EPISTOLAE

Ad Atticum:

i. 1, 2 457
i. 1, 3 285
i. 12, 3 386
i. 13, 3 . 376, 386, 387, 388
i. 14, 1 . . . 387, 388
i. 14, 5 . . . 387, 437
i. 16, 2 388
i. 16, 3 388
i. 16, 4 . . . 388, 494
i. 16, 5 388
i. 16, 10 388
i. 19, 4 567
ii. 1, 8 . . . 334, 422
ii. 1, 10 126
ii. 4, 1 458
ii. 24, 2 485
ii. 24, 4 467
iii. 1 364
iii. 3 365
iii. 4 . . 364, 365, 366
iii. 7, 1 . . . 366, 511
iii. 12, 1 . . 324, 366
iii. 15, 4 360
iii. 15, 5 . 316, 360, 361, 362
iii. 15, 6 . . 324, 366

Ad Atticum (*cont.*):

iii. 23, 2 366
iv. 1, 4 521
iv. 15, 4 . . . 448, 458
iv. 15, 9 461
iv. 16, 5 458
iv. 16, 8 498
iv. 16, 9 447
iv. 15, 9 454
v. 2, 3 106
v. 11, 2 409
v. 11, 6 511
v. 16, 2 125
v. 20, 1 129
v. 21, 6 117
v. 21, 9 129
v. 21, 11 . 95, 119, 127
vi. 1, 2 119
vi. 1, 8 . 27, 136, 161
vi. 1, 15 . . 118, 120, 121, 122, 284, 285
vi. 1, 16 . . . 121, 126
vi. 1, 23 522
vi. 2, 4 117
viii. 11, 2 573
viii. 16, 2 445
ix. 14, 2 513
x. 4, 3 360

Ad Atticum (*cont.*):

x. 8, 8 . . . 399, 402
x. 13, 1 100
xi. 6, 2 105
xii. 5, 3 420
xii. 5, 4 493
xv. 16 a 39
xvi. 8, 2 568
xvi. 15, 2 . . 242, 243

Ad Familiares:

i. 9, 4 491
i. 9, 7 491
i. 9, 19 491
ii. 15, 4 131
iii. 8, 2 135
iii. 8, 4 . 87, 119, 121, 129
iii. 8, 5 129
iii. 8, 6 129
iii. 11, 2 423
iv. 12, 3 372
v. 2, 3 430
v. 2, 4 430
vi. 5 568
vi. 6 568
vi. 7, 4 568

Ad Familiares (*cont.*): PAGE
vi. 9 568
vii. 12, 2 . 203, 204, 205
vii. 13, 2 215
vii. 21 . . . . 88, 214
vii. 30, 2 71
vii. 32, 1 . . . 59, 238
vii. 32, 2 . 55, 59, 164
viii. 6, 2 461
viii. 8, 1 . . 424, 457, 458, 475
viii. 8, 2 . . 427, 459, 466, 471, 503
viii. 8, 3 . 416, 459, 470, 496, 497, 498, 503, 504
viii. 8, 5 . . 393, 445
viii. 8, 8 573
viii. 9, 5 573

Ad Familiares (*cont.*): PAGE
ix. 16, 7 280
x. 32, 3 . . 311, 414
xi. 16, 2 334
xii. 30, 5 285
xii. 30, 7 . . 130, 131
xiii. 11, 3 . . 100, 103
xiii. 19, 2 . . 127, 511
xiii. 26, 3 292
xiii. 27, 1 166
xiii. 30, 1 100
xiii. 66 568
xv. 16, 3 215
xvi. 12, 3 573

Ad Quintum fratrem:
i. 1, 7, 20 . . 129, 131
i. 1, 7, 22 . . 110, 289

Ad Quintum fratrem (*cont.*): PAGE
i. 1, 11, 32 . . . 126
i. 2, 2, 5 . 411, 428, 506
i. 2, 2, 6 . . 125, 412
i. 2, 3, 10 98
ii. 3 341
ii. 3, 1 346
ii. 3, 2 346
ii. 3, 3 346
ii. 3, 5 . . . 458, 459
ii. 3, 6 . . . 431, 458
ii. 7 346
ii. 13, 2 . . 458, 466
ii. 16, 3 . . 450, 471
iii. 1, 7, 24 . . . 430
iii. 3, 2 476
iii. 3, 3 430
iii. 4, 1 . 396, 447, 475, 498

OPERA PHILOSOPHICA

Academica Priora:
ii. 30, 97 . . 232, 291
ii. 47, 146 . 274, 276, 481

De Amicitia:
11, 37 . . . 383, 403

De Divinatione:
i. 18, 34 395
i. 45, 102 137
ii. 35, 74 347

De Finibus:
ii. 12, 36 276
ii. 16, 54 . . 381, 420
ii. 19, 62 487
ii. 22, 74 . . . 84, 97
iv. 1, 1 395
iv. 28, 77 420
v. 22, 62 420
v. 29, 88 166

De Legibus:
i. 4, 14 167
i. 5, 17 . . 83, 87, 90
i. 15, 42 314
i. 21, 55 . . . 40, 196
ii. 8, 19 137
ii. 9, 22 . 299, 300, 378
ii. 12, 29 137
ii. 15, 37 300
ii. 19, 47 26
ii. 19, 48 286
ii. 23, 59 27
iii. 1, 2 79

De Legibus (*cont.*):
iii. 1, 3 80
iii. 3, 6 . 43, 264, 289, 321, 332, 343, 347, 414
iii. 3, 8 . 22, 25, 83, 397
iii. 4, 11 . . 312, 317
iii. 11, 26 325
iii. 12, 27 345
iii. 16, 36 . . 99, 350
iii. 19, 44 . 312, 313, 317
iii. 19, 45 . . 316, 317, 361, 362
iii. 20, 46 82

De Natura Deorum:
i. 23, 63 420
iii. 30, 74 . 63, 83, 165, 167, 178, 203, 350, 379, 420, 432
iii. 33, 81 298

De Officiis:
i. 13, 40 300
i. 25, 88 299
i. 25, 89 80
ii. 12, 41 80
ii. 12, 42 . . . 80, 81
ii. 21, 75 419
iii. 10, 43 270
iii. 10, 44 270
iii. 11, 47 425
iii. 14, 60 . . 179, 429
iii. 15, 61 . . 196, 202, 203, 205
iii. 16, 66 . . 204, 206

De Officiis (*cont.*):
iii. 17, 70 . 64, 203, 204
iii. 17, 71 32
iii. 19, 77 . . . 54, 266
iii. 20, 79 351
iii. 31, 111 . . . 300
iii. 31, 112 . . . 39

De Re Publica:
i. 3, 6 . . 325, 350, 351
i. 13, 20 . . . 76, 217
i. 38, 59 276
i. 38, 60 19
i. 40, 62 308
ii. 1, 2 7
ii. 10, 18 4
ii. 14, 26 23
ii. 17, 31 19
ii. 24, 44 20
ii. 31, 53 . . 308, 319
ii. 31, 54 . 20, 305, 312, 318, 319, 321
ii. 32, 56 25
ii. 34, 59 74
ii. 35, 60 . 309, 327, 335
ii. 36, 61 . 317, 569, 571
iv. 8, 8 . . . . 4, 40
iv. 10, 12 207
v. 2, 3 . . . 18, 23, 24

Tusculanae Disputationes:
ii. 24, 57 385
iv. 1, 1 21
v. 37, 108 . . 509, 511

www.ingramcontent.com/pod-product-compliance
Lightning Source LLC
Chambersburg PA
CBHW032108110726
47902CB00003B/507

9781616194734